A History of Recent America

A History of Recent America

Paul K. Conkin

UNIVERSITY OF WISCONSIN

& David Burner

STATE UNIVERSITY OF NEW YORK AT

STONY BROOK

THOMAS Y. CROWELL COMPANY · NEW YORK · ESTABLISHED 1834

Manufactured in the United States of America

1 2 3 4 5 6 7 8 9 10

Photo research by Elizabeth Bidwell Bates

Library of Congress Cataloging in Publication Data
CONKIN, PAUL KEITH.
    A history of recent America.

    1. United States—History—20th century.   I. Burner,
David, 1937–   II. Title.
E741.C55   973.9   73-22490
ISBN 0-690-00293-9

Over three years ago we began this text with all the hopes, and many of the illusions, of a beginning pilgrimage. Finally, after a great deal more travail than we ever expected, we have at least paused long enough to get a tentative version into print. Of course, we did not complete all the work we envisioned, achieve the masterpiece we contemplated. But as we worked we did become more and more aware of three very traditional and very challenging goals of historical writing—*accuracy, clarity,* and *fairness.*

The problem of accuracy is almost overwhelming in a book of this length and scope. We shudder at the number of factual errors that undoubtedly still remain. Yet several chapters represent not only a culling of rich secondary works but a goodly amount of primary research, particularly in government documents. We have tried to tell the truth about the domestic and foreign policies adopted by our national government, to survey the major policy alternatives that vied for political acceptance, and, much more hazardous, to suggest the motives and goals and even the intellectual assumptions that influenced policy makers. The book is most interpretive in this sense—in revealing varied perspectives, in showing how quite diverse Americans reacted to events. It is more a history of interpretations than our own interpretation.

Clarity is as important as accuracy, and scarcely separable. The difficulty of communication always haunts the historian. We have tried to avoid easy labels and categories, such as the unending liberalisms and conservatisms, the imperialisms and racisms, that confuse and obscure so much of our present political discourse. We have searched for ambiguous words that cry out for definition, for grouping categories that require careful qualification, for issues that beg detailed analysis. Our aim has been a very serious, conceptually sophisticated account, one that escapes the easy stereotypes, the loose caricatures, the simplistic theories that the average college student has already learned and now most needs to quality and revise. We have, however, tried to tell the story as simply as often complex issues allow. We want the student to understand exactly what was at stake in critical policy decisions. Unless we have spoken clearly, yet without oversimplification, we cannot have spoken truthfully. A failure to communicate as precisely as possible is really complicity in deceit.

Fairness, and a type of balance, is a quite different sort of goal. At least

Preface

today, historians are a heterogeneous group. Students are even more diverse in their tastes and basic beliefs, and thus in their moral preferences. Because of common methods of inquiry and common canons of verification, historians may reach agreement on certain necessary conditions for a New Deal policy, or agree on some of the consequences that clearly flowed from it. But both historians and students often profoundly disagree on whether the policy was good or bad for the country, for they have quite varied images of an ideal society, of what they want America to become. For one historian, the adoption of "beneficent" welfare measures saved the country from an awful socialism; for another such "hypocritical" measures prevented the country from attaining a glorious socialism. To us, fairness meant that we should try to discover, and sympathetically describe, as many valuative perspectives as space permitted. When analysis required it, we have included even small minority views. We have achieved our goal if we have uncovered, understood, and successfully communicated all major evaluative perspectives, and if we have treated all with the seriousness that sincere conviction and moral earnestness deserve. In these valuative areas, we have tried to avoid coercing student judgment, even though our language may reveal, or more often misleadingly seem to reveal, some of our dearest preferences. But we have tried only to inform judgment, to provide students with a broad and reliable foundation for the exercise of moral criticism, particularly in the area of federal policy making.

Although we endlessly crticized each other's work, we divided up the writing task and accept individual responsibility for designated chapters. David Burner wrote chapter 3, and chapters 26 through 32. Paul Conkin wrote the other chapters, plus the Introduction and Epilogue.

We cannot begin to acknowledge all the help we received, particularly from critical students, from colleagues who read chapters, from wives and children who edited and read proof and above all shared our frustrations, and from several excellent typists who corrected so many of our errors and oversights. Paul Conkin particularly acknowledges the invaluable, extremely conscientious contribution of Anne Boylan, a research assistant for one busy summer. David Burner is especially grateful for help from James Moore, Tim Patterson, Paul Ehrlich, and the circulation department of the Stony Brook library. We both appreciate the conscientious work of Joan Greene, the press editor, and Elizabeth Bidwell Bates, who did most of the photographic research. Both gave of their time and talents well beyond the call of duty.

PAUL CONKIN
DAVID BURNER

Contents

MAPS

CHARTS AND TABLES

MAJOR NEW DEAL AGENCIES

AAA	Agricultural Adjustment Administration
CCC	Civilian Conservation Corps
CCC	Commodity Credit Corporation
CWA	Civil Works Administration
FDIC	Federal Depositors Insurance Corporation
FERA	Federal Emergency Relief Administration
FHA	Federal Housing Administration
FSA	Farm Security Administration
HOLC	Home Owners Loan Corporation
NIRA	National Industrial Recovery Act
NLRB	National Labor Relations Board
NRA	National Recovery Administration
NYA	National Youth Administration
PWA	Public Works Administration
RA	Resettlement Administration
REA	Rural Electrification Administration
RFC	Reconstruction Finance Corporation
SCS	Soil Conservation Service
SEC	Securities and Exchange Commission
TNEC	Temporary National Economic Committee
TVA	Tennessee Valley Authority
USHA	United States Housing Authority
WPA	Works Progress Administration

INTRODUCTION

Domestic Challenges in an Age Called Progressive

When the new century began in 1901, the United States was still a very young nation. A few old people could remember vividly the simultaneous death of John Adams and Thomas Jefferson that occurred almost miraculously on July 4, 1826, or fifty years to the day after the signing of the Declaration of Independence. For almost everyone, particularly Southerners, *the* war was the horribly cruel Civil War, not the delightfully successful skirmish with Spain in 1898. Change was omnipresent. Everyone talked of progress. Yet, from our perspective, the continuities with the past seem just as striking. A majority of Americans (60 percent) still lived in rural areas. Almost all blacks lived in poverty on southern farms. The latest immigrants formed strange, parochial enclaves in our largest cities. Agriculture employed approximately one-third of our workers; factories less than a third. And in most areas of national life—politics, education, industrial management, the Protestant churches—older American families, with professional or entrepreneurial positions and above average incomes, retained the predominance of power and status.

All was not idyllic. Behind all the centennials and expositions, the popular celebrations of new technology, the endless talk of reform, the surface smugness of the Victorian Age, lurked plenty of strains and stresses. For a Henry Adams, so morbidly aware of an older America, of its lost ideals and promises, the future seemed so foreboding that he could scarcely reject suicide. To some sensitive writers, from a cynical Mark Twain to a fatalistic Theodore Dreiser, our society offered either a vast panorama of absurdity or an example of impersonal forces totally beyond human control. More hopeful novelists and journalists would soon begin raking through the muck of national degeneration—special privilege in high places, monopolies of economic power, horrible living conditions in cities, and the oppressive insecurity and servility of factory employment. Behind the publicized litany of evils, the middle-class guilt and fear, the first varied and confused efforts at reformation, was a widely recognized gulf between heralded American ideals and developing realities. We had somehow betrayed the promise of American life, the earlier confidence engendered by our enormous resources and by what we still desperately hoped was the most enlightened form of government in the world.

The Challenge of Old Ideals and New Realities

The new century invited, even required, new governmental initiatives in several areas. Initiatives would come, but without any consensus on goals or on policies. Older political ideals remained, at least in their verbal form, but often with unclear or transmuted meaning in a country that had changed so drastically since the Civil War. These ancient ideals provide a convenient point of departure.

The preamble of the Declaration of Independence celebrated the two most compelling ideals of the American Revolution—popular government and human freedom. Governments, to be legitimate, must rest upon the consent of the governed and must secure rather than threaten life, liberty, and property. Americans soon created the techniques to give substance to the idea of consent. They perfected the constitutional convention and almost ritualized methods of ratifying and amending constitutions, which formed a special type of fundamental law. Through their constitutions, the people retained a power above that even of their own elected legislators. But election was second only to constitutional process as a guarantee of consent. If the vague word "democracy" denotes government by the majority of citizens, or by elected representatives, Americans adopted a modified form of it. The people are free to elect, officials free to act, only within limits set by constitutions and also by fundamental freedoms that all individuals possess as a moral right. Thus in America we have a mixture of democracy, or of policy determined through elective bodies, and of a government by law, or by a more remote form of authority expressed in constitutions and in reserved rights.

The imagery of freeman versus slave dominated the controversy with Britain and much of the rhetoric of the American Revolution. Slavery meant servitude or dependence. Freedom meant independence or personal autonomy. Americans had several examples of what they feared—the lowly Negro slave in America, the dependent serf or peasant in Europe, the wage laborer of English factories. To be free one had to have security for his person (clear laws and an exemption from all arbitrary criminal procedures), for areas of personal expression (religion, speech, press, assembly), and above all for property (access to the God-given resources of nature and a secure claim on the products of one's own labor).

Property was the key. More than today, the eighteenth century conception of freedom had an economic meaning. If one did not have access to the means of production, if he did not make his own economic decisions, if he did not control his own labor, then he could hardly be free. Such economic dependence made other types of freedom (to believe in any god one preferred, to publish any book one wrote) a poor substitute, for a slave may have religious freedom and still have someone else control his labor. Given economic independence, these other freedoms may become all-important. This concern for economic freedom clarifies the most dangerous and treacherous aspect of government—its power to take property as well as protect it. If a government can tax or otherwise take property or labor without limit or without some form of popular consent, then it is tyrannical and has the power to enslave. Here was the most feared power of the British Parliament over the colonies. Fears of government abuse of individual property led, very early, to the slogan of the Jeffersonians—"Equal opportunities for all, special privileges for none." Presidents as late as Woodrow Wilson and Herbert Hoover still reiterated this slogan, and found in it the moral heart of any legitimate government policy.

The same focus on property helped define the ideal American. As a freeman, he would be a type of entrepreneur, with complete control over productive property and his own labor, and free to use both in behalf of his own happiness. Wage employment undermines this ideal, for it places one person under the domination of another. Thus, the ideal American could accept wages only as a means to move on to ownership and self-direction. Equal opportunity entailed a political and economic environment that allowed everyone a chance for ownership and the type of responsibility and citizenship that derive from a "stake in society." This did not mean that everyone would start with the same advantages; varied talents and a different inheritance precluded this. Nor did it promise an equality of wealth; choice, ability, and a head start for some would always allow variations of both income and wealth. It did mean that anyone should be able to pursue his economic desires or potential without governmental impediments of any sort except those necessary to protect the property of others.

In this sense, early Americans idealized a classless society. Without an understanding of what they meant by it, it is impossible to make much sense of their efforts to reform our institutions in the early twentieth century. It may seem paradoxical today to talk of a classless society without meaning an equality of income or wealth. But in the eighteenth century, economic egalitarianism seemed inimical to freedom, for its achievement would require coercive control over the labor of the most talented and industrious people and unearned gifts to the least talented or industrious. Classless meant that in America there would be no artificial privileges and no permanent, frozen economic groups, no class of owners paired against a class of wage laborers. Work and talent would continually redistribute real property, and the status of families would shift with changes in their character or their application to the tasks of life. At any one time large and prosperous farmers might exist beside small, impoverished homesteaders; prosperous shop owners beside struggling apprentices; wealthy merchants beside back-country peddlers. But no one would have to give up on the expectation of eventual ownership and management; no one would have to accept a role as a permanent wage laborer.

Much in nineteenth-century America sustained this entrepreneurial vision. The expanding frontier of virgin land seemed to guarantee it, even as the reality of entrepreneurship all but disappeared for millions of people. The small, personal nature of commerce and manufacturing also supported it. The farmer was, and remains, the most characteristic example of the free entrepreneur, in full control of real property. But merchants and shop owners, craftsmen and professionals, also exemplified the ideal. Every early American president, in what became a virtual ritual, blessed the workman and celebrated his three main fields of labor—agriculture, commerce, and manufacturing. The ever-present threat to entrepreneurship was the factory system, only marginally significant in America before 1830, still fledgling even by 1860. Factory labor, the ogre of men like Jefferson, simply could not exist alongside the prevalent conceptions of freedom or of private property. England, with its large factories and crowded cities, already exhibited a permanent class of servile wage laborers, most with virtually no chance of becoming owners and managers even of the tools they used. Foreclosed from property and economic independence, these nonmen were not only pitiful but also dangerous. Out of despair or bitterness, the workers might rise up against their owners and managers, destroying not only the special privileges that make possible such large enterprise but also types of legitimate property. Meanwhile, these desperate wage slaves fell into vice and crime, filled hospitals and poorhouses and prisons, and lived at a mere subsistence level in inhuman city slums.

Before the Civil War a majority of white Americans probably realized the entrepreneurial dream, or at least believed that it was an option. The centers of economic activity remained the farm, the store, and the small shop or workhouse, with a loose, personal supervision of apprentices or wage laborers. Most homes retained an economic function, even as children very early performed productive tasks. Despite the wide range of wealth and achievement, a common body of economic aspirations helped create a sense of social solidarity so often remarked by European visitors. With few exceptions, Americans at every economic level felt an obligation to work, a compulsion rooted in Protestant conceptions of a calling or vocation. The New England Puritans elevated work to the status of art, or even prayer. One who did not work lived on the labor of another, a clear example of unfair privilege. Those who did the most menial tasks probably saw work only as a necessary discipline, but those in more rewarding vocations easily celebrated its intrinsic value and creative potential. Rich and poor alike condemned idleness and conspicuous luxuries, and honored hard work, ingenuity, and thrift. But again, the honored form of work was for oneself, not at the command of others, and the image of work was not that of specialized, boring tasks performed under the compulsion of a foreman and a time clock. As late as the Civil War, Lincoln still insisted that all Americans could become their own employer, and that America would never have a class of hired laborers.

The American of the nineteenth century dreamed of a classless society, with each man his own entrepreneur. The farmer best characterized this dream, for he controlled the land. Many blacks of that era, however, still worked in virtual peonage on Southern farms. *Library of Congress*

New York City's Lower East Side was a haven for East European Jewish immigrants during the late nineteenth and early twentieth centuries. Despite poverty and congested living conditions, the people were hopeful and anxious to make a better life. *Library of Congress*

The American dream of entrepreneurship and classless society extended to blacks as well as whites. A middle-class black family outside their home (left), a picture used in the Paris Exposition of 1900 to depict American life. Below, a black-owned turn-of-the-century print shop in Richmond, Virginia, is printing the Virginia Baptist newspaper. *Library of Congress*

Families such as the Walshes and the McLeans realized the American dream—they acquired wealth, prestige, and were the leaders of society. Here Evalyn Walsh McLean, owner of the Hope diamond, and her son are shown vacationing at Palm Beach, Florida, which even in 1913 was a vacation spot for the very rich. *Library of Congress*

No industrial revolution occurred in America; the label obscures more than it reveals. Industrial techniques change continuously. In nineteenth-century America better techniques of farming helped transform our largest and most basic industry and in the process freed labor for the further processing of the products of farm and mine. The limited liability corporation became the legal basis for the gradual shift from individual or small-group production to large, highly specialized collectives. In fact, liberal chartering privileges in several states represented the most significant form of legal benevolence to economic enterprise in all of American history.

The corporation, blessed by a charter and able to gain the full protection of property for its collective privileges, soon threatened the competitive position of less-favored individuals and small shops. First in New England textiles, then in milling, shoemaking, iron smelting, arms, and railroads, the corporation became the dominant means of capital formation and of organizing labor. It almost always separated work from ownership and management, and thus threatened the traditional right to own property. But the corporate form and the factory were never dominant in the nineteenth century. Even in 1901 a majority of Americans, although employed, worked outside factories. But by then the future was clear. Ex-

Challenges and Risks of a Corporate Society

THE RECIPROCITY SITUATION.   LA SITUACION DEL ASUNTO RECIPROCIDAD.

This 1902 cartoon sug-
gests that big business
had become big enough
to influence government
foreign-policy decisions.
The early part of the
century witnessed an enormous increase in corpo-
rate wealth and power.
Library of Congress

cept for farming and small merchandising, it seemed likely that a corporate or collective form of production and distribution would eventually
prevail. Its promise of efficiency, of higher levels of consumption, of
greater national power, overrode its threat to the quality of the work experience and the creation of a class of dependent, nonpropertied workers.

The ramifications of highly collective forms of production lay behind
almost all the perceived problems of the new century that began in 1901.
The corporation, or new refinements on concentration (trusts and holding companies), joined commercial need in facilitating population cluster-
ing and the growth of large and often grimy cities. They provided most
of the job opportunities for an endless stream of immigrants, created
economic power so massive as to bypass or corrupt traditional political institutions, incited the growth of retaliatory labor unions and a degree of
class consciousness and conflict, provided early models of bureaucratic efficiency and paternalistic welfare, and by sheer competitive advantages,
political manipulation, or market controls posed a dire threat to farmers.

Concern over these effects did not await a new century. Beginning
with the Age of Jackson, various would-be reformers sought answers to
the problems of economic servility. How could we preserve the economic
advantages of collectivism without suffering all the penalties, which
Americans usually identified by reference to Europe? Could we have fac-

tories without class conflict? The proposed solutions varied immensely. One appealing answer was the magical power of education to produce alert and intelligent citizens even among the laboring class. Post-Civil War reformers tried to ameliorate the servility of a corporate system by cooperative ownership schemes, by new devices to reopen the land to workers, by profit-sharing and stock-purchase plans to transform laborers into minor capitalists, and by all manner of paternal welfare schemes for employees, including planned factory towns.

These schemes failed. As a result, by 1901 middle-class Americans were often morbidly concerned with the problems of "industrialization" and the specter of class conflict. But they rejoiced in economic growth, and accepted some of its imperatives—a foreign market for goods, greater international involvement, and better supportive institutions at home. The past decade had revealed an alarming amount of industrial strife, and a virtual revolt by farmers who felt cheated by governments that seemed to favor the corporations and the banks. Already obvious were some of the internal abuses of the corporate world—the graft and bleeding of stockholders, the threat of monopoly and price gouging, the possibilities of bought politicians and a narrow political oligarchy. Early muckrakers pointed out some of the hidden horrors of urban life, particularly for the most deprived class of factory workers—immigrants from Europe or from the American South, both uprooted and vulnerable. Special interests flagrantly bought local governments and at least swayed the federal government. Corruption and a highly personal, boss-type rule characterized most large cities. Vulgarity and greed seemed to reign everywhere.

The first two decades of the new century offered a congenial time to combat these problems. Even before 1900, the depression of 1894 slowly yielded to a sustained period of economic growth (the gross national product rose at an average rate of 5 percent from 1899 to 1919). Except for a severe banker's panic in 1907, only brief recessions arrested the economic gains. With growth came the consolidation of large corporations, and a turn away from the gaudy, reckless speculation and aggressive competition of the post-Civil War decades. The second generation of corporate managers often seemed a world removed from such mavericks as a Fisk or a Carnegie or even a more conventional Rockefeller. College-trained, concerned as much with image and respectability as with quick profits, often moved by the revelations of muckrakers or responsive to the pleas for social concern expressed by many ministers (the "Social Gospel"), at least a minority of well-placed executives sought not only order and efficiency but also more moderate personnel policies. The splurge of mergers that marked the turn of the century and the seeming threat of monopoly through various pooling devices eased after 1904, not so much because

POST-MORTEM FOOD.

In heaven all eat angel food,
  And nectar 's served to most;
But in the regions down below
  They give us all a roast.

HIS FIRST BEE-STING.

David Henry, aged three, not being acquainted with the peculiarities of the insect, took a half-frozen bee into his hand one day recently, and soon thereafter was wailing vigorously. His mother ushed to the door.

"Oh, the poor child has been stung by a bee!" she exclaimed.

"T-t-tain't a b-b-bee-e-e," sobbed the victim; "it's a b-b-bear-r-r-r!"

LAUGHLIN

FOUNTAIN PEN

The Best at Any Price

Sent on approval to responsible people.

A Pocket Companion of never ending usefulness, a source of constant pleasure and comfort.

To test the merits of JUDGE'S LIBRARY au an advertising medium we offer **your choice** of these popular styles superior to the

$3.00

grades of other makes for only

$1.00

Unconditionally Guaranteed
Pre-eminently Satisfactory.

Try it a week, if not suited, we buy it back, and give you $1.10 for it (the additional ten cents is to pay for your trouble in returning the pen). We are willing to take chances on you wanting to sell; we know pen values—you will when you have one of these.

Finest quality hard Para rubber reservoir holder, 14k. Diamond Point Gold Pen, any desired flexibility in fine, medium or stub, and the only perfect ink feed known to the science of fountain pen making.

Sent postpaid on receipt of $1.00 (Registration, 8c extra.)

This great Special Offer is good for just 30 days. One of our Safety Pocket Pen Holders **free of charge** with each pen.

Remember—There is No "just as good" as the Laughlin: insist on it; take no chances.

State whether Ladies' or Gentlemen's style is desired. Illustrations are full size of complete article. Address

LAUGHLIN MFG. CO.

194 GRISWOLD ST.,
DETROIT,   MICH.

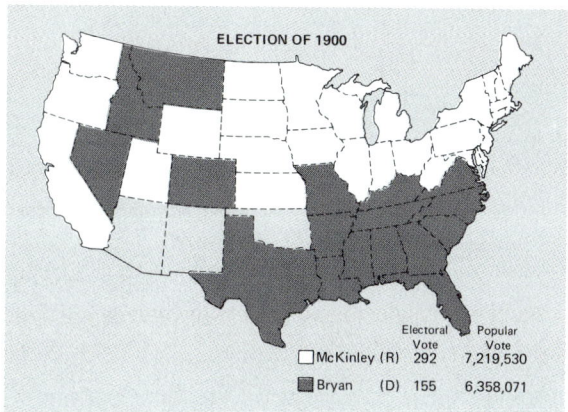

of government pressure as because of changed industrial priorities. There would be no more Standard Oil monopolies (one company controlling 90 percent of all petroleum) or railroad pools.

The farmers were also in no mood to fight more political battles against corporate privilege. Midwestern and southern populism was dead, for neither its morally sophisticated analysis nor its conspiratorial fantasies could survive prosperity. Improved foreign demand insured a decade of high prices for most farm commodities (these prices later provided a yardstick for agricultural support prices). Farmers returned to their traditional political alignments (most often Republican outside the South), and worked for more modest economic goals through a variety of farm organizations.

Even the leaders of organized labor made their peace with the developing corporate system. Earlier, a few laborers, dreaming of a cooperative commonwealth and an end to wage slavery, had flirted with socialist politics. They won few followers. The most moderate labor unions only grew slowly and against great impediments. Unskilled workers, in 1901 and even in 1920, remained mostly unorganized. Samuel Gompers, a cigarmaker who immigrated from London to rise to the top of the American Federation of Labor (AFL), adopted what became the enduring strategy of large labor unions in America. He began with an acceptance of corporate ownership and management. Organized laborers would not seek such traditionally American goals as worker ownership of the means of production and control over management decisions. They would forsake the

An advertisement from
Judges magazine, 1902.
Library of Congress

entrepreneurial dream for a more modest but more realistic goal of bargaining rights, better working conditions, shorter hours (the eight-hour day was the most unifying goal of all), and higher wages. To get these, Gompers eschewed separate political parties, but emphasized solidarity and such economic weapons as the strike. These policies led to waves of union growth, particularly in the skilled trades (the AFL, a federation of craft unions, was not enthusiastic about organizing unskilled workers for whole industries). By 1920 close to one-fifth of wage workers belonged to unions, most to the AFL.

Gompers's successful tactics revealed a gradual accommodation to a highly centralized, yet privately managed economy. Implicit in the AFL strategy was a major transmutation of American values. Now continuous employment, which even Lincoln had excluded from the American dream, became an acceptable choice for self-respecting men, even as it was in fact a necessary choice for many. Soon celebrations of opportunity merged with pleas for full employment. The right to work replaced the right to own in the American hierarchy of values. The heralded goals of individual entrepreneurship—independence, responsibility, and all the joys and hazards of setting one's own goals, of doing one's own thing— gave way to the lauded delights of consumption and high living standards and even to a celebration of leisure. Not everyone accepted large-

Samuel Gompers (1850– 1924), the labor leader responsible for the success of the American Federation of Labor, is pictured here on the steps of the Capitol. He helped perfect such present-day labor negotiating tactics as the strike. *Library of Congress*

scale economic organization, or the reduction of labor to a specialized function within a bureaucratic structure. The farmer remained the classic opponent of such collectivism. A few socialist unions, and the more anarchistic Industrial Workers of the World (IWW), accepted collective production, but struggled to gain worker control over the tools and decision making. After 1901 these small, radical groups represented the only politics of conflict and confrontation in America, and they frightened almost everyone else.

The abatement of economic conflict accompanied a form of political ferment at every level of government. By the valuative standards of those "good citizens" who sought changes in policy, it was a period of "reform" or of definite improvements. Critics judged differently. But to the enthusiasts, reform meant progress, and those who supported "constructive" change became, by their own definition, "progressives," while their opponents gained such opprobrious labels as "standpatters," "stalwarts," and "conservatives." The word "progressive," so useful as a flattering badge of identity, and so indicative of the undying hopefulness of varied reformers, never attached to any single ideology, class, or program. Contrary to the simple categories of historians, there was never a "progressive

A Decade of "Reform"

THE OLD CONUNDRUM.
MISS RIVERSIDE DRYVE—" She refuses to marry him unless he resigns from Tammany hall."
HE—" Well, which will it be—' the lady or the tiger '?"

A cartoon from *Judges* magazine, 1903. It is not unusual in the cartoons of this era that the caption have no direct bearing on the accompanying picture, the caption making the point and the picture acting merely as an illustration. Here, Tammany Hall and boss rule are subjects of mirth for a wealthy couple. They could afford to joke about such things, for they needed only to buy their way around Tammany rule. *Library of Congress*

movement," for a movement requires, at the minimum, a unifying goal. It does make some sense to expand a widely shared badge of identity into a "progressive era." There was a Progressive party in 1912, but competitors never surrendered to it their equal claim to the label. Thus, the term has no single institutional reference. Ambiguities in a label does not mean either vagueness or confusion on the part of those who adopted it. Several strategies for reform competed, and possibly at the most general and abstract level shared a pervasive and unifying moral fervor. By drawing fine enough distinctions, one can identify almost as many progressive movements as he wants. By muting almost all distinctions, he can reduce a complex body of phenomena to a single but amorphous whole.

The muckraking journalists focused the best of their investigative reporting on corporate abuse and on the social and political maladies of the cities. Lincoln Steffens, by later assessments the most influential reporter, turned an often cynical eye on *The Shame of Our Cities*. In large cities all across America he found similar patterns of corruption and misrule, but he slowly lost all faith in the possibilities of lasting improvement by conscience-pricked, middle-class citizens. Ironically, he ended with more admiration for the bosses than the do-gooders. But the good citizens had their day in the sun and, whatever value one places on their work, they did make some enduring changes in urban life.

The impetus for city reform came either from such dynamic mayors as Samuel "Golden Rule" Jones of Toledo or Tom Johnson of Cleveland or, more often, from such organized civic associations as numerous City Clubs. Vice, crime, poor amenities, corrupt private utility companies, tax inequities, and graft-ridden political machines offered the major targets. The constituency for reform had to be broad, for most efforts failed if they engendered basic conflict. The bywords of change were public interest and efficient government; the dangers were special interests and narrow partisanship. Reform groups in city after city repudiated "politics" in behalf of such nonpartisan schemes as city managers (trained ex-

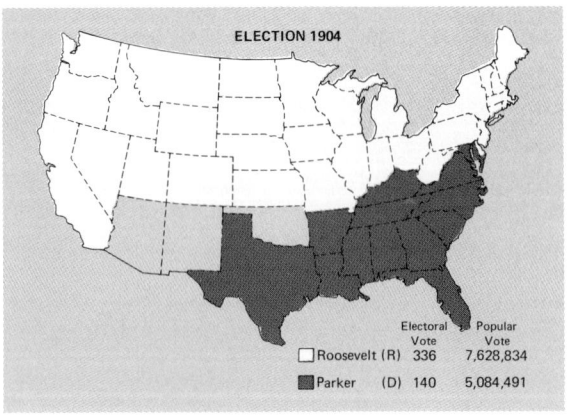

ELECTION 1904

	Electoral Vote	Popular Vote
□ Roosevelt (R)	336	7,628,834
■ Parker (D)	140	5,084,491

perts above politics) or the elimination of all party labels in city elections. Business leaders, educators, socially active ministers and priests, and even labor leaders gathered in civic clubs, set committees onto elaborate fact-finding investigations (often aided by social scientists from the universities), lobbied for home rule and enabling legislation in rural-dominated state capitals. They usually gained some of their objectives in more consensual areas. Everyone but utility magnates agreed on the need for good services and fair prices, and accepted municipal regulation or even ownership ("gas and water socialism"). How could anyone publicly oppose noise and smoke abatement, improved streets and trolleys, better trained police and firemen? The first zoning of property, and the earliest city planning commissions date from the pre-World War I era. The ideal was a city government staffed by experts, committed to the public interest, responsible to the total electorate, and at least powerful enough to police corrupting special interests.

Quite similar reform strategies spread to the states. At least at the level of services—health and education—these reforms affected practically all the states. But in only ten or twelve states, such as Wisconsin or Oregon, did the public-service image lead to major institutional changes. These included a more zealous regulation of business enterprise, early welfare legislation (most notably workmen's compensation and child labor laws), and numerous efforts to make state government more efficient and more representative. The political reforms seemed to pull in two opposing directions—toward government by experts or by an elite, as reflected in higher civil service standards, research and bill-writing services for legislators, and a wide array of regulatory commissions; but also toward a more directly democratic government, as reflected in petition or referenda devices which allowed citizens to select candidates by direct primaries, to initiate legislation, to force a vote on legislation, or even to recall offending officials. Both strategies reflected a common purpose—to bypass competing special interests, to defuse powerful lobbyists, to keep government honest, to bring government up to date, to force it to serve the public interest.

At the national level, President Theodore Roosevelt best exemplified these concerns for an effective yet neutral government. President from 1901 to 1909, he illustrated these themes by his political slogan—"a square deal." In both foreign and domestic policy he fought for what he perceived as a transcending national interest. Roosevelt illustrated a new type of political leadership—youthful, vigorous, supremely competitive, sensitive to popular images, but loosely tied to a political party. Only the assassination of President McKinley in 1901 enabled such a party maverick to become president. He easily dramatized and glamourized policy is-

Theodore Roosevelt (1858–1919), a symbol of youth and vigor, is shown here as a colonel of his Rough Riders in the Spanish-American War. He succeeded to the presidency in 1901 on the death of William McKinley. As president, Roosevelt formulated aggressive policies for curbing trusts, regulating business, and conserving natural resources. *Library of Congress*

Although intelligent and conscientious, William Howard Taft (1857–1930) lost popularity when he signed the controversial Payne-Aldrich Tariff Act in 1909. He demonstrated unwise political judgment in settling controversies, generally placing too high a priority on political expediency. Taft is pictured in Portland, Oregon in 1909 after having addressed Portland school children. *Library of Congress*

sues, standing confidently above the various competing interests in society as an intensely moral referee with a quick whistle. He blew it on monopolistic or arrogant holding companies, and gained the favorable label of "trust-buster." He also supported consumer legislation (the Pure Food and Drug Acts) and a drastic extension of Interstate Commerce Commission (ICC) regulation of railroads. Yet, he permitted mergers that he believed to be in the public interest, and found friends and fervent political support among "enlightened," nonvulgar, and nongrasping corporate leaders. Roosevelt helped spur the shift toward corporate respectability, and accepted large, collective production units under centralized management as inevitable. The task was to keep them honest.

Roosevelt tried to be fair to all sectors of the economy. In a famous 1902 coal strike, he intervened in behalf of the miners and horrified the mine owners, not as an expression of any favoritism to unions (they could be as self-serving as corporations), but in behalf of equity. A lover of the outdoors and forests, Roosevelt popularized conservation, moving millions of acres into national forest and mineral reserves to insure a balanced and rational harvesting. To aid farmers, he called a famous Country Life Conference in 1908 that practically initiated the serious study of rural sociology. As much as anyone of his day, Roosevelt revealed a fervent commitment to our existing institutions, including the new corporate system, but also an equally fervent desire to use governmental power to refurbish them, supervise them, and thus make them function effectively.

In 1909 Roosevelt turned his whistle over to his chosen successor, William Howard Taft, and took off for a much publicized game hunt in Africa. Taft, fat, affable, conscientious, let the game get out of control. He did not have the force of personality or the energy to dominate party leaders in Congress, or the flair needed to win public sympathy. Taft blew the whistle more often and more effectively on business combinations than had Roosevelt, yet, after a mild compromise, he signed and lamely defended one of the most controversial, privilege-reeking tariff

ELECTION OF 1908

		Electoral Vote	Popular Vote
☐	Taft (R)	321	7,679,006
■	Bryan (D)	162	6,409,106

bills in our history. The debate on the Payne-Aldrich tariff had immense political significance, for it split the Republican party and almost assured a Democratic victory in 1912. A group of Republican insurgents, mostly from the Midwest, led a detailed, embarrassing, but largely unsuccessful item by item fight against the new tariff schedules, revealing the collusion between corporate interests and obliging, usually Republican congressmen. Taft even seemed to betray the sacred cow of conservation in a legally correct but misunderstood handling of a complex policy struggle within the Department of the Interior.

The insurgents, led by Robert La Follette of Wisconsin, planned to take over the Republican party in 1912. Roosevelt came home and dramatically "threw his hat into the ring." But even his prestige was not sufficient to unseat Taft and the party regulars at the Republican convention. The mavericks convened their own "Progressive" convention, nominated Roosevelt, and went out to do battle with all the fervor of religious crusaders.

The Wilson Administration

The Democratic party, with victory virtually assured in 1912, floundered in a prolonged effort to choose a candidate. The compromise choice, Governor Woodrow Wilson of New Jersey and formerly president of Princeton University, was a man of commanding eloquence and exceptional moral fervor. He gained political prominence for his political integrity in New Jersey, where he bearded the very political bosses who picked him as governor. Like Roosevelt, he had long espoused strong executive leadership and governmental ascendancy over all special interests. For the imperceptive, his promise of a "New Freedom" seemed almost indistinct from Roosevelt's call for a "New Nationalism." Taft, stuck with the stalwarts of his party, had to defend an unpopular record and despairingly avow his own "progressive" credentials. To further confuse one of

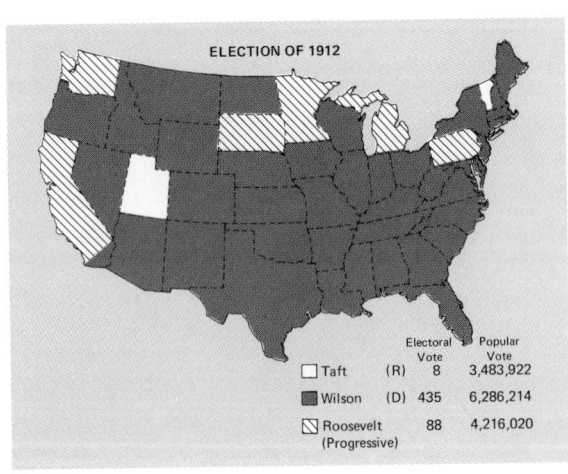

ELECTION OF 1912

		Electoral Vote	Popular Vote
☐ Taft	(R)	8	3,483,922
■ Wilson	(D)	435	6,286,214
◩ Roosevelt (Progressive)		88	4,216,020

EVINRUDE

Summer Vacations that Never End

Those who own an "Evinrude" Detachable Rowboat Motor enjoy endless vacations for they carry their "Evinrude" with them wherever they go. It clamps to the stern of any rowboat, yours or a rented one, and makes an eight-mile-an-hour motorboat. These features are found only in the "Evinrude:"

The Only Portable Motor with a Built-In Reversible Magneto
The Evinrude Magneto is built within the fly-wheel and therefore protected from injury. It has no brushes, bearings or commutators and is not effected by rain, waves or even complete submersion.

The Only Portable Motor which does not require a Rudder
The propeller steers freely in either direction and there is no rudder to become entangled in the weeds, fouled or damaged by rocks and driftwood. The propeller turns the boat within its own length.

The Only Portable Motor Equipped with a Maxim Silencer
We can now supply Maxim Silencers for 1913 and 1914 "Evinrude". The Silencer eliminates practically all noises. No similar motor can use the Maxim Silencer as it is an exclusive "Evinrude" feature.

The Only Portable Motor with a Compensating Steering Device
The tiller is controlled by a shock absorbing, Compensating Device which allows it free range in either direction and permits steering without the exertion of strength which is necessary with a rudder.

It is on sale at Sporting Goods and Hardware Dealers Everywhere. Have you seen it?

EVINRUDE MAGNETO MOTOR, 2 H. P. . . . . . . $80.00   EVINRUDE BATTERY MOTOR, 2 H. P. $70.00
ILLUSTRATED CATALOG SENT FREE ON REQUEST

EVINRUDE MOTOR COMPANY, 256 F STREET, MILWAUKEE, WISCONSIN

An advertisement from the humor magazine *Life*, 1914 that uses one of the same advertising techniques that is popular today—sex appeal. *Library of Congress*

the most significant political campaigns in our history (it offered more realistic alternatives than most), a growing Socialist party, led by a charismatic Eugene Debs, gained 6 percent of the vote and seemed to be making a successful bid for major party status after significant achievements in Milwaukee and in a few cities in New England. But only Debs's leadership held together a variously splintered coalition of factions, which later shattered over the issue of intervention in World War I.

Wilson's New Freedom speeches, delivered so forcibly by the former history professor and son of a Presbyterian minister, constituted a seminar on the undying principles of American government. Much more than Roosevelt, Wilson feared the new corporate society. It had matured on the foundations of special privilege, and he doubted that any amount of government discipline could turn industrial trusts into public servants. Free Americans should not have to live under any managerial elite, or even the most benevolent trustees. Such idealism had a traditional ring. Wilson's opposition to high tariffs, his sincere deference to state rights and localism, and his emphasis upon restored justice rather than governmental paternalism, helped to appease the South and to unify disparate elements in the party. It also pleased farmers and small businessmen, whom Wilson eulogized. His enmity to monopoly joined that of Roosevelt, but he sensed monopolistic tendencies in all large, market-dominating corporations and wanted no working partnership between government and large enterprise, no foreclosed opportunities for individual entrepreneurs or small corporations. With his usual eloquence he insisted that "the strong should not prevent the weak from entering the race. America stands for opportunity. America stands for a free field and no favor. America stands for a government responsive to the interests of all." The promise was clear. He favored a restoration of an older America, when the avenues of economic opportunity were open for all, and when a free, competitive market kept everyone honest. His eloquence helped win him an easy victory over Roosevelt, with Taft finishing third in the popular vote.

Events forced Wilson to make endless compromises in his professed goals. He began his administration with the two best symbols of a new freedom—tariff reduction and stronger antitrust legislation. He proved to be a brilliant legislative technician, using a public exposure of intense corporate lobbying to intimidate protariff congressmen. The resulting Underwood-Simmons Act lowered tariff rates for the first time since the Civil War, and thus eliminated a considerable tax on American consumers. In the same act, Congress approved a small income tax as an alternate revenue source (the states ratified the enabling amendment, the Sixteenth, in 1913). But only World War I made clear the enormous potential of income taxes. Wilson achieved less in antitrust action. The Clayton Act, an amendment of the older Sherman Act, broadened the definition of "restraint of trade" to encompass forms of interlocking directorates (the same person on several boards of directors). The change was minor, while a separate section designed to protect labor unions from in-

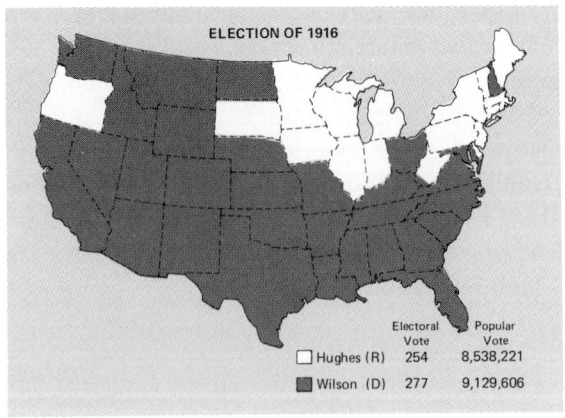

ELECTION OF 1916

	Electoral Vote	Popular Vote
☐ Hughes (R)	254	8,538,221
■ Wilson (D)	277	9,129,606

junctive action under the antitrust laws proved ineffective. Instead of the promised war against bigness, which rural congressmen still demanded, Wilson tried more stringent regulation and, in effect, adopted Roosevelt's strategy. Congress created a new Federal Trade Commission (FTC) as the second major regulatory agency of the federal government (the ICC was first). Empowered to police interstate business enterprise, the FTC could investigate unfair trade practices and issue cease and desist orders, but Wilson did not use it for any rigorous control over corporations. By 1914, beleaguered by a recession, he proclaimed the achievement of his New Freedom. Yet, his commitment to freedom and his antipathy to special interest legislation restrained him in other areas. Only the political pressures of the 1916 election forced his support for minor but innovative labor legislation—one measure gave federal protection to seamen, another set hour regulations for railroad crews, and a third, later voided by the courts, prohibited several types of child labor.

The major legislative achievement of the Wilson administration—the Federal Reserve System—was too complex to exemplify any one reform strategy, such as regulated bigness or restored competition. Even the roots of new banking legislation lay in different directions. A banking panic in 1907 stimulated a minor banking act, and led to extensive investigations by a National Monetary Commission. From a strictly economic perspective, the difficulty seemed to be the lack of a central bank, of coordinated credit policies, and of a flexible currency system. But to Wilson the key problem was a near banking monopoly by a few large, New York-based banking houses, symbolized by the empires of J. P. Morgan and John D. Rockefeller. Wilson wanted to break their power over a family of credit-

The millionaire and banker, John Pierpont Morgan (1837–1913), became the American symbol of wealth, arrogance, and control. He is, perhaps, best known for his railroad reorganization and his formation of the United States Steel Corporation in 1901. *Library of Congress*

dependent corporations. The resulting Federal Reserve Act was a clever compromise of many contending views, an artful hybrid of centralized versus decentralized, governmental versus private control.

Twelve regional reserve banks, owned jointly by private bankers and the federal government, carried out the work of the new system, effectively breaking the monopoly of New York City. These twelve operating banks were under the loose control of a Federal Reserve Board in Washington. Each reserve bank served member banks in its region, providing a source of credit and such vital services as check clearing (used also by nonmember banks). All nationally chartered banks had to join the system. Only the reserve banks could now issue bank notes. These notes were legal tender and continue to make up most of our circulating currency. In effect, the supply of notes expanded to meet credit demand, limited only by the categories of paper (debt instruments, such as notes and mortgages) that they could discount (accept and hold as security for loans to banks) and by the legally established percentage of gold that each reserve bank had to hold as reserves. The eligible paper included types of agricultural loans and thus met a demand of farmers for easier credit, while the flexible note issues satisfied their long-standing demand for an increase in the monetary supply. Finally, the twelve regional banks had one important control over the use of credit, and thus over the level of economic activity in the whole society. They could change their rediscount rates (the interest they charged member banks for loans), thus largely determining the interest rates for private borrowers whenever local banks had to discount paper in order to expand their loans and profits, or in times of high credit demand.

The stream of domestic legislation that began with Roosevelt and climaxed with Wilson's first term never resolved a critical policy issue—how government would accommodate itself to large corporate enterprise. Regulation still vied with antitrust efforts, and both competed with the yet powerful belief that the federal government should do nothing at all in the economic sphere. Also, the adopted strategies completely bypassed other reform goals voiced by minorities unable to gain any political leverage. For example, socialists repudiated either a return to small economic units and fair competition, or attempts at regulation by any government committed to corporate capitalism and vulnerable to the overweening political power of entrenched wealth. The long-range socialist goal—government ownership of all major industries—was so radical that socialist candidates rarely campaigned for much more than a beginning on this path.

Another vague goal remained only a minor chord in the period before World War I. Its adherents also laid a claim to the label "progressive."

From the settlement house movement, from social workers, from a few academics, and from several socially concerned ministers came a demand for special governmental favors to the poor and exploited. In a society permeated by privilege, why not give a few more to the weak and helpless? Those who thought along these lines represented the earliest proponents of a welfare state, and often gained inspiration from the social welfare schemes of Europe. They organized a lobbying organization to promote a broad form of social insurance in America, but achieved success only in the minor area of workmen's compensation. Their efforts continued until the enactment of social security in 1935. The same reformers supported class legislation, such as laws regulating the hours worked by women, and also tried to upgrade the forms of charity traditionally dispensed to the poor, the aged, and the disabled. Implicit in their early crusade was a belief that an impersonal, urban-centered industrial

One perennial reform goal in America had been women's suffrage. As early as the 1840's a small group of women argued that they should have the right to vote. By 1912, when this picture was taken, suffrage had become an election issue. It was not until 1919, however, that the states ratified the Nineteenth Amendment, which granted women the vote. *Library of Congress*

society created many types of unmerited insecurity, and that society as a whole should assume responsibility for alleviating it.

For the politically concerned American Negro, the easy celebration of progress and reform must have seemed a cruel mockery. In the South the very architects of a so-called progressive society, of dramatic improvements in education, in the regulation of business, and in agricultural techniques, always concurred in, and often led, efforts to achieve a "great race settlement." This meant the segregation of all public facilities and a near blanket disenfranchisement of blacks, under several more than clever devices that met loose court interpretations of the Fifteenth Amendment. Roosevelt gained Negro favor by a few daring appointments of Negroes and by a highly publicized, and almost universally condemned, luncheon meeting with the reigning ambassador of the Negroes to white America, Booker T. Washington. Later, as the Progressive candidate, Roosevelt followed a well-established Republican pattern—a "lily white" policy in exchange for southern support. Even the Socialist party, despite its ideology of racial equality, practically ignored the Negro and condoned separate black units in the South.

Woodrow Wilson, although not personally hostile to blacks, still reflected his southern background and its racial beliefs. He did not conceive of social equality. He also brought a large group of white Southerners

A class in algebra at Tuskegee Institute, a black industrial school in Alabama headed by Booker T. Washington (1856–1915). Washington believed that blacks should be educated in good manners and in the trades, so schools like Tuskegee prepared them for agriculture, domestic service, and lower-paid factory jobs—the only ones open to them at that time. *Underwood & Underwood*

into the federal bureaucracy. With his seeming complicity, most federal agencies adopted a rigid segregation policy, all the way down to separate black and white toilets. Separation, in many cases, paralleled sincere if paternal efforts to improve black schools. It lessened conflict, opened new avenues of white benevolence, and accompanied considerable economic gains even by southern blacks, particularly in moving up from tenancy to farm ownership. Blacks, themselves, divided sharply on political strategy if not on the eventual goal of complete equality. Booker T. Washington, a masterful schemer and politician, believed it expedient for blacks to accept limited social goals, and at least temporary racial separation, in order to gain the economic improvements that would mean political power. But the youthful W. E. B. DuBois, a brilliant, ultrasensitive son of affluent Negro parents, with his Ph.D. from Harvard, would accept nothing but full equality. He was one of the founders, in 1909, of the National Association for the Advancement of Colored People, which was for the next forty years the main instrument of black efforts to attain legal equality.

Because of the exigencies of war, Wilson accepted a degree of national economic direction and control never even dreamed of by Theodore Roosevelt. The fervor and almost hysterical patriotism of World War 1

War and Reform

W.E.B. DuBois (1868–1963) eventually adopted different tactics than Booker T. Washington. He became a militant on the subject of equal rights and a radical in politics. For over fifty years he was the nation's leading black intellectual. DuBois ultimately became an expatriate in Africa. *Library of Congress*

eroded most of the traditional fears of a large and expensive government. For those who admired the new order, the result seemed to be a wonderful example of a unified people sacrificing local and selfish goals in behalf of one clear, national purpose. As never before, the national interest prevailed over all competing private interests. But what beguiled some only galled others, and by war's end many of the controlling agencies were so bitterly resented that Congress rushed to disband them.

The ultimate coercion was the draft. For the first time in American history, young men had to serve in the armed forces without qualification (in the Civil War one could buy replacements). Even conscientious objectors donned a uniform and performed noncombat duties or went to jail, usually for ninety-nine-year terms (commuted after the war). The government also took over full control of the railroads, operating them in behalf of the war effort. Less direct coercion included the use of suasion and bribes by federal administrators to get producers to meet governmental quotas. The major directive agency, the War Industries Board, under the forceful direction of financier Bernard Baruch, won voluntary compliance for its detailed controls over what corporations produced, over resource allocation, and indirectly over many prices. This eliminated needless duplication and wasteful competition. In return for such a loss of managerial leeway, the corporations could expand plant facilities and earn large profits. Herbert Hoover, as head of a Food Administration, used many of the same tactics with farmers, enticing expanded food production through guaranteed prices and using the food to feed a devastated Europe in 1919. Other agencies—for fuel, transportation, shipping, and labor—tried with mixed results to coordinate specific economic activities, all in behalf of an early victory.

The war experience had its obvious lessons. Under the artificial stimulus of war, most Americans had worked together for a common cause. For a time, the older fears of class conflict abated. This happened under a new and frightening economic strategy: the president and Congress determined the long-range goal of victory; government experts and bureaucrats worked out the specific economic priorities, and then imposed those upon private producers. Instead of contending interest groups (farmers versus manufacturers, labor versus management), and an ever more powerful group of private collectivities (the corporations), the national economy functioned very much as a single, coordinated unit. It revealed in two brief years an undreamed of productive potential, even as it made suggestive innovations in such areas as wartime housing and shipbuilding. Such federal direction threatened individual initiative and a voluntary market approach to economic decision making, but it may have insured a larger economic return and possibly a higher level of social justice for the vast majority. It promised great grief only to the uncooperative, to the courageous conscientious objector who "refused to do his part" or the corporation president who refused to accept federally imposed priorities.

As a partial and incomplete experiment, the war illustrated the benefits and the pitfalls of a centrally planned economic system. The government made the most basic managerial decisions but left legal ownership in private hands and permitted a large degree of private management within the overall priorities. While short of the socialist demand for government ownership, yet it was much more than the regulatory state advocated by Roosevelt, for the government went beyond rules to the most critical decision of all—who produces what. Herbert Croly, in his influential book, *The Promise of American Life*, had already advocated such a consolidated economy. In the twenties he and his disciples espoused economic planning in an influential journal of opinion, the *New Republic*. They would have marginal influence upon the New Deal. But even the planners disagreed on details. The general idea lent itself to the ultranationalism of Mussolini in Italy, to forms of technocracy, or to the brilliantly defended group democracy heralded by America's most eminent philosopher, John Dewey. But in each case the planners looked back to World War I as a brief, golden age in an otherwise dismal history of a country torn and splintered by selfish interests.

From War to Depression

pansion, a European type of colonialism. This led to a small empire—
the Philippines, Cuba and Puerto Rico, and a protectorate over the states
of the Caribbean. The highly successful and gratifying war with Spain
seemed to foretell a new approach to American foreign policy—we
would belatedly join France and England in an effort to gain either colonies or protected spheres of influence around the world. By and large,
Republicans, best typified by Theodore Roosevelt, supported this policy.
A majority of Democrats, led by William Jennings Bryan, the three-time
contender for the presidency, opposed it and referred to themselves as
anti-imperialists.

When elected in 1912, Wilson had more emphatic commitments in domestic than in foreign policy, but he selected Bryan as his secretary of
state and easily adopted the moral imperatives that lay behind anti-imperi-
alism. In fact, in Mexico and the West Indies, he found it difficult to live
up to these imperatives, or even translate them into policies. And, much

The ardent socialist, Eugene V. Debs (1855–1926), was one of Wilson's
most outspoken critics on the subject of entering the war. Between 1900
and 1920 Debs made five unsuccessful bids for the presidency as the candidate of the American Socialist party. He is seen here speaking at a labor
convention in 1910. *Library of Congress*

more than he realized, the two sides were not that far apart. Although Republican in origin, the open door policy for China, based on existing realities and opportunities, bypassed classic colonialism in behalf of territorial integrity and commercial equality for the United States. Our commercial dreams required new strategies, and the open door nicely blended idealism and self-interest.

Wilson judged nations much as he judged individuals—he expected a high level of responsibility and exemplary behavior. He found the world full of people who easily rejected these standards; of selfish states that used power to gain their own myopic ends. The ideal answer for wayward individuals was a demanding social order, with lawful obligations and legally protected individual rights. The ideal answer for the world of nations was likewise a constitutional order, and a willingness on the part of nations to act cooperatively, in concert, in behalf of the greatest realized benefits for all, for peace, profitable trade in goods and ideas, and wide areas of freedom for individuals. Wilson desired constitutional, multiparty, popular governments for all nations, or a political system he called "democratic."

With war in Europe in 1914, Wilson asked for American neutrality. He wanted to use his agencies to restore peace and a world order less conducive to conflict. He reflected a widespread and highly traditional American belief—that most European governments were callous or corrupt or even sinful. The governments in Germany, Austria, and Russia were autocratic. Militarism flourished in Germany and to an extent in France. European politicians had long schemed and plotted secret alliances, or unholy bargains involving other peoples and other lands. Selfish, grasping, they refused to cooperate in developing the colonial world and continuously scrambled for special advantages.

Despite this distaste, Wilson eventually chose sides, although not completely. He asked for war against one side in an unholy war, and often included France and Britain in his idealistic hopes for a world finally beyond war. He believed the Allies less guilty than the Central Powers, but not guiltless. And in the heat of war, he tried to be fair and what he believed to be generous toward Germany, hoping always to ease her into an armistice and cooperative participation in a postwar league of nations after due penance and an exorcism of autocratic government, militarism, and all expansionist goals.

Wilson demanded for America all the traditional rights of a neutral nation, including the right to trade with both sides. He also demanded a rigorous adherence to a body of custom somewhat optimistically called international law. But these policies, traditional and easily accepted by Americans, in effect aided the Allies. Most of our trade would be with

France and England, both because of traditional lines of commerce and effective Allied blockades of Central Power ports. Our insistence on full commercial freedom allowed us to send valuable material to the Allied armies. Because of British superiority in surface ships, Germany could effectively counter the blockade only by using a relatively new weapon, the submarine, which depended on surprise and had little room for survivors. Thus, it could not operate effectively under the traditional rules of war, which required warnings and evacuation of personnel from merchant ships. The unique imperatives of submarine warfare eventually created the occasion for American involvement. But this involvement also reflected developing policies both in Germany and the United States,

DUSTING OFF THE OLD PROPS.

This 1915 cartoon depicts William Jennings Bryan (1860–1925) getting ready to go out and fight for yet another cause—American neutrality. As Wilson's secretary of state, he tried to keep the U.S. out of the war, but finally resigned because he disagreed with Wilson's policies after the sinking of the *Lusitania*. *Library of Congress*

The sinking of the *Lusi-
tania* on May 7, 1915 by
a German submarine pro-
voked the first major
American confrontation
with Germany. Although
the Germans did warn
people not to get on the
ship, many Americans
sailed anyway, believing
that a passenger ship
would not be attacked.
The ship, however, car-
ried both arms and am-
munition. *Library of
Congress*

policies tremendously influenced by clever British propaganda and diplomacy.

Britain violated Wilson's conception of neutral rights as often as Germany, but usually without loss of life and almost always with effective
diplomatic apologies. Britain diverted and searched our ships, confiscated
mail and cargo, and even blacklisted American corporations that traded
with Germany. The United States protested each violation. Meanwhile,
German submarines tried to isolate Britain by sinking all Atlantic merchant ships delivering needed supplies. Germany proclaimed a war zone
around Britain and made all British merchantmen targets, and warned
that neutral ships could be misidentified. As early as April 1915, an American went down on a British ship.

On May 1, 1915, a German submarine sank the British luxury liner, *Lusitania*, which we now know was an armed passenger ship loaded with war
cargo (Wilson concealed such facts from the public). Among the hundreds
of dead were 128 Americans. Even though Germany had warned prospective passengers, the sinking shocked Americans. Ultranationalists such as
Theodore Roosevelt demanded war. But Secretary Bryan believed we had
erred in allowing passengers on a belligerent ship, and backed efforts to
find a peaceful compromise. Complicated negotiations, punctuated with
other less shocking sinkings, ended in an informal German concession in
May 1916. Her submarines would henceforth try to obey the "rules of
war," including a search of unarmed merchantmen before sinking. For al-

most nine months this agreement held, providing an interlude for intensified peace efforts by several Americans.

During the winter of 1916–1917, Germany seemed close to victory. She had new offensives planned in France. The Russian front was in a shambles. Attempts at negotiation had failed. Germany then made a calculated decision—to wage total war in behalf of an early victory. In January 1917, Germany resumed unrestricted submarine warfare, which posed a direct challenge to a proud Wilson, already bitter at his failure to mediate a settlement. Beleaguered by nationalists and interventionists, he had already broken with leading neutralists (Bryan left the cabinet after the *Lusitania* affair) and had come close to accusing German-Americans of a lack of patriotism. He had also prepared America for war, through military preparations, a careful orchestration of news, and the exploitation of events, or the strategy of any administration seeking public support for a major departure in foreign policy. Past accusations of German atrocities, expertly exploited by British propagandists, helped create a clear partiality to the Allied cause. An intercepted message to the German minister in Mexico (the Zimmerman note) was especially helpful. In case of war with the United States, the envoy in Mexico City was to invite Mexico to join the Central Powers. He was to exploit the intense Mexican antipathy to the United States in the immediate wake of armed American excursions into Mexico (in 1916) and over a decade of intervention in her domestic affairs. The strategy, although an obvious one, horrified Americans. Then, on March 18, German subs sank three American ships. The gauntlet was down. Wilson spoke of honor and pride, lamented the inevitable cost, but asked Congress to declare war.

The submarine issue was only one condition for war, and far from sufficient. To speak of causes usually involves an historian in ambiguities; proximate events, underlying motives, practical considerations, and even well-developed habits often serve as causes in different contexts. Without the new submarine offensive, Wilson would not have requested a declaration of war. And it was not his decision alone. Congress gave its assent, and in many ways a whole nation went to war, gladly for the most part. Millions of people had diverse motives for supporting war, even as a minority had strong reasons for opposing it. The numerical preponderance on the side of war heightened the enthusiasm; the vocal opposition helped turn the enthusiasm into a frenzied crusade for conformity and loyalty.

Close institutional and cultural ties with the Allies swayed many interventionists. The March revolution of 1917 in Russia allowed Wilson and others to make a more persuasive moral distinction between the contending sides—one clearly represented autocracy and militarism, the other "democracy." Since our commercial opportunities and private war loans were all with the Allies, their defeat would have meant a great economic loss to Americans. Although he opposed German Americans, Wilson had great sympathy for Slavic Americans and gladly worked for their "liberation" in Eastern Europe, even as he easily overlooked Allied colonialism in Africa and Asia. And so the list grows.

Never had a country entered a war with such a strange body of rationalizations (the term is not a derisive one, for the reasons given were cogent and sincere). To Wilson, the United States was an innocent and threatened outsider now able to bring new-world rectitude to the relief of a corrupted old world. We were not only foes of the Central Powers but also of the whole continental political system, which Germany most and England least exemplified. America would stand above the petty and selfish bargains, the greedy aspirations of European states, and fulfill a peculiar mission because of our lofty impartiality and superiority. We entered the war, said Wilson, without a selfish desire, with no demands for any territory, any payments, any special advantages. All we sought was a just settlement and a new world order that would prevent the recurrence of such wars and all the suffering they entailed. We were the agents, almost it seemed divine agents, of peace and justice, the last great hope for mankind, as we fought "to make the world safe for democracy."

Today, most of us are too cynical to accept Wilson's idealism as other than a camouflage for some ulterior designs. It was not that, although some critical analysis places the idealism in a less innocent context. Wilson was a moral man—that is, on all issues he wanted to embrace a moral dimension, calculate what was right and wrong in the situation. He reflected the intense moral seriousness of his parents and of other Calvinists. But Calvinists are not alone moral. Surely most Americans were in the same position as Wilson; they too wanted righteousness in all areas of policy, including foreign policy.

Wilson was neither a diplomatic innocent nor a fool. As president he wanted to serve the best interests of his country, and in fact had a constitutional obligation to do just that. In the context of world politics, he simply believed righteousness and national interest coincided. Contrary to the intense nationalists who wanted us to play the game of power politics, he believed our long-range national interest was identical with that of all the peoples of the world—a legal, constitutional, peaceful world order. He was quite aware that our interests in the larger world were in large part economic, or profitable trade and investment. Unlike more recent moralists, he found nothing sinister in this. A godly merchant really can enter the heavenly city. Wilson hated monopoly, a foreclosing of economic opportunity. He wanted fair competition. Talent and virtue could win in such a fair contest. At home he tried, despite necessary compromises, to keep the economy open. Abroad he wanted to lower trade barriers, insure freedom of the seas, settle colonial claims by arbitration and with due regard for colonial peoples (because of his belief in their racial or cultural inferiority, he did not envision early and complete independence for all colonial people).

Wilson wanted American businessmen to compete in foreign trade, to seek markets and profits, but to do so fairly and without any special privileges. In its worst manifestations, colonialism gave foreign countries just such a special advantage. He believed American businessmen had much to offer the world—better and cheaper materials and products, a high ethical standard in commerce, and first-hand acquaintance with our free economy and our superior political institutions. One can make this position seem hypocritical. After all, our immense resources, and the tremendous addition of wealth and competitive advantage assured by the war itself, meant that Wilson's orderly and open world best insured our own continued prosperity and security. We had no fear of our ability to compete, only of our chance to compete. But what options do a cynical reading of his motives suggest? Surely not a president turning away from national interest and espousing a world that, in some ways, worked to our national disadvantage. His most vocal critics certainly did not challenge his support of pro-American policies, but only the adequacy of his means or the arrogance of his moralistic rhetoric. The one exception was a few American socialists, who wanted to destroy the existing political and economic systems in behalf of revolutionary changes in all Western countries.

One could allege that Wilson indulged fantasy and illusion. Maybe a dream of marrying power and morality always expires sooner or later in the hard realities of international politics, or succumbs to one or another of the old litany of pitfalls—human nature, original sin, demonic fate. Surely these always manage to turn idealism into ashes. Power and morals do not fit together. Power always corrupts. This seems to suggest that to be moral one must remain futile. But Wilson was a Calvinist. To be moral always entailed to him the righteous use of power, not a retreat from the battlefield. He wanted to implement as well as celebrate his political and economic ideals. This is why his commitment to the war did involve a sacrificial element and a bit of missionary zeal. It was our destiny to save the world.

Wilson knew the perils of war. He predicted a horrendous cost— intolerance, coercion, economic dislocation, and, saddest of all, the innocent boys who would have to die. These costs surely bore on his mind.

His unending stress on the good that would come from it all, the almost apocalyptic celebration of a new era aborning, alone assuaged his guilt, redeemed all the brutality. From ancient Israel to the present, rulers and peoples have tried to find an ideal vindication for their national goals and exertions, using them to rise above the mundane level of mere interest or selfish desires, to humanize politics and take it away from the jungle. But the problem has always been to live up to the ideals, to realize the most lofty visions. Only in this is there redemption. And in this Wilson ultimately failed, and knew that he failed. He did not secure the world order he celebrated. But he always believed that he had been right in his choices, and that other people had failed him. He died with this consolation.

Behind the scenes in France, September 29, 1918. World War I was an extremely destructive war, in the loss of both property and human life. Here soldiers of the 3rd Division march through the ruins of a small French village. *Library of Congress*

The Price of Victory

Apart from the tragic aspects of Wilson's frustrated hopes for redemption in a future league, the war was a roaring success for the United States. It was also a lot of fun for many Americans. In an economic sense, we had won the war even before we joined it. The profits accrued to America.

By joining, we brought the war to an earlier close, saved Europe from greater destruction and most likely from major revolution. We also preserved Europe and the parts of the world it controlled for continued American intercourse of a profitable sort. We would even profit from its reconstruction. Before 1917 we had become creditor to the Allied governments, and during the war we increased our near monopoly on hard currency. Our economy soon boomed from war-related purchases. Private individuals received high interest rates on Allied bonds. By war's end the United States was clearly the most powerful country in the world. And at what cost? In comparison to European nations, very little. We suffered no domestic destruction, but instead built up our capital resources at an unprecedented pace. We primarily provisioned foreign troops, and even after we joined the war we did this, not by gifts, but by credit. This we would hold as a postwar asset and insist upon early repayment. We came to the rescue of Europe and had no war booty to vindicate our efforts. And contracts are contracts.

But there was a financial and human cost which only slowly became apparent. War bond drives became patriotic orgies. Doughboys marched off as blissfully as they had in 1898. Never had people felt so American,

Although this fighter plane seems primitive, the Great War used very modern fighting techniques— poison gas, submarines, and, toward the end of the war, the airplane. *Library of Congress*

so caught up in a grand crusade. For many, life took on new meaning and purpose. We mobilized efficiently. We drafted young men, carefully orchestrated propaganda, enlisted academics and intellectuals to provide much of the promotional literature. The war cost about $33,000,000,000, or what seemed an astronomical figure in 1918. Income, excise, and estate taxes, although low by present standards, seemed shockingly high.

Until the spring of 1918 American troops provided backup support for the veteran British and French divisions. In the spring selected American units moved into the lines, and by war's end had taken over a major sector of the front. American divisions participated fully, and successfully, in the final offensive that preceded the armistice of November 11. American boys experienced the rigor of trench warfare and the terror of poison gas. We lost approximately 100,000 men, many from nonmilitary causes. This was a token loss in comparison to every other major belligerent. In retrospect, America contributed so little for so much gain. Instead of a distant, even if profit-gorged spectator, we went to the peace conference as more than an equal. Wilson, most responsible for the armistice on November 11, would also be the principal architect of the Versailles treaty. Germany had some confidence in him, and chose to turn from the declining fortunes on the battlefield to negotiation. A constitutional revolution and the dethroning of the emperor met Wilson's minimal demands.

The Treaty

The end was the beginning for Wilson, the time for vindication. He had to prove to the doubting, to German Americans, to American socialists, to critical intellectuals, that the war had not been a crass thing, a way of

During the war post cards such as this inspired chauvinism in Americans and helped finance the efforts of volunteer groups. *Library of Congress*

further enriching the wealthy or joining an unholy entente with France and Britain to rule a world now safe from effective competition. Wilson carefully planned the peace. Earlier he summed up his idealism in fourteen famous points (Clemenceau of France grumbled that God had only ten). Five of the more general points reflected the vague aims of most humanitarian supporters of the war—free trade, disarmament, self-determination, freedom of the seas, and an end to secret alliances. Eight, more concrete and more perilous in detail, related self-determination to various countries or nationalities. The last point expressed Wilson's grandest goal, a league of nations to insure both collective security and the implementation of all the other points.

The stereotype of an innocent Wilson going to Versailles to do battle with the wolves and losing everything is absurd. Wilson went to Europe with unprecedented prestige, virtually as a conquering hero, and took with him a staff unprecedented in size and ability. He had superb intelligence briefing and the results of endless academic inquiries that encompassed almost every conceivable problem and every area of the world. No delegation was ever better prepared. On factual issues the American delegation often provided needed information for European negotiators. And Wilson was not innocent. Despite misleading public statements, he knew most of the specific commitments that the European Allies had made to each other, the spoils that they expected. Wilson fought skillfully, even petulantly, for all he could gain. Despite all the compromises—this is what negotiation is all about—he gained as much in the bargaining as anyone else. Yet, the end result was disillusioning when contrasted to all his hopes. He had to moderate his idea of freedom of the seas in deference to England, postpone tariff and armament reductions until later conferences, and deal with colonial claims under a transparent mandate system that, in effect, permitted France and Britain to collect their German spoils in Africa. Drawing national boundaries in Eastern Europe proved divisive. Two of the Allies, Japan and Italy, felt cheated by the paucity of their spoils.

France, and to an extent England, did not share Wilson's vision of an open world. Both countries wanted to enlist the United States in an enduring system of Allied hegemony. The conflict of goals met head on in the case of Germany. Wilson was ambivalent toward Germany. He wanted to punish the country, cleanse it of its old leadership, its military proclivities, its aggressive aims toward central Europe. He reflected some of the wartime propaganda, the image of Germany as a renegade among nations. But after the deserved cleansing he hoped Germany would become an equal member of the League of Nations. France, much more vindictive, wanted to cripple Germany by taking away much of her territory and by assessing a huge reparations bill. Wilson moderated French demands, at one point by a threat to quit the conference. But the verdict was still harsh. Germany lost territory and German-speaking people to a restored Poland and a new Czechoslovakia, gave Alsace-Lorraine to France, accepted league supervision of the Saar for fifteen years, and lost all rights to maintain military forces in the rich industrial heart of Germany, the Rhineland. She could maintain only a token military force, and had to accept a clause that attributed full guilt for the war to the Central Powers. France even demanded up to $120,000,000,000 in reparations, although the exact figure was left for later determination (it would be much less). The harsh terms shocked and embittered Germans, lost Wilson all the respect he had earlier gained, and created the psychological conditions for renewed hostilities. Yet, even France and Britain were unhappy with the truce terms. They wanted more security from a revived Germany, disliked Wilson's righteousness, and despaired at his unwillingness to join them in a pact of victors.

The Germany settlement left a complicated economic situation for the twenties. The United States accepted the burden of critical food relief at war's end, but did not offer to rehabilitate Europe. There was no Marshall Plan. We asked repayment of Allied war debts. They in turn expected to cover these with reparations from Germany. Private American investment would underwrite German recovery after a near disaster early in the decade. This recovery allowed a scaled payment of reparations to the Allies and of war debts to the United States. But instability remained. We had the gold and the soundest currency, but such a privileged position actually threatened us. We had to sell as well as buy, and thus maintain some balance in international payments. Lacking balanced economies, the war-scarred countries of Europe became dependent on American fiscal policies and vulnerable to any diminution of American credit or any rapid liquidation of existing loans. The American stock market crash of 1929 slowed the loans and forced the recall of others. The European economy collapsed in 1931 and helped push the United States into deep depression.

The Russian Revolution

One final circumstance very much conditioned the controversies at Versailles—the November revolution of 1917 in Russia, which led to the formation of the Soviet Union. This was, for Wilson and for many leaders in the West, the most disillusioning and threatening development of the war. In March 1917, the first Russian revolution led to the Kerenski government, which seemed comparable to Western parliamentary systems, with a constitution, one elected assembly, multiple parties, and protection of individual rights. Wilson exulted, and Americans never loved the Russian people more than in their moment of victory over czarist tyranny. This accounted for the intense disappointment at the Bolshevik victory in the fall, at the termination of the constituent assembly in early 1918, and at the first large official purges after a threat to Lenin's life. Early attempts to alleviate the harshness of the new regime, and also to get Russia back into the war, gave way by the end of 1918 to open opposition to the Bolshevik government. To Wilson, it seemed a new form of barbarism, a dictatorship of a few people, a threat to personal freedom and legitimate property, a denial of a government of law. The new regime also seemed an international rogue, exporting its form of revolution to other countries and finding a broad following in the war-torn countries of Europe—temporary communist rule in Hungary, near takeover in Germany, and strong Communist parties in most of Eastern Europe.

In the perspective of time, we know that the "Bolsheviks" changed the whole contour of international relations. Their hatred of the Western state system and of existing economic arrangements, their desire for early, apocalyptic revolution to establish a new socialist order, added a new political alternative to the world. Wilson, the apostle of the distant American Revolution, finally close to a conversion of Europe and the world to his form of order and peace, was now, even though he could not recognize it, the advocate of a middle way in the world, a posture that defined what would soon become, in loose jargon, the "Right" and the "Left."

Wilson of course did not recognize the Lenin government; in fact, through 1919 it was not clearly going to prevail. Russia was in turmoil, with large areas controlled by anti-Bolshevik factions of different persuasion. It seemed to Wilson almost inevitable that, sooner or later, the vast majority of Russian people would overthrow the communists and reaffirm a "democratic" order. He frequently and sincerely expressed his sympathy for the Russian people. He wanted to preserve their real revolution, not the new reign of terror. He reflected perhaps a general inability to believe in the possibility of such a radical and extreme alternative to our beliefs and institutions.

Wilson was quite open to democratic socialist parties in Europe, or to Marxist parties that functioned in a constitutional setting and cooperated with other countries. But how assimilate the idea of such an intense, ideological, expansive movement as that in Russia? It seemed a threat to his plan for a league, to commercial cooperation, to orderly government, to law and order in the world. It threatened the very heart of his moral vision—individual opportunity, private property, and civil liberties. Soviet communism also promised to feed on extreme discontent, with the focus then on a devastated Europe. Lenin condemned the exploitation of the underdeveloped world by Western commercial and manufacturing interests, and suggested that the maintenance of the private economies of the West had been possible only because much of the burden of economic growth had been transferred to colonial areas. Again, Wilson could not grasp the range and depth of the Leninist critique. He was too much in love with Western political and economic institutions to want more than a perfecting of them, eliminating their distortions and injustices.

American troops fought in Russia under the disingenuous rationalization that we would not involve ourselves in her internal affairs. In 1918 American troops joined an Allied force in north European Russia, or around Murmansk. During 1919 Wilson withdrew most of these American units, which had helped support a White Russian, anti-Communist regime in the raging civil war. The Allies claimed a military objective —to prevent German penetration and to salvage war materials—but clearly had political goals. Wilson, as much as he wanted to be rid of the "Bolsheviks," rightly feared the effects of intervention, for it only helped rally support for Lenin. He also suspected French-British motives, and found many anti-Bolshevik leaders much too autocratic for his taste. Again, he was squeezed in the middle.

In Siberia the United States intervened in a much more unilateral way. Although it joined with Japan, in part to limit possible Japanese expansion, it contributed a majority of the troops. The episode began in 1918 with Czech soldiers fleeing across Siberia, where they fought against freed German prisoners and Red Army units. Japan asked us to join in aiding them. American and Japanese troops guarded the trans-Siberian railroad, fought against armed brigands, and brought in relief supplies. A White Russian general organized an anti-Communist government in Siberia, and in 1919 advanced toward the West to battle with the Red Army. We did not use our troops in direct support, but in effect secured his rear and offered transportation and economic support. He was not an ideal ally, more of a czarist than a constitutionalist. He also lost. But even before that Wilson began withdrawing American troops. During 1919 he also sent an envoy to Moscow to discuss peace terms, sent a food mission (under Herbert Hoover) to aid the Russian people, and still hoped either for a drastic moderation on the part of Lenin or a return to the "true" revolution of March 1917. In all these hopes he would be disappointed.

**The U.S. and
the League**

Considered as a whole, Wilson's efforts in Europe could only depress him. The League of Nations, dutifully included as a part of the final treaty, alone consoled him and preserved the redemptive possibilities of the war. In form the league paralleled the present United Nations. Its Executive Council had five permanent members (Britain, France, United States, Japan, and Italy) and four elected. Its Body of Delegates included all members, each with one vote. At the Geneva headquarters it had a permanent Secretariat, a Bureau of Labor, and several humanitarian and administrative divisions. Its greatest challenge was to keep peace. Notably, two major powers—Germany and the Soviet Union—were not members, but both would become eligible later by a two-thirds vote of the delegates.

The heart of the League Covenant was Article X, which bound members to protect and preserve against aggression the territory and political independence of all member states. All members pledged to submit disputes to inquiry or to arbitration by a separate but related Permanent Court of International Justice. If worse came to worse, the council could ask members to contribute military forces to uphold its principles. There was no compulsion. In actual fact, the league did not use the sanctions,

REFUSING TO GIVE THE LADY A SEAT.

Wilson's greatest diplomatic goal was ratification of the Treaty of Versailles, which provided for a League of Nations. Although cartoons such as this tried to stir up sympathy for the league, the United States never ratified the covenant. *Library of Congress*

but became more of a forum with some degree of moral suasion over the action of nations. The idea of "collective security" all too easily became a cliché, for different people used it differently. But it sounded good. The nations of the world would join in a pact, mutually commit themselves to nonaggression and disarmament, and join to put down any international immorality by members or nonmembers. This would end the hostilities of the past and provide the effective machinery for peace. No wonder Wilson so desperately clung to this one last chance for peace and for mankind.

He faced his greatest perils at home. Here his pilgrimage ended in personal tragedy. In 1918 the Republicans gained control of the Senate, and thus of the vital Senate Foreign Relations Committee (two-thirds of the Senate have to concur in all treaties, and the League Covenant was part of the Versailles treaty). The chairman of the committee, Henry Cabot Lodge of Massachusetts, was a longtime antagonist of Wilson and, with Roosevelt, had led the old "imperialists" in their opposition to Wilson's brand of idealism. Wilson had proved tactless in the 1918 congressional elections, when he asked for the choice of Democrats in order to insure a successful conclusion of his quest for a new world order, implying a lack of patriotism on the part of Republicans. He gave the Republicans no real voice in the peace negotiations. His prickly personality, his self-righteousness, angered Republicans and made it difficult for him to work with anyone who disagreed with him. Wilson, on the borderline of severe illness throughout his presidency, became even more tense and uncompromising at the end of his European negotiations. The treaty offended ethnic Americans, particularly Italians, Irish, and Germans. Finally, the covenant raised important issues about America's role in the world. Aware of pitfalls, Wilson renegotiated some provisions to clarify the voluntary nature of any military action by member states, and also secured clauses protecting the American position in Latin America (the Monore Doctrine). But even as amended the league appeared to commit the United States to a form of alliance system, and also threatened to diminish the role of Congress in committing American troops.

The early opposition seemed to come from all sides. Many socialists and academic intellectuals who had only reluctantly supported the war now followed the lead of philosopher John Dewey, who saw the league as a tool of the victor and who pleaded for an organization that would represent the people of the world, not governments. Some feared all types of entanglement aboard, and warned that the league committed us to a status quo that favored France and Britain. Old fears of Britain reappeared and shaped some near absurd amendment proposals. But Congress focused on Article X, and on the threat to their own control over mili-

tary commitments. Lodge and his Foreign Relations Committee proposed amendments that gave Congress the power to withdraw from the league and to veto any commitment of troops to defend the territory of another country. These amendments would not have affected the subsequent role of the league as a debating society and mediator (it never had the power to restrain great powers and never used force against small ones), but at the time they seemed to Wilson a direct threat to the whole principle of collective security and a return to an antiquated form of nationalism.

Wilson could have had a modified league. A majority in the Senate wanted it; so did the public according to some less than reliable polls conducted in 1919. Wilson chose to gamble for a virtually unchanged league, and made the issue one of highest principle. By his request, loyal administration Democrats voted against all reservations or fundamental amendments and against any compromise treaty that contained them. Joining them in votes against an amended league were twelve absolutists (led by Senator William E. Borah of Idaho) who opposed American participation in any international organization. Wilson employed an old strategy—a direct appeal to the American people, bypassing their representatives in the Senate. He hoped his superb oratory would persuade Americans of the correctness of his position. To him, a weakened Article

Wilson's last cabinet meeting. In 1919 Wilson suffered a severe stroke, which left him a near invalid. By 1921 he was aware that the United States would never join the League of Nations. He left the presidency embittered and disillusioned, living in retirement until his death in 1924. *Library of Congress*

X threatened the heart of the treaty, while he did not want to return to Europe for additional negotiations. He felt pride of authorship and believed the honor of the United States at stake. Consistent with his belief in the importance of presidential leadership, he denied to the Senate the right to undermine his difficult negotiations abroad.

In order to gain the needed votes, Wilson set forth on a nationwide speaking tour on September 4, 1919. As he spoke in city after city, he sounded like a prophetic Jeremiah of old. "I can predict with absolute certainty that within another generation there will be another world war if the nations of the world do not concert the method by which to prevent it." "If you want to keep your boys at home, you will see that boys elsewhere are kept at home. Because America is not going to refuse, when the other catastrophe comes, again to attempt to save the world, and having given proof once, I pray God we may not be given occasion to prove it again." "The next time will come; it will come while this generation is living, and the children that crowd about our car as we move from station to station will be sacrificed upon the altar of that war."

Wilson collapsed at Pueblo, Colorado on September 25, 1919. Shortly thereafter he suffered a severe stroke, and would never be completely well again. On November 18, as he lay abed, the Senate accepted the Lodge reservations by a simple majority vote, made up mostly of Republicans. But loyal administration Democrats had the necessary one-third vote to prevent approval of the amended treaty. Moderates from both parties worked out additional compromises, which Wilson rejected from his sick bed. On March 19, 1920, the treaty, with these compromise amendments, actually received a majority but failed the needed two-thirds by seven votes. Ironically, the major opposition came from Wilson's most devoted followers. Wilson asked that the 1920 election be a referendum on the league (it was not that), and even dreamed of being the Democratic candidate. The Republicans won, but their candidate, Warren G. Harding, equivocated on the league and gained the support of many proleague Republicans. By 1921 no chance of American ratification remained. The league was a lost cause.

The Legacy

What is the end of this story? In the short term, Wilson failed. He failed to get treaty approval, and thus the United States pursued a unilateral foreign policy until World War II. Wilson died still bitter over his defeat, still sure of his wisdom in trying for the whole loaf. In retrospect, he greatly overestimated the importance of the league. For a nation as powerful as the United States, the league could have served as a useful tool of foreign policy. It might even have given some of our policies the sanction of "collective security," as for example the United Nations did in Korea in 1950. But even as a tool it had its dangers. Without it we risked fewer involvements. We could be more selective in our choice of issues, and would in fact be quite selective and quite effective in our foreign policy in the twenties. Finally, the same lack of will that kept us from using force to uphold "collective security" from the outside might well have kept us from upholding it from within.

The United States, with or without the league, had the power to guarantee the wartime settlements for an indefinite period of time. All we had to do was support France and Britain, arming their desires with additional power. Had we supported the status quo in Europe, there would have been no World War II as we now know it. And in Asia we could have contained Japan, not an easy but an achievable goal given our military power. We could, in other words, have stymied the ambitions of the aggrieved states—Germany, Italy, Japan, and the Soviet Union. At least Germany and the Soviet Union had abundant reasons for their unhappiness with the wartime settlements. They waited for the opportunity to rectify what they viewed as past injustices. The United States could have denied them their best opportunities and thus assured their continuing acquiescence. But at what cost? As it turned out, much more than we were willing to pay, particularly in the depression thirties. We had pressing domestic problems. Many Americans did not believe the cause of France and Britain was a just one. No one could foresee the magnitude of the coming holocaust.

We eventually joined World War II, too late to restore the status quo, but soon enough to become, once again, the main architect of the postwar settlements or nonsettlements. Of all the revisionist powers, only the Soviet Union gained its territorial and political objectives, although at a horrible cost. Only it survived the war in a position to challenge our desire to fashion a world to our esthetic, moral, and economic taste.

Such a realistic analysis may sound too cynical, particularly when searching out the consequences of Wilson's policies. It reflects hindsight. Today, it is hard to view even the purest of international organizations as other than instruments of big-power decision making. Such organizations depend upon the active concurrence of the large powers, or else become instruments for big-power hassles. Voluntary membership allows only this, however useful such an organizaton may be in facilitating negotiation or in disciplining small states.

But Wilson also succeeded. We did not join the league. This negative decision, so well dramatized by Wilson, so lamented by disciples, shaped our foreign policy all the way down to the present. The martyrdom of Wilson became a history lesson often posed in its profundity with Washington's Farewell Address. In most of the world the weakness of the league, its easy prostitution to the interests of a few victors, brought appropriate disillusionment to advocates of that ambiguous nostrum, "collective security." Not so in the United States. Here it seemed only to prove Wilson a prophet. Had we but joined, the league would surely have behaved differently. It was our fault, our cowardice, our irresponsibility that made it fail.

By World War II we were finally willing to make restitution for our mistake. Prodded by such latter-day Wilsonians as Cordell Hull, we belatedly tried to undo our earlier failures. In the midst of a horrible war, it seemed clear that our absence allowed the league to become a tool of Britain and France, yet made it too weak to stand as an effective barrier to German, Japanese, and Soviet aggression. It did not restrain the nations that dared nonpeaceful territorial or ideological expansion, that threatened constitutional and libertarian institutions, or that tried to create areas of the world that were closed to international trade and comity. At the end of World War II we had to redeem our failures of 1919, take a more active responsibility for order and morality in the world, and join with all other "peace-loving and free countries" to achieve that end. But as Wilson had so well understood, the leadership had to be ours. We could not disengage, could not hide behind neutrality. Other countries did not have the will or the high purpose. Only our active commitment to world order could end the threat of war and preserve our national interests, which of course were roughly synonymous with international morality.

In this sense Wilson continued to haunt us from the grave. We had refused his burden and reaped his predicted whirlwind. In the thirties, so goes the myth, we fell for the lures of pacifism and neutralism, swayed by the siren voices that urged us to leave Europe to fight its own wars. By 1945 "isolationism" became a term of abuse, as did the term "appeasement." Now, finally, Wilson had his way. The Roosevelt administration had so sold the idea of a new League of Nations that few congressmen dared oppose it. According to public opinion polls, the American public overwhelmingly supported the United Nations, although few knew very much about it. A second lesson accompanied the first. This time we would not suffer political partisanship in foreign policy. We would have no Borahs and Lodges. The few dissenting voices were completely ineffective. Foreign policy was consensual.

We now live in the glorious world shaped by our commitment to a form of "collective security," by an America fully responsive to its mission to save the world. For at least two decades after World War II, this form of collective security meant a complex Western alliance system largely collected and mostly secured by the United States. As always, in the complexity and dilemma of any policy implemented, the dream had its unexpected elements of horror, and good men often failed the vision, or possibly the vision betrayed them. Thus even in his years of vindication, old Woodrow Wilson, so moral, so driven by a noble dream, surely did not rest peacefully in his grave.

2

Few interludes in our history have such precise boundaries as the years between World War I and the stock market crash of 1929. Few decades have received so much loving attention from historians, journalists, and even movie and television script writers. As a result, the "twenties" has become a much valued imaginative creation, much more a possession of later Americans than of those who experienced the decade.

The twenties, as an historical construct, has a romantic, unreal character, for the memorable aspects of the decade seem not only larger than life but also full of paradoxes. The rebellious twenties rise above conventionality and orthodoxy; religious skepticism jostles with Christian fundamentalism; extremes of intolerance accompany the revolt against something called puritanism. The final domestication of corporate enterprise paralleled an unprecedented, eloquent repudiation of the vulgarity and commercialism of American life. Even as academic intellectuals, writers, painters, and musicians took part in a lively ferment of ideas and expressive experimentation, middle Americans fought a desperate holding action on behalf of traditional verities and against a frightening array of alien gods. When most beleaguered, they added to their counterattack some of the fanaticism spawned by paranoia. Many of the more colorful events of the decade hardly touched upon government policy, but nonetheless the prosaic affairs of government, and the complex maneuvers of diplomats, deserve our careful attention. In the long run they had more to do with our present fate than most of the excitements of a jazz age.

If we rely only upon our folk memories, we should have only pity for Warren G. Harding, even as we spare a random smile for the pleasant and innocuous image of "Silent" Cal Coolidge. Poor Harding. Undone by his cronies, too aware of his own limitations, he died an early and mysterious death under the shadow of scandals he unwittingly caused. He seemed peculiarly inept except in one titillating respect—the brilliant deception he used to conceal his sexual encounters at the White House with the last in a series of mistresses. Calvin Coolidge enjoys a less exciting image in our heritage. We usually remember the simple or inane generalities attributed to him ("the business of America is business") or note

Harding

56

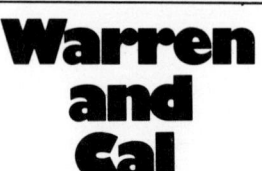

that he was most eloquent in what he did not say, politically most successful because of what he did not do.

Harding only in part deserved his image of weakness and incompetence, or his unenviable reputation as the "worst American president."
An Ohio senator, a former small-town publisher and civic promoter,
Harding was genial, good-natured, kindly, strikingly handsome, and in
most contexts a persuasive politician, but conventional in beliefs and quite
limited in intellectual ability. He won his nomination out of a deadlocked
convention, and as a result of bargaining by party leaders in an endur-
ingly famous "smoke-filled room." No doubt he was a very appealing, for
in no sense threatening, candidate for the large financial and corporate interests that provided so much financial support for the Republican party
in 1920. Harding conducted a low-key campaign and captured a postwar
yearning for a period of calmness and private indulgence by his promise

Warren G. Harding
(1865–1923) greeting
Shriners at the White
House. Harding enjoyed
the ceremonial duties of
the presidency and per-
formed them well. But
in appointing often in-
competent cronies to
political office he left the
way open for the scandals
that were to taint his
administration. *Library
of Congress*

of a return to "normalcy." He won before he began his noncampaign.

The Democrats also nominated an Ohioan, the uninspiring James Cox. Even the most compelling candidate could not have overcome the handicaps of a demoralized and divided party. Wilson's ill health had deprived it of effective leadership for almost two years. The Democrats had to take responsibility for a treaty that fully pleased almost no one. The wartime controls still rankled, as did the high postwar prices. Yet farmers resented earlier price management, and in 1920 suffered a sharp decline in prices as European agriculture recovered. Harding swept all except the southern states, winning overwhelmingly by 16 million to 9.

Harding appointed able and independent men to the major cabinet posts; often incompetent friends to most other offices. These cronies were the source of the public corruption and much of the private excess (girls and "booze"), that left such a negative image for the whole administration. Under Harding, the responsibility for policy determination shifted to cabinet heads. Charles Evans Hughes, the Republican candidate for president in 1916, and before that a judge on the Supreme Court, proved an exceedingly able secretary of state. Herbert Hoover, deservedly famous for his food and relief activities during the war, converted a young and formerly minor Department of Commerce into the most active and innovative branch of the government. Hoover would be the most able Republican of the decade, yet was so little identified with partisan politics that the Democrats had considered him as a possible candidate in 1920. Secretary of Agriculture Henry C. Wallace, an Iowa agricultural journalist, used national conferences and a new Bureau of Agricultural Economics to probe the "farm problem." From his largely academic appointees would come almost all the agricultural programs of the New Deal, when his son, Henry A. Wallace, would also serve as secretary of agriculture. Finally, Andrew Mellon was a conscientious and forceful secretary of the treasury. Himself a millionaire, and practically forced upon Harding by the large corporate interests in the party, he

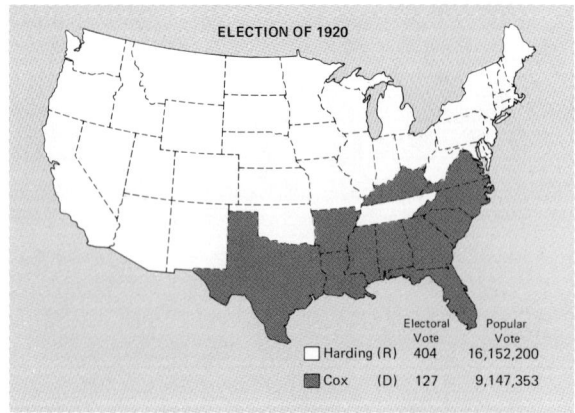

pursued a consistent but very controversial fiscal policy that favored investment and capital growth. To many Democrats he became the prime symbol of an administration they believed controlled by wealth and special interests.

The war and the new Republican era, according to a well-established theory, marked an end to reform or even to that elusive phenomenon called "progressivism." Such a theory is valuative, not descriptive. Concerns certainly shifted after the war. Many pre-World War I causes became minority efforts in the twenties, lacking both in political appeal and in publicity. Some earlier crusades had ended in victory, most notably the century-old struggle for women's suffrage (the required three-fourths of the states ratified the nineteenth amendment by 1920). But there was no lack of prominent crusades in the twenties, some as broadly supported as any in the preceding two decades. Millions of Americans labored to secure an apparent victory of wartime, the achievement of national prohibition. No campaign against a social evil had engaged as many people over as long a period of time, and no issue seemed more important in the twenties. A minority fought just as fervently for repeal, either to expand individual freedom or to restore respect for the law. Other Americans struggled for immigration restriction, either to protect laborers from an inundation of low-wage Europeans or Orientals or to preserve racial purity. Serious, even frightened Christians tried to keep Darwinism out of the public schools and thus protect their children from some form of atheism. It is apparent that as we look to our past, we dignify with the label "reform" only those crusades that match our own preferences. More historians attribute the label to trust-busting than to prohibition, revealing their own sympathies and exemplifying how easily those sympathies shape their vocabulary.

Obviously lacking in the twenties was the type of leadership offered by Roosevelt and Wilson. Neither Harding nor Coolidge dramatized a major legislative program, or offered a compelling moral leadership. They lacked either the talent, the commitment, or the energy. The most important legislation of the decade did not carry their personal stamp. Possibly the people did not want forceful leaders; perhaps they tired of the tension and moral rigor of a Wilson. But the argument is still circular. Since the Democrats offered no real alternative, one cannot say how Americans would have responded to a more purposeful and dynamic candidate.

Another shift is much more difficult to chart. Both Roosevelt and Wilson, with somewhat different strategies, not only increased the power of the federal government, but more often than not used it as a check upon large concentrations of private economic power. Both tried regulation and discipline, while Wilson at least made verbal attacks on bigness itself. But they were not against business or against "capitalists," if one can give any precise meaning to such ambiguous and overused labels. If a businessman is one who owns or manages productive property, and who uses it to provide goods or services in expectation of profit, then short of anarchists and a very few socialists, no one in America was antibusiness. The farmer, the owners of the local pharmacy or bank, or the managers of a local factory were all businessmen by this definition. To protect individual entrepreneurs, or small corporate enterprise, Wilson battled with financial and manufacturing oligarchs. The almost universally hated stereotypes of "Wall Street" or "trusts" fit only the largest industrial empires, or identified the few men at the top who controlled (and usually did not own) large economic collectivities with enormous power over production and prices. Roosevelt hoped that, with a bit of governmental discipline, even large, consolidated enterprises could be good public servants. Wilson thought not. But neither man desired class legislation. Their battle against monopoly was not a crusade against business, but was for business. They opposed unscrupulous competitors or unjust rules in the marketplace. Wilson only reluctantly supported legislation favoring laborers or farmers, and only then as a necessary corrective for past injustice.

Whatever the shift from Wilson to Harding, it was not from hostility to favoritism toward business. The change lurked behind the word "business," and all the various images that attached to it. For surviving Progressives, for many Democrats, the problem with the Republican regime was that it had departed from the principle of a neutral government, from a commitment to equal justice for all producers, call them businessmen or not. Quite simply, they charged that Harding and his successors favored large corporate enterprise, or in fact the very forms of production that least fit the entrepreneurial ideal. Republicans denied this charge. Even Harding and Coolidge, and most of all Hoover, continued to talk of neutrality, of equal concern for the welfare of all producing groups. In their perspective, they certainly freed enterprise from all the detailed controls of World War I. They also proudly took responsibility for the favorable environment for investment and profits, and saw growth and prosperity as the greatest achievement of the decade. They would have no diverting and demagogic crusade against imaginary monopolies (they saw none) or against honorable and conscientious corporate executives (almost all of them, as they knew from firsthand experience).

What had changed most dramatically during the war years was the popular image of the large corporation. The Republicans exploited this changed image, and gained votes so long as it remained intact. Those who still nourished deep and dark suspicions of Wall Street made up a dwindling and ineffective minority. For large corporations, the wartime achievement in production, the consumptive promise of the twenties, the joyful public acceptance of such new products as the radio and such assimilating products as the automobile, new forms of "enlightened" business management, and perhaps above all the flowering of corporate public relations and institutional advertising, created the benevolent image of business and insured a useful ambiguity in the word. Harding and Coolidge, as well as congressmen, helped popularize the new status of businessmen as benefactors, as the ones most responsible for a new era of plenty. The prestige of "business," whatever the reference, gained from the contrasting image of organized labor. In the reconversion from wartime, wages suffered. Over 4 million workers joined strikes in 1919 alone, and a few radical labor leaders managed to create fears of a massive, general strike. Some strikers won wage increases, and then seemed responsible for resented higher prices paid by consumers. One irony of public relations was that huge corporations, the epitome of collective enterprise, managed to adapt to themselves the older icons of individual property and entrepreneurship, and to indict labor unions as an un-American form of collectivism.

Harding was not a simple stooge of large corporations. His own proclivities lay with small-town businessmen and farmers, with the mentality of the Chamber of Commerce and not that of the more sophisticated National Association of Manufacturers. He cooperated with a newly formed farm bloc in Congress on several agricultural measures made urgent by a 1920 collapse in food prices. Four different acts increased government control over exchanges and commodity markets, aided farm cooperatives, and opened new avenues of credit. This was far from what farmers wanted, but still represented an unprecedented number of gifts. Even the Fordney-McCumber tariff, the most emphatic Republican repudiation of Wilson's policies, provided new protection for farmers, although overall it was a carefully drafted sop for manufacturers and a tax on consumption.

Because of intraparty divisions in Congress, the Republican ascendancy did not smooth the way for legislation. The Republican party contained a minority faction of rural-based insurgents or old Progressives willing to merge with congenial Democrats to block what they conceived as special interest legislation. This split surfaced in tariff and tax legislation, but found its most enduring symbol in a relatively minor but unresolvable controversy over a government-built dam and power plant at Muscle Shoals, Alabama. Already, under Wilson, the survivors of the Progressive party had lost in a bid to retain the war-induced federal ownership of

railroads, accepting instead a fairly strict form of federal regulation (the Esch-Cummings Act of 1920). The Muscle Shoals controversy agitated an issue that dated from the turn of the century—the relative merits of federal versus private ownership of hydroelectric power. The uncompleted project on the Tennessee River also included a nitrate plant built to manufacture explosives but now with great potential in the production of fertilizers. Led by an eloquent public-power advocate, Senator George Norris of Nebraska, the rebellious Republicans and congenial Democrats blocked several administrative schemes to sell or lease the facilities to private companies, including one highly publicized but improbable scheme announced by Henry Ford. Yet, later congressional bills providing for federal development, all direct predecessors of the later Tennessee Valley Authority, succumbed to vetoes by Coolidge.

Thomas Edison (sleeping in foreground), Henry Ford, and President Harding (right) at the Ford-Edison camp. Edison and Ford were the very symbols of American ingenuity, with Edison's many inventions ranging from the phonograph to the microphone to the incandescent electric lamp. *Library of Congress*

One almost hidden achievement of the Harding administration gained neither the attention nor the debate that it deserved. In 1921 Congress passed the Budget and Accounting Act in a deliberate effort to bring business efficiency to the federal government. The bill established the Bureau of the Budget and the General Accounting Office, and for the first time required planning and strict accountability in government spending. In the long run, the act rivaled the Federal Reserve Act in its impact on government fiscal policies.

Although he was never the source of great new programs or decisive governmental action, Harding and "normalcy" proved an excellent although largely unwitting antidote for hysteria. The wartime crusade had created intense animosity toward nonconformists and dissenters, with German ethnics, antiwar socialists, and the long-feared IWW the most conspicuous. A federal sedition act, and even more stringent state laws backed by organized loyalty committees, supported a virtual reign of terror against domestic "traitors." The war's end, accompanied by frustrating problems of reconversion, a divisive debate on the league, intense labor strife, major race riots in Arkansas and in many northern cities (a consequence of southern blacks who moved to jobs in the North during the war), did little to diffuse the internal conflict. But the hostility did shift away from German-Americans to a brand new ogre—the "Bolsheviks." Many assumed that they were behind all the tension. The Soviet revolution spread fear throughout the Western world, particularly in the wake of Communist successes in Hungary and Germany. Two new, small Communist parties in America received both inspiration and help from Russia. For a brief time, diverse radicals sensed the possibility of an early revolution in America. A few violently acted upon this hope. Their reputation suffered because most Communist party members and a good share of socialists were "ethnics," concentrated in large cities, particularly New York. For varied reasons, many of these immigrants had not become naturalized citizens, and thus faced all the legal disabilities of aliens. These ingredients combined to produce the "Red Scare" of 1919–1920.

The near hysteria of 1919 fed upon events and their subsequent exploitation by politicians, especially Wilson's attorney general and presidential hopeful, A. Mitchell Palmer. The spreading labor problems were real enough. Most frightening were a brief, abortive general strike in Seattle, and a much publicized police strike in Boston (Governor Calvin Coolidge began his move to the White House with a belated condemnation of all strikes against "the public safety"). More serious was an unsuccessful but violent steel strike in September 1919, by newly organized steel workers seeking relief from a twelve-hour day, and a bituminous coal strike in November led by a United Mine Workers Union headed by a youthful militant, John L. Lewis. Palmer eventually led troops into the coal fields. A wave of mysterious violence frightened even more people. In April 1919, someone mailed bombs to at least thirty-six prominent Americans, leading to several serious injuries (everyone assumed the "Bolsheviks" were responsible, since May Day was approaching). In June bombs exploded in eight cities. An apparent assassination attempt ended in front of Palmer's Washington house when a man tripped and blew himself to bits. Finally, on Armistice Day 1919, American Legionnaires and an IWW local fought a deadly pitched battle in Centralia, Washington.

63

The federal response, led by Palmer, included a continued investigation of radicals by a newly reorganized Bureau of Investigation (headed by a youthful J. Edgar Hoover), the gathering of a long file on suspects, but few arrests and convictions. Often aliens provided the only vulnerable target. Palmer, not by any means a bigot or unconcerned with civil liberties, slowly intensified his battle against "undesirable" radicals and began to deport those who were aliens, with enthusiastic public approval but often without adequate hearings and with great suffering by individuals or by separated families. Billy Sunday, the leading Christian evangelist of his day, at one point suggested lining up Bolsheviks and shooting them to save room on ships, or sending them to sea in "ships of stone with masts of lead." Immigrants from Russia, including many Jews, fared worst. Membership in a radical party or club, or even a suspicious appearance, made an alien a likely passenger on a ship to the Soviet Union. The deportees included several persons later famous in radical circles, including the anarchist Emma Goldman. On January 2, 1920, federal agents rounded up four thousand alien suspects in thirty-two cities. It tried to deport as many as possible, but faced delays from an assistant secretary of labor, Louis Post (the commissioner of immigration was in the Department of Labor), who insisted upon fair procedures, so glaringly absent in earlier deportation hearings. Only about six hundred of this last group had to leave the country.

Attorney General A. Mitchell Palmer (1872–1936) became the symbol of government repression of radicals and aliens during the "Red Scare" in the last years of the Wilson administration. He was responsible for deporting many immigrants. *Library of Congress*

The excesses of Palmer, better publicity for the more inhumane effects of deportation, residual concerns for civil liberties even for noncitizens, and possibly a sense of basic decency, finally ended the "Red Scare." Clergymen, attorneys, even veterans condemned threats to free speech. Senator Warren G. Harding joined Charles Evans Hughes to denounce the expulsion of five elected socialists by the New York Assembly. When Palmer incorrectly predicted a new wave of bombing for May 1920, he faced ridicule and laughter. Economic problems and an election contest helped divert attention from "Bolsheviks." By 1921 the scare was all but over. Harding helped further deflate the fear of radicals by pardoning the grand old man of American socialism, Eugene Debs, who left prison on Christmas Day 1921, after serving part of a sentence because of his opposition to World War I.

In a less hysterical context, the concern over aliens continued. The fear of radicals only added one additional, although minor, support for immigration restriction, an issue that had slowly gained political strength from the late nineteenth century. Ethnic Americans revealed, by their wartime allegiances, how slowly they melted in our magical pot. Two main concerns fed the crusade for restriction. Laborers had long resented the competition from job-hungry Eastern and Southern Europeans, who fled to America at the rate of over a million a year before the war, and who took

John L. Lewis (1880–1969), head of the United Mine Workers, is pictured here at the Capitol discussing the coal situation with Representative Nolan, chairman of the House Labor Committee (April 1921). Lewis remained an influential member of the AFL until 1935. He then helped organize the Committee for Industrial Organization, which in 1936 became a separate union federation, the Congress of Industrial Organizations. *Library of Congress*

IMMIGRATION TO THE UNITED STATES, 1900–1930

Year	All Countries	Europe	Asia
1900	448,572	424,700	17,946
1905	1,026,499	974,273	23,925
1910	1,041,570	926,291	23,533
1915	326,700	197,919	15,211
1920	430,001	246,295	17,505
1925	294,314	148,366	3,578
1930	241,700	147,438	4,535

Source: *Historical Statistics of the United States: Colonial Times to 1957,* prepared by the Bureau of the Census with the cooperation of the Social Science Research Council.

IMMIGRATION QUOTAS, 1924–1930

Country	Under the 1924 Act (2 percent of 1890) *	Under the National Origins System (1930)†
Germany	51,227	25,957
Great Britain **	34,007	65,721
Ireland **	28,567	17,853
Sweden	9,561	3,314
Norway	6,453	2,377
Poland	5,982	6,524
Italy	3,845	5,802
Russia	2,248	2,784
Greece	100	307
Asia	1,300	1,323
Africa	1,200	1,200
All Others	621	600
Total	164,667	153,714

* From 1924 to 1930 the annual quota equaled 2 percent of foreign-born residents in the United States as determined by the 1890 census.
† From 1930 on the annual quota equaled one-sixth of 1 percent of the number of white inhabitants in the continental United States in 1920.
** All Ireland included with Great Britain prior to 1925; thereafter, Northern Ireland only.
Source: *Historical Statistics of the United States: Colonial Times to 1957.*

the most menial jobs or served as effective strike breakers. Even the Socialist party, with its egalitarian ideals, had to overcome strong union opposition in order to maintain its support of unrestricted immigration.

Perhaps even more determinant were widespread fears of cultural or racial contamination. It is difficult to do justice to the range of these concerns. Some were completely practical—the social problems created by immigrants, particularly those ill-equipped for jobs or too poor to get a start in America. After 1890 the majority of immigrants came from southern or eastern Europe, or areas generally with people of darker hair and skin than the blondes of northern Europe. Religiously, they were Catholic, Greek Orthodox, or Jewish, headed for a predominantly Protestant America. As a whole they reflected greater economic and cultural

deprivation than early migrants; they had less education, less money, and
fewer skills.

New, detailed theories about race spread from Europe to America, and
here found many popular and academic spokesmen in the new century.
The old game of trying to categorize the varieties of mankind had a resurgence of popularity. But much more than in earlier and later racial ty-
pologies, the purportedly "scientific" classifications merged physical traits
with cultural achievements. By most accepted theories, Slavs and Latins
were less intelligent, less open to abstract ideas, and less gifted in the arts
of government than their less emotional and often less artful northern
cousins. For a time, the carefully articulated distinctions within the
larger Caucasian family eclipsed the usual concern over Negroes or
Mongolians. The implications of this racial theory were quite clear. As
inferior European immigrants mixed with the older American stock (unlike with Negroes or Indians, intermarriage was a common occurrence),
the beautiful Aryan civilization of America would inevitably decline.
Madison Grant, a popularizer of "scientific racism," epitomized this idea
by the title of a 1916 book, *The Passing of the Great Race*. Such "experts" as Grant testified before congressional hearings on immigration, and
usually received a warm hearing from most congressmen. Thus, racial
theories not only supported restriction, but almost alone determined the
distribution of new quotas.

Restrictive legislation touched a sensitive nerve, for it challenged a valued self-image of America as a refuge for the exploited of Europe. Wilson
refused to surrender that image, and vetoed restrictive legislation in 1917.
But in 1921 Congress passed, and Harding signed, an emergency act that
established a rigid quota on immigrants. Each country could, in any one
year, send only 3 percent of the number of their nationals in America in
1910. In 1924, under Coolidge, Congress enacted a much more complex,
permanent quota system. The National Origins Act (in amended form
still the basis of our immigration policy) provided for both a temporary
and a permanent quota system calculated to maintain the existing ethnic
balance. Both excluded East Asians, a much resented insult to Japan. The
temporary provision set a 2 percent quota for European countries, based
on the number of Americans of that nationality listed in the census of
1890. This meant that most of the 164,000 eligible for immigration would
live in northern Europe, for 1890 was early enough to discount most of the
new immigration. The permanent provision, based on the current census
and on elaborate calculations of genetic fractions, took effect in the Hoover
administration and achieved the same racial goals. It simply apportioned
immigrant quotas according to the proportion of Americans who could
trace their origin to any given country, and thus favored the British Isles
and Germany. Since the quotas did not apply to the Americas, the new

restrictions had the unexpected consequence of attracting a new mass of Latin American immigrants. They also helped create new economic opportunities for blacks in northern cities.

Harding never had to suffer the great public embarrassments that began to surface in 1923. During a summer trip to Alaska he agonized over carefully concealed scandals that he already knew about. Upon his return to Seattle he suffered an apparent heart attack, and died a few days later in San Francisco. His totally unexpected death helped nourish rumors of suicide or murder. Harding died with undiminished popularity and received a hero's burial. Then broke the storm.

The scandals involved either friends that Harding had trusted, or appointees of his friends. Attorney General Harry Daugherty caused many of the afflictions. One of his appointees in the Justice Department, Jesse Smith, fixed suits involving tax frauds and even deposited some of his illegal fees in a joint account with Daugherty. When Harding learned of this, he ordered Smith out of Washington; instead Smith committed suicide. Charles Forbes, a chance acquaintance whom Harding appointed as head

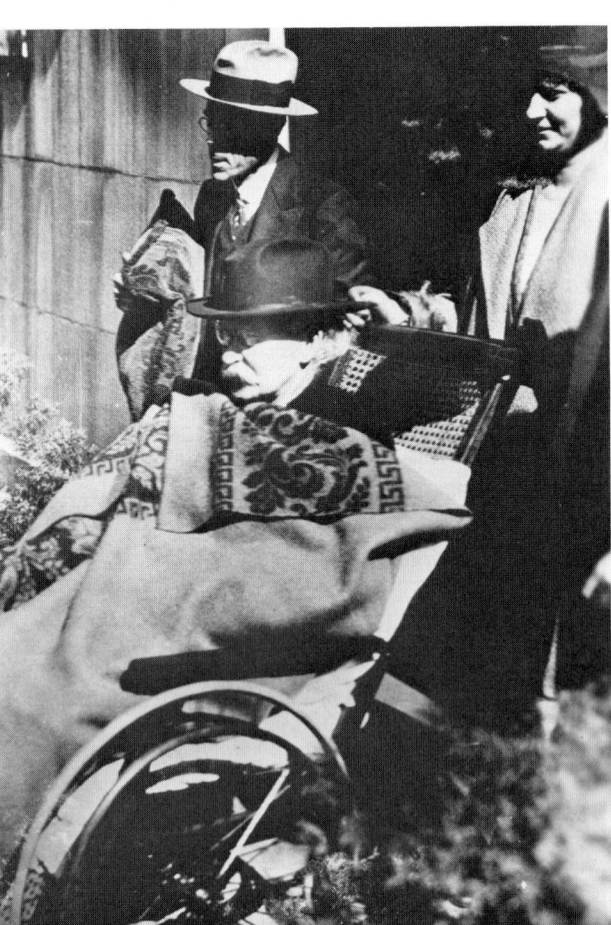

The Teapot Dome oil scandal was the culmination of a series of scandals that surfaced after Harding's death. Secretary of the Interior Albert Fall (1861–1944) was convicted and imprisoned for accepting industrial bribes. He is seen here leaving the courtroom after being indicted, October 12, 1929. *Library of Congress*

68

of the Veterans' Bureau, defrauded it of over $200,000,000 and eventually received a fine and a two-year jail sentence. Another subcabinet official, Thomas Miller, the custodian of alien property, served an eighteen-month sentence for gifts he collected after virtually giving away German chemical patents. Again, a joint bank account implicated Daugherty, who refused to testify before a congressional committee. Coolidge fired him as attorney general, but some doubted any direct guilt. He lived frugally and possibly only tried to protect Harding's reputation by using secreted funds to finance Harding's sexual escapades.

The most sensational scandal made famous a small oil reserve in Wyoming called Teapot Dome. Secretary of the Interior Albert Fall, lacking as much in discretion as in intelligence, leased government oil reserves in both California and Wyoming to two different oil companies. From one he received an unsecured loan of $100,000. For the Teapot Dome lease he received $85,000 in cash and a herd of cattle as gifts from Harry Sinclair. After a detailed congressional investigation, which delighted Democrats, Fall was indicted and eventually received a one-year sentence (the first cabinet officer in our history to go to jail).

The scandals did not hurt the Republican party as much as the Democrats hoped. The Teapot Dome inquiry unveiled suspiciously high legal fees paid by another oil company to William G. McAdoo, Wilson's son-in-law and a prime contender for the Democratic nomination in 1924. The revelations hurt the reputation of a dead man, not Calvin Coolidge, who was in every way the opposite of a gullible, lovable Harding. The most sensational revelations came early in 1924; by summer other news items completely dominated the headlines. Coolidge replaced Daugherty with a distinguished law professor, Harlan F. Stone. He also appointed a "nonpartisan" investigating body, and stressed his own desire to punish all culprits. He even shifted some of the implied guilt to the Democrats, who seemed to pursue the investigations in order to develop a desperately needed campaign theme for 1924.

Coolidge and Hoover

Coolidge was an unusual president. Although he came to the vice-presidency from a successful career in urban Massachusetts, he always retained the image of his rural Vermont childhood, of thrift, perfect integrity, and small-town democracy. He disliked conflict and avoided problems. As few other presidents, he followed a policy of drift, of letting problems solve themselves. He achieved no clear goals simply because he had none. It is difficult to associate him with a single major legislative initiative. He tried to work with all wings of the Republican party, and gave important appointments to acknowledged Progressives. Yet, he won the respect of large business interests, more because of his personal concern for governmental economy and his friendship with several corporate executives than from any understanding of complex economic issues. He usually reduced complexity to simplicity. Against his inclinations, he fought continually with Congress, vetoing agricultural and tax and power bills that he considered unorthodox or dangerous. Congress even blocked his second nominee for attorney general, an almost unprecedented action and one that angered Coolidge almost beyond endurance.

Coolidge, always popular even if not loved, won easily in 1924, and practically without campaigning (he left that to his vice-presidential partner, Charles Dawes). In this election the Democrats reached the lowest ebb in their history. For seventeen sweltering days in June, their New York City convention struggled to complete a platform and nominate a candidate. The delegates divided almost perfectly between the urban Northeast and North (wet, anti-KKK, prounion, and almost unanimously for Al Smith of New York) and the rural South and West (dry, Protestant, susceptible to Klan influences, and determined to nominate McAdoo). Because of the two-thirds rule for nomination, both Smith and McAdoo had to withdraw in behalf of John W. Davis, a mild, honest corporation lawyer without a national following. The spark in the campaign, and the main object of Republican abuse, was a revived Progressive party. The insurgents had their second go at it, with Robert La Follette as their candidate. The party represented a hopeful but largely unsuccessful effort to unite the labor and farm vote, and in its platform combined a traditional attack on monopolies with support for more direct democracy, collective bargaining rights, and government ownership of the railroads and certain power facilities. Such planks drew Republican charges of socialism and communism. Coolidge won more popular votes (15 million) than Davis (8 million) and La Follette (5 million) combined. The Progressive party did not long survive the defeat, and for good reason many wondered if the Democratic party could endure. It came in a dismal third in most nonsouthern states.

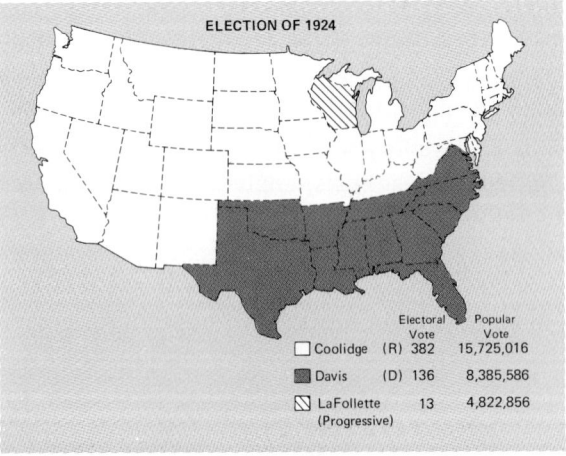

ELECTION OF 1924

		Electoral Vote	Popular Vote
☐ Coolidge	(R)	382	15,725,016
■ Davis	(D)	136	8,385,586
◩ LaFollette (Progressive)		13	4,822,856

Unlike the ephemeral Progressives, the Democratic party had the strength of an established tradition. It only awaited new issues and new leadership to resolve or conceal its inner tensions. It secured neither in 1928, but moved well away from the abyss of 1924. The 1928 convention marked a completed shift of power; the urban factions now had a majority. Without the deep divisions of 1924, it nominated Al Smith, a versatile, colorful Tammany politician from the streets of New York City. Unlike an earlier Cox or Davis, he invited attention and either love or hostility. Yet, Smith was still a desperate gamble in a bad year. Roman Catholic in religion, he had worked to relax the Volstead Act, and in accent and concerns symbolized the distinctive parochialism of New York City. Thus, he suffered from a damning array of liabilities in the Protes-

Calvin Coolidge (1872–1933) succeeded to the presidency on the death of Harding in 1923, then won an easy victory for a term of his own in 1924. He is seen here on a poster announcing the opening of the baseball season. Secretary of State Frank Kellogg, of Kellogg-Briand fame, is raising the flag in the lower right-hand picture. *Library of Congress*

tant hinterlands, but had vote-getting assets for Catholics and ethnic minorities. Smith had proved an able administrator as governor of New York, and was in the forefront of American politics in such areas as conservation and the planned use of resources. He supported both city and regional planning in New York. On national economic policy he was not far from the Republicans. He had deep sympathies for organized labor, but certainly did not share the Progressive fear of economic concentration, and gained a large share of his support from corporate executives. The nomination of Smith reflected an unusual shift by a major party toward at least a symbolic extreme, and almost necessitated a more harmonizing candidate in 1932. But the shift then would not be back to the rural and southern elements of the party, although these groups retained their dominance over key congressional committees.

In 1928, a year when the Democratic party faced a tenuous future, it nominated Governor Al Smith (1873–1944) of New York as its presidential candidate. Smith was a very controversial candidate because he was Catholic, supported the repeal of Prohibition, and was a Tammany Hall politician. *Library of Congress*

In 1927 Coolidge, with the willing complicity of party leaders, had taken himself out of presidential contention by a typically terse statement: "I do not choose to run." The early scramble for the nomination ended in an anticlimactic, first ballot nomination of Secretary of Commerce Herbert Hoover, the obvious heir apparent because of service and party leadership. In a near vacuum of presidential leadership, he had served as the leading Republican policy maker, using his post to fashion a consistent economic philosophy. He had as much to do with labor and agriculture as the secretaries in those departments. But Hoover was not a voluble politician. He remained an intensely private man, overly sensitive to criticism, and lacking in public charm or persuasive ability. Because of his food and relief activities in the war, and his success in commerce, he enjoyed immense prestige as a Quaker humanitarian and person of great integrity. As much as Smith, Hoover was a self-made man, moving from an orphaned childhood in Iowa to Stanford to enormous success as a mining engineer. In his views on both foreign and domestic policy he was close to Woodrow Wilson, whom he would eventually honor by an appreciative biography. Party leaders neither understood nor trusted him. Business interests feared him, not because of any hostility on his part toward ethical businessmen (he was one), but because he promised strong presidential leadership and reflected an inviolate honesty, both of which meant an unresponsive attitude toward special interests.

Two factors helped Hoover win an overwhelming victory—his proud blessing upon Republican prosperity and the early end of all poverty in America, and the urban, Catholic image of Smith. Hoover endlessly sang the praises of a free economy which, at worst, only needed a few fiscal repairs and a higher level of social responsibility. His plaudits went to all sectors of the economy—to farmers, to factory workers, to the various types of businessmen. All contributed to the success story, and all would share in its benefits, even farmers (Hoover was sensitive on the farm issue, for his strategy of cooperative marketing ran counter to

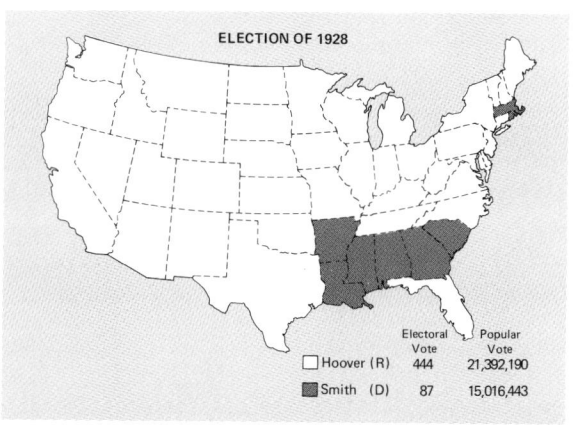

price-fixing schemes advocated by most farm organizations). In fact, co-operation was a key word in his speeches. As secretary of commerce he had tried to get both farmers and businessmen to cooperate in trade and marketing associations, dedicated to product quality and fair competitive rules. He believed the federal government, as a servant of its people, should provide a favorable environment for all producers, without mo-nopoly, unfair privileges, or slanted rules. Above all, the government, in establishing minimal rules or in its necessary regulatory role, should never

Herbert Hoover (1874–1964), here pictured with his family, posed as the godfather of prosperity, believed in a free econ-omy, and wanted the fed-eral government to be a servant of all the people. Although he tried to show favoritism to no sector, the terrible depression and his lack of persuasive ability helped lead to his defeat in 1932. *Library of Congress*

invade the area of private choice and responsibility. In his celebration of economic opportunity he echoed a moral idealism that went back to Jefferson. He failed to appreciate all the subtle changes in those ideals forced by large, corporate enterprise, and did not perceive the pitfalls that always threatened the equilibrium of a delicate market system. But his glowing praise of Republican economic policies made sense in a prosperous 1928, and the economic boom gave substance to his prediction of a coming consumer's paradise.

The Hoover landslide (21 million to 15 million) was not surprising. But the election returns still invited a careful analysis. Smith's total vote almost duplicated that of Coolidge in 1924, and almost doubled that of Davis. Part of the gain came from former Progressives, even more from new voters enticed by a fervent, often ugly election campaign. The most sensational shift occurred in the South, where Hoover carried such improbable states as Florida, North Carolina, Tennessee, Virginia, Texas, and Oklahoma. But this proved a one-time defection, an understandable reaction to rum and Romanism. Smith gained the reverse vote in the conflict of religion and life-style, for Catholic voters turned out in record numbers and much of his campaign financing came from those opposed to prohibition. More enduring was a shift to Smith in almost all large cities, and in such heavily manufacturing states as Massachusetts and Rhode Island. Hoover carried the Midwest, despite his less appealing farm plank. But Hoover's greatest asset—prosperity—soon became his Achilles' heel. It was the personal tragedy of Herbert Hoover that, within six months of his inauguration, the alluring god of plenty began to withdraw her winsome but fickle favors. Thus, the story of the Hoover administration does not fit the jazz age.

3

Republican prosperity paralleled a general economic recovery in Europe and a gradual reduction in international tensions. It seemed, for a brief golden era, that the armistice might ripen into an enduring peace. Old hostilities, such as those between France and Germany, eroded a bit at numerous conference tables, and even a roguish Soviet Union finally joined the League of Nations and tempered its early enthusiasm for revolution with the prosaic dullness of negotiation. As if to belie all the lamentations about the United States not joining the league, the Republican administrations played a critical role in the relaxation of tensions. In no sense did America retreat within its shell or isolate itself from world events. The growing scope of its economic interests, its potential military strength, and the interdependence of the Western market system assured some level of involvement.

Charles Evans Hughes, secretary of state between 1921 and 1925, gave diplomacy a more favorable public image. Hughes had a reputation for intelligence and integrity. Even his physical appearance—he wore a white Edwardian beard—commanded confidence. The secretary put to work his extensive executive and intellectual talent to brace up the demoralized Department of State. In foreign policy he emphasized workable compromise rather than large theoretical formulas. Yet his kind of practicality did not mean secrecy and manipulation. He usually pursued an open diplomacy, free of tortured, private negotiations. Though President Harding, inexperienced and uninterested in foreign affairs, largely ignored the State Department, the president's charm and his knowledge of the Senate sometimes eased the way for Hughes's policies.

The Harding administration had two immediate tasks: to end the technical state of war with the former Central Powers and to determine the relationship of America to the League of Nations. The refusal of the Senate to ratify the Versailles treaty left the United States diplomatically adrift. Hughes quietly approached the Senate Foreign Relations Committee and suggested a *de facto* settlement of the war, a method that would avoid the wastefulness of renewed negotiations. On July 2, 1921, Congress

76

When Swords almost Became Plowshares

adopted a series of peace treaties that Hughes negotiated with our former enemies. They reserved for America the rights we would have had under the Versailles settlement. But to reconcile the anti-Wilson forces, Hughes had to make each agreement specifically reject our membership in the League of Nations.

For some months the State Department simply ignored communications from the Geneva headquarters of the league. This nonapproach threatened national interests—the council would shortly discuss mandates, for example—but official participation would only provoke an angry response from the Senate. Initially, Hughes had to address every message to the league with a rude reminder that we were "not a member," and had to negotiate with each power individually rather than with the league council. This formality and awkwardness could not continue. Hughes decided to dispatch "unofficial observers" to league meetings that involved United States interests or dealt with humanitarian questions. These "observers" fully represented the government; only the connection with the league was "unofficial." Through this device, the United States ended its isolation from events in Geneva, yet remained outside the formal structure of the league.

Hughes gained enduring diplomatic stature from the Washington Naval Conference of 1922. Renewed shipbuilding programs in Japan and the United States, together with Britain's determination to maintain its superiority at sea, augured a new naval race. The war had created something of a power vacuum in the Far East, a dangerous situation that threatened possible clashes between Japan and the United States. Precisely because of this possibility, England anxiously sought to escape from its alliance with Japan, scheduled for renewal in 1922. Prospects for a negotiated solution were good, for such was in the interest of each of the three nations.

**The Washington
Conference**

Although the most compelling impetus to a conference was Britain's desire to abrogate the Anglo-Japanese alliance, Hughes seized the leadership. An end of the London-Tokyo axis and a naval truce would benefit the United States and at the same time satisfy a growing domestic demand for disarmament, based partly on a public belief that the mere existence of arms imperiled peace. A conference would also counter Senator William E. Borah by substituting a sensible international plan of disarmament for his desired disengagement from the world. Accordingly, Hughes invited major European and Far Eastern nations—Britain, Japan, France, Italy, China, the Netherlands, Belgium, and Portugal—to a conference in Washington to discuss disarmament and the political and military problems of the far Pacific. All the powers agreed to come, though

16798--11/9/31
American Delegates leaving D.A.R. Hall.

The American delegation leaving D.A.R. Constitution Hall in Washington, D.C., during the Washington Naval Conference. The principle architect of the conference was Secretary of State Charles Evans Hughes (1862–1948), bottom right, who later became chief justice of the Supreme Court. *Library of Congress*

not with equal enthusiasm. Should the conference arrange a halt to naval construction, the French navy would be frozen at its inferior size. Japan seemed certain to lose important advantages, notably its alliance with England and its naval freedom. Yet, Tokyo could not force a clearly reluctant Britain into renewal of the alliance and, in any event, domestic opinion opposed a continuation of naval spending, then consuming one-third of Japan's national budget.

The Washington Conference formally convened on November 12, 1921. The day before, on the third anniversary of the armistice, the delegates had attended the burial of America's unknown soldier. If moved by Harding's words that "the millions of dead shall not be in vain," the diplomats were unprepared for Hughes's opening speech. Instead of hearing the expected routine welcome, the delegates listened to the secretary's startlingly specific plan for a naval truce: the United States would scrap thirty capital ships, already built or under construction, totaling nearly 850,000 tons; England would halt construction on its four new *Hoods*, as well as other ships, thus disposing of almost 600,000 tons; Japan would forfeit 450,000 tons. On hearing this, the first lord of the admiralty, David Beatty, "lurched forward in his chair like a bulldog who had been poked in the stomach." The secretary also suggested a ten-year holiday on new construction of capital ships and a replacement tonnage thereafter not to exceed 500,000 for the United States and Britain, 300,000 for Japan, and 175,000 each for France and Italy. Individual ships might be replaced only when at least twenty years old and only by vessels not exceeding 35,000 tons.

Hughes's implicit object was the termination of the Anglo-Japanese alliance, which neither Britain nor America liked. Hughes hinted at a nicely balanced detente: America would abandon, as Britain and Japan wished, its huge and ultramodern naval program; and Japan, reasonably well satisfied with this, would have to release the British from the alliance. Without British backing, the Japanese were isolated. Within twelve weeks the conference had drawn up three major treaties, all subsequently ratified. The Five Power Naval Treaty, valid for fifteen years, followed Hughes's original scheme. The United States, Britain, and Japan agreed to scrap almost two million tons of naval vessels and thereafter to maintain a tonnage at a ratio of 5 for America, 5 for Britain, 3 for Japan, and 1.75 for France and Italy (neither France nor Italy had to scrap ships). The treaty also limited capital ships to 35,000 tons with guns of no more than sixteen-inch caliber; light cruisers could not exceed 10,000 tons and eight-inch caliber weapons. In addition, the ratio applied to aircraft carriers, though at reduced total tonnages. France's pique at its enforced inferiority prevented Hughes from extending the agreement to destroyers or submarines. All the powers accepted a moratorium on further military fortifications in the Pacific between the parallels of Hawaii and Singapore.

One effect of this settlement was to preserve American naval dominance in the Western Hemisphere, Japanese supremacy in the western Pacific, and British preponderance elsewhere. Its implementation required two more treaties, both essentially political. The Four Power Treaty, signed by the United States, Britain, France, and Japan, specifically abrogated the Anglo-Japanese alliance and provided a collective guarantee for the signatories' possessions in the Far East. Britain escaped the dreaded eventuality of supporting Japan in a controversy with the United States. Washington's price for adherence to the agreements was the Nine Power Treaty, drafted by former Secretary of State Elihu Root. Accepted by each participant in the conference, this treaty sought to elevate the open door principle into international law. It pledged respect for the "sovereignty and territorial integrity" of China and proclaimed equality of commercial opportunity, specifically outlawing spheres of influence.

Neither the disarmament provisions nor the political treaties lived up to their promise. In the early 1930's all three agreements collapsed. In 1931 Japan invaded Manchuria, in direct violation of the Nine Power Treaty. The failures led critics to denigrate the original effort. Certainly the Washington Conference reflected and reinforced the popular conception in Britain and the United States that armaments themselves, rather than international tensions or conflicts of interest, are primarily responsible for war. That belief nourished an oversimplified moral: if only arms cause war, and arms are abolished, then no sustained participation in world affairs is necessary. The treaties also produced a false sense of security. London and Washington assumed an enduring stability in the Far East. In reality, the distribution of power there was in constant flux. Critics have also pointed out that without effective enforcement procedures the agreements were pointless from the outset. But the United States Senate, which happily ratified the treaties with only one dissenting vote, would surely have defeated any treaty incorporating bold enforcement measures. Also, it was subsequent events rather than any inherent weakness that undermined the work of the Washington Conference. Any international arrangement is very much at the mercy of national interests and emotions; and these run a shifting course beyond the calculations of treaty-makers and other men.

Latin America

Less spectacular was Hughes's reorientation of United States policy toward Latin America. The secretary hoped to restore normal diplomatic practice in the Western Hemisphere, and to remove the resentment created by Theodore Roosevelt's direct intervention and by Wilson's moralistic recognition policies. Under increasing pressure from American oil interests, the State Department negotiated new agreements with Colombia and Mexico. Colombia still burned over Roosevelt's intervention in Panama, which insured its successful secession from Colombia and provided us with favorable terms for an isthmian canal. The new agreement paid Colombia $25,000,000, as a concealed form of retribution, a tacit admission of error, and a bid for easier access to her mineral wealth.

Mexico had many bitter memories. The United States had intervened in her internal affairs for over a decade, climaxing in the Villa affair of 1916 and American troops on Mexican territory. A thaw began in 1923. Mexico acknowledged its foreign debt and tempered its constitutional provisions for confiscating property, which had included the property of American firms in Mexico. The United States agreed to recognize the revolutionary government in return for a settlement of private claims and an exemption of American oil properties acquired before 1917 from subsequent confiscatory laws. We also recognized Mexico's rights to unexploited subsoil minerals. This decision, which severely disappointed the oil companies, foreshadowed an important shift from economic to political priorities in United States relations with Latin America.

Hughes also renounced Roosevelt's self-proclaimed right to police the Western Hemisphere, and promised that his government would use the Monroe Doctrine not as an expedient for American encroachment but as a means only of self-defense. The secretary refused to abjure the right of intervention: during the Pan American conference of 1923 in Santiago, Chile, he insisted that "special interests" of the United States might conceivably require unilateral action. But even as he maintained this theoretical option, he withdrew Wilson's military missions from Cuba, the Dominican Republic, and Nicaragua. Relations with the Caribbean nations worsened after Hughes left office (as a result of renewed intervention in Nicaragua in 1927), but Hughes's policy of nonintervention continued under the Hoover administration. Then we finally removed our last troops from Nicaragua and the Dominican Republic, and began recognizing *de facto* governments that fulfilled their international obligations. We also renounced any interpretation of the Monroe Doctrine that justified unilateral intervention by the United States into the internal affairs of other American nations. This "thaw" in Latin American relations continued in the thirties under the inflated title of the Good Neighbor policy.

Economic Diplomacy

The most frustrating problem in Europe was the tangle of reparations and war debts left by World War I. Germany had little means to pay the huge reparations the victors demanded, and the Allies owed America heavy debts they could not comfortably meet without the payments from Germany. The United States took the lead in complex economic negotiations, at first to calm international tensions and then to sustain the German economy and protect huge American investment. Despite long, often tedious discussions, the dilemmas surrounding payments were never effectively resolved.

Wilson outlined a policy for war debts. Wartime and reconstruction loans, the Democratic president had insisted in Paris, were legitimate obligations that had to be repaid. These debts in no sense depended on German reparations. Recognizing the popularity of this approach with American taxpayers, Congress early in 1922 instructed the newly created

World War Foreign Debt Commission to negotiate a stringent repayment schedule. Particularly unrealistic were congressional requirements for a minimum interest rate of 4.25 percent and a maximum repayment period of twenty-five years. The commission, composed of Hughes, Secretary of the Treasury Andrew Mellon, Secretary of Commerce Herbert Hoover, and members from each house of Congress, negotiated with America's debtors from 1923 to 1926. When Europe simply rejected Congress's original terms, the commission reduced interest rates and extended repayment schedules according to a "capacity to pay" formula, but adamantly insisted upon full reimbursement of the principal. England would begin its installments immediately upon a debt carrying interest at a little over 3 percent; Italy's payments would not begin for five years and then at less than 1 percent interest. In every case, payments were to extend over a sixty-two year period. The total debt of roughly $11.5 billion was funded at an average 2⅛ percent interest; the debtors would repay an aggregate of over $22 billion.

This settlement shocked Western Europe, long accustomed to the British precedent of canceling war loans upon the conclusion of peace. Europeans complained that the United States wanted to profit from the war; since Europe had contributed its blood, America might at least contribute its dollars. Europe could repay its debts by only three methods. The easiest would have been a transfer of gold, but Wilson's "cash and carry" policy for war purchases between 1914 and 1917 had denuded European treasuries of bullion; what little remained was necessary for currency cover and as a base of domestic credit. The sale of more European goods and services to the United States than bought could, in effect, repay the debt, yet trade balances continued to favor the United States, in part because of American tariffs. The only remaining option was to repay the debts to America with reparations receipts from Germany. Although the European countries repeatedly attempted to link debts and reparations, Washington consistently rejected any connection.

In April 1921 the Reparations Commission, representing the Allies, demanded $32 billion from Germany, partly to reimburse Allied expenses, partly to prevent a German revival. Although Berlin paid the initial installments, political disorder and growing inflation in Germany during 1922 clearly necessitated a halt in payments, with the attendant risk of Allied reprisal. Fearing that events would soon involve the United States, Hughes privately suggested to Paris and Berlin that "nonpolitical fiscal aid" might avoid a clash. Financial experts, the secretary said in a speech late in 1922, should develop a plan for reasonable reparations within Germany's capacity to pay. Unfortunately, within a month the French had occupied the Ruhr in a fruitless effort to collect overdue reparations. Together with a subsequent hyperinflation in Germany, the invasion delayed Hughes's plan for nearly a year. But Great Britain, unhappy with the French action, revived Hughes's suggestion in late 1923. On January 14, 1924, a panoply of experts from Britain, France, Belgium, Italy, and the United States opened talks that resulted four months later in the famous Dawes Plan—named after the American delegate, Charles Dawes, who presided over the meetings. Essentially an interim device, the plan assumed that the restoration of a strong German economy would be necessary for the renewal of German payments. The powers greatly reduced reparations for the moment and approved an international loan to stimulate German industry. They postponed negotiations for a permanent settlement until 1929. After prolonged talks in that year, the Young Plan, again named after an American delegate, Owen Young, reduced the total German liability to a little over $2 billion exclusive of interest, payable over fifty-nine years, and promised an early evacuation of the Rhineland, occupied by the Allies since 1919.

The Dawes and Young plans initiated and then sustained a jerry-built structure that temporarily eased the problem of reparations and war debts. Beginning in 1924, American and British investors, attracted by high interest rates, lent large sums to Germany, which in turn used part of this capital to rebuild its industry and to pay reparations. With this source of income, the Allies could repay their war debts to America. Entranced by the huge flows of capital, neither American lenders nor German borrowers questioned the long-range soundness of the arrangement. By the end of 1928, the German government had borrowed $1.5 billion and paid $1.25 billion in reparations; local governments and private citizens in Germany had borrowed an additional $4.5 billion from abroad, over half from the United States. This circular flow of capital required increasingly larger loans, since Germany often committed its resources to nonproductive public works or to increased living standards rather than to capital growth. Beginning in mid-1928, the bull market in New York began to attract more American capital into domestic investment and away from Germany. By 1930 a developing depression drew foreign money increasingly out of Germany, revealing the delicate economic interrelations that had existed among the countries.

If the prosperity of the late 1920's obscured the pitfalls of international finance, it fostered an important peace movement that culminated in the Kellogg-Briand Pact to "outlaw" war. The success of recent diplomatic negotiations, particularly the Washington Conference and the Dawes Plan, allowed American pacifists to hope that their goals were not only

**The Kellogg-
Briand Pact**

feasible but shortly to be realized. On April 6, 1927, the tenth anniversary of American entry into World War I, the French foreign minister, Aristide Briand, addressed a message to the American people, proposing that the two nations mutually renounce war. Briand hoped to counter France's militarist image in the United States. Such a maneuver promised a "negative alliance," and a strengthened French position in Europe. But peace groups ignored the rather obvious political implications and enthusiastically launched a massive campaign to secure United States acceptance.

Briand's message irritated Frank B. Kellogg, who succeeded Hughes as secretary of state in March 1925. A self-made man, Kellogg had served a single term in the United States Senate before his appointment as ambassador to Britain by Harding. He had to respond to public opinion, now heavily in favor of Briand's proposal. Yet the secretary recognized that such an agreement would antagonize other powers, almost certainly provoke serious opposition in the Senate, and undermine his own efforts to negotiate bilateral arbitration treaties. Senator Borah offered a way out of the dilemma. When Kellogg appeared before his Foreign Relations Committee, Borah suggested that all nations renounce war. No one could ob-

A Senate Foreign Relations Committee hearing on disarmament. Seated, from left to right are: Secretary of State Henry L. Stimson; Senator Frederick Gillett; Senator Hiram Johnson; Senator William Borah, chairman; Senator Thomas Walsh; Senator Claude Swanson; Senator Joseph Robinson; Senator James Reed. Standing, left to right are: Secretary of the Navy Charles Francis Adams; Senator Pat Harrison; Senator Robert La Follette; Senator Arthur Vandenberg; Admiral William Pratt; Senator Key Pittman. *Library of Congress*

ject to such a course, and the idea electrified pacifists. Since no power could risk defending war, negotiations proceeded rapidly on a formula to outlaw war "as an instrument of national policy." Dozens of powers eventually subscribed to the resulting Pact of Paris (also known as the Kellogg-Briand Pact), a thoroughly innocuous document lacking enforcement machinery and without credibility in most foreign ministries. The diplomatic historian J. B. Duroselle has called the Kellogg-Briand Pact a "policy of illusion," for it created a psychological security without the collective guarantees or reconciliation of interests necessary for a lasting peace.

Intimations of Armageddon

The economic collapse that began in 1929 destroyed the fragile diplomatic and political structures of the twenties. Depression undermined the balance of peace in the Far East, vitiated the movement toward disarmament, and more intimately involved the United States in European affairs. During Hoover's presidency, the mood of America's foreign relations changed abruptly, from the equanimity of the twenties to a crisis mentality appropriate to the first intimations of a coming Armageddon.

The man who grappled with these perplexities, Henry L. Stimson, proved to be one of the most skillful of our secretaries of state. Exceedingly wealthy—his annual income normally surpassed $1 million—the new secretary had the independence and certainty of the very rich. He was also aloof and legalistic. His State Department subordinates thought him cold and stubborn. He largely ignored his permanent staff, a thoroughly competent and qualified group. Clashes in taste and opinion even marred his relations with President Hoover. The two men irritated each other from the beginning. The aristocratic New Yorker loathed Hoover's early morning exercise sessions at the White House: Stimson's brief workday and frequent vacations annoyed the indefatigable president. Stimson's inclination toward the use, or at least the show, of force frightened a president determined to avoid war. The secretary of state usually ignored the domestic ramifications of foreign policy, a luxury denied Hoover. The two respected each other, however, and a reasonably efficient but impersonal working relationship gradually emerged. After 1930 deepening internal crises preoccupied Hoover, yet Stimson always understood that the president's wishes, not his own, would determine the main configurations of our international affairs. The result of all this was a peculiar mix, a Hoover-Stimson foreign policy.

Two persistent problems dominated American policy during the early 1930's: the breakdown of peace in the Far East and the world economic disaster. The Far Eastern crisis crashed down upon the new administra-

tion almost immediately. The disintegration of China had created a fundamental imbalance of power throughout East Asia. Under Chiang Kai-shek,
the Chinese revolution degenerated by the 1920's into a factional contest
for personal power—if indeed it had ever risen above that. Corruption
and intrigue destroyed Sun Yat-sen's ideals; war lords kept the nation in
disunity and wasted China's strength. The national government in Nanking employed foreign policy as a weapon in domestic politics. This shattered relations with China's two powerful neighbors, the Soviet Union
and Japan, and subverted the essential prerequisite for the Anglo-American open door, a self-sustaining China. Stimson initially miscalculated the
Far Eastern situation and soon blundered into ill-considered and embarrassed commitments.

In the summer of 1929, an intensely nationalistic Chiang seized the Rus-
sian-owned Chinese Eastern Railroad in Manchuria. He wanted to encourage national feeling in central China and undercut the power of a
local warlord. The Soviet Union broke diplomatic relations. Stimson immediately tried mediation. The Soviets had not signed the Nine Power
Treaty and were not yet members of the League of Nations. Thus, Stimson suggested that the great powers remind both China and Russia of
their obligations under the Kellogg-Briand Pact, the only applicable
agreement. Relieved of responsibility, Europe gratefully supported this
gesture. Then, without consulting the interested countries, Stimson also
proposed an international "committee on conciliation" to negotiate a settlement. The idea did not sit well; Japan, fearing the establishment of a
disadvantageous precedent, rejected the proposal outright, while Britain
and France clearly disliked meddling in Asian complexities. Fortunately
for Stimson, neither China nor Russia wanted war and negotiated a *status
quo ante* settlement in private. Nevertheless, this episode placed the
United States in the unwelcome role of guaranteeing the Pact of Paris
and revealed that European countries would hesitate to challenge Japanese ambitions in Manchuria.

In 1931 Japanese troops occupied large parts of Manchuria, directly violating the two Washington Conference treaties. This invasion launched
fourteen years of war between Imperial Japan and the Republic of China.
War was not altogether unexpected. China had continued to drift, internal struggles draining its power. Economic depression diverted Britain
and America from the Far East and, at the same time, sharpened the Japanese interests in mainland Asia as a market for manufacturers and a source
of raw materials. Asia was more than an economic issue for Japan; territorial expansion would fulfill the nation's destiny and the honor of its
people. The fertile soil and mineral wealth of relatively underpopulated
Manchuria in particular had attracted Tokyo since the nineteenth century.

The needs of the early thirties convinced many Japanese, especially soldiers and businessmen, that a propitious opportunity had arrived.

It all began on September 19, 1931. After falsely announcing that Chinese troops had "attacked" the Japanese-owned South Manchurian Railway, the Japanese assaulted a 200,000-man Chinese army stationed along the railroad. Incredible Chinese incompetence, together with Japanese tactical sophistication, led to an early Chinese defeat, even as Chiang attended to a Communist challenge in central China. The victorious Japanese Kwantung Army moved south toward the important city of Chinchow, the industrial center of Manchuria. Army headquarters in Tokyo supported the move. Accountable only to the emperor, the military effectively overruled the outraged civilian government. Prospects of glory and empire provoked initial public enthusiasm. The inflationary effects of deficit spending and government borrowing partially revived Japanese prosperity and sustained the army's adventure. In the fact of public fervor and military stubbornness, the civilians lost control over events.

An early picture of Chiang Kai-shek (1886–). Chiang began his political career as a member of the revolutionary party of Sun Yat-sen in 1911. He created the Kuomintang army in the early 1920's and led it to victory at Nanking, where he established the seat of government in 1927. Chiang became president of the Chinese Nationalist government in 1928, a position he has held since. *Library of Congress*

International reaction was immediate but indecisive. The Western powers were preoccupied by a financial crisis that eventually forced the British off the gold standard and Germany into something approaching international receivership. But Japan's action clearly required a response, and the issue rapidly resolved itself into a simple question: who would lead an effort to halt Japan—the League of Nations or the United States? Since Hoover steadfastly rejected any policy likely to result in war, and the economic troubles proscribed military action by other powers, the prospects for successful action seemed remote. Stimson first tried to cooperate with Europe. Mistakenly assuming full American support, the League of Nations Council urged Japan to evacuate occupied territory by November 16, 1931, the date of the next scheduled council meeting. This impetuous action risked league prestige, and when it became clear that the Japanese army would ignore the deadline, the November meeting assumed great significance. On November 20, the Japanese government, perhaps hoping to employ the league in its struggle against the army, proposed a temporary military truce and a neutral investigation. After three weeks of complicated maneuvers designed primarily to force Chinese acceptance, the council adopted Tokyo's proposal and immediately dispatched the famous Lytton Commission to Manchuria.

The solution never materialized. The army refused to honor the truce and a new Japanese cabinet had already approved the occupation of all Manchuria and the neighboring Chinese province of Jehol. When Chinchow surrendered to Japanese troops on December 23, Tokyo's intentions could no longer remain hidden. Angered at the guile of the Japanese and frustrated by the apparent failure of the league, Stimson decided that America must take independent action. Following a suggestion of President Hoover, he dispatched a reminder to both Japan and China that the United States would not recognize any situation impairing its rights in China. In practice, nonrecognition—the so-called Stimson Doctrine—meant that Washington considered the Japanese annexations to be illegal. Although Stimson had intended his declaration to be unilateral, he was pleased by international support. In February 1933 the league requested Japanese withdrawal from Manchuria; instead, Japan withdrew from the league.

Within its American context, nonrecognition represented a limited but firm response, a clear and forceful assertion of United States interests in Asian affairs. But the Stimson Doctrine did not halt Japanese expansion. Indeed, as a tactic of passivity, nonrecognition was a retreat from the arbitral and conciliatory procedures outlined in the League Covenant. In late January 1932 Japanese naval officers, apparently jealous of army successes in Manchuria, attacked Shanghai in central China. Unlike the earlier incidents, however, this act frightened everyone in Tokyo, particularly the army, and the government ultimately disavowed Admiral Shiozawa. Fighting continued for over a month, since Japan could "save face" only by taking the city and then abandoning it. The Western powers, however, did not know this. Tokyo rejected Anglo-American mediation. Stimson then wanted to invoke the Nine Power Treaty, an audacious proposal that could result in collective sanctions against Japan and possibly war. The British foreign secretary agreed in principle but confronted an extremely hostile cabinet. The resulting delay, which Stimson mistook for evasion, persuaded him to undertake another unilateral act. Unable to deal directly with the principals, he addressed a public letter to Senator William F. Borah, chairman of the Foreign Relations Committee. The "Borah letter" hinted that because Japan had undermined the Washington treaties, the United States might fortify Guam and the Philippines. It was America's good fortune that Tokyo, already having decided to withdraw from Shanghai, did not call Stimson's bluff.

International Finance

The ineffectiveness of the Western response to the Manchurian crisis resulted chiefly from problems elsewhere, particularly the international financial crisis. By 1931, two years of price deflation and contraction in credit had brought intolerable pressures against the weakest links in the world economy, particularly Germany. That nation, which was dependent upon semipermanent renewal of its short-term commercial papers and continued export surpluses to pay its bloated debts, had responded to depression with price and wage deflation in an effort to maintain a favorable balance of trade. In May 1931 the collapse of Austria's largest bank, the *Kreditanstaldt*, set off a distrust of printed currencies and a demand for gold throughout central Europe. When British and American investors withdrew capital, finances suffered further; Germans themselves, fearing a downward revaluation of the mark, converted their paper money into gold, thereby threatening the entire banking system. If unabated, the dual pressures threatened to bankrupt Germany and, since extensive foreign capital would be frozen, menace British and American solvency as well. Initially the Bank of England propped up the tottering German-Austrian economy; its resources, however, were insufficient to reverse the accelerating demand for gold. France attached unacceptable political conditions to its offer of economic aid. Europeans anxiously turned to the United States.

Since enveloping European crisis threatened disaster for the American banking system, Hoover responded with a broadly conceived rescue operation. As the crisis expanded, the president unilaterally proposed—the world by now was getting used to such pronouncements from Washington—the famous Hoover Moratorium, a twelve-month suspension of war debts and reparations payments. Hoover hoped that the moratorium on reparations would enable Germany to cope with its private debt payments and forestall repercussions elsewhere. The president included war debts in his moratorium proposal both to induce Allied acceptance and to relieve the drainage of sterling out of Britain. France, which was financially secure, balked for nearly three weeks over the surrender of reparations, hoping to gain political concessions. This delay undermined the psychological benefits of Hoover's proposal. In the interval, a devastating run on German banks developed. Even governmental intervention, international loans, and exchange controls could not prevent technical insolvency. In response to this new crisis, the resourceful Hoover initiated a "standstill conference," which met in London during July 1931. Germany's major creditors quickly extended Hoover's moratorium to include short-term commercial paper.

Hoover's imaginative diplomacy had several unexpected results. Since the Bank of England held large amounts of frozen German bills, a speculative drive developed against the pound. Drained of public confidence by unfounded fears of mutiny in the British navy and the cumulative nature of such runs, by September the bank had exhausted its gold reserves. Britain had to abandon the gold standard and devaluate the pound. The three months of uncertainty, followed by continued fluctuation in the exchange value of the pound, further weakened confidence. Speculators next attacked the dollar, but immense American gold reserves thwarted the effort. Partly to halt this monetary chaos and restore confidence, but largely to capitalize upon the implications of Hoover's moratorium, the European powers met at Lausanne in July 1932. The Allies reduced German reparation liabilities to a token $700 million but connected this settlement with a reduction in the war debt owed to the United States.

For those who like to seek out the most intriguing but necessary conditions for momentous events, the debt issue provides a perfect occasion. The Lausanne Conference tried to force an American concession on debts in behalf of canceled reparations. But by 1932 Hoover did not have the political leverage even to renew the moratorium, let alone cancel the debts. Since Hitler gained power in Germany in 1933 by narrow margins, these varied concessions could well have alleviated the chauvinistic bitterness that fed his campaign. In other words, a more generous debt policy on our part might, in combination with a thousand other causal conditions, have averted the Third Reich. But obviously no one could foresee all of this in 1932, and neither Hoover nor a later Roosevelt had the political leverage for doing much about the debts. With minor exceptions they would never be collected. Save for Finland, even the countries that resumed payments in 1932 resorted to token payments in 1933, and canceled all payments thereafter when Congress forbade private American loans to defaulting countries. The lack of eventual collection thus compounds the tragedy of our policy, for the debt issue had tremendous negotiating value late in 1932, none by 1934.

With financial crises and a war in Asia, the old dreams of disarmament slowly faded. When the World Disarmament Conference finally convened in Geneva on February 2, 1932, it only began two years of delay and frustration that led to an almost inevitable failure. In spite of the economic crisis and Japanese expansion, there was much popular hope that disarmament, promised in the Versailles treaty, might soon occur. The statesmen gathered in Geneva were much less sanguine. Differences of purpose divided the major powers from the outset. Stimson believed, for example, that the conference should concentrate on peace, settling European problems capable of provoking war. In contrast, the French emphasized disarmament itself and argued that the Geneva talks should augment the security of France. Britain wanted to reduce military expenditures immediately, and thereby to ease the pressure upon the delicate English financial situation. Germany saw in disarmament a method to achieve parity. Exceedingly complex technical complications emerged, principally the familiar "yardstick" problem and the distinction between offensive and defensive weapons. The fundamental dilemma was political. The French demanded either an international police force or Anglo-American guarantees before disarmament. Neither London nor Washington would issue France a blank check, and the United States argued that in any event only disarmament could insure security.

This question of timing—whether disarmament or security should take precedence—together with technical complexities and divergent purposes soon deadlocked the talks. Despite several ambitious plans, notably Hoover's dramatic suggestion for an immediate reduction by one-third in all existing armaments, and British Prime Minister MacDonald's much milder approach, which was simply to strengthen the league by maneuvering the United States into its consultative machinery, the conference could neither escape nor resolve its dilemmas. When inconclusiveness became only a method to preserve the status quo, notably the military predominance of France, Germany withdrew from the interminable talks late in 1933, rendering success impossible. At an ever accelerating pace, Europe would now turn its plowshares back into mighty swords.

4

For those who grew up or became young adults in the twenties, the decade will remain the most memorable of their lives. Those who remember Lindbergh's famous flight or the Scopes trial are now grandparents, fully deserving of all the indulgent pleasures of nostalgia. Old albums, with slightly faded snapshots, reveal the confined and straightened curves of the flapper, and hint at the exuberance of the Charleston. In a few ancient attics, ponderous old Atwater-Kent radios gather dust beside the stereoscopes and Victrolas that they largely replaced in fashionable parlors. Until antique dealers grabbed them up, ancient T-model Fords rusted in barns or garages, often in unspoken witness to Grandpa's inability to master the clutch that an inconsiderate Henry Ford placed in his 1927 concession to competition, the A-model.

It is testimony to the ferment and diversity of the twenties that the shared memories encompass mainly the externals, the sensational, the fashionable, or the superficial. Americans of all persuasion could cheer the athletic exploits of Babe Ruth or Jack Dempsey, or lament the senseless killing of Bobby Frank, or condemn the gang wars in Chicago, or join in such fads as Mah-Jongg or crossword puzzles. But they divided on the merit or even the morality of jazz, both applauded and lamented the sensuality of such movie heroes as Rudolph Valentino or Clara Bow, cheered and rebuked the ephemeral antics of rebellious college students, celebrated and condemned all the talk about Freud and sexual liberation or even a "new" woman. At one point only, the sensational also touched deeper chords of sympathy and a common loyalty, and renewed an insecure belief in the possibilities of heroism and authentic greatness—the thrilling flight to Paris by a youthful Charles A. Lindbergh in 1927. His exploit received more publicity than the armistice of 1918 (one Sunday paper devoted 100 columns of text and pictures to Lindbergh). President Coolidge sent a naval ship to retrieve him and his *Spirit of St. Louis*. He returned for a triumphant tour unrivaled before or since.

The diversity of taste in the twenties reflected wide differences of heritage, belief, and experience. No simplified typology, such as rural versus urban, or low-brow versus high-brow, can do justice to the complex is-

Strange Interlude—The Memorable Twenties

Earl Carroll, Broadway producer, providing "make up" instructions for some of the Washington, D.C., dancers selected for the Vanities (January 1925). Such shows, which would have scandalized Victorian grandparents, symbolized the gay and carefree mood of the twenties. *Library of Congress*

Organized crime enjoyed its heyday during Prohibition. George "Bugs" Moran, chief of the North Side Gang in Chicago, established his headquarters in a garage on North Clark Street. On St. Valentine's Day, 1929, six of his gang were in the garage waiting for a shipment of liquor. A touring car pulled up; five men, three in police uniform, got out and entered the garage. They lined up the Moran men facing the wall, and sprayed them with machine-gun bullets. Bugs Moran escaped by a few minutes, for as he approached the garage he saw the supposed policemen and, thinking it was a raid, stayed clear. *United Press International*

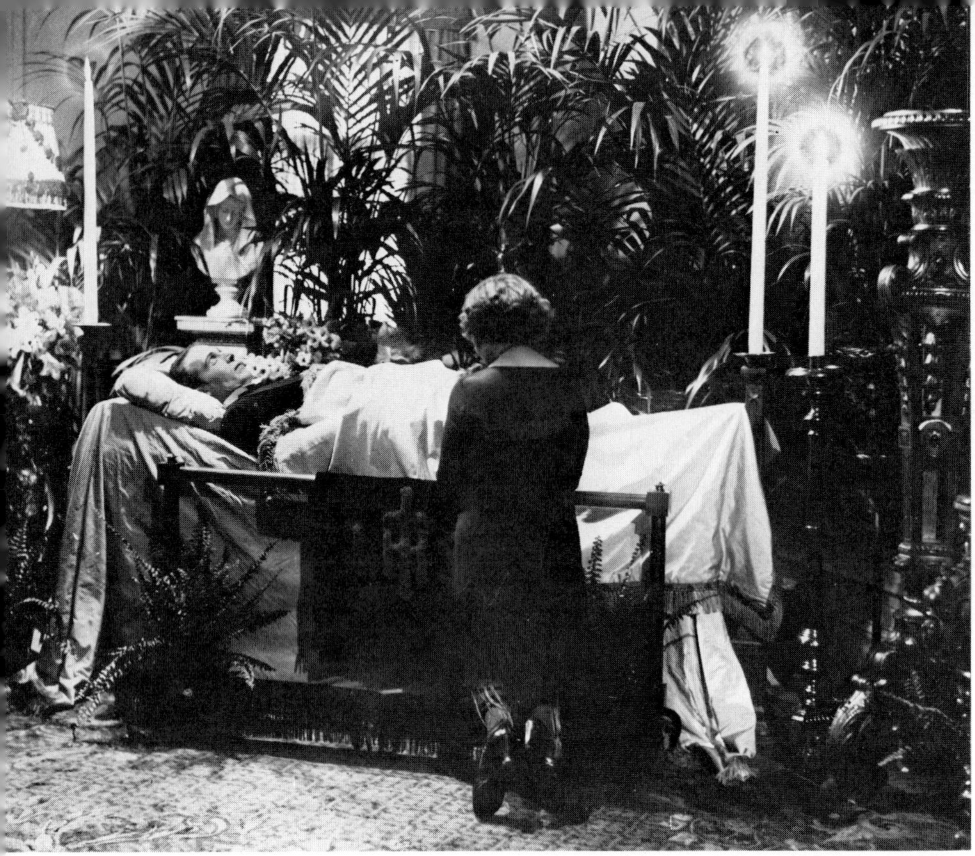

When Rudolph Valentino died, all of American womanhood mourned. Valentino, star of the silent screen, lived in an age when Americans created larger-than-life-size idols to worship. *United Press International*

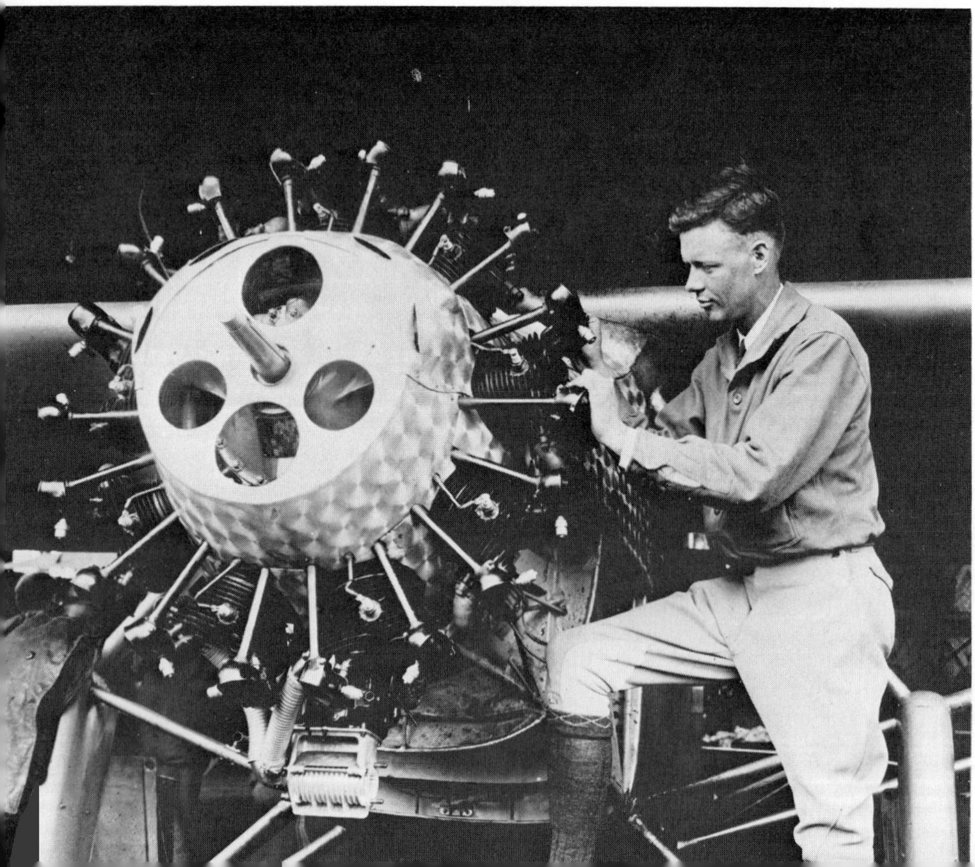

Charles Lindbergh with his plane, the *Spirit of St. Louis*. Lindbergh was the prototype American hero. His boyish good looks captured the hearts of all Americans. *Library of Congress*

sues that divided people. It would be so simple if all rural or small-town Protestants struggled for Biblical literalism against egg-headed Darwinists, or to enforce prohibition against whiskey moguls or undisciplined Irish Catholics, or to preserve puritanical mores against libertines on campus or in the bohemias or Gomorrahs of large cities. Or that the same type of people, when most threatened or fearful, joined the Ku Klux Klan, adding to their defensive strategies a virulent hatred of Catholics or Jews or Negroes. Such a simplified pattern breaks down in all directions. Protestants fought as well as supported prohibition; so did Roman Catholics. Klans formed in cities as well as villages. Religious fundamentalism flourished among city dwellers who came from such a religious tradition, and it still does. And some of the very people who fought prohibition, including Roman Catholics, fought for the most puritanical standards in the areas of sex and the family.

Prohibition was the most fractious issue of the decade. It was also a very old issue. Legal prohibition existed at the state level before the Civil War, when temperance vied with abolition as the most compelling moral issue in America. The organized crusade against the manufacture or sale of spiritous beverages flowered in the late nineteenth century, led by the Women's Christian Temperance Union and, later, by the more militant Anti-Saloon League. By World War I almost half the states had statewide prohibition; others had local option. The war provided the final stimulus for the Eighteenth Amendment and national prohibition, and thus one more extension of federal regulatory power. The need for alcohol in the war, the widespread hatred of Germans (and thus of breweries and beer), and the spartan and sacrificial idealism of war made ratification easy. By January 1919, the required three-fourths had approved. Congress responded with a strong enforcement bill, the Volstead Act, which it passed over a presidential veto. Neither the amendment nor the act made drinking a federal crime; both prohibited the manufacture, sale, or transportation of alcoholic beverages (defined as more than .5 percent alcohol).

The focus upon manufacturing and sale helped broaden support. Many who personally drank alcoholic beverages still condemned the commercial exploitation of human weakness, and willingly sacrificed a personal indulgence in behalf of ridding society of the high costs of alcoholism. Socialists often saw prohibition as one blow against an immoral capitalist system. An analysis of prohibitionist literature reveals a strong paternalist emphasis, a concern for the welfare or the sober industry of laborers or, in the South, of blacks. The powerful religious ingredient more nearly related to ethnic background than to theology or Biblical authority (the

The "Noble Experiment"

Bible only condemned drunkenness). The most abstemious denominations, and particularly the Methodists, were English in origin and always insistent upon a high level of personal purity. Prohibition, on the whole, proved a unifying cause for most major Protestant denominations, for it appealed both to modernists and to the orthodox. Contrary to the stereotypes of "wets," the religious crusaders always emphasized the dire social consequences of drink, or of institutions that it supported (the saloon), and did not condemn it because it was pleasurable. Only the theologically naïve saw alcohol as an evil (orthodox Christians believed all that their God created was intrinsically good). Christian prohibitionists saw alcoholic beverages as dangerously addictive intoxicants for some people, and at best a nonnutritional and diverting vice for others. Notably, those who viewed drink as a moral or religious issue did not incorporate any form of alcoholic drink into their normal life pattern, and thus imbibed, if at all, in guilty defiance of local mores or to find escape through intoxication.

A government so quick to pass the Volstead Act never effectively enforced it. Perhaps no one foresaw the difficulty. In the early twenties less than 3,000 Internal Revenue agents had to guard all our coasts and borders, check on the diversions of industrial or medicinal alcohol, and locate and destroy thousands of private stills. From the beginning, illicit liquor reached either the more affluent or the well-situated customer. Yet, although we have no measure of "bootleg" whiskey, we can easily exaggerate it. In areas with strong popular support for prohibition (geographically, most of the country), the sources did dry up. The saloon disappeared. The overall consumption of alcoholic beverages dropped drastically (possibly by several times its previous level), the incidence of alcoholism went down, and the drinking habits of the common people altered for a lifetime. After repeal, the American consumption of such beverages remained low for at least two generations. The most enthusiastic prohibitionists attributed almost miraculous effects to the Volstead Act; economic prosperity seemed to them direct products of a much greater sobriety. But it was a quite different story in areas where local opinion divided, or even opposed prohibition, as in large cities and in certain ethnic communities, rural or urban. There federal officials were helpless and local law enforcement authorities totally uncooperative. The "wets" fought either for revision of the act (to allow beer or wine) or for complete repeal.

The problems of enforcement undermined prohibition more than the minority desire for accessible drinks. Those willing to ignore the law helped undermine respect for all laws, and also provided a lucrative, relatively safe market for large, organized criminal syndicates, particularly in wide-open cities such as Chicago. Al Capone became one of the prime

symbols of the age, as prohibitionists even in small towns somehow suspected his mythical hand behind every local bootlegger. An easy, but absurd, contention was that prohibition failed because the government tried to legislate on a moral issue, as if murder or robbery or practically any acts proscribed by law are not moral issues. It failed locally because of a lack of public consensus on moral issues. No one denied the terrible social effects of alcoholism, but many doubted that prohibition reduced these. They viewed moderate drinking as an innocuous pleasure. In certain national traditions, beer and wine, or the beerhall and tavern, fulfilled a vital communal need. For rebellious youth, or for urban sophisticates, defiance of prohibition became a treasured game. In some social circles, prohibition actually increased the consumption of alcohol, and helped break down earlier barriers to social drinking on the part of women. To all such people, prohibition seemed a form of cultural imperialism, a challenge to a beloved way of life, or an intolerant expansion of government authority into areas of private freedom. They neither respected the law nor those

The Volstead Act, passed in 1919, made the manufacture, sale, or transportation of alcoholic beverages a federal crime. Here, federal agents are destroying $1 million worth of beer, champagne, and whisky in Brooklyn, New York. The agents found the whisky in the U.S. Army warehouse pier in Brooklyn. *Underwood & Underwood*

who tried to enforce it. Where such attitudes prevailed, enforcement proved almost impossible and terribly costly. In the long run, the advocates of repeal won their battle almost as easily as prohibition won in 1919. The depression helped defuse the issue, and created appealing economic reasons for reopening breweries and distilleries. But repeal, which came in 1933, did not end prohibition. It simply restored local option, and allowed a diversity of answers to the as yet unsolved problems of drink and alcoholism.

While prohibition united most Protestants, very fundamental theological and doctrinal issues divided them. The division became visible soon after the Civil War, although its roots went back much farther. The higher criticism of the Bible, theories about the evolution of species, the earliest returns from cultural anthropology all challenged Biblical literalism and even very basic Christian doctrines. Professors in leading theological seminaries, and a minority of parish ministers had to cope with these new ideas, even as a majority of pastors and parishioners continued to ignore or simply to reject them well into the new century. By 1900 it was possible to divide Protestants in a very loose way as "modernists" versus the adherents of older forms of orthodoxy. The modernists made at least a weak accommodation with newer scientific knowledge; the orthodox held firm to ancient doctrines and either denied the relevance of scientific knowledge to Christian doctrine or, more hazardous but more honest, frontally challenged it at all points of apparent conflict.

In 1910 two California laymen funded a series of pamphlets to defend the traditional doctrines of the church, published under the title of *The Fundamentals*. Serious, scholarly works, written by eminent English and American theologians, and in many cases intellectually equal to the very best of "modernist" literature, these pamphlets gave a new name to a type of holding action in the churches. The label "fundamentalist" would always have an insecure semantic position somewhere between orthodox (a reference to belief or doctrine) and evangelical (a reference to religious feeling or to the quality of religious experience and commitment). By the twenties the label gained an opprobrious meaning in many circles. It usually referred only to those among orthodox and evangelical Protestants who led a desperate, often political, and usually anti-intellectualist crusade against modern scientific theories and against all theological modernism. These "fundamentalists" defended an "old-time" religion, which usually entailed a central concern for redemptive experience and only a secondary interest in the "social" evils that so often preoccupied "modernists." For such fundamentalists, a stereotyped Darwinism came to symbolize the most critical issues at stake, even as the public schools and state legislatures became the battleground.

In many ways the fundamentalists were prophetic. They defended not only certain treasured religious beliefs but a whole way of life. The values of a largely rural America were under attack. Evangelical Protestantism had underwritten the old culture. Now it was in jeopardy. It seemed that urban cynics, the connoisseurs of despair and decadence, the insensitive and arrogant scientists, the brash college kids, and the novelists and critics all wanted nothing more than to ridicule and destroy the old Biblical beliefs, the moral verities, the simple virtues that fundamentalists still loved, and that they correctly sensed still had great appeal for the majority of common people. Something almost maliciously called "Christianity" might survive all the elitist revisions, but it would really be a new and alien religion, in most of its essentials different from what they knew and treasured.

Darwinism was an excellent focus for some of the critical issues, but few of the contenders on either side understood its subtleties or some of its implications. Charles Darwin in his *Origin of Species* (1859) did not originate the idea of evolving species. He did offer a new understanding of species, and a theory about how new life forms develop in nature. He noted the normal variations from generation to generation, and how animal breeders take advantage of these to develop desired characteristics in domestic animals. This is artificial selection. The variations (explained in detail only by later geneticists) provide the possibility of organic change but do not in themselves determine the direction of change. Darwin, as he observed the beautiful differentiation of species in such isolated environments as the Galapagos Islands, suspected that variant environments shape the course of organic change and insure the slow evolution of more complex or more highly adaptable species. In a loose sense, an environment selects, although not as quickly or as neatly as animal breeders. This is natural selection. Certain inherited characteristics adapt an organism to an environment and increase its likelihood of survival or procreation. Since variation is continuous, and selection always at work, the word "species" only refers to relatively stable organisms, and not to a created, hierarchical order of beings. Using these hypotheses, Darwin speculated that all present organisms evolved through variation and natural selection from primitive life forms, although he could not possibly provide anything close to a complete fossil record of this long process.

At a very unsophisticated level, Darwin not only challenged the Biblical story of creation but, more critically for Protestants, the veracity of Holy Scriptures, both as to events and as to chronology. Much more important, he threatened one of the major foundations of Christian belief

—that a deity was the creative and intelligent source of all things, including all forms of life. If Darwin's view of natural history were correct, then biology reveals no intelligent design or purpose at all, and certainly requires none as an explanation of present organic diversity or a wonderful ecological harmony. One may, of course, still affirm such creative purpose behind nature, but he cannot use organic complexity to support the belief. In short, Darwin undercut one of the most pervasive, and most used, defenses of theism—from design to designer. Of course, he offered no explanation of ultimate origins. No one can. A biologist who assumes the eternality of nature joins the Christian who assumes the eternality of God. But the implication was clear—Darwinism was inimical to very basic assumptions heretofore held by Christians.

For one who took seriously the empirical foundations of Darwin's theories but continued to affirm Christian creationism, the alternative position was a subtle variation on Darwin. Louis Agassiz, a prominent American naturalist, accepted the continuous alteration of organisms by variation and a form of natural selection, leading to major changes in life forms within a geological age. But he did not believe such changes account for major breakthroughs in nature, such as the transition from plants to animals, or from fish to amphibians, or from nonverbal primates to intelligent man. He assumed several periods of creativity in the long evolution of species. Subsequent work in paleontology has only somewhat weakened this position and strengthened that of Darwin. Not the fossil record, but characteristics of Darwinism itself generally recommended it to almost all biologists.

Ironically, few Christians, even among the most radical, ever tried to cope with Darwin in the honest way that Agassiz did. In almost every case they joined him in discarding a literal interpretation of Genesis, but then turned to a non-Darwinian and purposeful form of evolution, which they now saw as God's method of creation. They reinserted design and purpose into a process. Despite all their claims and all the fundamentalist accusations, they came no closer to Darwin than fundamentalists except in the minor area of Biblical interpretation. But fundamentalists did not worry about the niceties of biological theories. They saw a clear tendency in modernists—to hedge on any Biblical truth as soon as scientists presumed to undermine it. This would eventually mean a rejection of all Biblical miracles, and an undermining of the one central doctrine of Christianity—that Jesus was the Christ. Miracles such as the virgin birth provided the proof of this claim. On such issues the fundamentalists were at one with Roman Catholics and with other less aggressive Protestants, who preferred to fight the doctrinal issues away from the glare of publicity and the hazards of the political arena.

In American mythology, the fundamentalist controversy reached a climax in a sweltering Dayton, Tennessee, in the summer of 1925. Nothing could be more erroneous, although it is possible that a small element of fundamentalism received its last national publicity as a result of the Scopes trial. The trial was contrived. Tennessee, along with several other states, passed a law that prohibited the schools from teaching that man "descended from a lower order of animals," a restriction that needed careful qualification to fit Darwinism, and which in loosest form fit several competing theories of evolution. Partly for commercial reasons (to put Dayton on the map and to help local business) and partly to test the validity of the law, a cooperative young teacher in the Dayton high school, John Scopes, arranged his own arrest after reading an offending passage to some baffled students. The state dutifully prosecuted, and journalists quickly made the trial the big show that Dayton wanted, particularly after William Jennings Bryan volunteered to assist the prosecution, and Clarence Darrow, a famous defense lawyer and religious agnostic, joined an already able defense panel.

Bryan and Darrow stole the show even as they obscured the legal issues. Bryan had become the most prominent spokesman for antievolution laws. On this as on earlier economic issues, he backed the majority position. His own religious and humanistic convictions led him to defend the uniqueness of man, which he believed under attack by what he called the "monkey theory." He beautifully caricatured many of the most absurd claims by self-professed Darwinists (a baby wiggles its toes because it used to hang in trees), and suspected a form of sophistry in much of what scientists advertised as the gospel truth. He also identified Darwinism with a callous "survival of the fittest" ethic that he had long battled in his war against corporate power and aggressive, arrogant nationalists. The version of evolutionary theory that he attacked seemed to deny God as well as any purpose and design in the world. If widely disseminated, it would persuade man and literally fulfill its own prophecy by turning him into an insensitive animal. Ironically, Bryan was not a doctrinal fundamentalist. He lacked in theological sophistication, and could not be doctrinaire. He defended a rather ecumenical and vague Christianity, but loved the Bible and assumed its truth, although he was open to variant translations or plausible interpretations. At Dayton, his very lack of theological sophistication often left him defenseless, for when pressed he felt burdened to defend noncontextual passages of the Bible that he had undoubtedly never even tried to puzzle out before.

Darrow, a clever lawyer, was not nearly as adept as Bryan in such a setting. He did not represent any form of Christian modernism, but rather a type of humanistic agnosticism that occasionally bordered onto a deep

William Jennings Bryan culminated his long political career as a prosecutor at the Scopes Trial in Dayton, Tennessee, July 1925. He died at the end of the trial. *Underwood & Underwood*

Clarence Darrow (1857–1938) headed the team of defense attorneys at the Scopes Trial. He was a clever lawyer, and attempted to try the law rather than the specific case. He is seen here reading a portion of the daily sack of mail that he received at Dayton. *Underwood & Underwood*

cynicism. To fundamentalists, he seemed a living demonstration of the effects of evolutionary doctrines. Politically, Darrow had long joined with Bryan in the defense of underdogs and in opposition to special privilege. With only limited success, Darrow tried to place the Tennessee law on trial, and to argue the merits of a generalized form of evolutionary theory as against the Biblical story. He revealed only contempt for the beliefs of Bryan and most of his courtroom audience. The most sensational point of the trial came when Darrow questioned Bryan, whom he invited to the witness stand as an expert on the Bible. Under the pressure of Darrow's questions, and his ridicule of a "fool religion," Bryan defended the Adam and Eve story, the restrictive chronology required by Biblical literalism, and the account of Noah and the flood. The trial developed into a delightfully newsworthy farce. It made Dayton the news capital of the world and led to an endless flow of articles and radio broadcasts. But the trial fueled religious passions on both sides without a single redeeming feature. The main contenders, unfortunately, were equally devoid of theological insight or understanding. The trial ended in a type of draw. The state easily proved its case—Scopes violated a state law. But it misassessed the $100 fine, which allowed the State Supreme Court to reverse the verdict without ruling on the constitutional issues. It thus frustrated the one justifiable goal of the defense.

A tired and exhausted Bryan died at the end of the trial. Fundamentalism did not die. It had a new martyr. Orthodox doctrines and an evangelical emphasis remained dominant in a large share of American churches, and most of all in black churches. If anything, the more traditional versions of Protestantism retained more vitality than the "modernist" forms, which faced overwhelming intellectual problems in the succeeding decades. But the fundamentalists would never again receive such publicity. Gradually they would withdraw from the political arena, relinquishing their early hope of using majoritarian democracy to insulate their beliefs and preferences, as was so well illustrated in their battles against evolution and for prohibition.

Klansmen and Agrarians

The new and improved Ku Klux Klan of the twenties provided a vulgar caricature of older American prejudices. This new Klan had only a sentimental tie to the KKK of Reconstruction. The new organization began at Stone Mountain, Georgia in 1915, but remained a small, local organization until after World War I. Then, aided by an aggressive recruitment strategy (each recruiter kept part of the new member's fee), it zoomed into a politically powerful national organization, able to sow seeds of dissension in the Democratic party and in several labor unions. By 1924 it claimed over 2,000,000 members, drawn mainly from laborers, farmers, and small businessmen. Yet most members remained active only for a short time, and some enticed into paying the original fee never became active at all. Locally, the Klan was often respectable, but the national organization suffered continuous criticism from major newspapers and from the intellectual community. For some, membership could be an embarrassment, and the white sheets used in parades a protection of anonymity. Most local Klans were little more than fraternal lodges for families, with an elaborate regalia and ritual. The appeal was nativist, Protestant, and racial, although regionally the Klans often denied religious intolerance or even any special animus toward blacks. Except in a few areas of the South, the KKK was never primarily an antiblack organization. Everywhere it stressed patriotism and religiosity, or the flag and the cross. It gained gullible members because of these conventional and normally respectable themes.

What was the Klan against? Verbally, anything un-Christian and un-American. Each Klan filled in the details, which varied from an intense fear of racial contamination, to concern for violations of local sexual mores, to exaggerated fears of immigration, to a zeal for prohibition, to efforts to close Catholic parochial schools, to fantastic allegations about sinister conspiracies by Jewish bankers. Yet, most local chapters rarely had the strength to do much more than talk. Their monthly meetings reinforced their fears, as they chanted the litany of advancing evils. They received most of their publicity from parades down Main Street, or infrequent regional meetings with great burning crosses. A local Klan might offer its welcome or unwelcome services to local police in order to enforce prohibition or to clear prostitutes from hated ethnic neighborhoods. In their most brutal guise, Klansmen formed vigilante committees and took the law into their own hands, harassing or driving away undesired and nonconforming citizens, or carrying out concerted attacks on Catholics or other resented minorities. In a few states, particularly Indiana and Oklahoma, the KKK gained immense political power. But its very undoing was its state and national leaders, who over and over turned out to be callous promoters, traitors to the Klan's own narrow standards. An early grand dragon fell sway to drink; a later one sexually assaulted a young girl. Several leaders played loose with funds. After 1925 the Klan steadily declined in numbers and lost almost all its political influence.

Fundamentalists and Klansmen offered extreme and often unlearned resistance to aspects of modernity, to new moral standards, to the erosion of older religious beliefs, to the very heterogeneity of American life. But their vague apprehensions did not have to take such a crude form. Down in Nashville, a group of Vanderbilt University professors framed an ex-

tremely subtle, philosophical defense of southern provincialism and agrarianism against the false gods of factories, commercialism, and ugly cities. Their perspective was essentially esthetic (most were poets or critics), and only derivatively economic. They believed man could not find fulfillment in large, impersonal organizations or collectivities, or apart from traditional roots in a regional culture. Their avowed goal was to persuade Southerners to resist the corporation and the factory system, or the lure of big government and a large federal bureaucracy, and to retain its agricultural economy and its rural folkways, including its existing religious and racial institutions. Economically, they hated all forms of modern corporate capitalism and yearned for a Jeffersonian world of propertied entrepreneurs. Their goal was radical—the early redistribution of real property, so that once again each person would own the means of production and have direct control over his own fate. Their romantic glorification of farm life, and of a largely subsistence form of agriculture, joined with a perceptive analysis of the loneliness and experiential bareness and growing ugliness of a society committed to profits, consumption of artless and tasteless products, a larger and larger gross national product, and endless but unrewarding labor.

A float from Cape May, New Jersey, shows that Klan membership became nationwide after a recruitment drive in the 1920's. The Klan enjoyed a surge of popularity in the early 1920's, but by 1925 it began a rapid decline. *Underwood & Underwood*

The southern agrarians seemed to glorify what was all but unrecover-able—small traditional communities and a simple life uncomplicated by greed and excessive ambition. Even as they perfected their argument (in a 1930 book, *I'll Take My Stand*), streams of young people fled the countryside and county seats of rural America for the larger cities. In part, they moved out of economic necessity. But, lured by their own vision of a good life, most left without regrets. This shift from farm to city constitutes an epic in our history, even as the tension between rural and urban values still haunts us. By 1920, for the first time, cities and towns of over 2,500 contained slightly more people than villages or the open countryside. By 1930 the balance clearly favored the towns and cities. The southern agrarians, and a few kindred voices (a Catholic Rural Life Conference, a few small back-to-land clubs) made up only a tiny mi-nority crying in the wilderness. And their moral and esthetic perspective, their emphasis upon subsistence and self-help, did not even match the dominant concerns of despairing farmers, who also lamented the plight of agriculture but in commercial terms. They complained of prices and poor profits, and lamented their inability to consume as much as city workers.

Artistic Ferment

The other side of the ageless rural-urban feud was what a perceptive liter-ary critic characterized as a "revolt against the village." It preoccupied several writers. Sherwood Anderson first exploited the theme in his semi-autobiographical short stories, collected in 1919 as *Winesburg, Ohio*. He began the literary exploitation of Freudian theories, and tried to probe the psychic depths of people in a small town. He found anything but a sim-ple and happy community, although he showed as much pity as contempt for people afflicted by all manner of guilt and neuroses. Sinclair Lewis of-fered a less psychological but just as foreboding a picture of village or small-town life in two of the best sellers of the decade—*Main Street* (1920) and *Babbitt* (1922). In small towns and large, educated young women identified with Carol Kennicott, who tried in vain to bring some-thing resembling culture and enlightenment to Gopher Prairie, Lewis's version of small town, U.S.A. Carol failed, and finally bowed before the banality of the complacent citizens and the boredom and ugliness of everyday life. Lewis's Babbitt would enter our vocabulary as the stereo-type of a superficial businessman in a small city. Yet, as so many refugees from the village, Lewis revealed his own ambivalence, and hinted at vir-tues in a world he never completely rejected. In later years he even ac-knowledged his affection for it.

H. L. Mencken never qualified his revulsion for most facets of American life, and particularly for small towns, Protestants, farmers, Southerners, and all provincials, by which he meant almost all Americans. He became the darling of college students, the very epitome of sophomoric rebellion. Personally, Mencken was a Baltimore newspaperman, an expert on the American language, and quite conventional in his own life-style. He made his national reputation as editor of two iconoclastic journals—*Smart Set* and *American Mercury*. Here he cultivated the best of young writers, and crusaded for greater literary freedom against the hated remnants of Victorian prudery. In his magazines, and then in a series of books appropriately entitled *Prejudices*, Mencken carried on his own vendetta against low-brow America. He had an epigrammatic insult for everyone, for the pompous and the sentimental, for the sincere and the idealistic. His prejudices often contradicted one another, and in total reflected no clear commitment except, possibly, to a vague sort of elitism. Mencken's vituperation reached its apogee in his commentary on the Scopes trial, on the *homo boobiens* of the hills, the gaping primates of the mountains, who were only part of the anthropoid rabble or peasants who largely populated our country. He sneered at all religions, but particularly Methodists, or Baptists, or Presbyterians. He unmercifully ridiculed politicians. His vitriolic pen never weakened, but in time his audience tired of iconoclasm, and in the committed thirties was quick to condemn him as an apostle of negativism.

In one sense, Mencken typified so many of the ablest writers in the decade in being virtually apolitical, contemptuous of mass politics or the inanities of majoritarian democracy. Nothing was more hopeless than entrusting one's fate to the people. Except for the problem of censorship, he found few political causes worthy of his efforts, no ideology to enlist in, no exploited people worth saving. He was the tired radical, with the post-rational resignation that follows the last battle. To the moralist, his non-constructive debunking suggested cowardice or a form of decadence. But other writers also felt, or at least celebrated, an empty world without reason or purpose or even hope. They gathered in Greenwich Village or as soon as possible fled a vulgar, commercial, unappreciative, and conformist America for the imagined freedom, the elevating conversation, the stimulating new art forms of Paris. Gertrude Stein called them a lost generation. Two young novelists, two of the "beautiful and the damned"—Ernest Hemingway and F. Scott Fitzgerald—achieved the highest rank among American writers. Hemingway seduced a thousand imitators by his terse style, and at least in the twenties reflected a fatalistic view of a world that allowed only the nobility of a heroic moment or the pleasure of open sensuality. The publication of both his *The Sun Also Rises* (1926) and his haunting obituary to World War I, *A Farewell to Arms* (1929), created a literary sensation; no one had ever written prose like this, although Hemingway borrowed from that long-term exile, Gertrude Stein. In *The Great Gatsby* (1925), Fitzgerald created the antihero of the decade, for Gatsby was a pathetic although somewhat successful and sentimental and corrupt capitalist, cheap and vulgar but with elements of nobility. He was, like the proverbial emperor, an American entrepreneur with no clothes on.

Our two most innovative poets, Ezra Pound and T. S. Eliot, chose permanent expatriation. They did not play games with their alienation, or mix their repudiation of American culture with self-conscious posturing. Pound came from Idaho, experimented with several new poetic techniques, tremendously aided young poets, and found his own journals, cults, and disciples. Eventually he moved from London and Paris to Rome, becoming a disciple of Mussolini's new corporate state. His ablest protégé, T. S. Eliot, hailed from St. Louis and studied philosophy at Harvard. In 1914 Eliot found his spiritual home in England, and eventually in high-church Anglicanism, in a structured, traditional, and Christian world. Close to Pound in his poetic experimentation, he was ideologically closer to the southern agrarians in his classical tastes. His exceedingly difficult poems, *The Waste Land* (1922) and *The Hollow Men* (1925) came to symbolize, at least in title, his critique of much of modernity. But no American writer, not even Eliot, captured the extreme disillusionment, the sense of despair, the boredom, the possibilities of senseless violence that haunted so many European writers in the wake of World War I.

If the young writers seemed daring, so surely did many painters and composers. Just as the older realistic and naturalistic tradition in letters survived into the twenties (Theodore Dreiser published *An American Tragedy* in 1925), so did a form of realism among painters. At the turn of the century a small circle of painters tried to reveal, in hurried but vivid portraits of slums and boxers and prostitutes, the harsh realities of urban America. Except for their near fatalistic acceptance of a raw reality, they were the muckrakers of the canvas and gained the appellation "Ashcan School." Two of these painters, John Sloan and George Bellows, reached the apex of their careers in the early twenties (a youthful Bellows died in 1924). In 1913 they had also helped stage the most famous exhibit in the history of American painting and sculpture, the Armory Show. Here the layman often first glimpsed the daring charms of French impressionism (now perhaps the most popular genre of painting in America), and the then totally incomprehensible challenge of complete abstraction, particularly cubism. The new forms became commonplace in the twenties, and a few young painters at least experimented with a combination of the two innovations, or with abstract expressionism. In music, jazz moved up river from its Negro and southern origins in New Orleans and Memphis to

Evangelist Billy Sunday (1862–1935) zealously attacked radicals and aliens while defending Prohibition and high moral standards. Ironically, Sunday, a former professional baseball player, is seen here in a chance meeting with actress Mae West, who symbolized sexual license. *Wide World Photos*

take center stage, thrilling young people even as it shocked their parents. Such composers as George Gershwin and Aaron Copeland even incorporated elements of jazz into their most serious work.

New Intellectual Horizons

Any brief and necessarily superficial survey of the fine arts can only witness the openness, the promising ferment, in the intellectual life of the decade. This ferment was just as evident outside the arts. A small but influential minority of Protestant clergymen or lay leaders not only continued, but daringly expanded, the earlier social gospel. In one area—peace—the concern touched almost all segments of church life. With some of the promotional excesses of business, Americans flocked in 1920 to the support of an Interchurch World Movement, but long before the movement raised its projected billion dollars it fell prey to internal divisions and a widespread evangelical fear of "liberal" domination. It was small social action committees in the large denominations, small interdenominational action groups, or seminary professors and students that kept up a radical witness. While a majority of Protestants echoed Billy Sunday's strident attack on radicals and aliens, or spent most of their crusading zeal on prohibition, Reinhold Niebuhr and other prominent clergymen advocated Christian socialism (in 1930 they would form a Fellowship of Socialist Christians), while others, led by Quakers and Methodists in a daring Fellowship of Reconciliation, pledged their support to complete pacifism. Such small organizations directly intervened in labor disputes, defended convicted radicals, and even spoke out in support of black equality, although this was rarely an issue of focal concern.

For six years these radical Christians joined academic intellectuals, civil libertarians, and shocked literary figures to champion the innocence of Sacco and Vanzetti. Their case became the cause célèbre of the decade, much more the symbol of repression and injustice than the deportation of aliens or even the continued lynching of blacks. In 1920, in the midst of the Red Scare, two armed men killed a paymaster and a guard and stole the payroll of a small shoe factory in South Braintree, Massachusetts. Eventually, on indirect evidence, the local police arrested Nicola Sacco, a shoemaker, and Bartolomeo Vanzetti, a fish peddler. Both were Italians, both anarchic socialists, both draft evaders, and both fearful of arrest for their radical activities, and thus evasive when arrested for the murder. The trial involved several procedural errors or questionable decisions by the trial judge, the admission of prejudicial evidence about the defen-

IF IT HAD NOT BEEN FOR THESE THING, I MIGHT HAVE LIVE OUT MY LIFE TALKING AT STREET CORNERS TO SCORNING MEN. I MIGHT HAVE DIE, UNMARKED, UNKNOWN A FAILURE. NOW WE ARE NOT A FAILURE. THIS IS OUR CAREER AND OUR TRIUMPH. NEVER IN OUR FULL LIFE COULD WE HOPE TO DO SUCH WORK FOR TOLERANCE, FOR JOOSTICE, FOR MAN'S ONDERSTANDING OF MAN AS NOW WE DO BY ACCIDENT. OUR WORDS-OUR LIVES-OUR PAINS NOTHING! THE TAKING OF OUR LIVES- LIVES OF A GOOD SHOEMAKER AND A POOR FISH PEDDLER-ALL! THAT LAST MOMENT BELONGS TO US- THAT AGONY IS OUR TRIUMPH.

Ben Shahn (1898–1969) was a leading social protest painter. In memory of two anarchists unfairly executed for murder, in 1958 he made a serigraph, *Passions of Sacco and Vanzetti.* The unique lettering is by Shahn, a master calligrapher and typographer. *Philadelphia Museum of Art; Purchased from funds given by Dr. and Mrs. William Wolgin.*

dants' political views, and misleading evidence by experts about the identity of the murder weapon (recent ballistic findings apparently support the guilt of Sacco). By contemporary standards, their subsequent conviction was invalid. At the very least they deserved a retrial on the basis of an array of new evidence and even other possible suspects. But all such appeals failed. The judge refused all motions for a retrial, and the Massachusetts Supreme Court, in a decision on very narrow grounds, refused to find any prejudice on the part of the judge. In 1927 the state executed Sacco and Vanzetti, who had eloquently pleaded their own innocence to the very end and who had enlisted the sympathy of people around the world. The case provoked at least three novels, led to long and impassioned pleas from European intellectuals and to endless demonstrations at home, but all to no avail. Those who had fought so long felt only emptiness and helpless despair at the end, and a deep bitterness toward many of their countrymen who applauded both the conviction and the execution.

An advertisement from the humor magazine *Life*, 1929. *Library of Congress*

Marcus Garvey (1887–1940) in his uniform as president of the Republic of Africa. Garvey dreamed of the day when all blacks would return to Africa. From the time he came to this country from Jamaica in 1905 until he was deported for mail fraud in 1923, he worked to achieve this nationalist goal. *Wide World Photos*

Much of the intellectual ferment of the decade defies any brief analysis. A full story would have to encompass the many, often desperate efforts to find a more fulfilling style of life. So much of the creativity of the twenties turned inward, to nuances of experience and away from political causes. It led not to legislation but to personal wisdom or to some new appreciation. Not only were there significant changes in the family but a whole literature on such changes. Whether sexual behavior changed or not, there was a new frankness and openness about the subject, and in the talk about companionate marriage a hint of shocking changes about to take place. A feminine self-consciousness would hardly be duplicated until the sixties; the first stirrings of black nationalism among urban Negroes climaxed in the pan-African movement led by a puzzling Marcus Garvey. The decade saw a new synthesis in physics, as scientists made the first marginal tests of Einstein's general theory of relativity and introduced a complex element of indeterminacy into a maturing quantum theory. Even as laymen read the fascinating social map of *Middletown*, Hoover commissioned an elaborate study of social trends in the United

States. The institutional approach to economic theory, pioneered by a still active Thorstein Veblen, flowered in the academies. Finally, American philosophy reached a new level of influence and technical achievement in the work of John Dewey, the single most commanding intellect of the decade.

In 1925 Dewey published *Experience and Nature*, a strong candidate as the most significant book by any American philosopher. By far the most comprehensive of all his books, it alone included a searching inquiry into ontology or theories about reality. In it, Dewey combined his earlier interest in theories of knowledge and value, in the philosophy of science, and in educational theory, with a growing concern for the quality of immediate experience and the nature of art. With deep personal piety he celebrated nature, by which he meant not the conceptual creation of the scientist but the existential given that men directly encounter, and thus the subject of all our experience. By the use of language symbols, man variously characterizes this experience of nature. Some appreciative characterizations reflect well the quality of experience, or the uniqueness and particularity of each moment. Others designate common elements and

John Dewey (1859–1952), the great American educator and philosopher, in his library. *Wide World Photos*

regularities, and these collectively constitute our empirical knowledge or our sciences. They enable us to predict and control future experiences, and aid man in achieving practical goals. Such knowledge is gained by very rigorous inquiry, or by what Dewey called the scientific method. Although inquiry is a delightful and self-fulfilling art for the expert, it has an adaptive function in a biological context. Knowledge is power. Until professionalized and specialized, inquiry originates in doubt, perplexity, and behavioral futility; it eventuates in understanding and successful action.

Dewey believed the ultimate good for man was good experience, or those moments that are so beautiful that they are self-justifying. The good is intrinsic, not extrinsic. It is in the having. Such experience has an esthetic quality, or a unifying and harmonizing content. Activity that contributes to such experience, or even more that which is accompanied by it, is artful. Knowledge, not a photograph of reality but a useful abstraction fitted to the experienced aspects of reality, guides us in much that we do. But as all instruments, it justifies itself by the end it serves. If a society is able to foster inquiry, to develop abundant knowledge and technique, it has only the potential of widely realized fulfillment. Just as important is appreciative awareness, openness to new experiences, and a developed taste for those that bring us delight and joy.

After World War I, and intense disillusionment over its disappointing consequences, Dewey tried to apply these insights to American society. In industrial processes and in education he found dull routine, subservient behavior, purely instrumental goals, and an appalling lack of artfulness along with a near monopoly of good experiences by a dominant class. Children verbally celebrated the delights of democratic participation even as authoritarian teachers made all the important decisions. A few men made the important decisions in factories, while lower managers, clerks, and laborers worked artlessly and meaninglessly at routine tasks that contributed only to the industrial goals of other people. They had to work for such extrinsic goals as wages and consumptive pleasures. Out of his desire to merge knowledge and art, technique and moral sensitivity, Dewey began a searching critique of the deficiencies of corporate capitalism, a critique that culminated in the thirties and led him into the American Socialist party.

For Dewey, as for so many others, the depression of the thirties would both focus and narrow concern. Economic issues came to the fore and dominated all others. As a consequence the intellectual life of that decade, so serious and so practical, would never exhibit the luxuriant variety, the sense of intellectual possibility, the occasional playfulness, and the haunting hint of sadness and despair that made the twenties so distinctive.

5

The depression of the thirties warped almost all subsequent perspectives on the economy of the twenties. The horrible malaise that settled upon America by 1931 begged for explanation. Both historians and economists found clues in the preceding decade. But knowledge of what came later insured a pathological bias, a search for clues to a developing cancer. The assumption was that, for such grave diseases, an ounce of prevention is worth a pound of cure, and that somehow the Republicans flunked a test in preventive medicine. What this bias conceals are the healthy aspects of the economy, or almost all the elements apparent to those who lived through Republican prosperity (it was no mirage), to those who knew the economy to be "fundamentally sound" rather than "inherently weak."

Many features of the economy in the twenties offered a preview of the long, sustained but problem-plagued growth that followed World War II. The depression thirties was the aberrant decade, the great hiatus in our economic history. During the twenties the federal government provided many services for private producers, and posed few threats either to continued private ownership or to management. The supportive role of the government remained small compared to today, but vital. The volume of goods and services expanded at a moderate rate; so did the monetary supply (currency and demand deposits). The concerns seem strikingly contemporary: technological disruption, shifts in consumer demand, frequent threats of growing unemployment, a complex "farm problem," an insecure international market, and continued problems for most small business. The major innovations of the decade would soon become commonplace: large, industrywide trade associations, a new emphasis upon a more efficient use of labor, and a wide array of corporate welfare schemes. Two characteristics decisively separate the decade from today —the weakness of organized labor, and the comparatively minor role of government fiscal operations, or of its buying, spending, and taxing.

Had presidents and congressmen foreseen the coming depression, they would have had the will to try and prevent it. Pathetically, they would still have lacked the requisite knowledge, and by earlier interference would probably have incited an even earlier depression. The only possible

Governmental Policy and Economic Performance

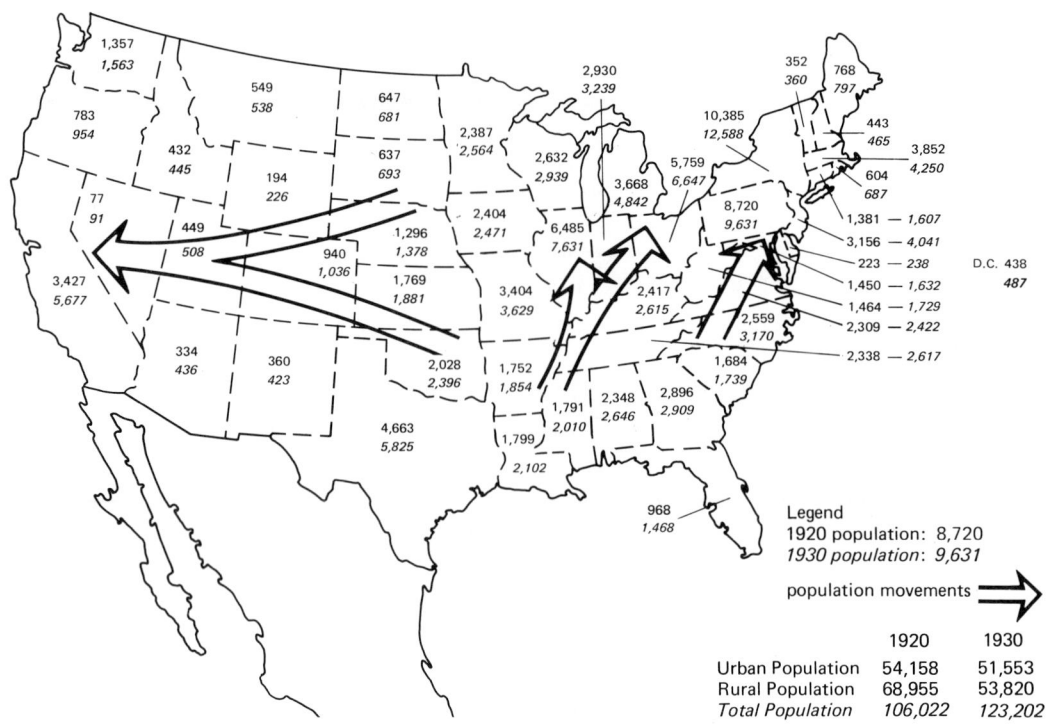

consolation is that it might have been less severe, and less dangerous in its international effects (the depression was the most prominent cause for the breakdown of the 1918 armistice, and thus of events that culminated in World War II). A more likely time for effective governmental action was in the earliest stages of depression, for then very vivid and frightening events created the political will. But the knowledge was still lacking, as both Congress and President Hoover vainly sought early cures for what they expected to be a temporary disease. At this point, as hopes and dreams slowly crumbled, their failure was more than pathetic. It took on tragic dimensions, as good but helpless men suffered an undeserved fate.

By 1931 the disease had fully developed. Again, neither Hoover nor Roosevelt found a ready cure. From a strictly economic perspective, one can fashion a persuasive argument that recovery would have come even sooner without Hoover's and Roosevelt's special recovery legislation. But their efforts to repair the economy did lead to a dramatic expansion in the economic role of the federal government, to a very rapid assimilation of new economic knowledge if not economic wisdom, and to a greatly reduced probability of any future depression of the same magnitude. When the depression was over, we had a different political economy. To the despair of many critics—socialists, advocates of planning, or, most radical of all, those who wanted to return to a free, competitive market—it was not as different as it should have been. It remained a highly collectivized but still private economy, despite a much broader array of government supports and indirect controls. And, as in any collective and highly productive economy, there remained grave problems of equity in distribution, of servility in work, of special privileges for a favored few, and of enormous environmental destruction, or problems much more apparent today than in the twenties and thirties.

The federal government made a limited although vital contribution to the economic growth of the twenties, but it had precious little to do either with creating or erecting safeguards against the much heralded weaknesses of the private sector. These included certain built-in domestic and foreign pitfalls that insured, once a downfall began, a domino effect, or an escalation of corporate failures and international monetary crises. The reason for its restricted role was twofold: few people in government, from either major party, believed that the federal government should intervene in a detailed way in the operations of a market system; also, the low level of governmental economic activity had small impact and yielded few options. Throughout the twenties the federal budget remained in the $3 billion range, or less than 3 percent of the gross national product (this compares with a budget today of approximately 25 percent of the gross national product). The largest budget item was interest on the national debt, largely incurred during World War I. Such a low level of government spending minimized the impact of government fiscal operations, of taxation, debt funding, and budget management.

The Republican administrations made their greatest contribution to

**Republican
Fiscal
Policy**

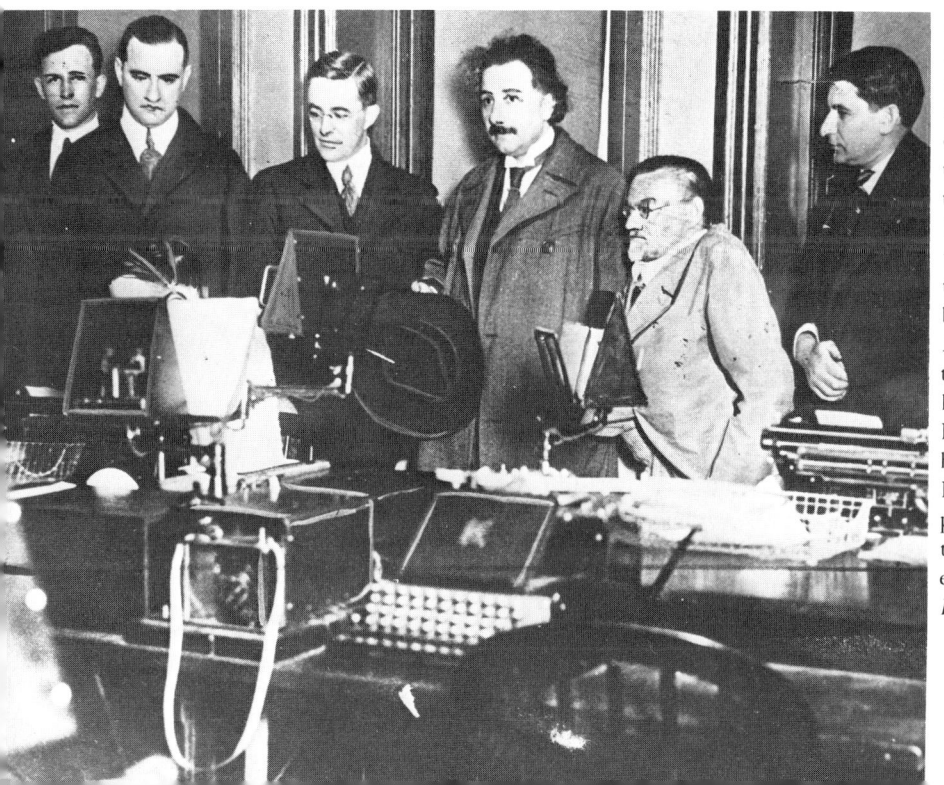

Albert Einstein (1879–1955) with Charles Steinmetz (1865–1923) (next to Einstein, right) at a demonstration of wireless transoceanic communication. Einstein came to the United States in 1933, a victim of Nazi persecution, and became a member of the Institute for Advanced Study, Princeton. The introduction of his Special Theory of Relativity in 1905 and his General Theory of Relativity in 1916, were part of the many scientific achievements of the early part of the century. *Library of Congress*

As secretary of commerce Herbert Hoover participated in the World War Foreign Debt Commission (1922), which was authorized to deal with monetary obligations of foreign governments to the United States. The members of the commission included (left to right), Assistant Secretary of the Treasury James W. Wadsworth, Congressman Theo E. Burton, Senator Reed Smoot (1862–1941), Secretary of State Charles Evans Hughes (1862–1948), chairman of the commission and secretary of the treasury, Andrew Mellon (1855–1937), and Hoover. *Library of Congress*

economic growth by something a great deal more elusive than legislation. They helped reinforce the favorable, even eulogistic image of the private producer or businessman that so captivated the public imagination (Henry Ford was the greatest hero). The epitome of this was a much publicized comparison, by advertising pioneer Bruce Barton in a best-selling book, of Jesus and modern advertisers: "He picked up twelve men from the bottom ranks of business and forged them into an organization that conquered the world . . . ;" His parables were "the most powerful advertisements of all time . . .," and thus "He would be a national advertiser today." Such a valuative perspective seemed hopelessly vulgar to horrified intellectuals.

More important, Harding and Coolidge offered no threats to those responsible for the production and distribution of goods and services, and generally sided with business in its disputes with organized labor. Hoover often stressed partnership, or a new symbiotic relationship between government and enterprise. In a decade smothered by a cult of efficiency, and usually negative in attitudes toward "politicians," the Republican presidents supported an expansive and hopeful mood, an expectation of continued harmony and cooperation. Since the critical economic decisions still rested with private managers, such a sense of government-business partnership provided a vital psychological support for the expansion of plant, production, and consumption. Any concerted government hostility toward any major segment of the economy might have incited an

118

even earlier depression. In fact, by 1929 the economic equilibrium was so precarious that government officials were afraid to make any pessimistic analysis of economic prospects or to identify any developing maladies in the private sector. A type of forced optimism sustained the last days of prosperity.

The continuing supportive services of government added fuel to the steady expansion of the mid-twenties. The Department of Agriculture had the most complex bureaucracy in Washington, and sponsored a vast, nationally distributed system of research and education (experimental farms, county agents, vocational education in high schools), and in Washington coordinated a mass of marketing information and research. The major policy debate of the decade was over what further support the government should provide farmers.

Under Hoover, the Department of Commerce expanded its services to large and small business enterprise. Hoover set up what amounted to a second consular service to promote foreign markets for American products and investments, provided leadership and helpful guidelines for voluntary trade associations that established codes of ethics and standardized production for whole industries, expanded market research, and used the Bureau of Standards to help raise product quality and to eliminate unnecessary duplication. These services joined the highly protective Fordney-McCumber Tariff of 1922, continued subsidies for ships and airplanes, and more amenable appointees to the two regulatory agencies (FTC and

ICC). Already, such commissioners usually came from within the regulated industry, and often worked more assiduously to bring order and rationality to their area of responsibility than to champion the interests of consumers. During the decade the Republican administrations, out of compelling need in both cases, established the beginnings of two additional commissions to regulate radio transmission and commercial airlines.

If there were any major options in economic policy, any choices that might have arrested the later depression, they had to be in the overall management of the federal budget. Here the Republicans have generally fared badly in the hands of historians. Yet, the budget goals of Hoover and Mellon (the two principal architects of economic policy) came close to a political consensus. Most Democrats and Republicans supported governmental economy, lowered expenditures, lower taxes, but still enough taxes for a gradual retirement of the national debt, or a policy of reconversion from the artificially high expenditures, taxes, and deficits of wartime. This policy ordinarily would be deflationary, for the government retired almost $8 billion of its debt through taxes taken from the people and not spent by the government for goods and services. In fact, such an economic policy, because of a high level of private demand and the expansion of credit (particularly in installment buying), led to stable or slightly higher prices as the decade advanced.

In a nonpolitical sense of the word, there were "options" to this overall strategy. Had there been support for it, the government could have maintained the existing debt (not large by present standards), retained the high wartime taxes, and continued a high level of government expenditure. In the absence of economic controls, such a policy would have spurred inflation. But what could the government have used the money for? Since such questions invite highly speculative answers, one might draw upon subsequent experience and suggest rearmament as the most likely expedient, and the one least likely to stimulate corporate hostility or to run aground on congressional opposition. But the breadth and depth of pacifist sentiment would have required, as justification, either a clear foreign threat or a successfully propagated illusion of such a threat. The naïve might suggest expenditures in what goes under the vague rubric of "social need," but this would be to ignore the almost total lack of any perception of such need, any developed plans to meet it (a lag of several years), or any sense that the federal government, rather than the states, should meet it. If one wants to be really utopian, to parade all the vivid lessons of hindsight, he might suggest that the higher taxes should have replaced and excused all debt payments from Europe, and that all budgetary surpluses should have gone to Europe as an early version of the Marshall

Plan, thus restoring a balance of trade and averting the international collapse of 1931 that contributed so much to an enduring depression and to the coming of World War II.

Lower expenditures meant lower taxes. The political controversy swirled around the nature of the cuts. Secretary of the Treasury Mellon followed a consistent tax policy throughout the decade—to lower all income, excise, and estate taxes, private and corporate; to insure strict enforcement of tax laws; and to flatten out the progression in rates. This meant major tax relief for very high incomes (including his own); he believed most investment, and thus most growth in productive capacity, came from the savings of the more affluent. He desired at least a small tax liability for people of average or below average incomes, arguing that only such direct taxes insured popular support for governmental economy. In a version of the "trickle down" theory, he assumed that only productive growth could assure full employment, rising wages, and higher living standards for all. For the economy of the twenties, his assessment was essentially correct. Almost all new capital came from the reinvested earnings of corporations or from the savings of the affluent. The reduced taxes at the top did increase the quantity of investment wealth, and at least a share of it funded plant growth.

Congress only slowly conceded Mellon's tax goals. In a series of controverted revenue bills, Democrats joined insurgent Republicans to force the earlier tax cuts at the lower levels, either by broader income tax exemptions or cuts in excise taxes. In 1922 Congress repealed the excess profits tax, slightly raised corporate income taxes, increased estate taxes, and lowered the surtax (this refers to progressive additions to a flat income tax rate, which was 8 percent in 1922) from 65 percent to 50 percent. Mellon had wanted it at 40 percent. More important, it exempted most heads of families from any income tax at all, since it granted them a $2,500 exemption plus $400 for each dependent (in 1922 the average factory worker received less than $1,400 a year). Families of average or well above average income now paid only federal excise taxes, on admissions, telephone rates, automobiles, tobacco, and a few other products. In 1924 Congress reduced many of these excise taxes, even as it pleased Mellon by reducing the maximum surtax to 40 percent. In 1926, with annual budgetary surpluses providing the opportunity, it lowered the income tax rate to 5 percent, raised the family exemption to $3,500, and in effect limited the income tax liability to single people of average income (they had only a $1,500 exemption) and to affluent families (by comparison to present in-

come levels, only families with incomes over $25,000 would pay taxes).
After a further reduction in excises, Congress conceded Mellon's main
point—it lowered the maximum surtax to 20 percent, which meant a
maximum tax liability of only 25 percent for the very wealthy. In 1928
Congress removed the excise tax on automobiles, leaving the laboring person with only two conspicuous federal taxes—on tobacco and movie
admissions. Finally, Congress lowered corporate taxes by a very small
amount, in part fulfilling the last of Mellon's tax goals.

These major revisions, and particularly the one in 1926, freed investment funds for a variety of uses. Mellon had won his way largely by default. Either the government had to cut taxes, spend more, or retire the
debt at a more rapid and more deflationary pace. Since interest rates on
the debt represented the largest single federal expense, several congressmen from both parties wanted to pay it off quickly. Such a policy would
have slowed the economic growth of the decade. Democrats and Progressives, by 1926, had all but won their goal—relief at the bottom. Only
token taxes remained here. Thus, the only remaining issue was the distribution of the income tax burden between corporations and private individuals, or between the very rich and the comfortably affluent (sometimes
called middle class in the twenties, but by income levels in the upper 20
percent). Higher corporate taxes or very high surtaxes promised a slight
reduction in savings and investment; a wider spread of income taxes into
the comfortable middle class assured a slight reduction in consumption of
such luxury or expensive items as homes and automobiles. Affluence and
low government needs made possible a tax policy that pleased almost
everyone, and that left almost no margin for tax cuts calculated to have a
major impact on the economy.

The exact consequences of Republican tax policy involve quite complex calculations about what happened to the tax savings, and almost impossible guesses about the possible effects of a different distribution of the
tax burden. The lowered progression in income taxes increased the
amount of savings among people able and willing to take high risks. By
1928 this added zest to the stock market. By then the annual amount of
savings for individuals and corporations totaled approximately $12 billion.
Almost two-thirds of this was in the hands of the very wealthy. Less than
half of these savings went into new capital, but quite enough to meet
market needs in almost every area. By 1929 the stock market began to
draw a disproportionate amount of savings away from plant expansion,
but the crash came too soon to allow many effects of this diversion to be
felt. After the crash, we had a redundancy of productive capacity. Even
in 1929, our plant capacity still exceeded production by about 20 percent.
Thus, a more rapid expansion of capital required more markets, and these

were simply not available at home or abroad. Tax policies alone could do little to increase the demand for goods. The lower income people, those normally most anxious to buy, paid almost no federal taxes. For tax policy to contribute to consumer demand, it had to join with more radical forms of income redistribution, such as welfare subsidies to the unemployed or to underconsumers among laborers or marginal farmers. Such welfare remained taboo for both major parties. It took a depression to make it politically acceptable and, ultimately, even orthodox.

Trade and International Balances

The final complexity in fiscal policy is the one most easily overlooked. In effect, our tax policy facilitated a fragile solution to the problem of international balances in trade and payments. Our tax policies helped free the private American investments which underwrote a foreign market for American exports, and particularly for critical agricultural exports, even as our tariff laws made the underwriting costs (or rewards) even higher. One alarming result of this was the dependence of Europe upon private decisions in America, and the vulnerability of the perilously balanced system to any serious maladies in the American economy. More than anything else, these international perils would help transform our stock market crash into a world depression.

Again, it is difficult to suggest any easy or politically appealing answer to this international dilemma. Even drastically lowered tariffs would not, alone, have restored European trade and currency balances; they would have threatened production and jobs in a few key American industries. Debt forgiveness remained politically anathema. Direct subsidies to Europe were simply beyond comprehension. Again, the most serious problems would not respond to conventional fiscal policies. Given the narrow context of decision making, the proinvestment stance taken by Mellon and Hoover helped keep an ingeniously contrived market going for as long as it did, postponing some of the uncollected accounts of war for over a decade. When it all fell, it fell hard. And there was no built-in necessity of it falling. Even 1929 was not too late for beginning major and costly repairs, had any of the Western countries possessed the will or the knowledge to begin them. None did.

Of course, one may object that domestic growth and a rather general prosperity, or even a functioning international exchange system and the diplomatic harmony this helped insure, are not sufficient goals for economic policy. Functional success may conceal moral dilemmas or camouflage terrible injustices. Both major parties, and presumably the vast majority of the electorate, supported such concrete goals as secure jobs and higher living standards within the existing economic system. Constituencies varied, and they helped account for the bitter debates over tariffs, taxes, and farm policies. But few of the debates involved major conflicts over institutions and goals. Yet, as an earlier survey of opinions among artists and intellectuals so well illustrated, there were very different minority perspectives on America. Some of these revealed acute moral reservations about either the structure or the functioning of our economy. Such reservations ranged from the esthetic horror of artists confronted by what they perceived as little but ugliness and vulgarity, to the agrarians who found modern industrial organization destructive of humane feeling and the quality of work and leisure, to Communist party members who noted correctly that the rich got ever richer, and who wanted to overthrow the power and privileges of a capitalist ruling class. It is impossible to survey all the moral perspectives and the ideal images of America that provided the basis of such negative evaluations. Just as politicians and economists, struggling to keep an economy working, could become blind to the all-important question—Where are we going?—so the more alienated critics could ignore hard economic realities. As a matter of simple justice, some believed we should "soak the rich" by near expropriative taxes. Such a moral imperative easily obscured the complex economic role played by the savings of the affluent, or the economic pitfalls that awaited any but the most intelligent tampering with an economy that, righteous or evil, beautiful or ugly (these are matters of taste), was enormously complex and vulnerable.

Business

Most sectors of the economy gained strength in the twenties. The complex area all too loosely called "business" included all production outside agriculture, all transportation, all wholesale and retail merchandising, and even financial institutions. Within this large whole, interests varied immensely (iron versus aluminum, trucks versus railroads, banks versus manufacturing, large corporations versus individual entrepreneurs). Beyond the generally favorable image for the label, and the modest gains in total production (the gross national product rose from $73.3 billion in 1920 to $104.4 in 1929, adjusted to 1929 prices) and dramatic gains in overall profits (up 76 percent from 1922 to 1929), the detailed economic story was checkered and much too complex for any simple summary. In New England, textile mills barely survived southern and foreign competition; conditions in the small, highly competitive coal fields of Appalachia remained horrible. Electric utilities suffered from financial manipulation and bleeding on the part of holding companies. Small merchants felt the effects of chain store competition. But growth industries— automobiles, electronics, aluminum, rubber, and a hundred others— boomed as never before in peace time.

In the major corporations (the 200 largest owned almost one-half the corporate wealth), the major institutional change was in the use of labor. As a whole the production of workers rose by almost 25 percent in the decade, and in some key industries by over 50 percent. These increases supported a slight decrease in hours worked, a gain of almost 20 percent in wages, and a steady increase in corporate profits. In part, the gain reflected improved tools or techniques, such as the assembly line in automobile factories. Even more, it reflected a more careful attention to work and work conditions. Under the label of "scientific management," managers of nonunion factories experimented with soothing plant environments, a careful spacing and planning of tasks, carefully timed procedures, piece work or production bonuses, and even the placement of toilets and water fountains.

The well-established trend toward large, national corporations continued. This meant a continued shift away from family control to a professional managerial elite, from stockholder domination to bureaucratic rules, and from external to internal financing, which meant a decline in the power of investment banks except in such areas as electrical utilities. These shifts entailed a less speculative mentality in corporate management. Consolidation continued at a moderate pace. In relatively new industries, such as automobiles, there was a wringing out process, with marginal companies merging with larger ones or going bankrupt. Integration and size often moved well beyond any possibilities of increased efficiency in production, but permitted greater political power and market control, or the ability to carry out long-range plans and to insure stable profits. The growth at the top was reflected in the assets of the largest 5 percent of corporations, which in 1920 had 78.9 percent of the total compared with 85.2 by 1930. The assets of the 200 largest corporations climbed from $43 billion in 1919 to $81 billion in 1929.

Even as carefully designed factories helped increase work effectiveness, a growing number of corporate executives tried to win the loyalty and improve the morale of their workers. Their motives differed: to prevent rapid turnover or slowdowns or sabotage on the job, to avert labor unions, to improve worker performance, and to fulfill humanitarian goals of their own. The large corporation was a small government, or a feudal fief, sovereign within its empire, and with a body of subjects bound to it by economic need. Although wages rose during the decade, the quality of the work experience may well have suffered from the very increases in efficiency that underwrote improved wages. Corporate paternalism, or welfare capitalism, became the goal of a few highly profitable firms with benevolent managers, such as Sears, Roebuck and Eastman Kodak. These companies experimented with substantial benefit programs—profit sharing, stock purchase options, and ambitious health, retirement, and recreational programs. Their schemes succeeded both in increasing loyalty and in avoiding unions. Possibly many workers would have preferred such gains as a result of independent bargaining. At times they surely resented a form of bribery, but they still gladly accepted the more authentic gifts. Many employers made a travesty of the whole idea, using company unions to block employee bargaining, hiring company nurses to check up on absentee employees, or ballyhooing ill-funded softball teams as an artificial morale booster. In the depression thirties, few corporations could afford to continue welfare schemes. But all the publicity for welfare, by corporate public relations officers or in institutional advertisements, surely helped win public acceptance of the idea of welfare benefits, and thus prepared the way for federal welfare programs in the New Deal.

Wage workers hardly constitute a sector of the economy, since they exist in every industry, including agriculture. Thus, it is misleading to talk of them as a unified group, and in fact almost all statistical data on workers is skewed by a lack of information on certain categories of agricultural workers. In 1920 the United States had a nonagricultural labor force of about 27 million; this grew to 31 million in 1929. In manufacturing (only a part of the above), the work week averaged 51 hours in 1920; by 1929 this had dropped to only 50 (the average hours worked per week was much lower, because of unemployment or temporary employment). Factory workers on the whole received an average of 57 cents an hour in 1922 (about $1,300 a year) and 64 cents in 1926 ($1,473 a year). Unionized workers, for the most part an elite of skilled craftsmen, fared much better (only a 45-hour work week in 1920, and wages that moved up from 88 cents in 1920 to $1 an hour in 1926). Labor turnover remained high (almost 50 percent a year), but unemployment moderate—down from a temporary high of 11.9 percent in the depression of 1921 to about 4 percent in such good years as 1923, 1925, 1926, and 1928.

The modest gains by laborers did not parallel any gains in union power. Just the opposite. Union membership, which was over 5 million in 1920, dropped to about 3.3 million in 1930. The Red Scare and the major strikes of 1919 helped reinforce long-standing popular fears of unions, and fed a crusade by industrial managers in behalf of what they called the American Plan, a euphemism for individual bargaining with employers. It rested upon the assumption that both collectivism and class consciousness were un-American, yet conveniently ignored the fact that corporations were huge, legally sheltered collectivities. The hostility also reflected a lingering suspicion of an exceptionally militant AFL at the end of the war, when it championed governmental ownership of the railroads and launched effective strikes in major industries. But union decline reflected several other contributory causes—the successes of welfare capitalism and company unions, governmental policies, and the decline in militancy among AFL leaders. The AFL, now under the leadership of a cautious Walter Green, simply did not continue militant organizing campaigns, and practically ignored the large mass of unskilled workers. Desperate efforts by labor militants, and particularly by Communist party members, met overwhelming public resistance and floundered in either employee apathy or cruelly effective corporate suppression. After 1926, when the AFL national convention excluded Communists from its leadership, Green moved closer to an accommodationist position with receptive corporate executives, stressing the mutual benefits of recognized unions and harmonious labor relations.

To a man, the Republican leadership claimed to be prolabor. They meant it, for in American politics this commitment was roughly the equivalent of being promotherhood. But they were either divided or ambivalent in their attitudes toward unions. Under Harding, Attorney General Daugherty was overtly hostile to striking unions and frequently used injunctions to settle labor disputes. Hoover best illustrated a moderate position. His principle of voluntarism encompassed the right of organization, and for a period he hoped to win union support for the Republican party. Yet, he leaned toward mediation and cooperation as against strikes and labor conflict. He hoped to use persuasion and conferences to avoid these. Since the abortive steel strike of 1919 left only bitterness, Hoover helped secure voluntary settlements by 1923 that secured the eight-hour day for steelworkers. In their long battle with steel executives, the workers had gained much public support, even as the major steel companies had become an embarrassment to other industries because of their tenacious support of twelve-hour shifts and a seven-day week. Hoover exploited public feelings, assembled expert opinions on the benefits of an eight-hour day, and called meetings of steel executives, putting the greatest pressure on Judge Elbert H. Gary, head of giant United States Steel. Although angry at governmental intervention, Gary capitulated and carried the lesser companies with him.

Unfortunately for Hoover, such mediation did not always work. In 1922 both coal and railroad unions walked out in what turned out to be the last major strikes of the decade in such vital industries. When Hoover's conferences failed to get an early settlement, Harding lost patience and asked the federal courts for a sweeping injunction against the railroad unions. It provided for federal prosecution of rail union executives who continued the strike. Actually, the injunction did not end the strike; after mutual concessions, the contenders achieved a settlement in the fall, be-

FARLOW TWIN SPRING
DRAFT GEAR
STEEL COUPLER 5×7

METAL BRAKE BEAM,
W. A. BRAKE.
K1 TRIPLE VALVE

fore the chill of winter created a coal emergency. The Harding injunction, and his intemperate charges against unions, pushed labor leaders toward a more sympathetic Democratic party at least after the Progressive failure of 1924, and also added the injunction to the blacklist and yellow-dog contract as the most potent symbols of labor exploitation. The Republicans, in a clearly political and largely unsuccessful effort to undo the Harding damage, in 1924 advocated, and in 1926 enacted, a Railroad Labor Act which guaranteed collective bargaining rights in this closely regulated industry.

Generally, labor unions preferred to win their goals through collective bargaining rather than through governmental paternalism. But most workers were not in unions, and welcomed wage and hours legislation. This legislative strategy first flowered in the Wilson administration. The states even won court approval for special legislation to protect women in factories. But there would be no such legislation in the twenties. In 1923 a divided Supreme Court, in *Adkins* v. *Children's Hospital*, denied the constitutionality of a minimum wage law in the District of Columbia, and by implication any such general regulations at the state level. Already, in voiding a child labor law passed during the Wilson administration, the

The reaction of Harding and the Republicans to the outbursts of labor violence in 1919 and 1922 revealed their ambivalence toward unions. *United Press International*

Court practically excluded such federal legislation except in special areas, like the railroads, that clearly came under the interstate commerce power. Corporations had long since gained the legal status of persons, coming under the protections of the Fourteenth Amendment, originally a civil rights amendment which, among other provisions, prohibited the states from depriving any person (or corporation) of life, liberty, or property without due process. The Court found minimum wage laws a form of unconstitutional deprivation of property, and precluded such regulation until the Court was willing to reverse *Adkins* (it did this in 1937).

Agriculture

Out on the farm, all the celebration of prosperity had a distinctly hollow ring. Large numbers of unhappy farmers in the twenties reflected a growing bitterness. Contrary to a myth they propagated almost as successfully as corn and wheat, farmers as a whole did not suffer an economic depression during the decade. Able farmers, in most commodities, enjoyed modest prosperity and considerable gains in productive efficiency, or a quite muted replica of the economy as a whole. Yet, psychologically, farmers experienced something like a "depression." This experience was an inescapable reality in the politics of the period, as major debates on agricultural policy punctuated every congressional session, and posed the most aggravating problem faced by the Coolidge administration. Many of the roots of farm bitterness were noneconomic. Farmers sorrowfully watched their children leave for cities, either for better economic opportunities or the bright lights. They defensively praised farm life in a decade more attuned to cities and to business enterprise, and resented the caustic insults of a Mencken. They rightly feared an erosion of a valued and familiar way of life, of revered religious beliefs and institutions, of the mores and easy familiarity of the village, of character and manliness as they understood it. Beleaguered and defensive at the cultural level, they even more resented what they perceived as economic injustices.

The war years had a lot to do with farm discontent. Extraordinarily high government-supported prices in 1919 and 1920 had stimulated unwise purchases of land and equipment and had encouraged farmers to produce in 1920 a crop that turned out to be disastrously large, since the government ended its price supports in that year. A precipitous further decline in agricultural prices in 1921, and only a partial recovery of wartime prices in subsequent years, joined with a complementary fall in land values and a rise in industrial prices. Farmers felt cheated, particularly in a time of vaunted prosperity and continuously pleaded for higher prices. Actually, the prices of farm products in the twenties, compared not with the inflated ones of the war years but with the purchasing power of those in the prosperous base period from 1909 to 1914 ("parity" prices) did not look bad. They ranged from 80 percent of parity in 1921 to 95 percent in 1925, with 92 percent in 1929. Indeed, per capita farm income rose after 1921 at a slightly faster rate than wages, reflecting slight improvements in seed and in farming techniques, and a considerable sophistication in labor-saving equipment (the tractor was making its first major impact). Efficient farmers made profits and continued to expand operations.

For some people on the farms, however, the depression was very real. Price levels varied immensely from one crop to another. Wheat suffered precipitous price cycles and grave problems of surplus; tobacco and dairying flourished. Cattle and hogs fluctuated, but generally remained below parity. Shifts in consumption (away from breads, toward dairy products) and in international demand (away from wheat and cotton in particular) threatened special groups of farmers, as did unusually severe droughts or flooding.

In the twenties, as today, fewer than one-half the farmers produced over 90 percent of the agricultural product. In an economic sense, only the 50 percent could be called professionals. The lower half owned small farms, sometimes on submarginal land, or were tenants or sharecroppers. The real bottom of agriculture, and a huge one, included farm laborers, and particularly migratory workers. Many of these were deficient in skills, unable to adjust to new tools or changed demands of the market. In either case, farm laborers or marginal farmers had no means of attaining the efficiencies in production that would compensate for the drop in farm prices. Some lived in a social and cultural poverty as great as their economic distress. They constituted a grave social problem, also a rural problem, but hardly an *agricultural* problem. They simply exemplified the human surplus created by a very "successful" American agriculture, a surplus that, by choice or economic necessity, remained in rural areas. But those small farmers who were relatively well off—able tenants and owners of small farms with fairly good soil—provided in the twenties a large and vociferous constituency for higher prices. On most economic issues, they joined with the larger farmers.

All politically successful ideas for agricultural reform in the twenties promised one thing—higher price levels. Every farmer wanted these, yet without direct subsidies and without mandatory controls in production. Three plans dominated the congressional debates of the middle and late twenties: a protected domestic market through government controlled foreign marketing; a rationalized domestic market through large marketing cooperatives; and a controlled domestic market through some form of domestic allotment.

The first proposal—controlled foreign marketing—gained the loyalty of most farm organizations, including the powerful American Farm Bureau Federation. Its authors were George N. Peek and Hugh S. Johnson, two farm machinery manufacturers of Moline, Illinois. In the form of several, slightly divergent bills (all called McNary-Haugen after congressional sponsors), this proposal remained before Congress from the mid-twenties to 1929. Two such bills passed both houses of Congress only to be vetoed by President Coolidge.

The McNary-Haugen bills provided for a government-owned marketing corporation to purchase all surplus agricultural production in major crops at a set price level. In its earlier form the plan defined that level as an established "parity" price, while in a later version it called for a level equal to that of the world price plus an amount equivalent in percentage to the existing tariff rate on imports. The price paid by the federal corporation would, in effect, be a floor price since the government remained willing to buy all surpluses at the set price. To compensate the government for all losses incurred in selling surpluses abroad, the farmers had to pay an equalization fee. Tariffs would protect the farmer against foreign competition. The higher domestic prices would be paid by consumers because of the protected domestic market and the artificial scarcity. The plan could have worked in an expanding world market; in a contracting one it might well have forced retaliatory tariff action by foreign governments. The government corporation would then have suffered enough losses to cancel many of the benefits for such heavy export crops as cotton and wheat, or the very ones most penalized by surpluses and low prices.

The Coolidge and Hoover administrations supported a second proposal—cooperative marketing. In fact, this became a pet idea of Hoover's. He wished not only to leave all managerial decision to the farmers, but also to leave price determination to the free market. He consistently opposed the artificial price-fixing provided for by the McNary-Haugen bills. Yet Hoover wanted farmers to rationalize their production and control their marketing in behalf of both higher and more stable prices. For this purpose, he advocated governmental aid for large marketing cooperatives—similar to trade associations in other industries—made up in each case of farmers producing a given commodity. He hoped that each major cooperative could successfully recommend annual production quotas to individual farmers, make marketing agreements with purchasers, rationalize marketing by calculated storage and by better processing, and possibly even expand markets by advertising.

The third scheme, a domestic allotment system, dealt more directly with production, although it skirted any compulsory acreage controls. The McNary-Haugen bills alerted farmers to the problem of their surplus production; and effective cooperatives could make predictions of market prospects and advise farmers about specific acreage reductions. But would this be enough? In the later twenties a group of farm economists thought not, and worked out an allotment plan as an improvement over McNary-Haugen. Under one version, the Bureau of Agricultural Economics would estimate, on the basis of predicted consumption, how much of an agricultural product could be put on the domestic market without an undesirable slump in prices. It would then distribute to farmers market certificates or debentures covering this amount. Farmers or processors could sell on the home market only the crops covered by debentures. They could only dispose of additional production by exporting it and receiving lower world prices. The government would neither buy commodities nor dispose of them abroad. The farmer would have a clear indication, even before planting, of his domestic allotment, the only portion of his crop for which he could expect decent prices during periods of world surpluses. During the depression, Milburn L. Wilson, a farm economist from Montana, revised and simplified the domestic allotment scheme, replacing the debentures with special processing taxes and direct payments to those farmers who contracted to control their production according to domestic quotas. In this revised form it directly shaped the New Deal agricultural program.

6

A decade of economic optimism ended during a few hectic days in late October and early November 1929. The memorable days came in pairs: October 23 and 24, October 28 and 29, November 4 and 6. The New York stock market collapsed in a series of catastrophic losses after brief and partial rallies. A severe economic depression was still over a year ahead. But the great bull market was now a sustained bear market, and the national mood, despite all the optimistic cant, one of growing gloom. Whatever the complex causes, the stock market failure was a prelude to economic disaster for the whole Western world.

Even in the simple beginnings of the corporation in America, common stock represented a peculiar form of property, if property was the correct word for it. Most early American corporations were local, chartered for some needed public service (a road, a bridge, a canal), and with only a few, local owners. But after 1800 the corporate form became the preferred means for collecting industrial capital. Normally, the word property entailed not only exclusive possession of land or tools or products, but also full control over their use and complete responsibility for any claims against them (taxes, debts, penalties). Not so with corporate shares. As a legally privileged collective person, the corporation was alone responsible for claims, not the holders of its stock. Most early owners of stock did participate directly in management. To this extent stock still functioned as a form of joint property, for the owners controlled the fate of the enterprise and directly contributed to its policies.

As corporations grew larger, the vast majority of shareholders had such inconsequential blocks of stock, or were so far removed, that they rarely tried to influence policy. Few even conceived of managerial rights as one of the benefits of "ownership." When this change occurred, stock became, functionally although not legally, a special form of investment, posing greater risks than bank savings but with open possibilities for both dividends and capital gains. By 1920, for most stockholders, a share was a piece of negotiable risk paper that gave them a legal claim to a percentage of corporate profits and a residual claim on corporate assets in the rare case of liquidation. In this form, stock served few of the social functions

The Market for Common Stock

133

The Awful Taming of the Bull

earlier attributed to property—an education in individual responsibility, a challenge to initiative and ingenuity, a mandate for prudence and good citizenship. In fact, it often fostered the quite opposite qualities of the gambler, of one who wants to earn not only a normal interest on his savings, but who seeks unearned speculative gains based either on luck, on the work and ingenuity of others, or on the growth and increased values of the total economy.

Despite the loss of almost all property attributes, corporate shares still served one social purpose—the collecting of capital for building new productive capacity. In the nineteenth century our industrial plant grew as a result of stock purchases, often by Europeans. Early in the nineteenth century, the New York Stock Exchange became the principal market for the buying and selling of corporate securities. Those with access to such markets became the middlemen or brokers in such transactions, collecting fees for their services and thus anxious to increase the number of transactions. With the buildup of our industrial plant, and the maturation of large corporations, the largest body of stock transactions involved not new issues, but trade in older ones. Such trade, as carried out on stock exchanges, has only a peripheral economic function—it facilitates a type of investment mobility, or the easy movement of high-risk capital from existing enterprises to appealing new ones. In the late twenties even a large share of new issues did not underwrite new productive capacity, but only investment trusts or holding companies. By then, large and profitable corporations rarely financed growth by stock issues; they simply reinvested their own earnings.

Such a fluid market in corporate securities allows a sometimes fickle demand to determine the price of stock, without any close correlation with corporate assets, earnings, or early growth prospects. Thus, the value of stock on the exchanges has always fluctuated much more erratically than the assets or realistic earning prospects of corporations. This permits the type of speculative boom and collapse that occurred in 1929. Such booms and busts directly affect production, for the stock market not only serves as an index of economic confidence but also contains a large portion of the private assets of individuals, assets available for other uses either by sale or as security for credit. A dramatic drop in stock values depletes the amount of potential credit and purchasing power, lowering the level of economic activity.

The Early Boom

After the doldrums produced by the recession of 1921–22, stock prices began a steady advance in a prosperous 1924. By contemporary standards, stock was underpriced. Realistic economic prospects justified all the early gains. To make comparative judgments easy, the *New York Times* index of twenty-five industrial stocks (a rough gauge of the overall market) moved above 100 in 1924, and up to 134 by December 31. In 1925 the get-rich-quick investors enjoyed a hectic Florida real estate boom much more than the mundane stock market, which rose slowly but undramatically to 181. In 1926 the market moved lower, then back up at year's end, closing at 176. So far, there was no indication of unwarranted speculation. The first intimations of a boom came in 1927, perhaps in part as a response to very low interest rates. By the end of 1927 the *Times* index stood at a dazzling 245, perilously close to the upper limits of any prudent investment outlook, although key stocks still sold at a comparatively safe ten or twelve times their annual earnings. The economy seemed to justify the new faith in its future performance, although a growth in production of only 15 percent had paralleled an increase of 145 percent in the *Times* list. Clearly, low prices in 1924 had made the stock market an excellent investment opportunity. By early 1928 the market was ready to take off on a speculative binge. From this point on only illusory hopes, not realistic economic forecasts, justified the increases.

One question rightly arises in any discussion of the stock market: Where does the new wealth come from in a boom, and what happens to it in a bust? The value in either case seems somewhat mythical. Farmers continue to farm, laborers to produce, and such substantial resources as factories and mines and fields remain unharmed by any "shenanigans" on Wall Street. Demand creates the value; decreased demand cancels it. But demand only establishes the price; it does not pay the broker. Someone buys every share of stock sold, drawing from two possible sources: disposable income and wealth, or from an expansion of credit. The commitment of income or existing wealth means that individuals bid up stock even as they postpone other investments or consumptive goals. In a free market, as demand drives stock values up, the relative value of other goods should drop. Of course, real economic growth and not sheer demand may underwrite higher stock prices without any depressing effect on other values. But in 1928 and 1929, almost all the new value added to stock came from increased demand, not productive growth.

And now a bit of magic much indulged and much appreciated by speculators in the twenties. Credit can cancel at least part of the apparent cost of stock. If borrowing meant only a transfer of funds from one person to another, there would be no magical expansion. But by the rules of our banking system, bank credit has a flexible, expandable feature. A bank that maintains minimal reserves (set by law) can lend many times the amount of deposits it holds, for it accepts as security the paper it accepts, and can rediscount this at Federal Reserve Banks to get extra currency. In

effect, a person with a good credit rating can write a promissory note for
$1,000, pay a 10 percent discount on it at a bank, and walk off with $900
in Federal Reserve notes (cash), courtesy of the banking system and the
Bureau of Engraving.

In 1928, as the great bull market began its dizzy twenty-month spiral
toward eventual disaster, one could borrow about 50 percent of the value
of stock. This moderate credit possibility—called margin—varied but
little during the boom, for brokers remained cautious. Margin buying was
simple, beguiling for investors and completely safe for brokers and bankers. It worked this way: banks, or other primary lenders (after 1928 it
would increasingly be corporations and private individuals), furnished
credit lines to brokerage houses, accepting stock certificates as security.
The broker then advanced the credit to stock buyers. The margin requirement determined the amount of collateral a buyer had to have; if at
50 percent he had to have $5,000 to pay down on a $10,000 stock purchase. The broker or bank actually held the stock. With a 50 percent
margin, such loans were ironclad, for the market never dropped so precipitously as to endanger them. As stock prices dropped, brokers asked for
additional collateral to maintain the margin (thus the term "call loans"). If
the buyer could not supply it, the broker exercised his authority to sell
the stock, collected his $5,000 plus interest and fees, and paid the remain-
der to the purchaser. For the speculative investor on a rising market, marginal buying, even at 50 percent, almost doubled his chances of profit. Of
course, one had to pay a high interest on the loan (at least 6 percent after
1928, and usually much higher; in periods of spectacular advances, call
money occasionally commanded 20 percent). Dividend rates on most stock
remained much lower than this, but speculators, then and now, were little
concerned with dividends. They looked for early capital gains, and in one
good day on Wall Street could make enough to pay a year's interest on a
broker's loan. By frequent selling and buying, a lucky or knowledgeable
speculator could get rich in a few weeks during the bull market of 1929.

Despite credit expansion, the tremendous accretion of stock values in
1929 still reflected a major diversion of capital from other uses. The margin rate required at least 50 percent cash, while many investors never
bought on margin. Brokerage loans from corporations and individuals bypassed the credit expansion possible for banks. In a minor way, this diversion of capital had much the same economic effects as the liquidation of
capital when the market later fell. The high returns either from stock or
from brokerage loans diverted American investments from Europe, and
attracted European capital to Wall Street, which posed a threat to the
debtor states of Europe. Had the diversion continued, it would have
forced upon Europe many of the same strategies that followed the crash

This picture shows Wall
Street as it looked at the
end of World War I. The
people celebrating the end
of the war expected a mild
postwar depression, but
after the prosperity of
the twenties were totally
unprepared and helpless
in the face of the cata-
strophic depression that
came in the thirties. *Library of Congress*

—higher tariffs or import quotas. These directly threatened a major market for American farm products. As the stock market lured away corporate earning from capital expansion, it threatened the continued growth of our productive plant. As affluent Americans used more and more of their disposable income for stock purchases, they stopped buying automobiles or homes. Most of these implications were long-term ones; they did not terribly distort the economy even in 1929, for most people did not gamble on the stock market. But they did contribute to a recession that began in the summer of 1929, and to a severe drop in private home construction.

Throughout 1928 stock prices and brokerage loans climbed in tandem. Brokerage loans moved up from $3.4 billion in January 1928, to a then astounding $6 billion in January of 1929. Stock prices boomed in March, fell off in the early summer, and soared again during the fall (the election market). During the year the *Times* index rose from 245 to 331 (from just above 100 in 1924). On one day the market gained 25 points. On two days the New York Stock Exchange sold over 6 million shares (a slow day in 1974, but unprecedented for the twenties). Regional markets, or the curb market (over-the-counter) ballooned with the higher sales, capturing almost 40 percent of stock sales by 1929.

The Climax

By the end of 1928 the orgy was in full swing. Everyone seemed to forget the relationship of stock to earnings, or even to any reasonable prospect for growth in the near future. Al Smith's campaign manager, John J. Raskob, predicted, with a straight face, that everyone in America could get rich. An investment of $15 a month in stock, for twenty years, would yield $80,000, a small fortune in 1929. From all the publicity for the stock market, it seemed that everyone believed him. Not so. The market never became a casino for the poor. With few exceptions, it remained an indulgence of the affluent. By the crash, about 1.5 million Americans owned stock (others indirectly owned it through retirement funds or insurance equities), or possibly one person in every twenty families. This was not a drastic increase over earlier years. Less than 1 million Americans bought for purely speculative purposes, and only about 600,000 bought on margin. But the interest in the market was much broader than investment, as it is today. And by 1929 a heretofore unnoticed type of corporation began to make much of the news.

Unlike earlier speculative frenzies, the stock market did not exploit any popular faith in nostrums. The boom made it easy for old and new companies to float new stock, and for corporate directors to rake in quick profits in their early sales of new issues obtained at a privileged price.

Some minor chicanery of this sort marked the bull market. And a few new industries—notably radio and aviation—were so attractive that new companies easily accumulated capital on the basis of little more than grandiose plans. But most of the trading was always in quite legitimate securities, including that of the blue-chip companies. The major exception to this was the growing subscription to the newly issued stock of investment trusts, which accounted for about $3 billion in stock value before the crash. The number of investment trusts ballooned from 160 in 1927 to 751 in October 1929.

Investment trusts functioned as do more closely regulated investment funds today. They raised capital by selling their own preferred and common stock, and after deducting costs (often scandalously high) invested their capital in the stock market. Their only product was capital gains. In ordinary circumstances such trusts had a justifiable role—to offer small investors the presumed knowledge of experts and the stability of a diversified holding. In the bull market, all but a few of the older, respectable trusts became market parasites, the prime example of greed and duplicity at work. Brokerage houses or other sponsors initiated the trusts, and used their leverage to push up selected stocks (they would buy strongly in a company, force its prices up, and then sell at the highest point). This made their own stockholders happy. But increasingly the trusts pyramided into trusts that largely owned other trusts. The board of a parent trust would charter a new one and channel most of its capital into it. Soon there developed a complicated maze of trusts, surviving on the rapidly rising market and buying each other's stock. Sponsors milked the funds by high administrative salaries while investors remained content so long as they realized capital gains. The magic of the boom concealed the chicanery. The weak funds (most of them) represented the most vulnerable stock on Wall Street. As the market later declined, their authentic holdings in productive corporations often barely covered their preferred stock, leaving no assets to support common stock. When this became apparent, their stock fell precipitously, even as some trusts used the last of their resources in suicidal purchases of their own stock. Some investment funds fell close to the ultimate limit on stock prices—0.

The boom climaxed in early September 1929. The *Times* index peaked at 452; brokerage loans peaked at over $7 billion, with over half of that provided by corporations and individuals. But the boom had invited fear and tension. Many who talked of a coming collapse received the scorn reserved only for traitors. In fact, the terrible danger of pessimism intimidated most people within and without government. Somehow, the most brilliant financiers and economists persuaded themselves and the public that the market was sound, that our glorious economy justified the high stock prices, that if skeptics would only remain silent our economic growth would sustain the existing price levels. There even seemed some hope of deflating the bubble without bursting it in September and early October, for the market drifted downward without panic, and with many good days alternating with the bad ones. New issues still sold well and brokerage loans increased.

The Crash

The first clear intimation of disaster came on October 21. In a near frenzied sale of over 6 million shares, the market broke sharply, only to recover at the end and make new gains the following day. The first enduring break came on October 23. Losses for the day amounted to 31 points on the *Times* index (down from 415 to 384). Worse came on the morning of October 24 (black Thursday), as everyone seemed anxious to sell. By noon the ticker tapes were far behind the sales; sheer panic gripped the market. A hurried meeting of bankers, and their conspicuous buys on the floor, rallied the market in the afternoon. Despite an unbelievable sale of nearly 13 million shares (double any previous day), the market closed with a loss of only 12 points and, encouraged by a steady ballyhoo of optimistic predictions, would remain steady on Friday and Saturday of this first week of disaster.

A weekend of reflection apparently led only to morbid thoughts. On Monday, October 28, the market dropped 49 points on 9 million shares, or the single worst loss of the whole depression for the stock averaged by the *Times*. On Tuesday the losses continued unabated during the darkest day of all. Over 16 million shares set a new record, wrecked the machinery of the market, and left people dangling until midnight to learn whether they were bankrupt. Only a final rally prevented a loss of over 50 points (it closed off 43). During the day several offerings found no buyers. But the lowered prices finally brought buyers back on the market. Averages were up 31 points on Wednesday (October 30) and gained again on Thursday. On this hopeful note, the New York Stock Exchange, which had considered closing, suspended trading for a long weekend to enable its fatigued clerks to catch up on all the paper work.

The extent of the disaster was not yet clear. Small investors or the more reckless speculators had been forced out. They usually lost all. Large investors had suffered severe losses but stayed in the game. Brokers remained solvent and the banks sound, although none were now willing to try and rescue the market. Optimists concluded that the wringout had been necessary, even worthwhile, but surely it was over. Not so. On November 4 the market dropped 22 points, as investment trusts struggled to survive. It dropped 37 points on November 6, and continued downward on November 11, 12, 13, leaving the *Times* averages at 224, or just under half the level of two months earlier. Once again the market seemed near the bottom. Prices stabilized and even rose during December, and again in the early months of 1930. This seemed the ideal time to get back in a low market and to reap the heady profits of recovery. But once again even the most prudent investors lost. The market collapsed a second time in June 1930, and would continue its periodic downward cycles until 1932, when the *Times* index stood at 58, just slightly more than the market lost on October 29, 1929.

Almost a half-century later, several questions remain unanswered. Why did the market collapse when it did? It is easy to chant the weaknesses that pushed it downward once the huge losses began, and particularly the role of margin buying and investment trusts. What is not clear is why the boom eased off in September, or why people rushed to sell on October 21 and 23. Given the behavior of investors, one is inclined to look for frightening events. There were none of demonstrable significance. The economy slowed in late summer. Inventories built up, production eased, and a cyclical recession seemed in the offing. The bull market contributed to the decline, but there is nothing to indicate that the decline discouraged speculators. Economic prospects had long since ceased to have very much to do with stock prices. Dividends were not that im-

Impressions of Magazine Offices.
The Wall Street Journal.

This cartoon is from the November 29, 1929 issue of *Life* magazine. *Library of Congress*

portant. The only visible clues were minor ones—a particularly pessimistic forecast by a well-placed American economist in early September, and the failure of an English investment trust. The buildup of tension as the market moved downward in September probably had a great deal to do with the sharp break in October. But who can say? A few critical sales may have reflected a few acute cases of indigestion rather than any dark clouds on the economic horizon. One is left only with that gem of false wisdom—what goes up has to come down.

The Government Response

A more useful question is why the government did not prevent the crash. In fact, Presidents Coolidge and Hoover, Congress, and such independent agencies as the Federal Reserve System did very little to arrest the speculative boom, even as they apparently did nothing to light the fatal fuse in October 1929. The securities markets were not under federal control. Besides, it was largely poor judgment and not overt chicanery that produced the boom. There were few hidden conspirators, no easy scapegoats, and, as later investigations revealed, a surprisingly small number of crooks. The lessons of the crash led to the later Securities and Exchange Commission, and detailed controls over stock issues. It is unclear whether such controls would have prevented the crash, since most of the trading was with legitimate issues. At best, securities regulation would have prevented the worst abuses of the investment trusts. Had Coolidge asked for such regulation in 1928 or Hoover after March 4, 1929, the implied accusation of unsoundness would have caused a severe break in stock prices. Instead of preventing a crash, this could easily have provoked it a bit earlier.

The Federal Reserve System had some controls over credit, and thus quite indirectly over the interest charged for call loans. It did not have one critical power that it gained in the thirties—the power to set margin requirements for all stock purchases. In retrospect, it appears that higher margin requirements at the takeoff point, possibly in the fall of 1927, might have retarded the speculative boom. But at the time no one foresaw what was coming or sought such authority. In the midst of the boom it was too late, for controls then probably would have meant a collapse on Wall Street.

Of two indirect Federal Reserve controls over interest rates, one had small possibilities in the twenties. The New York Reserve Bank, as a normal banking function and without specific authorization, bought and sold securities (government bonds and notes) on the open market, and in a sense served as broker for the other eleven banks. By buying securities from private banks, it increased their cash reserves and their lending authority, thus fostering lower interest rates. By selling such securities it diminished bank reserves and made credit more dear. By 1928 it recognized the need for credit restrictions and began selling. Its problem was that it had only a small inventory of securities (only $617 million), the largest share of which it sold in 1928 with no visible effect on interest rates.

The other weapon—the rediscount rate—was at least in theory more powerful. Under less than energetic leadership, the Federal Reserve banks lowered the rediscount rate in 1927 to 3.5 percent. This encouraged low interest rates and an increase in brokerage loans. The Federal Reserve Board desired low interest rates both as a spur for domestic investment and as a gesture of support for Europe (low interest rates here made our bonds poor investments for Europeans, but helped persuade Americans to seek more lucrative rates abroad, thus underwriting the precarious system of balanced payments). With the growing boom of 1928, the Reserve Banks raised the rediscount rate back up to about 5 percent (it could vary among the twelve banks). This at least raised the floor on the interest charged for call loans, but it also placed a heavy penalty on those who needed installment debt, on farm mortgage rates, and on the prime rates charged businessmen. It helped slow the economy in 1929. But it did not slow the pace of brokerage loans. In the boom it was hard to find any connection between interest rate and demand for loans. The fever was too high to let such mundane issues intervene. Finally, in August 1929, after earlier opposition from Hoover, the banks raised the rediscount rate to a very high 6 percent (banks would have to charge at least 8 percent, and probably more to make lending profitable). Again, there was no immediate effect on the stock market, although the bull market peaked within a few weeks. Ironically, if the new rates did influence the market break, then the Federal Reserve System helped produce the crash in its futile effort to dampen down a boom. After the crash, the system reversed its priorities, lowered rediscount rates, and tried to encourage more borrowing and more buying.

All of this does not mean that the federal government was helpless. The bull market was exceedingly sensitive to government policies. In early 1929 the mere fact of secret meetings by the Federal Reserve Board sent tremors through the market and prices tumbling. Had either Hoover or the Federal Reserve Board disavowed speculation or suggested new, stringent legislation, the market would have responded almost immediately. A threat was as powerful as action. Instead of being helpless, the government found itself in an awful dilemma and chose inaction as the best course of action. Anyone in government who bearded the bull on Wall Street had to be ready to accept responsibility for causing a panic. In the middle of the boom the government simply did not have the subtle tools or the finesse to puncture the bubble without breaking it. It was in this sense that the government was so helpless. At a certain point in a speculative boom there were no longer any good answers.

The relationship between the crash and the subsequent depression remained the most complex issue of all. It is difficult even to date the beginnings of depression. A drop in production preceded the crash, and did not revive after it. Yet, the crash directly affected only an affluent 2 percent who held stock. It did not lead immediately to severe unemployment or to sharp losses in production. Few people sensed a depression in late 1929 or early in 1930. Prices and wages, outside agriculture, held up to earlier levels. Only in the fall of 1930 was it clear that America would experience a depression as serious as the one in 1921. And this depression, clearly, derived from the crash. Hoover, who later distinguished three depressions, admitted that the first one came as a direct product of the stock market problems. The crash accelerated the downturn that preceded it, even as the economic problems of 1930 helped spur further, cyclical declines in the stock market. Investors, who had blissfully ignored economic realities in 1929, became morbidly sensitive to them. The market that precipitated a depression finally became a casualty of what it so recklessly began.

The stock market losses were real enough for those who suffered them. Of course, exaggeration is always a danger. The early accounts of mass suicides, that one could not safely walk the streets of New York because of falling bodies, were demonstrably false. Rare was the former person of wealth who ended up selling apples on the streets. Few established corporations failed (the rate of corporate failures only went up 50 percent by 1932), although many went for years without profits. Almost no new corporations were chartered between 1930 and 1933. For the investor who held on to his stock portfolio, the loss was almost unbelievable—over 80 percent of the value as of September 1929, had dissolved by 1932. Others lost even more, as they kept selling during each decline and reentering the market with each temporary stabilization.

The economic impact of these losses turned out to be much more than Hoover or almost anyone else expected. Hoover correctly celebrated the sound aspects of the economy, the fecund farms and factories, the awesome technology, the willing workers. But the problem was demand, for goods and services or for new capital improvements. This demand dropped sharply after the crash. The diversion of income into the boom market cut consumption; the complete loss of much of this investment cut it at a much faster pace. Because of the distribution of income in America (the top 10 percent received more than one-third of all income), the very people who lost all their savings on Wall Street had been the ones who sustained the market for luxury and high-priced goods and who normally financed new industry. Their losses, and their destructive loss of confidence in the economy, took away a major stimulant in the economy.

House construction, already declining in 1929, almost ceased in 1930. The record production of automobiles in 1929 led to a glut on dealers' lots. Those who had planned new enterprises gave up both plans and hope. The extreme illusions that fanned the boom gave way to pessimistic fantasies just as extreme. Even the eventual price of stock was as irrationally low as it had been high on the bull market; a halfway intelligent investment of $5,000 in common stock in 1932 would insure one of being a millionaire today.

As a result of the international complications created by the crash, farmers suffered most of all and led the gloomy march into depression. The crash practically destroyed all American sources of private loans for Europe, threatening the whole, fragile financial system so carefully erected in the twenties. Germany was most vulnerable. In 1930 European countries had to react both to the fiscal impact of the crash and to higher American tariffs. They first tried higher tariffs or import quotas. In 1931 they had to try a more extreme remedy—currency devaluation. Overall, the United States seemed quite well insulated against the effects of a trade war, of a resurgent economic nationalism. Our exports of goods in the twenties made up barely 4 percent of our total production, and thus seemed a marginal support for prosperity. But in agriculture the situation was quite different. In the years before the crash we exported almost 17 percent of our farm products, and for several commodities the export market and world prices determined domestic prices. We exported about 40 percent of our tobacco, about 28 percent of our cotton, and about 12 percent of our wheat (much more in good years).

The overall economy drifted into depression over a two-year period; agriculture plunged in abruptly in 1930. The cold statistics at least hint at the despair and suffering in rural America. The cash income of farmers dropped almost $2 billion in 1930, or by 20 percent; in 1931 it dropped another 30 percent. In 1930 farm prices fell to the depressed levels of 1921, and then plummeted in 1931. Heavy export crops best revealed the magnitude of loss. Cotton dropped from 20 cents a pound in 1927 to 16 cents in 1929 to only 9 cents in 1930; wheat dropped from $1.19 a bushel in 1927 to $1.03 in 1929 to only $0.67 in 1930 and a dismal $0.39 in 1931. Tobacco dropped from 20 cents a pound in 1928 to 12.8 cents in 1930 to 8.2 cents in 1931. Corn, although not an export crop (animal products were), dropped from $0.79 a bushel in 1929 to $0.59 in 1930 to $0.32 in 1931.

In the two years following the crash farm prices fell by up to two-thirds, or many times as rapidly as most manufacturing prices. The reason was not a drastic drop in domestic consumption of foods and fibers, but export barriers and drastically reduced world prices. Farmers, with large

"You've no idea, folks—what a marvelous time everybody's having!"

Although only a small percentage of the population was affected by the stock market crash itself, the suffering of farmers was apparent even by 1930. In the wake of the crash, Hoover tried to convince people that all the country needed was confidence in itself. This cartoon, from *New York Life*, December 27, 1929, illustrates this psychological campaign. *Library of Congress*

domestic surpluses, had no alternative but to dump them on world markets. With no effective control over production, farmers even increased their planting in 1930 and 1931 in futile hopes of maintaining incomes and meeting debt payments. The most efficient and specialized farmers suffered most. Marginal farmers, with small sales and a near subsistence livelihood, and already desperately poor, had been unable to avail themselves of credit. Their meager lives went on much as before. But able farmers had enjoyed the magical and normally wise indulgence of the twenties—credit. Mortgage debt declined only slightly during the decade and remained at about $10 billion in 1929. The collapsed price structure on basic commodities simply could not sustain these debts, facing expert farmers with the horror of foreclosure and a lapse into the growing class of farm tenants. Not only the farmer suffered. Those who worked on our 6.5 million farms made up almost a third of our labor force and supported a population of about 35 million. They provided a vital market for goods and services which sustained millions of jobs in manufacturing.

The disruption of normal trade patterns (American exports dropped from 5.1 billion in 1929 to 2.9 in 1931), of payments balances, and the related plight of agriculture help explain why the crash so directly contributed to the worst depression in history. Insofar as the international market had been a fool's paradise, it had seemed that Europe, not America, had enjoyed the fruits of illusion as they postponed a final accounting of the costs of war. Surely they would be the ones to suffer later. The

United States, with its near self-sufficient economy, and a near monopoly of world gold supplies, seemed ideally situated to weather an international crisis. Yet, because of the peculiar role of our stock market, the United States did the most to precipitate a crisis and then suffered most from it. Since the European countries, in desperate defensive maneuvers, helped undermine the market for farm products, they made American farmers pay the first of the bills accrued by reckless gamblers on Wall Street. As so often, the most innocent spectators suffered the most.

The authentic suffering of farmers supported an appealing myth for Democrats. A drastic reduction in consumption by farmers certainly helped convert a Wall Street panic into a severe depression. But instead of seeing the agricultural collapse as a first casualty of the crash, Democrats and farmers themselves easily referred their problems back into the twenties, when controversies over agricultural reform had continuously inflamed the political arena. The blurred image of a long-term agricultural depression simply turned the crash into an added stimulus in an ongoing process of impoverishment sustained by callous Republican policies. Actually, the crash was a dramatic turning point in the fortunes of farmers, and none of the politically acceptable strategies for higher farm prices in the twenties would have done very much to save the farmers in 1930 and 1931. Only rigid controls over production or vast subsidies were potent enough weapons against the new ills.

The Republicans had their own beguiling myths. Hoover endlessly emphasized psychological factors, or the loss of confidence. Of course, this contributed to the developing depression. The loss of hope may have been the most intractable problem with the economy after 1930. But too much emphasis upon this could so easily camouflage the direct and authentic impact of stock market losses on demand, and the nonpsychological maladies in agriculture. It could also divert attention from such hard issues as the distribution of income and wealth, the critical role of consumer demand in sustaining prosperity, and the demoralizing effects of open chicanery or low business ethics in corporations or on the stock exchange. Even if these issues had a minor role in precipitating the crash, they certainly helped magnify its economic impact and also contributed directly to the pessimism that Hoover tried to counteract with continual and increasingly forced cheers for the soundness of our economy and optimistic predictions of an imminent recovery.

All the interpretations, all the political charges and countercharges, could not obscure one political fact—the Republicans had posed as godfathers of prosperity, and now had to accept the primary responsibility for its horrible offspring. Hoover accepted this responsibility, and forcefully even if joylessly set about putting all the pieces back together again.

7

When Herbert Hoover took office in March 1929, he seemed the very epitome of a confident, humane benefactor. He committed his administration to the perfection of a successful economic system. He promised that he would try to eliminate the remaining pockets of poverty and to reduce private selfishness and special privileges, even as he encouraged a wide array of private, cooperative efforts to increase employment, foster home ownership, insure against illness and old age, and above all help the farmers. In fact, he almost immediately called Congress into a special session to enact a new program of farm cooperation and to raise certain selected tariff rates on agricultural products. As if in mockery of all his confidence and optimism, his farm bill was the only part of his program enacted before the stock market crash created a whole new list of priorities, and slowly shifted the aim of his administration from the perfection of our economic system to desperate efforts to save it.

Although he never so intended it, Hoover's new farm bill became the first recovery measure. The Agricultural Marketing Act of 1929 established a Farm Board of eight members to dispose of a revolving fund of $500 million (Hoover loved such loan funds, which in theory could go on working forever, helping people help themselves without any direct federal subsidy). The fund was to help farmers form cooperative marketing associations for each major crop, and thus develop greater efficiency in production, control their own marketing, and even establish advisory production quotas. Before most cooperatives could even organize, the crash and an early collapse in farm prices magnified one minor provision of the act, and one closer to earlier congressional plans for price-fixing than to Hoover's emphasis upon cooperation and self-help. The Farm Board established stabilization corporations for cotton and wheat. Hoover accepted them as aids to rational marketing, not as means of establishing minimum prices. They were to purchase enough commodities to sustain level prices during times of cyclical decline, and then sell when prices were high. This would exempt individual farmers from the vagaries of widely fluctuating prices. But, in fact, falling prices became the rule and not the exception. The corporations bought but could not sell except at a great loss. They thus offered the farmer the first price support system in our peacetime history, yet at a tremendous cost. Throughout 1930 the

Hoover
and
Depression

corporations purchased enough cotton and wheat to keep our prices slightly higher than world prices, but their $300 million of available funds proved completely inadequate. By the harvests of 1931 the two corporations were effectively bankrupt, with warehouses full of almost unsalable wheat and cotton worth less than half their cost.

From a contemporary perspective, Hoover's immediate response to the crash was brilliant, although not predicated upon present economic theories. In light of budgetary surpluses, he supported a rather drastic cut in taxes, which Congress enacted in December 1929. The act lowered income rates by more than half at the lower levels (or to less than 1 percent on incomes of less than $5,000). Unfortunately, the tax rates were already too low for such drastic cuts in rates to have much economic impact. For a relatively affluent family with an income of around $5,000, the cut amounted to only a few dollars a year, and meant nothing for the masses of workers who paid no income taxes.

Hoover combined the tax cut with a request for over $400 million in expanded public works, and also asked state and local governments to speed up public construction. As commerce secretary Hoover had tried, without success, to get approval for a $3 billion public works fund to underwrite economic stability. Had such a fund been available, along with matured plans for public projects (roads, new federal court houses, office buildings, and post offices, or marine, park, and conservation facilities), Hoover might have been able to offset much of the slackened private demand that followed the crash. In the absence of such funds, federal agencies could only increase the pace of existing projects or begin the slow planning of new ones.

As a complement to tax cuts and increased spending, Hoover launched his psychological crusade. He had long relied upon the good will and public spirit of citizens, using persuasive appeals and publicity to mediate labor disputes and to raise the level of business ethics. Now he used the same tactic to inspire confidence. He endlessly noted the soundness of our productive economy, despite obvious maladies in banking and in the securities market, and promised reduced spending and greater efficiency in government (this was an almost sacred litany, and very important in inspiring business confidence). Finally, he convened a series of highly publicized White House meetings with businessmen and representatives of labor and farmers. He asked corporate executives to continue production and maintain employment and wages, which many tried to do at least into the summer of 1930. But persuasion was not enough. In June the stock market resumed its downward spiral. Agricultural prices continued their plunge, and many businessmen had such large, unsold inventories that they had to cut production. Growing unemployment made the cities as well as the farms feel the full impact of depression in the winter of 1930–1931. As always, the decline fed on itself, as every drop in employment reduced the potential market for the very products that sustained employment. Hoover had to form a committee to seek work for the unemployed, and again asked for increased public works spending.

Trade and Fiscal Policies

In April 1930, a Republican-controlled Congress passed a controversial Hawley-Smoot Tariff, and a reluctant Hoover signed it. A year earlier Hoover had asked only for higher rates on vulnerable agricultural products. All the prominent plans for agricultural relief required tariff protection. Any price-fixing mechanism required rigid tariff walls at least as high as the differences between artificial domestic prices and world prices. Even Hoover's milder program of stabilized marketing required protection against erratic and cyclical declines in world prices. Obviously, the stabilization corporation for wheat could not work effectively if Canadian wheat growers flooded our market whenever our stabilized prices exceeded world prices. In addition, a few agricultural commodities had always required tariff protection to survive (most notably wool and both beet and cane sugar). Eventually, Congress enacted more than the needed agricultural rates, and simply used these as an excuse for major tariff revision. By 1930 our glutted marketplace created intensive demands from manufacturers for additional protection, demands often echoed by laborers in beleaguered industries. As usual in tariff debates, regions and interests clashed. The end result was the highest rates in our history (50 percent) and a major impediment to international trade. There were a few balancing features—a careful calculation of many rates by the Tariff Commission, and a reciprocal provision that permitted Hoover to negotiate mutually lowered rates with cooperative countries.

The Hawley-Smoot Tariff placed the United States in the forefront of countries that desperately tried to preserve a healthy national economy in a period of international instability. We curtailed imports to boost domestic production and jobs. Other countries retaliated, and by 1931 a type of trade war threatened the whole Western market system. The remarkable thing is that Hoover, a declared disciple of Wilson and of responsible internationalism, signed the tariff. Much as Taft in 1910, he gave in to congressional Republicans rather than dominating them. Paradoxically, the tariff revision, predicated on the needs of agriculture, ended up as a prime contributor to falling farm prices. After 1930 Hoover tried in every possible way to move back to an internationalist position. He used the debt moratorium of 1931 (agreed to when Congress was not in session) to cancel some of the disruptive effects of our trade barriers (see pp. 89–90). By then he was willing to make major American sacrifices in order to sustain European economies, and at great political risk refused to devalue the dollar and go off the gold standard, even though such moves could have aided our domestic recovery (devaluation is a stronger weapon than tariffs, for it not only impedes imports but boosts exports). After 1931 Hoover viewed the depression as an international calamity, and believed that any enduring recovery as well as continued world peace depended upon renewed international cooperation and trade. It would be the new Roosevelt administration that would briefly reject this international magnanimity and experiment with an extreme form of economic nationalism.

In November 1930, the American voters expressed their growing fears and their disenchantment with the Hoover administration. The depression had already changed voting habits. By a slim majority the Democrats carried the House and came within one vote of controlling the Senate, where insurgent Republicans gave them an effective majority. Hoover thus faced a hostile Congress in his last two years. The Democrats, delighted to exploit the depression to gain political power, still did not sabotage Hoover's efforts at recovery. The crisis was so serious, the need for effective solutions so obvious, that both parties sought realistic compromises on legislation, and both contributed in important ways to recovery measures. The most important legislation always represented a joint presidential and congressional program, although after plenty of bickering and political posturing. Hoover often resented the role of Congress and suspected the worst of motives. Yet, in retrospect, the major recovery legislation, which rarely pleased either side, probably gained from the conflicts. Congress as a whole had no recovery plan, and thus usually responded to Hoover's proposals or to individual measures offered by congressmen with firm ideas about the economy. In reality, no one knew what to do about the depression, even as dozens of people sponsored their own pet cures. By the vaunted economic knowledge of today, most had built-in contradictions.

It seemed to Hoover that the stock market depression bottomed out in the winter of 1930–31, thanks in part to his own vigorous policies. Indeed, in the spring of 1931 the economic indicators moved upward, as if recovery were underway. Then, in May, the European economy began to collapse, first in Austria and Germany, then in Britain. England had to leave the gold standard. This collapse imperiled trans-Atlantic trade and also imperiled private American loans in Europe (many of those in Germany would never be paid in full). The American stock market broke once again. By fall a banking crisis threatened. Industrial production again declined, with devastating effect on employment. A defensive Hoover, with some justification, defined this as a second depression, rooted not in domestic weaknesses but in international problems that traced back to World War I. He particularly deplored European devaluation and desertion of the gold standard. His early response was at the international level, as he negotiated the debt moratorium. But when the frustrated new Congress finally met in its regular session in December 1931, Hoover was ready to propose a major legislative program, one which began a long series of recovery measures enacted both in 1932 and 1933 under two separate presidents.

On several critical issues, Hoover and a vast majority of congressmen in both parties were in complete agreement. They agreed on two general economic goals—maintenance of the gold standard and the existing value of the dollar, and on the need for a balanced budget and strict governmental economy. These ancient economic truisms, given their hold upon the popular mind, were also necessary supports for that elusive angel called "confidence." But, by the time Congress met, gold had become a pressing problem. After European devaluation, our dollar was overvalued in relationship to other currencies and to gold. Europeans fortunate enough to hold dollar credits during the summer of 1931 began converting them to gold, forcing us to ship it out of the country to maintain the dollar. This led to the first of two reserve crises during the Hoover administration.

The Federal Reserve Act required the twelve Reserve Banks to hold gold reserves amounting to 40 percent of outstanding Federal Reserve notes. The other 60 percent of currency reserves could be in certain narrowly defined types of debt paper (notes and mortgages). In fact, from World War I on our near monopoly on gold had meant excessive gold reserves. Even in 1931 gold made up not 40 percent, but close to 70 percent of the reserves backing our monetary supply. But the gold drain, and the low demand for high quality credit, and an even lower demand for rediscounts by banks now blessed or cursed with excessive cash reserves, caused a crisis. There was simply not enough eligible paper to replace the fleeing gold. If the drain continued, the Reserve Banks would be unable to print additional notes, and thus unable to rediscount paper, drying up the sources of credit. To avoid this calamity, the Reserve Banks began raising their rediscount rates (and thus interest rates) in 1931. Nothing could have been more absurd. The Federal Reserve System was in the embarrassing position of discouraging borrowing in a declining economy, thus reducing effective demand and worsening the depression.

One solution to the crisis, but one anathema to Hoover, was devaluation of the dollar. This would entail a reduction of its gold content, or, stated in other terms, an increase in the dollar price of gold. If such deval-uation raised the dollar value of gold above world prices, it could reverse the direction of flow. Short of such devaluation, Hoover proposed an easy solution, and in so doing began a process of revamping the Federal Reserve System that continued until 1935. In February 1932, Congress passed the first banking act called Glass-Stegall. It broadened the categories of paper eligible as currency reserves to include government bonds, and thus immediately freed additional gold to back up the dollar and allowed the Federal Reserve Banks to lower rediscount rates and once again encourage borrowing. Yet support of the overvalued dollar remained a burden on the domestic economy, a costly form of expiation for the Hawley-Smoot Tariff. In late 1932 our gold reserves finally sank so low as to threaten the 40 percent requirement. On the last day of the Hoover administration, and in the midst of the severe banking crisis of 1933, two Reserve Banks had to raise their rediscount rates to protect their reserves. This terrible bind helped stimulate dramatic new gold policies in the Roosevelt administration.

The widely praised goal of a balanced budget also required attention by 1932. Because of additional government spending (notably for public works and the farm program), and drastically reduced revenues, the federal government incurred a deficit of approximately $900 million in 1931. In an economic sense, the deficit spending helped stimulate the economy. But the idea of a deficit in a depression horrified most Americans. They had long understood that, in bad times, one retrenched—cut expenses to the bone, stopped borrowing, and tried to balance budgets. Since the level of government spending could not decline in 1932 (congressmen even more than Hoover were pressing for new programs), the only alternative was new taxes. This was almost beyond controversy. Up in New York State, Governor Franklin D. Roosevelt made headlines by accusing Hoover of spending too much, thereby endangering the country. When, in the midst of debate on a tax bill, a House leader made a moving speech in behalf of balanced budgets, every single congressman stood up in a solemn rededication to this hallowed ideal (actually, a handful of congressmen indulged a normal form of hypocrisy, for they had already accepted the necessity of deficits in such an emergency). The only controversial issue was not a tax increase, but who should pay it. As we view depression legislation from present perspectives, nothing horrifies us so much as tax increases. However assessed, they almost have to lower the demand for goods and services and thus for jobs. Here we glimpse a pathetic dilemma of the thirties. A policy necessary to appease orthodox beliefs, or even to stimulate business confidence, directly threatened the recovery everyone desired.

The debate on the Revenue Act of 1932 revived all the controversies of the mid-twenties. Treasury Secretary Mellon, soon to leave Hoover's cabinet, wanted increases at all levels, and particularly at the bottom, with both cuts in personal exemptions and a sales tax on manufactured goods. The original tax bill provided for a sales tax, which led to most of the controversy. The proposed tax increase was a whopping $3 billion, or the largest proposed increase in peacetime history, quite large enough to have a major economic impact. Congress, led by Democrats, emasculated the sales tax (leaving it on only selected items), but reduced family exemptions from $3,500 to $2,500. Against the advice of Mellon, it also raised the maximum surtax rate from 20 percent to 55 percent as a direct slap at the wealthy.

The Second Hoover Recovery Program

During the summer of 1931 Hoover tried to organize a voluntary pool of private credit to sustain beleaguered banks, railroads, and insurance companies. When private efforts failed, he asked Congress for a federal lending agency. In January it authorized a Reconstruction Finance Corporation (RFC), a government-owned finance agency with $1.5 billion of authorized loans. Most would go to banks. The RFC, probably the most effective of all federal recovery agencies, soon gained additional programs, and remained the major government finance agency until World War II. It easily attracted critics both within Congress and without. Democrats recklessly publicized the names of some of its clients, thereby in part nullifying its effort to avert public fears. To people suffering from unemployment, such major aid to banks and to the wealthy, with none for relief, seemed unfair, an example of administration callousness. But Hoover correctly perceived the immense economic effects of major bank or corporate failures; the ones who suffered most would be small depositors or thousands of discharged workers. Behind the RFC was an as yet unarticulated understanding, although one later well assimilated. The largest financial and manufacturing firms, although legally part of the private economy, are really "public" enterprises because of their immense economic role. Their services, the jobs they provide, are vital to the total economy; their failure an unbearable threat. Thus, the federal government either has to rescue and sustain such giants or directly manage and operate them. Hoover, as well as his successors, chose to rescue and sustain. But, more than most of his successors, he limited his aid to well-secured loans.

Agriculture remained as the most aggravating of problems, with no real prospect of improved prices so long as production so much exceeded domestic needs. In the crisis, Hoover's dream of self-imposed production quotas seemed completely utopian. Even his own Farm Board proposed some type of government restrictions on production, and bills to this end circulated in Congress. Hoover would not buy them. He did not believe the government should invade the area of entrepreneurial decision making, and once again turned to credit devices, and these mainly to relieve drought conditions in the Southwest. The most conspicuous gap in Hoover's otherwise comprehensive recovery strategy was any proposal for major new farm legislation.

Farmers were not the only people with mortgages. Urban homeowners often faced foreclosure. In response to their needs, Hoover asked Congress for a new home financing program, a pioneer effort that expanded, in 1933 and 1935, into the Home Owners Loan Corporation and the Federal Housing Administration. The Home Loan Bank Act of 1932 set up a miniature federal reserve system for mortgage lenders. Instead of foreclosing mortgages to gain needed reserves or to pay off depositors, banks and savings-and-loan associations could now rediscount mortgages in the home loan banks. This not only helped people retain their homes, but kept lending institutions from closing because of the immense loss of value on the property covered by their mortgages, and the dismal prospects of a good sale on foreclosed homes.

The most emotional controversy between Hoover and the Democratic Congress involved public works and relief. The debate involved principles. Hoover wanted to use government resources in a supportive way. His varied recovery program stressed such devices as public works (the government fulfilled a need, and actually profited from increased construction in a time of low prices), or revolving loan funds, which insured a full return of value to the government, usually with interest. He disliked subsidies and tried to maintain a difficult middle position between a government that took no responsibility at all for the private economy, and one that so directly intervened in it as to diminish the primary responsibility of individuals for their own welfare or their leeway for free and responsible choice. He gained criticism from both sides. Many economists, and even Secretary Mellon, decried the degree to which Hoover was willing to intervene in the economy. They believed recovery would come more quickly if politicians let the course of liquidation run its limits, and allow a natural restoration to take place. Possibly they were correct, for the different, often contradictory strategies may have retarded recovery.

But Hoover, too committed to supportive services to do nothing, wanted to help people help themselves. In a complex economic system he believed such governmental roles necessary. But in normal times he did not want any agency of government telling a farmer what or how much to produce, or a worker where or how long to work, or a corporate executive what to produce or how much to charge for the product. He believed no private groups could gain, in the long run, from direct governmental subsidies. They would become dependent and lose all private initiative. In time the government would become a huge bureaucratic trough from which powerful interest groups would try to drink all they could. Neither could he accept government doles or direct relief payments. Despite the suffering of the depression (an overly serious Hoover suffered his share of anguish), he would not violate these moral scruples. The appearance of callousness, which Democrats exploited, also drew support from a few highly symbolic events. World War I veterans (the Bonus Army) marched on Washington in the summer of 1932 to seek congressional approval for an early payment of their bonuses, due in 1945. After the Senate defeated a bill to that purpose, a portion of the veterans (perhaps not many more than 2,000) set up a shantytown along the Anacosta River. After a small melee involved in the evacuation of vet-

Members of the Bonus Army are shown here in their Washington shantytown. The gravestones single out Secretary of the Treasury Mellon and President Hoover as responsible for the death of the bonus. *Underwood & Underwood*

erans from government buildings (this alone Hoover ordered), the secretary of the army used the excuse of a "riot" to order an army unit to clear the area and burn the shacks. Hoover gained all the blame.

Democratic congressmen, who were often less concerned than Hoover with the ultimate implications of relief, responded to the immediate suffering of their constituents and proposed a variety of schemes for work projects or direct relief expenditures. However much Hoover relied upon private agencies, such as the Red Cross, or upon local governments, these organizations were simply not prepared for the magnitude of distress caused by a sustained depression. Up to one-fourth of urban workers were unemployed; others worked only part time. None had unemployment insurance and few had savings. Many local governments exhausted dwindling tax resources and had no sources of credit. The immense drop in local governmental expenditures more than balanced the increase of federal expenditures. By 1932 the long bread lines, the soup kitchens, the endless stream of hoboes, the temporary shan-

General Douglas MacArthur (1880–1964) used four troops of cavalry and four infantry companies to break up the Bonus Army in 1932. MacArthur is shown here with one of his junior officers, Dwight D. Eisenhower. *United Press International*

tytowns ("Hoovervilles") at the outskirts of cities all testified to the amount of suffering. Farmers, stripped of almost all income, forced often to sell crops at a net loss, and faced with mortgage foreclosures, began some rather effective organizing and tried limited withholding actions.

Hoover, aware of the compelling need for federal assistance, wanted to exhaust local resources before offering aid, and wanted to be very scrupulous about the method of giving it. He vetoed a bill for direct relief, but approved almost the same amount under a lending arrangement. This compromise relief bill permitted the RFC to lend up to $300 million to local relief agencies. It had expended only part of these funds when Roosevelt became president. He created a separate funding agency, the Federal Emergency Relief Administration, which continued to make loans to state agencies. Later, rather than continue such an indirect dole, he substituted a form of work relief.

The final controversy concerned public works. Most Democrats wanted a new public works program under a special agency. Hoover resented what he considered the continuous political exploitation of human suffering, and the steady undermining of his own recovery program (his suspicions were exaggerated). He also had a proprietary claim to public works. In 1932 he wanted a new agency to coordinate existing works programs, but insisted that further large appropriations would either require a lead time of months and years, thus nullifying relief goals, or fund some form of wasteful and unplanned work, resulting in only a concealed form of dole. He was correct. Yet, he again compromised, and in July approved a bill that allowed an expanding RFC to loan up to $1.5 billion for self-liquidating projects, including nonprofit housing developments. By the very rules of such a program, few applications had gone beyond the planning stage before the inauguration of Roosevelt in 1933. In turn, Roosevelt added funds to public works, created a separate agency to administer them, but also had to wait years for most of the returns. The first housing projects, begun under Hoover, were only completed in the mid-thirties.

The Hoover Legacy

This varied body of recovery and relief legislation, always proposed in some form by Hoover, but often modified by Congress, was as innovative but not as well-funded as later New Deal programs. The legislation differed more in scale than in conception. It never seemed as daring as that which came later, largely because of Hoover's moral scruples, his low-keyed personality, and his lack of flamboyant leadership. At least in an embryonic way, for good or for worse (that depends upon one's political commitments), the federal government in only a three-year period had begun a limited program of price supports for farmers, had tremendously expanded expenditures for public works, made daring efforts in the area of international currency stabilization, provided the first meager funds for relief, initiated a major lending agency to prevent business failures, cured one grave weakness in the Federal Reserve System, and established pioneer programs in both home financing and public housing. Because of later agency shifts and new labels, much of the credit and almost all the blame for these innovations soon attached to Roosevelt, who had the advantage of a warm personality, an overwhelming public mandate from the election of 1932, a willing and cooperative Congress, and above all a total exemption from responsibility for the depression. A bitter election campaign also helped obscure the continuities of policy and magnify the very real shifts that occurred under Roosevelt. To a much greater extent than contemporaries realized, the long battle for recovery was a single story, beginning in 1930 and only ending in World War II. Its most remarkable aspect was the endless frustration and failure. Even the most effective programs paralleled other, counterbalancing failures.

Hoover completed his recovery program just as political conventions signaled an election campaign. This was unfortunate for him. His plans either bore fruit in the New Deal, or became obscured in the election and its aftermath. Any judgment on their effectiveness would have to extend into the mid-thirties—did the RFC save much of the economy from disaster? How much worse would the economy have fared without federal public works? Were all the loan programs in agriculture, for housing, for local relief completely ineffective, or simply inadequate? By the most obvious of reasoning, it is easy to prove either that Hoover did not do the right things or did not do enough, for recovery did not come. Many of the same circular arguments could be applied to Roosevelt's 1933 recovery legislation, which was more successful only in agriculture. But all such attributions of failure probably assume too much—that there were available and even remotely acceptable governmental strategies that could have assured early recovery. Instead, built-in beliefs and commitments severely limited the options, the most obvious being the demand for economy and balanced budgets.

As if to confound his numerous critics, Hoover always insisted that the legislation of 1932 was both effective and sufficient, for there was a brief upturn in early 1933. He believed the insecurities of an election campaign, the normal temptation of businessmen in particular to await its verdict before committing themselves to expanded production, arrested the early gains. The Republicans nominated Hoover for a second term without enthusiasm, for they had small chance of winning the election. This meant that the Democratic nominee, Franklin D. Roosevelt, would be president, and this made his speeches and personality a vital factor in business confidence. As Hoover saw it, Roosevelt's vague speeches contained frightening hints of economic planning and gold devaluation, thus stimulating a third economic collapse or a "Democratic depression." Such an interpretation seemed persuasive only to the supporters of Hoover, ridiculous to the more numerous supporters of Roosevelt. But Hoover did identify one final complication in the desperate search for recovery. The

A vigorous young **FDR** is pictured here in about 1920, when he was assistant secretary of the navy. The photograph is one of the relatively few taken before he contracted polio in 1921. *Library of Congress*

depression reached its climax during an election campaign and the long interregnum that followed, or during the time when the country lacked strong presidential leadership.

Hoover never gave up on his program or on the promises of the American economy. Amidst all the gloom and suffering, he always believed it could be put back together again. He always worked for one central goal—recovery, which focused his efforts on the business community, on a restoration of confidence and economic activity at the very centers of power. He would not admit any deep economic maladjustments, any permanent insecurities, any but a temporary cessation of growth and new productive possibilities, and thus any need for major institutional changes (such as central economic planning, or the nationalization of major industries) or for permanent, redistributive welfare programs. To essay such changes was to admit the failure of the American dream, of our commitment to opportunity and free participation by all in an open system. If we could only rebuild faith in our institutions, then all Americans could once again find fulfillment in a classless and humane society, and finally realize the glorious promises that Hoover had so eloquently expressed in 1928.

Very much as Woodrow Wilson on the issue of the league, Hoover tenaciously, at times dogmatically and uncompromisingly, held his ground and fought his fight to a final, embittering conclusion. The people no longer seemed to comprehend his dream, see the moral grandeur of his endlessly reiterated principles, or respond to his conscientious but undramatic leadership. In his final political campaign, Hoover continued to write most of his own speeches, to attempt a debate on political principles as well as on political expedients. For one so sensitive to criticism, so temperamentally unfitted for political campaigning, the final defeat was a great deal more crushing than even the one-sided election returns indicated. Sorrowfully, with declining hopes for America, for a continuation of freedom and self-reliance, he turned his awesome responsibilities over to a "happy warrior," who approached the presidency with an exuberance and an adolescent delight that seemed all but "blasphemous" to Hoover.

Bibliography

Studies touching the Red Scare of 1919–1920 include Stanley Coben, *A. Mitchell Palmer: Politician* (New York: Columbia University Press, 1963) and Coben, "A Study in Hysteria: The American Red Scare of 1919–1920," *Political Science Quarterly* (1964); Robert K. Murray, *Red Scare* (Minneapolis: University of Minnesota Press, 1955); Robert Friedman, *The Seattle General Strike* (Seattle: University of Washington Press, 1967); William M. Tuttle, Jr., *Race Riot: Chicago in the Red Summer of 1919* (New York: Atheneum, 1970); Arthur Waskow, *From Race Riot to Sit-In* (Garden City, N.Y.: Doubleday, 1967); David Brody, *Labor in Crisis: The Steel Strike of 1919* (Philadelphia: J. P. Lippincott, 1965); Julian F. Jaffe, *Crusade Against Radicalism: New York During the Red Scare, 1914–1924* (Port Washington, N.Y.: Kennikat Press, 1972).

A number of excellent books now clarify the issues and events surrounding the Versailles Conference: Arno J. Mayer, *Politics and the Diplomacy of Peacemaking* (New York: Alfred A. Knopf, 1967); N. Gordon Levin, *Woodrow Wilson and World Politics* (New York: Oxford University Press, 1968); Ralph Stone, *The Irreconcilables* (Lexington: University of Kentucky Press, 1970); Lawrence Gelfand, *The Inquiry* (New Haven: Yale University Press, 1963); Arthur Link, *Wilson the Diplomatist*, rev. ed. (Baltimore: The Johns Hopkins University Press, 1963); and Joseph P. O'Grady *The Immigrants' Influence on Wilson's Peace Policies* (Lexington: University Press of Kentucky, 1971).

Politics in the 1920's

The best recent surveys of the twenties are the first section of George Mowry, *The Urban Nation, 1920–1960* (New York: Hill and Wang, 1965); William Leuchtenburg, *The Perils of Prosperity, 1914–1932* (Chicago: University of Chicago Press, 1958); John D. Hicks, *Republican Ascendancy, 1921–1933* (New York: Harper and Row, 1960); and Arthur Schlesinger, Jr., *The Crisis of the Old Order, 1919–1933* (Boston: Houghton, Mifflin, 1957). Another good introduction to the decade is by way of the varied and up-to-date essays contained in John Braeman, et al., *Change and Continuity in the Twentieth Century: The 1920's Revisited* (Columbus: Ohio State University Press, 1968). *Middletown* (New York: Harcourt Brace, 1929) by Robert S. and Helen M. Lynd, is a very important book on the twenties. Still current are Henry F. May, "Shifting Perspectives of the 1920's," *Mississippi Valley Historical Review* (1956) and Arthur S. Link, "What Happened to the Progressive Movement in the 1920's?" *American Historical Review* (1959).

On the presidents see Randolph C. Downes, *The Rise of Warren Gamaliel Harding, 1865–1920* (Columbus: Ohio State University Press, 1971); Robert K. Murray's now standard *The Harding Era* (Minneapolis: University of Minnesota Press, 1969); and for certain points Andrew Sinclair, *The Available Man* (New York: Macmillan, 1965) and Francis Russell, *The Shadow on Blooming Grove* (New York: McGraw-Hill, 1968). Burl Noggle, *Teapot*

Dome (New York: W. W. Norton, 1966) is a good treatment of the Harding scandals. On Coolidge the best book is Donald B. McCoy, *Calvin Coolidge: The Quiet President* (New York: Macmillan, 1967), but see also the perceptive William Allen White, *A Puritan in Babylon* (New York: Macmillan, 1938). On Hoover there are his own *Memoirs* (New York: McGraw-Hill, 1952); Harris Warren, *Herbert Hoover and the Great Depression* (New York: Oxford University Press, 1957); Albert U. Romasco, *The Poverty of Abundance* (New York: Oxford University Press, 1965); and Jordan A. Schwarz, *Interregnum of Despair: Hoover, Congress and the Depression* (Urbana: University of Illinois Press, 1970).

The Democrats are treated in David Burner, *The Politics of Provincialism: The Democratic Party in Transition, 1918–1932* (New York: Alfred A. Knopf, 1968). J. Joseph Huthmacher published a pathbreaking monograph on ethnic voting, *Massachusetts People and Politics, 1919–1933* (Cambridge, Mass.: Harvard University Press, 1959). See also John M. Allswang, *A House for All Peoples: Ethnic Politics in Chicago, 1890–1936* (Lexington: University of Kentucky Press, 1971). Nancy J. Weiss examined *Charles Francis Murphy, 1858–1924: Respectability and Responsibility in Tammany Politics* (Northampton, Mass.: Smith College, 1968). Edmund A. Moore studied the Al Smith campaign of 1928 in *A Catholic Runs for President* (Gloucester, Mass.: Peter Smith, 1956); La Follette is covered in Kenneth McKay, *The Progressive Movement of 1924* (New York: Columbia University Press, 1947).

Individual political biographies of note include Frank Freidel, *Franklin D. Roosevelt: The Ordeal* (Boston: Houghton, Mifflin, 1954); Richard Lowitt, *George W. Norris: The Persistence of a Progressive, 1913–1929* (Urbana: University of Illinois Press, 1971); Leroy Ashby, *The Spearless Leader: Senator Borah and the Progressive Movement in the 1920's* (Urbana: University of Illinois Press, 1972); Oscar Handlin, *Al Smith and His America* (Boston: Little, Brown, 1958); Arthur Mann, *La Guardia* (Chicago: University of Chicago Press, 1959). For political figures of the South see the relevant chapters of George Brown Tindall, *The Emergence of the New South, 1913–1945* (Baton Rouge: Louisiana State University Press, 1967).

The Economy

The economy of the 1920's is treated in George Soule, *Prosperity Decade* (New York: Holt, Rinehart, 1947). See also James Prothro, *Dollar Decade: Business Ideas in the 1920's* (Baton Rouge: Louisiana State University Press, 1954). An important study of businessmen as reformers is Marguerite Green, *The National Civic Federation and the American Labor Movement, 1900–1925* (Washington, D.C.: The Brookings Institution, 1956). John Kenneth Galbraith, *The Great Crash* (Boston: Houghton, Mifflin, 1955) is a brief and entertaining account of the stock market plunge and early Depression; Galbraith is working on an extended book on the Depression. Milton Friedman and Anna Schwartz's *A Monetary History of the United States, 1868–1960* (Princeton, N.J.: Princeton University Press, 1963), pp. 240–419, is thesis-laden;

the section covering the Hoover-Roosevelt period has been published separately by Princeton in paperback as *The Great Contraction* (1964). See the interesting Robert Sobel, *The Great Bull Market: Wall Street in the 1920's* (New York: W. W. Norton, 1968).

On agriculture there are John D. Hicks and Theodore Saloutous, *Agricultural Discontent in the Middle West, 1900–1939* (Norman: University of Oklahoma Press, 1954); George C. Fite, *George N. Peek and the Fight for Farm Parity* (Norman: University of Oklahoma Press, 1954; and James Shideler, *Farm Crisis, 1919–1923* (Berkeley: University of California Press, 1957). The essential labor history is Irving Bernstein, *A History of the American Worker, 1920–1933: The Lean Years* (Cambridge, Mass.: Harvard University Press, 1960). Ronald Zeiger, *Republicans and Labor, 1919–1929* (Lexington: University of Kentucky Press, 1969) is also important. Preston Hubbard, Jr., examines the power controversy in *Origins of the T.V.A.* (Nashville, Tenn.: Vanderbilt University Press, 1961), and Donald Swain explores natural resources in *Federal Conservation Policy, 1921–1933* (Berkeley: University of California Press, 1963).

For social history Frederick Lewis Allen, *Only Yesterday* (New York: Harper, 1931) is still excellent. Paul A. Carter surveys intellectual life in his bibliographical *The Twenties in America* (New York: Thomas Y. Crowell, 1968). See also Don S. Kirshner, *City and County: Rural Responses to Urbanization in the 1920's* (Westport, Conn.: Greenwood Publishing Co., 1970).

Society

On the Ku Klux Klan see Kenneth T. Jackson, *The Ku Klux Klan in the City, 1915–1930* (New York: Oxford University Press, 1968); David Chalmers, *Hooded Americanism* (Garden City, N.Y.: Doubleday, 1965); Charles C. Alexander, *The Ku Klux Klan in the Southwest* (Lexington: University of Kentucky Press, 1965); and Arnold Rice, *The Ku Klux Klan in American Politics* (Washington, D.C.: Public Affairs Press, 1963). The liveliest account of prohibition is Andrew Sinclair, *Prohibition: Era of Excess* (Boston: Little, Brown, 1962). Interesting also are James Timberlake, *Prohibition and the Progressive Movement, 1900–1925* (Cambridge, Mass.: Harvard University Press, 1963); and Joseph Gusfield, *Symbolic Crusade* (Urbana: University of Illinois Press, 1963). John Higham, *Strangers in the Land, 1865–1920* (New Brunswick, N.J.: Rutgers University Press, 1955) is still the best general account of nativism. See also Thomas Y. Gossett, *Race: The History of an Idea* (Dallas, Texas: Southern Methodist Press, 1963). On fundamentalism an important corrective to older works is Ernest R. Sandeen, *The Roots of Fundamentalism* (Chicago: University of Chicago Press, 1970), and see the excellent Lawrence Levine, *Defender of the Faith: William Jennings Bryan 1915–1925* (New York: Oxford University Press, 1965) as well as Norman Furniss, *The Fundamentalist Controversy, 1918–1931* (New Haven: Yale University Press, 1954).

Blacks in the twenties are treated in Gilbert Osofsky, *Harlem: The Making of a Ghetto* (New York: Harper and Row, 1965) and Theodore G. Vincent, *Black Power and the Garvey Movement* (Berkeley: Ramparts, 1971). William L. O'Neill studies feminism in *Everyone Was Brave: The Rise and Fall of Feminism in America* (Chicago: Quadrangle, 1969); see also especially for the period 1916–1920 David Morgan, *Suffragists and Democrats: The Politics of Woman Suffrage in America* (East Lansing: Michigan State University Press, 1972).

A review of the decade's literary productivity is Frederick Hoffman, *The Twenties: American Writing in the Post War Decade* (New York: Viking Press, 1955); Charles Angoff studies *H. L. Mencken* (New York: T. Yoseloff, 1956); Arthur Mizener, *F. Scott Fitzgerald in the Far Side of Paradise* (Boston: Houghton Mifflin, 1951); and Mark Schorer *Sinclair Lewis* (Berkeley: University of California Press, 1960). Thomas R. West, *Flesh of Steel* (Nashville, Tenn.: Vanderbilt University Press, 1967), examines literary responses to the machine in the 1920's. Other monographs on important topics include the study of a marriage reformer, Charles Larsen, *The Good Fight: The Life and Times of Ben B. Lindsey* (Chicago: Quadrangle, 1972); Clark Chambers on the social welfare movement, *Seedtime of Reform* (Minneapolis: University of Minnesota Press, 1963); and Herbert B. Ehrmann, *The Case that Will Not Die: Commonwealth vs. Sacco and Vanzetti* (Boston: Little, Brown, 1969).

Foreign Policy

Important studies of foreign policy in the twenties include L. Ethan Ellis, *Republican Foreign Policy* (New Brunswick, N.J.: Rutgers University Press, 1968); Allan Nevins, *The United States in a Chaotic World: 1918–1933* (New Haven: Yale University Press, 1950); Selig Adler, *The Isolationist Impulse* (New York: Abelard-Schuman, 1957); Selig Adler, *The Uncertain Giant, 1921–1941* (New York: Macmillan, 1965); Jean-Baptiste Duroselle, *From Wilson to Roosevelt* (New York: Harper and Row, 1968); Thomas H. Cukley, *The United States and the Washington Conference, 1921–1922* (Nashville, Tenn.: Vanderbilt University Press, 1970); Peter Filene, *Americans and the Soviet Experience, 1917–1933* (Cambridge, Mass.: Harvard University Press, 1967); Carl P. Parrini, *Heir to Empire: United States Economic Diplomacy, 1916–1923* (Pittsburgh: Pittsburgh University Press, 1969); Herbert Feis, *The Diplomacy of the Dollar: First Era, 1919–1932* (Baltimore: The Johns Hopkins University Press, 1950); and Joan Wilson, *American Business and Foreign Policy, 1920–1933* (Lexington: University of Kentucky Press, 1971).

For the Hoover period see the standard Robert Ferrell, *American Diplomacy in the Great Depression: Hoover-Stimson Foreign Policy, 1929–1933* (New Haven: Yale University Press, 1957); Akira Ireiye, *After Imperialism: The Search for a New Order in the Far East, 1921–1933* (Cambridge, Mass.: Harvard University Press, 1965); Raymond G. O'Connor, *Perilous Equilibrium: The United States and the London Naval Conference of 1930* (Lawrence: University of Kansas Press, 1967); George E. Wheeler, *Prelude to Pearl Harbor: The United States Navy and the Far East, 1921–1931* (Columbia: University of Missouri Press, 1963); Alexander DeConde, *Herbert Hoover's Latin American Policy* (Stanford, Calif.: Stanford University Press, 1951); and Robert Freeman Smith, "American Foreign Relations, 1920–1942," in Barton Bernstein, ed., *Towards a New Past: Dissenting Essays in American History* (New York: Random House, 1968).

PART TWO

The
New
Deal

8

An unsuspecting speechwriter, hoping for an emotional response from a convention audience, gave a name to an era—the New Deal. Franklin D. Roosevelt, by strength of personality and unprecedented political appeal, gave enduring content to the label. But the New Deal, both in the thirties and in retrospect, always meant many things to many people. It still labels a decade and an administration, but not a single coherent philosophy, a unified and consistent program, or a distinct achievement. The ambiguities should not obscure dramatic changes in our political and economic life between 1933 and 1938, for during that time Congress approved more important legislation than in any comparable period in its history. Many programs proved ephemeral. Many survived. We can still find in the thirties more clues to the nature of our political economy than in any other single decade.

A severe depression assured the dominance of economic issues in the politics of the 1930's. The national government faced one supreme challenge—to adopt the policies necessary to restore economic well-being and if possible also make the institutional changes necessary to alleviate long-term economic inequities and to prevent future depressions. For many reasons, this challenge could not be met in the thirties or even afterward. But the very effort led to enduring changes in our economic policy and in prevalent conceptions of the rightful economic role for the federal government. Both norms and actualities shifted, and perhaps more abruptly than in any comparable period in our history.

To stress the magnitude and the permanence of change is not, of course, to evaluate it. But if one now loves our economic system, he will have to direct a goodly share of his gratitude back to the New Deal. If he hates it, then no decade will seem more mistaken, more a betrayal of possibilities. Also, to suggest important and enduring changes is not to respond to that most puerile and simplistic issue: Was it a revolution? The word allows such a range of meanings that either any change, or almost no change, can be so labeled. The often contradictory changes made in the thirties did not further one clear goal, serve any one class, eradicate any one evil, or finally solve any one great national problem. The more

First Fruits of the Roosevelt Era

enduring changes reflected an implementation of old ideals, the fruition of earlier crusades, the realization of past hopes, and the strengthening of existing institutions. The more ephemeral programs often essayed more striking change, and at least provide us with still persuasive alternatives.

In 1928, as Al Smith suffered overwhelming defeat by Herbert Hoover, Franklin D. Roosevelt won an upset victory as governor of New York. Returning to active politics after years of struggle against the effects of polio, he made himself the most appealing and best placed Democratic presidential prospect for 1932. Overwhelming victory in 1930 enhanced his prospects, while the deepening depression assured a Democratic resurgence. Roosevelt carefully calculated and dramatized his achievements as governor, particularly in relief, conservation, agriculture, and public power. His alter ego, the dutiful Louis Howe, cleverly wooed diverse national support. Roosevelt's search for relief from crippling polio had led him to a farm and vacation home in Warm Springs, Georgia, where he became the leading benefactor of a healing foundation as well as a part-time resident. His growing concerns with southern problems, particularly agriculture, and his easy rapport with southern politicians, helped secure support from the only solid bloc in the party.

In 1932 Roosevelt conducted a quite conventional campaign for nomination. He cultivated the moneyed patrons of the party, muted issues to please almost all factions, and bargained future patronage. He turned to academic experts for advice on very complex issues, as well as for speech-writing assignments. Journalists publicized these advisers as the celebrated brains trust. Assembled and coordinated by a Columbia University political scientist and an expert on the administration of justice, Raymond Moley, the trust included at various times about a dozen academics, but continuously only two others: Columbia economist Rexford G. Tugwell, and Adolph A. Berle, Jr., an expert on corporate law and co-author of one of the most influential books of the decade, *The Modern Corporation and Private Property*, published in the campaign year. Tugwell pressed Roosevelt toward broad economic planning and toward temporary budget deficits in behalf of restored purchasing power. Berle supported planning but with greater detachment and perhaps more sensitivity to political obstacles. Moley, who wrote often brilliant speeches, desired a recovery coordinated by the federal government but clearly retained his hopes for voluntary business-government cooperation. All three desired coordination, saw no hope for a return to a competitive and decentralized economy, and rejected easy inflationist theories. Surely Roosevelt learned from his dinner-table academicians, yet rarely followed their prescriptions, because of disagreement, lack of full understanding, or his own assessment of political possibilities. In politics he remained the expert.

By the time of the Democratic convention in Chicago, Roosevelt had a majority of delegate votes. He needed two-thirds by convention rules—a provision he would get repealed in 1936—and bargained successfully for the extra votes, among other things accepting John Nance Garner of Texas as his running mate. Pursuing his usual flare for dramatic gesture, he flew from Albany to Chicago in stormy weather (a daring act in 1932) and delivered a flamboyant acceptance speech charged with optimistic promise. He emphasized the symbolic heart of his coming campaign—a break from the past, new hopes, and resolute, unprecedented action. He gave only a few hints of actual programs. In fact, he as yet had only the vaguest outline of what he wished to accomplish and could not have given full details had he wanted.

The Democratic party had the most effective candidate in its history. Roosevelt would win four presidential elections, one by an unprecedented majority, and dominate a decade as no other leader in our history. Whatever critics perceived as the failures of his programs, the limitations of his ability, the unfairness of his methods, all could agree that he effectively communicated concern and hope in the midst of gloom. A majority so responded to his personalized leadership that the New Deal often became a political success as much in spite of, as because of, its concrete achievements.

In background, in personality, Roosevelt was hardly a typical American politician. An only child of indulgent and socially prominent Hudson Valley parents, he grew up with ease and luxury on a large Hyde Park estate perched on a high bluff overlooking his beloved river. Servants and tutors accompanied him on several boyhood trips to Europe and on many vacations at Campobello Island, New Brunswick, in the Passamaquoddy Bay just off the Maine coast. He had outstanding educational opportunities at Groton Preparatory School and at Harvard. He absorbed a strong sense of duty, and strong loyalties to the soil and the sea, to church and college, to a beloved state and nation. Economically and emotionally secure, intellectually versatile but never brilliant, he early displayed an engaging personal warmth and obvious talents for leadership. After an undistinguished academic career at Harvard, he completed enough law school at Columbia to pass his bar exams, and settled into a comfortable life as a New York lawyer, an upriver gentleman, and a rising figure in state Democratic politics. Here, as with so much else, his fervent support for the Democratic party came as a family tradition; it did not detract from his youthful adulation and later emulation of cousin (and uncle by marriage) Theodore, the greatest of the Republican branch of the family.

Even as a youth, Roosevelt loved competition. He never quite attained his own goals as an athlete, but continuously exhibited a rousing partisanship, both in college and in politics. Yet, unlike most men, he never had to compete for a living, for economic power, even for love. He would always remain casual about finances and about personal friendships. To his political battles he brought the self-assurance of an established patrician, confident but benevolent in victory. He never had the brilliance of a Wilson, the moral intensity of a Hoover, even the varied intellectual achievements of a Theodore Roosevelt. But more than any other American president he would always reflect a sense of confident mastery.

Much of Roosevelt's appeal lay not in his common touch but in his upper-class attitudes and manners, as well as his personal warmth. In a country of mobile, displaced, rootless people, Roosevelt was a product of tradition, of ancient roots. His celebrated Harvard accent and almost English manners symbolized an uncommon man. In spite of his sensitive response to other people's attitudes and hopes, Roosevelt retained an aloof detachment, a social distance. He was clearly lord of the plantation, captain of the ship. Few presumed on his station or refused proper deference, which he graciously received. He did seem to be concerned about those

Four generations of the Roosevelt family are represented in this portrait made during Franklin D. Roosevelt's term as governor of New York. Front row: Franklin D. Jr. and John A. Roosevelt, the governor's youngest sons. Second row: Mrs. Curtis B. Dall and Anna Eleanor Dall; Eleanor Roosevelt; Franklin D. Roosevelt; Mrs. D. D. Forbes, the governor's aunt; Mrs. James Roosevelt, the governor's mother. Back row, standing: Curtis B. Dall and James Roosevelt, the governor's eldest son. *Wide World Photos*

beneath him. He reached down, and the gesture, for such a one, was more beguiling by far than false attempts to be one of the gang, and far less vulgar than aggressive leadership by one's peers.

Roosevelt's only natural vocation was politics. He showed no dedication, no compelling interest, no real skill in either law or business, both part-time pursuits in his nonpolitical interludes. Despite his interest, he really only dabbled in agriculture. His early political career in the New York legislature showed a flair for effective campaigning, a proclivity for avoiding such controversial issues as prohibition, a growing ability to manipulate rather than surrender to such political machines as Tammany Hall, a command of exceptionally able political advisers, and at least a fashionable commitment to such causes as conservation and public power. His achievements in New York won him an appointment as assistant secretary of the navy in the Wilson administration. Although frustrated by his subordinate role, and by his stateside duties (he wanted to be in the thick of the fight, to win his battle at San Juan Hill) he enjoyed the ceremonial duties of his office and proved adept as an administrator of the civilian branches of the navy, particularly in labor disputes. As a young man seeking military or imperial glory, ever-anxious for a larger navy, he proved a trying but appreciative protégé of his chief, Josephus Daniels. In 1920 Roosevelt received the vice-presidential nomination of his party, and campaigned as a Wilsonian disciple in a losing cause. He remained out of office until 1928.

But not by choice. In 1921 he was stricken with polio while on vacation on Campobello Island. The disease left him permanently crippled, although he tried for years to regain strength in his wasted legs. Much of the burden of his illness fell on his wife, Eleanor. A distant cousin, also a Roosevelt, Eleanor had been an ungainly, sensitive, overly shy bride and was a dutiful, subservient mother for five energetic children. More sensitive than her husband, Eleanor suffered most of the emotional responsibilities for the family. She now assumed added duties for her husband, nursing, giving confidence, and prodding him back to an active political role. Eleanor profited from the reversal in role. From retiring wife, she became a committed activist, a conscience for her husband and his party, and an often irksome and nagging but needed "do-gooder" among Roosevelt's circle of male cronies.

Polio diverted but hardly changed Roosevelt. It did change his image. It gave him the added appeal of an underdog, one who had faced and overcome great adversity, although not quite so completely as most Americans imagined. As one who always tried to project an image of strength and mastery, Roosevelt minimized or concealed his disability. He exploited the mercifully nonvisual radio for communication. In public appearances he usually concealed his difficult, assisted entrances, and appeared strong and capable on a podium. His crutches and wheelchair rarely appeared in newsprints or films. He reentered politics with the same outward show of confidence, the same zest for meeting problems head-on and conquering them.

At his nomination in 1932, Roosevelt neither symbolized nor voiced any clear position on political economy. He never would. He presided over tremendous changes in our economic system, arbitrated many policy struggles within his own administration, but on the most subtle or complex issues remained either vague or uncommitted. His New Deal never had the policy content of Wilson's New Freedom, Theodore Roosevelt's New Nationalism, or even the later Harry Truman's Fair Deal with its avowed welfare orientation. Roosevelt simply did not make his political contribution at this level. As a result, the word New Deal, like almost all labels in American politics, still functions in many contexts, and with quite divergent meanings—planning, welfare policies, class-based politics, and Keynesian economics. It has about as much clear policy meaning as the word "liberalism," and remains as pointless as a label. To refer to someone as a "New Dealer" means almost nothing ideologically or programmatically.

But to say that Roosevelt did not resolve policy issues is not to say very much. Such were the divisions among Americans—class, interest, ideological—that no president could have won overwhelming support by adhering to a consistent and exclusive program, such as national economic planning, government ownership, dramatic fiscal incentives, artificial monetary devices, decentralization of production and restored competition, or aggressive foreign adventuring. Roosevelt would, at various times, embrace many of these, and in so doing accept varied and conflicting goals as well as a diversity of means. His expedient policies helped win him unprecedented political support, not as adjuncts of an appealing political philosophy but of a successful personal appeal.

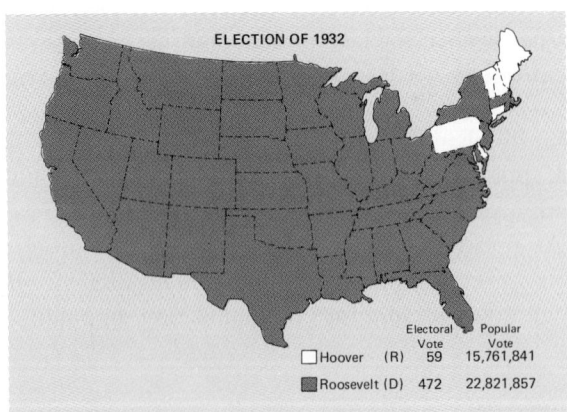

ELECTION OF 1932

		Electoral Vote	Popular Vote
☐	Hoover (R)	59	15,761,841
■	Roosevelt (D)	472	22,821,857

Roosevelt's 1932 campaign speeches were important to millions of increasingly anxious Americans. He confused almost everyone, not because his speeches lacked content, but because they seemed to point in so many different directions. His targets, beyond the Hoover administration, seemed to be financiers or bankers, convenient because they had been rather thoroughly disgraced in the popular mind. In a key speech at Oglethorpe University in Atlanta, he called for "bold, constant experimentation," and hinted at inflationary tampering with the dollar, a particularly frightening idea to people of means. Yet, later in the campaign, he offered vague promises of maintaining the gold standard. And so it was on other issues. He promised new relief efforts even as he continuously committed himself to governmental economy and balanced budgets. In a few speeches he seemed to embrace a quite significant commitment to major economic planning, but ordinarily he sounded much more conventional. Ambiguity was a political strategy. It worked. He defeated Hoover with 57.49 percent of the total vote, and carried the electoral college by 472 to 59.

Roosevelt's cabinet revealed a careful balancing of political interests. Four members served throughout the thirties: Secretary of State Cordell Hull of Tennessee, a Wilsonian internationalist; in agriculture, Henry A. Wallace of Iowa, a farm editor and son of a former secretary of agriculture; in labor, the first woman cabinet member, Frances Perkins, whom Roosevelt already knew and respected as an industrial commissioner in New York; and in interior, Harold L. Ickes, a Progressive Republican from Chicago. His first secretary of the treasury, William H. Woodin, a Republican businessman, suffered through many of Roosevelt's early monetary gambits and, because of illness, gave way to Roosevelt's New York neighbor, Henry Morgenthau, Jr.

The Interregnum

Although elected in early November, Roosevelt had to wait until March for inauguration. The long interval proved so disastrous that it helped prod final state ratification of the Twentieth Amendment, which moved the inauguration back to January 20 for subsequent elections. The depression reached its climax in the winter of 1932–33. Hoover, a lame duck thoroughly discredited by the election, but still doggedly sure of the correctness of his recovery measures, struggled hopelessly with a hostile Congress. He felt sure that Roosevelt's campaign, with its vague innuendos of deliberate inflation, dramatic spending programs, and some form of economic planning, had frightened insecure business and financial leaders and worsened any chances of recovery. In this estimate he was undoubtedly correct, and a less ambiguous, more revealing campaign by Roosevelt could only have frightened them more. Hoover further believed that his own policies had begun to take effect by the fall of 1931, and that the Roosevelt campaign and election sabotaged his own best efforts. This contention remains unproven and possibly unprovable.

Despite the bitterness of defeat, Hoover tried to work with Roosevelt in behalf of a smooth transition at least in foreign policy. In company with Raymond Moley, Roosevelt met with Hoover in December. The main issues at that Washington meeting were foreign debt payments and plans for an upcoming international monetary conference. This meeting, and subsequent, more relaxed meetings between Roosevelt and Hoover's secretary of state, Henry L. Stimson, failed to achieve any common agreement. The careful and meticulous Hoover, by now full of facts and details about international economic matters, developed only contempt for what he believed to be a complete lack of intellectual comprehension on the part of Roosevelt. Roosevelt resented Hoover's condescension, and would neither agree on joint policies for debt adjustments nor cooperate effectively on any plans for the upcoming conference. Roosevelt revealed his suspicion of Hoover's faith in multilateral or international solutions to depressions. These contacts between two administrations had little long-range effect on either foreign policy or domestic recovery.

Yet, closer cooperation became vitally important by February and the country suffered when this cooperation did not materialize. An unprecedented banking crisis developed that winter, one that could have been mitigated by effective cooperation between Hoover and Roosevelt. Bank failures had a contagious effect; by late February it seemed that the whole banking system might collapse, in part from the growing fears of depositors. Lacking adequate federal machinery to remedy the situation, Hoover first wrote Roosevelt asking for help in averting disaster. But he suggested, in all too much calculated detail, that Roosevelt promise to maintain a sound currency, a balanced budget, and unimpaired governmental credit, all in order to restore public confidence. Hoover was not being disingenuous. He realized such a commitment from Roosevelt would be an endorsement of Hoover's own policies and of his view that restored confidence was the only route for recovery. Unwilling to fall into such a political trap, or to foreclose new strategies in his coming administration, Roosevelt did not even respond to Hoover.

This political maneuvering continued until inauguration. Roosevelt not only refused to cooperate with Hoover, but, much more significant, took no action on his own, even to the extent of reassuring statements. He insisted upon Hoover's full responsibility, and probably did not know what he should do. In the dying days of his administration, Hoover asked Roosevelt to take joint responsibility for closing all banks under the somewhat suspect authority of an old World War I trading-with-the-enemy act. Roosevelt refused. Hoover would not act alone. The tragedy played out to its bitter end. Already, Hoover's Treasury Department was at work on the emergency banking legislation that Roosevelt would use just after his inauguration, taking all credit for the subsequent improvement.

The banking panic, added to the depression, gave high drama to Roosevelt's inauguration and increased his leverage for quick action. It was an opportunity to produce almost immediate and quite visible results. In his optimistic inaugural address, he promised to seek broad executive powers to wage a war and, in consoling but misleading words, declared his belief that the only thing Americans need fear was fear itself. Roosevelt apparently had no premonition of his own long and often futile efforts to defeat the depression, which proved only a little more amenable to his medicine than it had to Hoover's.

Following the inauguration, Roosevelt immediately convened Congress in emergency session. In the next hundred days it approved a flood of legislative proposals, some hastily drafted and sparingly debated. As a result, the legislation did not have quite the enduring significance of that approved by Roosevelt's second Congress. Special recovery legislation for both agriculture and manufacturing received the most detailed congressional attention, and proved most lasting. Much of the other legislation also represented a direct and varied response to an emergency. But not all. With little controversy, Congress approved both a new beer bill and the Twenty-First Amendment, thus ending the noble but difficult experiment in national prohibition.

The first item of business had to be the reopening of the banks. In one day, Congress introduced, debated, and approved an emergency bill that permitted federal inspection of all banks, and the subsequent reopening of all sound ones. Since the crisis in part had resulted from a frenzied demand for deposits, the inspection invited the needed confidence.

But the banks also had long-range problems. The Banking Act of 1933 (the second Glass-Steagall Act) attempted to remedy these abuses and to check strong demands for a completely nationalized system. The act required all commercial banks to divest themselves of all investment affiliates and to stop all purchases of speculative securities, such as stock. No officers or directors of Federal Reserve member banks could remain in the employ of a securities firm, such as a brokerage house. No loans could be given to bank officers. The act also prohibited interest payments on demand deposits, and gave the Federal Reserve Board authority to set the maximum interest rates allowed on time deposits in member banks.

Most important, the act provided insurance protection for small depositors, under a Federal Depositors Insurance Corporation (FDIC). A temporary plan protected the first $2,500 of deposits, and financed it by a .5 percent assessment on all insured deposits. In 1935 Congress gave up a more ambitious program and extended the temporary scheme with an enlarged $5,000 limit.

A related area of special concern had to be the securities market itself. After all, the whole problem of depression dated back to the great stock market crash. In the Securities Act of 1933 Congress placed limits on security issues and required strict accounting by stock issuing corporations. A Securities and Exchange Act of 1934 required all new issues of stock by interstate corporations to be registered with the newly established Securities and Exchange Commission (SEC). Incomplete or false statements made corporate officials liable for severe penalties. In addition, corporations had to file periodic reports to the SEC, and make open revelations about the financial interests of all officers and directors. All exchange operations came under SEC regulation. The act also placed margin requirements for stock purchases under Federal Reserve Board control.

In his campaign, Roosevelt made two rather contradictory pledges: to increase direct federal relief and, at the same time, to economize on gov-

This Clifford Berryman cartoon of 1938 comments on Roosevelt's "alphabetical solution" to the problems of the depression. Roosevelt was often pictured as a father dispensing hope and cheer to a troubled century. *Library of Congress*

ernment expenditures. By a $500 million appropriation, Congress enabled him to set up the Federal Emergency Relief Administration (FERA). From his earlier position as relief administrator in New York State, Harry Hopkins moved to Washington to supervise a vastly expanded federal program. The FERA allocated its funds to the states for direct distribution to the needy or for special work projects. The decentralized control allowed some imaginative innovations, including a special rural rehabilitation program in several states. Roosevelt believed his recovery programs would quickly end any need for such relief. But by the winter of 1933 recovery still remained utterly unattainable. Hurriedly, Roosevelt and Hopkins set up an ambitious, federally directed works program, the Civil Works Administration (CWA). Hastily employed, wastefully engaged, the four million CWA workers quickly generated a flood of political criticism, some based on substantiated claims of political favoritism. In the spring Roosevelt forced its disbandment, only to refurbish the idea in 1935 with a vastly better organized work relief program (WPA).

In 1933 Roosevelt wanted a balanced budget. He always would. His Economy Bill, actually the second item presented for the new Congress, reduced veterans bonuses and federal salaries, often extensively enough to cause hardship. Not only in 1933, but later, Roosevelt tried to reduce ordinary government expenditures and loved small economies, even as he was forced to request endless emergency appropriations.

Roosevelt brought to the presidency a conviction that our national resources needed more careful management. His seeming affinity for planning more often than not entailed support for advisory city planning or improved reclamation and conservation programs, and not a commitment to detailed federal supervision over production, prices, wages, and profits. Back of his concern lay the powerful influence of Theodore Roosevelt, an emotional affinity for wilderness and untamed nature, a fascination with America's great scenic diversity, a concern over soil erosion and the suffering of small farmers. Almost as soon as his inauguration was over, Roosevelt or sympathetic congressmen began flooding the hoppers with conservation bills. An Emergency Conservation Work Act passed in fulfillment of commitments made in Roosevelt's acceptance speech at the Chicago convention. It gave Roosevelt the authority needed to establish a long-planned Civilian Conservation Corps (CCC), one of the most popular New Deal agencies.

The act gave Roosevelt great leeway in organizing the CCC. It was to provide a militarylike, encamped work program for single young men, ages eighteen to twenty-five. They had to be from relief families, and had

Resource Management

to allot $25 of their $30 monthly salary for family support. The army enrolled the boys and, after some early confusion over administration, took complete charge of the camps and controlled all internal discipline. The Forest Service of the Department of Agriculture and the National Park Service of the Department of the Interior supervised most of the work. The boys lived in austere barracks, and worked in almost every conceivable area of forestry, soil and wildlife conservation, and park management. Eventually over two and a half million men served in the corps. Congress consistently renewed the authorization and appropriated funds until 1942. It then refused Roosevelt's plea to make the CCC a permanent agency, the nucleus of a postwar youth labor organization.

Civilian Conservation Corps workers in Beltsville, Maryland (1935). The CCC contributed not only to forestry and wildlife preservation but also to the development of recreational facilities. *Library of Congress*

The CCC represented only the most dramatic of New Deal conservation programs. Beginning in 1933, with public works funds, Roosevelt made unprecedented additions to the national forest, with up to four million acres acquired each year. In fact, he more than doubled our forest reserves. Under congressional authority granted in 1934, he set aside fish and game sanctuaries and increased by twentyfold the acreage in federal wildlife refuges. Two flood control acts enormously extended the dam and dike program of the Army Corps of Engineers. In addition to the varied soil conservation programs (some with flood control provisions) developed in the Department of Agriculture, Congress in 1934 approved major new policies concerning western grazing lands. The Taylor Grazing Bill, a product of earlier regional experiments, and an outgrowth of intense congressional bargaining between affected interests and equally persuasive administration pressures, set up grazing districts under the Department of the Interior's supervision, and permitted controlled grazing and range improvement under a quite modest fee system. These varied conservation programs led to an extended jurisdictional battle between the Departments of Agriculture (Forest Service and Soil Conservation Service) and the Interior (National Park Service, public lands, and grazing programs), a battle that only increased public interest in conservation.

The TVA

The most significant innovations in resource management, and possibly in the whole New Deal, occurred in the Tennessee Valley. In May of 1933, Congress approved the Tennessee Valley Authority Act, which initiated a more diverse program than even Congress could have anticipated. At the time, the act seemed only a fitting climax to the congressional battle that raged throughout the twenties. Endorsement by Roosevelt of Senator Norris's plan for government operation of Muscle Shoals, together with the impaired reputation of private utilities and a more friendly Congress, ensured his victory in early 1933. Other influences helped turn his beloved project into a multipurpose program for the whole Tennessee River watershed.

Consistent with Roosevelt's own conservation interests, and in response to a normal regional interest in internal improvements, the first listed purposes of the Tennessee Valley Authority (TVA) were flood control and improved navigability (these also provided constitutional justifications). And, in fact, the TVA would eventually control the disastrous valley floods and create a navigable channel for the whole length of the Tennessee, or over 600 miles. Other listed purposes included reforestation, proper use of marginal lands, agricultural and industrial development, and even national defense. The TVA itself would be a government-owned corporation with a three-member board of directors and autonomous personnel policies. The TVA could produce and distribute fertilizers to farmers, and could produce, sell, and distribute surplus electrical power (a necessary by-product of Wilson Dam and other new dams), with preference to states, municipalities, or other nonprofit distributors. It could build transmission lines into areas either without power or without inexpensive power, and study new ways to use electricity, particularly for local industries. Most tantalizing, the act authorized general plans for the whole Tennessee basin, in behalf of a controlled development of the physical, economic, and social resources of the region, and for the general welfare or social well-being of the people of the basin. This seemed a blank check for almost any program the TVA might devise.

These last references to planning or to overall social uplift reflected the ideas and the direct influence of Arthur E. Morgan, the innovative president of Antioch College, a renowned engineer and flood control specialist, and a long-time advocate of regional planning and community development. Roosevelt's early choice for TVA board chairman, he helped draft the act and select the early staff. Although in favor of using electrical power as part of a broad program of regional development, he did not conceive of the TVA as a major public power agency, or as a crucial participant in the long-ranging battle between private and public power advocates. Clearly, in this, he disagreed with Norris, and almost alone tried to expand or even divert the TVA toward a much broader and more diffuse program. In the early TVA, Morgan took responsibility for

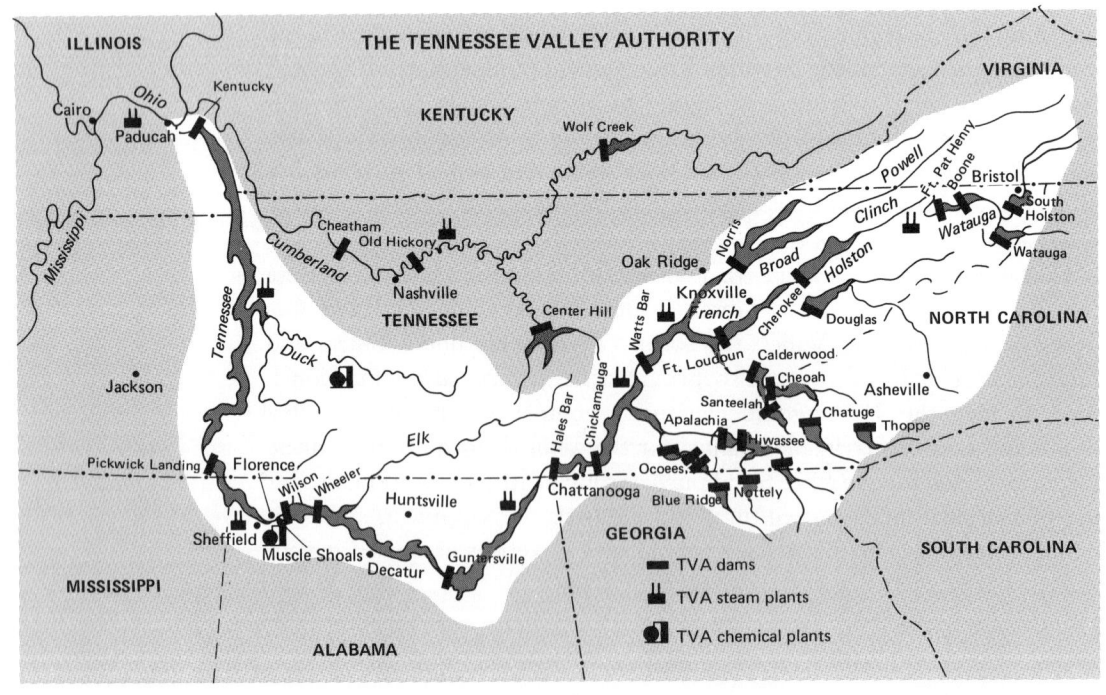

the engineering and construction program, including an early dam on the Clinch River (to be named after Norris). A second director, Harcourt Morgan, a respected southern agriculturalist and then president of the University of Tennessee in Knoxville, took major responsibility for the several agricultural and forestry programs. These soon included not only fertilizer distribution, but special demonstration farms, conservation assistance, and organized rural community building, all closely coordinated with the Agricultural Adjustment Administration (AAA), the Agricultural Extension Service, and the Soil Conservation Service. Finally, the last director, youthful David E. Lilienthal, a former Harvard law student and protégé of Felix Frankfurter, and just out of an aggressive stint on the Wisconsin Public Service Commission, took over the exacting job of managing the continued power program of the TVA.

The TVA matured through four years of increasing controversy. Lilienthal, already hardened by past battles with private utilities, suspicious of their every tactic, soon became an able antagonist in a developing battle with Commonwealth and Southern, the largest and most threatened of the utility holding companies in the seven-state Tennessee basin, and ably led by an equally competitive Wendell L. Willkie. As the struggle developed, both sides resorted to unfair tactics. Commonwealth and Southern harassed the TVA through the courts, marshaled immense lobbying strength, and wooed public sympathies, even as it pushed the palm leaf of cooperative agreements and power pools. Lilienthal used misleading propaganda about early and astonishingly low TVA rates, which could never be calculated with enough precision to serve as a reasonable yardstick for private rates, and later joined with Harold Ickes and the Public Works Administration (PWA) in a virtual blackmail of private utilities unwilling to sell to TVA (the PWA, on request, would conveniently promise loans to municipalities in order for them to construct duplicate facilities, and by this destroy all the value of private holdings). TVA won the power fight, but not before interminable court delays. Lilienthal also proved, even to the benefit of private utilities, the economic returns from much lower rates and greatly increased usage (TVA customers consumed double the national average). The TVA eventually completed all possible dams with significant hydroelectric potential on the Tennessee and its tributaries, bought out the needed facilities of all competing private companies, and furnished power at regulated and exceptionally low rates to customers in virtually the whole watershed. It more than fulfilled its defense role at the main Atomic Energy plant at Oak Ridge during World War II, and built an increasing number of steam plants to meet all the war's demands.

Meanwhile, Arthur Morgan assembled an excellent technical staff, pushed Norris Dam to completion (characteristically building a model town at Norris to demonstrate the virtues of planning and cooperation), and at least dreamed of a future, almost utopian valley, verdant beside the dark blue lakes, with revived folk arts and handicrafts, communal cooperation, prosperous farms, and new industrial employment. The dream in part depended upon electricity, but to Morgan it did not matter overly much whether private companies, won over by a convincing TVA demonstration of lowered rates, or the TVA itself actually distributed the power. In any case, the TVA should eschew partisan politics (the act required this), try in good faith to work with private companies, and never risk the broad planning objectives, or the crucial commitment to the overall welfare of the valley people, in any long battle over something as secondary to the TVA as electricity. Morgan's open enmity to Lilienthal, his critical published articles, soon undermined TVA's fight with the utilities. In 1937 Roosevelt, capitulating to public power advocates, fired Morgan.

In time the TVA became the New Deal's greatest concrete achievement and its most potent international symbol. Collectively, the fifteen major and many minor dams had no rival among other public works, although both the Hoover Dam and the Grand Coulee project far exceeded in size and in engineering difficulty any single TVA project. Such a broad scheme of internal development seemed quite instructive to underdeveloped countries, and helped account for the steady stream of high-ranking foreign visitors. With the resignation of Morgan, the completion of the major dams, and the achievement of a power monopoly in most of the valley, the TVA became, essentially, a government-owned electrical utility.

As few New Deal programs, the TVA invites evaluation. Did it succeed? This, of course, begs a clarification of valuative standards or realistic expectations. It failed Arthur Morgan's dream, and even in the beginning probably lacked the tools for any major transformation of a whole region. The Tennessee Valley area still contains some of the most impoverished counties in the country, with many parts of the Cumberland Plateau comparatively worse off today than in the thirties. This deterioration in no sense occurred because of the TVA, but rather in spite of it. Electricity is a pitifully inadequate tool for dealing with grave economic and social ills, and for most residents of the valley the TVA meant only cheap electricity and good fishing.

As a major public power project, the TVA succeeded beyond any possible early expectations. It became a model of productive efficiency, of fair personnel policies (except for blacks), and of pricing innovations. The low rates probably represented the most important government subsidy to

the Tennessee Valley area, despite TVA claims of paying its own way. The accounting problems are impossible in such multipurpose projects; how much of original costs should go to flood control, to navigation, to electrical production? Inexpensive electricity became one condition among many for a rapid build-up of manufacturing in the more favored parts of the valley. But it is at least arguable that many of the new corporations, as in so much of the South, were exceptionally exploitative, and that economic growth has created as many problems as it has solved, problems again well beyond the control of the TVA. Flood control in the valley could not be more complete, but it could involve a less expensive and a less ecologically disastrous series of smaller dams and levees (one old, and in part unfair, joke is that the TVA stopped valley floods by permanently inundating the whole flood plain).

One of the major TVA projects, the Hiwassee Dam on the Little Tennessee River. Despite the achievements of the TVA, local private interests fought the spread of such regional planning to other areas of the country. *Franklin D. Roosevelt Library*

The transition in the TVA mirrored similar changes in the Roosevelt administration. Arthur Morgan represented, or almost caricatured, many of the hopes of March 1933. He wanted broad economic and social planning carried out in an atmosphere of social harmony and cooperation; he tried to mute competition and partisanship and gain a true concert of interests in behalf of highly idealistic dreams. His was a nonpartisan, generous utopianism, the all too typical dream of the engineer, the architect, the planner. His technical skill lies embodied even yet in the TVA dams; his vision proved tragically unrealistic, but even Roosevelt shared it for a time. The future lay with politically ambitious yet idealistic young lawyers such as Lilienthal. They assayed much less, but more often achieved their limited goals. They never minimized the hard realities of power politics, and never bent an inch to accommodate those individuals or interests that stood in the way of their ambitions and their goals.

9

Beyond everything else, the campaign commitment implied by the vague slogan, a New Deal, meant economic recovery. Almost continuously in the campaign Roosevelt had placed the blame for depression on the Republicans, and by implication committed his administration to remedial action. If he could have fulfilled this commitment, it would have forestalled most of the legislation we now identify with the New Deal. The vast relief programs begun in 1935, and the welfare agencies approved the same year, would have been redundant.

Today, to talk of recovery even from a mild recession is to talk of a resumption of normal economic growth. Even a stagnant economy is tantamount to a sick economy. But in 1933 the idea of recovery rarely implied growth. To most, it meant a level of economic activity (production, consumption, employment, prices, and profits) equal to, or even close to, that of 1929, the last "normal" year. In fact, many believed that 1929 represented the apex of economic activity, and that recovery would actually fall somewhat short of that unusual year. With such modest expectations, the Roosevelt administration, even by 1936, could take credit for something approximating the possible. Loyal Democrats not only blamed Hoover for the depression but consistently denigrated the economy of the twenties. They saw in those years of steady growth not true prosperity, but some artificial substitute, steadily undercut and tarnished by gross inequities and untreated defects, particularly in agriculture. The "bogus" growth of the twenties, therefore, scarcely invited emulation. In fact, that type of economy, with all its expansion, seemed over, a part of our fading past of frontiers and immigrants and rapid population growth and abundant resources. This idea of a mature economy, expressed in one of Roosevelt's campaign addresses ("Our industrial plant is built;. . . . Our task now is not . . . producing more goods. . . . It is the soberer . . . business of administering resources and plants already in hand. . . ."), echoed from advisers and from a surprisingly large contingent of Democratic congressmen.

The Elusive Search for Recovery

Both economic realities and well-entrenched myths insured a continuing New Deal concern with agricultural recovery. Of all major industries, agriculture suffered the most from the depression. Throughout the twenties farmers had sought political remedies for what they conceived as unfairly low prices, and had successfully established the myth, for such it largely was, of an agricultural depression. By 1933, Roosevelt, most of his advisers, and a wide array of congressmen in both parties accepted as undisputed fact that the depression resulted in large part because of long-time agricultural distress and a resultant lack of consumption by farm families. Effective recovery as they conceived it required, first and above all, major programs to restore the purchasing power of farmers.

Special concern for farmers reflected more than an interpretation of economic realities. The farmer remained the archetypal example of the individual entrepreneur, the last repository of traditional American dreams. Roosevelt idealized farm life in direct proportion to his relative detachment from the hard economic realities of twentieth-century agriculture. Perhaps even today we can recapture some of the agrarian mystique that Roosevelt so unself-consciously reflected. But not all. Two generations separate us from the early thirties. No change seems more dramatic than our loss of immediate contact, in experience, fond memories, or inherited folklore, with a fecund land and with the multiple skills of husbandry and self-provenance. And such have been the changes in agriculture that few of our vague images of farm life fit the present reality.

Today any successful farmer is a highly skilled and quite specialized producer. His very skills isolate him. Ignorance of his ability is at one with a growing ignorance about all types of production, for all are largely hidden from public view. Such ignorance removes the possibility of appreciation and sympathetic understanding. Only extensive vocational education (correctly understood, not a teaching of skills but a teaching about skills), could remedy this ignorance. But lack of immediate appreciation must not conceal the significance of different types of production, or of the public policies that set limit conditions for their organization and change. In 1930 approximately 12 million Americans worked as farmers, or 20 percent of all employed persons; by 1970 there were only 3 million farmers, or 4 percent of workers. But today, as much as in 1930, agriculture is the most basic of industries, and will always remain so. All manufacturing depends on farm or mine, and is, in effect, only a processing of such products. Thus, governmental policies toward agriculture directly affect us all. And New Deal agricultural policies have added importance because they proved so enduring. More than in any other area, the recovery policies for agriculture, although justified as temporary measures, became permanent.

Dorothea Lange, 1936. *Library of Congress*

188

Except for details, all important innovations of agricultural policy had been proposed in the twenties (see pp. 130–32). The New Deal pioneered in implementation, not conception. Even at the level of basic policy, most New Deal agencies still celebrated ancient loyalties—to the entrepreneurial ideal, to the moral values of farm experience, to the desirability of small, privately owned enterprise, to an atmosphere of open opportunity, to local, decentralized decision making. Yet, in what seems contradictory but in fact is only ironical, the major New Deal farm programs (acreage control and price supports) involved a greater degree of central coordination and control, more hard economic planning, a greater departure from uncoerced private enterprise and open market control, than in any other industry. By 1933 a free competitive market, made up of small producers, existed in few industries save agriculture. Farmers, unlike large corporations, did not have the concerted means to control their own market, either by limiting production or coordinating marketing. Yet, the very survival of small, family-owned farms seemed to necessitate some degree of central and, most probably, governmental coordination. The degree of market freedom had to be narrowed in order to insure the survival of traditional institutions. Strange as it sounds, only a degree of coordination could preserve a degree of decentralization; only severe limits on competition could preserve competition. And, finally, only agricultural programs that fostered improved technology and greater efficiency would lower relative prices for food, insuring that governmental agricultural programs served not only farmers but also the larger public.

By 1933, almost all farmers were poor, or rapidly becoming so. Never had a major industry suffered quite so much from a depression. From 1929 to 1933 farmers absorbed a 57 percent decrease in gross income (back to the level of 1909). Their net income in 1933 was only one-third what it had been in 1929. Farm prices, as a whole, dropped an astonishing 63 percent. Farm production dropped only 6 percent by 1933, then 15 percent by 1934 under government controls and in the wake of an unprecedented drought. Meanwhile, the cost of farm implements dropped only 6 percent while their production dropped 80 percent, illustrating a high degree of market control and the limited role of price competition. The unprecedented squeeze on farmers threatened most with bankruptcy. And no general statistics can reveal the suffering of farmers in some crop regions, although stories of corn used for firewood and sheep carcasses thrown into western canyons represent the extremes.

Dorothea Lange, 1939.
Library of Congress

After extensive debate, agonizing amendments, and diversionary detours into complex monetary issues, Congress finally approved an Agricultural

The AAA

Adjustment Act in mid-May of 1933, well after most crops were in the ground. The act represented a compromise among various relief proposals of the twenties. It passed with the active support of the Farm Bureau, the National Grange, and smaller farm organizations. The more militant Farmers' Union alone opposed it, seeking in vain a cost-of-production formula that came closer to an income-maintenance system and appealed particularly to small and marginal farmers.

The Agricultural Adjustment Act can best be understood as an enabling act which left major policy decisions to the Roosevelt administration and to the one authorized action agency, the Agricultural Adjustment Administration. The least important program was land retirement. A Land Policy Section of the AAA bought some submarginal farm land and converted it to nonagricultural uses such as state parks, but not significantly enough to reduce production. Much later, the idea of land-leasing (or soil bank) became a mainstay of production control. The act also, in a final echo of McNary-Haugenism, provided for export subsidies to aid in the disposition of surplus crops (including some already in government possession). George N. Peek, the author of "parity" and long-time supporter of the export principle, became the first head of the AAA and tried to push subsidized exports. He met almost unanimous opposition in the AAA and, eventually, from Roosevelt. Thus, he was able to use this provision only for wheat, and only in 1933, although the Department of Agriculture resumed export subsidies later in the thirties.

The act permitted farmers in a given crop to work out another device favored by Peek—marketing agreements with processors. These included guaranteed prices. The AAA could also license and variously supervise all processors of agricultural commodities, and in this way exercise some control over unfair practices by middlemen. Peek favored price-fixing agreements over detailed supervision (the act exempted such agreements from antitrust laws). By a marketing agreement, tobacco farmers in 1933 received higher guaranteed prices for their product. Early attempts to attain a fair and workable system failed in the dairy industry. Since the direct payment provisions of the act applied only to seven basic crops, the marketing agreements and licensing control represented the only available weapons for most small crops.

Finally, the act authorized something close to a modified allotment plan. Within a few months this became the principal AAA program for basic commodities, and was the only one to receive wide publicity. For basic crops, the AAA could negotiate production agreements with individual farmers. As an incentive for signing a contract limiting production, the farmer received a direct monetary payment, proportioned to his achieved production level in the preceding years, and sufficient to bring

Dorothea Lange, 1936.
Library of Congress

his expected returns on allotment crops closer to the parity level. A processing tax reimbursed the government for the payments, passing the burden of higher prices to consumers. Not only were such contracts voluntary, but local farmers joined in committees to gain compliance and to apportion the quotas. This much publicized revival of "grass-roots democracy" enlisted stronger local support, but also gave control to large landowners and made the program susceptible to local prejudice, whether racial or class.

In the first year the AAA struggled to implement, in ever greater haste, some of its new programs, and also to resolve internal conflicts in policy. In 1933 the production controls could work only retroactively, or not at all. In two critical commodities, cotton and hogs, farmers signed agreements during the summer and then destroyed growing surpluses. Plowing up fields of almost mature cotton seemed shocking enough; the massive slaughter of pigs was a scandal to many Americans, particularly since most of the pigs were too small for efficient meat processing and had to be used for fertilizer and grease (soap), neither very critical in a time of breadlines and desperate need. In the fall of 1933 and the spring of 1934 the AAA successfully extended its production agreements to other basic crops, including wheat, corn, and dairying. In 1934 Congress used two additional bills to establish mandatory (rather than voluntary) production controls for tobacco and cotton, with AAA payments still the reward to farmers.

In 1934 a severe drought began throughout much of the trans-Mississippi West. It continued for the next three crop years (the age of the great dust bowl), and effectively reduced production in such crops as wheat, transforming the agricultural problem there from one of surpluses and low prices to no production and fearful wind erosion. It helped boost some farm prices back to the relative levels of the twenties as early as 1935. The AAA payments, since they were based on past production records, often provided the only cash income for drought-stricken farmers, and served an insurance and relief role scarcely contemplated in 1933.

By the end of 1934 Secretary of Agriculture Henry A. Wallace was able to resolve two major policy conflicts in the AAA. George N. Peek, ever seeking marketing agreements and exports, disliked mandatory production controls and had to be eased into a face-saving advisory role outside the AAA. Much more divisive were class and ideological differences, both in the Department of Agriculture and in the AAA, but especially in the AAA's legal staff. The representatives of such large organizations as the Farm Bureau, as well as the extension agents and land-grant college graduates, upheld one position generally supported by Wallace. They were industry-oriented, and desired programs to aid established family farmers, their main constituency. They wanted rapid agricultural recovery, but feared a diverting, class-based emphasis upon internal reform, especially elaborate efforts to change the status of small farmers and share-croppers.

The legal staff of the AAA, led by such class-conscious lawyers as Jerome Frank and Lee Pressman, abetted in some of their aims by Under-secretary Rexford G. Tugwell, tried to protect consumers' interests by forcing a stricter accountability from processors. Such concern usually delayed Peek's beloved marketing agreements. More importantly, the re-formers tried to force farm owners to live up to the letter of the produc-tion agreements and fairly divide benefit payments with tenants and share-croppers, particularly in the South. Often, they seemed more concerned about curing the gross inequities in agriculture than in gaining a rapid re-covery of agricultural prices. Their concern jeopardized the main action programs of the AAA, and threatened to convert it from an interest-ori-ented recovery agency to one devoted to major and surely economically disruptive structural changes. Wallace, who wanted a broader and more direct control program than Peek and many large farmers, and who also desired, within practical bounds, to alleviate some of the inequities in the administration of AAA agreements, still conceived of the AAA as a main-stream agricultural agency. He fired the reformers but later supported Tugwell's desperate efforts to do something for rural indigents.

In many ways the AAA fulfilled farmer expectations. It not only raised farm income by payments but also helped push farm prices higher by both psychological effects and by artificially created scarcity. Even in an-ticipation, farm prices rose dramatically in the summer of 1933. Unfortu-nately, the higher farm prices often only matched higher prices for manu-factured goods, induced in part by the National Recovery Administration (NRA). As for the larger goal of overall recovery, the AAA contributed little. It improved the status of farmers and thereby helped rescue small-town banks and merchants. But this improvement came largely at the ex-pense of consumers, who now paid more for food and retained less for other purchases.

In January 1936, the Supreme Court, in U. S. v. Butler found unconsti-tutional the processing taxes of the AAA and thus destroyed the main in-centives in the crop control program. The decision neither outlawed mar-keting agreements and acreage control nor dissolved the AAA. But it did force new, and rather hasty, legislative action for the 1936 crop year. By clever strategy, Congress amended a soil conservation act of 1935 and re-placed it by a Soil Conservation and Domestic Allotment Act. Under the constitutional guise of preserving and improving soil fertility, the AAA paid farmers for conservation practices, which in effect meant converting a portion of their crop acreages to grass or other nonsurplus crops. The act provided for basic-crop allotments, for a continued local committee system, and specifically protected the rights of tenants and sharecroppers. It also made the conservation payments serve the old parity principle. Finally, it even permitted continued market operations and the disposition of surpluses. Since the payments to farmers came directly from federal funds and not from processing taxes, the new program gave a much greater boost to recovery and provided more protection of consumer interests.

Finally, in 1938, Congress approved a new Agricultural Adjustment Act, which consolidated and improved several existing programs. In effect, it merged acreage control, conservation, and support prices. It strengthened the local committee system, extended the crops covered by price supports, reinforced and expanded the parity system, and authorized national production quotas for five basic commodities whenever any suffered surpluses. One-third of the affected farmers, in a special referendum, could reject quotas. Subsequent congressional amendments made support prices directly dependent on acceptance of such quotas. The act continued payments for certain types of conservation practices, and for the first time set up a Federal Crop Insurance Corporation (at first only for wheat, but later for most commodities). Except for the increased use of acreage leasing after World War II (soil bank and feed grain programs), the frequently amended second Agricultural Adjustment Act long remained the principal legislative base of our agricultural program.

Supplemental Agricultural Programs

The AAA was the major recovery program for farmers; it was far from being the only program. In an almost desperate attempt to arrest further price declines in the fall of 1933, Roosevelt began what would become the second base of American agricultural policy—direct price supports. The original act creating the Reconstruction Finance Corporation (RFC), back in the Hoover administration, had contained a congressional amendment authorizing direct loans to farmers. Roosevelt now implemented such a program. He created, under the RFC, a Commodity Credit Corporation (a second CCC). It worked in cooperation with the AAA, but in 1933 used $220 million in RFC funds to support corn and cotton prices. Technically, the device was a "nonrecourse loan." To farmers it seemed simple: the government purchased their crops when domestic crops fell below the support level. Legally, the CCC lent the farmer money on the security of his crop, which the CCC acquired and eventually sold. But if the CCC suffered eventual losses, it did not have recourse to the farmer. If marketed at a profit, it had to distribute the extra return to farmers. By supporting minimum prices, the CCC could manage farm prices to the limits of its lending power.

The CCC remained a secondary program during the early New Deal. Acreage controls and drought reduced or ended surpluses; rising prices insured profitable disposal of most loaned crops. Under the second Agricultural Adjustment Act (1938) the CCC moved to the foreground as a twin to production controls. After World War II huge surpluses in such crops as corn, wheat, and cotton, combined with relatively high support levels, made the CCC the largest commodity storage and marketing agency in world history. Its annual losses on loans (i.e., purchases) then mounted into the billions, making its supports the largest direct subsidy ever given to a single industry. But Roosevelt did not foresee such a large program or particularly want it in 1933.

In 1933 Roosevelt consolidated all federal farm credit agencies into a new Farm Credit Administration, with new authority to grant production loans and to loan money to cooperatives (the New Deal replacement for Hoover's Farm Board). The TVA carried out an extensive agricultural program, with fertilization, demonstration farms, and new conservation techniques. With FERA funds, but in coordination with the AAA, a Federal Surplus Relief Corporation distributed surplus foods to the hun-

Roosevelt in Mandan, North Dakota, visiting a farmer receiving drought relief. The combination of prolonged drought and economic depression caused severe suffering among farmers *Library of Congress*

gry. A later Federal Surplus Commodities Corporation in the Department of Agriculture bought surpluses, supported export sales of some, and used most for domestic relief needs, exchanging gifts for a much heralded food stamp plan in 1939. These surplus programs directly supplemented the work of the CCC.

In 1933 Roosevelt established a Soil Erosion Service in the Department of the Interior. It carried out demonstration projects on private lands. In the wake of the dust storms of 1934, Congress replaced it by a permanent Soil Conservation Service (SCS) in the Department of Agriculture. The SCS, which worked through decentralized soil conservation districts, provided not only plans but also technical and financial aid to private farmers. With separate relief funds, Roosevelt established a very special conservation project on the Great Plains. At about the one hundredth meridian, the government funded the planting of erosion-preventing bands of trees (a shelter belt), and then turned them over to cooperating farmers for private management. To the surprise of many skeptics, the idea worked.

Not only did New Deal programs for commercial farmers succeed by sheer endurance; they also succeeded by stimulating efficient production and relatively low prices. American consumers still spend a smaller percentage of income for farm products than those in any advanced country in the world. But such an evaluation does not include such hidden costs as taxes to support farm prices, or to pay for the welfare costs incurred by displaced agricultural workers, or for the yet unpaid social cost of farm pesticides and ecological distortions. By tying subsidies to production, and by controlling acreage rather than the amount marketed, our system of agricultural planning provided every possible incentive for maximum production per acre. Labor costs, escalating skills, and a tremendous capital requirement (in scarce land and sophisticated tools) encouraged work efficiency. This led to increased mechanization, the merging of small farms into larger ones, almost impossible capital requirements for entering farming, and various lines of dependence between farmers and related businesses, from banks and appliance dealers to processors. The small farmer had to specialize in the few remaining high-work, low-capital specialty crops, work as a contract supplier of a large processor, or accept the status of a tenant or farm laborer. By every indication, the number of farmers will continue to decline while the skills and profits of those remaining will continue to increase.

Rural Relief

Other New Deal programs benefited rural people but had only marginal relationships to commercial agriculture. In 1933 Roosevelt helped secure legislative authority for a very special program that he and Eleanor had long supported in principle. With $25 million he established, in the Department of the Interior, a Division of Subsistence Homesteads. It was to construct small rural communities to house unemployed people (particularly stranded miners) who, he hoped, could find part-time factory employment, and who could also work part time on the land in order to provide most subsistence (gardens, orchards, hogs, a cow). The division actually began construction on thirty-three communities or towns, but gave way in 1935 to an expanded rural housing and resettlement program under a new agency. The Division of Subsistence Homesteads reflected, better than any other agency, the romantic glorification of rural and farm life, and paralleled a considerable back-to-the-land movement that peaked in the early depression.

The Federal Emergency Relief Administration, in recognition of the special problems of indigent rural people, established a Rural Rehabilitation Division, and formed government-owned but locally administered Rural Rehabilitation Corporations in most states. Some early rural relief funds had to go into direct doles, but many of the corporations tried to use funds for special, supervised loans. Insofar as they were successful, the loans could help the very poorest farmers get enough food to work and enough tools and seed to resume production. Repayments funded new loans. In a few more daring innovations the state corporations, at federal urging and under uniform standards, initiated rural-industrial colonies comparable to subsistence homesteads except that some were entirely agricultural and in the others the expected employment involved agricultural processing or strictly rural crafts.

In 1935 Roosevelt used relief funds to establish the Resettlement Administration (RA) and appointed the controversial Rexford G. Tugwell to head it. Tugwell had lost his Department of Agriculture battle in behalf of the most lowly farmers and now welcomed the freedom of a special agency, unhampered by the special interest orientation of the AAA. He had long lamented the effect of the AAA on southern tenants and sharecroppers; not only did production cuts leave many stranded, but AAA payments never reached all too many tenants, particularly southern blacks. Since he inherited the rural rehabilitation program of the FERA, he continued the supervised loans but provided more central direction. Soon RA agents in each county operated a second extension service for the most exploited or untrained farmers. Tugwell also inherited the two community programs with projects still abuilding. He deemphasized the subsistence goal and added new communities based entirely on commercial agriculture. He tried to use such communities to demonstrate better rural housing and new forms of cooperation. In the approximately one

hundred completed communities the RA also experimented with collective farming, long-term leases, exceedingly detailed supervision, prepaid
cooperative medical plans, and unprecedented recreational and crafts projects. In a separate program, the RA began a number of migratory camps,
mostly in California.

A former Arkansas
woman, as photographed
by Dorothea Lange, was
in a camp near
Westley, Calif. (1939).
Library of Congress

The RA invited controversy. Created without specific congressional authority, innovative in programs, ambitious in hopes and dreams, exceedingly class conscious in many of its operations, it soon had a broad spectrum of enemies. Neither the Extension Service nor the Farm Bureau appreciated its particular class bias or the reformist bent of its leadership. After Tugwell (a political liability to Roosevelt) retired at the end of 1936, and after Henry Wallace toured the South and gained a greater enthusiasm for rehabilitation programs, the RA moved to the Department of Agriculture as a permanent agency. After new legislation added a special tenant-purchase program, the RA became the Farm Security Administration (FSA), but with few basic changes in its programs. The tenant-purchase plan, even though small, adhered closely to the old entrepreneurial ideal and won greater congressional enthusiasm than any other FSA mandate. In World War II, after severe congressional criticism and a long investigation, the emasculated remains of the FSA became the Farmers' Home Administration, the present title of its mild successor.

Contrived Inflation

The Agricultural Adjustment Act of 1933 contained one important section, the Thomas Amendment, which seemed strangely out of place. It gave Roosevelt authority to inflate our currency in order to raise price levels, with farm prices the prime consideration. The depression had revived an old panacea for hard times—deliberate inflation by governmental control over the monetary system. From colonial paper issues to greenback crusades to the free silver movement, this magical remedy in one form or another had a perennial appeal not only for cranks or eccentrics but for realistic politicians and even astute professors. Almost in desperation, Franklin D. Roosevelt fell for the lure in 1933. It never worked quite as he hoped. Thus, he gave up on it in 1934, but not before significantly transforming our monetary system.

In the Emergency Banking Act of 1933, Congress restricted all monetary gold to the Federal Reserve System and licensed its use for commercial purposes. On April 19, 1933, Roosevelt refused to free additional gold for export, thereby allowing the overpriced dollar to find its own competitive exchange level. In other words, the effective gold value of the dollar declined and the dollar price of gold soared (as it would again in 1971–73 when the Nixon administration allowed the dollar "to float"). This floating meant an informal devaluation of currency, and immediately bettered the competitive position of the United States in world trade (it lowered American prices as stated in other currencies, and thus encouraged exports, and increased the dollar price of foreign goods, and thus discouraged imports and certain forms of consumption). In the international realm, it had the same effect as an increase in tariffs, yet without any of the political hazards of new tariff laws for a Democratic president. But Roosevelt did not seek such competitive advantages. Instead, he hoped for a rapid rise in our domestic prices and new and stable foreign exchange rates based on rising international prices. But because of international price instability, declining markets everywhere, and competitive monetary warfare by other countries, the devaluation did not open up significant markets for our surplus products and thus provide much competitive pressures for higher prices at home. Devaluation, in itself, did not increase domestic monetary supplies (currency and demand deposits in banks).

This original devaluation had some justifying economic effects. It protected us from low world prices and made possible such price-fixing devices as agricultural marketing agreements. More important, it freed the Federal Reserve System from the restraints of an artificially low dollar price for gold. Under the Hoover administration, the Federal Reserve Banks had to export gold to maintain the statutory dollar (see pp. 152–53). At two critical points they had to tighten credit and restrict monetary supplies in order to maintain minimum gold reserves. Or, in other words, the maintenance of the gold standard forced deflationary central banking policies at the worst possible time in our whole history. Devaluation reversed the outflow of gold and allowed such easy credit policies as lowered rediscount rates. Also, under mandate from Congress, the Federal Reserve System began open market purchases, a direct inflationary stimulus. Unfortunately, the easy credit policies had small impact on prices. Reserves accumulated, interest rates dropped to unprecedented levels, but few people sought loans or proved willing to take the easy credit path to new purchases.

By the fall of 1933 agricultural prices began to fall, at great peril to the administration's hard-won political capital with farmers. Instead of leaving exchange rates at competitive levels, the administration tried to force higher prices by arbitrary and artificial increases in the dollar price of gold. It hoped to force prices back to predepression levels, and then maintain them by varying gold values rather than allowing domestic prices to fluctuate. For over two months the United States steadily raised its bids for gold, often setting a new price each day. This blunt strategy did force the dollar down in foreign exchange, a rare example of a country laying siege to its own currency values. The policy further demoralized the international exchange system, made the United States vulnerable to charges of selfishness, and, most important, did not lead to higher domestic prices. Effective demand remained low. Even Roosevelt lost faith in such forced inflation. Instead of returning to a competitive dollar (or un-

Depression and Recovery (The Base of 100 Fits Each Index for 1929)

Source: U.S. Bureau of the Census, *Historical Statistics of the U.S.*, Washington, D.C., 1960, Series D 46, p. 73.

•••••• Employment   — •• — Corporate profits   ——————— Wholesale commodity prices

—— ——GNP   — • — • Agricultural prices   — — — — Dow–Jones industrials for
1929 = 100   August of each year

UNEMPLOYMENT	
1929	1,550,000
1930	4,340,000
1931	8,020,000
1932	12,060,000
1933	12,830,000
1934	11,340,000
1935	10,610,000
1936	9,030,000
1937	7,700,000
1938	10,390,000
1939	9,480,000
1940	8,120,000
1941	5,560,000
1942	2,660,000
1943	1,070,000

pegged gold prices), Roosevelt asked Congress for stabilizing legislation in early 1934. The Gold Reserve Act set the price of gold close to its final arbitrary level (at $35 an ounce versus the pre-1933 price of $20.63)—or gave formal approval for a 40 percent inflation of the dollar. Despite a modest executive leeway for further inflation, this price remained fixed until 1971 despite wide shifts in gold supplies and, after 1965, intense pressure for new dollar devaluation.

There was a final inflationary binge. It involved silver, the older monetary panacea. In December 1933, Roosevelt generously implemented an international agreement on silver. He pegged the official value at a then astounding $1.29 an ounce, and committed the government to purchase all domestic silver at one-half that price (still an increase over competitive prices and a subsidy for silver interests). The Treasury issued new silver certificates, not on the official value, but only on the purchase price of the silver. Since our gold stock was zooming upward, the silver backing was already redundant. The Federal Reserve System could already more than meet currency demands by printing reserve notes.

Congress wanted more inflation. By large majorities in both houses it passed a Silver Purchase Act in June 1934, long after the administration ardor for forced inflation had cooled. The act directed Roosevelt to nationalize silver supplies and to issue silver certificates to cover the cost of all purchased silver, domestic or foreign. The buying of silver was to continue until silver became 25 percent of our monetary base or until world silver prices reached our arbitrary valuation of $1.29 an ounce. Until April 1935, the United States bought all available silver and drove international prices up to $0.81 an ounce. It then stopped such aggressive buying, exploded the great silver bubble, and watched world prices decline to $0.45 an ounce. The increasing gold stocks never allowed silver to reach the mandated 25 percent. The Treasury issued silver certificates only to cover the purchase of silver, and not, as authorized, to match the arbitrary value of the silver. Thus, the administration thwarted the inflationary purposes of Congress, except for the effect of governmental purchases of silver bullion. The purchases amounted to a major subsidy for both domestic and foreign holders of silver. The high silver prices meant a forced deflation of foreign currencies based on silver (China had to leave the silver standard). At the time, the governmental credit used to purchase unneeded silver could have been spent on pressing domestic needs, with greater impact both on prices and on overall recovery.

The Origins of the NRA

Some still remember it with nostalgic affection. But anyone who can vividly recall the Blue Eagle is now old enough to be a grandparent. Almost every factory flew its flag. Laborers proudly wore it on their lapels. The Post Office dutifully issued a stamp. Like proud soldiers off to war, thousands marched in its honor in a New York parade. In the somber yet hopeful summer of 1933, loyal and patriotic Americans enlisted in a great campaign, abetted by all the propaganda and the manufactured enthusiasm of a war. Surely the depression was crisis enough, and recovery noble enough, to engender such commitment. But all too soon the crusade proved ephemeral, the enthusiasm futile, the emotional rituals too much a promoter's imposition.

Yet, a tinge of nobility still savors the remembered futility. The National Recovery Administration (NRA), which the Blue Eagle symbolized, surely deserved better. And for a few brief summer weeks the mirage of recovery did grace the land, and millions sincerely cheered the magic of FDR and NRA director, Hugh Johnson. And even later, in months of decline and disillusionment, discriminating critics had to acknowledge the lofty dreams, as well as the confused goals, that informed the NRA. Even its sheer daring and magnitude invited respect. Never before had a peacetime American government essayed such a precedent-shattering and grandiose economic program.

Congress approved an omnibus National Industrial Recovery Act on June 16, 1933. Its first section authorized a major industrial recovery program, centered on a coordinating federal agency (this would be the NRA), and on a type of supervised industrial self-government. Simply stated, Congress hoped to increase purchasing power and thus begin a spiral of recovery. It stressed the emergency nature of the act (unless renewed, the NRA would expire after two years), and the need for an early and drastic increase in production and jobs. The Roosevelt administration expected the act to bring an early resumption of normal production, large-scale reemployment, and an increase in wages paid. The paychecks would provide a growing market for the newly produced goods. The success of the plan depended on the decisions of private businessmen. In payment for renewed production and employment, they were to receive, under a system of industrial codes, protection against unfair competition and against other sources of industrial instability. Under a close, business-government partnership, they could expect secure profits and rapid recovery.

The National Industrial Recovery Act, in Title II, authorized a $3,300 million public works program, a great expansion over Hoover's earlier efforts. This government investment held out a promise of a vastly increased market for goods and for an immediate expansion in the moribund construction industry. It did not so work. Roosevelt placed the public works program not in the NRA but in the Department of the Interior under Secretary Harold Ickes. This left the NRA with no action funds to support its code program. In fact, it also meant no close coordination between Ickes' Public Works Administration (PWA) and the NRA. Two different New Deal coordinating committees, established to coordinate several recovery programs, never functioned effectively. Ickes went his own way. He insisted upon carefully planned, efficient projects, which often entailed a lead time of two or three years before actual construction. Within the first two years he could not commit the total appropriation, and lost part of it to other programs. Yet, Ickes spent well in such diverse areas as public housing, highways and bridges, municipal power facilities, innumerable government buildings, even ships. The only trouble was that his efforts contributed almost nothing to early recovery.

In conception, the NRA seemed close to the AAA. In both cases the government assumed a coordinating role, offering to producers a more secure market, higher assured returns, but at the cost of more supervision and imposed rules. In both cases the government worked closely with producers, more nearly providing the tools for self-regulation and planning than imposing such plans. Just as the farmers worked through local committees, so nonagricultural producers would cooperate in the drafting of industrial codes. In both cases, at least in theory, the government retained enough power to protect the larger public, and promised to use its police power to enforce the collective rules against selfish, individualistic industry mavericks. But the AAA applied to only one industry, the NRA to hundreds of quite divergent ones, ranging from retail trades dominated by family-owned businesses to heavy manufacturing dominated by a few large corporations. The AAA developed from a near consensus of policy among at least the more successful farmers; an always ambivalent NRA reflected a conspicuous clash of policy goals. Finally, the AAA enjoyed many continuities with past policies or policy proposals; the NRA, in so many ways, seemed a sharp break with the past.

The Conflict over Policy

Policy clashes among Roosevelt's advisers dominated even the earliest attempts to outline a recovery act. Members of his brain trust clashed with major business advisers. Men like Tugwell wanted to duplicate World War I planning; businessmen wanted to extend the trade associations developed in the twenties. An impending compulsory thirty-hour week proposal in Congress forced Roosevelt to mature the National Industrial Recovery Act, which at least smoothed over differences of policy. Yet the supporters all agreed that the United States had outgrown a competitive economy, and most particularly price competition and class rivalry. The word was hardly popular, but in effect they agreed that our economic system was already collectivized, with large and efficient productive units already dominant in most fields. In the language of Tugwell, we now needed a true "concert of interests"; business and labor should work toward common national goals. Only by cooperation could we have recovery and a shared prosperity. Divisive and distorting competition, between classes, between industries, and within industries, was now counter to the public good.

Such a general agreement concealed the critical issue: who would determine the public good, who would draft the codes, who would have ultimate powers of enforcement? The businessmen assumed that they would make the major decisions, subject to governmental guidelines. After all, they were public-spirited and, more important, alone knew the needs of their own industries. In the twenties corporations in several industries had joined in trade associations, both to improve product quality and image and, sometimes, to form an effective front against labor unions. Such trade associations had often been able to set rules about product standards and probably had much to do with the determination of prices.

Such voluntary associations were fragile; recalcitrant corporations could refuse to join or flout agreements. Quite divergent businessmen saw in the NRA a device that could enforce industrywide rules and rationalize production and marketing. In effect the consolidated industry would now become a more important economic unit than the individual corporate unit (some called this pooling or cartelization). In the distant past a type of wide-open competition had stimulated economic innovations and permitted a few men to amass great wealth but had also made almost all businesses vulnerable and insecure. Since the government in the NRA would function more as a paternal protector than a dictatorial boss, businessmen would lose little managerial leeway under the codes but still have assured profits. A system of industrial government, under their own enlightened trusteeship, would bring business confidence, new investment, and a sound recovery. They so badly needed this in 1933 that they dared risk governmental supervision.

Here Roosevelt visits "Tugwell town" or Greenbelt, Maryland, with Rexford G. Tugwell, a member of the "brains trust." *Franklin D. Roosevelt Library*

For academic advisers such as Tugwell (Moley came close to the business view), the threat of business trusteeship seemed even more ominous than a continuation of wasteful competition. Whatever their self-image, businessmen would govern themselves, not in the public interest, but in behalf of corporate profits. And not because they were businessmen, but simply because they served a limited constituency. Laborers or farmers would be equally myopic if they exercised code-making authority. Thus, if public ends were to dominate, the coordination of a national economy had to be under strict governmental control, an instrument of national economic planning. Tugwell wanted long-range economic goals, governmental supervision of the allocation of national resources, and possibly wage, price, and profit controls. Without nationalizing property, the government still could force national goals upon private producers (nationalization might become a final weapon against the noncooperative). The planning could be two-tiered. Congress, as spokesmen for the people, would establish general goals and values. Detailed implementation would require trained experts, working closely with the president. The NRA would be the first of such planning agencies. The critical problem was to make planning both democratic and informed. The planners kept the business emphasis upon national purpose and centralization and the hatred of competition. They also had no illusions about labor unions. Although they wanted to use governmental power to redress the balance between capital and labor, they had no desire to create another divisive and short-sighted interest group. Coordination meant a great deal more than arming the lambs and then refereeing a fight with the wolves.

Both business trustees and insistent planners seemed to reject the entrepreneurial ideal. This made either position seem radical and threatening to all who still affirmed our traditional political economy. By an elitist, distant bureaucracy, by an overpowerful central government, the planners would force individuals to become functioning units in ever larger wholes, and strip from them any remaining opportunity to find fulfillment in their own schemes, or in truly private and free *enterprise*. The business trustees seemed bent on creating a few large cartels or monopolies in behalf of their own profits and in order to destroy all small business enterprise or, more critical, even the environment that allows opportunity for such enterprise to originate. But those who feared collectivism did not, of necessity, argue for uncontrolled competition. The AAA proved the possibility of governmental coordination, even to the extent of administered prices, yet all in behalf of small, decentralized producers who retained a very large sphere of managerial freedom, and who met locally to influence national agricultural policy. Why could not the NRA serve a similar role for business? Instead of ending competition, it might so regulate it as to protect small concerns against the large monoliths. It might equalize the odds between small and large enterprise, and in one sense of that hydra-headed word, "competition," even increase the competitiveness of our economy. Such "fair competition" would reward the honest and inventive and bring once again to consumers the benefits of a free market.

Such an anticollectivist view had the strongest appeal in Congress and provided a vantage point for unending criticism of the NRA. Congress had included in the National Industrial Recovery Act a specific, and almost contradictory, requirement that codes not allow monopolistic practices or give advantages to large businesses over small. Yet, the act as a whole suspended the antitrust laws and, by every clear intention, opened the way for integrated cartels. Obviously, the language of the act allowed varying interpretations. Thus in the NRA, as in the AAA, the most important policy decisions had to come after Congress acted. The NRA could be many things. In practice, at any one time it had to be something quite specific.

The Operation of the NRA Codes

The early history of the NRA consoled only the business trustees. In 1933 the administration sought quick results, not major structural changes. Hugh Johnson, the first head of the NRA, tried to enlist the support of business leaders. A tremendously energetic and colorful man, he was a retired general and a former assistant to Bernard Baruch on the National War Industries Board of World War I, perhaps the closest governmental precedent for the NRA. Most of his early staff, save specialists on labor or consumer affairs, either had business connections or a sympathetic understanding of the problems and goals of private businessmen. In almost all major disputes within the NRA over major policies, Johnson and his main staff members defended their business constituency. When he had to force a governmental priority, he tried to win support by persuasion rather than force.

Even as industrial representatives gathered to draft the first codes, Johnson launched his first and greatest propaganda campaign. He urged each industrial firm to accept what he called the President's Reemployment Agreement (PRA), a type of precode contract. He authorized each voluntary adherent to fly the Blue Eagle flag (later it would also signal compliance with the industrial codes). In the PRA pledge a corporation promised to end child labor, to pay a minimum wage to all employees (from $.30 to $.40 an hour), and to limit hours for certain specified employees to either forty or thirty-five a week. Replacements for children and for shorter work weeks should, in theory, have expanded the adult

Hugh Johnson (1882–1942), the colorful director of the NRA, is shown here in 1934. Since the early NRA codes proved difficult to enforce, Johnson launched a vigorous propaganda campaign in behalf of compliance. *Franklin D. Roosevelt Library*

work force; the minimum wages should have maintained or increased paychecks. It worked briefly but an expected spiral of recovery proved illusory; higher summer prices dropped in the autumn. Since the PRA agreements did not come under the code authority of the NRA, they did not have the force of law. Thus Johnson depended on a tremendous propaganda drive to bring sufficient social pressure for general agreement. He used all the techniques of World War I bond drives, including four-minute speakers. Few resisted. The Blue Eagle became a new badge of patriotism, necessary for public respect and patronage.

The code-making amounted to an unprecedented legislative process through complex bargaining. Representatives from trade associations, composed of all the firms in that industry that chose to join, drafted the original codes setting up what they believed to be desirable rules to insure fair competition. An NRA administrator usually checked the early draft for obvious statutory violations before submitting it to a required public hearing. In the hearing, consumers or other interested parties could offer complaints or suggestions. Since there would be over 500 primary codes, arranging and publicizing such hearings was no easy task. By consultation, the NRA administrator secured any revisions indicated by the hearings and then submitted the final draft to General Johnson. If approved by him, it went to the president for a pro forma signature which made it part of the law of the land, enforceable in federal courts. At the president's discretion, the NRA could now demand certain reports and accounts from code firms in order to monitor their compliance. But rarely did the NRA administrator have enough detailed information about an industry at the time of code making to suggest any major changes. In a sense, it was industrial self-legislation.

What did the codes provide? For one thing, the original act required all to contain certain labor provisions. Each code had to guarantee the right of workers to organize and bargain collectively and also prohibited any compulsory membership in company unions (it did not specifically outlaw company unions). More directly related to recovery, each industry code had to include maximum hours and minimum wage provisions, and most would also include codes governing working conditions. In this way, the codes resembled miniature labor contracts, since the labor provisions had to be negotiated by labor and management. Except in those industries with established and strong industrial unions, this often meant little more than consultation. Although the collective bargaining code did not require independent unions, it did seem to invite more effective organizational drives; the American Federation of Labor so interpreted it. Finally, it seemed, the federal government was on the side of organized labor. But the NRA scarcely fulfilled this early promise.

The labor clause of the National Industrial Recovery Act (Section 7(a) of Title I), led to endless controversy and, eventually, to a good share of the business disillusionment with the NRA. Since management had the dominant role in drafting and enforcing codes, only determined governmental efforts could secure labor rights. Johnson believed that the end of cutthroat competition, and code provisions on wages and hours, would remove most of the grievances of workers, and also lessen the antagonistic relationship between labor and capital. Under the codes, all could work together in harmony and enjoy the fruits of recovery. From this perspective, company unions did not seem a grave threat to employee rights. Consequently, the NRA interpreted Section 7(a) quite loosely and in such a way as to accommodate its principal clientele, the employing corporations. A separate NRA Board, the National Labor Board, was to mediate any dispute over wage and hour codes. Because of prolabor members, the board struggled to uphold collective bargaining rights, but consistently met firm resistance from NRA administrators. Thus in the spring of 1934, Roosevelt replaced the National Labor Board with the National Labor Relations Board, independent of the NRA but still restricted to the ambiguous authority provided in Section 7(a). It tried to defend labor rights both in the drafting and enforcing of codes, antagonizing businessmen. But its statutory weaknesses and its inability to overcome NRA jealousy helped create a demand, by Senator Robert F. Wagner and other prolabor congressmen, for new and stronger labor legislation, or for what became the National Labor Relations Act of 1935.

Apart from the mandated labor codes, most of the substantive codes at least related to prices. Yet, only a few approved codes ever legislated explicit prices. NRA approval of these had to be based on truly exceptional circumstances. Instead, over two-thirds of the codes prohibited "unfair" competition, usually defined as sales below cost with various formulas for determining costs. In effect, most codes tried to use this device at least to keep prices high enough to insure profits for all or most of the firms in the industry grouping. Eventually, under pressure from congressmen, the NRA avoided such price provisions in all new codes. Other codes required open prices, or a system of published price levels, with changes only after notification to competitors. These helped reveal any code violations and made enforcement easier. Finally, some codes either governed conditions of sale, and thus standardized such things as credit, premiums, trade-in-allowances, and quality, or placed limits on productive capacity.

The price-related codes, even as labor codes, engendered a running controversy. The proclamation of codes accompanied rising price levels, yet triggered no appreciable recovery. The higher prices affected everyone, or that most nebulous of economic classes, consumers. Just as the early National Labor Board challenged the dominant business mentality of the NRA, so a Consumers' Advisory Board tried, without great success, to protect the neglected interest of buyers. It received support from antibusiness congressmen, from agricultural groups, from small business defenders, and from other administrative agencies. The higher prices, without clear public returns, seemed evidence of the dangerous monopolistic capacity of the NRA. A hostile National Recovery Board, led by Clarence Darrow, investigated the NRA in 1934, and reinforced the monopolistic charge by detailed if one-sided evidence. Under such pressure, the NRA by 1934 at least promised to curtail overtly anticompetitive practices, a promise frightening to businessmen and one scarcely consistent with the very purpose of most of the approved codes.

Finally, the approved codes contained provisions for code authorities to administer and enforce the industrywide rules. Most code authorities simply duplicated trade associations, and most remained almost completely under business control. Less than 10 percent included labor members, and no more than 2 percent any consumer representatives. At least one representative of the NRA had either voting or nonvoting membership on the authorities, but few government representatives even attended all meetings; at first few represented a point of view divergent from the industry representatives. But in 1934 and 1935 the NRA at least tried to exert more influence on the code authorities, and insisted on a broader, more representative membership. To back up or supplement the code authorities, the NRA formed a compliance division that often worked at odds to the National Labor Board and the Consumers' Advisory Board.

The Downfall of the NRA Codes

Many businessmen, in theory the greatest gainers from the NRA, became dissatisfied with its policies by 1934, in part because of tighter federal monitoring, in part because of administrative complexity and overlapping codes. Small businessmen, in particular, claimed that they suffered under the domination of large firms. By the summer of 1934, Johnson was under attack from all quarters, and under intense pressure to reassert the competitive idea. In August Roosevelt eased Johnson out of the NRA, and replaced him with an administrative board of five men. Under the chairmanship, first of S. Clay Williams, a tobacco executive, and then Donald Richberg, a former labor lawyer, long-time assistant to Johnson, and an able politician, the NRA played out its last, most peaceful months. In May 1935 the Supreme Court unanimously ended its main role, codemaking (*Schechter Poultry Corp.* v. *United States*), finding no constitutional basis for such a delegation of legislative powers and no justification in the interstate commerce clause for such a broad use of federal regulatory power. Its demise, regretted by few except Roosevelt and NRA officials, necessitated both a new policy toward business enterprise and toward organized labor.

In one sense, the NRA was the most ephemeral major agency of the New Deal. The industrial codes and the elaborate code authorities disappeared forever. Under intense pressure, the very idea of large, government-coordinated cartels had eroded even in the NRA, and similarly in the Roosevelt administration. The favored policy by 1935 was antimonopoly and antibigness. Competition regained rhetorical fashion. Admittedly, the NRA became the crucible for a new labor policy, but this was quite incidental to its main purpose. Yet, some of the problems that engendered it still remained in 1935.

If the public interest required government coordination and protection in agriculture (and it did if it encompassed the survival of family farms), then it also required it in several other industries made up largely of small producers or retailers. There, destructive competition threatened unending disorder and the probable elimination of very small enterprise. And where security did not exist, and where profit margins remained small or nonexistent, there was also the most antisocial behavior, the most kicking and gouging, the cruelest treatment of labor. Ironically, it was in such unstable industries, either without strong trade associations or without strong unions, that the NRA codes were both more needed and less-easily administered, particularly the labor and consumer codes. There, in spite of codes, vicious competitive practices continued and instability threatened to continue even after 1935. In the wake of the NRA the Roosevelt administration had to find substitutes for this category of industries.

After the *Schechter* decision, Roosevelt won from Congress a nine-month extension of an emasculated NRA. It helped over thirty industries formulate voluntary trade practice agreements. Of much greater significance, Congress began in 1935 to enact little NRA's for highly competitive, unstable, or sick industries. After long litigation in the courts, Congress provided for regulated competition in bituminous coal by the Guffey-Vinson Act of 1937, for retail merchants by the Rayburn-Pitman Act of 1936, and for drug stores in the Miller-Tydings Act of 1937. It used marketing acts to support state controls over petroleum production, broadened Interstate Commerce Commission powers to encompass interstate trucking, and gave extensive regulatory power to new commissions to supervise airlines and the merchant marine.

For industries dominated by large corporations there would be no substitute for the NRA, but rather a complex and subtle government-business relationship. The NRA experiment in direct partnership had not pleased any constituency. Corporate executives, anxious in the crisis of 1933 to obtain governmental aid, then hopeful of dominating NRA policies, knew all the pitfalls by 1935. Big business could do better on its own. The government by then had responded to other interests, such as labor and even occasionally to aggrieved consumers, and threatened to inundate business with bureaucratic controls and detailed supervision. In the long run, the government would again harmonize its relationship to the large corporations. In 1935 there seemed little more than bickering and countercharges.

But did the NRA aid recovery? The question scarcely permits a competent answer. Within the lifetime of the NRA the economy, by almost every conceivable index, did show distinct if limited improvement over the depths of 1933. The gross national product rose from $56 to $72 billion, industrial output increased by 28 percent, unemployment dropped by something like 2 million, and the average earnings of factory workers went up by 20 percent. In no major area did the economic gains restore the 1929 level. In the literal sense of the word, there was no full recovery. And the NRA may even have hampered this limited recovery and impeded the effectiveness of other measures. It is at least easier to relate the limited economic gains not to the NRA but to other New Deal programs, such as relief expenditures and to banking and investment reforms.

10

The depression of the thirties had a more enduring impact on Americans than any war of this century. By good fortune, America escaped bombing and internal destruction in either of its wars. Those who fought abroad often had life-shattering experiences. Most stayed home and knew war only at an insulated distance. But almost no one could escape the depression, although a minority profited by it. The adults who lived through it, the children who grew up in its midst, became very different people because of it. Their very self-image, their identity, would forever carry with it an indelible brand—"depression made." They knew by immediate experience, and would remember for a lifetime, what it was like when the American economy mocked all its widely acclaimed possibilities of unending growth and great affluence. Those who suffered the most still have their nightmares, still carry the marks of extreme insecurity, still participate with mixed guilt and exultation in present prosperity, still nourish the pecuniary caution and almost apocalyptic forebodings so typical of a scarce and meager economy.

The Direct Economic Impact

The depression rewarded a few people—those with assured, fixed incomes, those with savings still to invest, those who could still command cheap labor or cheap money, those in the rare areas of the country, or the few industries, not severely curtailed by depression. But because of severity and length, the hard times affected people at all levels of income. Bank or corporate failures, as well as stock market losses, could reduce the mighty to near poverty, although only a minority probably suffered so much. More important, prudent and able farmers and small-town businessmen often suffered most, in part from their own ability and enterprise. In the twenties, as today, the most capable farmers and merchants used credit in order to expand operations, adopt new technology, or ensure long-run efficiency and profit. The depression bankrupted a large proportion of such able entrepreneurs. The best farming areas of Illinois and Iowa often endured the worst distress; in some counties over half the farmers lost their land under the impact of ruinous prices, drastically reduced land values, or the failure of local banks. And many of these people had been community leaders, the "best" people, the ones most in love

216

Depression America— A Profile

John Vachon made this haunting study of an unemployed youth in 1938. Vachon, like Dorothea Lange, Russell Lee, and Ben Shahn, sought to illustrate the mood and spirit of depression America. *Library of Congress*

By 1933 a quarter of Americans usually employed were out of work, but the psychological costs of the depression cannot be measured. These men are registering for unemployment relief. *Franklin D. Roosevelt Library*

with the American economic system and now most effective in demanding restorative government action.

In the large cities the depression hurt the bottom more, the middle and top less. Throughout the twenties, despite the overall growth, unemployment had remained a serious problem, particularly in such declining regional industries as coal or textiles. The only salvation had been new growth industries, particularly automobiles. A worker, even if unskilled, could usually find work in some city, at least for part of the year. The depression all but eliminated new job opportunities for unskilled workers, and in many cases even for skilled craftsmen (in the moribund construction industry, for example). By early 1933 one out of four normally employed or job-seeking Americans were without work. Another one out of four suffered underemployment, or severely curtailed working hours. The unskilled and the unlucky, the untenured and newly hired, soon had to depend on private or public charity, since these more marginal workers rarely had either home or savings.

For those workers who had skills, seniority, and adequate support from craft unions, the depression did not mean family disaster. Industrial wages often fell less than wholesale prices. The city breadlines included primarily the unskilled or semiskilled laboring class, long insecure and vulnerable, ethnically divided, unorganized, and politically ineffective, and now so numerous as to break down all institutional forms of charity. Lower level white-collar jobs also evaporated, forcing beginning store clerks, stenographers, bookkeepers, and even low level executives out of their jobs, and leaving them little prospect for reemployment. Self-employed professionals, such as lawyers and physicians, suffered from their inability to collect fees, and in some areas from a sharp drop in demand for their services. Their economic condition thus closely matched that of their neighborhood clients.

Public employment showed a mixed picture. Local governments often had to default on obligations, leaving municipal employees without work, and forcing public schoolteachers to accept less or a deferred salary. But apart from such area disasters, lower level governmental jobs, such as public schoolteaching, became desperately sought sources of security in a desert of depression. The custom of firing married or pregnant female schoolteachers forced thousands of young women to delay marriage, or to remain secretly married for years. The one great area of job expansion in the thirties would be in the federal government. Ordinary federal positions, such as in the post office system, became great prizes, eagerly sought by those who wanted security. The largest single source of opportunity for young people with skill or college training (would-be teachers, welfare workers, lawyers, secretaries, architects, engineers) were the varied New Deal agencies. While most of America lay in economic doldrums, Washington, D.C., almost exploded with new activity. The enthusiasm, the idealism, the unwavering zeal of the new bureaucrats always contained an element of gratitude.

Frozen or declining enrollments foreclosed most new positions on college faculties, but if anything increased the prestige of established professors. Even with stabilized salaries, professors could live better, relatively, than ever before. The expanding New Deal programs also attracted academics to Washington. Perhaps more significant, the New Deal accelerated the use of outside, largely academic, consultants and advisers. The use of university talent first peaked in the wartime Wilson administration, had long existed in the Department of Agriculture, and expanded rapidly in the depression. Hoover, for example, launched several significant research projects. Although the government could not yet afford the luxury of pure research, practically every New Deal program demanded a great deal of practical investigation. Most agencies set up research divisions. Congressional committees, in order to monitor the new level of federal activities, also had to add more academic experts to their committee staffs. From this use of trained experts would come a symbiotic relationship between campus and government, or what could be called a governmental third estate (the sometime members of advisory councils, boards, committees, and task forces, who move between campus and Capitol Hill, transferring to government agencies a bit of their idealism and of their specialized myopia). But a jealous Congress kept Roosevelt from completing a formal, institutional structure for expert advising. As an adjunct to his early public works program, Roosevelt established a National Planning Board, and in 1934 elevated it to an independent National Resources Committee, staffed by leading American economists and city planners. The committee tried to carry out far-ranging studies on resource use, and also to coordinate the work of various agencies in behalf of overarching, longer-term objectives. Members often dissented rather dramatically from congressional opinion, and often recommended daring or far-reaching policies. But during World War II the committee fell before the concerted wrath of Congress, which forced Roosevelt and subsequent presidents to work through less formal, ad hoc committees (the later Council of Economic Advisers today came closest to a formal, academically related planning agency).

Basic Beliefs and Intellectuals

The effect of depression upon basic American beliefs, or upon that vaguest of categories, "intellectuals," cannot be charted. One is always left, at best, with suggestive impressions. It is all too tempting to speak about national moods or attitudes, or of a national character or even an American mind, as if diverse Americans somehow coalesced into a larger, animate, self-conscious whole. They do not. In reality, almost all summary judgments about a whole people in any period of the past is a partial judgment, usually based on the articulated views of a few fashionable critics, novelists, scholars, or journalists. Every age, every decade, soon gets its stereotypes of mood and belief, and these often live on as historical caricatures.

Hungry people think about food and, insofar as they analyze public issues, this focus conditions their political behavior. In the thirties, over 2 million Americans eventually wrote letters to Roosevelt, to Eleanor, or to highly placed New Deal officials. These letters revealed the range of personal misfortune, the illusory hopes for rapid and almost magical improvement, and often pathetically naive strategies for recovery. The letters did not reveal any general, emerging new conceptions in political economy, no massive rejection of traditional beliefs, no emphatic mandate for change in any one direction. Although certain highly charged political controversies of the thirties, particularly the Court fight of 1937, touched on basic political institutions and theories, and possibly provoked a wider consideration of such issues, the New Deal as a whole looked to immediate practical goals and appealed to proximate needs or to existing and scarcely articulate beliefs. Politics, as usual, had an immense personal element, and the more so as traditional institutions seemed inadequate. The institutional changes that came from depression politics, rather than reflecting any changed popular understanding at any level of generality, instead required decades of intellectual adjustment. The broadly understood rationale, the general policy agreement, came later in the fifties and sixties, even as a small minority of critics had already moved to a rather emphatic rejection.

Perhaps mood stereotypes predominate, but at least the conventional image of the thirties, viewed almost always against the contrasting backdrop of the twenties, is that of at least an intellectual community overburdened with moral seriousness, deeply traditional in its search for roots and meaning, aggressively nationalistic in its revived love affair with America, and almost unrelieved in its preoccupation with class relationships and with economic problems. The daring innovations, the deep questioning, the sparkling originality, the luxurious playfulness, and the biting criticism of American institutions and culture, all so typical of the twenties, either disappeared or lost any following. The expatriates came home, joined the fight for a new America, and discovered a lost and inspiring national past, one with more radical content than they had before realized. Intellectuals, like Mencken, who continued their carping criticism, suffered condemnation as dilettantes or cultural saboteurs. Solidarity and unity became the rallying cry for a new, positive outlook. The effect appeared as both a concentration of cultural energy and a seeming narrowing of intellectual possibilities. These stereotypes all have some merit. In total, they best fit certain literary figures, or somewhat more loosely the provincial world of letters that has always centered on New York City. Most people who lived through the thirties, even the majority of academic intellectuals, would find some of the stereotypes highly amusing.

Our more basic beliefs change very slowly, and have often ancient roots. Most Americans did not alter their beliefs about supernature (about their Gods), about nature, or about man in the thirties. And surely an economic depression is not a sufficient catalyst to force such changes; on the contrary, hard times may send men to the most literal experiences of the past—there they might regain steadiness of vision and renewed faith in the future. It makes no real sense to talk about depression philosophy or theology, or a New Deal science or psychology, although one may well talk about philosophy in the thirties, or the role of scientists in the New Deal.

But even to introduce serious scientific or philosophical issues into a text is necessarily to vulgarize ideas that have all their beauty and merit in subtleties and in complexity, or it is merely to list names and catalogue movements. At the level of public policy, serious inquiry in the physical sciences became important only in World War II, and from then on has received major federal subsidies. Serious philosophical inquiry remained in the academies not only in the thirties, but ever since.

Both the physical sciences and philosophy gained immense resources in the mid-thirties as exiles from the fascist countries of Europe flocked to this country (Einstein is only the best-remembered). By World War II the United States had the largest collection of top-ranked physicists and chemists ever assembled in one country. Unfortunately, less eminent Europeans could not override our immigration laws, and neither the president nor Congress had enough solicitude for European Jews to press for wider quotas. By 1941, Hitler's ovens began to consume Jews who earlier tried, without success, to gain refuge in America.

The concerns of the depression, and the goals of New Deal welfare programs, both gave added importance to the social sciences, particularly economics and sociology. Many of the ablest economists served directly or indirectly in the New Deal, while all the major competing theories swirled through the endless debates. The prevalent concern for "social problems," even the popularity of the vague word "social" in all manner of contexts, suggested the importance of sociology. Yet, no outstanding new social theories characterized the thirties. Instead, in both academies and in government, sociologists of various types developed new techniques of data collection and interpretation and carried out diverse studies on social mobility, urban change, racial attitudes, patterns of poverty, and regional differences.

The same concerns affected historians. Economic determinants and class conflict received more historical attention than before or since. Charles Beard, who pushed this theme to the fore in the twenties, now had numerous disciples. The first major historian of American thought, Vernon L. Parrington, ended his career and his masterpiece, *Main Currents in American Thought*, much as he began it—with a vast indictment of economic privilege and a glorification of a type of Jeffersonian "democracy." As more and more historians viewed our past, Jefferson and Jackson, populists and socialists, emerged as heroes; Hamilton and Hoover, bankers and businessmen, as villains. A popular historian, Matthew Josephson, apotheosized this theme in his dramatic attacks on *The Robber Barons* and *The Politicos*. Walter P. Webb, reviving and extending an environmentalist and frontier hypothesis first developed at the turn of the century by William Graham Sumner and Frederick Jackson Turner, used it as an effective weapon to indict the imperial aggression of eastern capital against the South and the West.

Religion

Unlike most academic thinking, religious thought has a direct, easily distinguishable institutional expression. At this level the depression surely had visible effects, although it is still impossible to determine exactly what they were. Organized religion, both Christian and Jewish, seemed to decline slightly in the thirties; but always unreliable membership and attendance figures reflected in part economic incapacity rather than doctrinal disillusionment. Orthodox Protestants kept intact their belief in the inerrancy of Scripture, the certainty of ultimate judgment, and in salvation only through a special faith in Christ. More militant fundamentalists remained as at least minorities in most Protestant denominations, often continued to splinter off into smaller sects, and made up a majority in areas of the white South, and probably a majority of blacks nationally. They successfully proselytized new members, and probably grew more rapidly in the thirties than any other wing of Protestantism. At least by impressionistic evidence, orthodox and often enthusiastically evangelical (an emphasis on the quality of feeling in religion as well as on energetic efforts at proselytizing) groups received new, almost escapist fervor from depression suffering. Itinerant ministers also seemed to multiply; loud and enthusiastic preaching offered a decent living.

Middle class urban or suburban congregations moved toward a type of flaccid ecumenism in the thirties. They deemphasized clear and distinguishing dogmas and affirmed a broad consensus of vague religious generalities, or a type of public religiosity founded on humane impulse or theological cliches. Cooperative community churches, without theological distinction, grew rapidly. Anti-Catholic feeling among Protestants seemed to lessen before a nondiscriminating toleration. Closely related, the major Protestant denominations, loosely joined in a Federal Council of Churches, espoused a revived social gospel, largely stimulated by the suffering and obvious injustices of the depression. Both the Federal Council and social action wings of most denominations urged the churches to seek significant social change, and cast a hearty "amen" for New Deal relief and welfare measures. A few ministers, organized in small interdenominational action groups, tried to get more radical reforms, committed themselves to pacifism, to forms of socialism, and even to revolution. Many Reform Jewish rabbis, and some Catholic priests, backed the social action if not the ecumenism.

The lack of theological or psychological depth in so much "liberal" Protestantism, and its pervasively uncritical and often overly optimistic acceptance of American institutions (even when refurbished by a New Deal), led in the thirties to a growing reaction, best symbolized by Reinhold Niebuhr, a former parish minister in Detroit and then a professor at Union Theological Seminary in New York City. Niebuhr came to a harshly realistic social theory, in part influenced by Marxist thought, and to a revived and penetrating theological orthodoxy. Rejecting any easy optimism, seeing the human and historical impediments to utopia or to anything but piecemeal reform, he found new inspiration in the sublime biblical idea of grace and in the Christian expectation of heaven as a form of redeeming experience, not a perfected social order. By his emphasis upon man's sinfulness, or his separation or alienation from God or reality, and thus on his need for grace, and in his pessimistic estimates of the possible returns from either reason or science, he helped revive the basic themes of early Protestantism. Reinforced by more systematic European theologians (Karl Barth and Paul Tillich), this new orthodoxy captured most theological seminaries by the forties, and soon sparked a revival of serious dogma and theology in the churches. It placed social action in a new context, and often armed it with more realistic and even radical tools of criticism. But in the orthodox perspective, social action is a necessary outcome of religion, not its essence. The goal of religion remains human redemption, more an esthetic than a political objective.

Most of the stereotypes of American life in the thirties, even as in the twenties, draw inspiration from literature. The epic has almost parabolic dimensions. The exiles came home from Paris. They took up their peculiar weapons and set about creating, not just novels and poems, but that grandest work of art, a new society. And in the early thirties many must have felt the truth of the parable. For those who had condemned a consumer and business culture, and had rather self-consciously nourished their own alienation, the depression came as a cleansing and deserved purge of "capitalism," now in focus as the most un-American of institutions. The depression destroyed the old and left the new to be built. Writers turned from psychological probes, to social protest, to a new version of muckraking, even to the revolution. These "leftist" or "radical" writers included such critics as Alfred Kazin, Edmund Wilson, Michael Gold, Granville Hicks, and Malcolm Cowley; the novelists John Dos Passos, James T. Farrell, Jack Conroy, John O'Hara, and Erskine Caldwell; the poets Stephen Vincent Benét, Archibald MacLeish, Edna St. Vincent Millay, even Carl Sandburg. But the enduring literary symbol of the decade became John Steinbeck's epic of the Okies, *Grapes of Wrath*, and playwright Clifford Odets's radical play about trade unionism, *Waiting for Lefty*.

To list only the "radical" writers, or those devoted to an overwhelming transformation of America, is to capitulate too much to a stereotyped mood, and in no sense amounts to a survey of the diversity, or an estimate of the quality, of literature produced in the thirties. In literary criticism, the greatest long-range impact came not from socially conscious writers for the *New Masses* or the *Partisan Review* but from a group of critics who tried to isolate purely esthetic criteria (the "new criticism" of Allen Tate, John Crowe Ransom, Kenneth Burke, or even an earlier T. S. Eliot), and who often came out of the southern agrarian movement, whose social creed, albeit radical enough in implication, harkened back to a nation of yeoman farmers and excluded all forms of collectivism. Important novelists included a much diminished Sinclair Lewis and F. Scott Fitzgerald; an eccentric and brilliant William Faulkner, who narrated the declining fortunes of an always depressed Mississippi, and who reached a career peak in the thirties without fullest recognition; an exuberant, irrepressible, romantic Thomas Wolfe; the superb stylist Ernest Hemingway, still fixed on wartime themes of disillusion and heroism; and a triumvirate of excellent women writers: Ellen Glasgow, Willa Cather, and Edith Wharton. It is not easy to forget that the most popular novel of the decade was a romantic and cruelly stereotyped Civil War epic, Margaret Mitchell's *Gone With the Wind*. Finally, the less polemical plays of Robert E. Sherwood and Maxwell Anderson proved more enduring if not

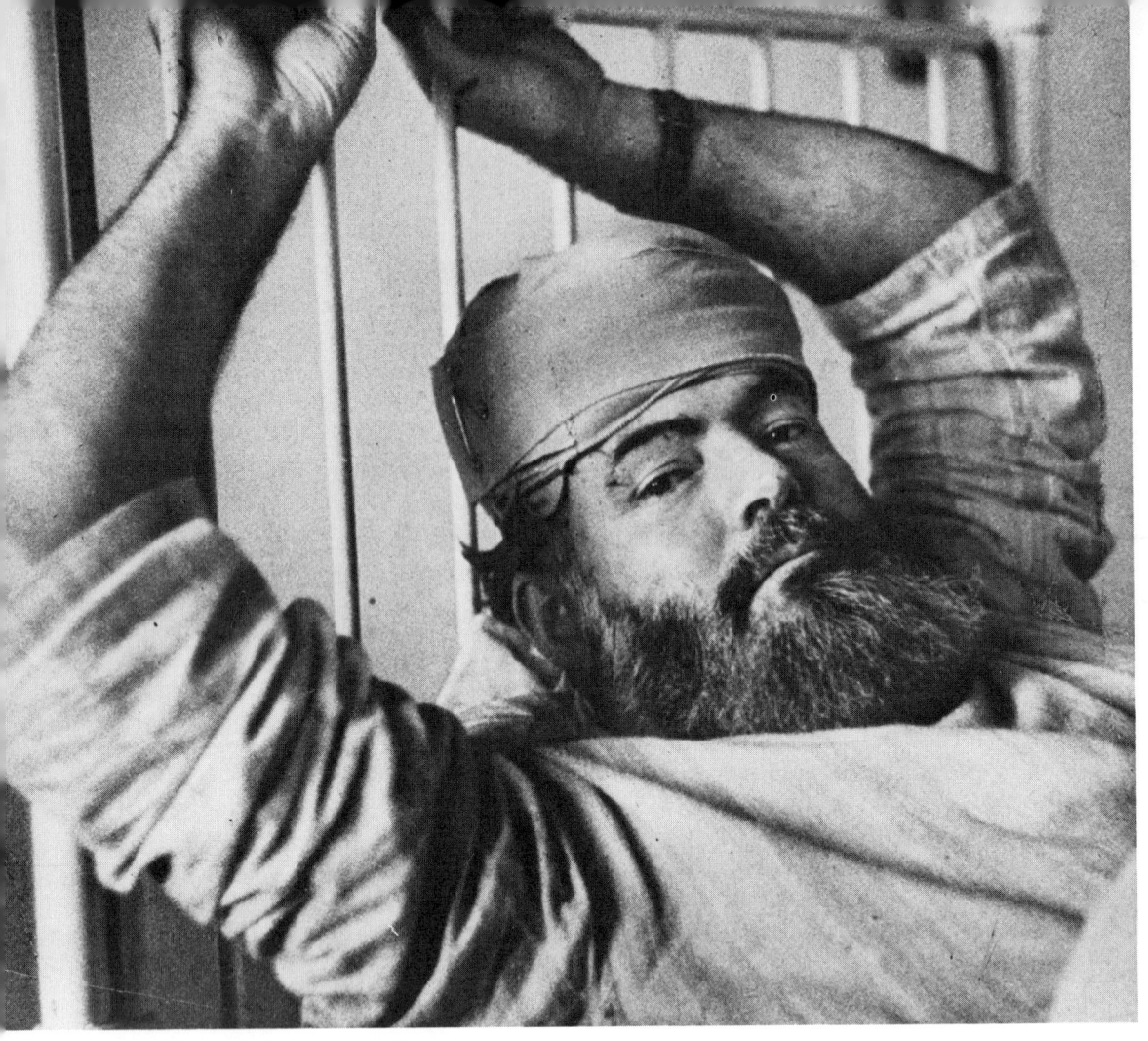

more topical than those of Odets. Unfortunately, such a listing of names can only stir memories or reawaken an appreciation based on past reading.

The plastic arts, although much less influential in America than literature, reveal some of the same themes. A wide group of painters and sculptors rediscovered America, and tried to fashion a socially conscious realism. Many young painters, often penniless in the dearth of fashionable private patrons, resolved finally to banish artificial European influences, develop an authentic national art, abolish the fashionable and elitist beauty parlor art condemned by John Dewey, and finally bring beauty to the people, to merge art and life, or to dedicate their lower art forms to the higher forms of beauty represented by a just and harmonious social order. This strategy could mean an often-demanding change in form, from abstract simplicity to pictorial realism, and also in subject matter, from the penetrating and often very personal psychological insights of

Ernest Hemingway recuperating from injuries suffered in a plane crash in Africa. In the thirties Hemingway's concern with heroism centered on the Spanish Civil War. *Magnum*

earlier expressionism to the less subtle but honest portraits of Americana. The range and diversity of talent, the subtle array of esthetic theories, simply defy any brief summation. If our enduring image of the thirties contains the vivid indictments of exploitation in Farm Security Administration photographs by a Dorothea Lange or a Ben Shahn or a Walker Evans, or the regional and lovingly nationalistic realism of a Thomas Hart Benton or Steuart Curry, the harsh urban themes of New York's Fourteenth Street School, the often sentimental unearthing of folk arts and traditions, the often insipid American themes impressed on too many post office murals, we also have to recall that it was a formative decade for a Jackson Pollack (he too worked for the WPA) and a Willem de Kooning, neither realists nor regionalists.

In music, the depression helped create some new interest in native composers and in our own musical heritage, but the impact was not the same here as in most other art forms. Even in WPA projects, most compositions were European, and by a strange, perennial reverse snobbery, performing musicians still found European acceptance the best entree to American fame. Even the popular George Gershwin or a more talented Aaron Copland, received little critical acclaim, perhaps because they did not copy European themes or techniques, but instead exploited native American materials, including ethnic and black. The radio, even more than the phonograph, opened a national audience for good music of all types, from the still-heralded National Broadcasting Company Symphony to Nashville's then authentic Grand Old Opry. Jazz, although now identified with the twenties, developed in technique and popularity throughout the thirties, which was also the decade of "swing" and of the great popular bands. Early collectors journeyed to the Ozarks and the Appalachians to record folk music, but even by the end of the thirties neither folk nor country music had attained respectability, and the national debate still raged over the authentic musicality of jazz.

The thirties was a great age for both movies and the radio, in part because of their escape value. From the gangster craze of the early thirties, to the often-absurd humor of Charlie Chaplin or the Marx Brothers, to many variants of social criticism and social uplift, to the popularity of G-men and United States marshals in the mid-thirties, to *Gone With the Wind*, the greatest spectacular of them all, the movies reflected many of the popular moods of the decade: impotence in the face of vast, impersonal events, the need for escape, a growing awareness of social ills, and the widespread placing of hope and trust in the benevolent and powerful federal government, best exemplified by a hero of the decade, J. Edgar Hoover, and by his FBI. Swamped by the views of scriptwriters, many movies by the mid-thirties reflected subtle or overt political themes, some much too radical in intent to fit the mild programs of the New Deal, but many representing good propaganda for relief and welfare. The radio included everything—news, pop music, a steady diet of midafternoon soap operas for women (Helen Trent, Ma Perkins), late afternoon cereal operas for kids (Jack Armstrong, the All-American Boy), and for the whole family in the evening the inescapable "Lum N' Abner" and "Amos N' Andy." Weekly there were the great comedians (Fred Allen, Jack Benny), the bands, amateur hours, the Saturday afternoon opera, sports, and even experiments in good radio drama. The radio enormously influenced national tastes, provided wide news coverage, and gave to Roosevelt an effective forum for his wooing of public support for varied New Deal programs.

The unflagging cheerfulness of child movie princess Shirley Temple distracted depression audiences from their economic troubles. Here she is with FBI director J. Edgar Hoover (1895–1972) during a visit to Washington. *Wide World Photos*

Here a Communist is hustled away by police at a New York City demonstration protesting widespread unemployment in 1930. The word "Communist" symbolized a wide variety of social and intellectual protest during the depression. Communism referred both to a fashionable intellectual stance and to a political party, both to an undefined sense of injustice and a rigorous form of Marxism. *Associated Press Photo*

The "Left"

The pervasive economic themes that characterized so much of the thirties, infused so much of the scholarship, pervaded so many of the movies and radio scripts, lurked in so many proletarian paintings, also flavored the intellectual life of the decade. And the number of writers, at least, who preached Marxist theories and joined the Communist party, further contributed to the "radical" or "leftist" image of the thirties. Those "radicals" with access to the media had some impact on popular opinion and probably helped reduce the resistance to types of social change. In this way, they offered political solace to the Roosevelt administration. And by the very extremes of their aspirations, by their early alienation from the New Deal and its mild alphabetical remedies, they also dramatized the essential moderation, the conventional and traditional aspects of the New Deal, and thus helped disarm criticism from other directions.

If one gives specific content to the word "left" (such as a clear commitment to the interests of the working class, hatred of corporate capitalism, and a desire for some type of cooperative commonwealth), then the range of leftist opinion in the thirties almost defies definition. The American Socialist party, only vaguely Marxist in origins, and with more of a practical than an ideological appeal, had a resurgence in the early thirties. Its candidate, Norman Thomas, won 882,000 votes in 1932. In a general sense, such Marxist themes as class conflict and economic determinism pervaded a large share of the creative thought of the decade. But even by then the exegesis on Marx rivaled that on the Bible, and made impossible any test of orthodoxy.

The word "communism" also had broad appeal, but varied nuances of meaning. Among writers in New York City and some students on eastern campuses, being a communist became at least an obligatory fad, a means to social or intellectual acceptance. The label symbolized a more egalitarian economic system, stood for idealistic political goals, and linked self-conscious, middle class intellectuals to the heroes of the labor movement, to romanticized IWW martyrs and revolutionary leaders around the world. It also reflected a broad and friendly interest in the Soviet Union. Was that "experiment" a success? Glowing, uncritical praise mingled with a flood of disturbing reports of Stalinist suppression and purges. Some wanted desperately to believe in its success, in a new way for the world. If one believed in the Soviet way, and wanted somehow to emulate it in America, then he could proudly claim to be a communist, even as other Americans, some highly placed, found somewhat different reasons to applaud Mussolini's experiment in corporatism in Italy.

Finally, there was the American Communist party, alive, legal, active, with ill-supported candidates in each national election (only 103,000 votes in 1932; 80,000 in 1936) and organized party groups in at least the major cities and in most major labor unions, where it found its most enduring constituency. Few academic intellectuals, even including avowed Marxists, ever joined the party, but students, labor organizers, and a quite long list of prominent writers and performers did join, at least for a few years in the early or mid-thirties. The postwar Red Scare now lay in the distant past, the Roosevelt administration recognized the Soviet Union, Congress had other problems to absorb its full attention, and in the thirties narrow ideological distinctions lost their importance in politics as well as in religion. Small Communist party cells even existed, with at least official sufferance, in New Deal agencies. But the party proved a poor vehicle for radical idealism. It lacked able intellectual leadership and remained subservient to Soviet domination, serving as a source of petty Soviet espionage and propaganda. It easily changed policies, moving from a rigorous condemnation of mild reform in the early thirties to a "popular front" alliance with "liberal" parties in the mid-thirties, only to have to backtread desperately after the Nazi-Soviet Pact of 1939. The most vital forms of dissent remained outside the party.

The expectation of early recovery proved the most enticing and elusive mirage of the thirties. As the early mood of crisis and desperation passed, the Roosevelt administration confronted renewed bitterness and incipient violence, a resurgence of despair. To satisfy many competing interest groups, it had to sacrifice such nationalistic and consensual agencies as the NRA. In 1933 Roosevelt exploited a mood of crisis and a widespread willingness to trust in some form of salvation. The sense of impending catastrophe had briefly bound people together, heightened their loyalties to old and familiar institutions, and created a willingness to join in large, national efforts. By 1935 the depression was more like a chronic disease, susceptible to efforts to alleviate some of its worst symptoms yet still resistant to any final cure.

In conformity with the recently approved Twentieth Amendment, a new, more Democratic Congress assembled in Washington, not in March but in early January of 1935. In a single session it approved more significant legislation than any former Congress in our history, and in so doing reoriented the economic program of the New Deal. It initiated a virtual revolution in labor union policy, began an unprecedented relief program, and initiated a welfare state. Much more than in 1933–34, Congress assumed a major role in legislative innovation, helping to shape administrative policies as often as it dutifully followed Roosevelt's lead.

The Expanded Relief Program

By 1935, an improving but still depressed economy required additional federal relief expenditures and invited a new intensity in political conflict. For direct relief, the new Congress appropriated the largest single sum in its history ($4,880 million). By the budgetary standards of the thirties (total federal expenditures for 1936 amounted to only $8,493 million), this was an enormous amount and seemed to portend a major redistribution of income by government fiat. It also constituted a tremendous stimulus to economic recovery, since an increased governmental debt, rather than significantly increased taxes, immediately funded the appropriation (the deficit for the year almost equaled this single appropriation and made up more than half the total budget). It also reflected a sober acceptance even by Roosevelt that full recovery lay far in the future.

A More Partisan Deal

Roosevelt could use the relief funds largely as he saw fit. He used a portion to fund the Resettlement Administration; another to revitalize the Public Works Administration. But the largest single grant went into a reorganized relief agency, the Works Progress Administration (WPA), the successor of the FERA. In the dark days of 1933 the hurriedly organized FERA had to work through the states, and by sheer necessity used much of its funds for direct subsistence grants ("the dole"). But increasingly the state relief administrators had tried to develop work programs, and during the winter of 1933–34 the politically vulnerable Civil Works Administration set a precedent for a huge national work force. Demand for such national work programs went back at least to Coxey's Army and the depression of the 1890's. As a solely work relief effort, the WPA, however, did not provide direct relief funds, either leaving this burden unmet or forcing it upon states or municipalities (often generously aided by federal grants from other sources).

The WPA became one of the best-remembered symbols of the thirties, personified now by the pick and shovel. The concept behind the WPA received wide support. Direct governmental doles threatened self-respect. Honest, constructive work could maintain pride and avoid the worst stigma of "being on relief." Moreover, the government funding would be justified by socially useful projects. The WPA employed up to three million people a year until World War II on conservation and public works (roads, bridges, airports, and numerous buildings). Wage rates varied regionally. To the despair of organized labor, they were below those in private industries. Yet, they were high enough to provide a greater degree of economic security than most direct relief grants, which had usually been based on minimal subsistence budgets. Overburdened by unskilled workers, too often forced to proceed without careful and prior planning, and on occasion afflicted by low morale and a slow pacing of work, the WPA represented a terribly inefficient use of labor. Yet efficiency had to take second place to massive employment and the rapid distribution of wages to those in desperate need. From the perspective of WPA administrators, the real problem was never the poor utilization of labor but the lack of enough funds and projects to utilize a larger portion of the unemployed.

A mere recitation of its scope fails to convey the distinctive character of the WPA. The Washington office attracted more than its share of imaginative and highly dedicated men and women. The former social worker, Harry Hopkins, proved an astute director, dedicated to humane goals, yet enough of a politician to bargain effectively for his full share of limited administration funds. Although less marred by overt political scandal than the ephemeral Civil Works Administration, the WPA none-

By 1935 Roosevelt and the Congress realized that large-scale relief programs were desperately needed, and at the same time opposed any type of dole. Thus, they created the WPA. By 1937, when this photo of protesting WPA workers was taken, massive work relief was a normal part of American life. *United Press International*

theless clearly carried an unstated message—"This is a gift of the New Deal." However scrupulous in hiring policies, the WPA often exuded a bit of the flavor of its more idealistic administrators—a proletarian bias, contempt for business or for the shibboleths of "capitalism," and an emphasis upon equally vague countersymbols, such as cooperation, community, and democracy. Few agencies invited more caricatures or overt contempt. Despite the "honest" work, the WPA always carried some of the stigma of relief and induced resentment from those who managed to find employment and make it, often marginally, on their own, or from small employers who felt that the WPA, despite its wage scales, undercut their supply of compliant laborers.

The most distinctive and revealing WPA programs aided artists and professionals, although these consumed only a small fraction of the expended funds. The Civil Works Administration allocated over a million dollars for an art acquisition program in the Public Buildings Administration of the Treasury Department, a program that continued under new funds long after the demise of the CWA. As chairman of an advisory committee, Edward Bruce, both a corporation lawyer and a painter, became the real director of this Public Works of Art Project, carefully using his limited funds to commission murals, canvases, and other art works for newly completed public buildings, including many post offices. Although the commissions had to be low, this early effort was no relief project. It permitted competitive demonstration of skills and allowed a discriminating selection of artists. By the conditions of selection and employment in the Treasury Department, the content of murals and of other works could be controlled. Bruce screened out the least competent, but a desire for optimistic and inspiring subjects helped insure mild and noncontroversial productions. In 1935, the WPA adopted this project and made available through the Treasury Department funds for virtually unscreened artists drawn directly from relief rolls and paid only relief wages.

The WPA, on its own, attempted a much more daring form of patronage. It used an original grant of $27 million to establish work projects for four broad categories of artists: Federal Theatre, Music, Writers', and Arts Projects. Each project broadly defined its categories. For example, the Arts Project included not only such fashionable crafts as painting and sculpture, but practically the whole gamut of plastic skills. In all the programs, neglected national achievements and our own enormous folk art received long-due recognition. But the Arts Project is now best remembered for its aid to a coterie of young painters who would later achieve international fame. Most would then drop some of the socially conscious, politically involved themes that so often characterized depression painting. Since the Four Projects could not be narrowly discriminating in selecting clients, they subsidized a great deal of junk.

The Writers' Project encompassed not only novelists and poets but also journalists and historians. A Local Records Division left an enduring legacy of county-level research materials for later historians. The Music and Theatre Projects subsidized not only writers and composers but full-fledged performing companies. The Theatre Project, daring in its stage experiments or in its political content, attracted vehement congressional criticism, an almost sure gauge of considerable intellectual and esthetic achievement. Although somewhat centered on New York City, where a large part of their clientele lived, the two performing projects tried to bring good music and live theater to all sections of the country. In fact, the WPA temporarily made all the fine arts the property of millions of people. Such major subsidies for the fine arts raised a still widely debated question: Does governmental support for creative endeavors inevitably influence subject and style, and even subtly bend art to the service of a beneficent state, and thus to the established or prevailing political order?

For young people, the WPA supported a subsidiary National Youth Administration (NYA), under the direction of Hopkins's assistant, Aubrey Williams. The NYA primarily supported high school and college students, paying them for part-time campus work (akin to later work-study jobs) to keep them in school and off the job market. Summer work camps, at least to a limited extent, allowed the NYA to imitate European youth movements and possibly permitted some degree of political education.

The total relief program was temporary, a phenomenon only of the thirties. In the forties, federal defense and war purchases created enough new governmental and industrial jobs for everyone, allowing the WPA to wither and die. The cultural subsidies also ended. After World War II defense spending and major public subsidies for highways and education helped maintain a high level of employment without recourse to work relief programs.

Business and the Sources of Class Conflict

By the huge relief appropriations of 1935 and by supplemental appropriations in succeeding years, the New Deal shifted its tactics for overcoming the depression. In the first two years, behind at least the rhetoric of planning, Roosevelt had used pricing and monetary tactics, neither requiring extensive governmental funding. Now, acting in behalf of sheer need, and counter to his own economic commitments, he in effect shifted the greatest effective emphasis to such fiscal weapons as spending, taxing, and borrowing. These policies, new and often misunderstood in their political implications, led to increased apprehension on the part of business leaders.

By 1935, businessmen were not alone in their apprehension or growing anger. Many interest groups, some with long-term grievances—the aged, the poor, the ill, and organized labor—developed new, often unrealistic and frustrating expectations. In rhetoric, and to an extent even in programs, the New Deal would try to meet their demands. But in doing so, it would further alienate a large share of the business community, including not only executives in large manufacturing, commercial and banking firms but often also owners and operators of small plants and merchandising firms.

The increasing alienation of at least some well-placed businessmen from Roosevelt and from New Deal programs, and the president's increasing distrust of the organized business community, represented the major source of political conflict in the thirties. It lent to later New Deal politics a distinct class bias. Despite the NRA, a lasting alliance of large business enterprise and the Roosevelt administration seemed unlikely even in 1933. Most businessmen had long been Republican. Most sought the restoration of traditional economic policies, and normally resisted increased governmental economic roles, from mild regulation, increased governmental expenditures and taxes or deliberate inflation, to such major threats as direct governmental planning or ownership. Much early New Deal legislation (TVA, SEC) stimulated excessive fears, as did the mild New Deal flirtation with organized labor. With the toughening of NRA supervision of codes, and more demands from both consumers and labor, businessmen even seemed to be losing their only New Deal benefice. By August 1934, large businessmen joined with many dissenting Democrats in the bitterly anti-New Deal American Liberty League, to the embarrassment and anger of Roosevelt. Recrimination increased throughout 1935, and climaxed in the presidential election of 1936 and the Court fight of 1937.

On his side, Roosevelt had and retained the friendship of several corporate executives, easily charmed them in social contexts, and always shared many of their assumptions about political economy. As he frequently lamented, he never intended any radical changes in the American economy and could scarcely understand or forgive so strenuous an opposition to him and the New Deal by those who really profited most from its policies. But even if he did not deserve businessmen's scorn, by the summer of 1935 he began to use it very effectively. Thoroughly disillusioned with corporate leaders and what he interpreted as their lack of public spirit, pushed by those who wanted what he perceived to be much too radical measures, he added an increasing class emphasis to his speeches. He lambasted the anti-New Deal interests, the powerful monopolistic royalists who operated the large corporations for their own private benefit, and who now became the devils or conspirators in a New Deal morality play. Roosevelt directed his appeal to that vaguest of entities, the "people," common, hard working, loyal Americans. This class rhetoric won more enthusiastic support from labor and from the older warriors against privilege and against monopoly, particularly Wilsonian Democrats and insurgent Republicans.

The growing business-administration split worsened during three critical legislative battles of 1935—over an administration-supported Public Utilities Holding Company Act, a National Labor Relations Act conceived entirely in the Congress, and a new tax bill that seemed to threaten large wealth. The Holding Company Act remained before Congress from February to late August and attracted the most lobbying heretofore devoted to a single bill. The background was complex. Private companies produced and distributed most of the nation's electricity, usually under some type of public franchise and regulation. Since such utilities were monopolies, their prices were not competitive. The electrical utilities, with large capital investments and continuously refunded debts, had many of the attributes of public agencies. Particularly in the twenties, large holding companies acquired local electrical companies, forming them into large interstate systems. Such consolidation fostered needed coordination in production and distribution but invited financial chicanery. A pre-New Deal Federal Trade Commission investigation of holding companies revealed a complicated but frightening situation, and helped sway public opinion against the larger companies. Instead of operating companies united by one primary holding company, the FTC found several pyramided systems, with several levels of ownership, exaggerated capitalization, multilayered profit-taking, and scandalously inflated prices for individual consumers.

Roosevelt, drawing on brilliant new legal advisers largely furnished him by Felix Frankfurter and the Harvard Law School, sponsored a bill not only to end the abuses but to end many holding companies. The original bill authorized the Federal Power Commission to integrate operating companies into regional systems, and the Securities and Exchange Commission to simplify and rationalize holding companies, even to the point of abolishing any that could not prove their usefulness (the "death sentence"). This bill followed in the wake of several direct confrontations between public and private power advocates in the conflict between the Tennessee Valley Authority and perhaps the most economically justifiable of the holding companies, Commonwealth and Southern, headed by Wendell Willkie, probably the ablest and most honest of the utility leaders. The persuasive testimony of Willkie and others turned the holding company issue into a symbol of governmental opposition to free enterprise and private business. The bill eventually passed Congress with only a slightly weakened "death sentence" and left a legacy of bitterness among other corporate executives who now expected other New Deal intrusions.

In reality, neither Roosevelt nor many of his officials intended any crusade against free enterprise, whatever symbolic meanings the term had. Roosevelt had long backed either rigorous public regulation or public ownership of utilities, neither an unusual nor a radical position. He never supported complete government ownership and control of either electrical production or distribution, and restrained more militant public power advocates who did. He long espoused an all-too-pat idea—that limited government ownership would provide a yardstick on costs and prices needed for effective public regulation. In 1935 he used Reconstruction Finance Corporation funds and his own executive authority to create a Rural Electrification Administration. Always interested in the welfare of farmers, he noted that only 10 percent then had electricity. Few private companies believed it economically feasible to construct power lines very far into rural areas. In its first phase, the REA could loan funds to private companies. Few companies responded to this opportunity, reinforcing Roosevelt's belief that they lacked public dedication. He happily greeted congressional action in 1936 that gave the REA permanent status. Its funds, in most cases, would go to local electrical cooperatives. Only in later years, when rural markets proved profitable, would many of these come into direct competition with privately-owned companies. The REA succeeded on two counts—it brought electricity even to remote areas, and in most cases at lower rates than even city-dwellers paid to private utility companies.

Roosevelt's efforts to control utilities did not presage any broad attack on either private ownership or management. It did launch a growing administration battle against concentrated economic power and monopolistic practices. This was of course an old battle, and one sure to win broad support in Congress and out. Who could be for monopoly or for privileged industrial giants? To attack monopolistic business was to vindicate free enterprise, or the conditions necessary for it. Despite the NRA, Roosevelt now committed himself to a quite conventional, competitive, but more responsible private system, with widespread economic opportunity. For small, vulnerable producers, like farmers or small miners, he would still support enough direct governmental supervision to preserve fair rules and insure adequate returns. But with the end of the NRA, Roosevelt turned to more detailed regulation of large corporations (the Federal Trade Commission regained its pre-NRA role, now with appointees distinctively suspicious of business), and, in cases of overt monopoly or abuse, to an older trust-busting. The antitrust division of the Justice Department slowly came back to life, and after 1938, under the able and articulate Thurman Arnold, pushed its investigation and prosecution to an unprecedented level. The very emphasis on regulation, the insistence on fair rules and public responsibility, although galling to many corporations, still marked a mild policy in comparison to the worst business fears—increased governmental ownership or direct controls.

The New Deal and Organized Labor

Even as the Roosevelt administration adopted a more overtly antibusiness rhetoric, and favorably moved toward stricter albeit indirect regulation, it also responded to the pressures of organized labor. This seemed a final insult to business, but the prounion policy had immense political benefits for the Democratic party. And, in the long run, it surely aided some financially secure corporations for it helped institutionalize a near-uniform, formalized bargaining relationship in most large industries. As always, a legal order, however antagonistic the bargaining process, provides security. Further, despite all the fears to the contrary, powerful, established unions contributed to industrial peace, not strife; order, not disruption.

A new labor policy evolved from the NRA. Senator Robert F. Wagner of New York, one of the most successful legislators of the decade, had participated in the complex bargaining that went into the National Industrial Recovery Act. He approved the idea of industrial codes, but fought tenaciously for Section 7(a). As a result of his advocacy for organized labor, he became chairman of the courtlike National Labor Board within the NRA. During the first year he became an effective critic, if not of the NRA idea, at least of its administrative favoritism toward business. Seeking both wage gains and collective bargaining rights, he served as a virtual ombudsman for aggrieved labor interests. From often frustrating experience on the National Labor Board, he came to believe in the rights of workers to organize and to select their bargaining unit by secret elections. In March 1934 he wrote and introduced a Labor Disputes Act. This, the forerunner of the National Labor Relations Act of 1935, suffered from administrative reluctance and such crippling amendments that it failed to pass.

Without a glimmer of White House support, Wagner introduced a National Labor Relations Act in February 1935. It paralleled the Utility Holding Company Act, and elicited only a bit less lobbying opposition from organized business groups, particularly the National Association of Manufacturers and the U.S. Chamber of Commerce. It received intense support from the American Federation of Labor. Although Roosevelt at first refused any support, he never tried to block the bill in the Senate, where it passed in May by an overwhelming and surprising 63–12 vote. Since it now seemed sure to pass in the House, Roosevelt had to make a crucial decision. He still supported the NRA principle and had never had any close contacts with or natural sympathies for labor unions. His natural approach to labor had been in the direction of welfare policies—wage, hour, and insurance provisions—rather than in revitalized, competitive unions, which invited what he assumed would be increased labor conflict. But his growing anger at business, a keen appreciation of future political harvests, and finally the need for a new labor policy after the Supreme Court invalidated the NIRA in late May, all propelled him into open and even enthusiastic support. The bill passed the House without a roll-call in late June, a mark of acceptance that completely belied its importance or controversial content.

The National Labor Relations Act, or Wagner Act, gave employees in interstate industries an ironclad right to organize independent unions, and to bargain collectively with management through representatives of their own choosing. Unlike all past legislation in behalf of union rights, this one had no loopholes. The act created a new National Labor Relations Board (NLRB) with full authority to implement its provisions. The board had the authority to prevent unfair practices by management, to certify the bargaining agent for labor, and, if requested, to conduct elections to determine that agent. The act defined several unfair practices—refusing to bargain collectively with elected union representatives, interfering with an employee's right to organize, dominating or subsidizing a union (a company union), discriminating against union members in hiring or tenure or against any laborer for filing charges under the act. The board could investigate charges of unfair practices, hold hearings, subpoena witnesses, and force compliance through federal courts. Employers could appeal all decisions to higher courts; they received no other concessions.

In effect the Wagner Act equalized, or attempted to equalize, the bargaining strength of management and organized labor. The Wagner Act also gave indispensable rights to working men. By redressing the balance of power in industry, it would finally allow fair competitive bargaining, a position long advocated by most unions. The NRA labor codes, with the status of law, had amounted to government supervised contracts; their enforcement anticipated something close to governmental arbitration. The Wagner Act avoided such direct government interference and thus backed away from detailed governmental management of the economy. Instead, the government at most determined the conditions and rules for private negotiations.

A resurgence of union activity had preceded the Wagner Act, but the act helped insure final union victories in such major industries as steel, rubber, and automobiles. In part abetted by the NIRA, John L. Lewis of the United Mine Workers began massive organizing drives in 1933. He sought industrywide unions, made up of all employees, skilled and unskilled, and powerful enough to secure significant benefits for all workers. Such industrywide unions challenged the ancient ideal of the American Federation of Labor—strong and usually skilled trade or craft unions, at best only joined on a factory or industry level by loose federation. But the emerging jurisdictional battles between trade and industry unionism surely intensified the organizational efforts on both sides. In the past, the American Federation of Labor had conspicuously failed to organize basic industries dominated by large numbers of unskilled workers. Lewis and other advocates of industrial unionism first formed a recalcitrant committee within the AFL, but upon expulsion in 1936 became the independent Congress of Industrial Organizations (CIO), by far the most dynamic of two large, competing union organizations. The CIO developed new organizational tactics, embraced a larger, more direct political role, and attracted wide support and effective talent from such organizations as the American Communist party.

The organized drive by unions met powerful opposition from management. As early as 1935 sporadic labor outbursts punctuated the debates over the Wagner Act, which had appealed to some as a means of ending violence. The climax came in 1936 and in 1937. A series of 1936 sit-down strikes (the worker occupied the factory and refused to work or to leave) made national headlines, and frightened businessmen even the more by a failure of governmental action or condemnation.

Meanwhile, the new National Labor Relations Board received hundreds of charges of unfair practices, charges investigated and, after favorable Supreme Court rulings in April of 1937, usually upheld. In the climactic spring of 1937, the two greatest symbols of successful union opposition, United States Steel and General Motors, granted recognition. By 1938, almost all major corporations (Ford held out until 1940) had either recognized unions or held elections (a few prosperous and traditionally generous corporations retained enough employee loyalty to avoid union organization). In more critical holdouts (such as the other main steel companies) National Labor Relations Board findings favorable to unions often aided the militant labor organizers. By 1939, the unions claimed over 9 million members, a three-fold increase from 1933. Although still representing a minority of workers, the unions now dominated the most basic nationwide industries.

The rapid reversal of traditional governmental policies toward unions paralleled an equally sharp shift in public sympathies. Even extreme new

tactics, such as sit-down strikes, enlisted more sympathy than condemnation. Businessmen felt betrayed by it all. They suffered through NLRB investigations, felt persecuted by decisions rendered by prounion bureaucrats, and challenged the whole structure of administrative justice that seemed abuilding in Washington. In 1938, Senator Robert M. La Follette, Jr., led a congressional committee investigation of civil liberties violations which, in fact, largely exposed widespread antiunion activities throughout the country. The volume of damning evidence did not conceal a strong

Although at first Roosevelt rarely responded to the requests of labor unions, by 1935 he accepted the NLRA. In this picture deputies fire on strikers in the Chalfont Seamless Tube Company Strike (1933). *Library of Congress*

prounion, antibusiness bias on the part of most committee members, and the frequent hearings, the badgering of witnesses, often with broad public exposure, all seemed to businessmen an unfair governmental technique for punishment without fair trial or due process.

The many pronged New Deal attack on corporate bigness and on business prerogatives helped win an enduring constituency for the Democratic party, particularly on the part of organized workers. But at a high cost. The political clash impeded economic recovery. Alienated and embittered businessmen still managed the private sector of the economy (or almost the entire productive plant). With economic planning dead by 1935, and "concert of interests" already becoming an archaic expression, there seemed no prospect of enough increased governmental controls to force higher levels of private production. The political battles had a demoralizing effect on corporate managers, who, out of fear or uncertainty, chose to postpone plant expansion and to defer productive increases. In retrospect, much of the battle was futile, more sound than substance. But

Robert M. La Follette, Jr. (1895–1953) used radio to great effect in his congressional investigations of antiunion activities. One effect of the investigation was to exacerbate antagonism between government and business. *Library of Congress*

the participants certainly took it seriously. And, at the very least, it helped shape much of American political behavior for the next thirty years. To balance the escalating rhetoric, the New Deal had to do more in the public sector to obtain needed increases in economic activity than it would have needed had Roosevelt retained some degree of rapport or even effective communication with the majority of business leaders. At times he tried. He never really succeeded, and always found political attack personally more appealing and politically more effective.

The class rhetoric of 1935 and 1936 both promised and threatened more than the New Deal could ever attain. Businessmen would never lose as much as they expected, either in power or in wealth. And various aggrieved groups could never receive as much as they often hoped and expected. But the very identification of internal devils, of entrenched privilege and exploitation, did imply a major realignment of both political and economic power. And Roosevelt, and even more emphatically many members of Congress, did want this and even tried, usually with inadequate weapons, to attain it. Roosevelt may have indulged in exaggerated rhetoric, but he intended no deceit when he promised to slay the financial and business dragons and free their victims. The outvoted advocates of national planning believed they had the only sufficient economic tools for such a task and that, short of dominant and coercive governmental power, short of mandated prices, wages, and profits, the private sector could never be reliably bribed or browbeaten into serving humane social ends. But having rejected such a direct, managerial role, the New Deal had to work with other weapons—it could still try to force fairer rules (as had the National Labor Relations Act), and it could extract more of the final economic product for its benevolent purposes. Instead of the central coordinator, the federal government could still become a more effective referee and a more obliging servant.

Tax Policy and Income Redistribution

In June 1935, Roosevelt, with great fanfare and in strong language, proposed what even he believed to be a drastic revision in our tax system. This measure, soon identified as the "soak the rich" or "wealth" tax, seemed calculated as much or more for desired social ends than for revenue. Roosevelt lauded small enterprise and condemned large accumulations of wealth and large concentrations of economic power. Past taxes had not penalized such bigness. By convincing statistics, Internal Revenue officials showed the increasing tax burden on the poor and on consumers, a matter of injustice as well as lost purchasing power. Roosevelt made this tax proposal his clinching weapon in his emerging battle against economic giants. Yet, the actual proposals scarcely seemed adequate to the task. He wanted a higher graduation on incomes in excess of $50,000, increased inheritance and gift taxes, a corporate income tax graduated according to the size of the business, and a tax on intercorporate dividends in order to weaken holding companies. The bill unleashed a violent debate both in Congress and out. His sharp attack on concentrated business enterprise seemed pleasing to many older Progressives and also to a coterie of influential new advisers, who slowly replaced the early brains trust. Vaguely labeled as neo-Brandeisian, these included Felix Frankfurter, then a Harvard law professor and later a Supreme Court appointee, and two of his students, Thomas (Tommy the Cork) Corcoran and Benjamin Cohen.

Under intense lobbying pressure, Congress reduced the graduation at the higher levels, practically halved the graduation feature on the corporate income taxes, added a small increase in the excess profits tax, retained a small, 10 percent tax on intercorporate dividends, and slightly raised top rates on estate and gift taxes, or a total increase of only $250 million in annual revenues. Since the Social Security Act (see below, pp. 251–53) had just passed, its regressive taxes on workers' income would, when they took effect in 1937, more than outweigh the progressive features of the "wealth tax" (by 1940 Social Security taxes had taken more than $3.5 billion from workers' payrolls). Both taxes retarded recovery by reducing investment and consumption.

By 1935 the idea of income redistribution had gained a fervent national constituency. Huey Long, more energetic and charismatic than Roosevelt, built a political empire in Louisiana and increasingly wooed a national following. By concerted attacks on real or mythical privileges, and by an economically daring promise to make everyone veritably rich by a massive sharing of the wealth, the colorful Long exploited older, popular resentments against Wall Street and millionaires, and fostered a widespread illusion that there was enough cream at the top to sweeten the whole pot if only it could be forcibly mixed. Working out of California,

INCOME DISTRIBUTION IN AMERICA, 1910–1937

Percentage of national income received by highest and lowest deciles of population

Year	Highest		Combined		Lowest	
	Highest 10%	Next 10%	Highest 20%	Lowest 20%	2d lowest 10%	Lowest 10%
1910	33.9	12.3	46.2	8.3	4.9	3.4
1918	34.6	12.9	47.5	6.8	4.4	2.4
1921	38.2	12.8	51.0	5.2	3.2	2.0
1929	39.0	12.3	51.3	4.4	3.6	1.8
1934	33.6	13.1	46.7	5.9	3.8	2.1
1937	34.4	14.1	48.5	3.6	2.6	1.0

Dr. Francis E. Townsend recruited an army of older people in support of a massive federal old age pension program for everyone over sixty ($200 a month with a requirement that it be spent), financed by what amounted to a complicated 2 percent national sales tax. Since the tax could never come close to underwriting the high level of benefits ($200 a month was a considerable sum in the depression), Townsendites eventually settled for variable pension levels to match the actual tax income.

The Townsend Plan was deliberately inflationary. And inflation remained the principal goal of the most effective, and in many ways the most enigmatic, of the popular agitators—Father Charles E. Coughlin, a Catholic priest who was pastor of The Shrine of the Little Flower, in Royal Oak, Michigan, just outside Detroit. He used his resonant voice and dramatic prose to build an enormous national audience for his weekly "Golden Hour of the Little Flower" radio broadcasts. An avowed enemy of "capitalism," and more particularly of callous individualistic international bankers who controlled it, he avidly backed Roosevelt and the

Huey Long's (1893–1935) initial support for the New Deal was tempered by what he saw as an insufficient effort to share the wealth of society. Here he is shown after his fifteen-hour filibuster in the Senate in support of an amendment to the NRA. *Wide World Photos*

early New Deal. Then, in bitter disillusionment over its failure to follow his more radical prescriptions (nationalized banks and utilities, redistributive taxes, radical monetary inflation, and free silver), he slowly broke with Roosevelt and by mid-1935 came to detest him with the passion reserved only for apostates. In addition, he began to preach a violent anti-Semitism.

By 1936, Coughlin was able to coalesce (he never really unified) the followers of Huey Long (after Long's assassination in 1935 in Baton Rouge, an opportunistic Protestant evangelist, Gerald L. K. Smith, assumed nominal control of his national movement), of a more reluctant and suspicious Townsend, and of a much less flamboyant inflationist, William M. Lemke. Lemke, a North Dakota congressman of Populist and Non-Partisan League fame, was best known by 1935 for his unending attempts to get mortgage relief for farmers (the Frazier-Lemke bills). Under

Like Huey Long, Father Charles Coughlin was convinced that the New Deal had not gone far enough to dethrone "bankers and millionaires." Here an elderly woman in Royal Oak, Michigan, reads Coughlin's newspaper. *Library of Congress*

the banner of a Union party, but one ever more splintered by divergent factions, Lemke hopelessly waged an anticlimactic campaign for the presidency in 1936. He received only 890,000 votes.

But no one would have predicted such a debacle in the spring of 1935. By then variously hued native radicalisms flourished as never before. The movements were too eccentric, too much flavored by colorful leaders, to allow any simple political categorization, such as right or left. But they did meet at one point—they all expressed a deep hatred of massed wealth and privilege, of almost mythologized bankers and millionaires. This class-conscious partisanship, and the often bizarre programs it spawned, represented an extreme pressure on certain congressmen and on the New Deal as a whole.

From this perspective, Roosevelt had to play not a divisive role, but a unifying one. He had to moderate tensions, lower the level of conspiratorial suspicions, and eventually utilize New Deal programs or appealing rhetoric to co-opt all the rage and the undisciplined demands. However much his war on corporate power imperiled recovery, it had a pacifying role politically, and even helped avert programs that would be much more radical—radical both in the economically disruptive extent of property redistribution, and also in political techniques more directly responsive to deliberately massed and controlled opinion and thus less restricted by law, tradition, or respect for minorities. In this sense, the emerging partisanship of 1935 served not as a means for destroying harmony or national consensus, but as a device for preventing much worse polarization.

12

Permanent welfare measures provide some degree of economic security to those who, for various reasons, cannot compete successfully in a private economy. They also mute the incipient hostility, or even revolutionary anger, of those who would otherwise feel cheated by the distribution of rewards in such an economy.

The Roosevelt administration always conceived of, and defended, the relief programs as exceptional emergency measures, unnecessary in ordinary times. But even before the depression, Americans had suffered from unexpected illness, temporary unemployment, insecure old age, dictatorial and inhuman conditions of labor, and terribly inadequate housing. Some of these problems had worsened as increasingly mobile Americans moved to cities and took jobs in factories, often leaving behind traditional and compassionate family and community concern for the weak and the old.

By 1935, simple justice seemed to demand some governmental response to seemingly permanent sources of individual insecurity and suffering. Over the long run New Deal fiscal and monetary policies would provide increased economic security for large producers and for most organized laborers, and at a minimal cost in managerial freedom. Subsidies, price guarantees, direct purchases, and governmental insurance programs would continue to underwrite corporate profits and farm prices. Such welfare at the top suggested compensatory welfare at the bottom. A failure to provide such could only increase the political demand for more radical policies, such as state planning, governmental ownership, or the redistribution of existing wealth.

A lasting security system surely required unemployment, old age, disability, and health insurance, major federal housing efforts, and a wide spectrum of legal protections for unorganized laborers and minority groups. Each of these welfare measures had powerful proponents and a growing political appeal. Most already existed in western European countries, an example that often proved instructive in the thirties. But despite their appeal, the precedents, and even bipartisan support, welfare policies still seemed heretical to many Americans, insidious and diverting to others.

249

An Enduring Welfare State

Governmental paternalism challenged the oldest and noblest of American economic ideals—individual entrepreneurship in an environment of open opportunity. The ideal early American had access to nature, and was a free and responsible producer, beholden to no one. A welfare state seemed to assume permanent employees and many citizens without realistic opportunity to own and manage productive property. To opt for a welfare state meant a drastic lowering of social vision, a dramatic confession of national failures. Instead of active participation, of a viable economic role for everyone, some citizens would become wards of the community, even as many were already virtually wards of corporations. The first real model for welfare came from a few large corporate experiments in the twenties. Whatever their degree of security, recipients of either corporate or governmental patronage would surely become less independent and responsible, more servile and obliging. Many opponents of welfare asked for a harder, more radical solution to economic insecurity—they wanted restored entrepreneurial opportunity for all, and even a redistribution of private property.

A small minority of critics condemned governmental patronage as too mild and too diverting. Either through socialist ownership or state planning, they wanted a new economic democracy with more radical answers than minimal bribes to the dispossessed. Through some form of co-operative commonwealth, all presently dependent workers could become owners and managers of capital, gaining thereby the intrinsic values of work (responsibility, artistry) rather than the mere extrinsic value (consumption). Welfare programs would only camouflage the injustices of the existing system, and keep alienated people from seeking the harsher tactics necessary to overthrow injustice and exploitation.

But such a theoretical analysis of welfare leaves unanswered the concrete question: What were the New Deal programs and how much welfare did they really provide? A detailed answer to the first answers the second: not very much. But to those who believe in the humaneness of a welfare approach to social problems (the more problems, the more welfare), the New Deal had inestimable significance, and however critics might minimize the scope of a program, the proponents could always quite correctly reply that "at least it was a beginning." And, in principle, beginnings are very important and allow a steady build-up of later benefits. To critics, the limited nature of New Deal welfare programs did not atone for the sacrifice of principle; later accretions scarcely changed the principles. Either way, the extent was not as significant as the fact of a program. Only for accepting and perhaps thankful recipients could the extent be the main issue.

The Social Security Act of 1935, perhaps as much because of its name as of its provisions or even the number of people affected by it, became the prime symbol of a welfare state. The act culminated a long crusade for various types of social insurance, and support for it in part reflected the growing appeal of the Townsend movement. Beginning in 1911, a privately organized movement for publicly financed social insurance worked for a variety of different programs, workmen's compensation, unemployment insurance, dependents' bonuses, health care, and retirement security, a system of care reaching from birth to the grave. It achieved only one goal before 1933; most states had at least some form of workmen's compensation.

As president-elect, Roosevelt promised Frances Perkins that he would support some type of unemployment insurance. In June 1934, after Congress had considered bills both for unemployment and old age insurance, Roosevelt created a Committee on Economic Security, headed by Edwin E. Witte. It reported in January 1935 and included a draft of an Economic Security Bill. After introduction and rather severe congressional amendment and rewriting, this emerged as the Social Security Act. The committee, and probably Roosevelt, had considered unemployment insurance the bill's most important provision; Congress wrangled more over old age security, particularly under the stimulus of critical Townsendites. The amended act, despite sharp criticism in committee, received bipartisan support and passed Congress overwhelmingly (it was perilous for a congressman to oppose it): in the House, 371–33; in the Senate 77–6.

The Social Security Act initiated several programs. The unemployment compensation provision not only answered a pressing need, but also promised another weapon against depressions. Since loss of purchasing power became the favorite New Deal explanation of the depression, it seemed only logical that continued income in periods of layoff could maintain a market for goods and help moderate the length and severity of a recession. The act provided for a cooperative federal-state program, financed by a federal tax on employers. But by an offset provision, states with their own program (eventually all states) could really collect 90 percent of the tax and set up their own compensation schedule within federal guidelines. This meant different compensation rates for various states, perhaps in part justified by regional wage rates but not nearly to the extent of actual differences. A minority in both the committee and in Congress fought for a centralized, federal system, with uniform rates. Congressional amendments also exempted from coverage agricultural and domestic industries, employers of less than eight workers, and all public or nonprofit organizations.

251

Old age insurance became the best-known program administered by the new Social Security Administration. By a special payroll tax (shared equally between employer and employee), the government collected an old age reserve fund for all eligible workers (with the same exemptions as above). Roosevelt insisted upon actuarial soundness, ample reserves, and a noncharitable, self-supporting system. Congress removed from the early bill all provisions for government grants to get the program started, and substituted higher beginning taxes. The administration advertised the program as a good old American effort at self-help, or as a large, cooperative insurance program. This concealed the taxing and redistributive features that remained in the program, but probably helped gain political support.

Francis Townsend (1867–1960) is shown here with his well-wishers. His plan for old-age assistance and his "army" of elderly people contributed to the passage of the Social Security Act in 1935. *Wide World Photos*

The original tax rates (1 percent in 1937), although necessary for eventual reserve needs, represented a taking and freezing of workers' income at the expense of overall purchasing power. As most people now know, the bill provided for a variable retirement income at age sixty-five, based on past earnings, but with a then-maximum rate of eighty-five dollars a month and a variable minimum based on past earnings (later changed to a set minimum). It excluded farmers, the self-employed, and most categories of public workers. Congress has since expanded coverage, rates, and benefits several times; for example, the coverage now includes almost all Americans except those under special governmental or railroad retirement systems with equal or better benefits.

The other provisions of the Social Security Act, which are not usually as well known, variously underwrote a system of public welfare at the local level. These included direct grants to support approved state old-age assistance programs (a minimum of thirty dollars a month for elderly people not under the new retirement program, which meant all needy old people in 1935), grants to states as aid for dependent children (still a basic ingredient in all public welfare programs), special grants for maternal and child-care services in rural areas, and special aid for the blind. The Committee on Economic Security studied health insurance, reported separately on it to the president, but left any such proposal even for the aged out of the bill because of expected political and medical opposition. The act restricted itself to authorized grants to states for public health, administered by the U. S. Public Health Service. A later effort by Senator Wagner to get congressional approval for a national health plan also failed in Congress.

Housing

Next to basic economic maintenance, housing was possibly the second most acute, long-term social problem to receive New Deal attention. The story has two main themes. One involved governmental support of private housing activities; the other, direct, subsidized public housing.

The housing industry, as well as construction in general, is acutely sensitive to business fluctuations. By 1933, home building had practically ceased (less than 100,000 housing starts for the whole country); foreclosures on mortgages consistently outnumbered new construction. Despite the repossession of rural shacks and filthy tenements, new homes remained empty, virtually unsaleable commodities in a glutted market. Lack of funds and lack of confidence combined with stringent mortgage requirements (the banks had been burned once and would not take even the slightest risk again) deterred any revival even by the mid-thirties. Both would-be homeowners and even more the various business and banking interests involved in home building and financing begged for governmental help. The Roosevelt administration, in recognition of the critical role of construction in overall recovery, proved quite responsive to various aid schemes.

As in so many other policy areas, rapid changes in home financing began in the Hoover administration. The depression proved the vulnerability of traditional, private financing (high down payments, five-year renewable mortgages, and inevitable waves of foreclosure and eviction with every depression as banks refused to renew mortgages at the very time repayment or refinancing was most difficult). Hoover, aware of these deficiencies, sponsored a 1931 Conference on Home Building and Home Ownership which asked for a complete overhaul of home financing. The National Association of Real Estate Boards, always anxious to sell more homes, also lobbied for long-term financing and a federal mortgage discount bank (or for what amounted to a Federal Reserve System for home lending institutions). In 1932 Congress approved such a discount bank, establishing Federal Home Loan Banks to provide loans to insurance companies, local banks, and particularly savings and loan associations. At the very least, lending agencies could now renew mortgages if they so desired. But all too few could or would in 1932 and 1933, particularly after the banking crisis.

In the summer of 1933 Congress initiated a rescue operation for both defaulting homeowners and desperate lenders. The Home Owners Loan Corporation (HOLC) purchased or refinanced imperiled home mortgages with a temporary moratorium on payments, longer terms (fifteen years), and lower interest rates. For lenders, HOLC purchases of mortgages meant a welcome governmental subsidy; for harassed owners, it meant retention of their homes.

In 1934 several New Deal financial experts drafted a National Housing Act, the most significant housing act in our national history and even today the basis of most government support for home financing. The act created the Federal Housing Administration (FHA) with one primary purpose—to insure home mortgages. Buyers with FHA-approved loans had to pay a small monthly fee to fund the program, and still do. Lenders received a government guarantee of repayment and so could safely lend for longer terms with smaller down payments and to higher-risk applicants. By the first FHA standards mortgages had to have twenty-year terms and could require only 20 percent down; the period would later be extended and down payments lowered. The FHA, in order to insure a mortgage, also demanded certain standards in construction, and in this indirect way helped control the quality of housing in America. Unfortunately, even these incentives did not entice many borrowers in the thirties, a decade in which home ownership actually decreased. But in the forties, and afterward, the FHA, joined with a Veterans' Administration insurance program even more liberal in its terms, achieved a veritable revolution in home financing and home ownership. By 1950, for the first time, over half of American families owned their homes. Liberalized loan policies (private lenders soon duplicated FHA terms for high risk borrowers) made home ownership available for every family with near-average or above-average income, or roughly from one-half to two-thirds of all American families.

But what about the lower one-half or one-third? In the thirties, even as today, many families could not afford private housing even under the most liberal terms. Some could not afford rent for any decent housing. (Of course, the criterion for adequate or decent changes through time, and always has an arbitrary aspect, being closely related to such other vague entities as average standards or normal expectations.) Aid for lower-income housing requires at least an outright rent subsidy and possibly some form of government ownership or construction, and thus more than self-liquidating financial support.

The first significant government public housing came as a temporary by-product of World War I defense spending. Out of this effort came planning innovations and a growing demand by reform groups for continued government involvement. The movement for public housing gained new enthusiasm and support in the thirties, a decade that practically discovered juvenile delinquency and became deeply enamored of environmental theories of social uplift (provide good environments, such as better homes, and *ipso facto* you have good, clean, obedient, middle-class people). The crusade paid off in 1932, when Hoover's Reconstruction Finance Corporation (RFC) made loans available to limited dividend corporations for the construction of low-rent housing. This began a public housing program that still continues but one which suffered early problems and numerous administrative shifts. Under Hoover, the RFC primarily screened an inflow of applications from local promoters but did lend a small sum for rural homes in Kansas and $8 million for a 1,593-unit in Manhattan, which could be considered the first authentic public housing project. Early in the New Deal, Roosevelt transferred these RFC applications to the newly created Public Works Administration. Under Ickes's rigorous scrutiny, the PWA rejected most of the over five hundred project proposals, approving only about twenty. All the early effort had led to depressingly little achievement.

In October 1933, Ickes tried to begin direct governmental construction. By December 1934, he could announce firm plans for forty-seven projects (21,000 units), but by then Roosevelt had transferred his funds to direct relief. Only in 1935, under new funds from the Emergency Relief Act, could Ickes proceed with actual construction. In 1937 he completed the 21,000 units. By then the PWA faced grave legal impediments to continued, direct federal construction, including a court prohibition against eminent domain procedures. This limitation, in particular, suggested the need for a more direct involvement of state and local governments, which had eminent domain authority under state law. As early as 1933, the Ohio legislature, followed soon by most other states, created municipal housing authorities. But fruition of federal-state cooperation required new federal legislation.

This came, after two years of effort and belated administrative support, in the Wagner Housing Act of 1937, which established the United States Housing Authority (USHA) in the Department of the Interior. The USHA used substantial federal funds to support slum clearance and construction of low-rent housing. Under strict federal regulations, the actual construction and administration of such projects came under local housing authorities. The federal government lent, for a sixty-year term, up to 90 percent of the cost of projects. The interest was nominal, making the loans in effect governmental grants. By 1949 the United States Housing Authority had completed 117,000 low-rent units, so small a number as scarcely to affect American slum conditions or to provide homes for more than a small percentage of those in need. Finally, the early United States Housing Authority worked under such rigid cost schedules ($4,000 a unit), and succumbed to so much local pressure that a majority of its completed projects (boxlike, bleak, stigmatized) became new slums within a decade or so. Only rare projects combined good landscape planning with imaginative architecture.

The most innovative New Deal housing occurred in a program so small that its lasting influence had to be educational. The Resettlement Administration, in addition to its rural community programs (these also could be classified as a type of public housing), supported a Suburban Resettlement Division. Its grandiose early plans shrunk to three special greenbelt towns, in the metropolitan areas of Washington, D.C., Cincinnati, and Milwaukee. Save for sources of employment, these were complete towns with all needed public facilities. Planned carefully, in conformity with the garden city or new towns idea so important in modern Britain, the towns demonstrated several planning and architectural principles: a belt of parks, farms, and woods surrounding each town and restricting its size; large city blocks with internal parks, infacing homes, and pedestrian underpasses; cooperative retail outlets and intensive community organization; careful retention of trees and adaptation of building sites to terrain features; and a diversity of architectural styles even in small, inexpensive apartments. But the public facilities and extensive land made the overall cost much higher than in the USHA projects, and helped provoke congressional opposition to any extension of this imaginative form of public housing.

Labor standards represent a third area of significant and overt welfare legislation in the thirties. The National Labor Relations Act of 1935 aided labor unions and gave organized workers the means to compete more effectively with management. If organized in powerful unions, laborers could now bargain for safe and fair conditions of employment. But most laborers in America were not members of unions, and were thus unable to force demands upon employers. Beginning with the crusade to end child labor, agitation to end the exploitation of workers led to state unemployment compensation laws, to a revitalized United States Employment Service in 1933, to the unemployment insurance features of the Social Security Act, to the mandatory wage and hour codes in the NRA, to special Resettlement Administration efforts to aid migratory workers, and even to the incidental retraining and rehabilitation programs in several relief agencies. This continuous increase in labor protection climaxed in 1938 in the Federal Fair Labor Standards Act.

What the NRA codes achieved by hearings and negotiation—minimum wages, maximum weekly hours at regular pay, prohibitions against the employment of children—the Federal Fair Labor Standards achieved by law. It rested, as did so much New Deal economic legislation, on the interstate commerce clause, and applied only to interstate trade and production. This exempted most local retail businesses, domestic help, and agriculture, or the very people most afflicted with extremely low wages. The original act abolished child labor, established a forty-hour week after a three-year transitional period, and an immediate twenty-five cent minimum wage to be raised slowly to forty cents. The category most affected were southern factory workers, particularly in small textile mills. Large, mature corporations already exceeded these standards and often supported the legislation. Entrenched labor unions did not need it.

With the completion of such a repertoire of relief and welfare measures, the federal government now played a direct role in the detailed, day by day existence of millions of Americans. In fact, it was on the way to replacing state governments as either the principal dispenser of public services or as the prime source of funds for such services. This direct contact immensely expanded the federal responsibility for dealing with minority groups, particularly with blacks. The relief agencies also made contact with truly destitute Americans, mired in poverty long before the depression. Over and over again, conscientious government employees of agencies such as the WPA developed understanding and real concern for the special problems of minorities or the hidden poor. But such notice remained almost incidental to New Deal programs and to the type of political support that lay behind them. The welfare programs, for example, almost always excluded the very bottom of the social scale (even new slum housing had such stringent eligibility requirements that it rewarded only the abler of low-income workers) and included no special provisions for racial or ethnic minorities.

The Indians, largely isolated in the West, required and received special relief and welfare programs. They also received a new degree of independence in the thirties. For decades, and most particularly from the early twenties, the Bureau of Indian Affairs had worked to assimilate Indians into the white culture. Under this policy, Indians lost much of their tribal government, their communal lands, and their native religion and art. The change began during the Hoover administration. Daring investigations helped cleanse the bureau of often unscrupulous agents and essentially anti-Indian policies.

In the thirties, Harold Ickes appointed as head of the bureau a long-time advocate of Indian tribal and cultural autonomy, John Collier, and quickly settled some pending land conflicts in favor of the Indians. Through direct consultation with Indian tribes, Collier prepared for Congress a monumental fifty-two-page Indian Reorganization Bill, by far the most significant Indian legislation of this century. Passed in amended form in 1934, it recognized the importance of the Indian tribe and the integrity of varied Indian cultures. It also authorized restored tribal self-government and rejected the policy of assimilation. By its terms, reorganized and near autonomous tribes could become federal corporations for the purpose of holding land and other economic undertakings. The bill also gave added protection for existing land holdings, established a specially trained Indian civil service, and provided subsidies for tribal agriculture and industry. Congress rejected a separate system of Indian justice and any consolidation of now-scattered Indian lands (whites had purchased the best lands on most reservations). The legislation paralleled an unprecedented popular and scholarly interest in Indian culture.

Black Americans presented insuperable problems for the New Deal. The real dilemma came in the distribution of benefits and the frequent conflict between local patterns of discrimination and often courageous attempts by New Deal agencies to apportion benefits fairly. Of all New Deal cabinet members, Ickes showed the most aggressive concern for Negro rights. He enlisted Clark Foreman, a white southern civil rights advocate, to coordinate Negro affairs in the Roosevelt administration. He also made every possible effort to include blacks on an equal even if a necessarily segregated basis in the PWA and in all the public housing projects. Although frustrated by local pressures, particularly in the state-operated FERA phase of relief, Harry Hopkins and many on his staff suffered intense political criticism in order to open the WPA to blacks. Au-

brey Williams did even better in the National Youth Administration, making a Negro, Mary McLeod Bethune, its deputy administrator of Negro affairs. The Resettlement Administration and Farm Security Administration duplicated this record in their agricultural and rehabilitation programs. But other agencies capitulated almost completely to local pressures; these included the NRA, the AAA (particularly vital to the South), and even the TVA. Although the CCC, under military discipline, integrated some of its camps in New England, and enrolled close to a 10 percent quota of blacks, it generally adhered to regional racial taboos and never advanced many blacks to administrative posts.

But the struggle within agencies probably had less impact on Negro opinion than highly symbolic, even if largely empty, gestures by Roosevelt or by leading congressional Democrats. The large expansion of federal agencies, plus bureaucratic concern, enabled a dozen or so Negroes to

Although Franklin Roosevelt's attitude toward blacks was, like that toward labor, paternalistic, his wife's concern went much farther. Here, during the war years, Eleanor Roosevelt greets Mary McLeod Bethune (1875–1955), president of Bethune-Cookman College. *Library of Congress*

find prominent positions in Washington. Professional blacks entered civil service jobs on a near-equal basis and began a process that would make Washington, D. C., a haven for middle-class Negroes. Perhaps most effective of all, Eleanor Roosevelt continuously stressed equal opportunities for all, and on several well-publicized occasions broke social segregation patterns.

Roosevelt apparently did not share his wife's intense commitment, although political exigencies dictated much of his behavior. He hinted at equality but never proclaimed it. Loved and respected throughout the white South, directly dependent upon southern congressmen, he never dared jeopardize that support and politically had no need to. In the campaign of 1936, the blacks (in the border states and the North—they could not vote in the deep South) flocked to the Democratic party. On the one major civil rights issue of the decade, a series of antilynching bills, Roosevelt withheld any direct support, apparently for political reasons. But strong efforts by Democratic congressmen helped offset the possible effects of this reluctance. Roosevelt believed that outstanding economic problems were more important, even for Negroes, than any possible legal or social or political gains. In his personal life, he reflected the same paternal concern for Negroes that he exhibited for labor.

Because of the omnipresence of racial issues in the last two decades, it is very easy to overestimate their importance in the thirties. The black revolution began, at best, in the World War II period. Few people in the thirties saw race as a major issue. Negro militancy had been greater in the twenties. The overwhelming importance of economic issues helped suppress legal and social goals even for blacks. To get a WPA job, even in a segregated and stigmatized work crew, seemed a real achievement. Paternalism still worked and very effectively. At a popular level, racial stereotypes remained pervasive, not just in the South but nationally. One only has to review the absurdly humorous or subservient role of Negroes in the movies of the decade to appreciate this. Only a limited circle of white intellectuals had yet come to any appreciation of black cultural contributions, and these mostly in music. Yet, the most limited New Deal concern seemed terribly significant and won black support. It also triggered almost unbelievable hostility from whites.

The class legislation, the relief and welfare measures, paid off in the election of 1936. So, of course, did the political appeal of Roosevelt, who always remained more popular than his programs. With the various congressional acts of 1935, the New Deal had clearly alienated only one major interest group—business—and had offered tangible benefits or

**The Election
of 1936**

appealing symbols to most others. The Democratic party, already well entrenched among urban ethnic groups, now had the near-unanimous support of organized labor. Farmers, even when habitually Republican, often voted Democratic in gratitude for the dramatic improvement in agricultural prices and the varied government response to severe drought. Negroes, pleased even by small rewards or dramatic gestures, now enthusiastically supported Roosevelt. The Social Security Act, although a bipartisan measure, stood as a New Deal gift to the elderly; relief swayed the poor.

Although Roosevelt conducted a sharp, pointed, and very extensive campaign, he offered no dramatic new programs for the future. The Democratic platform, in addition to adopting a pending public housing proposal, largely promised more of the same—a stronger war against bigness and improved labor and farm legislation. Roosevelt emphasized over and over again the success of his New Deal, and asked help and support to expand it. He implied that more reforms were in the offing. But the enemies of the New Deal and of the "people" remained strong, even as large numbers of Americans remained exploited and impoverished. In suggestive hints for the future, he also lamented the role of federal courts in frustrating New Deal programs. But at this time he refused to take frequent Republican lures and openly attack the courts.

The Republicans faced an almost impossible task in 1936. They still suffered unfair blame for the "Hoover" depression. Roosevelt's popularity, and the broad acceptance of many New Deal programs, made it difficult to launch an effective campaign. Hoover had carried out a searching but often embittered attack on almost every New Deal measure. He unraveled every contradiction and sought the underlying and vital principles at stake. But such a political Jeremiah hurt the party politically; he was a moralistic nay-sayer in the midst of a crusade. Even if a majority of solid Republicans agreed with Hoover, he certainly could not win the independent and undecided voters.

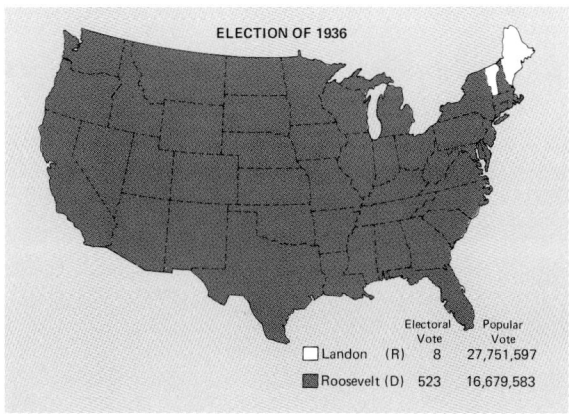

ELECTION OF 1936

		Electoral Vote	Popular Vote
☐	Landon (R)	8	27,751,597
■	Roosevelt (D)	523	16,679,583

Seeking a candidate ideologically closer to Roosevelt, the Republicans nominated Governor Alfred M. Landon of Kansas, an old insurgent, "Bull Moose" Progressive. Landon had a less conventional and less orthodox political past than Roosevelt and a greater claim to the Progressive tradition. But what could such a Republican do with the New Deal? Criticism of New Deal methods on economic or constitutional grounds, or of its obvious contradictions, seemed weakened by Landon's clear sympathy with many of its goals and programs. Landon, less dynamic and less gifted on the platform than Roosevelt, too often seemed to be quibbling, or else promising "me too." He lost overwhelmingly (16,674,665 to 27,-752,869), carrying only Maine and Vermont.

13

In the exuberant aftermath of his victory in 1936, Roosevelt seemed poised for a confident and relaxed second term. As 1937 began, most economic indexes finally approached 1929 levels and moved upward more rapidly than at any time since 1929. A more cautious and less divisive extension of taxing, regulatory, and welfare measures seemed a safe and easy goal. By his magical coattails, Roosevelt pulled into office young, often surprised congressmen from districts that had never voted Democratic. The Republicans, with only sixteen in the Senate, only eighty-eight in the House, and out of power in most states, simply could not offer effective opposition. Many people, apparently including even Roosevelt, had some apprehension over the survival of a two-party system. Perhaps no president in our history ever faced a new Congress with greater prestige, more political leverage, and fewer effective enemies (their very ineffectiveness bred bitterness).

But the power proved vulnerable, the electoral and congressional support fickle, the enemies persevering and clever. In what proved to be a terrible blunder, Roosevelt decided to launch a frontal campaign against the one still effective source of opposition, the federal courts. Only if he could be victorious on that front, all flanks secured, could he go on with a new legislative program. He lost. And of all the administrative proposals considered by the New Deal Congress, Roosevelt's court bill raised the most crucial theoretical issues, implicated and threatened the oldest and most fundamental traditions. It also rallied an effective coalition to oppose Roosevelt, any further extension of his powers, and any further extension of New Deal fiscal and welfare policies.

On February 5, 1937, Roosevelt unveiled his court "reform" bill. He and his attorney general, Homer Cummings, had secretly drafted it. The bill, on the surface, seemed constructive enough, but in the context of 1937 it shouted its ulterior purpose. The bill included several minor reforms in inferior federal courts, some important jurisdictional changes, and the following vital change applying to the Supreme Court: if a federal judge, on the bench for ten years, did not retire within six months of age seventy, the president could appoint an additional judge to the same court, provided the increase of membership through this device did not exceed six in the Supreme Court and two in inferior courts. Although

263

The Supreme Court

Roosevelt disingenuously pointed to overwork and delays in the federal courts, everyone understood the political purpose of the act: to get new and more amenable judges on the Supreme Court. At stake was the vast and vulnerable body of New Deal legislation passed in 1935, and already under litigation in lower courts.

As a backdrop to the court bill, and the extended, often brutal controversy that swirled around it during the hot summer of 1937, one has to turn to certain American political traditions and institutions. In its opening phrase the Constitution of 1787 reaffirmed a then well-established idea—popular sovereignty, or a compact theory of government. By this theory a legitimate government rests on the will of a sovereign people, and derives all powers from the people acting in a special capacity, as makers of compacts or constitutions. A compact of government, approved by representatives of the people in special constitutional conventions, and endorsed by them in ratifying votes, becomes a form of privileged law in the society. It apportions the powers of sovereignty to various governments or various branches of the government, and reserves to the people rights and privileges beyond the legitimate scope of any government, however representative. Within their allotted authority, the branches of government are free to act as they deem desirable (and, if democratic in form, as the people instruct). But no change in the compact can be legitimate unless the people covenant once again in a special constitutional capacity, and thus amend the Constitution. Such constitutional processes, special in importance, slow in execution, require something close to a mature consensus of the community, and thus more than the simple majority gained by political processes.

By implication and by determined assertion of its power, not by any clear mandate of the Constitution of 1787, the Supreme Court became the main interpreter and protector of our basic charter of government. The individual states early competed for the role, but lost. Variously both Congress and the president have chafed at the power and have tried to gain more control over it. But at least the right of the Supreme Court to nullify congressional and presidential action, on constitutional grounds, has been sustained by nearly two hundred years of experience. Such a role, just as the functioning of political parties, has become an unwritten addition to our basic compact. At any one time the Supreme Court can frustrate the will and desire of the other two branches of government, or a vast majority of demanding citizens. It can do this in behalf of small, unpopular minorities, or simply in behalf of legitimate procedures. When so frustrated, the other branches of the federal government have to resort to the sovereign people, and rely upon a more complete consensus, or else await such a development. But, of course, neither the Constitution nor the exact intent of its drafters is crystal clear, and the members of the Court are not omniscient. On quite concrete and clear constitutional issues, only amendments permit any basic change in federal powers. On other issues that engage more ambiguous sections of the Constitution, the Supreme Court has simply reinterpreted the Constitution, and often thereby registered a clear change in consensual understanding. But, in theory, such interpretive changes must spring from the honest and uncoerced opinion of judges, and must not reflect the coercive pressure of either public opinion or other branches of the government.

But, one may protest, God does not appoint judges. They come to the courts via an often quite political process, and in their decisions cannot remain aloof from their own moral and political biases. Presidents nominate judges by ideological or party affinity, and the Senate uses such criteria in approving. The great constitutional protection of judicial integrity in federal courts is thus life tenure, subject of course to what the Constitution calls "good behavior." Through time, a president may make enough appointments to the Supreme Court to change its basic outlook, but he can never be assured of such options or be able to exercise them at will. Congress, by the Constitution, has power to change the makeup of the Court. But either some attempt by the president to force his own appointees on a court, or of Congress to alter the number of judges, all in behalf of immediate changes in orientation and decisions, particularly on pending cases, directly violates the traditional independence and integrity of the third branch. Such politically motivated changes in the membership of the Court had occurred in the past, but never in as charged a context as 1937, and never with as direct a threat to a given group of judges.

The Supreme Court is a nondemocratic branch of government, and the only surviving one from the early Constitution, since both the Senate and the president became popularly elected, responsive officers. The very idea of a special, constitutional law, accessible only to an elaborate constitutional process and supreme even over the actions of legislatures, embodies the idea of a special, long-term, nonwhimsical, rational will of the people, deeply embedded in hallowed forms and internalized ideals, and thus something more traditional, authoritative, and much more stable than electoral politics.

In the thirties it was easy to ignore or detest such nondemocratic and authoritarian features of American government. Democratic ideas dominated. In a period of crusades and of charismatic leadership, the immediate will of the people seemed self-legitimizing. Roosevelt, as a popular president, with an overwhelming electoral victory, easily expressed his belief in the immediate popular will and his resentment of authoritarian impediments and restraints. He easily personalized opposition, and thus often viewed Court opposition, not as a quite normal expression of institutional checks, but as the obstructionism of reactionary judges. As he saw it, the conflict between himself and the Court involved not great issues or principles of government, not dangerous precedents, but a form of political conflict. The situation thus did not require new amendments either to circumscribe judicial review or to extend governmental powers, or a patient wait for new appointments, but the only immediate, legislative remedy—changing the number of judges. By doing it in this context, and for such clearly partisan but popular goals, Roosevelt attempted, in effect, to give the president and Congress (or the people in their elected capacity) more direct control over the Constitution, and to take part of that power from the Supreme Court (or from the people in their special constitutional capacity).

The New Deal Context

The New Deal background to the Court bill deserves very careful, and exact, understanding. As few other issues in the New Deal, commentators have distorted the role of the federal courts by ill-fitting political labels, such as "liberal" and "conservative." The New Deal Congress turned out an unprecedented volume of new legislation, some ill-drafted and hasty, some calculated for extreme, emergency situations. The legislation invited a veritable flood of litigation from those adversely affected by new laws. As a result of such appeals to the federal courts, New Deal agencies continually suffered adverse decisions or frustrating injunctions. Finally, in several critical cases, the New Deal lost in the Supreme Court. There is no doubt but that the frustration became almost unbearable to several agency heads and to Roosevelt, particularly when decisions involved narrow subtleties of interpretation or narrow 5–4 verdicts on the Court. The tantalizing feature was here; a shift in one or two judges could often make the difference. And surely, Roosevelt believed, no grave constitutional principles could be present in such split decisions.

Most New Deal legislation had an economic function. It tremendously expanded the scope and extent of federal governmental power over individuals, most often under either the justification of the general welfare or interstate commerce clauses of the Constitution. Litigants usually claimed a deprivation of rights (life, liberty, or property) without due process, occasioned by governmental violations of contracts, by illegitimate delegation of legislative authority to the president, by usurpation of regulatory powers reserved to the states, and by illegal regulation or taxation. The Court decisions thus focused on the general welfare and interstate commerce clauses (Article I, section 8), the Tenth Amendment (reservation of powers to the states), the Fifth Amendment (due process requirements for the federal government), and for closely related state regulatory action, the Fourteenth Amendment (requires due process of states). Almost all the New Deal cases involved civil liberties, and particularly the right to some form of property. The often privileged position of litigants should not conceal the legal issues involved. Property, as legally defined, has the same constitutional protection as life or expressive freedoms, and is as vital to some individuals, or often more vital, than any other right, since livelihood and any possible happiness may rest on property. Also, in the thirties as later, the people who sought protection in the courts were members of unpopular minorities, particularly distraught businessmen or stockholders, just as later they would be blacks or extreme dissenters.

The most critical decisions of the thirties involved constitutional issues that remained in a state of flux. Thus, opposing judges could marshal equally relevant precedents on both sides of crucial issues. For example, the scope of federal authority under the welfare and interstate commerce clause had received extensive attention by the Court during the twenties. Under the leadership of William Howard Taft, the Court had often, but not unanimously and not conclusively, broadened the meaning of interstate commerce to encompass production of goods involved in interstate movements. At the same time the broader issue of judicial function and the constitutional role of the Supreme Court had long concerned not only reflective judges but many legal theorists. Judges remained sharply divided over strict versus latitudinarian interpretations of the Constitution, or over an active versus a restrained use of judicial power to nullify acts of Congress.

The Supreme Court inherited by Roosevelt (he was able to make no appointments in his first term) reflected rather inflexible divisions on certain constitutional issues, but had able and extremely conscientious men on both sides. Four judges (Willis Van Devanter, Pierce Butler, James C. McReynolds, and George Sutherland) generally concurred in condemning all dramatic extensions of federal power (all four, notably, had served over ten years and were over seventy). Sutherland, able and respected even by those who disagreed with his opinions, most often wrote the dissenting opinions of the four. They felt that the interstate commerce clause of the Constitution, by any reasonable interpretation of either the intention of the framers or of the brief words themselves, did not sanction the federal regulation of anything other than commerce in a strict sense, and then only for items clearly and directly involved in interstate movements. They also discounted emergency justifications for the centralization of power in either the federal government or the person of the presi-

dent, or any erosion of the due process safeguards for the person (corporate as well as in the flesh), particularly through attacks on contracts and obligations. If the Roosevelt administration wanted to expand the regulatory functions of the federal government, it should use the amending process and not the dangerous precedent of emergency legislation. They thus interpreted the Constitution quite rigorously and refused to make any concessions to popular will, to emergency conditions, or to overwhelming legislative desires. They stood squarely athwart the New Deal crusade, and at times did not hesitate to lecture the Congress or the administration for constitutional lapses or for adopting constitutionally unsound legislation or administrative procedures. Personally, their constitutional apprehension matched their own horror of the new structure of federal power abuilding in Washington.

Three judges almost always disagreed on these same economic issues (Louis Brandeis, Benjamin N. Cardozo, and Harlan F. Stone). They gained the label of "liberal" and consistently approved the extension of federal regulatory powers, but not always the extension of presidential

In this 1935 photo three Supreme Court justices testify before the Senate Judiciary Committee on a case involving injunctions against federal agencies. In 1937 the same committee would consider the Court bill. From left to right: Senators Warren Austin, George W. Norris, William E. Borah, Henry F. Ashurst (chairman of the committee), and Pat McCarran; Justices Willis Van Devanter, Charles E. Hughes, and Louis D. Brandeis. *Underwood & Underwood*

powers, and tried to uphold most New Deal economic legislation. This did not mean that they would not disallow legislation that clearly violated unambiguous sections of the Constitution. They usually (Cardozo almost always) responded positively to the administration claim of emergency conditions and the grave need for new powers, and particularly to a compelling need for an expanded interpretation of interstate commerce. Just as the united four (the so-called "conservatives") faced the continuous charge of letting personal bias against the New Deal govern their decisions, so these three judges seemed, to New Deal critics, lackeys of Roosevelt, willing to bend an overly flexible Constitution to fit anything coughed up by the administration. But their very flexibility often rested on a viable juristic principle—judicial restraint. In a tradition brilliantly expressed by Oliver Wendell Holmes, Jr., and then most consistently defended by Felix Frankfurter at Harvard University, they argued that the Court should not impede legislative will (or the popular will) without a completely clear constitutional mandate. In every case the Court should exercise restraint, finding every possible constitutional leeway to uphold legislation, whether the judge personally agreed with it or not. Nine men should not substitute their wisdom for that of the people. If the people voted themselves into hell, without directly violating the Constitution, then the Court had to say "amen." This emphasis also lessened a judge's interest in the distant intentions of the drafters, and focused it more on contemporary realities.

Two judges (Chief Justice Charles E. Hughes and Owen J. Roberts) fit no easy pattern. They voted with either side, and revealed no clear bias for or against New Deal legislation. Hughes showed more openness to an extended definition of interstate commerce, and to more detailed governmental regulation of industrial processes. Roberts often decided cases on quite narrow and subtle technical distinctions, and thus became the best, but often the most unfathomable, key to how the Court would go on a given issue.

The continuous and quite predictable Court divisions on New Deal economic legislation did not carry over into other issues that came before the Court. In the thirties all civil liberties issues did not involve either property or action by the New Deal. Consistent with their rigorous concern for procedure and for individual rights, the so-called conservative four often took the lead in expanding the scope of federal protection over individual rights at the state level, even as on other legislative issues they insisted upon the reserved power of the states. Their expansion of the scope of the Fourteenth Amendment to prevent state economic regulation carried over into other areas, and would have tremendous significance in the post-World War II period. But on these issues the "liberals"

Here cartoonist Clifford Berryman satirizes Roosevelt's attempt to alter the composition of the Supreme Court. *Library of Congress*

usually agreed, while a moderate Hughes consistently provided leadership. In a series of unheralded cases the Court began its first detailed scrutiny of southern justice for blacks, expanded the scope of both freedom of the press and of speech, and by 1938 entered its first wedge against school segregation.

There are many ironies in the Court battle. One is that even from Roosevelt's perspective, the battle might have been futile even from the beginning. The Court continuously ruled in favor of major New Deal legislation from 1937 on; also, within three years, Roosevelt was able to appoint an almost new Court. Apart from the Court battle, and defensive action by elderly judges, the election of 1936 and the simple, liberalized noncontroversial retirement provisions approved by Congress in March of 1937 might have encouraged even earlier retirements. Moreover, a series of pro-New Deal votes by Roberts may have reflected his already changed commitments, his response to the overwhelming electoral mandate of 1936, or no fundamental shift at all, but only a reaction to quite technical differences in the legislation considered. But apart from a seeming shift in interpretation, only possibly tied to the Court fight, the Supreme Court even before 1937 did not comprise a record quite as threatening to the New Deal as Roosevelt imagined.

Many of the earliest critical New Deal cases involved contract modifications seemingly necessitated by the depression. On this issue, the New Deal won substantially in the Court. Beginning in June 1934, the Court upheld (though 5–4 in all such cases) the principle of an imposed modification of contract terms, such as extended repayment rights, as long as the lender suffered no eventual loss of property (*Home Building and Loan Association* v. *Blaisdell*). Since the Frazier-Lemke Farm Mortgage Act of 1934 actually permitted a reduction in the face value of mortgages, the Court unanimously voided it in 1935 (*Louisville Joint Stock Bank* v. *Radford*). During the Court fight the judges unanimously upheld the well-drafted Farm Mortgage Act of 1935, which provided for a moratorium but no diminution of obligation (*Wright* v. *Vinton Branch of Mountain Trust Bank of Roanoke*). With great reluctance and in each case only by 5–4, the Court earlier upheld (the Gold Clause Cases) a 1933 act of Congress that canceled the gold clause in all public and private contracts (a promise to pay in gold).

In another category of cases the New Deal lost decisively. But here the blame could not be placed on old or reactionary judges; no victory could be won by added appointments. The Court, by unanimous or near-unanimous decisions, refused to accept a broad expansion of presidential powers, particularly of a legislative nature. Except for Cardozo, the Court in 1935 overturned presidential executive orders, under NIRA authority, which prohibited the interstate shipment of oil ("hot oil") produced above state-set production limits. To the Court, this presidential regulation clearly involved an unconstitutional delegation of legislative powers (*Panama Refining Co.* v. *Ryan*). The same reasoning led the Court to a unanimous invalidation of all NRA codes, in perhaps the most famous decision of the decade (*Schechter Poultry Corp.* v. *United States*). The decision in the *Schechter* case also repudiated the NIRA for an illegitimate extension of the commerce clause to cover indirect effects of interstate transactions, properly a function only of the states. The Court also, on the same day as *Schechter* (May 27, 1935), unanimously declared unconstitutional an earlier presidential dismissal, without any charge or proof of malfeasance, of a by-then deceased member of the Federal Trade Commission, and awarded back salaries to his estate (*Humphrey's Executor* v.

United States). This decision affirmed the independence of regulatory agencies from arbitrary presidential power. Since the invalidation of Frazier-Lemke came also on the same day (Black Monday), Roosevelt spoke out bitterly against the Court. But he spoke against a unanimous Court.

The other significant cases involved three other principal issues—the limits of taxing power, the limits of regulatory power without violating due process, and the extent of federal jurisdiction under the interstate commerce clause. Here the Court, and particularly individual judges, seemed a great deal more inconsistent. However analyzed, the decisions of Roberts either involved quite subtle distinctions between seemingly similar or closely related cases, or a later switch in his own convictions. He revealed this on federal taxing power. In the AAA decision (*United States v. Butler et al.*), Roberts wrote the majority decision (6–3), which argued that the processing tax was not a true tax under the taxing authority of the Constitution, but a means to take money from one group and award it to another. Also, the AAA used the tax money to coerce the behavior of farmers, and thus to regulate agricultural production, a power not bestowed by the Constitution upon the federal government. Both means and ends were thus unconstitutional. The decision threatened unending claims against the government for taxes already collected (blocked by quick congressional action), and invited a sharp verbal exchange among the judges. No subsequent case involved the exact issues, for the New Deal never again resorted to such a processing tax for regulatory purposes. The most likely comparison could be the two forms of taxes collected under the Social Security Act, both of which Roberts approved during the Court fight (*Steward Machine Co.* v. *Davis; Helvering* v. *Davis*). But here the details are at least distinct enough to challenge, and forever leave mute, either charges of inconsistency or, much worse, of a politically motivated switch in order to help defeat Roosevelt's plan.

The most confusing cases of all involved the limits of both state and federal governmental regulation. In an early decision in the New Deal period, the Court upheld by 5–4 (*Nebbia* v. *New York*) a New York Milk Control Law that set minimum prices for milk. Roberts wrote the majority opinion, and argued that the milk industry had sufficient public interest to warrant regulation, and that reasonable and nonarbitrary regulations to this constitutional end did not violate due process as required by the Fourteenth Amendment. This seemed to place Roberts (and also a majority of the Court) clearly on the side of broadened regulatory legislation, although it left open the problem of state versus federal jurisdiction. But in May of 1935 Roberts wrote the majority opinion (5–4), which overturned the Railroad Pension Act (*Railroad Retirement Board* v. *Alton Railroad Co.*) for violating the due process provisions of the Fifth

Amendment. In this case Roberts did not censure the purposes of the act, but rather the inequities involved by treating all carriers involved as one conglomerate (the majority also denied federal jurisdiction under interstate commerce). Then, on June 1, 1936, Roberts concurred in a 5–4 invalidation of a New York minimum wage law for women workers (*Morehead* v. *New York ex rel. Tipaldo*). This seemed to be a direct reversal of his stand in the *Nebbia* case, and for the Court a return to much earlier restrictions on almost any type of economic regulation. The decision also seemed to challenge almost any state or federal regulatory legislation, particularly since the federal acts would face the same problem of due process plus other hazards based on jurisdiction. It also provided excellent ammunition for Roosevelt and seemed to support his claim of a need for Court "reform."

In the New York case, the state supreme court had invalidated the minimum wage law under the precedent of a 1923 Supreme Court case that overturned such state legislation (*Adkins* v. *Children's Hospital*). In its appeal, New York asked the Court to distinguish their act from *Adkins*, and in this way reverse the lower court. The argument, therefore, revolved around not the substantive issue but the technical one—did the case have enough distinguishing features to exempt it from *Adkins*. The appeal did not allow a reversal of *Adkins* unless the Court went beyond the issues actually presented. By his decision in *Nebbia*, and by subsequent decisions, Roberts seemed quite willing to reverse *Adkins*, but on the technical question joined the recalcitrant four, who agreed that it came under *Adkins* and also felt that the Court should continue to uphold the *Adkins* precedent. In dissent, Justice Stone also agreed that the case did fall under *Adkins*, but wanted to argue it on its merits. Hughes, Cardozo, and Brandeis tried to distinguish the act from *Adkins*, but also defended it as a legitimate use of state power.

The sequel came six months later, or in December 1936. At that time eight judges (Stone was ill) considered a quite similar minimum wage law in the state of Washington, which had also been challenged under the due process clause of the Fourteenth Amendment (*West Coast Hotel Co.* v. *Parrish*). But in this case the appeal asked for a reversal of *Adkins*. Roberts joined with Hughes, Cardozo, and Brandeis on reversal, using the same substantive arguments as Hughes included in his dissent on the New York case, thus leaving a 4–4 tie. When Stone rejoined the Court he made a majority in favor of the minimum wage law, and the Court announced its decision on March 29, 1937, in the very midst of the Court fight. Almost everyone at the time interpreted the result as a crucial switch by Roberts, when in actuality the decision conformed to Roberts's record all during the New Deal. His December vote to overturn *Adkins* left no impediment to a Court that would continuously rule in favor of broader regulatory power for the states.

Thus, as Roosevelt plotted his Court bill, one critical juristic issue remained unsolved—the possible extent of federal jurisdiction over interstate commerce (still ambiguous was the limit of federal taxing power). On the interstate commerce issue a divided Court had consistently and clearly opposed New Deal legislation. In the NRA decision the Court tried to distinguish between direct and indirect involvement in interstate commerce, and consistently thereafter a majority (Hughes and Roberts as well as the four) denied federal jurisdiction for indirect involvement, which seemed a near-blanket permit for centralizing and federalizing almost any conceivable activity. In several cases, and most notably in the Carter Coal Company decision, the Court majority had gone back beyond rather clear precedents in the twenties, and had refused to consider production, or anything tied directly to production, as involved in interstate commerce. This seemed to preclude any federal jurisdiction over labor disputes in factories.

The issue came to a head during the Court fight in an extremely significant test of the Wagner Act (*NLRB* v. *Jones and Laughlin Steel Corp.*). The act hung upon the interstate commerce clause, for only under its authority could the federal government grant the extensive new rights to labor unions. The Court, by 5–4, upheld the NLRB, and in so doing gave a license for other such sweeping legislation. In the majority opinion, Hughes insisted on the direct involvement concept, but argued that labor disputes in companies such as Jones and Laughlin had a direct impact on interstate commerce. Such disputes also involved plant production, not the movement or sale of products. Although Hughes did not specifically reject earlier distinctions between production and trade, the decision nevertheless had that implication. With better logic on their side, the four dissenters lamented what they believed to be an inconsistent departure from the NRA and Guffey precedents. To them the Court had clearly reversed itself. They were correct. The decision would be a landmark in the history of the Court. It permanently expanded the meaning of interstate commerce and finally opened to the federal government an unambiguous and tremendously broad sphere of economic authority. So pervasive was the authority that in 1964 Congress used the interstate commerce clause as a constitutional justification for a major civil rights act.

It is at least possible that the Court fight helped sway Roberts on the interstate commerce issue, and thus contributed to a major constitutional shift. Apart from this one issue, it is now clear that the Roosevelt administration and the Court moved rather steadily toward a degree of accommodation. Congress and the administration accepted the unanimous ver-

dict against undue delegation of powers to the president and also the
Court's demand for more carefully drafted legislation. Most of the 1935
legislation reflected a new legal sophistication. On its part, a five-member
majority of the Court bent over backward to accommodate New Deal
policies whenever dire national consequences awaited Court vetoes (such
as in the Gold Clause cases) and tried in several cases to clarify guidelines
for redrafting legislation. But even when the accommodation process occurred before the Court case, its effects only became clear afterward, and
thus had little effect on Roosevelt's decisions in 1937.

However motivated, the decisions of the Court in March and April of
1937 very much influenced the battle in Congress, as did Justice Van Devanter's retirement in May and a crucial letter from Hughes defending
the capability and efficiency of the Court. Roosevelt already suffered
from his own strategy—secret preparation of the act, disingenuous
early arguments for it, and intense pressure that he brought to bear on
wavering Senators. His own action lent credence to charges of excessive
executive power, and helped provide a convenient lever for already du-
bious congressmen to move into active opposition. Consistently, Roosevelt
refused any compromise proposals, insisting upon the whole package or
nothing at all. The fight opened up Supreme Court issues to broad public
discussion; books and articles informed or misinformed millions. Since the
bill had to be viewed as a possible precedent for subsequent changes
when other popular issues ran into Court obstacles, and thus judged not
alone on the merits of immediate issues pending in the Court, many senators soon had second thoughts, including even as loyal New Deal supporters as George Norris or Robert Wagner. Everyone vitally concerned
with civil liberties could see the dire implications of such a capitulation to
majoritarian democracy. As the debate went on, Roosevelt also failed to
gather his expected support from the broader public or from organized
pressure groups of farmers and laborers, who often responded to pro-
Court rather than proadministration propaganda. Roosevelt's majority
leader in the Senate, Joseph Robinson of Arkansas, unrelentingly sought
enough support to pass the bill, but since almost everyone assumed he
would get the first vacant seat on the Court, even his leadership seemed
tainted. Worn out by the struggle, Robinson died just eight days after the
bill moved from stormy committee hearings onto the floor of the Senate.
There, on July 22, the Senate voted (70–20) to recommit, and in this
way to kill the Court bill.

The only legislative result of Roosevelt's "reform" bill was minor
changes for the lower federal courts. Even these reflected overt and de-

As it turned out, by 1946, when this picture was taken, the Court had fully endorsed a broad spectrum of federal economic regulations. Here members of the Court are shown at the funeral of Justice Harlan F. Stone (1872–1946). They are, left to right: Justices Hugh L. Black (1886–1971), Charles Evans Hughes (1862–1948), Stanley F. Reed (1884–   ), William O. Douglas (1898–   ), and Wiley Rutledge (1894–1949). *Acme Photo*

vious political purposes. One section allowed the attorney general to become a party to cases in the lower courts, thus helping the New Deal avert delaying injunctions at that level. Another provision required a panel of three federal judges to issue any injunctions impeding the implementation of congressional action. In part drafted by TVA lawyers, this had an immediate purpose. A hostile federal judge in Alabama had already issued an injunction against the extension of TVA electrical power, and now waited to retry the same case when remanded to him by an appeals court. The "reform" bill removed it from his solitary jurisdiction and, in the first application of the provision, secured a 2–1 verdict in favor of TVA. Rarely had Congress so conveniently interfered to change a court judgment on a pending case.

The Court fight helped dissipate any of the lingering spirit of 1935. Roosevelt not only lost on the bill itself (a tremendous bitter pill for his ego), but would never regain his earlier prestige and influence in the Congress. The Court issue also allowed his bitterest enemies to steal some of his own tactics. Now they, and not Roosevelt, could appeal to old and revered American traditions, and for the first time add substance to their charges that he was a "political royalist," seeking near-dictatorial powers, and unwilling to tolerate opposition or effective dissent. The Court battle marked the beginning of the end for an effective New Deal, at least in the sense of innovative and far-reaching legislative achievements.

The controversy had brought the Supreme Court into the public limelight as never before. The highly partisan issues, the seeming political skills of Hughes, surely helped dissipate some of the popular awe that still attached to a remote and almost sacrosanct institution. But the Court hardly suffered any loss of prestige or power. If the Court battle is viewed as a conflict between two branches of the government, then the Court clearly won. And not for a long time would either Congress or a president dare try such blunt tactics in order to bring the Supreme Court to heel. In this sense, the acrimony and conflict strengthened the Court for a later, more positive, innovative, and controversial role in our society.

14

Roosevelt's defeat in the Court fight seemed to unleash a tide of adversity. Late in 1937 the growing economy suddenly collapsed. An economic crisis returned, not only mocking New Deal claims of recovery but lending some substance to long-standing business charges against the administration. Roosevelt had to respond to this new panic and invest almost all of his remaining political capital in new spending programs. Increasingly beleaguered by opposition in his own party, he tried in 1938, without success, to purge his leading Democratic opponents. By then Congress not only refused him new legislation but more closely scrutinized and often denied adequate funds for existing programs. The New Deal was over. Almost in relief, Roosevelt turned more and more to pressing issues in foreign policy, and postponed his domestic goals in behalf of a new congressional coalition willing to support his initiatives in Asia and in Europe.

The Court fight ended in late July 1937. An increasing rate of economic growth also peaked in July. A new economic disaster began in August. Within a few months unemployment jumped by approximately four million, or back to the levels of 1934. Other millions suffered intermittent layoffs. The stock market fell off by 43 percent, industrial production by 33 percent, profits by 82 percent, payrolls by 35 percent, income and prices by approximately 10 to 12 percent. In only a few months the economy reversed about half the gains made since 1933, and declined even more rapidly than in the Hoover administration.

The economic gains of 1936 and early 1937 were much more fragile than they seemed at the time. Relief expenditures, at their peak in 1936, certainly provided an indispensable but politically vulnerable condition for the gain. The very rise of price levels, and a hint of future inflation, encouraged advance purchasing and, unless growth could be maintained, an inevitable future slack. The paying of veterans' bonuses, against Roosevelt's opposition, also gave only a temporary impetus to spending. Behind the stimulants, the economy still displayed grave maladies: unemployment remained at six or seven million, construction hardly reached half its level in the mid-twenties, and demoralized and cautious businessmen, angry at sit-down strikes and at an undistributed profits tax, proved reluctant to spend.

278

Denouement and Legacy

In this context governmental economic policies in early 1937 proved disastrous. Overreacting to the economic boomlet, Roosevelt drastically curtailed relief programs and terminated all appropriations for the Public Works Administration. He rejoiced in the opportunity to balance budgets, to get back to normal. Too easily overlooked, the new Social Security tax began in January to cut into incomes, slightly curtailing purchasing by workers. Profits leveled off early in 1937, even as raw material prices rose. At least as businessmen viewed the economy, there was no reason for optimism. Their reluctance joined that of consumers, and left the economy with no stimulants to substitute for lowered government expenditures.

The Magic of Spending

The critical situation in 1937 provided the first real test for a complex of new fiscal policies that we now identify with the New Deal. In 1935, as an expedient reaction to events, Roosevelt had finally accepted massive budgetary deficits. But not gladly. He had already reluctantly accepted permanent welfare programs, and begrudgingly forged a political alliance with organized labor. In every area, the pressure of events seemed to override his ancient loyalties. He hoped the budgetary deficits could be temporary, and justified them by the extraordinary emergency of depression, which he compared with that of war. This is why he welcomed a briefly balanced federal budget in early 1937; this is why he supported the retrenchment in federal expenditures which, more than anything else, abetted the new economic crisis.

Many administration advisers saw no heresy in an unbalanced budget. They identified this fiscal strategy with the theories of John Maynard Keynes, an English analytical economist. His theories became fashionable in the late thirties. By the end of World War II they entered, in a more precise and sophisticated form, the established orthodoxy of major economics departments in large universities, and through the advisory role of economists have largely dominated our economic policies since World War II. In 1946 Congress in effect accepted the main bent of Keynesian theory in a now-famous Employment Act. It directed the federal government to use all its plans, functions, and resources to foster and promote both free competitive enterprise and full employment, production, and purchasing power, with special emphasis on employment opportunities. Keynes could hardly have expressed his goals more clearly—to maintain an open, privately owned, privately managed, publicly policed economic system, but one rescued from radical instability, and thus from depressions and intense human suffering, by adequate welfare measures and by stabilizing, compensatory governmental policies, including both short-term monetary policies and, most crucial, long-term fiscal policies. In a general way, his prescriptions now seem almost obvious: as economic growth slows, the government compensates by liberalized credit, possibly by tax cuts, and finally by increasing its expenditures over its revenues. In an overheated economy, the government should try to do just the opposite, although this has proved perilous. There are, of course, subtleties. For example, some tax cuts have different effects than others. So do some government expenditures.

Government spending, particularly for relief, clearly stimulated the economic growth of 1935 to early 1937. WPA employees could not afford to stash their meager wages away in a can or even deposit them in a bank. They spent and would have spent more could they have earned it. Their limited spending could create more spending, just as bank deposits, in a period of reasonable demand for money, support more loans and thus more deposits. In fact, consumer spending has a very rapid expansionist potential. Every extra WPA dollar bought that many extra goods and thus allowed retailers to procure replacements, profited wholesalers, reduced the inventory of factories, helped finance the production of replacements, gave a bit of extra employment to workers, whose wages might begin the whole process over again. Meantime, WPA projects required materials and in this direct way also stimulated other spending. In theory, a penny could end the depression if it multiplied its effects long enough. But at any point the process could stop. The retailer, with a large supply, might simply reduce his inventory and bank his meager profit.

The irony of spending is that, in good times, with an expansive mood everywhere, a little bit has a great multiplying effect, but in hard times it may have only small effects, simply because of the number of people in the producing-buying chain who have neither the hopeful expectations nor the will needed to increase their economic activity. For these psychological reasons, it is never possible to chart the exact amount of government spending necessary to insure a given effect on prices or on production, or to estimate the exact effect of a given amount of spending after it has occurred. Obviously, only a slight increase in the level of private spending or investment, spread over the whole country, would have exceeded the relief appropriation and had greater economic effect. Inversely, any New Deal policies or frightening proposals, or even a Roosevelt speech, might have enough of a depressing effect on private decisions to offset the effect of the WPA. One recent criticism of New Deal policies has been that Roosevelt did right to spend but spent too little. In one sense, that he spent too little is a truism, for he never attained full recovery. But this assumption isolates the amount of governmental spending from the level of private spending; the private sum is itself a variable and directly influenced by governmental policies. Even the WPA, as a testimony to severe economic maladies, may have frightened some individuals and increased their pecuniary caution.

The indirect and supportive nature of such governmental spending, and the minimal institutional changes required by it, allowed one group of New Deal critics (socialists in particular, but also the disillusioned planners of 1933) to argue, in their own pet labels, that Roosevelt turned "right" or "conservative" by 1935. His class rhetoric and the limited welfare benefits only camouflaged the retention, or even the strengthening, of a "capitalist" system. It had gross inequities and so concentrated economic power in a few private hands as, in every crunch, to insure that the federal government granted the largest share of its patronage to the prosperous and powerful, not to the weak and exploited. Thus, the compensatory government spending was largely of a wasteful variety. These critics included various examples of Marxists, all anxious to convert our economy to some form of state ownership, as well as academically accredited economists who urged more direct planning and less reliance on indirect fiscal methods.

Other economists rejected the Keynesian approach in behalf of purely monetary controls. Many monetary theorists seemed to be the heirs of Adam Smith or economic godfathers of a form of incipient anarchy. They maintained that the main role of government is to insure a completely free market and to provide an adequate, stable, but growing supply of money, largely through central bank policy and a careful and cautious management of government finances. They viewed governmental regulation as self-defeating (it is always coopted by the interests being managed), saw much welfare as needless or economically distorting, and condemned most fiscal policies, including deficits, as foolish and harmful when not carefully correlated with monetary objectives. The object of their criticism was a reduced economic role for government, a major decentralization of economic power, expanded initiatives for private corporations and private individuals, and more real competition. If the old label "laissez faire" still had any meaning, they probably adhered to it as closely as any identifiable group. Their pungent critique of a welfare state, or of "regulated" capitalism, rang with the brilliance of a William Graham Sumner, and had increasing appeal for Americans disenchanted with the new economic innovations.

Monetary Policy

Even Keynes recommended credit controls through central banking policies. In 1933 Roosevelt, in a sense, stole monetary supervision from the

Federal Reserve System and placed it in the Treasury Department. After the Gold Reserve Act of 1934 he returned much of the authority to the Federal Reserve System. Then in 1935 he supported a major reorganization of the Federal Reserve System, a reorganization that further centralized and nationalized the system and made it a potential instrument of a coordinated national economic policy, yet one with a degree of independence from local politics. The Banking Act of 1935, originally the handiwork of Federal Reserve Board Chairman Marriner Eccles, a former Utah banker, suffered several moderating but nonessential amendments in the Senate. As passed it gave a renamed Board of Governors virtually complete control over open-market operations, permanent control over reserve requirements within established limits, full veto power over rediscount rates, which were still set by the twelve Reserve banks, and power to veto the selection of presidents and vice-presidents of the reserve banks. Following earlier precedents in the Hoover administration, it further broadened the classification of eligible paper.

Despite its new repertoire of credit controls, the Federal Reserve System remained virtually helpless. The rediscount rates meant little, since excessive reserves insured that practically no banks wanted to borrow. Likewise, liberalized reserve requirements had no effect except to increase excessive reserves in member banks, and thus make it even more difficult to tighten credit should this ever become desirable. Finally, open-market purchases lost all their potency (after 1933 the Federal Reserve System stopped all buying), since they could only increase reserves. Even if, in theory, federal bank policies and stabilized monetary supplies could have prevented a depression, they clearly could not cure it.

In 1937 the newly reorganized Federal Reserve Board flunked its first big test. Throughout 1936 it had used every available tool to encourage easy credit. By mid-1936 excess reserves (the amount beyond those required by the Federal Reserve System to back up demand deposits) reached $3 billion. The slack was so great that the Federal Reserve Board had no effective weapons to curtail inflation should such control become desirable. Thus, in August of 1936 the Federal Reserve Board raised reserve requirements of member banks by about 50 percent. This halved the excess reserves but did not raise credit rates, since the banks still desperately needed borrowers to maximize their own income. Since the reserves continued to rise, the Federal Reserve System in January 1937 again increased reserve requirements. This again only halved excess reserves, and left banks as a whole with an excess of about $1 billion. For this reason the action could not be interpreted as any attempt to cool the economy, raise interest, or curtail monetary supplies. But it had that psychological effect. Some banks, accustomed to large reserves, sold bonds to increase them. Government bond prices dropped, and this tremor combined with the other, major causes of the late summer recession. The Federal Reserve System had a red face.

Could it reverse its damage? It could try. Its Open Market Committee bought enough bonds to stabilize bond prices, and in so doing increased bank reserves. It also cut margin requirements on stock purchases and lowered rediscount rates, both rather futile gestures under the circumstances (no banks needed or wanted to rediscount when they had ample reserves). More significant, the board reversed itself on reserve requirements, lowering them again in April and allowing excess reserves to mount. Obviously, such reserves had no real effect in a lifeless credit market, with already rock-bottom interest rates. As of 1938 the Federal Reserve Board was in a truly unfortunate position: its quite reasonable efforts to gain more leverage over monetary supplies helped, for few rational reasons, to stimulate a severe recession, while it had no reverse leverage to cure it, and would not have so long as excess reserves and low interest rates continued.

The cure, at least by the government, had to be fiscal—more spending. But Roosevelt resisted this. Just as he gained a semblance of recovery, he hated to start the long ordeal of relief and deficits all over. Involved was a loss of face and some regained status for his critics. Roosevelt blamed businessmen for the economic reversal. They refused to spend. He even called it a "strike of capital," and saw it as a deliberate conspiracy by businessmen to embarrass his administration. His anger led him to new condemnations of concentration and monopoly; a few powerful businessmen could still frustrate government and public goals and plunge the country into depression for political reasons. He stepped up antitrust activities in the Justice Department and urged a willing Congress to create the Temporary National Economic Committee (TNEC) to investigate monopoly power. The committee, made up of members of both the executive branch and of Congress, spent a year and a half in a monumental study of economic concentration. Its thirty-one-volume report did not reveal any business conspiracy against New Deal recovery, but it more than documented all of Roosevelt's charges of concentrated power, and helped destroy forever any lingering illusions about an America made up of small producers. But the committee could not offer any potent, politically acceptable remedies for what it saw as a problem (not all Americans believed concentration in itself to be undesirable), and rather lamely emphasized increased antitrust action.

Neither charges, investigations, nor legal action against monopoly could reverse the economic plunge in 1937. In fact, too many threats could only worsen it. Having few alternatives, influenced by a growing

group of pro-Keynesian advisers, Roosevelt asked Congress in 1938 for increased relief appropriations, which he used to reinvigorate the WPA and
to revive the PWA. By mid-1938 the economy responded and began to
move upward, although slowly until given new stimulus by defense expenditures in 1941.

Tax Policy

Business leaders, generally hostile to deficit spending, insisted upon tax
cuts and fiscal orthodoxy as the appropriate cure for the new depression.
Except for the symbolically important repeal of an undistributed profits
tax, and a slow gain in prestige, they received very little. But one must
note that tax cuts are possible corollaries of spending. Either increases
purchasing power among some classes of consumers, depending in each
case on whose taxes are cut or how the government spends its money.

New Deal tax policy was never Keynesian or well-adapted to promote
recovery. In theory, often in intent, but rarely in effect, it was redistributive. In the early New Deal Roosevelt had proposed no major tax policies,
and probably did not realize that the AAA processing taxes amounted to
a regressive sales tax on food. In an even more hidden way, gold devaluation had added a tarifflike cost to imported goods, to the detriment of
those with low incomes. A minor tax revision in 1934 made the income
tax more progressive, but note that only relatively affluent people yet
paid income taxes. The controversial wealth tax of 1935, before congressional emasculation, did contain clear and emphatic progressive features.
But all tax increases were deflationary, and thus retarded recovery. The
only tax policy that could have matched the inflating effects of deficit
spending would have been major cuts, particularly for reluctant corporations and low-income consumers. Save for excise and social security taxes,
only local governments were in a position to make the cuts most stimulating to consumers, and they were usually too pinched for funds to cut
taxes.

One minor New Deal tax change dominated the long debate over the
causes of the depression of 1937. In 1936 Roosevelt had asked Congress
for a graduated tax on undistributed corporate income. Either way, this
promised new federal revenue and also an increased level of economic activity. Despite the depression, many corporations had accumulated sizable
surpluses during the thirties, surpluses they never distributed to stockholders nor used for immediate expansion. The tax, if it forced distribution of funds, would mean increased personal income tax revenues and
also would force more corporations to seek bank loans, bringing them
under the control of central banking policies. If the corporations held on
to the surplus funds they would have to pay 30 percent on the first $10,-

ooo and 42.5 percent on all amounts over $10,000. Although such taxes had been used before and proposed even by Andrew Mellon in the twenties, the proposal seemed like salt on a wound to frustrated and bitter businessmen who predicted the direst of consequences if it passed. They won sympathy for their charge that it would unduly penalize small, beginning businesses that needed surplus capital in order to grow and become competitive. To meet this criticism the administration agreed to exempt small corporations. Congress finally passed a mild measure providing graduated rates from only 7 percent to 27 percent. But the bitter criticism continued, and allowed businessmen to blame the tax, unfairly, for the depression of 1937–38. Congress virtually repealed it by substituting a rate of only 2.5 percent and repealed even that in 1939.

In retrospect, New Deal tax policy was full of irony and contradictions. Roosevelt's tax goals clearly worked against recovery by fiscal means and testified to his own resistance to Keynesian-type theories. Roosevelt sought both a much more progressive tax system with penalties on large wealth and concentrated economic power, and also enough tax increases to prevent large governmental deficits. He achieved limited tax increases, in part through such incidental means as social security, but scarcely achieved from a reluctant Congress any significant redistribution of the tax burden. In fact, counting social security and other hidden taxes, lower income groups probably fared worst of all. But more important, tax increases of any type impeded his recovery goals and the fighting rhetoric that accompanied his 1935 bill only reinforced this unwanted effect. Thus Roosevelt lost on his social goals, fell into contradiction in his recovery policies, and gained, if at all, only the political returns from sharp controversies with the wealthy.

The 1937–38 panic had unusual educational value. Its inescapable relationship to government spending added new stature to Keynesianism. But it also documented the importance of psychological factors, of consumer and business confidence. The early thirties left a legacy of fear and caution. Almost everyone expected another crisis comparable to 1933. Workers saved for it. When lay-offs came, they accepted them as normal. Businessmen tried to build their own nest eggs, and thus resisted undistributed profits taxes. In this context government relief expenditures sustained the economy but could not create the magical demand needed for sustained expansion in the private sector, particularly when government expenditures declined. By later example, the consumers proved they had (or could be induced to have) an almost infinite number of unfilled wants, although no dramatic new product in the thirties pushed people over the threshold of spending and borrowing. When war came it created the demand.

Congress obliged the administration in 1938 on the new relief expenditures, but not without searching criticism. It also approved the new AAA, the Federal Fair Labor Standards Act, and aided consumers by a mild tightening of governmental controls over food, drugs, and cosmetics (it rejected much more stringent measures proposed as early as 1933). But senators almost tortured several agency heads in appropriation hearings, showed a more detailed and critical interest in executive programs, completely rejected a new Executive Reorganization Bill, and directly defied Roosevelt on tax policy. All this resistance and independence came from the most overwhelmingly Democratic Congress in history.

The opposition either to Roosevelt or to particular New Deal officials or programs fits no neat pattern, and permits no single analysis. It obviously crossed party lines. The beleaguered Republicans, of course, had less difficulty maintaining party discipline than the Democrats, and often joined in near-unanimous opposition to the administration. By their very numbers the Democrats risked internal division, and more so because of the diverse interests now represented in their party. In 1936 several new congressmen ran on a strictly pro-Roosevelt platform, and in Congress usually followed administrative policies wherever they led. But they had no seniority and little power on any committees. By 1938 Roosevelt's most effective support came from older, urban, labor-oriented Democrats, and from a handful of former Progressive Republicans, such as Norris or Robert M. La Follette, Jr. On many, but not all issues the president steadily lost support from a powerful group of southern congressmen, and most particularly from such powerful senators as Millard Tydings of Maryland, Harry F. Byrd of Virginia, Walter George of Georgia, and Kenneth McKellar of Tennessee.

This Democratic opposition reflected several points of conflict, all of which merged in a Harry Byrd. In part, it involved power. Individual congressmen resented the shift of power to a strong executive and to academically sophisticated bureaucrats. Congressmen were often quite conventional in belief, and reflected regional and class bias. If from the South, they avidly defended segregation; if from rural areas, they remained spokesmen for the hallowed ideals of agrarianism. The very confusions of economic policy in the administration made loyalty an exceedingly personal matter, and invited defection by the more established and independent congressmen. At a more ideological level, many southern congressmen adhered to the ideal of state rights, either as a protection for individual rights and privacy or as a protection against future federal intervention on civil rights. Not only southern Democrats, but others as well, joined Republicans in opposition to overt class legislation, or legislation that seemed to threaten major producers in their home states. For

286

such reasons, Democrats increasingly voted against new administration legislative proposals, and helped prevent an enlarged New Deal.

Such opposition meant treason to Roosevelt. Just as he had seen his leadership and the expressed will of the people thwarted by the Supreme Court, so now Democratic members of Congress became the effective saboteurs (he accepted Republican opposition as normal). But why did they dare express such opposition? One answer inheres in the nature of our political system, the other in the nature of the New Deal. Our congressional system, with its two houses and a separate executive, does not merge interests of the president and a congressional majority, even when both belong to the same political party. Our two-party system, an unwritten part of our Constitution, does insure some degree of adhesion between the president and congressional members of his party. But despite patronage and party roles, the president cannot overcome either strong regional interest or ideological dissent by "his own" congressmen. We do not have a parliamentary system. Our government does not rise or fall as a unit; the political fortunes of a congressman often dictate opposition to his president. Also, neither of our major parties has ever reflected single interests, regions, or ideologies. No two monolithic parties could encompass our national diversity. By their very role, each political party always reflects a loose coalition of some sort, and maintains only a minimal and ambiguous average or distinguishing position, often scarcely enough to discriminate it very clearly from its opposition. In this context, party discipline is impossible and political predictability rare.

The New Deal itself invited intraparty fragmentation. By personal appeal, Roosevelt helped to gather quite diverse interests. But their diversity showed through in Congress. The weakness of the Republicans, the very size of the Democratic majority, removed one support for party loyalty —the weakness or vulnerability of a party in national elections, or the insecurity of congressmen in local elections and their need for patronage and presidential campaign support. Finally, Roosevelt moved in too many directions, stood for too many divergent programs, to establish any clear New Deal orthodoxy. Thus, his desire for party loyalty, such as on the critical Court issue, amounted to little more than an appeal for personal loyalty. The more the New Deal stood for anything espoused by the Roosevelt administration, and not for a coherent point of view or specific program, the more difficult it was for Roosevelt to insist upon loyal support. After all, congressmen did not like to be pulled into contradictory positions any more than they wanted to lose their sense of integrity and autonomy.

The net effect of all this was that by 1938 Roosevelt faced concerted opposition within his own party. And short of a new emergency, or some tremendously new and widely appealing program, he could do little about it. His personal prestige did not provide the capital needed for altering local voting habits or local beliefs, to which congressmen responded more effectively than did any president. Yet, he wanted to try just this. Eschewing an old policy of wooing all elements in the party, he gave calculated support to acclaimed friends, to those he called "liberals," in several state primaries, and opposed entrenched incumbents who by now rather consistently joined the Republican opposition. Vilified as Roosevelt's "purge," his efforts usually backfired. In Maryland (Millard Tydings) and in Georgia (Walter F. George) it placed Roosevelt in the position of invading state rights, and possibly boosted his opponents. At least it gave them a diverting political issue.

Behind his primary effort lay an idea that tantalized Roosevelt until his death. Why not rationalize the American party system? A small minority of "liberals" should leave the Republican party, a rather large contingent of Democratic "conservatives" should join it. Then the popular will, as expressed in national presidential elections, could be effectively achieved. A "conservative" president would have behind him a conservative Congress, and could quickly fulfill platform commitments. Roosevelt, of course, conceived of himself as head of a liberal or progressive party, and, characteristic in such plotting, gained a near-corner on virtue, for in his rhetoric the useless labels stood for everything good. But, in theory, a "conservative" would only have to play the same definitional game to reverse the odds. Behind Roosevelt's hopes lay some concrete justification. On certain issues party lines meant very little, and by careful attention to detail either "liberal" or "conservative" could be given specific content. But national issues were much too varied to fit into any two rational groupings, whatever the labels implied. And individual politicians could come up with a whole spectrum of positions. Roosevelt soon found his best allies in foreign policy to be the very Southerners who had always loved his farm program, distrusted his labor policies, suspected his racial proclivities, and often opposed his "excessive" spending. On close analysis the only solid, unambiguous glue for a "liberal" party in 1938 or afterward had to be personality; the only true test of party orthodoxy had to be personal loyalty.

In 1939 Roosevelt faced even more congressional hostility. The Republicans began their long road back to political equality, increasing their House membership in 1938 by eighty-one and their Senate by seven. Congress approved new flood control programs but refused seriously to consider six more valley authorities, an idea Roosevelt began pushing in

Harry Hopkins (1890–1946), right, with Harold Ickes (1874–1952), center, and Frank C. Walker, left, in 1935. Hopkins played many roles in the Roosevelt administration; works progress administrator, secretary of commerce, head of Lend-Lease administration, and personal assistant to Roosevelt. Ickes, another close adviser, was variously secretary of the interior, administrator of public works, and petroleum administrator. *Franklin D. Roosevelt Library*

1937. As a direct slap at Roosevelt, and at the role of relief officials in the preceding election, Congress passed the Hatch Act, which severely curtailed the political role of federal employees. Congress also decisively defeated an expanded home financing bill, new taxes, and new wages and hours legislation. Finally, and most important, it approved a watered-down Governmental Reorganization Act.

In 1937 a top-level presidential commission recommended extensive changes in the organization of the executive branch, a reorganization necessitated by the rapid and haphazard accretion of federal programs. The resulting bill, as defeated by Congress in 1938, contained political dynamite despite its seeming reasonableness. It gave the president extensive and unilateral authority to investigate, change, consolidate, or abolish governmental agencies, excepting only cabinet-level departments, the congressional fief in the District of Columbia, and the still prestigious Federal Reserve Board. It also provided for a drastic expansion of civil service jobs, again with great presidential discretion. It provided for internal Treasury authority over accounts, an overall Auditing Office, and a Joint Congressional Committee on Public Accounts, or a considerable dilution of congressional budgetary supervision and a clear attempt to open the way for more effective governmental action. In direct anticipation of the later Department of Health, Education, and Welfare, the act authorized a Department of Social Welfare, plus a Department of Public Works. To please Ickes, it would have renamed Interior as the Department of Conservation. Finally, and possibly most frightening to Congress, it established a permanent planning agency, a National Resources Board of five presidential appointees, approved by the Senate, and with a mandate to develop the facts needed for planning the development and utilization of the nation's human and natural resources.

The problem of reorganization would not go away. Congress would not give Roosevelt and his advisers much leeway, but in 1939 it did give him broad authority to save money through the consolidation of related agencies, but with very strict congressional controls. The Reorganization Act allowed six new presidential assistants (part of a new, formalized White House staff), but refused any departmental name changes and exempted many old-line agencies from reorganization. More significantly, the president had to forward all reorganization plans in detail to both houses of Congress, estimate the savings achieved, and subject them to a veto by a joint congressional resolution. If Congress did not act, the reorganization took effect in sixty days. Under the scheme Roosevelt placed both the Division of the Budget and the National Resources Planning Board within a new Executive Office of the President, and created a Federal Security Agency, a Federal Loan Agency, and a Federal Works Agency, achieving the consolidation of agencies he earlier sought by new executive departments. But nothing in the new act, or in the changes made under it, gave any congressional approval for a permanent planning agency. In the whole debate over reorganization Congress showed a keen sensitivity to its own power and a jealous resentment of any executive hegemony.

The mild Reorganization Bill marked the last major domestic legislation of the thirties, and what might be called the legislative ending of the New Deal. By 1940 defense problems occupied most congressional attention, although Congress still performed its annual rite of rejecting antilynching bills and willfully chopping away at domestic appropriations. New taxes underwrote defense, while the intensely controverted Selective Training and Service Act began a "peacetime" draft. Drawn by lot, relatively unsuspecting young men began their one-year military service. Few returned to civilian life until 1945. By 1940 Roosevelt simply had no congressional leverage for any significant extension of class or welfare legislation, or for effective control over concentrated private economic power. Always quick to perceive political obstacles, he realized that he could not move ahead on the domestic front. In these areas he could only fight a holding action, trying to protect new programs but not trying to extend them.

Roosevelt's new role as internationalist helped him win the unprecedented third-term election of 1940. His decision to accept but not seek renomination gave a political weapon to Republicans, and severely strained his relationship with many Democrats. Why he made such a bid remains, like all questions of motivation, open only for plausible speculation. The simplest explanation fits his own justification. The fall of France in June, the beginning battle of Britain, persuaded Roosevelt that not only the ultimate security of the United States, but all Western civilization, was at stake. Domestic issues became secondary. Bolstering Britain, defeating Hitler, became Roosevelt's one great goal. As usual, he rose to a challenge. His ego became deeply involved. He wanted to lead America, help shape its policies so that it could provide more aid to Britain (he still hoped to avoid war, but surely saw it as one possibility). With these commitments, Roosevelt easily assumed that no one else had the experience and prestige to provide effective leadership in this new crusade. After all, he had already directed our foreign policy in the critical early years of the European debacle. Could any new leader, however able, pick up at that point and carry on as well? Of course Roosevelt may have been wrong in his assumptions; any number of Americans might have been better equipped for wartime leadership. Such speculation, in any case, is pointless. Roosevelt simply revealed the assurance of a very able politician, and typically saw himself as the person most needed at that time.

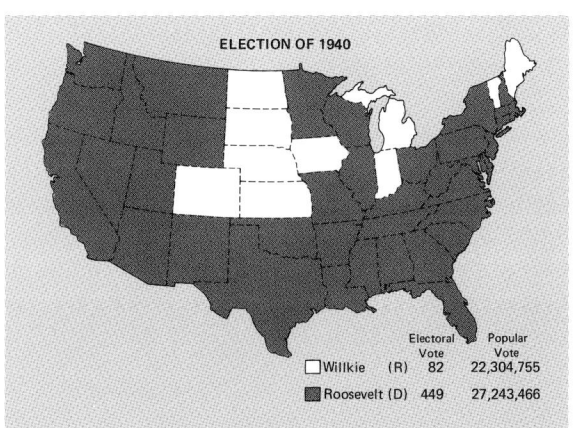

ELECTION OF 1940

		Electoral Vote	Popular Vote
☐	Willkie (R)	82	22,304,755
■	Roosevelt (D)	449	27,243,466

But there were surely other considerations, and some much more suggestive to Roosevelt's critics. For example, by 1940 Roosevelt had failed to develop any favored successor, and in fact had led several men to believe that they would be his choice for the nomination. This strategy created a vulnerable party in 1940, and increased the likelihood that it would press Roosevelt for a third term. Also, as much or more than most presidents, Roosevelt had been continuously besieged by the crassest of flattery. From his ambassadors abroad, from his own immediate advisers, from old friends such as Frankfurter, he heard unending praise of his brilliance, eloquence, and ability, of the success of his speeches and programs, of the rightness of his commitments. It was easy for him to believe that he was the savior of democracy in a chaotic world and more indispensable than ever in the deepening chaos. His overwhelming electoral victory in 1936 had greatly enhanced his self-esteem.

The Republicans, in a surprise move at their earlier convention, nominated Wendell Willkie, in all ways an attractive candidate. Youthful in appearance, appealing as a speaker, an internationalist in foreign policy, he promised a more effective campaign than Landon. As a result of his long crusade against New Deal business policies, he had a large national following, and could begin his campaign with a lead over any conceivable Democrat except Roosevelt. This meant that Roosevelt's candidacy might be necessary to insure victory. Finally, even though many party leaders opposed his third term, a large number of close friends, or dependent members of his administration, fervently supported it, and thereby reinforced Roosevelt's own inclinations.

Roosevelt easily capitalized on his advantages as an incumbent. At the convention he further rankled party bosses by forcing the nomination of Henry A. Wallace as vice-presidential candidate (Garner had opposed the third term). Wallace was an effective symbol of the now-completed New Deal, and a pledge to the large constituency for New Deal programs. This was Roosevelt's gesture to what he now called the "liberal" wing of his party, a wing that he loved. But he launched a noncampaign that deliberately appealed to a more diverse audience. From July until September he did not make a single campaign address. Instead he gave all his time to an unending series of diplomatic and defense issues, helping create the image of an experienced leader, giving of himself to a great national cause, and much too involved to enter into vulgar, political discourse. This strategy left Willkie defenseless. He continued his attack upon New Deal domestic policies, but from sincere conviction had to give general support to Roosevelt's interventionist foreign policy. Only belatedly did he attack Roosevelt's defense posture, and then most often to indict his fumbling and inefficient attempts to rearm. Both candidates supported an

A campaign poster for Wendell Willkie (1892–1944), the GOP nominee for president in 1940. Willkie was an Indiana lawyer, who, as president of Commonwealth and Southern Corporation, had national exposure for his anti-New Deal politics. His youthful appeal made him an attractive candidate, and although he did well against Roosevelt, he lost the election. *Library of Congress*

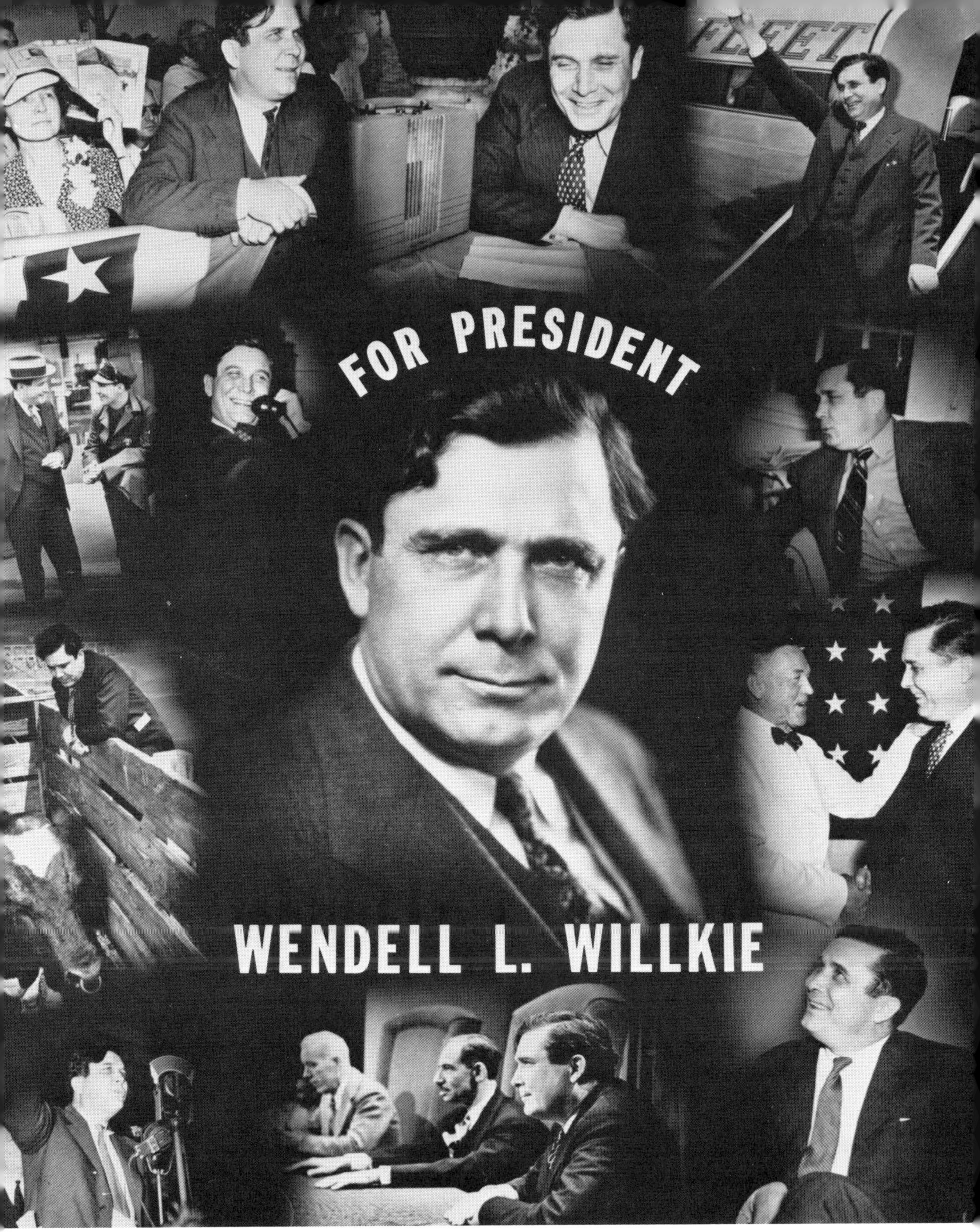

FOR PRESIDENT

WENDELL L. WILLKIE

Allied victory; both pledged to avoid war, with Roosevelt's strongest rhetoric later coming back to haunt him ("Your boys are not going to be sent into any foreign wars . . ."). After a belated but rather nasty campaign, Roosevelt won more easily than even he expected (roughly 27 million to 22, and 449 electoral votes to 82).

In his third term Roosevelt had to devote almost all time and attention to war and diplomacy. But the very necessities of war seemed to fulfill some of his earlier domestic commitments. It brought full economic recovery and more, ended the unemployment problem, allowed a significant downward redistribution of income, and helped reestablish his political prestige. The war also seemed, at least on the surface, to vindicate deficit spending as a weapon against depression. (In reality, it did not, for the massive expenditures of World War II so flooded the economic pump as to require, not the finesse of fiscal tools, but strict governmental controls.) These results of war have abetted those Roosevelt critics who believe, but cannot document, that a conspiratorial Roosevelt, desperate because of the economic ineffectiveness of his recovery measures and because of the increasing effectiveness of an anti-New Deal coalition in Congress, deliberately and cleverly maneuvered the United States into war as a final solution to his dilemmas. In their perspective, the war represented the real culmination and climax of the New Deal.

Roosevelt surely felt differently. He either sacrificed or postponed what he called "social" goals in order to gain the consensual unity needed to win a war. He wooed businessmen rather than railed at them. He dropped all demands for increased welfare. During the war he had to sacrifice his beloved Civilian Conservation Corps, see Congress emasculate the Farm Security Administration, and give up his National Resources Planning Committee. By 1940 a majority in Congress, including a good share of Democrats, perceived the "New Deal" as a bad word, evoking images of dangerous radicalism. The war practically forced Roosevelt to establish a new image for himself as a truly national, wartime leader. Only a handful of men identified with major New Deal agencies—a Hopkins and a Wallace—remained in the limelight. Because of the demands of war production, he had to sanction immense business consolidation and underwrite both profits and spectacular capital growth. Even the redistribution of wealth occasioned by war taxes scarcely reflected a clear social goal, but only the effect of war financing and attempts to control inflation. Roosevelt even moderated some of his political partisanship, and often successfully sought agreement on basic issues. These aspects of his wartime leadership, if at all related to the New Deal years, hearkened back to the honeymoon of 1933, to the idea of a concert of interests, but contrasted sharply with the class legislation and rhetoric of 1935.

With the perspective of time one can identify the more enduring legacy of the New Deal years. By indirection as often as by plan, by accident as often as by choice, the Roosevelt administration eventually adopted new fiscal and monetary policies well calculated to avert serious economic cycles. It complemented these by an array of new welfare programs to succor some of the victims both of an exceptional depression and also of the more permanent insecurities of a complex production and distribution system. Finally, it dramatically increased the federal subsidies and regulations affecting most categories of producers. Politically, in an atmosphere of intense partisanship, often with ideological and class content, Roosevelt used persuasion or programs to unite to the Democratic party an even larger share of wage laborers, a surprising number of small producers, particularly farmers, most of a growing black electorate, and large numbers of journalistic and academic intellectuals (including most of those who wrote early histories of the New Deal). He also helped create among these groups a new, often undoubted, belief in the benevolence of federal power and in the desirability of strong presidential leadership.

Just as important is what the New Deal did not do. This list reflects not all the unlimited possibilities, but stated goals of Roosevelt or his advisers, or purported achievements claimed by New Deal fans as well as purported crimes condemned by its critics. In this perspective, the New Deal did not significantly increase government ownership of the means of production, did not lead to direct governmental economic planning, did not redistribute income or wealth, did not arrest the pace of business consolidation, and did not provide many gifts to the people at the very bottom of the social and economic scale. Perhaps most important, it did not bring the federal courts under the control of large, popular majorities.

Such a summary in no way reflects the understanding of people in the thirties. Only later eventualities, unknowable, even inconceivable in the thirties, allow such sweeping judgments. Our present emphasis upon such fiscal devices as deficit spending, or upon a new welfare state, must not lead to a false perspective. The issues proclaimed, the passions engendered, the events experienced in the thirties hardly reflected either the abstractions of Keynesian economics or any mass acceptance of a still frightening welfare state. The focal issues then seemed very different. Also, such enduring results of the New Deal years can hardly be equivalent with the label "New Deal." Admittedly, the label may function in a strictly historical context, or as a typical product of the historian's workshop. As a convenient historical stereotype it may come to stand only for the more enduring programs, or even for the unanticipated effects, of the Roosevelt administration. But in the thirties it functioned, not in the selective perspectives of historians, but in the passionate political arena. It at least vaguely symbolized Roosevelt, his retinue of advisers and officials, and almost any administrative program. Many efforts proved ephemeral. Thus, one must surely see the NRA as a key New Deal agency, yet may argue persuasively that it had little to do with any enduring legacy of the Roosevelt years. In a history of the thirties the immense passions aroused by the so-called "wealth tax" of 1935 must loom large. Yet, it neither redistributed income nor significantly influenced our tax policies.

Bibliography

The literature on the Roosevelt administration is already as extensive as for any comparable period in our history. The flood of historical monographs shows no sign of slackening. Thus, the following bibliography has to be narrowly selective.

General and Political

Despite the volume of writing, we do not yet have a single, brilliant history of either the Roosevelt administration or the domestic New Deal. The task may well be beyond the ability of any scholar. So far, the most ambitious effort remains conspicuously incomplete. Arthur M. Schlesinger, Jr., *The Age of Roosevelt*, 3 vols. [I, *The Crisis of the Old Order, 1919–1933*; II, *The Coming of the New Deal*; III, *The Politics of Upheaval* (Boston: Houghton Mifflin, 1957–1960)] carries the story only to 1935. These volumes are vivid in characterization but imprecise in concepts, exacting in scholarly detail but enthusiastically partisan toward Roosevelt and the New Deal. The best brief survey is by William E. Leuchtenburg, *Franklin D. Roosevelt and the New Deal* (New York: Harper and Row, 1963). Other briefer surveys include Mario Einuadi, *The Roosevelt Revolution* (New York: Harcourt, Brace 1959); Dexter Perkins, *The New Age of Franklin Roosevelt, 1932–45* (Chicago: University of Chicago, 1957); Edgar E. Robinson, *The Roosevelt Leadership, 1933–1945* (Philadelphia: Lippincott, 1955); Paul K. Conkin, *The New Deal* (New York: Thomas Y. Crowell, 1967).

Several members of the Roosevelt administration left revealing diaries or wrote perceptive books. The best of these are by two members of the original brains trust: Raymond Moley, *After Seven Years* (New York: Harper and Brothers, 1939), and *The First New Deal* (New York: Harcourt, Brace and World, 1966); and Rexford G. Tugwell, *The Democratic Roosevelt* (Garden City, N.Y.: Doubleday, 1957), and *The Brains Trust* (New York: Viking Press, 1968). *The Secret Diary of Harold Ickes*, 3 vols. (New York: Simon and Schuster, 1953–54) is full of intimate gossip and revealing insights into New Deal policy making. Less perceptive is John Morton Blum's edition, *From the Morgenthau Diaries*, Vol. 1 *Years of Crisis, 1928–38* (Boston: Houghton Mifflin, 1959). Robert E. Sherwood, himself a New Dealer as well as a playwright, wrote a revealing account in his *Roosevelt and Hopkins: An Intimate History* (New York: Harper and Brothers, 1950). Felix Frankfurter was surely one of the most trusted advisers of Roosevelt. Yet, Max Freedman, ed., *Roosevelt and Frankfurter: Their Correspondence, 1928–1945* (Boston: Little, Brown, 1967), reveals both men at their worst, and provides surprisingly little insight into New Deal policies.

The most extensive and complete biography of Roosevelt is by James M. Burns, *Roosevelt: The Lion and the Fox* and *Roosevelt: The Soldier of Freedom* (New York: Harcourt, Brace, 1956 and 1970). Frank Friedel's more detailed and more extensive biography remains uncompleted for the crucial New Deal years, but provides a wealth of information on most of Roosevelt:

297

Franklin D. Roosevelt, 4 vols. (Boston: Little, Brown, 1952–73). Daniel Fusfeld helps explain New Deal economic policy in his *The Economic Thought of Franklin D. Roosevelt and the Origins of the New Deal* (New York: Columbia University Press, 1956). Francis Perkins, *The Roosevelt I Knew* (New York: Viking Press, 1946) not only reveals an intimate perspective, but best exemplifies the several biographies of Roosevelt penned by his admirers.

A few excellent books are topical, yet pertain to the New Deal as a whole. Among these are Otis Graham's *Encore for Reform: The Old Progressives and the New Deal* (New York: Oxford University Press, 1967), and James T. Patterson, *Congressional Conservatism and the New Deal* (Lexington: University of Kentucky Press, 1967) and *The New Deal and the States: Federalism in Transition* (Princeton: Princeton University Press, 1969). The following three books critically examine our recent political economy in a way that directly encompasses the New Deal: Henry Dariel, *The Decline of American Pluralism* (Palo Alto, Calif.: Stanford University Press, 1961); Theodore Lowi, *The End of Liberalism* (New York: W. W. Norton, 1969); Grant McConnell, *Private Power and American Democracy* (New York: Knopf, 1961).

Populistic movements in the thirties defy ideological classification. Most of these are treated by David H. Bennett in *Demagogues in the Depression: American Radicals and the Union Party, 1932–1936* (New Brunswick, N.J.: Rutgers University Press, 1969). Also revealing are Abraham Holtzman, *The Townsend Movement: A Political Study* (New York: Bookman Associates, 1963); Charles Tull, *Father Coughlin and the New Deal* (Syracuse, N.Y.: Syracuse University Press, 1965); and T. Harry Williams, *Huey Long* (New York: Knopf, 1969).

Conservation and Natural Resources

There are no histories of the total New Deal conservation program. Edgar B. Nixon edited *Franklin D. Roosevelt and Conservation, 1911–1945*, 2 vols. (Washington, D.C.: Government Printing Office, 1957), which includes a broad distribution of source materials. Marion Clawson and R. Burnell Held have written a general history of soil conservation: *Soil Conservation in Perspective* (Baltimore: Johns Hopkins University Press, 1965). Phillip O. Foss's *Politics and Grass: The Administration of Grazing on the Public Domain* (Seattle: University of Washington Press, 1960) contains a full account of the Taylor Grazing Act. The most comprehensive story of the CCC is in John A. Salmond, *The Civilian Conservation Corps, 1933–1942: A New Deal Case Study* (Durham, N.C.: Duke University Press, 1967). This can be supplemented by two older and specialized studies: C. P. Harper, *The Administration of the Civilian Conservation Corps* (Clarksburg, W. Va.: Clarksburg Publishing Co., 1939), and Kenneth Holland and Frank E. Hill, *Youth in the CCC* (Washington, D.C.: American Council on Education, 1942).

The Tennessee Valley Authority is a story in itself. The best account of its origins is in Preston J. Hubbard, *Origins of the TVA: The Muscle Shoals*

Controversy, 1920–1932 (Nashville, Tenn.: Vanderbilt University Press, 1961). The best single history of the TVA is C. Herman Pritchett, *The Tennessee Valley Authority: A Study in Public Administration* (Chapel Hill: University of North Carolina Press, 1943). Topical studies include Philip Selznick, *TVA and the Grass Roots: A Study in the Sociology of Formal Organization* (Berkeley: University of California Press, 1949); William H. Droze, *High Dams and Slack Waters: TVA Rebuilds a River* (Baton Rouge: Louisiana University Press, 1965), a history of navigational policies; Norman I. Wengert, *Valley of Tomorrow: the TVA and Agriculture* (Knoxville: Bureau of Public Administration, University of Tennessee, 1952); Thomas K. McCraw, *TVA and the Power Fight, 1933–1939* (Philadelphia: Lippincott, 1971); and Thomas K. McCraw, *Morgan vs. Lilienthal: The Feud Within the TVA* (Chicago: Loyola University Press, 1970). David Lilienthal's *TVA, Democracy on the March* (New York: Harper and Bros., 1953) is little more than a propaganda piece.

Agriculture

There is no overall history of New Deal agricultural policy. The origins of the AAA, and of domestic allotments and price supports, receive attention in Russell Lord's meandering *The Wallaces of Iowa* (Boston: Houghton Mifflin, 1947); in Gilbert Fite, *George N. Peek and the Fight for Farm Parity* (Norman: University of Oklahoma Press, 1954); and most perceptively in Richard S. Kirkendall, *Social Scientists and Farm Politics in the Age of Roosevelt* (Columbia: University of Missouri Press, 1966). Van L. Perkins provides a detailed and revealing picture of the first year of the AAA in *Crisis in Agriculture: The Agricultural Adjustment Administration and the New Deal, 1933* (Berkeley: University of California Press, 1969). The economic implications of farm policies are treated in Donald C. Blaisdell, *Government and Agriculture: The Growth of Federal Aid* (New York: Rinehart and Co., 1940); and Edwin G. Nourse, *Government in Relation to Agriculture* (Washington, D.C.: The Brookings Institution, 1940).

The problems of poverty and exploitation in agriculture have received as much attention as the mainline programs. Sidney Baldwin has written an excellent history of the FSA: *Poverty and Politics: The Rise and Fall of the Farm Security Administration* (Chapel Hill: University of North Carolina Press, 1968). This special area of agricultural reform is also treated extensively in Bernard Sternsher, *Rexford Tugwell and the New Deal* (New Brunswick, N.J.: Rutgers University Press, 1964), and in Paul K. Conkin, *Tomorrow a New World: The New Deal Community Program* (Ithaca: Cornell University Press, 1958). The very lowly farmers have their due in Carey McWilliams, *Factories in the Field: The Story of Migratory Farm Labor in California* (Boston: Little, Brown, 1939); David Conrad, *The Forgotten Farmers: The Story of the Sharecropper in the New Deal* (Urbana: University of Illinois Press, 1965); and John L. Shover, *Cornbelt Rebellion: The Farmers Holiday Association* (Urbana: University of Illinois Press, 1965).

By far the most complete and balanced history of the American worker in
the New Deal is Irving Bernstein, *The Turbulent Years: A History of the
American Worker, 1933–1941* (Boston: Houghton Mifflin, 1970). This supplements his much earlier monographs on *The New Deal Collective Bargaining Policy* (Berkeley: University of California Press, 1950). Milton Derber and
Edwin Young have edited a group of short articles on *Labor and the New
Deal* (Madison: University of Wisconsin Press, 1957). A more narrow economic study is Harold W. Metz's *Labor Policy of the Federal Government*
(Washington, D.C.: The Brookings Institution, 1945).

More specialized monographs on New Deal labor policies or on the history
of labor unions in the critical thirties abound. Many were reports close to the
actual events, such as William H. Spencer, *Collective Bargaining under Section 7 (a) of NIRA* (Chicago: University of Chicago Press, 1935); Selig Perl-
man, *Labor in the New Deal Decade* (New York: International Ladies Gar-
ment Workers Union, 1945); Herbert Harris, *Labor's Civil War* (New York:
Knopf, 1940); and Edward Levinson, *Labor on the March* (New York: Harper and Brothers, 1938). More scholarly monographs include Jerald S. Auer-
bach, *Labor and Liberty, the La Follette Committee and the New Deal* (Indianapolis, Ind.: Bobbs-Merrill, 1966); Sidney Fine, *Sit-Down: The General
Motors Strike of 1936–1937* (Ann Arbor: University of Michigan Press, 1969);
Walter Galenson, *The CIO Challenge to the AFL* (Cambridge, Mass.: Harvard
University Press, 1960); and Philip Taft, *The AFL from the Death of Gompers
to the Merger* (New York: Harper and Row, 1959).

By far the best book on New Deal policies toward business, and also the
most comprehensive account of the NRA, is Ellis W. Hawley, *The New Deal
and the Problem of Monopoly* (Princeton, N.J.: Princeton University Press,
1966). Hugh S. Johnson left his own memoir of the NRA in *The Blue Eagle
from Egg to Earth* (Garden City, N.Y.: Doubleday, Doran, 1935). An early
economic appraisal of the NRA was Leverett C. Lyon, et al., *The National
Recovery Administration: An Analysis and Appraisal* (Washington, D.C.:
The Brookings Institution, 1935). The relationship between Roosevelt and
business leaders has to be gathered from the general histories of the New
Deal, or from topical economic studies, such as Sidney Fine, *The Automobile
Workers Under the Blue Eagle* (Ann Arbor: University of Michigan Press,
1963).

There is no adequate economic history of the thirties. Broadus Mitchell,
Depression Decade: From New Era through New Deal, 1929–1941 (New
York: Rinehart and Co., 1947) is now dated and often quite inaccurate. Stan-
dard works of broader scope contain sections on the New Deal; these include
the monumental text by Milton Friedman and Anna Jacobson Schwartz, *A
Monetary History of the United States, 1867–1960* (Princeton, N.J.: Prince-

ton University Press, 1963); a chapter in Herbert V. Prichnow, ed., *The Federal Reserve System* (New York: Harper and Row, 1960); and a very brief survey of New Deal policies in Lewis H. Kimmel, *Federal Budget and Fiscal Policy, 1789–1958* (Washington, D.C.: The Brookings Institution, 1959). Adolph A. Berle, Jr., and Gardiner C. Means, *The Modern Corporation and Private Property* (New York, 1932), is still a good introduction to the modern American economy. It can be supplemented by Berle's *The 20th Century Capitalist Revolution* (New York: Harcourt, Brace, 1954) and by Means's *The Structure of the American Economy* (Washington, D.C.: National Resources Committee, 1939). Other general works are Andrew Shonfield, *Modern Capitalism: The Changing Balance of Public and Private Power* (New York: Oxford University Press, 1965), and Arthur E. Burns and Donald S. Watson, *Government Spending and Economic Expansion* (Washington, D.C.: American Council on Public Affairs, 1940).

The best starting point on fiscal policy is John Maynard Keynes, *A General Theory of Employment, Interest, and Money* (New York: Harcourt, Brace, 1936). Robert Lekachman analyzes the impact of Keynes in *The Age of Keynes* (New York: Random House, 1966). Marriner Eccles, the head of the Federal Reserve System, was the most articulate administration spokesman for indirect fiscal devices, and has left an able record of New Deal fiscal policies in *Beckoning Frontiers* (New York: Knopf, 1951). For tax policy, see Randolph E. Paul, *Taxation for Prosperity* (New York: Bobbs Merrill, 1947).

For the details on monetary policy see Arthur W. Crawford, *Monetary Management under the New Deal* (Washington, D.C.: American Council on Public Affairs, 1940); Allan S. Everest, *Morgenthau, The New Deal, and Silver: A Story of Pressure Politics* (New York: King's Crown Press, 1950); E. A. Goldenweiser, *American Monetary Policy* (New York: McGraw-Hill, 1950); James D. Paris, *Monetary Policies of the United States, 1932–1938* (New York: Columbia University Press, 1938); and Joseph Reeve, *Monetary Reform Movements* (Washington, D.C.: American Council on Public Affairs, 1943).

Relief and Welfare

As yet we have no full history of the New Deal relief efforts. Three older, topical studies provide at least an abundance of factual detail: Donald S. Howard, *The WPA and Federal Relief Policy* (New York: Russell Sage Foundation, 1943); Betty and Ernest K. Lindley, *A New Deal for Youth: The Story of the National Youth Administration* (New York: Viking, 1938); and Arthur W. Macmahon, et al., *The Administration of Federal Work Relief* (Chicago: Social Science Research Council, 1941). The best introduction to the major relief program is in Searle F. Charles, *Minister of Relief: Harry Hopkins and the Depression* (Syracuse, N.Y.: Syracuse University Press, 1963). Jane D. Mathews, *The Federal Theater, 1935–1939* (Princeton, N.J.: Princeton University Press, 1967) provides an excellent account of one of the special WPA projects; Francis V. O'Connor has edited *The New Deal Art Project:*

An Anthology of Memoirs (Washington, D.C.: Smithsonian Institution, 1972).

Of all New Deal welfare programs, social security was probably the most important, and by all odds the most symbolic. It has received considerable historical attention. The long battle for social insurance, up to 1935, is summarized in Roy Lubove, *The Struggle for Social Security, 1900–1935* (Cambridge, Mass.: Harvard University Press, 1968). Grace Abbott, in *From Relief to Social Security: The Development of the New Public Welfare Services* (New York: Russell and Russell, 1966) stresses the public assistance features of the Social Security Act. An older work is Paul Douglas, *Social Security in the United States* (New York: McGraw-Hill, 1936). Lewis Merriam provides an economic analysis in *Relief and Social Security* (Washington, D.C.: The Brookings Institution, 1946). Edwin E. Witte, one of the principal architects of the Social Security program, has written the detailed legislative history in *The Development of the Social Security Act* (Madison: University of Wisconsin Press, 1962). Theron F. Schlabach's biography, *Edwin E. Witte: Cautious Reformer* (Madison: State Historical Society of Wisconsin, 1969) includes an account of the social security movement.

Housing is the second great area of New Deal welfare efforts. An overview is in Robert M. Fisher, *Twenty Years of Public Housing* (New York: Harper and Row, 1959). C. Lowell Harriss, in *History and Policies of the Home Owners Loan Corporation* (New York: National Bureau of Economic Research, 1951) evaluates the first New Deal venture into home financing. The PWA directed the first major effort in public housing. Harold I. Ickes, its director, wrote an early brief in its defense: *Back to Work: The Story of the PWA* (New York: Macmillan, 1935); John K. Galbraith and F. F. Johnson, Jr., reviewed its housing efforts in *The Economic Effects of the Federal Public Works Expenditures, 1933–1938* (Washington, D.C.: National Resources Planning Board, 1940). For the all-important public housing act of 1937, see Timothy McDonnell, S. J., *The Wagner Housing Act: A Case Study of the Legislative Process* (Chicago: Loyola University Press, 1957). The only scholarly biography of Wagner, the architect of so many welfare measures, is by J. Joseph Huthmacher, *Senator Robert Wagner and the Rise of Urban Liberalism* (New York: Atheneum, 1968).

The special problems of the Negro in the thirties has received attention in articles, but in few books. Raymond Wolters critically examines the Negro's lot in the early recovery program, *Negroes and the Great Depression: The Problem of Economic Recovery* (Westport, Conn.: Greenwood, 1970). Beyond this, see Bernard Sternsher's anthology, *The Negro in Depression and War* (Chicago: Quadrangle Books, 1969), and Richard M. Dalfiume, *Desegregation of the U. S. Armed Forces: Fighting on Two Fronts* (Columbia, Mo.: University of Missouri Press, 1968).

The Supreme Court

There is no adequate history of the Court fight. Most general histories of the New Deal emphasize the political implications of the struggle, but ignore or minimize juristic issues. The most enduring reportage is in Joseph Alsop and Turner Catledge, *The 168 Days* (Garden City, N.Y.: Doubleday, 1938). Beyond this there are biographies of individual judges, and a general study of *The Roosevelt Court* by C. Herman Pritchett (New York: Macmillan, 1948).

Life and Thought

By far the best social and cultural history of the thirties is Charles C. Alexander, *Nationalism in American Thought, 1930–1945* (Chicago: Rand, McNally, 1969). Frederick Lewis Allen, in *Since Yesterday* (New York: Harper and Row, 1940) provides a lighter overview. Arthur A. Ekirch, Jr., *Ideologies and Utopias: The Impact of the New Deal on American Thought* (Chicago: Quadrangle, 1969) is most perceptive on the governmental patronage of the fine arts.

Three excellent books survey American religion in the thirties, each with particular attention to social issues: Paul Carter, *The Decline and Revival of the Social Gospel* (Ithaca: Cornell University Press, 1956); Donald B. Meyer, *The Protestant Search for Political Realism, 1919–1941* (Berkeley: The University of California Press, 1960); and Robert M. Miller, *American Protestantism and Social Issues, 1919–1939* (Chapel Hill: University of North Carolina Press, 1958). For Roman Catholics, see David J. O'Brien, *American Catholics and Social Reform: The New Deal Years* (New York: Oxford University Press, 1968).

Literature has received extended treatment for the thirties as well as for other decades in the twentieth century. A good starting point is Robert E. Spiller, ed., *A Time of Harvest: American Literature, 1910–1960* (New York: Hill and Wang, 1962); and an interpretative classic, Alfred Kazin, *On Native Grounds: An Interpretation of Modern American Prose Literature* (New York: Harcourt, Brace and World, 1942). More directly related to the thirties are Daniel Aaron, *Writers On the Left: Episodes in American Literary Communism* (New York: Harcourt, Brace and World, 1961); Maxwell Geismar, *Writers in Crisis: The American Novel, 1925–1940* (Boston: Houghton Mifflin, 1961); and Edmund Wilson, *The Shores of Light: A Literary Chronicle of the Twenties and Thirties* (New York: Farrar, Straus, and Young, 1952).

The best overall history of the plastic arts is Oliver Larkin, *Art and Life in America* 2d ed. (New York: Holt, Rinehart and Winston, 1960). For painting, the earlier references to the relief arts projects can be supplemented by Edgar P. Richardson's encyclopedic *Painting in America: From 1502 to the Present* 4th ed. (New York: Thomas Y. Crowell, 1965). So far, there is no comprehensive history of the popular arts. The older classic, Lewis Jacobs, *The Rise of the American Film* (New York: Harcourt, Brace and World, 1939) covers most of the New Deal years. So does Francis Chase's *Sound and Fury: An Informal History of American Broadcasting* (New York: Harper and Row, 1942).

PART THREE

Foreign Policy in a Disordered World

15

The European truce arranged so hopefully in 1918 ended in renewed conflict as early as 1935. The war in China continued. More ominous, in 1933 Hitler and the Nazi party began their own New Deal in Germany. Roosevelt never had a respite from diplomatic tensions. He faced crucial decisions from 1933 on. The United States had played a leading role in securing the years of respite in the twenties. In the early years of the depression, it refused to make the major commitments necessary to avert or at least postpone the coming tragedy. But American choices, in at least marginal ways, influenced the course of European and Asian events.

The Roosevelt administration continued Hoover's cautious policies in Asia, expanded his new overtures to Latin America, but reversed much of his economic internationalism in Europe. Even before the inauguration, Roosevelt consulted extensively with Hoover's secretary of state, Henry L. Stimson. He gladly accepted the Stimson Doctrine, or nonrecognition of Japanese conquests in China. Roosevelt had a developed affinity for China, a sympathy in part rooted in cherished family memories. His secretary of state, Cordell Hull, shared Roosevelt's apprehensions about Japanese expansion. Hull held to the Wilsonian ideal of collective security and American opposition to all clear violations of existing treaties. But such was the press of economic issues that the American role in the Far East would have to take the form of continued and increasingly meaningless protest.

Economic Nationalism

The most immediately pressing issues in foreign policy in 1933 were trade, debts, and currency. Hull wanted lower tariffs and, as the other side of the same coin, stabilized currencies, all in behalf of increased international trade and with it better understanding and enhanced prospects for enduring peace. These themes may seem like empty and pious cliches today; Hull believed them and at least never vulgarized them. His own traditional internationalism, fortified by sincere idealism and moral preachment, ran counter to prevailing administration concern for nationalist policies to overcome depression. Hull would be disappointed, and at times even horrified, at some of the New Deal domestic programs. Young men in the administration often had little more than contempt for the courtly, slightly archaic Tennessean. They terribly underestimated Hull. He would suffer endless setbacks in implementing his ideals. Roosevelt

307

Depression Diplomacy

often seemed to betray him or to follow other advice. But Hull kept to his "mission," doggedly overcame obstacles, and eventually won most of his points. By his perseverance, he gave Roosevelt's foreign policy a greater consistency, and a greater continuity, than seemed ever to exist in the domestic New Deal. Despite the president's early flirtation with such "heresies" as a more insular economic nationalism or with neutrality in a morally divided world, he eventually concurred with Hull's commitment to collective security. And Hull's traditional loyalties, even the flavor of his rhetoric, helped gain him enormous prestige.

Before the inaugural stands fell, Roosevelt began receiving an unending stream of foreign delegations, all seeking some new economic concessions from the United States. These ranged from one led by the British prime minister, Ramsay MacDonald, to prestigious French and German economic missions, to an unending stream of VIPs from small countries. The major European countries all hoped for debt, tariff, and currency concessions, and tried desperately to gauge the new administration's economic policies. Most carried home illusions of one sort or another, including what they interpreted as early Roosevelt pledges of tariff reduction and stabilized currency exchange. These impressions bolstered hopes for significant achievements at the upcoming London Economic Conference in June of 1933. The depression led to a more than usual brutal competitive scramble among commercial nations, each desperately trying to gain some edge over the others. By June, Roosevelt justifiably felt a bit cynical about the various pleas for collective action in behalf of recovery, for clearly each country wanted such action on its own best terms. But, of course, so did we.

Roosevelt, who had refused any close cooperation with Hoover in planning for the London conference, faced this, his first major diplomatic test, with what seemed growing confusion. He consistently vetoed even discussion of war debts, thereby successfully removing one illusion of European delegations. He initially supported Hull's efforts for reduced tariffs and trade restrictions, and even made this one of his instructions to the American delegation. But by the time the conference convened in London he had reversed himself, in effect dropping tariff reform from his congressional program. This left currency issues as the only significant diplomatic bargaining point in London.

On this issue, the delegates themselves had ambiguous instructions and divided loyalties. In fact, the delegation as a whole was ill-fitted for any significant negotiations. Hull led it and gave the Americans prestige, but when Roosevelt undercut his one great concern—tariff reduction —he had no substantive role to play (Hull apparently approved currency stabilization but refused to become personally involved with that issue at the conference). He did prove himself a brilliant diplomat in matters of internal organization, and in preventing an early adjournment of the conference. His fellow delegates, quite correctly, gave priority to domestic political concerns over any coherent foreign policy. They included a sincere but relatively uninformed Texas millionaire, a Tennessee senator incapable of playing any substantial role in technical negotiations, an able but nonexpert James M. Cox (Roosevelt's running mate in 1920), and Senator Key Pittman of Nevada, given to embarrassing intoxication at critical moments, and with only one word in his diplomatic vocabulary—*silver*. By tenacious singlemindedness, Pittman secured a new international agreement on silver, the only achievement of the American delegation or of the conference.

The issue of stabilization really complemented the issue of tariffs. Either by higher tariffs or currency devaluation a country could discourage imports. Devaluation could also lower prices of its exports, increasing foreign sales. In the economic warfare of the early depression, European countries had resorted to both trade restrictions and devaluation in order to gain a competitive edge. In April Roosevelt had joined them by leaving the gold standard. The European countries hoped that Roosevelt would agree to a stabilized dollar (possibly at its current value and not its earlier gold value), an International Stabilization Fund, and a permanent set of exchange rates between major world currencies, all tied to gold. This would surely lead to restored trade, create prospects of tariff reductions, and reverse the junglelike competition that pushed more and more countries toward insulated and managed national economies. By the conference, with its built-up expectations, the prestige of both France and Britain depended upon at least some temporary stabilization agreement. Both countries believed that Roosevelt had given them a rather clear commitment to such an agreement.

Since stabilization had to be at a set exchange rate, it could hardly help all countries equally. In the final accounting some would sacrifice and some gain. And no country wanted to make any sacrifices, or dared bargain away immediate prospects of national recovery. As the negotiations in London came closer to concrete proposals, Roosevelt became more apprehensive over any stabilization prospects. Even hints in this direction arrested domestic price increases. He also responded to the persuasive influence of inflationist theorists and sought leeway for further devaluation. Finally, he smelled a trap, ready to be sprung by France and England or self-seeking international bankers. With the American dollar already disadvantaged by earlier European currency manipulations, stabilization would in effect freeze us in a poor exchange position and possibly subsidize European recovery at our cost. In June of 1933 he decided to sabotage stabilization, a nationalistic position that promised him added prestige at home however much it horrified financiers.

To help unsnarl the conference, Roosevelt sent Raymond Moley to London, apparently as a messenger and observer and not with any special authority to negotiate over the heads of the delegation. But he came as a direct representative of Roosevelt; everyone simply presumed he brought dramatic new proposals. His trip, with some rather harrowing escapades in the last stage, attracted blazing publicity in the European press and created unwarranted hopes of early agreements. The exact story is impossible to reconstruct because of divergent accounts by various participants, but apparently Moley came with either Roosevelt's assent to, or at least a justified impression of his support for, some type of temporary stabilization. In high-level consultations (as Hull fumed) Moley communicated this assurance. By the end of June he could wire a tentative agreement to Roosevelt. It seemed innocuous enough—a commitment of gold-standard countries, such as France, to continue their existing exchange rates, and nongold countries such as the United States and Britain to work for the restoration of gold, and to do all they could to limit further exchange speculation. This implied, at most, some concerted efforts to prevent a further decline in the American dollar, possibly through export of gold.

In a private message received in London on July 1, Roosevelt rejected the agreement, reserving for himself freedom to seek further price increases (and further devaluation). He stressed domestic prices as America's first concern and deplored attempts by other nations to impose fixed standards. The president disingenuously suggested that the conference discuss permanent solutions for the problems of all sixty countries present, and not intrude on the domestic policy of only one. The next day he made public his final rejection of stabilization (the bombshell message). Again he suggested broader problems as proper to such a conference, and argued that the internal economic system of a country had to take priority over international exchange conditions (he would later insist that the 7 percent tail of foreign trade should not wag the hefty dog of domestic commerce). He blamed international bankers for adopting a selfish strategy. In the future, with balanced budgets and higher price levels, he granted the possibility of permanent stability backed by gold and silver. But not now, and not by temporary agreements. Let the conference treat the fundamental issues—increased trade, lower tariffs, and above all higher prices. In effect, but not in fact, this ended the London Economic Conference. And Roosevelt had to take responsibility for an effective wrecking job, although in behalf of what he perceived as American interests.

The conference helped reinforce Roosevelt's suspicions of our European "friends," particularly France. It reduced considerably any remote likelihood of American cooperation in resisting subsequent German rearmament and expansion. In Europe, while it created resentment toward America, it also created a type of respect, although a respect based on independence and power, not generosity. At home Roosevelt's action gained popular assent and reinforced a growing popular disenchantment with foreign involvements, collective security, and complicated international marketing and banking programs. It abetted what, in popular terms, paraded as "isolationism."

Some of the fallout from the conference came quite early, and on other than economic issues. In a circular letter Roosevelt sent to other heads of state on taking office, he emphasized his support for disarmament and, in the vein of the old Kellogg-Briand treaties, for collective efforts to prevent aggression. Characteristically, his new crew of ambassadors, including several old college cronies, deluged him with flattering letters about the wonderful effect of his pious generalities. In a vague sort of way Roosevelt seemed to be issuing a warning not only to Japan but possibly to Germany. Yet, by October 1933, when Germany withdrew from the World Disarmament Conference over a failure to attain arms parity with France, Roosevelt emphatically refused to join in collective sanctions against aggressive acts, the only support France needed to accept the parity principle. Burned by the London conference, he would soon give at least official support to stringent neutrality legislation.

Roosevelt's economic nationalism did not mean a retreat from an active and positive foreign policy. It did reveal what had to be the overwhelming priority in such policy—increased trade, to help in the recovery effort. Since Roosevelt perceived economic losses in stabilization, he rejected it. But other pending issues promised economic gains for America. Early recognition of the Soviet Union, for instance, promised to create what many industrialists and many cotton and corn and wheat farmers believed to be a large market for American goods. In negotiation in Washington in late 1933, the Soviet representatives met at least minimal American demands—promised abstention from propaganda, religious freedom for Americans in the Soviet Union, and settlement of the czarist debt. To help collect the promised windfall, we established the Export-Import Bank to loan the Soviet Union dollars to buy our products. Formal recognition at least restored lasting diplomatic relations, but did not profit the United States. Because of debt disputes, we never offered the anticipated credits or appreciably expanded our trade beyond the existing small trickle.

As for Germany, the State Department tried to find some way of collecting on private debts threatened with permanent cancellation by the

Nazis. The intense pressure from bondholders helped moderate our early diplomatic pressures on Hitler. Counterpressure came from American Jews, or less persistently from other morally concerned Americans, who reacted to the cruel anti-Semitism of even the early Nazi regime. Our official protests, at least in retrospect, seem quite weak (no one could then predict the horrors to come). The State Department helped block consideration of a liberalized immigration law in order to admit more Jewish refugees. Roosevelt seemed to feel that other goals—disarmament, moderated demands by Hitler, restored trade—outweighed in importance the immediate problems of a Jewish minority.

The "Good Neighbor"

Even as the United States backed away from economic agreements in Europe it tried to better its bargaining position in the Americas. In 1929 our export trade in the Western Hemisphere came very close to that of Europe, or about $2 billion. It fell off by nearly three fourths by 1932. Almost half of the loss involved Canada. Early in his administration, Roosevelt, with great enthusiasm, backed a joint St. Lawrence Seaway project, but it fell prey to too many counterinterests in the Senate, and waited almost two decades for realization. The only other major economic initiative toward Canada came later with successful attempts to forge reciprocal trade agreements.

As for Latin America, Hull helped complete a revision of American policy, a revision publicized by the label "Good Neighbor Policy." In the early years of the century the United States assumed a protectorate over several Caribbean countries, and exercised direct political and military control whenever necessary to protect American lives, property, or security. Both Hoover and Roosevelt recognized the harmful effects of such overt American domination. It created enmity in the helpless recipients of our "supervision" and fanned anti-American sentiments, particularly in Mexico, Brazil, Argentina, and Chile. It also drove these countries toward closer diplomatic and commercial ties with Europe, and often foreclosed our trade or our investment opportunities. The loss of American markets for raw materials during the Depression led to intense suffering in Latin America and greater possibilities of anti-American revolutions. Finally, our intervention was both costly and also morally offensive to many Americans who detested such blatant interference in the affairs of officially sovereign states. Freer trade and closer cooperation in any further war also necessitated a new policy.

Cuba provided the first real test of the new attitudes. Roosevelt inherited a new revolution there—one that threatened almost all major American investments. An unpopular dictator, Gerardo Machado, had

gained earlier American support and had worked closely with American financial interests, but succumbed to the distress of a depression in part rooted in the disastrous fall in sugar prices. Roosevelt tried to save the existing government by promising increased sugar quotas in exchange for major social reforms. Machado fell before any such agreements could be effected. The revolutionary replacement, Ramón Grau San Martín, proved a direct threat to the considerable American interests in Cuba (around $1 billion), especially American-owned sugar companies. In earlier times his ascendancy would have drawn immediate American military intervention. Even now Sumner Welles asked for such from his post in Havana, and many American newspapers expected it at any moment.

Fulgencio Batista (1901–) reached his position as the strong man of Cuba in much the same fashion as his successor, Fidel Castro. With encouragement from the U.S., Batista helped to overthrow Machado and Martín before becoming virtual dictator in 1933. *Wide World Photos*

Roosevelt chose to wait, and used special envoys (including Adolph Berle as well as Welles) to try conciliation. Under the excuse of instability we refused to recognize Martín. Our delegates apparently helped encourage a further coup, led by Fulgencio Batista. In any case, he overthrew Martín (today revered as a great Cuban hero) and set up a puppet government which we not only recognized but supported with a generous loan. Although our ships sailed close and our planes flew over, we had not used direct force. Batista would remain in power until overthrown by Fidel Castro in 1959.

But limited restraint in Cuba hardly persuaded Latin America. The first opportunity both to announce a clear new policy and to exploit its fullest benefits came in December 1933, at an inter-American conference in Montevideo. Here Hull achieved a sterling diplomatic victory. He came as an equal, solicited good will by visiting each delegation, and then dramatically supported a convention which, among other things, established the equality of all states in the hemisphere, their complete sovereignty, their right to de facto recognition, and their inviolability to intervention by other states (primarily meaning the United States). This concession successfully countered other anti-American resolutions, and produced at least a Latin American willingness to test American sincerity. We soon made good on most of our promises at Montevideo. Our last military forces left Haiti and the Dominican Republic, and would not return to either until 1965. We promised less intervention in Panama, although we were not about to give up our special position there.

Mexico, larger, more self-sufficient, had never been an American fief, though it had suffered often from U. S. "paternalism." Its successful and thoroughgoing revolution, completed in the twenties, led to intense conflict over oil properties. But the Good Neighbor Policy helped appease President Cardenas, and at least made possible reasonable negotiations on outstanding differences. After the final nationalization of American oil companies in 1938, Secretary Hull secured at least a minimal compensation from Mexico and subsequently negotiated a trade agreement. Despite the oil companies' loss, Mexico remained an excellent market for our products and for American capital willing to accept strict governmental controls.

In a global context, reciprocal trade complemented the Good Neighbor concept. Although deferred in 1933, Roosevelt backed Hull's pet program in 1934 when Congress approved the Trade Agreements Bill. It did not directly lower the existing Hawley-Smoot tariff schedules, but gave to the president full authority to modify existing rates as much as 50 percent in response to concessions by other countries. The recent currency devaluation had the effect of raising our trade barriers to their highest level in history. Now Hull could begin the long process of negotiating reductions with individual countries (twenty-one during the 1930's). As explained to Congress and the public, and most often in fact, the new agreements involved reductions by the United States on noncompetitive or only slightly competitive imports, and complementary reductions by other countries on our less competitive exports. The expected return was increased trade and a vital contribution to our recovery, as well as firmer diplomatic ties to cooperating countries. The agreements did help increase trade, though not spectacularly. Even by 1939 our exports remained at only 66 percent of the 1929 level, and imports at just over 50 percent.

Even as Japan prepared for excursions in China, and Hitler began to dismantle the Versailles agreements, a peace movement flourished in the United States. Widespread disillusionment over our participation in World War I, stimulated by critical historical writings, became pervasive by the mid-thirties. The war had been a horrible mistake, surely occasioned by one or another conspiratorial group. The most likely devils were the large corporations most directly involved in the munitions buildup, or the American investors whose loans gave them a stake in an Allied victory. In Congress, Senator Gerald P. Nye proved most receptive to antiwar sentiment and retrospective accusations. An able, tremendously conscientious North Dakotan, Nye had supported the economically radical Non-Partisan League. Earlier in the Teapot Dome scandal and in investigating election frauds, he had established himself as a determined exposer of concealed evils. In 1934 he introduced a resolution calling for an investigation of the munitions industry. All-out support from peace groups secured even reluctant administration support and Congress approved a committee made up almost entirely of congressmen committed to a rigorous American neutrality.

The Lure of Neutrality

The Nye Committee scarcely proved any corporate conspiracy to have been a cause of World War I, although some committee members certainly stacked their findings in that direction. But it did expose large wartime profits, a close, compromising relationship between corporations and the War and Navy Departments, corporate lobbying in behalf of military appropriations, and a callous exploitation of foreign wars as a source of profits for these corporations. However sinister it all sounded, these types of behavior could only be expected of such corporations. The hearings, continued into 1936, helped cement a belief that World War I had not involved American security or even our vital interests, but only emotional sympathies and our pocketbooks. While boys died on the battlefield, the Du Ponts doubled their profits.

Concern was most intense among youth. Even in 1933 a loose survey of over 20,000 college students revealed that 72 percent would not serve in the armed forces in wartime; almost 50 percent would not serve even in the unlikely case of a foreign invasion. In 1934 students organized a strike against war (no particular war): over 25,000 left their classes to participate in demonstrations and to cheer impassioned speakers. In 1935 a student strike in New York drew even more participants, with campaigns directed against naval appropriations and campus ROTC. This emphatic antiwar feeling pervaded many youth groups and churches, had abundant support from the clergy, and at least reflected a widespread sympathy among parents.

From this repudiation of the past, from the dramatic revelations of the Nye Committee, from organized antiwar protest, came some serious discussion of neutrality and of collective security. Neither concept is very precise. Those who wanted the United States to join in a world organization like the league, or even cooperate with other countries to resist early aggression, often wanted peace above all else. Could the United States most successfully avoid war by very positive international efforts to prevent its occurrence, or by concealed efforts to avoid involvement in foreign wars? Those who sought a truly complete or immaculate neutrality argued, cogently, that foreign wars could not be prevented by any American action, and that collective involvement could only pull us into such struggles. They spoke in the context of an undeclared war in China and emerging European conflict, and used such immediate examples to reinforce their position. But advocates of collective action against aggressors detailed the extreme difficulty of avoiding involvement in major wars; a complete severance of all trade relationships with belligerents, for instance, was too extreme a measure to secure popular support in America. Real neutrality had to be a positive program, involving major economic sacrifices and also the moral sacrifice of eschewing any active role in preventing or punishing such international outlaws as a Hitler. Since America would sooner or later be directly involved in major wars (our very economic commitments almost necessitated this), we should direct our energies to the prevention of such wars even at the expense of limited military engagements. We should, in other words, help police the status quo, demand only peaceful change, or work in such positive areas as international disarmament.

In the mid-thirties the advocates of neutrality and disengagement, abetted often by an ambivalent Roosevelt administration, won their way. The old issue of an arms embargo, debated in 1933, became in 1935 the basis of stringent neutrality legislation. Ironically, the policy drew strength from the deteriorating world situation, which aroused fears of American involvement rather than of any long-range threats to our security. Roosevelt even asked the Nye Committee to suggest new neutrality legislation. A reluctant Hull proved a master in delaying tactics, keeping legislation in committees for extensive State Department study. Nye wanted a complete embargo against all belligerents. But the most extreme congressional proposals stopped short of this, restricting only arms, contraband, loans, and foreign travel. The best the State Department could hope for was discretionary authority allowing the president to apply an embargo only against aggressors. On this they lost. The final bill, approved overwhelmingly in both houses and with at least tacit support from Roosevelt, imposed for the next six months a complete, impartial arms embargo, a ban on the shipment of munitions on American ships, a prohibition of travel by Americans on the ships of nations at war, and provision for a National Munitions Control Board. The bill left little leeway for further American cooperation with other countries, and rather decisively shifted the main guidelines of foreign policy from the president to Congress. He had discretion only in defining arms, or in applying the embargo to new states entering an existing war.

One irony of the first embargo act was that it gave Roosevelt the very authority he needed to aid beleaguered Ethiopia in the unequal Italian-Ethiopian War of 1935. He curtailed trade and travel with Italy. A second irony came when the league condemned Italy. Roosevelt's zestful use of the embargo then subjected him to neutralist criticism for cooperating with the league in what amounted to a collective action. This helped inspire added support for more stringent legislation. After a terribly complex debate, Congress compromised in early 1936 by extending the 1935 embargo and added a prohibition against loans to belligerents. In mid-1936 the administration could not use this against the competing sides in a brutal civil war in Spain (it did not apply to civil wars), but attempted a moral embargo based on persuasion. When this failed, Roosevelt easily secured from Congress in early 1937 a special embargo against both sides in Spain to the despair of a growing number of sympathizers with both sides.

By 1936 a major split developed in Congress. Administrative supporters of an embargo wanted discretionary authority for the president. He should be able to initiate it when he wanted. The advocates of complete neutrality tried to eliminate every possible leeway for presidential initiative, fearing above all a partial use of the embargo to aid a preferred side in war. Insofar as verbal distinctions are possible, the vast majority of neutralists were not isolationists; that is, they wanted to continue most American contact abroad, including at least the existing level of trade. Isolation threatened too many economic interests to gain broad accep-

Premier Benito Mussolini (1883–1945) with the sultan of Gimma, ruler of an Italian-annexed Mohammedan region of Ethiopia. Mussolini became the dictator of Italy in 1922 and remained the leader of fascism in that country until he was deposed in 1943. In 1935 he marched into Ethiopia, and by 1936 had annexed the country to Italy. *Wide World Photos*

tance. Only a persuaded antibusiness senator such as Nye wanted to go all the way and force severe losses on the economy at the cost of peace.

By 1937 the unresolved issue remained trade in nonmunitions. Would we forego profits in behalf of neutrality? Could a complete trade embargo even be a neutral act? What if it removed vital necessities from a country and assured its defeat while scarcely affecting the security of the other side? In this case an embargo would be tantamount to an act of war on our part (roughly, this would be the Japanese argument in 1941). The best answer (but far from a perfect one) seemed to be "cash and carry," even though it would reward the country with wealth and a large merchant marine. Roosevelt bought it, perhaps out of favoritism to the British. Again, as in 1936, the controversy involved the degree of presidential discretion in invoking cash and carry. Simply put, the Senate passed a permanent neutrality act that made cash and carry mandatory; the House made it discretionary. The House carried the issue in conference, but exacted a more rigid travel ban and also a ban against arming American merchant ships trading with belligerents. The bill required the president, when he found a state of war to exist (no great discretion here)—either between nations or a civil war—to embargo all arms (but not raw materials), to ban all except short-term commercial loans, to prohibit American travel on belligerent ships, and, if he so desired, to require cash and carry of all belligerents.

The 1937 act represented the climax of neutrality pressures on Roosevelt. There would be only one more dramatic effort—the Ludlow Amendment. Beginning in 1935, Lewis Ludlow of Indiana, a Democratic congressman as fully committed to neutrality (or even isolation) as Nye, pushed a new constitutional amendment requiring a national referendum before Congress could declare war except in cases of invasion. Passage, even in Congress (three-fourths of the states would have to approve), offered a distinct challenge to presidential leadership in foreign policy. Roosevelt avidly opposed it, but at a time of increasing congressional opposition to his programs. The House rejected Ludlow's resolution in 1938 by only 209 to 188. Even by 1939 Roosevelt would have little leeway for independent action in foreign affairs. But after the actual outbreak of a European war in September 1939, congressional neutralism slowly declined. At the very least, Congress cooled to any additional legislation.

Over and over again neutrality legislation, even though predicated on the highest of principles, had proved vulnerable to contextual sympathies or compelling interests. In the crunch, most people wanted neutrality only when they were emotionally neutral or when the legislation really worked for a favored belligerent. Abstractly, everyone wanted to avoid war. But few could consistently maintain a policy that forced the United States to foster a hated ideology or support aggressive acts. Thus, antiwar activists who in 1934 supported neutrality found it immoral in 1937 when they joined the Abraham Lincoln Brigade to fight the Republican cause in Spain. Italian-Americans could not tolerate the one-sided embargo in the Ethiopian war, but as Catholics could favor a rigid embargo against Spain. And so it went. In the long run, events in Europe and Asia, and careful persuasion by Roosevelt, so swayed American opinion that neutrality laws meant very little. They represented mood pieces, reactions of a moment, and never a matured and responsible consensus. America could not yet be either a Switzerland or a Sweden.

16

The climax of neutrality politics overlapped the first, faint tremor of a new, more active and critical involvement in international affairs by the Roosevelt administration. No single event provoked a change. No single act clearly exemplified it. No new aspirations lay behind it. Rather, threatening events in Europe and Asia required an American response, since they seemed to have grave implications for our future. Both the events, and our response to them, became gradually more significant. By degrees we joined the European war. With the excruciating disaster of Pearl Harbor we joined a related Asian war.

In retrospect, almost every foreign policy decision by the Roosevelt administration in the years from 1937–1941 invites critical scrutiny, and allows almost endless speculation about hidden motives and goals as well as ever-clearer alternatives. International politics is a tremendously complex game, involving not only the strategies of statesmen and diplomats, but also basic assumptions and beliefs of varied, human communities. Only an extended space of time allows an unraveling of much of the complexity and subtlety. Only hindsight, only living eventualities, permits any clear sorting-out of the momentous from the ephemeral. Only our present aspirations provide any basis for a critical evaluation of past policies. It is we who enjoy and suffer the consequences.

Thus, our criticism has in it the quality of a lament. The unending plaint directed at our progenitors is: "Woe is me." We know what our forefathers did not know. But our most crucial knowledge, being historical, could not be theirs. We may not share their aspirations. But this is simply to say we are different than they, and perhaps largely because of a lapse of time and a difference of experience. We can hardly condemn them for being what they inescapably were and even in a sense had to be. They affirmed themselves. We all do. They usually took responsibility for their decisions. We must do the same. We may pity their ignorance, lament their cultural limitations, note their inevitable mistakes of judgment, but we must not fail to see that such judgments always encompass ourselves.

Whatever it seemed, our pre-World War II diplomacy was neither bumbling nor naïve. The State Department staff, though small and almost chummy in comparison to today, did not lack expertise or sophistication.

On the Fringes of Catastrophe

Roosevelt, so typical of his personality, resented the caution, the bureaucratic slowness, of State Department employees. He rightly perceived the built-in myopia of area experts, the ponderous style of briefs and studies. But he had available to him as thorough intelligence estimates, as much linguistic and geographical knowledge as any head of state in Europe. Secretary Hull, who had the complete confidence of his department, had long since learned the need for careful staff work. Roosevelt offered a striking contrast to Hull's caution and often rejected Hull's moralisms. For more dramatic missions abroad, Roosevelt usually turned to Sumner Welles, the more volatile and daring undersecretary.

Roosevelt ran the show. He would have it no other way. As foreign-policy issues became paramount by 1937, he assumed full responsibility for them. This does not mean he failed to use or heed his subordinates. On most issues he had to. At his best, he wanted to. But he often did it grudgingly. He loved personal diplomacy. And whatever the varied constitutional systems, the major protagonists of World War II all came under the dominance of powerful individuals, of a Hitler, a Stalin, or a Churchill. Roosevelt early joined the club of personality and moved in it as an equal. He remained as unpredictable and as expedient as in domestic politics.

Whatever the merit of his foreign-policy decisions, Roosevelt won support for them. He took a unified nation to war. Events helped but the timing was his. From 1937–1940 he had to balance foreign initiatives and domestic opinion and often seemed to temporize. The European allies despaired of his delays and unbelievable caution. But somehow out of his apparent confusion and disorder came concentrated energy and victory. For those who wanted more internal mobilization on an earlier commitment to the allied cause, Roosevelt seemed terribly inept, captive to public whims and overly sensitive to congressional thinking. For those who wanted to avoid war, he seemed a clever conspirator, arbitrarily calculating events in behalf of a final disaster at Pearl Harbor. But either view ignores a much simpler explanation of his policies. Roosevelt as so often before led effectively because he never moved far ahead of conventional and majority opinion. Never far ahead, never far behind, he responded to opinion even as he helped organize it.

For anyone who wanted to preserve the existing world order, 1937 seemed a threatening and gloomy year. In Spain a fascist Franco pushed toward victory in the civil war. A year earlier Mussolini had completed his conquest of Ethiopia; Hitler had regained the Rhineland. Now Hitler made threatening gestures toward Austria and Czechoslovakia. In Asia, Japan moved beyond Manchuria to an all-out war against China. The new neutrality legislation seemed a deliberate effort to isolate America from all this chaos. It never had this effect. We had every reason to do all we could to influence events on both continents. Already in that ambivalent position of wanting to stay out of foreign wars, at the same time we tremendously wanted to influence or control events. Not wishing to be fully part of an evil, calculating outside world, yet we feared being left out of any critical decisions affecting it. Thus, even as a strange, have-your-cake-and-eat-it-too type of neutral, America was very much a participant in prewar diplomacy. Our position directly, and often crucially, affected the policies of other countries. Out of the experience of World War I, Europeans assumed that, sooner or later, the United States would join a general European war.

The Revisionist Powers

But in 1937, and for the next three years, we would remain at the fringe of events, ever willing to preach on territorial integrity, on the desirability of trade, disarmament, on peaceful change. On occasion we were ready to rush in where effective leverage or strong public support allowed, but usually we used our neutrality as an excuse for backing away from extreme sacrifices or tragically confusing ambiguities. Our firmest position remained the Stimson Doctrine. Japanese expansion in China also provoked the greatest unanimity in America. European events, even the escapades of Hitler, somehow seemed more ambiguous. The near-universal condemnation of Japan did not mean any readiness even for mild sanctions. The thirties would be punctuated by protests, each less effective than the one before, and all backed by one important but essentially weak possibility for action—suspended trade in strategic materials.

Japan had played a terribly mean trick on the West. Belatedly and reluctantly opened to Western influence and trade, Japan refused to play the normal game—to become a source of raw materials, a market for products. Instead, she quickly adopted Western forms of government and of industrial organization. In 1930 Japan equaled most Western countries in wealth and productive capacity. But not in international prerogatives. Crowded in population, restricted to small islands, short on farm land and vital resources, dependent on trade, Japan had no real empire (Korea hardly counted for that) and no protected trading sphere. European states had their colonies; America had its own near self-sufficient continental expanse and an especially protected and foreclosed Western Hemisphere.

The depression restricted Japanese markets and pushed her, even as Germany or the United States, toward a more self-sufficient nationalism. In the thirties the future looked bleak for an industrial, island country without some type of self-sufficient empire. For a time, a growing Japan shared many common interests with America. As latecomers to the imperial game, both needed to block a further expansion of European colonies or exclusive trading rights in Asia. Both wanted equal access. The open door, in China or elsewhere, coincided with Japanese interests so long as strong European states effectively blocked her own expansion. But with any opening for a Japanese empire in Asia, for a drastic revision of the status quo, the open door was bound to become the main obstacle to Japanese efforts to achieve equity with other industrial nations. If America insisted on an open door in China and on the status quo throughout Southeast Asia, then our policies were bound to conflict with those of Japan.

The conflict became critical only after 1931. The United States refused to recognize any change in Asia, even Japanese control over Manchuria. But in this the United States simply took the lead; the European states also feared Japanese expansion. And the long-range threat of an expansive Soviet Union added security motives to Japan's Manchurian adventure. China, so dear to American dreams, so skimpy in any real benefits (the elusive China trade kept moving, miragelike, into the future), also offered

THE EXPANSION OF JAPANESE POWER, 1931 to December 1941

a potential threat to Japanese supremacy. But not for the moment. Torn by revolution, not yet firmly unified under Chiang Kai-shek, it remained vulnerable, an opportunity more than an obstacle. The growing nationalism in China might, sooner or later, lead to an expulsion of all foreign influences, Japanese as well as Western. But in the thirties the Western powers (including the United States) remained in China, with special trading ports; separate, semiautonomous districts in large cities; even sizable military detachments to guard their enclaves. Thus, the Japanese invasion threatened real, tangible Western interests even in China, and beyond lay Indochina, Malaya, the East Indies, and great riches in rubber, tin, oil, and other minerals, resources quite vital even to the United States. These stakes gained Chiang Kai-shek allies in all the status quo countries and also in the Soviet Union. But not in the revisionist states of Europe—Italy and Germany. They wanted to build their own empires and break the monopoly of economic power held by the World War I victors. Thus while Germany diverted Britain, France, and the Netherlands, Japan had its best chance to build its own new empire in Asia. That is, if America would limit its opposition to continued protest, to enunciations

General George C. Marshall (1880–1959) visiting Madam and Generalissimo Chiang Kai-shek (right). In the years before the war Roosevelt and the American people were very sympathetic toward China, a feeling that was reflected in our foreign policy through trade and financial concessions. The Wellesley-educated Madam Chiang Kai-shek proved to be of great assistance to her husband in foreign policy as well as social and education matters. *Wide World Photos*

of high principles, and meanwhile continue its vital sales of petroleum products and scrap metals, upon which depended Japan's continued effort to "emancipate" China.

Hitler sought his living room in Central Europe. He gleefully wrecked the World War I settlements and challenged the peace, security, and prestige of France and Britain. But unlike that of Japan, Hitler's early expansion in Europe did not violate any American treaty agreements or as directly threaten significant American interests. Yet, the taking of territory by intimidation or force violated the same principles as Japan, and created a type of international insecurity that threatened almost every American interest in the world, whether economic, moral, or esthetic. Eventually, a Nazi empire might also pose a military threat. At the very least it promised subversion in Latin America and challenged our hemispheric dominance. Many Americans sympathized with German revision-

An early picture of Mao Tse-tung (1893–   ), right, with President Chang Kuo-tao. Mao was president of the first Chinese Peasants Union in 1927. He was well prepared to become chairman of the new Central People's Government in 1949, for he had spent the interim years in training and in leading the Chinese Communist forces in North China. *United Press International*

ism. They accepted the unfairness of World War I treaties and could
have supported even significant territorial realignments. But Hitler and
his Nazi followers effectively undermined the sympathy. Their plebeian
vulgarity and harsh racism, their grandiose and romantic ambition fueled
by arrogant nationalism, and their cruel repression and demagogic techniques made it difficult to judge their foreign policy on its merits, or to
see the harsh realities in the policies of those who opposed Hitler. The excesses of Nazism in Germany, the earlier ranting of Hitler in *Mein
Kampf,* helped create a conspiratorial myth about him. The West read his
every move as an unfolding of a great plan, and invested a quite vulnerable Hitler and a less than overpowering Germany with almost superhuman or devilish powers. In fact, Hitler often had to respond to events and
calculated many of his conquests on strategic grounds rather than on romantic visions or mad dreams.

Finally, there was the Soviet Union. It added a new and entirely
incalculable element to European diplomacy. Both Hitler and his opponents had to make adjustments for a seemingly transformed Russia. Stalin
haunted every conference, and forced compromises, adjustments, strange
new allies. Hitler had already effectively exploited a widespread, often ir-
rational fear of Soviet communism. Such fears abounded throughout Europe and conditioned the behavior of all European statesmen. The Soviet
Union, although not yet ready or anxious for any trial by arms, had its
own revisionist goals—to regain the lost fringes of the Russian Empire,
secure friendly Marxist governments in border states, and win some real
security in a world full of hostile "capitalist" states. For serious Soviet
theoreticians, there also remained the more idealistic goal of a world revolution. Stalin's revisionist goals matched those of Hitler but no one could
believe that the two could agree on how to divide Eastern Europe, or
that, owing to conflicting personalities and ideology, they could long remain peaceful neighbors. Yet, Stalin's distrust of the West as a whole precluded any effective anti-fascist alliance.

**Early American
Initiatives**

In July of 1937 Cordell Hull, primarily in reaction to the new Japanese
offensive in China, enunciated eight basic principles of American
foreign policy, including the usual emphasis upon disarmament, trade, and
peaceful competition. His statement, so in the vein of Wilson's
Fourteen Points, marked the limits of our response to what we considered
aggression. Then, on October 5, 1937, Roosevelt followed with an
important foreign policy address. He asked peace-loving nations to
make concerted efforts in opposition to treaty violations and inhumane
acts leading to international anarchy and instability. He in effect de-

nounced neutrality as a solution to inescapable and spreading political upheavals. By a confusing metaphor, he compared war to a contagious disease, and emphasized that a community joins to quarantine patients in order to protect health and prevent the spread of disease. Since the victim is quarantined, the metaphor invited varied interpretations. Apparently it was a veiled threat of some type of nonintercourse, or possibly an early hint of contemplated trade restrictions against Japan. But as a political balloon it drew so much deflating fire from neutralists that Roosevelt quickly had to deny any contemplated sanctions against Japan.

In late 1937 the president considered a grand conference, possibly in Brussels, to enunciate accepted principles of international behavior. There he hoped to use moral suasion against Japan and Germany. Prime Minister Neville Chamberlain of Great Britain had first rejected any such conference, since he was willing to offer concessions to get new agreements with Italy and Germany. Chamberlain would accept the Ethiopian conquest as a price for peace. He even believed the United States would swallow this pill as one condition of a conference and new agreements. He was wrong. Hull revealed a typical and recurring anger at what he considered such immoral compromises. Besides, in principle, a recognition of the new Ethiopia would undercut the Stimson Doctrine and the whole substance of our continued case against Japan. The absorption of Austria by Hitler in March of 1938 ended all hopes for any general conference, or of any brilliant peacemaking under American auspices. It seemed too late for pious abstractions, or for attempts to construct any new international law. But the old conference idea revealed one consistent trait of American foreign policy: although unwilling to make any political or military commitment to maintain the status quo in Europe, we were wrathfully censorious of Britain and France whenever they failed to live up to our moral principles. We took no risk of war but waxed righteous at every turn. France and Britain faced the prospect of war, and to avoid it often relented on principles.

From Munich to War

With Austria in the Reich, Hitler next demanded the Sudeten area of Bohemia, or what was the most heavily Germanic sector of Czechoslovakia. The United States could play no major role in the complex negotiations that led to the Munich Conference of September 1938. And no more than the participants could we predict that the conference would, in retrospect, be such a critical turning point in European history. Roosevelt lived at ease with the neutrality legislation throughout 1938, and made few significant remarks about foreign policy. On the eve of Munich, in messages to the participants, he emphasized the Kellogg-Briand Pact and

Adolf Hitler (1889–
1945) greeting Prime
Minister Neville Cham-
berlain (1869–1940) at
the Hotel Dressen at God-
esburg for the Night Con-
ference during the Czech
crisis of September 1938.
Following his policy of
appeasement, Chamber-
lain conceded the Sudet-
enland to Hitler in return
for "peace in our time."
Wide World Photos

pointed out the cost and danger of war. He wanted a peaceful settlement
and complimented Chamberlain for his success in winning a conference
from Hitler. He carefully hedged this involvement by emphasizing that
America had no political role in Europe and would assume no obligations
for any conference settlement. Apparently Roosevelt, in spite of his sympathy for Czechoslovakia, acceded even to the results of the conference
(Hitler's absorption of the Sudetenland), and hoped with Chamberlain and
most Britishers that this would end Hitler's requests and allow "peace in
our time." But Munich certainly did not gain American tolerance of Hitler. Subsequent and unprecedentedly cruel Jewish persecutions led to the
temporary recall of our ambassador and public demands for a boycott of
German trade. Also, in October, Roosevelt made his first request to Congress for special defense appropriations.

By the spring of 1939 the prospect of a European war had to be accepted in America. Roosevelt clearly planned to support France and Britain if war came, and he already believed that airplanes would be the most
critical weapon. In a mild speech to Congress he had suggested in
January that American neutrality should not reward aggression. Administration supporters in Congress pressed to repeal the arms embargo provi-

sion of the Neutrality Act. Unlike earlier years, Roosevelt now took a clear stand against neutrality legislation. But his case fell apart later that month when an air crash revealed that French officers had been flying in American bombers, familiarizing themselves with our secret equipment. Roosevelt had to reiterate our antipathy to entangling alliances. Neither Hitler's final seizure of Czechoslovakia in March nor Mussolini's invasion of Albania in April produced any congressional action. The threats of new expansion had occasioned almost pleading but hopeless American entreaties to Mussolini. On April 15, in the aftermath of the new aggression, Roosevelt used another letter to both Hitler and Mussolini to reiterate our objectives in foreign policy (trade, disarmament), and to ask each power to pledge that it would not, for the next ten years, attack any of thirty-one listed nations. We promised to work for greater equality in international trade, and so presumably relieve any possible need for expansion. Both Rome and Berlin received the message with near contempt.

In the summer of 1939 the European powers bargained for position. Hitler made demands on Poland and possibly considered moves against Rumania. Both sides wooed the Soviet Union and with equal cynicism. Both had an intense antipathy to the Soviet leaders, a contempt for its military capabilities, and a fear of its ideology and economic system. Stalin returned the cynicism with interest. He moved close to a defensive pact with France and Britain, and continued detailed military discussions with their representatives in Moscow throughout the summer of 1939. Meantime, Molotov bargained in Berlin. Hitler gave Stalin the best deal and also the promise of a few years of peace. On August 24 the two countries announced their startling agreement, the Molotov-Ribbentrop Pact. Overtly, the strange marriage amounted only to a simple nonaggression treaty. In secret, it provided the blueprint for a division of Eastern Europe, with the Soviet Union eventually either to regain or establish dominance over Finland, Estonia, Latvia (a later bargain also included Lithuania), and Bessarabia, then part of Rumania. This was much more than the Western allies had been willing to concede. More critical at the moment, Poland could now be divided between Russia and Germany. The United States, as much as France and Britain, looked on with ill-concealed and helpless horror. Not only did this give Hitler a secure Eastern flank, but it quite suddenly converted Western Communist parties from a crusade against fascism into a struggle for peace and appeasement. In France this considerably weakened the resistance to Germany.

Poland briefly played its major role, then exited. The Poles, who had joined Hitler in absorbing a portion of Czechoslovakia, had a quite over-inflated notion of their military prowess. Squeezed between the Soviet Union and Germany, they refused "bargain" offers from both sides, offers that in either case would have left its major territory intact (in the wake of Czechoslovakia, no one could expect such a bargain to be adhered to for long). By clever diplomacy, Poland gained a mutual assistance treaty with France and Britain in August. This committed the two allies to war in defense of Poland and helped strengthen the almost cocky confidence of the Poles. Hitler, who would not be deterred from his Polish invasion, tried almost desperately to prevent French and British intervention. His invasion on September 3 began what we now call World War II, for England and France honored their commitment. Poland fell in less than a month. The Soviet Union, at the last moment, grabbed its promised share. In midsummer Roosevelt had pleaded unsuccessfully with congressional leaders for a change in the arms embargo. Now he addressed appeals to both Poland and Germany, asking for mediation rather than war. He even tried a desperate message to King Victor Emmanuel of Italy in a futile effort to bring influence on Hitler through his Axis partner.

The American Response to War

The actual hostilities in Europe speeded our first major efforts to prepare for war and gained tremendous popular support for Poland and the Allies. Roosevelt never professed personal neutrality. He wanted to aid the Allies as much as possible and wanted early modification in our neutrality legislation.

The European war created immediate apprehension about our hemisphere. Germany had large military missions in several South American countries, and a lucrative trade with a few. Largely by United States initiative, the American states had met at Buenos Aires in 1936 and agreed on mutual consultation in case of a threat to the peace of the Americas. Then, in 1938 in Lima, the nations joined in a loose pact, promising collective action to defend any country in the hemisphere but leaving the final decision up to individual states. In the aftermath of Poland the same countries met in Panama to plan united action. Sumner Welles held out various American favors—trade and marketing agreements, eventual military aid—to win approval for sixteen resolutions assuring closer consultation and a degree of mutual defense planning. The Declaration of Panama, conceived by the United States, created an unprecedented "neutrality" zone around the Western Hemisphere (excluding existing European colonies) at an average distance of 300 miles from shore. United States ships began the hopeless task of patrolling the zone. All European belligerents protested the zone; Britain almost immediately violated it. But even in the early months of the war we muted our protest of British infringements. We allowed armed Allied merchant ships into our ports in order to ease the burden of cash-and-carry for nonmilitary goods, but refused any comparable sanctuary to German submarines and even used our "neutrality patrol" to inform on German submarine locations.

The neutrality zone set a pattern for American response to the European war. In a series of steps, each more daring than the last, the Roosevelt administration would flout almost every traditional conception of neutrality and violate many traditional precepts of international law. Our steadily growing support for the Allies represented no response to direct Axis provocations. There were almost none of these, and no such dramatic naval incidents as punctuated the 1914–1917 period. Hitler tried to avoid provocative acts against America. Our involvement simply reflected horror at Nazi excesses in Europe and sympathy with the Allied side. A Nazi victory seemed a dire threat to all our ideals and also to our long-range security, both in the sense of a world foreclosed to our trade and influence and of a monolithic and totalitarian Europe capable even of invading our hemisphere. In this situation, legalities seemed an expensive luxury.

In the aftermath of United States success at the Panama Conference, Congress repealed the arms embargo. William Borah led the opposition, correctly predicting an expansion of American initiatives in the future, and eventual war. The administration defended arms sales as a means to avoid war and to keep our boys off European battlefields. Since all of the other neutrality provisions, such as cash-and-carry and credit restrictions, remained intact, the repeal had only limited practical significance. We had few arms to sell. Symbolically, it represented a positive response to the Polish invasion. And at least momentarily Britain controlled the seas; Britain and France also had ample dollar credits. For a while Roosevelt was free to aid the Allies in almost the only way we were capable—the sale of strategic goods and very limited military supplies.

The Phony War

But in the winter of 1939–40 our limited aid seemed quite enough. Hitler did not invade France as expected; his submarine fleet, yet incomplete, seemed largely ineffective. The war was a phony. We now know that, despite his lightning success in Poland, Hitler had to regroup his forces before opening an offensive in the West. He wanted to invade France in November, but a group of cautious generals forced an indefinite postponement, even as various groups in Germany plotted his overthrow. Hitler also hoped for a time to gain peace with the Allies, believing they would surely offer a de facto acceptance of his "Polish solution." The American ambassador to Britain, Joseph Kennedy, ever ready to invest Germany with almost superhuman power, ever mindful of what he conceived to be the greater dangers of communism, tried to secure Roosevelt's support in negotiating such a peace. Roosevelt openly refused, though he might have acted in some capacity had Britain desired a settlement. The British people, and their officials, unlike large groups in France, almost unanimously opposed any settlement. Perhaps most crucial, the lull in the fighting and the restraint of Hitler helped stimulate quite illusory Allied hopes for an early military victory. Hitler, deeply offended by British contempt for his peace offers, soon lost any desire for negotiation and began preparations for "war to death." When Sumner Welles took a well-publicized fact-finding trip through Europe in February and March of 1940, he found absolutely no opening for a negotiated settlement, particularly in Germany.

The lull in Central Europe permitted more American attention to other parts of the world. Our protests continued against Japan. But Roosevelt was reluctant to go beyond protests. He clearly believed that Hitler offered the greatest threat to America and wanted to avoid a diverting war in Asia. The European conflict enhanced Japanese prospects in Asia. It neutralized British and French opposition and prompted them to make concessions, including even a de facto acceptance of the new era in China. Japan had announced a coprosperity sphere with Manchuria and China in 1938. This presaged the end of an open door and of Western influence. We responded by increased aid to China and in July 1939 gave the Japanese six months notice of the termination of our commercial treaty. This did not necessitate actual trade restrictions in 1940, but at least made them a possibility. In this sense the notice represented the first really concrete reaction to Japanese expansion. At the time it strengthened the militarists in the Japanese government. It also pulled Japan even closer to an active alliance with Germany and Italy, an alliance debated throughout 1939. But the German-Soviet pact insulted Japan, unleashed the Soviet Union at its very doorstep, and temporarily cooled negotiations with Germany.

After the outbreak of war in Europe, Japan tried to push on to an early victory in China. The Soviet Union and the United States both succored Chiang Kai-shek. In a major speech in Tokyo in October, our ambassador, Joseph C. Grew, frankly reviewed the hostility of Americans to Japanese aspirations in China and to any new, closed economic order there. Still insecure on its Soviet borders, anxious to preserve a vital American trade, Japan proved conciliatory. In late 1939 it offered such concessions as opening the Yangtze River, providing greater protection for Westerners, and ending the worst brutality against Chinese civilians. But no Japanese leaders would affirm the open door or promise Japanese withdrawal from China, which we insisted upon. Against the advice of Grew, who at least hoped to strengthen a vulnerable civilian government in Japan, Hull refused formal negotiations. But we did promise to continue trade with-

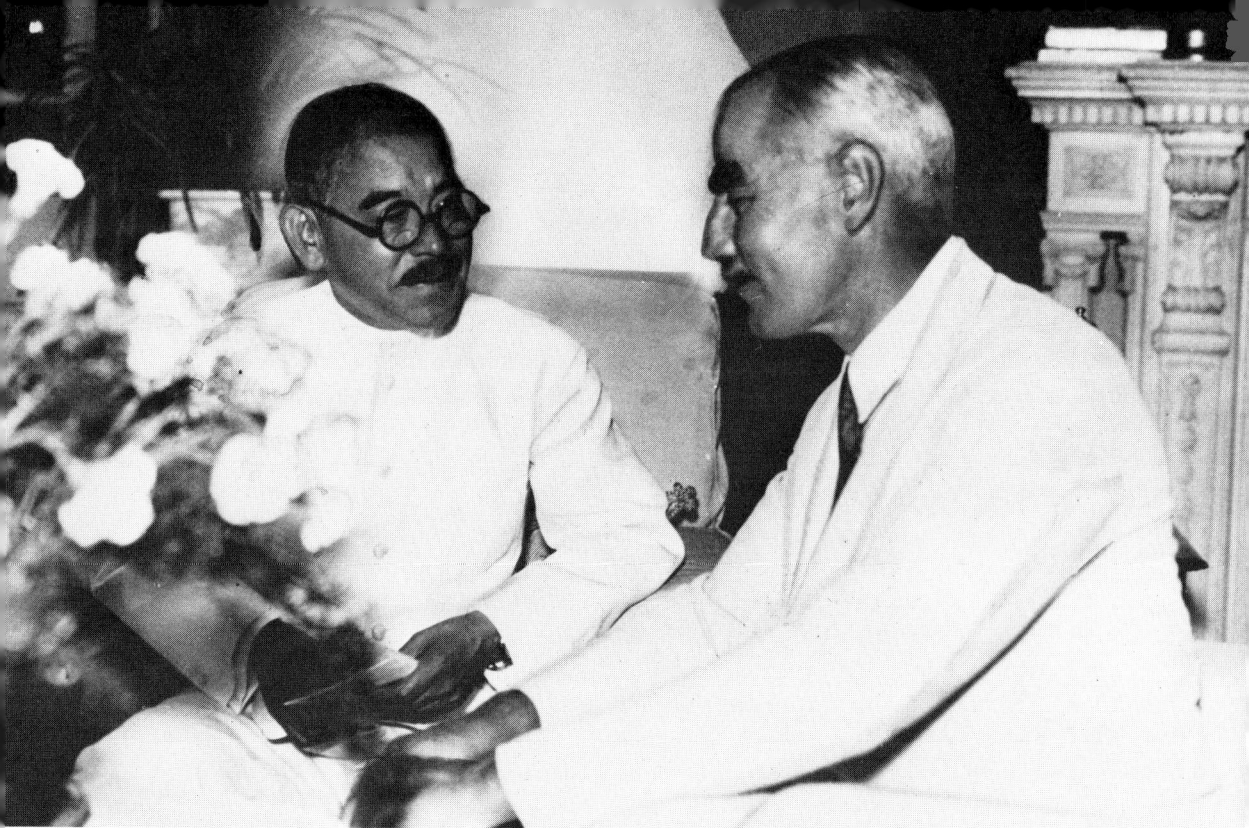

out restrictions beyond the expiration of the treaty. Instead of bargaining for a new trade agreement, or immediately canceling our exports of vital materials, we retained the threat of an embargo as a possible weapon in the future.

The small states of Europe existed at the sufferance of and often for the convenience of the great powers. The Versailles treaty had established a new European map particularly pleasing to France and Britain, obnoxious to Hitler's Germany and to the Soviet Union. The outbreak of war made each small state a pawn in big-power politics. It also cast France and Britain, the beneficiaries of the status quo, as the defenders of small states. When the western front stayed quiet, Western attention and sympathy shifted in the late fall of 1939 to Eastern Europe, particularly to Finland. In the wake of the division of Poland, the Soviet Union began a typically clever process of subversion in the Baltic states, transforming them into friendly puppets. In 1940 they became autonomous republics of the Soviet Union, which also grabbed off a chunk of Rumania. Finland, a former Russian province, represented a greater challenge. The first Soviet demands proved unexpectedly mild—access to one Finnish port city and enough valuable territorial grants to provide better defenses for Leningrad. Finnish compliance would have violated national pride, meant the surrender of its own vital defensive zones, and required the loss of valuable provinces and a difficult repatriation of citizens. In a desperate act

Foreign Minister Yosuke Matsuoka of Japan (left) and U.S. Ambassador Joseph C. Grew (1880–1965), right, discuss Japanese affairs in Tokyo in December of 1940. At this time, the U.S. was very concerned about Japan's attacks on China. *Associated Press Photo*

of courage, Finland flouted the Soviet ultimatum. Under the ruse of a puppet government, the Soviet Union invaded Finland on November 30, 1939.

America had long admired little Finland (she paid her World War I debts). The Soviet "rape" (Roosevelt's word) produced almost unanimous sympathy and concern, but we could do little in a tangible way to help Finland. We considered a break in relations with the Soviet Union, but did not want further to cement the Soviet-Nazi relationship. Roosevelt made available his good offices to get an early settlement, but under existing legislation could not even offer a helpful loan. He asked for a moral embargo on strategic materials to the Soviet Union, but since almost none existed this meant nothing. Eventually, and too late, Congress approved a loan. Meanwhile, virtually unaided, Finland fought brilliantly, and throughout the winter kept off an ill-prepared Soviet army. But in the spring her defenses broke and she had to accept a peace settlement. German concern, not Western threats, helped moderate the final Soviet demands. Finland gave up more territory than earlier demanded. But her great effort had intensified her sense of national pride. The bumbling Soviet effort created an unwarranted contempt, both in Germany and among the Allies, for Soviet military capabilities. The war pushed a desperate Finland, consoled but never significantly aided by the Allies, into a closer relationship with Germany.

The war in the West resumed on April 9, 1940. On that date Hitler marched through Denmark and invaded Norway. His timing placed much of the odium on Britain and France, for on April 8 Britain had begun mining Norwegian territorial waters. France, probably for domestic political reasons, had long wanted a dramatic new initiative and sought British cooperation for landing troops at vital Norwegian ports, directly aiding Finland, and intercepting Swedish iron exports to Germany. A reluctant Britain finally agreed to send a note to Norway and Sweden, asserting what amounted to a right to take necessary measures to counter German influence or conquests in Scandinavia. Norway pleaded for American protection but without avail. Mining the sea preceded a planned occupation of Narvik, and then more extensive occupation of ports and fiords in the face of almost certain German retaliation. The Allied plans gave a pretext for the carefully planned and brilliant German invasion. The Allies, totally outwitted, suffered a humiliating defeat. Norway resisted, but ineffectively. Britain landed troops and held on at Narvik until early June, but then had to withdraw its last conclave on the Norwegian coast in order to respond to the invasion of France. The

**To Counter the
"Blitzkrieg"**

United States could only console Norway and condemn such open aggression. It did assert a direct interest in Denmark's colony of Greenland (Britain meanwhile occupied Iceland), stating that it fell under the protection of the Monroe Doctrine and placing it under the protection of American naval forces.

Norway was only a prelude. The low countries (Belgium, Netherlands, Luxembourg) came next. Again, both sides rehearsed schemes for invading these small, neutral states. Britain and France at least planned a hasty occupation of Belgium should Germany move in that direction. They never had time to fulfill the plan. On May 10, with lightning speed, German divisions moved through Holland and into Belgium. The superb armored divisions and air superiority mocked ancient techniques of war and made the ineffectual Allied resistance seem almost pathetic. The invasion triggered cabinet crises in both France and Britain. A militant Winston Spencer Churchill came to power in Britain. France suffered near political chaos. The Allies still tried to defend part of Belgium, but a fast German thrust to the coast cut off and trapped the main Allied force by May 20, leading to a heroic but still humiliating British evacuation from Dunkirk. On June 5 Hitler launched his long-awaited French offensive. The demoralized French, angry at England and divided at home, offered scant resistance. On June 10 Mussolini joined the war. On June 14 Paris fell. On June 25 the French agreed to an armistice that took them out of the war, saved the remnants of their army and all of their large navy, but at a terrible cost of over half their territory. In a month of frenzied fighting Germany won a complete victory. Hitler, who had pressed his reluctant generals, seemed to vindicate his military genius and assumed almost unchallenged control of the German armies. Britain would be next, or so it seemed.

The pace of events in Europe astonished Americans. Hitler established an image of almost invincible power. Surely all Europe would fall under his sway. Many Americans reflected horror or near panic. One immediate result was increased appropriations for our meager army (only 280,000 men) and particularly for the Army Air Force (even by July of 1941 we had only 3,000 planes). Churchill dramatically requested full nonbelligerency status on our part, and received assurances from Roosevelt of massive aid. Most of this had to be strategic materials, not weapons of war. Under various legal ruses we even began the sale of materials already under War Department control. William Allen White and others began a campaign for increased American involvement. His perfectly-named "Committee to Defend America by Aiding the Allies" won support by its claim that Hitler threatened world domination. On the other side, Robert Wood of Sears-Roebuck led an anti-interventionist organization called

"America First." All polls showed Americans overwhelmingly wanted to avoid war, but growing numbers doubted we could. Finally, by the end of the summer, the United States joined Britain in efforts to improve relations with the Soviet Union, and if at all possible prevent its further complicity in Hitler's aggression.

In this hemisphere we used the Monroe Doctrine as a weapon to justify acquiring and holding assets of conquered states, and for insuring that the Nazis not acquire the American colonies of states such as France. In May we helped form, and finance, a pooling of strategic resources in the hemisphere. In June Congress authorized the president to buy or otherwise acquire islands in the Western Hemisphere. In Havana, in July, the American states jointly reaffirmed the Monroe Doctrine concept of no new colonies in this hemisphere, and set up a collective trusteeship to administer orphaned colonies. In August, at Ogdensburg, New York, Canada and the United States formed a joint board of defense and began joint staff planning.

The early victories by Germany created new possibilities for Japan. The complete defeat of France and the Netherlands, the critical siege of an isolated Britain, created an inviting vacuum in all of Southeast Asia. Unlike China, this region contained resources vital to the American economy, including tin and rubber. The threat of American embargoes increased the value to Japan of Indochina, Malaya, and the East Indies. By July Japan pressured the French Vichy government to cut supply lines to China. By September France agreed to a virtual occupation of parts of northern Indochina, including rights to move troops and occupy air fields. On July 25 the United States initiated the first, limited embargo on aviation gasoline and top grade scrap metal. Economically insignificant, it symbolized our concern and the likelihood of more severe restrictions later. Thus, in September of 1940 we embargoed all scrap metal but continued to export petroleum, fearing an embargo here would drive Japan toward the East Indies. Then, on September 27, Japan announced the Tripartite Pact with Germany and Italy. The new order in Asia would parallel the one in Europe. The pact applied most directly to the United States. It excluded the Soviet Union out of German deference to the Ribbentrop-Molotov Pact, but committed Germany and Italy to join Japan in any war against the United States.

In a darkened Europe a beleaguered Britain braced in the summer of 1940 for an almost certain German invasion. The British army survived Dunkirk, but now lacked adequate military supplies. Strangely, Hitler waited. Despite clear German military superiority, a cross-channel invasion posed frightful difficulties, particularly because of the British superiority in surface naval ships. Instead of invasion, Hitler unleashed the Luftwaffe for an unprecedented bombardment of British air fields and cities.

This, the now famous Battle of Britain, raged until autumn. Meanwhile, an increasing fleet of German submarines sank British shipping, threatening to isolate the British Isles. By now Britain lacked the credit to buy American goods and found ever greater hazards in carrying the goods across the Atlantic. In a time of desperate need Churchill used every conceivable strategy to pry Roosevelt into the war, or at least to get every conceivable type of military aid short of war. In particular, he wanted ninety-six of our older destroyers (to use against subs), and an unlimited number of smaller torpedo boats, large bombers, and rifles.

Roosevelt clearly wanted to provide the destroyers, but saw no clear legal justification for such an immense gift. But he could trade destroyers for American bases in this hemisphere. A private interventionist group first sponsored the idea; public opinion polls showed widespread support for it. General Pershing even came out of retirement to speak publicly in its behalf. Roosevelt's legal advisers found what they considered adequate authority without congressional action. In the midst of an election campaign, Roosevelt carried out the difficult negotiations. He secured at least tacit concurrence from Wendell Willkie. The final deal involved a ninety-nine year lease of American naval and air bases in Newfoundland, Bermuda, the Bahamas, Jamaica, Antigua, St. Lucia, Trinidad, and British Guiana. Despite earlier commitments to other categories of aid, including aircraft, the final bargain included only fifty destroyers. Churchill, realizing the poor bargain from a British standpoint, defended the deal as only in part a trade, and in the final document granted some of the bases as an unconditional gift. Roosevelt, on the other hand, used the idea of a great bargain to gain reluctant congressional and public support.

The destroyer deal marked the first dramatic retreat from the form of neutrality. Bargain or not, it was clearly a ruse to enable the United States to support Britain in its battle for survival. Despite much criticism, a majority of Americans seemed to support such a bargain. By almost any interpretation, the transfer from our navy of major warships violated almost any definition of neutrality and all well established international rules for neutral conduct. We rejected technicalities in behalf of what the Roosevelt administration considered hard reality. As of September 1940, if not before, the United States clearly became a nonbelligerent ally of Britain. Germany, if it had so desired, had every reason to interpret the deal as a hostile act of the United States, involving us in at least a type of limited warfare. In the next fourteen months we would gradually expand our role in that war, and avoid actual belligerency only by the sufferance of a calculating Hitler. Ironically, in Asia we would continue to insist upon the strictest legality in our relationship to Japan. Overtly hostile acts never prompted Hitler to a declaration of war. But our strict insistence upon treaty obligations triggered Pearl Harbor.

17

The election campaign of 1940 did little to clarify American foreign policy. The Roosevelt victory could not be interpreted as a clear mandate for anything specific. Or, perhaps more correctly, it seemed a mandate for quite contradictory goals. Both Willkie and Roosevelt promised a more determined buildup in defensive capacity and more aid to Britain. These commitments were clearly popular ones. But both candidates advocated peace, and in the last weeks of the campaign they recklessly tried to outdo each other in making more emphatic their pledge to avoid foreign wars. What remained unclear was how the United States could continue to support Britain, or to counter Japanese ambitions in Asia, without running an ever greater risk of all-out war, which most Americans clearly did not want. The candidates and the campaign seemed to support the illusion that we could have our cake and eat it too.

Fulfillment even of Roosevelt's commitment to Britain would soon require a congressional revision of our neutrality laws. Without such, the administration either would be severely frustrated in pursuing its undeclared economic warfare against Germany, or else sorely tempted to try some provocation to force an act of war by Germany, and by this tactic finally win overwhelming popular support. Secretary of War Stimson, closely seconded by Henry Morgenthau and Secretary of the Navy Frank Knox, was already committed to an all-out war effort, including eventual belligerency. Stimson continually campaigned to involve us more deeply in the war. From Britain, Churchill used every bit of persuasion, every possible diplomatic maneuver, every ounce of his superb acting skill, to gain the same objective. Hitler occasionally cooperated to the extent of making hostile speeches, but still carefully avoided any overt military provocations. He would never provide the excuse so badly needed by the more ardent interventionists.

Even though Roosevelt had determined interventionists among his closest advisers, there is little evidence to suggest that either in the campaign or later he worked step by step toward war. After an interval of time, however, he almost always came to accept the logic, and the concrete proposals, of men like Stimson. The lag in time paralleled the similar delay in the expression of vocal public and congressional opinion, even as his new initiative so often followed the careful preparatory propaganda of

Posters such as this were used to stir up prowar feelings by inspiring American pity for homeless war victims. *Library of Congress*

338

The Most Critical Year— 1941

interventionist organizations. To the opponents of war, this all lent credence to their belief that Roosevelt manipulated the public in behalf of concealed foreign policy objectives. For their part, interventionists had such deep moral commitments to the Allies that they could only believe that Roosevelt agreed with their objectives all along, but suffered the necessary frustrations and compromises of practical politics in order best to achieve them. Both tried to impose upon Roosevelt more coherent, long-run objectives than he usually displayed. It would be much more consistent with his personality, with his usual techniques of leadership, to accept his stated and apparent objectives, and to eschew all plots and schemes. In fact, Roosevelt most likely shared the somewhat ambivalent hopes of many Americans. He really wanted to avoid total war, and possibly refused to analyze all the long-range and even inescapable prospects that seem, at least to us, implicit in his policies. His hesitation and reluctance, as well as his eventual capitulation to interventionist schemes, could well have been his honest response. Such alone would be consistent with his usual habit of moving from one proximate issue to another. Of course, from one perspective he dallied too long. From another he capitulated too easily. But either way the series of decisions could be most fairly viewed as a result of inescapable illusions or foreshortened vision rather than clever deceit.

Lend-Lease

In the immediate aftermath of the 1940 election Roosevelt faced hard decisions about aid to Britain, decisions that he postponed until December. Just as the arms embargo had impeded earlier administrative desires to aid the Allies, and had forced congressional amendments, so now the neutrality legislation again threatened administrative goals. Britain had almost exhausted her liquid dollar assets, and could only temporarily continue to buy new American arms by very limited sales of private and corporate investments in America. Further, the Battle of Britain gave way to an equally desperate Battle of the Atlantic, as German submarines began to sink a disastrous tonnage of British merchantmen, threatening not only the Atlantic weapons trade but vital consumer goods as well. Thus, both sides of our cash-and-carry policy, earlier accepted by Roosevelt in part because it would surely favor Britain over any other belligerent, finally began to hurt, and made both Churchill and members of the Roosevelt administration reflect enviously on the World War I form of neutrality, in which our ships delivered credit goods to European ports.

Roosevelt sought in vain for some legal way to evade the cash requirement, and thus some brilliant new political strategy. We increased our arms sales to Britain and even included a few precious B-17 bombers. Still, the projected needs for 1941 seemed to exceed any British capacity for payment. The problem of British ability led to quite varying estimates, and to quite different beliefs about how many economic resources we should force a beleaguered Britain to sacrifice (to interventionists, she was fighting our war; we could not force her to drain away all her carefully accumulated wealth, leaving only an impoverished ally at war's end). In December Roosevelt took additional steps toward mobilization and first announced what would be called "lend-lease," a scheme suggested by the destroyer deal. In a famous December 17 press conference he suggested that we lease military supplies to Britain for the duration of the war. As usual, he used a simple analogy to make his point (or, as critics occasionally suggested, to oversimplify the issues): if a neighbor's house caught fire, and eventually threatened one's own, one would surely lend his hose to his neighbor in order to extinguish the blaze. Any gentleman would, of course, then return the hose. On December 29 he gave his "arsenal of democracy" fireside address, in which he made clear our desire to insure Nazi defeat, and in which he first discussed the lend-lease proposal. In his state-of-the-union address on January 6, 1941 he enumerated his four freedoms, or the first list of our always vague goals in World War II (freedom *for* speech and religion, *from* want and fear). Then, in the new Congress, the majority leaders of both houses introduced a lend-lease authorization act (suggestively entitled H.R. 1776). The bill occasioned one of the last sharp debates on the direction of American foreign policy, a direction that now pointed to the strong possibility of war.

In congressional hearings administration defenders of lend-lease stressed its defensive purpose, and even tried to show how it might prevent our full involvement in the war. Back of the arguments was a quite pervasive belief—that sooner or later America would come under attack from a victorious Germany, bent as it seemed to be on world conquest. British defeat would remove the main barriers against an invasion of the Americas. The necessity for self-defense therefore overrode any question of legality. Neutralist opponents were still numerous enough, and courageous enough, to marshal an able opposition, although soon a more coercive opinion in support of Roosevelt would silence most of the opposition. The America First Committee offered several arguments against lend-lease. Its most forthright spokesman, Charles A. Lindbergh, had already lost some of his hero lustre by anti-Semitic statements and a seeming favoritism toward Nazi Germany. He wanted the United States to remain neutral and do all it could to negotiate a peace settlement. He believed we should try to avoid a complete victory on either side that would leave a prostrate and vulnerable Europe. An armed America would be quite secure from any Nazi invasion, our further intervention in Europe could only increase bloodshed abroad and undermine democracy at home, and the United States was not strong enough to force its will on Europe and Asia. Senator Burton Wheeler called lend-lease a Triple-A type of foreign policy, since it would "plow under every fourth American boy."

An amended lend-lease bill rather quickly passed the House (260 to 165) but only after extended debate and neutralists' threats of a filibuster could it pass the Senate (60 to 33). The early votes were largely along party lines, despite the bipartisanship on foreign policy that Roosevelt so actively sought. In its final form (signed ceremoniously on March 11, 1941), the Lend-Lease Act specified no particular countries (this made the Soviet Union eligible later), and placed no restriction on the eventual amount of aid. But Senate amendments required detailed congressional control over the amount of aid granted by the president. In effect, the bill went much beyond the granting of credit; although it obligated our allies to return the leased equipment, much of the material would obviously be destroyed or obsolete at the war's end. Lend-lease thus came close to outright gifts. On March 11, Roosevelt asked Congress for $7 billion as the first installment. When Congress granted it within two weeks, Roosevelt appointed Harry Hopkins to administer it. This new spending, added to our own exploding defense requirements, finally placed our economy on a virtual war footing and soon necessitated imposed governmental controls over production.

By early 1941 Roosevelt had finally settled one critical point of strategy. In case America entered the war he would join Britain against Hitler, postponing any possible campaign against Japan. A series of secret high-level British-American staff conferences in Washington helped flesh out these strategic plans. Such staff work gave the military departments guidance for mobilization planning and for allocating industrial priorities. It also made it very desirable for the United States, if at all possible, to avoid war with Japan. In Asia Chiang Kai-shek made the same insistent demands upon the United States as did Churchill, but with much less response. Japan, still frustrated within China, desperately wanted to achieve a final victory. After 1940, Britain ended its earlier pattern of conciliation, reopened the Burma Road, and made quite clear its intention to defend Singapore. Churchill hoped that Pacific events would entice more American involvement, and vainly tried to get either American naval protection for Singapore or a firm American commitment to come to its defense if Japan attacked.

Although Roosevelt refused a common defense posture toward Asia, American military leaders did carry out low-level staff conferences with Britain and the Netherlands in Washington. We also continued our gradual squeeze on Japanese trade. In November 1940 Japan signed a treaty with a puppet Chinese government in Nanking, and by this strategy threatened Chiang's government as never before. We publicized a new, $100 million loan to the Chinese Republic, but could manage only a trickle of military aid (we lacked the materials, and had no easy way of transporting them to Chiang's capital, Chungking). By informal pressures on private exporters, we also gradually increased the scope of our economic embargo in the Pacific. Then, in December, the administration so tightened the licensing provisions as to curtail almost all exports except petroleum, which would continue until July of 1941. The economic weapons had an impact in Japan. They helped rally varied pro-American groups, including the emperor, several categories of bankers and businessmen, and even some of the naval commanders. Throughout most of 1941 these elements, supported by Prince Konoye, the Japanese prime minister, retained enough power in Japan to sustain a series of promising talks with the United States, talks that held real hope of formal negotiation and a practical détente.

The thaw, if it can be called that, began in December 1940. Konoye used informal contacts and two private messengers to propose new Japanese concessions in exchange for increased American economic aid and our influence upon Chiang Kai-shek in behalf of a Chinese settlement. Although never repudiating the Tripartite Pact, Konoye seemed willing to undermine it in behalf of such a settlement (the Tripartite required Japanese intervention against the United States if we attacked Germany). By February these overtures seemed betrayed by events. Japanese ship movements suggested an imminent invasion toward the south, possibly on Singapore. Churchill capitalized on the apparent threat, and as usual promoted a war scare to seek more American commitments. Hitler, likewise, urged the Japanese to attack British possessions. For once, both Britain and Germany could welcome a war in Asia (Britain to get the United States into the war; Germany to get Japan involved in the world conflict and insure an early victory before American intervention could be significant). We now know that the Japanese planned no new operations in February. In fact, they wanted to negotiate a settlement with the United States, perhaps as much or more than we wanted to avoid the war in Asia.

In Washington there was such a fund of distrust for Japan that our State Department only slowly yielded to overtures from Konoye. The informal proposals did not represent any official Japanese offer, and when made known might force enough hostility in Japan to endanger any ultimate negotiations. In addition, we knew that the Japanese foreign minister, Matsuoka, adhered closely to the Tripartite, admired Germany, and apparently had only contempt for the United States. Not surprisingly, the major Japanese overture came in April while Matsuoka carried out a much-publicized trip to Germany and Moscow, where he would negotiate a military pact with the Soviet Union. The Japanese ambassador to Washington, Admiral Nomura, transmitted a firm offer. Japan wanted the United States to persuade Chiang Kai-shek to accept a peace settlement, with a merger of the Nanking and Chungking governments and a united front against Chinese communism. After such a settlement Japan promised to withdraw its troops from China, to return all Chinese territory (excluding Manchuria), and to join the United States in negotiating what amounted to a new open-door policy. For these concessions the United States would end its aid to China, reopen normal trade, provide a loan, and aid Japan in securing needed raw materials. The final details would be settled in a meeting at Honolulu of Roosevelt and Konoye. The offer contained so many seeming concessions that the United States had to explore serious negotiations.

The Japanese offer led to over a month of hopeful talks between Hull and Nomura, to some vital exchanges of offers and counteroffers, and to all too many misunderstandings based on ambiguities of language and gesture. Matsuoka, after signing the neutrality pact in Moscow on April 13, returned to Japan quite prepared to do everything possible to undermine any agreement with America. An always skeptical Hull asked Nomura for better assurances that Japan would follow through with their proposed concessions, particularly the withdrawal from China. Quite typically, Hull also proposed four points of principle to which Japan would have to subscribe, and which in effect reiterated the open-door principle. Japan, unfortunately, interpreted this response as the opening of official negotiations. Under the influence of Matsuoka, they delayed a reply until May 3, and then considerably hardened their position (perhaps as an opening gambit in negotiations). For Hull, the new demands precluded formal negotiations. He continued the talks with Nomura because he wanted to avoid war in the Pacific, wanted to strengthen the Konoye factions in Japan, and wanted all possible time for our military preparations. Our final response to the modified Japanese offer came only on June 21, and with terms totally unacceptable to the Japanese. The moment of promise seemed over, although informal talks continued in Washington. Note that all these discussions concerned merely the conditions for formal negotiations, not the terms of any ultimate agreement. Japan in effect wanted to negotiate from the existing status quo, and seemed open to major concessions on this basis. We consistently made Japanese recognition in principle of the earlier status quo a basis of negotiation. Thus, Japanese acceptance of our demand would have left little more than small details and certain economic considerations for the formal negotiations.

In Europe Hitler once again moved from winter frustration to springtime glory. His air bombardment had failed to defeat Britain. His elaborate efforts to buy Franco's full support, and so secure a free path through Spain to Gibraltar and North Africa, floundered on Spanish caution (a victory for effective British diplomacy in Madrid). Even Vichy France held tenaciously to its African colonies, and used North Africa (it could fall so quickly to Britain or to Free French forces) as a weapon to secure some freedom of action. Finally, Italy performed as usual. An ambitious campaign into Egypt failed. Outnumbered British forces not only stopped the Italians, but by the end of 1940 came close to driving them out of Libya. In Greece, an Italian invasion led not to a glorious victory, but to an embarrassing stalemate, with the smaller Greek forces even launching an effective offensive into Albania. Hitler, already committed to an early invasion of Russia, first had to rescue his fumbling Axis partner. He moved into the Balkans and toward Suez.

Once again, everything seemed easy for Hitler. He thus helped augment the growing idea of German invincibility, but for the last time. On March 2, 1941, he moved troops into a cooperative Bulgaria. By March 25 he secured Yugoslavian agreement to the Tripartite, only to see it all undone by a *coup* and a new government prepared to defend its territory. Britain, long anxious to build an effective front in the Balkans by uniting the forces of Yugoslavia, Greece, and possibly Turkey, took heart from Yugoslavian resistance. But too late. From April 6 to April 17, German troops overran most of Yugoslavia and on the 17th began their attack on Greece, which surrendered on April 24. The British troops in Greece had to be evacuated in what amounted to a minor Dunkirk. Since Britain had moved them from Egypt, its defenses there crumbled before a surprising offensive by new German forces led by the most successful of Hitler's generals, Erwin Rommel. Thus, by May of 1941, Hitler controlled the northern Mediterranean. By sending his reinforcements to North Africa, he had attained effective control over Italy. He seemed poised for an almost certain victory in the Near East, particularly after the Vichy government permitted German air bases in Syria.

Once again Hitler had moved quickly, had kept his foes separated to the last possible moment, and had completed his conquest while they were off balance and disorganized. At no time had his armies engaged in

WORLD WAR II: THE EUROPEAN THEATER

Legend:

- ☐ Allied powers
- ■ Neutral nations
- ▦ Axis powers
- ▥ Axis allies
- ▭ Areas annexed by Russia, 1940
- ▥ German diplomatic gains, 1936–1939
- ▨ Areas occupied by Germany, 1942
- ▩ Areas controlled by Vichy France, 1942
- → Axis lines of invasion
- ⇢ Allied lines of invasion

prolonged battle with equivalent forces. The only Allied bright spots were almost tokens: the heroism of little Malta under bombardment, the successful defense of Tobruk against Rommel and a stalemate in Egypt, a rapid British and Free French occupation of Syria, and a successful effort to keep Turkey from cooperating with the Nazis. Yet, had Hitler decided to move on toward Suez he might well have succeeded. As everyone knows, he made a different, momentous, and disastrous decision to move first on the Soviet Union.

The United States could do almost nothing about the Balkan catastrophe. Even promised aid for the Greeks arrived too late. We did not see the Near East as being nearly as significant as did the British. The Battle of the Atlantic was quite another thing. By 1941 Roosevelt was firmly convinced, and had seemingly persuaded a majority of Americans, that Hitler's ultimate design included the Western Hemisphere, that the British Isles represented our first line of defense, and that our own security demanded whatever sacrifices necessary to provision Britain. In retrospect, this whole assumption seems somewhat less certain than it did then, but nonetheless it represented the basis of administration policies. By the spring of 1941 German subs were able to sink British shipping at twice its replacement rate (or at over 500,000 tons a month). The subs still scrupulously avoided any clash with American ships. Without our help, it seemed that the huge lend-lease commitment would never make it to England.

By several small steps, the United States in 1941 gave up all semblance of neutrality, directly moved supplies to England, and joined the naval war against Germany. In March 1941 Roosevelt seized German and Danish ships detained in American ports and subsequently converted them to our own use. He then considered outright American naval escorts of British ships but deferred to strong congressional opposition and took a milder step. At Churchill's urging, he extended our neutrality patrol to longitude 25° west, or to the mid-Atlantic. American ships patrolled to that distance, assiduously searching out and reporting German subs (now technically forbidden west of the line) to British warships. We also removed the Red Sea from our definition of a war zone, and used it to deliver American supplies in American ships directly to the British army in Egypt. In April an American ship and a German sub engaged in hostilities off the coast of Iceland, the very first such incident in the war and one clearly as much or more our fault than the Germans. But in May a German sub sank an American merchant ship, the *Robin Moore*, in the South Atlantic, apparently without direct provocation. In a fireside speech on May 27 Roosevelt carefully traced developments in Europe, hammered on the theme of our endangered security, stressed possible

German moves in this hemisphere, promised any means necessary to supply Britain, and proclaimed a national emergency. Finally, in July, the government of Iceland, a bit reluctantly, accepted 4,000 American troops as replacement for former British "protection." By this sleight-of-hand, Roosevelt in effect added Iceland to the Western Hemisphere. On July 11 we began escorting our merchant ships to Iceland. Britain could now pick up supplies close by and avoid the danger of an Atlantic crossing.

The long-planned German invasion of the Soviet Union on June 22, 1941, marked the major turning point of World War II, and the greatest strategic mistake ever made by Hitler. But this was not apparent in the summer of 1941, as Hitler's onrushing armies seemed destined to early victory. Although a minor thaw in United States-Soviet relations preceded the invasion, the Soviet Union remained nearly as unpopular in America as did Nazi Germany. The rape of Finland remained too recent for any great popular sympathy or remorse. But expediency outweighed sentiment. With British urgings, Roosevelt agreed to extend aid to the Soviet Union. Clarification of Anglo-American policy in the light of Hitler's new strategy became one of the justifications for the secret shipboard meeting of Churchill and Roosevelt from August 9–12, or what became known as the Atlantic Conference.

The Atlantic Conference would retain a great symbolic value, but would alter American policies only slightly. Even this early, Britain displayed a greater strategic interest than America in defending the Near East and the outer perimeter of its empire. Churchill also wanted to use air bombardment rather than invasion in Western Europe. By now Roosevelt believed the Soviet Union could survive until the winter (Harry Hopkins, after a daring flight to Moscow and extended talks with Stalin, made such a hopeful analysis), and that American aid would not be wasted. Since Churchill concurred in this evaluation, he and Roosevelt petitioned Stalin for an early planning conference to determine overall strategy and the correct allocation of scarce American aid. Already, the USSR wanted an early second front in Europe. Churchill and Roosevelt discussed the possible seizure of the Azores and the Canaries, and planned the content of a tough United States protest against new Japanese expansion in Asia, a position later somewhat muted in its actual transmission to the Japanese.

Most dramatic of all, Churchill and Roosevelt drafted the Atlantic Charter, a quite general and typically vague statement of war aims sure to have great propaganda value. Back of the actual declaration was Roosevelt's four freedoms speech and Hull's long concern for a free international marketplace. The British wanted qualifications on American advocacy of liberal trade; the United States would not join the British in an unambiguous commitment to another League of Nations. The Atlantic Charter, a compromise of the varied views, renounced any Allied territorial aims or desires for aggrandizement, and reiterated the old ideas of self-determination and nonaggression. Ironically, this pledge would be almost immediately violated by Anglo-Soviet occupation of Iran. With "due respect for their existing obligations," the two countries pledged free trade and equal access to the raw materials of the world, and asked for increased economic cooperation on behalf of economic growth and social security. They pledged, insofar as possible, a just peace, with free international travel and the freedom of all men from fear and want. Finally, without clarifying the nature of any enforcement machinery, they denounced force in international disputes and asked for widespread disarmament.

The American promise of aid did not satisfy Stalin. Fighting a life-and-death struggle for national survival, engaging practically the entire German army, absorbing all the force originally committed against England, abundantly suspicious of a Britain that he believed had betrayed the Soviet Union before the war, Stalin remained secretive, suspicious, and conspicuously ungrateful. He demanded a second front. In September W. Averell Harriman led a special war-supplies mission to Moscow to join the British in top-level conferences with Soviet leaders. By that date a desperate Stalin was willing to subscribe to the principles of the Atlantic Charter. Harriman committed the Western Allies to a $1 billion aid program over the next nine months. It is important to note that these supplies, shipped around Norway to Murmansk or Archangel, had to come out of potential allotments to Britain. Roosevelt first granted credit to the Soviet Union, and then under enabling legislation from Congress extended lend-lease. He did not feel free to implement such an aid program until widespread political and religious opposition subsided. This came about through effective propaganda, and also as a result of our increasingly direct and absorbing involvement in the European war. We needed the Soviet Union. Immediate military considerations dominated our policies.

Even as the United States made its first hesitant steps in big-power diplomacy, it steadily increased its role in the European war. After July 11 we escorted our own merchant ships to Iceland. On August 26, without formal announcement, British merchant ships first joined our convoys. In fact, certain convoys entirely under American naval protection soon contained only British ships. The problem was how to justify the de facto policy to Congress and to the American public. Here subterfuge had to suffice.

On September 4 a United States destroyer, the *Greer*, en route to Iceland, learned from the British that a German submarine lay submerged in its path. Since such subs had no orders to attack American ships, and had heretofore shown unbelievable restraint, the *Greer* had no reason for defensive action even though it was in a proclaimed German war zone. But American ships had long located and reported such subs in our "neutral" zone. Thus, the *Greer* searched out the sub, broadcast its location to the British, and trailed it for several hours. The harassed sub commander finally fired two torpedoes; both missed the *Greer*. Thereupon the *Greer* turned from observation to outright attack, dropping depth charges with unknown effect. Even before learning the full details, Roosevelt made this a *cause célèbre*. It marked, he suggested in a militant speech, the beginnings of a systematic Nazi plan to sink American ships. Because the sub fired first, without warning, and with intent to sink the *Greer*, he declared that its attack amounted to legal and moral piracy, and was part of a Nazi plot to abolish freedom of the seas and gain control of the oceans. The "deliberate" attack was thus a prelude to an attempted Nazi domination of the Western Hemisphere and of the United States. Roosevelt ordered our navy to eliminate the sub, and to preserve the two bulwarks of our national defense: freedom of shipping on the high seas and a line of supply to Britain. Henceforth, the very presence of German submarines in waters we deemed necessary for our defense would constitute an attack. Our ships need no longer await German action but could fire on sight. Our navy would now protect all merchant ships engaged in commerce within our defensive waters (all the western Atlantic and an area around Iceland).

Roosevelt's fire-on-sight order came close to a presidential declaration of war. He announced the policy in his capacity as commander in chief; he briefed only Democratic congressmen before his speech. Congress confronted a *fait accompli*, but one that brought prompt approval because of Roosevelt's claim of a highly provocative attack. The administration followed the *Greer* episode by a campaign against the remaining, effective provisions of our neutrality act, especially those that prohibited the arming of merchant ships and the entry of American merchant ships into war zones. The appeal to Congress paralleled a gathering momentum among varied interventionist groups. The American Legion, in particular, helped gain support for repeal. Neutralist organizations, notably America First, had already gained an unpatriotic image, an ever-worsening press, and a deserved reputation for occasional anti-Semitic and pro-Nazi statements. Even as early as 1940 Congress began its first attempt to control internal dissent (the first Smith Act, directed specifically against Communists); soon pro-Nazi groups would face congressional investigation, legal harassment, and public ostracism. Roosevelt had pushed so far by September that he surely saw full belligerency ahead, and now desired it as much as his advisers. Unprepared militarily for an expeditionary force, anxious to give Japan every possible chance to evade its commitment under the Tripartite, Roosevelt justified a policy of war by degrees; besides, strong naval aid seemed the best military contribution we could then make. As the neutrality debates revealed, he still did not have broad bipartisan support for outright war, and at this time could not have secured a congressional declaration of war. Hitler, unwilling to grab any provocative bait, would not cooperate by taking the last, necessary step of war, or even the proximate step of unlimited submarine warfare.

Even as Congress considered neutrality repeal, Roosevelt capitalized on another naval incident with even greater emotional possibilities. The American destroyer *Kearny*, while on patrol duty, engaged in battle with German submarines, dropping depth charges and then pursuing. In the midst of battle, it actually suffered a torpedo hit with a loss of American lives. Roosevelt, on October 27, announced that shooting had started and that history would record who fired the first shot. He proclaimed that "America has been attacked," and movingly announced that it was not just a ship, but that it belonged to every man, woman, and child of the nation. On the day after the attack (September 17), the House voted (259–138) to repeal the prohibition against arming merchant ships. Stunned by the *Kearny* episode, the Senate voted (50–37) to allow American merchant ships to enter combat zones. This bill passed the reluctant House by only 212–194, reflecting congressional hostility not only toward Roosevelt's exploitation of incidents but also toward his "generous" handling of labor disputes in defense plants. The narrow margin of support in the House paralleled public opinion (by one poll, only 61 percent favored direct carrying of supplies to England). Regionally, only the South gave near unanimous support to such interventionist legislation. But the act passed, laying aside forever the ghost of neutrality. American merchant ships now could carry lend-lease to England and to Russia. In fact, in November our ships completely convoyed two British divisions to North Africa, taking obvious advantage of Hitler's continued reluctance to attack our ships. Pearl Harbor would clear up the few remaining ambiguities in our road to war.

The Final Road to Pearl Harbor

Hitler's invasion of the Soviet Union again changed the situation in the Far East. Japan, at least for a while, had no need to fear the Soviet Union, but successfully resisted German urgings to attack in Siberia. The German-Soviet War coincided with the end of a promising period of negotiations between Japan and the United States. An uncompromising American note on June 21 disappointed those Japanese, and particularly Prime Minister Konoye, who still wanted some settlement with America. On July 2 an Imperial Conference voted to begin preparations for possible war with the United States. On July 12 Japan presented an ultimatum to the Vichy government, asking to occupy the southern part of Indochina. The French had eight days to cede eight air and two naval bases, to permit free troop movements, and to evacuate several French garrisons. Having no alternative, the French complied on July 21, giving Japan a strategic boost and a launching point for further expansion into Thailand and Malaya. The Japanese move into southern Indochina undermined the desultory talks that still continued in Washington, and triggered several counteractions by the United States. We froze all Japanese assets on July 26, closed the Panama Canal for "repairs," increased the speed of our defensive buildup in the Philippines, and added new trade restrictions (almost all trade with Japan had already ceased because of informal embargoes). The Japanese insisted that their "protectorate" in Indochina paralleled ours in Iceland. We, of course, argued that our occupation had been defensive, whereas theirs was clearly offensive.

The American reaction to the Indochina affair, with its clear threat of war, frightened Konoye. He decided to try once again for serious negotiations, for some form of détente. The hazards were great. Time was running out. Our unofficial embargo on petroleum and official embargo on all other vital materials threatened the long-term Japanese war effort in China, added to the militancy of army leaders, and would soon undermine the Konoye cabinet. In a sense, we had a noose around Japan, and slowly tightened it, hoping for capitulation but risking war. To our older demands for withdrawal from China, we now added our demand for a neutral Indochina, with an early evacuation of all Japanese troops. In the administration, Stimson, Knox, and Welles all desired a firm stand and offered only minor concessions. Hull used caution both ways—to moderate the bite of our position yet to resist any concessions. Finally, the United States broke the Japanese diplomatic code and gained rather complete information on all the crosscurrents of opinion in the Japanese government. Whatever advantage this information gave to our diplomats, it proved a disastrous impediment to successful negotiation. Over and over again our intelligence reports undermined the Japanese bargaining position and foreclosed the opportunity for good-faith bargaining. It was a situation comparable to a courtship in which a girl is privy to all the inner thoughts of her suitor. The odds against marriage are great.

The opening for new talks came with the resignation of Foreign Minister Matsuoka on July 16. This left Konoye with a moderate cabinet fearful of the consequences of the American embargo. In August Konoye relayed a new set of proposals, including a commitment against further Japanese expansion and a promise to withdraw from Indochina as soon as the China "incident" could be settled. But the other proposals contained obviously unacceptable qualifications such as United States recognition of a special Japanese position in both China and Indochina (a Japanese Monroe Doctrine). Konoye also asked for a special meeting with Roosevelt, and followed this with a message of good will on August 28.

In Washington the mood had been particularly hostile toward Japan. As a follow-up of the Atlantic Conference, Roosevelt had presented Nomura with a near-ultimatum against further expansion. Yet, Roosevelt's immediate and natural reaction to Konoye's generous overtures was quite favorable. He even began to select likely meeting places, and obviously welcomed a chance to use the personal diplomacy he so loved. From Japan, Ambassador Grew urged the earliest possible meeting. A hopeful Konoye readied a ship and selected a delegation. But an ever cautious Hull, abetted by the Far Eastern desk of the State Department, dampened all the ardor for an early meeting, insisting upon preliminary agreements on principles as a prelude. He kept the China issue in the foreground, feared Japanese hypocrisy (we knew of continued military preparations), and clearly felt that Konoye might not be able to implement any major concessions that he might offer.

Konoye's hopes soon lay shattered. News leaks from the United States incited Japanese press criticism and desperate efforts to undermine Konoye by Germany and by pro-German army factions. Our State Department remained evasive, neither rejecting a meeting nor fixing a firm schedule. Konoye tried to set the date for September 20, but Hull still insisted upon preliminary agreements. On September 4 Japan even submitted a draft agenda. Hull still demurred. From Japan, Grew urged negotiation as a last possible chance to avoid war, and probably the last moment when Japanese internal politics would allow any real concessions. Japan would have to decide in only a few months. Pride would not allow complete capitulation to Hull's principles. Without some compromise with America, Japan would eventually follow the military path. Many experts in the United States believed Japan would not soon be in any military position to open war against the United States, and that we had nothing to lose by a firm, uncompromising stand. In September the Japanese slowly lost hope for success from continued negotiations. An Imperial Conference on September 6 began new military planning, and, short of an early settlement, decided to ignore American protests.

In spite of all of the frustration, Konoye persisted until the bitter end. On September 22 he tried to clarify his position on Chinese withdrawal and other issues. On October 2 we responded with six pages of detailed qualification, which the Japanese read clear and true as a device for procrastination. Konoye offered new concessions that he probably could not have implemented. He even tried to gain support in Japan for a preliminary commitment to withdrawal of troops from China. On October 13 a Japanese envoy in Washington, in conversation with Welles, seemed to make every possible concession: no further Japanese aggression to the North or South, complete troop withdrawal, and nondiscrimination in the Chinese trade. The envoy stressed the need for haste, and even had a special code to use for telephone communications between Washington and Tokyo. The Welles conversations came too late. Konoye's concessions had alienated too many Japanese. Even as Welles talked, Konoye clashed in a cabinet meeting with Foreign Minister Tojo over his concessions on China. On October 16, Konoye resigned, his pro-American policies a confessed failure. Tojo replaced him, and in so doing dashed most prospects for peace.

But the shift was not immediate. The Tojo cabinet continued to reflect deep policy divisions. Moreover, the emperor still seemed to be against war and, in an unprecedented intervention into policy-making, insisted upon continued negotiations with America. Throughout October the Roosevelt administration played a guessing game, trying to predict the when and where of new Japanese moves. The State Department consistently underestimated both Japanese capabilities and their reckless courage. The Japanese could not be as sanguine. If they were to launch an offensive they needed to move by November or December. A despairing Nomura sought permission to return to Japan. Grew likewise lamented lost opportunities. He believed that we had been unduly rigid, that negotiations and avoidance of war remained our wisest choice. To force Japan into war made no sense, for Hitler's defeat would eventually take care of the Japanese problem. Tojo still had lingering hopes of a settlement, although an intransigent army, bent on early campaigns, left him ever less room for negotiation. By early November he had developed two negotiating plans, and won from the military only a few weeks delay for final diplomatic efforts. Most Japanese military leaders expected the talks in Washington to fail, and went ahead with their planning. After a Privy Council meeting on November 5, they gave the negotiators only until November 25. Already, the navy had planned an attack on Pearl Harbor as the opening move. Operational orders went out on November 5. The attack would be on December 8, Japanese time, or December 7 at Pearl Harbor.

For the final showdown, Tojo sent two negotiating plans (A and B) to Nomura. In addition, he sent a more experienced diplomat and a competent linguist, Kurusu, to Washington to assist the earnest but amateurish

Nomura. Neither negotiator knew the detailed military plans; both worked indefatigably to find some basis of settlement. Even Tojo reflected a bit of pathos, a pathos rooted in the gulf of misunderstandings between the two countries. He stressed that this had to be the last effort, that Japan had yielded and yielded, but America remained obdurate and unyielding to the point of dishonoring and humiliating Japan. Hull, meantime, felt confidence in his knowledge that we had honored all treaties and launched no aggression, whereas Japan had perpetuated one violation after another.

Tojo's Plan A reflected a slight retreat from the earlier offers of Konoye, but did focus on the critical issues. He would accept commercial nondiscrimination throughout the Pacific if the same principles applied to the rest of the world. He would not repudiate Tripartite, but wanted to avoid extending the war to the Pacific. On China, he promised withdrawal within two years to North China. Knowing the deadline of November 25, we tried to stall on our reply, and even introduced other time-consuming issues (a Hull query about possible Japanese-Chinese negotiations led to warranted and cruel hopes in Japan that we had relaxed our key demand). In his final response to Plan A, Hull stressed the Japanese violation of law and order in contrast to our own peaceful goals, and condemned the plan as an unacceptable ultimatum. He pointed to our inability to guarantee worldwide commercial equality, and to our need for much fuller assurances about Tripartite. If we had such assurances, we might begin serious discussions on Japanese evacuation of China. Thus, Hull revealed our reservations even on the two items Tojo had believed closest to settlement.

This left only Tojo's Plan B, or what amounted to a proposed freezing of issues or a *modus vivendi*. Our State Department had considered such an idea. Even before submitting Plan B, Kurusu explored a simpler scheme of his own invention—a mutual return to the status quo as of July 1941. This meant Japanese troops out of Indochina and renewed American trade. Plan B, as presented on November 20, provided for military stabilization in Southeast Asia, Japanese withdrawal from Indochina, an early end to the Chinese war, worldwide nondiscriminatory trade, American help in securing a Japanese market in the Dutch East Indies, United States release of Japanese assets and renewed petroleum sales, and a common effort for peace within Asia but without Japanese renunciation of the Tripartite. The terms could hardly please the United States; Plan B as much as Plan A revealed a slight hardening of the Japanese position. Besides, Plan B, as we knew from the intercepts, was a last-moment ultimatum, with neither the time nor the give for important amendations. Hull would later damn this final Japanese offer, and argue that acceptance of it would have meant a surrender to intimidation and a sacrifice of our rights and interests in the Pacific. But at the moment we did consider it, and came within an inch of submitting a modified counteroffer.

The United States never made a counteroffer. One proposed response met determined Allied resistance. The time was short. Newspaper leaks by China awakened popular fears of an ignoble capitulation. Internal disagreements in the State Department worked against an early response. Instead of a counterproposal, Hull offered Japan a tough ten-point declaration, originally drafted as an agenda for a long-range settlement. It could only be received by Japan as an insult. Hull never contemplated the document as a negotiable instrument, but only as a review, a vindication, a confession of faith, even a sermon. Its preface provided an excellent, by now almost nostalgic, summary of American hopes and dreams in Asia: territorial integrity, equality of commercial opportunities, and collective security.

Much irony surrounds the ten-point declaration. The two disappointed Japanese negotiators did not want to send it to Japan, but Hull insisted. The Pearl Harbor task force left Japan on November 26, or just before the ten-points arrived. Tojo, apparently, still had faint hopes of a favorable response to his Plan B, and of reversing the war plans before November 29. Our response, of course, dashed all hopes for peace. From the Japanese perspective it was an invitation to war, and helped win even moderates in Japan to a new militancy. American newspapers also saw it as an ultimatum, a take-it-or-leave-it response. Most applauded. On December 1 the Japanese Privy Council, joined by the emperor, gave final approval to the war plans, and asked assurance from Germany that it would honor the Tripartite. Nomura and Kurusu received instructions to continue the talks, now a camouflage for Japanese military operations (this they did not know). Stimson and Knox, usually so militant, now wanted more time. Both the army and the navy were unprepared for war. Hull, after clearing the air with his ten points, reverted to his usual caution. Thus, after the die had been cast, we began to search for a final *modus vivendi*. On December 6, Roosevelt, largely by his own initiative, revived an old idea—a note to Emperor Hirohito. He sent an uncoded appeal by way of Grew, asking the emperor for unspecified action to dispel the clouds of an impending war. Because of communication delays, it reached Grew after the Pearl Harbor attack.

During the last, confused week, Roosevelt and his military and diplomatic advisers tried to prepare for the war they now believed almost certain. Intelligence reports on Japanese ship movements persuaded almost everyone that the Japanese would move to the South. Thailand seemed the best prospect. And it presented a dilemma to Roosevelt. Would the

American people support our direct intervention in behalf of Thailand?

Throughout the week several advisers worked on drafts of a presidential
speech, trying to draw clear lines, or to find a formula by which we
could warn Japan of just when we would enter the war, and by such a
firm commitment also prepare the American people for intervention. But
Hull, as well as others, wanted no warning, preferring to avoid any possible incitement of Japan. No acceptable speech emerged from all the
drafts, and Roosevelt postponed his planned radio address to at least Monday, December 8. From November 25 on, the Roosevelt administration
booted around the problem of getting into war. The United States could
not open engagements without risking public support. The administration
could only hope that Japan would desist from aggressive action or, if not
this, fire first. They did.

The Japanese attack on Pearl Harbor remains one of the most brilliant
military actions in history. It caught the United States by complete surprise, despite much earlier warning by Grew, despite revealing intelligence reports, even despite an early, unbelieved sighting of the Japanese
planes. Everyone in Washington was so sure that the Japanese would attack to the South that our only marginal concern for American territory
focused on the Philippines. Hawaii, if ever contemplated, seemed an impossible target. In retrospect, both Washington and the field commanders
seemed derelict—Washington for not anticipating all eventualities and
therefore issuing more specific warnings; the commanders for not living
up to all the requirements of a general alert then in effect throughout the
Pacific. The carrier based Japanese bombers crippled or sank the largest
share of our Pacific battleships, which were so conveniently bottled up in
one harbor. This blow further threatened any successful resistance to simultaneous Japanese invasions in the Philippines and in Southeast Asia.
Politically, the Japanese erred. They might have moved into Thailand
without America entering the war. In any case, we would have been hesitant and divided. Pearl Harbor unified the country as never before. And
as so many Japanese appreciated, including the emperor, a war with the
United States was a desperate gamble, a gamble that had to succeed very
quickly or not at all. The very attack that seemed perfectly calculated for
maximum military effect helped insure the American will and fortitude
for a long war, which Japan could not win.

Pearl Harbor allowed a great release of tension. Germany had been unable to win its greatest goal—a Japanese attack on the Soviet Union.
But it now had an active ally in the Far East and a broad second front to
divert the Western Allies. Thus, both Germany and Italy honored the
Tripartite and declared war on December 11 (we responded the same
day). The Japanese, thoroughly rebuffed by the United States in what

they considered a sincere and even generous effort in negotiation, now risked war to save honor as well as to gain an empire. The Pearl Harbor success only reinforced their enthusiasm. Britain and China both welcomed Pearl Harbor, for it did what persuasion had failed to do. With America in the war an Allied victory seemed inevitable even if distant. Finally, American officials felt elated at the early news of Pearl Harbor (the extent of the military disaster quickly tempered their sense of relief). Japan fired the first shot. So many dilemmas evaporated—how to react to an invasion of Thailand, how to get more fully into the German war, how to win bipartisan support for Roosevelt's politics. After a week of indecision Roosevelt now had no difficulty in choosing the topic for his planned speech. On December 8, at noon, he asked a joint session of Congress to declare "that since the unprovoked and dastardly attack by Japan on Sunday, December seventh, a state of war has existed between the United States and the Japanese Empire."

18

We still live in the shadow of World War II. It reshaped our economy and drastically altered our role in the world. Almost every major foreign policy dilemma that the United States has faced since 1945 has roots in the policy choices made between 1941 and 1945.

World War II provoked less internal conflict than any war in our history. The divisions, the bitterness, the disillusioned stock-taking, all came after the war. By 1941 the moral issues seemed unambiguous. The hated characteristics of Nazism, the memory of Pearl Harbor, seemed to override any doubts. Communist party members, or other groups sympathetic to the Soviet Union, supported a war in which Russia was an ally. Because of their usual nationalist and patriotic stance, the avowed enemies of socialism and communism joined in a war to defend American security.

Crusades almost always lead to some injustices. Fortunately, there was no large, conspicuous minority in the war years to invite hostility and repression. We did not invest our enemies with the devilish qualities attributed to them in World War I. Generally, we maintained a clear distinction between Hitler, his party, and the German people. We never honed our wartime militancy on caricatured Huns, or launched domestic campaigns against German Americans or German culture. Although we did deal harshly with identified German agents, and also with a handful of pro-Nazi Americans, their small number scarcely invited public attention.

Unfortunately, we rarely maintained such a clear distinction between official Japanese policies and the Japanese people. The most distorted caricatures of World War II attached to the Japanese, particularly to their soldiers. A racial bias influenced (but did not dominate) our wartime propaganda against Japan. Thus, the greatest domestic repression affected a racially and culturally distinct group of American citizens—those of Japanese descent. Roosevelt capitulated to a near hysteria on the West Coast, to the popular but fantastic judgments of West Coast politicians and area military commanders, and ordered the relocation of over a hundred thousand Americans who lived in the three Pacific states. After losing much of their property in forced sales, these Americans of Japanese descent lived out either part or all of the war in interior concentration camps, surrounded by fences and armed guards. These camps invited terrible social problems and poor education. To the enduring credit of the

A Nation at War

Japanese Americans, many fought back, both in the camps and later in legal action. In Hawaii, Japanese-Americans suffered close surveillance, lost jobs in critical areas, received harsh treatment in military courts, and in the early years of the war were not eligible for military service. Late in the war some Japanese-American soldiers achieved brilliant military records—in Europe, but the proudest young men refused either to register as possible enemies of the state or for the draft.

The unanimity of purpose during the war years removed any need for special propaganda in behalf of loyalty. Instead, the wartime propaganda focused on such practical issues as devotion to work, enlistment, bond purchases, and economic restraint. Many of Roosevelt's advisers had wanted a "hard" propaganda effort before Pearl Harbor, a time when a divided public opinion and low morale seemed to impede defense efforts. Roosevelt never rejected their schemes but Pearl Harbor made their implementation unnecessary. The lame Office of Facts and Figures, tied closely to civilian defense, finally gave way during the war to an Office of War Information, which indeed gave an official slant to news, but at the same time helped secure relatively objective even if restricted information on the war. To provide greater security, both servicemen and civilians had to accept a rigorous censorship, which proved a bit less irksome than wartime rationing.

This photo, taken by Russell Lee (1941), of children playing in a vacant lot in the black ghetto of Chicago, is a reminder that although for many people the depression ended when the war started, most minority groups still lived under conditions of depression. *Library of Congress*

The war meant a considerable social upheaval. The draft or dislocations of war work affected almost every family. The military services forcibly mixed people of diverse classes and regions. Of all groups, the Negro both gained and suffered the most. The war enabled blacks to secure industrial jobs never before available. To an unprecedented extent, former black sharecroppers moved out of the southern countryside, increasing the ratio of blacks in large cities, northern and southern, and adding to the likelihood of racial tension. The new mobility and the absorption of national standards of taste and expectation, as well as the avowed purposes of the war, all helped to create Negro dissatisfaction. Blacks still suffered the indignity of segregation in all military branches, and for the most part provided domestic services for our forces. Despite Roosevelt's belated 1941 order forbidding job discrimination in defense contracts and establishing a Fair Employment Practices Committee, blacks still faced intense opposition from all-white unions and from many employers. Out of old frustrations, and new aspirations, blacks began serious efforts at united organization and protest. In many ways, the civil rights movement originated in World War II.

Riots at the Sojourner Truth Housing Project in Detroit, Michigan (1942). When blacks tried to move into the government housing project, they met signs reading, "White Tenants for Our White Neighborhood." After a confrontation, the blacks moved in. *Library of Congress*

After the economic doldrums of the thirties, the American achievement in production during World War II seemed almost a miracle. In only five years the industrial output doubled. In spite of the allocation by 1943 of approximately two-thirds of that production to the war effort, American living standards were on the rise. Apart from durable goods, and particularly automobiles, the total production for the domestic market actually rose even in the midst of war. Although at the time many Americans might have disagreed, we in fact never came close to full mobilization. We fought and won a war in the midst, not of dire hardship, but of comparative luxury.

The productive effort was neither a miracle nor a masterpiece of careful planning. Fortunately, at the end of the thirties the United States had a large surplus of plants and laborers, enormous material and intellectual resources, and out of the scarcity of depression a long pent-up hunger for work, wages, savings, profits. Just as important, from 1940 on Congress consistently even if reluctantly appropriated the money for the huge unleashing of energy. Finally, in a confusing and fumbling way, the federal government did a bit more than place its orders for goods and services; it tried with some belated success to coordinate production, manage priorities, control prices and wages, and generally to give aim and direction to the overall economic effort.

Economic planning for war began in 1938. From then until 1942 Roosevelt struggled with a confusing array of agencies, and tried without much success to assemble a capable team of administrators. Until Pearl Harbor, the administrative effort probably retarded mobilization more than it enhanced it. By Pearl Harbor we faced severe shortages in rubber, aluminum, steel, aviation gasoline, and railroad cars. In 1939 Roosevelt used the new executive reorganization scheme to bring both civilian and military procurement agencies into his White House staff. He appointed a beleaguered War Resources Board, largely under the direction of businessmen, and then dismissed it because of criticism from farmers and organized labor. Before its demise, it drafted a mobilization plan based on that of World War I. Roosevelt objected to any super agencies or industrial czars, and had Bernard Baruch revise the plan in behalf of greater flexibility and less coercive power. He would never implement even this, the so-called Baruch Plan, until 1942. Until then he made do with advisory committees and what slowly developed as a wartime cabinet, made up of the two military cabinet members (Stimson in War, Frank Knox in Navy), such influential assistant secretaries as James Forrestal of Navy, and the heads of major civilian agencies or programs, including Donald M. Nelson and Edward Stettinius for production, Leon Henderson for prices, and Chester Davis for food.

Money succeeded where bureaucracy failed. By 1940 Roosevelt devised a workable means of buying industrial expansion. Production remained in private hands, but the government underwrote both assured profits and the needed plant expansion. Throughout the war, most government contracts guaranteed profits beyond actual costs. Often without a day's delay, a transformed New Deal agency, the Reconstruction Finance Corporation, financed any plant expansion required to fulfill government contracts. Finally, and most important, the treasury allowed corporations a 20 percent annual tax writeoff on such capital expenditures. In five years the tax savings canceled the cost and left companies with new factories as a virtual gift from Uncle Sam. In all, the government underwrote over $20 billion in capital expansion, the greatest single gift to any sector of the economy. Finally, it eventually provided corporations with a refund of the portion of high, excess profits taxes needed to cover reconversion losses after the war ended (for example the cost for General Motors to convert from airplane engines to automobile engines, from tanks to trucks). Under these safeguards, the large corporations quickly, in a few cases even recklessly, expanded their production capacity.

By Pearl Harbor our war production still amounted to only 15 percent of our total, or just over $8 billion for 1941. War made the difference. In 1942 all heavy goods manufacturers, led by the automobile companies, converted either totally or largely to war production. In 1942, by conservative estimate, and based on 1939 price levels, war production reached $31 billion; in 1943, over $54 billion, or almost half of our gross annual product. It leveled off and even began to decline by late 1944 as we came close to victory in Europe and began to cancel certain long-range contracts. Also, the administration finally brought some order to the central management of production. Roosevelt, in effect, capitulated to the earlier Baruch strategy; in January of 1942 he consolidated all industrial controls in a War Production Board (WPB) under Donald Nelson. Lacking the forcefulness of an industrial czar, facing almost insurmountable problems, Nelson never successfully coordinated production with resource procurement, and often seemed overly intimidated by both the military procurement agencies and by the large corporations. Although maintaining the WPB, Roosevelt in October 1942, set up a Director of Economic Stabilization, James C. Byrnes of South Carolina, whom he often called his assistant president. Byrnes initiated a complete control over all materials flow, beginning with mining or farming and continuing through to final production. Most production snags ended in 1943, not only because of a matured administration in Washington, but because of clear strategic goals by the Allied military commands, more definite estimates of needed supplies, and the final adaptation of production tools to war products. Much of the

conversion had to be planned as well as achieved at the factory level, and
the final result depended as much on local initiative as on centralized
planning.

The most spectacular production achievements occurred in the shipbuilding and aircraft industries, in the rapid creation of synthetic rubber,
and in the supersecret Manhattan Project, which culminated in the
atomic bomb. In the war years, our merchant tonnage quintupled to 50
million tons, even as American shipyards supplied a large proportion of
Allied shipping and built up our navy. During the war we also built
over 250,000 airplanes, in large part because of the success of automobile
companies in converting assembly lines to airplane engines and other
components, as well as to tanks, jeeps, and army trucks. The rubber
shortage marked a failure of strategic stockpiling before the war. It led to
a severe rationing of tires and gasoline (usually in plentiful supply at low
octane levels) and to the national 35-mile wartime speed limit. A belated
crash program in 1943 led to an adequate synthetic rubber facility by
1944. In complete secrecy, the Manhattan Project commanded a great as-
semblage of physicists, who used vast public power resources in the state
of Washington and in the Tennessee Valley to extract uranium-235, and
in effect successfully hid a whole new city of 50,000 at Oak Ridge, Tennessee.

The industrial achievement depended, in part, on major research efforts. A small National Defense Research Committee of 1940 became, in
June of 1941, the Office of Scientific Research and Development. Despite
this degree of organization, we long lagged behind the British and Germans in critical areas of research and technology. Our belated work on
rockets led to such tactical weapons as the "bazooka," but seemed pitiful
beside the German missiles and jet fighters. It was the British who perfected radar. Our efforts paid off in less spectacular areas—in explosives, detonators, fire bombs, better communication, insecticides. Of
course, in the one greatest scientific race of all time—for the atomic
bomb—we won, but in large part because of the contribution of European scientists and our close collaboration with the British. To an extent,
the atom bomb was a gift of Nazi persecutions, which drove the best European physicists into exile in England and America.

The story for agriculture seems less dramatic—no drastic reorganization of agricultural agencies, only a 20 percent increase in production,
and a steady gain in farm prices and income. The increase came with a
reduction of one million in farm labor and an increase of only 5 percent
in acreage. As in manufacturing, the prime incentive was dollars, not patriotism or federal control. The Department of Agriculture remained
wary of future surpluses, and usually tried to reduce estimates of needs

made by other wartime agencies or those already planning massive post-war relief programs. It only dropped its crop quotas in 1943 (save for to-bacco). In 1942, to circumvent the ineffective secretary of agriculture, Claude Wickert, Roosevelt set up a War Food Administration, which simply worked through the existing agricultural agencies and particularly the AAA. The Department of Agriculture also had coordinating ties with other productive and pricing agencies.

An effective congressional farm bloc ably defended the interests of farmers, sometimes at grave cost to the overall war effort. Resistant in all cases to price controls, Congress repeatedly defied the administration in order to benefit farmers. In the original price control legislation of Janu-ary 1942, ceiling prices on agricultural goods could not be lower than 110 percent of parity (a ratio of prices received to the cost of goods pur-chased). Since farm prices even in 1941 usually ranged below 90 percent of parity, this in effect provided higher food prices and led to a spiral of inflation beginning in 1942. Wartime farm prices eventually doubled the 1935–39 average (food costs only rose about 45 percent, since other costs in food processing remained relatively stable). Farmers also received exceptional rights to purchase desperately needed machinery and retained exceptional deferment rights for farm labor. The War Food Administra-tion never imposed production controls, but instead used persuasion or guaranteed price supports. As a result, farm production never exactly fit war needs—too much cotton, too little oil-producing crops, and grave fluctuations in livestock supplies. In order to get desired production changes, Wickert tried to use incentive payments in 1943 but ran afoul of congressional displeasure. In 1943 Roosevelt finally forced Congress (by threatening to use his war powers) to lower farm price ceilings to 100 percent of parity for all crops still under that amount. Congress guaran-teed 90 percent parity support two years beyond the war. And Roosevelt, in order to relieve intense pressure from laborers and consumers, used over $1.5 billion of direct subsidies to farmers to lower food prices on eighteen items. Only by this technique could he maintain existing price levels to farmers, yet reduce prices to consumers. The farm leaders resisted the technique and insisted the subsidy really went to consumers. By war's end, food stocks remained ample for domestic needs but far short of for-eign needs. A severe food famine struck both Europe and Asia by the spring of 1946.

The federal government did not take over railroads or other transporta-tion facilities as it had in World War I. In early 1942 this seemed a re-grettable mistake. German submarines curtailed our coastal shipping, placing the full burden of transportation on overloaded railroads and trucks. Governmental pressures to build new rolling stock in 1940 and

1941 had gone unheeded by the Association of American Railroads; steel shortages prevented such an increase during the war. On December 18, 1941, Roosevelt set up an Office of Defense Transportation to supervise all domestic transport, with power to issue binding orders. Operating at maximum capacity under its control, the railroads and trucking companies realized profits without increased rates. Except for an early oil shortage, the railroads handled priority traffic without serious congestion, but not without restrictions on load sizes and a great deal of discomfort for the traveling public.

Manpower Policies

The curse of the thirties—unemployment—finally proved a bit of a blessing, for it provided a large labor surplus at the beginning of the war. In 1939 unemployment still approximated 10 million, including only those officially on the job market. There was also an enormous labor pool in nonworking women, in retired workers, in high school and college students, and in the possible use of overtime work. By Pearl Harbor defense preparation had absorbed approximately 5 million workers; the armed forces just over 2 million. Some pockets of unemployment remained even into 1942.

With war, change came rapidly, but without a total mobilization of manpower. The military forces enlisted approximately 15 million men and women during the course of the war, but never contained more than 12 million at one time. This loss of more than 18 percent of the potential civilian work force invited either a drastic increase of workers from other sources than military age youth, or a dramatic increase in working hours and labor productivity. Both occurred. The total work force, counting the military, expanded by approximately 10 million in just two years. That expansion represented student draftees, 3 million additional women who took jobs, many men over fifty-four who entered or reentered the job market, and possibly 4 million nonworking youth (fourteen through twenty-four) who left school for either the army or for full-time employment. Overtime work supplemented the added personnel. By 1944, the average work week advanced to 45.2 hours. Finally, work productivity increased steadily during the war, a result of accelerating technological innovation, high morale, and a very efficient use of scarce labor.

Even before the worst labor scarcities developed in 1944, the government used various indirect techniques to get laborers into, and keep them in, war-related industries, and into areas of the country with the greatest need. The only compulsory service was the military. A separate agency until April of 1942, the Selective Service then became part of the new War Manpower Commission under Paul V. McNutt. The Selective Ser-

vice System eventually registered all men between eighteen and sixty-five, with early expectations just after Peal Harbor that Congress would soon approve some type of mandatory labor service. The plenitude of laborers at this point postponed such a dire action, and this was the only frightened moment when Congress was receptive to such an extreme scheme. Yet, the Selective Service System tried to use occupational deferment as a powerful weapon to keep personnel in certain jobs. Local draft boards impeded this effort by favoritism for farm boys and a common

By 1943 labor was very scarce. More and more women were taking jobs outside the home, in all capacities. Here, a lady is welding pipe outlets for a ship in Baltimore, Maryland. *Library of Congress*

resistance to the drafting of fathers. The Selective Service System realized that the threat of the draft alone would force many fathers into essential civilian jobs. To an extent, the system had its way. By 1944 the military wanted only younger men. But for anyone occupationally deferred, an unapproved job shift meant an immediate call up, even when age and health conditions might otherwise have meant rejection. Of the 43,000 men drafted under these rules, most found, during basic training, that it would be much better to accept an enlisted reserve status and return to defense jobs. For men not subject to the draft, the War Manpower Commission requested, often without success, that corporations only hire men who had special certificates of eligibility, granted only to men who left essential industries for justifiable reasons. By referral, propaganda, or special recruitment drives, the commission usually managed to procure needed workers. In extreme cases the War Labor Board permitted special wage increases, the Selective Service System provided special deferments, or the army temporarily furloughed soldiers for industrial service.

During the war, nonsalaried factory laborers made up almost half of our work force. In most respects they fared very well indeed. They had

Wartime Washington overflowed with working people (primarily women), and with servicemen. The canteen was a place where the two could meet, with the proper supervision. Eleanor Roosevelt and singer Pete Seeger are seen here at the opening of a Washington, D.C., labor canteen, 1944. *Library of Congress*

secure jobs, higher wages, and enough overtime to boost their weekly income 60 percent above the 1939 level. By 1943 their wages were frozen, but not rigidly. Since the cost of living advanced about 15 percent after January 1941, the War Labor Board set a 15 percent maximum rise for wages during the war years. Laborers benefited from price controls, but received no benefits comparable to the special pricing and subsidies for agriculture, or the tax benefits and large capital gains for business. Finally, the higher wages had to compensate for major social dislocation—mothers absent from homes, families displaced from traditional communities, terribly inadequate housing, intense racial and cultural friction. Various incentives and pressures forced laborers to move to new areas of the country, such as California and the Pacific Northwest, and at times they must have felt like herded animals in the midst of wartime chaos.

Just after Pearl Harbor a national Conference on Labor Relations secured commitments from both management and large unions for a no-strike, no-lockout policy for the duration of the war. The agreement first floundered on the issue of closed or open shops. The new War Labor Board, created in the wake of the conference, and composed of representatives of labor, management, and consumers, became the final arbiter of all labor disputes, backed by presidential power to seize plants or even draft workers. It never imposed any closed or union shop requirements (new members could remain out of a union), but did require existing members to remain in unions for the duration of contracts, a moderate settlement of a terribly emotional issue on both sides. The real crunch was wages. Here the board tried to keep all contracts within the 15 percent limit. But several exceptions made its rule rather elastic—corrections of old inequities; of substandard wages (below subsistence); nonwage incentives, such as paid vacations; extra pay for night work or extreme conditions; and a few wage increases to get workers to more critical areas. Supplementing this were the administration efforts to roll back food prices.

Despite the responsiveness to union concerns, the War Labor Board could not appease on some issues. Strikes continued throughout the war, although most were short lived and local. The most famous strike of the war years, a general coal strike called by tough and able John L. Lewis in 1943, first led Roosevelt to seize the mines and then to threaten the drafting of miners. He had such extraordinary powers because of a Labor Disputes Act which an antiunion Congress passed over his veto in 1943. Despite the government, Lewis eventually achieved many of his demands, but only after Roosevelt had successfully turned intense public hostility toward him and the United Mine Workers. Lewis remained a virtual ogre to most Americans until well after the war, but a hero to his union.

Price rises affected the mobilization schemes. Inflation, so desperately sought in the thirties, became an overriding domestic problem in 1942. By and large, the Roosevelt administration solved the problem, for after 1942 prices, wages, and profits all remained stable except, again, for slight increases in farm prices. Under Leon Henderson, who headed the unpopular Office of Price Administration (OPA), selective price controls began in 1941, but foundered over and over again on farm prices and new wage demands. An act of Congress in January 1942 reorganized the OPA and gave Henderson full power to establish maximum prices, and to control rents in defense built-up areas. Eventually, after agonizing delays and an enormous accounting task (no computers then), the OPA put their price ceilings into dollars and cents lists and generally enforced them by the fall of 1942. Only food prices continued to rise. Meanwhile, wage guidelines and Federal Reserve System restrictions on borrowing also helped ease inflationary pressure. The controls over prices and wages worked hand in hand with the rationing of all scarce consumer goods and with special tax and borrowing policies.

Henderson and the OPA supervised the various forms of rationing, a problem almost as complex as price controls (both had to apply at every retail outlet in the country). First came tires and the organization of 8,000 local rationing boards. Then came sugar, coffee, gasoline, shoes, and most foodstuffs (all controlled through multicolored stamps). Excessive demands, preventive hoarding, problems of distribution, and, most important, increasing exports to our Allies, required some degree of control or central direction over consumer choices. Either local scarcity, or drastic shifts in consumer demands, could also force such pressures on the price controls as to insure black market operations, or at least permit informal favoritism by retailers. Only a fair, controlled distribution of available (and reasonably adequate) supplies could be fair to all, and also to our Allies. Both England and the Soviet Union forced their citizens to live on lower calories and much coarser diets, yet both contributed relatively more to the war effort.

The backbone of the war effort had to be government fiscal policies. The war had to be paid for. Just how we did it had momentous implications for the postwar world. The mobilization policies proved ephemeral, never yet revived even in our subsequent wars, and in large part because our economic growth made them unnecessary. That growth, in turn, rested in part on the fiscal policies first adopted during World War II.

In one sense, the war exacted its cost at the time. The necessary resources, the immense expenditure of human energy required, had to be

Controlling Inflation

Financing the War

370

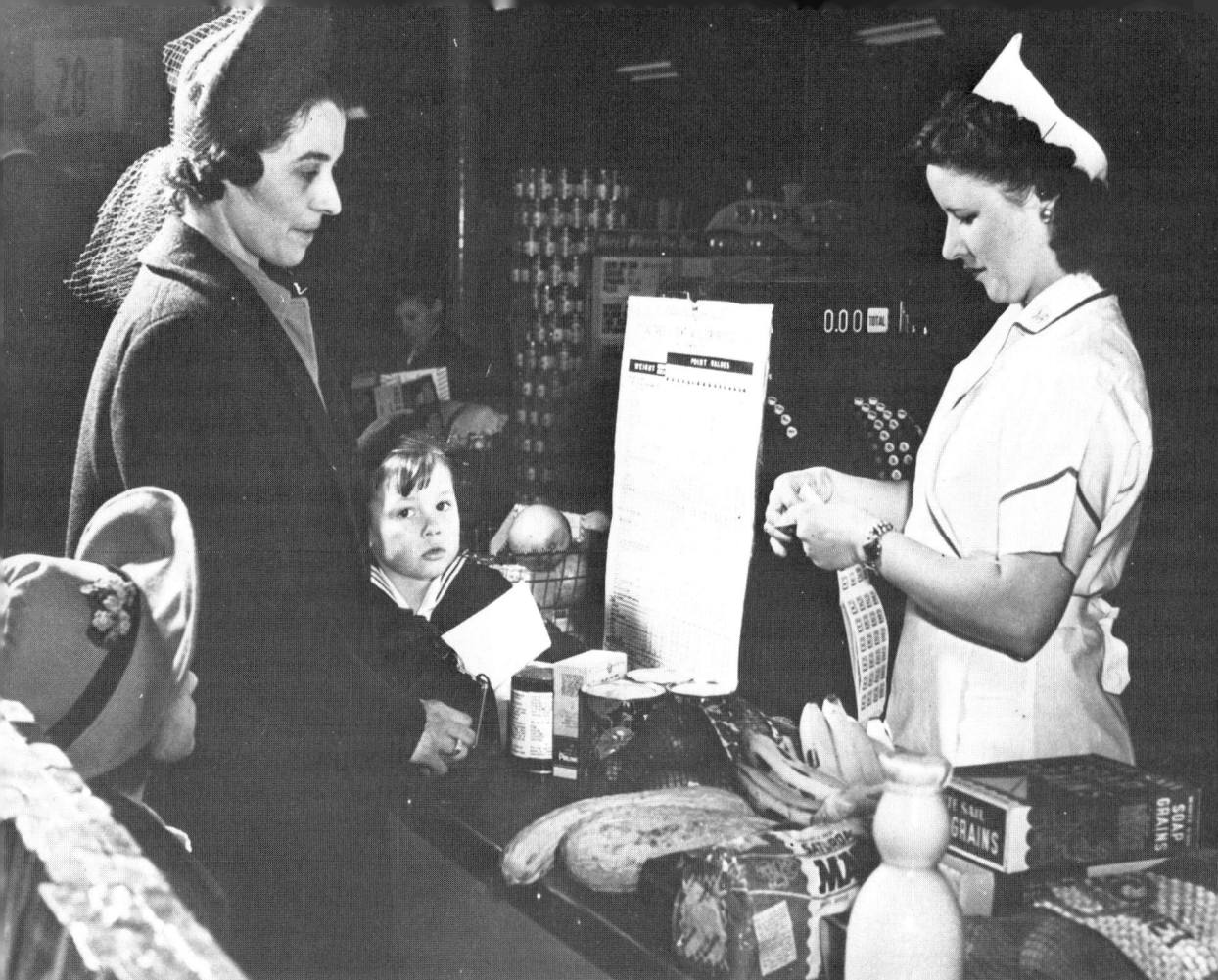

provided as needed. Some young men sacrificed their lives; others gave four years of underpaid work; practically everyone suffered a drastic loss in consumption from what all their extraordinary efforts ordinarily could have procured. The critical policy issue concerned the future. Would part of the cost be assessed against it, and collected later, in order to lessen the sacrifice of the present, or at least compensate for those sacrifices? If so, individuals during the war would have to collect assets redeemable at least in future consumption if not in present indulgence. The government chose such a course, paying for about 60 percent of the war through borrowing, about 40 percent by taxes. Roosevelt would have preferred a more equal mix.

As a general policy, the Roosevelt administration preferred persuasion or bribery to conscription, the military forces excepted. Private producers had to contend with priorities and allocations, ceaselessly procuring permits and quotas, but they still responded to the assurance of secure profits and the clear promise of immense profits in the postwar years, when they

While a shopper and her children look on, a clerk tears stamps from a war ration book to cover the processed foods being purchased (1943). Rationing brought the physically distant war close to home, and enabled those who could not fight to participate in the war effort. *Acme Photo*

could really cash in on all the bribes. Workers responded to the lure of overtime wages, increased family security, higher living standards, and accumulated savings that might bring a postwar cornucopia. The immediate gains and long-range promises brought zest to wartime efforts, and added the energizing leaven of self-interest to the weaker stimulus of patriotism. It could have been different. The government could have drafted factories and workers. By a virtual confiscation of all wartime savings, by high enough taxes, it might have paid for the immensely costly war (about $300 billion). But such a policy, apart from almost impossible efforts at propagandistic stimulants, would have lowered morale and inhibited the outpouring of creative energy, threatening the very productive base that won the war. Higher taxes would have reduced the level of wartime consumption (all spending was not for subsistence), eliminated the pressures for inflation and possibly the need for most rationing. In theory, this would have freed more workers and more factories for war production, but only if the same productive zeal had survived the coercion and civilian sacrifice. Finally, such a policy could only have threatened, not inflation, but depression in the postwar reconversion period. There simply would have been no built-up demand based on immense savings, no tax concessions to aid corporations through the reconversion period, no built-in inflationary forces to spur spending and investment.

The irony of all this: only by transferring much of the burden to the future, only by extreme government deficits, could the average individual in World War II actually profit from the war. His real spendable income went up, but over half of his production went for the war. A large share of that income had to be diverted from individual consumption into savings. Either directly by his own bond purchases or indirectly by bank purchases, these savings helped finance the war. Or, in other words, instead of turning these savings into taxes, the government instead issued claims for the future as its excuse for taking and using the money (or the energy). It also paid interest for the use. For the average person this seemed a good deal.

How good depended on postwar fiscal policies and the overall performance of the economy. In actual fact, the accumulated debt (approximately $260 billion by the end of the war, and so much larger than any earlier period as to defy comprehension) would not be repaid, but rather continuously refunded, a policy close to that of any business with assured income and growth potential. Since the economic growth of the war continued in the postwar era, this debt maintenance in itself never added a dire burden to postwar taxpayers, and certainly no burden remotely comparable to the sacrifice that would have been required by a cash funding of the war itself. But there are other aspects to the final accounting. One was inflation, particularly the unprecedented jump in 1946 and 1947, sanctioned by Congress and opposed by President Truman. This inflation, in effect, reduced the national debt by a third and also reduced the assets of those who held the debt. This meant that the tax bite was relatively less. But the holders of war bonds, as well as others who maintained savings accounts, lost money on their war-derived assets, for at maturity bonds yielded less purchasing power than the original cost, and thus to that extent served a concealed taxation role. Those who, against the plea of government, the claims of patriotism, used all their savings on real estate or corporate stock (stock prices remained low in the war) collected the greatest profits on their wartime investments.

The Federal Reserve System might have aided the battle against inflation; instead it supported government borrowing. The wartime inflation seemed to invite restrictive monetary policies. By maximum reserve requirements, the sale of all its open-market securities, high rediscount rates, and 100 percent stock margins, the Federal Reserve System could at least have forced higher interest rates. This would have checked some of the pressure toward spending, but not nearly all, since cash purchases increased so rapidly. Instead of these orthodox credit devices, the Federal Reserve Board did just the opposite, and apart from imposed restrictions on loans turned the whole problem of inflation over to the OPA. Meanwhile, from mid-1942 on, it pursued an emphatic inflationist policy—lowered rediscount rates and reserve requirements and unlimited open-market purchases. It enabled the money supply to triple. To understand the rationale for this requires some insight into the financing of the war.

From June 30, 1940 until the end of 1945, the federal government spent approximately $380 billion. Taxes covered only about $150 billion, leaving roughly $230 billion to be borrowed in a period of less than five years. Obviously, such a magnitude of deficit government expenditures would not only lead to almost irresistible pressures against prices, but to a drastic increase in interest rates as the government bid up the price of money by the very immensity of its demands. The Federal Reserve, rather than trying to add its inadequate bit to the holding of consumer prices, chose to anchor the price of money (interest rates) at the existing and very low level of the depression. If it had not done this, by 1942 several difficulties would have ensued. First, the prices on existing, low interest bonds and treasury notes would have plummeted, as investors looked to much higher returns through other means in the immediate future. Secondly, prudent investors would have withheld funds until interest rates soared, thus both delaying government bond sales and quickly forcing very high interest payments even on short-term treasury notes. By using the Open Market Committee to maintain existing bond prices (it bought all offered it), and by this and other techniques to expand bank reserves, the Federal Reserve maintained for the government a vast source of low-interest credit.

In simplest terms, the government financed 60 percent of its wartime expenditures by selling its securities (various promises to pay) to banks and to individuals. The income, in either case, went into government bank deposits, used to finance the purchases of war materials. A low private demand for credit meant that the banks had immense excess reserves, and every incentive to purchase government securities. The ballooning effect of government deposits meant a cycle of bond purchases, added deposits, excess reserves, and more purchases. The same was true for individuals with savings, since various U.S. bonds continuously out-yielded bank savings accounts. But since bank savings also ended up in the government bond market, the government secured its loans either way. In this manner, the government expanded the monetary supply in direct ratio to its need for credit, and in effect fed on its own credit needs. Finally, the Open Market Committee remained ready to buy government securities from banks, at a very minimal discount, and eventually held over $22 billion of the government debt itself. Such purchases directly increased bank reserves by an equal amount and further opened up credit resources.

The only flaw in this rather grandiose financing technique was the looming difficulty in getting off the accelerating system. By the end of the war, savings had accumulated; wants multiplied; money supplies tripled. How could we get out from under all these price controls and rationing without disastrous inflation, and then beyond that another disastrous and desperately feared depression? The answer was simple: we *could not* end the controls except by degrees, and then only over a long enough period of time for the Federal Reserve System to reverse policies and slowly bring monetary supplies under its control. At war's end, we hurried the process a bit and reaped severe but not ruinous inflation.

Taxes

Taxes represent the other side of fiscal policy. The purchase of redeemable E bonds, under the intense pressure of government propaganda and employer urgings, diverted potential consumer funds into the U.S. Treasury but often only for short periods of time. Taxes directly and permanently curtailed purchasing power, and were thus the most stringent anti-inflationary measure available to government, particularly when assessed on low-income families, or directly on goods purchased, as in excise taxes. Many groups, such as the National Association of Manufacturers, urged a national sales tax. Roosevelt seriously considered compulsory savings or an income limitation of $25,000. In fact, income and excise taxes provided the main weapons.

After the futility and contradiction of his tax policies in the thirties, Roosevelt now attained several social as well as fiscal goals. Consistently throughout the war years he fought for more sharply graduated personal income taxes, and for much higher taxes on corporate profits. Just as consistently, Congress responded to intense pressures from various, often regionally based private interests, including large war contractors, and either rejected or lowered administrative proposals. And even Roosevelt had to respond to the tremendous need for revenue and the necessity for curtailing consumption and inflationary pressures. Thus, he had to support excise taxes on all consumer goods except vital necessities, and new income tax rates that finally ensnared almost every family. During the war federal taxes grew to eight times their 1939 level.

This revolution in tax policies came by a series of steps, none nearly so radical or frightening as the cumulative result would have seemed in 1940. The first real war tax bill came in 1940 (it was called the Defense Tax), and raised revenues by about $600 million. In a pattern endlessly repeated, it lowered family exemptions from $2,500 to $2,000; individual exemptions from $1,000 to $800. By an old pattern, everyone paid a normal tax rate of 4 percent. Graduations affected only a surtax which, in the 1940 Act, remained at 4 percent on $4,000 to $6,000, ranging up to 75 percent on $5 million or over, or a 4–75 percent surtax rate. A slight rise in normal corporate income taxes retained a slight graduation (now 13.5–19 percent). Both corporations and individuals also had to pay a special 10 percent temporary defense tax, the largest source of new revenue and an across the board provision that made the tax bill regressive in its effects.

Widespread apprehension over high defense profits, or new war millionaires, revived in 1940 the issue of excess profits taxes, a form of tax in effect since World War I. The original Revenue Act of 1940 did not change the older rates (6 percent on net income above 10 percent of capital stock and 12 percent on net income above 15 percent), but it redefined excess profits on government contracts as actual profits earned, and set the maximum normal profit at 8 percent on competitive contracts, 7 percent on negotiated contracts, or on the type most often used for defense purposes. These new definitions horrified businessmen and almost stopped bids on government projects. Subsequently, in 1940, Congress redefined "excess profits" as either more than 8 percent above invested capital, or by a somewhat more complicated and often less demanding formula based on net income, but raised the tax rate on such profits from 25 percent at $20,000 to 50 percent on anything over $50,000. In addition, Congress then approved the 20 percent annual writeoff on all capital improvements required for government contracts, and by so sweetening the pill made contractors again anxious to get into defense work.

In 1941 Congress considerably upped the tax ante. It approved $3.5 billion in new revenues, and thus the largest single tax increment in our history. The Revenue Act of that year removed exemptions on federal securities, and increased excise taxes, particularly on luxuries. Family exemptions came down to $1,500; individual exemptions to $750. The act kept the personal income tax rate at 4 percent, but raised the surtax to 6–77 percent, and made it applicable to all taxable income, beginning at $4,000. It raised corporate rates to 31 percent, with a small surtax of 6–7 percent. Finally, it raised the excess profits rates to 35–60 percent.

The greatest single change in taxes came in the Revenue Act of 1942, which had a stormy congressional career. It raised approximately $7 billion in new annual revenue, and for the first time extended the income tax to a majority of American workers. Its huge return depended, primarily, on the broadened base of family exemptions of only $1,200 (a majority of families still had an income of under $1,500 in 1940), and individual exemptions of only $500. It raised the income tax rate to 6 percent and, more important, the surtax rate to 13–82 percent. It increased corporate taxes to 40 percent, and raised the highest excess profits tax to an astounding 90 percent (in part ineffective because of the still-liberal methods of computing profits). Most smaller taxes—estate, gift, excise—increased proportionately. Finally, Congress added a unique victory tax of 5 percent on incomes, collected at the time of earning (this came closest to forced savings and also began the withholding principle).

Throughout 1943 Congress wrangled endlessly over details, and did not pass a new Revenue Act until the spring of 1944. But before that it converted our income taxes to a current payment system, or the present withholding system. The heated issue in Congress involved the transition to "pay as you earn"—how much of past taxes should be forgiven? Roosevelt opposed and helped defeat a 100 percent exemption on due taxes, but signed a measure providing 75 percent relief. The new Revenue Act (passed in 1944, but for the 1943 fiscal year) reversed the increasingly progressive features of earlier years, and showed more solicitude toward business. Roosevelt vetoed it (the first revenue act ever vetoed), and an angry Congress overwhelmingly passed it over his veto, not so much because of its features as in resentment at presidential power. The act did not change personal income tax rates, but lowered the victory tax to 3 percent, canceled the promised postwar credits, and increased the excess profits tax to 95 percent even as it set up a special appeals board to appease war contractors with special tax grievances. Finally, late in 1944, Congress repealed the victory tax entirely and simplified tax returns. It reduced the normal tax rate to 3 percent, but set the surtax at 20–91 percent. Instead of separate family and individual exemptions, it established a $500 exemption for each family member. In 1945, and at the war's end, Congress began a rather hasty reduction of taxes, and repealed entirely the controversial excess profits tax. Except for it, our basic tax structure has remained very much as it became during the war.

Despite the increased burden of taxes on lower income families, the wartime taxes did achieve one of Roosevelt's goals—a leveling of income. To some degree the highest income groups lost in their percentage of the total income; lower income groups gained. Undoubtedly, the largest change came from the bottom, since full employment gave increased shares to families who had lived on relief in the thirties. The higher surtaxes and the excess profits taxes cut into higher level incomes, at least during the war. One detailed estimate on income distribution shows that in 1935–36 the highest 10 percent of our population controlled 39.4 percent of our total income; by 1943, the first year of big taxes, this dropped to 34.2 percent. Meanwhile, the lowest 10 percent moved up from 1.3 percent to 1.5 percent. After the war most of these shifts remained intact, but without any significant new leveling. In fact, in our century, the only major changes in the distribution of income, not of wealth (a quite separate issue), came in World War II, and in part as a result of tax policies. Yet, the highly progressive rates never led to the leveling of either incomes or of wealth expected by supporters and feared by opponents. This lack of profound effect on distribution reflects two major causes: loopholes in tax laws (and brilliant strategies of avoidance), and dramatic, offsetting increases in economic growth, and thus in salaries and profits for those at the higher levels of income.

19

Pearl Harbor came too soon. The United States was ill-prepared for full belligerency. It had not yet come close to economic mobilization. Besides, it had used much of its earlier production, not for its military forces but as aid for Britain and the Soviet Union. Thus, in the immediate aftermath of Pearl Harbor the United States could not do much to affect the military course of the war. The Pacific lay open to Japanese conquest and the United States Army could commit only a trickle of men to the European theater. For months a too scarce military production had to be rationed out in all directions to plug up deficiencies all around the world, and to provide enough support to Britain, the Soviet Union, Australia, New Zealand, and even China to slow or stop the many-pronged Axis advance. The Allies achieved this stabilization remarkably early, or by the late summer of 1942; by that fall and winter they were able to launch a counteroffensive.

Though weak militarily, the United States had long played a vital part in the European war. In cooperation with the British, it had already adopted major strategic guidelines, formulated war aims, and at least moved far toward combined staff planning. Also, it had almost unlimited resources. So far it had lacked only the will to commit them. Now it had the incentive. In a long war the United States contribution would be decisive. Churchill knew this; even the Japanese sensed it. Thus, despite all the crushing defeats that so depressed and shocked Americans in early 1942, all the odds now favored eventual Allied victory. How soon it would come depended, in part, upon the strategic planning of the three major Allies.

Outlines of Military Strategy

An exhilarated Churchill left Britain for America just after Pearl Harbor. In late December and early January he met with Roosevelt, while American and British military leaders worked out the details of a Combined Chiefs of Staff, to be located in Washington. The two countries also tentatively identified areas of primary responsibility in the world. Roosevelt and Churchill reiterated the idealistic if vague aims of the Atlantic Charter in a Declaration of the United Nations, to which the Soviet Union and other Allies later subscribed. More important, the two leaders reaffirmed an explicit earlier commitment to give first priority to the European war, and also an earlier implicit understanding that this would be

Strategy and Diplomacy

a war for total victory, or for the complete defeat of Germany and Japan.

The commitment to complete Axis defeat, to total war, represented no calculated decision, but a quite early emotional reaction to Hitler, to his internal policies, and to the type of war he waged. Particularly the Soviet Union, but also Britain, had suffered too much to contemplate any settlement or armistice. Regrets over German resurgence after World War I also precluded compromise. In the United States, the Pearl Harbor attack, the utter efficiency and seeming cruelty of early Japanese conquests, a total lack of understanding of Japanese culture, residual racial antipathies, and an effective barrage of wartime propaganda all helped to produce intense American hatred and with it a desire for a victory complete enough to eradicate Japanese political institutions, including even the emperor. A myopic, mild Hirohito became, in the war years, almost as potent a symbol of tyranny as Hitler. And the total war commitment, in itself, almost insured the defeat of a Japan with too limited resources for a sustained struggle. Japan fought for concessions, not for total victory. It could not invade or destroy America. But, as events proved, America could destroy Japan, and now intended nothing less.

The Soviet Union never became a part of the close Anglo-American partnership, particularly at the staff level. At least Roosevelt sought close cooperation with Stalin, but always with unclear results. The prominence of a common enemy, the courage of the Red Army, the tragic suffering in Russia won increasing American respect for the Soviet Union, and hopes that Russia would become a "democratic" country just like the United States. But old scars, and continued ideological differences, left an almost unbridgeable chasm. A marriage of necessity thrives only during a period of common adversity. During the war, at least, American-Soviet relations remained friendly even if cautious. The United States and Britain fought out the most serious disagreements on strategy and even on long-range political objectives. Roosevelt often had a greater sympathy for the Soviet Union than for an "imperialistic" Britain, and often acknowledged the disproportionate Soviet contribution to victory. Roosevelt tried unsuccessfully to use charm and alliance to soften the suspicions of Stalin, and also tried without success to win Churchill over to a Western strategy that would offer the greatest immediate solace to the Soviet Union.

The United States, despite its economic resources and potential military might, could do little to stop widespread Axis advances in 1942. By the Washington agreements, the United States had primary military responsibility in Asia. We had little to back it up. The Japanese pushed north to the Aleutians, east to Guam, Wake, and the Gilberts, and south to the Dutch East Indies and the Solomons (see maps on pp. 323, 380). The British and Dutch had no means to defend the rich resources of Malaya and the East Indies. The American navy, stripped of its capital ships by the Pearl Harbor catastrophe, decisively lost its only early challenge, off the coast of Java in January. The army, bereft of air support and naval supply, fought a futile holding action in the Philippines. During the spring of 1942, hopeful, then despairing Americans read about Bataan, the horrible death march, the flight of General Douglas MacArthur (with a typical flair for the dramatic, he promised "to return"), and the final surrender of a remnant force on Corregidor. As a gesture for morale rather than military purposes, a small force of specially equipped carrier planes, under General James Doolittle, bombed Tokyo on April 18, and then flew on to China (the famous "Thirty Seconds over Tokyo"). Then, in May, a reviving American navy, using carrier aircraft, stopped a Japanese invasion force off New Guinea at the battle of the Coral Sea, and in early June completely crushed a Japanese naval force intent on taking Midway Island. Closely allied to Australian and New Zealand forces, we were also

WORLD WAR II: THE PACIFIC THEATER

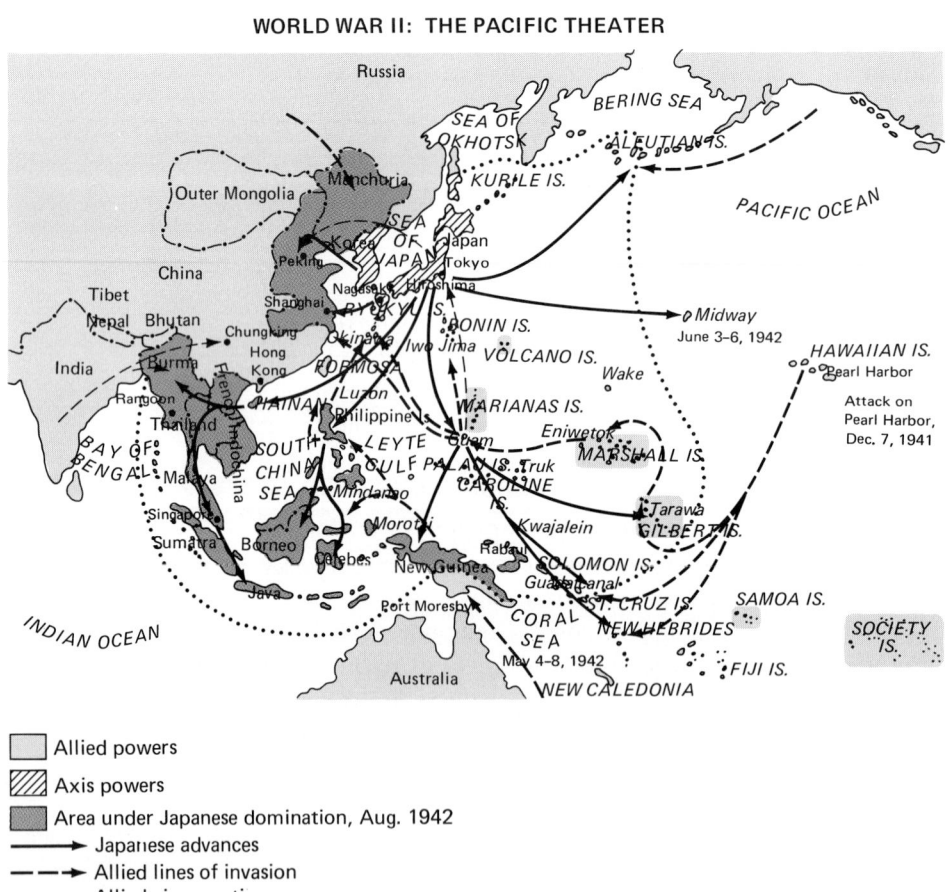

Allied powers

Axis powers

Area under Japanese domination, Aug. 1942

Japanese advances

Allied lines of invasion

Allied air operations

able to stem the Japanese southward advance in the steaming highlands of New Guinea and on Guadalcanal in the Solomons.

In Europe events were as frightening as in Asia. After the reverses of winter, Hitler resumed his offensive in Russia. Eschewing a further siege of Leningrad and Moscow, he sent his troops deep into the oil rich Caucasia and eastward to the Volga at the city of Stalingrad. There, after a series of rash strategic decisions, Hitler would meet the greatest disaster of the war, but this would only be clear in late 1942. In the Atlantic German subs, running in packs, sank the largest tonnage of shipping during the entire war. Now that American ships were fair game, the submarines seemed on the way to cutting all lifelines to Britain. Only our record-breaking production of destroyers and sub-chasers averted defeat. Finally, in the see-saw battle for North Africa, General Rommel picked the summer of 1942 for his greatest offensive. The British retreated to El Alamein, only seventy-five miles from Alexandria, and one of the last defensive positions short of the Suez Canal. Only exhaustion and overextended supply lines stopped Rommel's advance in August.

The Beginning Road Back

In the midst of such reverses, American military leaders developed their first detailed plans for a counteroffensive. In spite of our clear commitment to Europe first, we had to commit large forces to the Pacific even to save Australia. Since most Americans had a more intense hatred for the Japanese than for the Germans, such effort also strengthened morale at home. Much more than anyone had intended, Washington responded to MacArthur's and Admiral Ernest J. King's continual requests for men and supplies. We steadily increased our Asian forces throughout 1942 and 1943, in part because of a British refusal to accept our major strategic plans for Europe. We began the long road back well before we gained a clear superiority in Europe.

Our main effort was still in Europe. In Washington, General Dwight D. Eisenhower, then assistant chief of staff under George C. Marshall, supervised the preparation of our grand strategy. By it, Britain would become the launching pad for an early cross-channel invasion of Hitler's Europe. We wanted to go on the offensive, concentrate our energies on one clear objective, and get Hitler out of the war as quickly as possible so that we could turn to the Japanese. Both Marshall and Stimson believed that such an invasion would be the only way to defeat Hitler. It was also the best way to divert massive German forces from the Soviet Union, and thus relieve the beleaguered Russians. By April 1 Roosevelt had approved a major invasion by no later than the spring of 1943, and a smaller attack in September of 1942, particularly if the Soviet Union seemed on the

verge of defeat. Roosevelt approved these plans well before Molotov arrived in Washington in May to press for an early second front. We then promised him every possible effort, consistent with our ability to transport supplies to England and still continue aid to Russia. The Soviet reverses of the summer only reinforced our hopes for an early invasion. But the British demurred. Eventually, reluctantly, Roosevelt had to overrule his military staff and accept Churchill's proposal for an invasion of North Africa. But not until after a summer of Anglo-American wrangling.

In April 1942 Churchill and his staff agreed, although a bit reluctantly, to a cross-channel invasion. They qualified their approval by their concern over adequate preparations. In a June conference with Roosevelt, Churchill argued against any small, diversionary attack in the fall, but still backed a major invasion early in 1943 if it could be so strongly launched as to insure success. He wanted no second Dunkirk. The British reverses in North Africa made an attack there most appealing to Churchill. He was able to get Roosevelt to consider it as at least a substitute for the

General George C. Marshall, chief of staff, is greeted on his arrival in Paris after a nonstop flight from the U.S. in the first air transport command plane to make the trip. Left to right are: General Dwight Eisenhower, supreme Allied commander in Western Europe; General Marshall; James F. Byrnes, director of war mobilization; and Lieutenant General Omar Bradley. *Wide World Photos*

small invasion of Europe. But Marshall and Eisenhower would not give in so easily. They joined Harry Hopkins in London for a final showdown with the British. They also tried to get the mobilization effort under way. Even American naval officers joined the British in pointing out all the hazards. We simply lacked the ability for any remotely promising attack in 1942. So the only clear hope was a major operation sometime in 1943. Foreclosed in Europe, Roosevelt opted for an earlier action in Africa. Planning for an October landing commenced in August.

This critical strategic decision has left a bundle of historical puzzles. Eisenhower and Marshall, at least during the summer of 1942, felt that the British virtually sabotaged our plans. Americans thought they detected a myopic political motive in Churchill's advocacy of Africa. He wanted to save Suez, preserve the British empire, secure continued British domination of the Mediterranean, and only then move quickly to win the war or succor the Russians. Possibly he already looked to the postwar settlements, pursuing a strategy most likely to serve Western political goals and possibly frustrate Soviet political ambitions. He later employed these guidelines. The Americans remained military purists. They placed one goal above all others—a quick defeat of Hitler. All political issues had to be deferred until we achieved this goal. Even on strictly military grounds the British may have been correct. In retrospect, it seems that a limited invasion of France in 1942 would have been too pathetic to divert many Germans from the Eastern front. The earliest possible success had to be in 1943. But an impatient Roosevelt could not wait so long. Then, once in Africa, even a 1943 invasion of France became less plausible. In sacrificing the first plan, we ultimately lost both. And only a great deal of speculation about forever unknowable eventualities can say whose plans were best. But one can, in any case, sympathize with growing Soviet doubts about the good faith of their Western allies (if they ever had such faith in the first place).

The invasion of North Africa required great diplomatic finesse. The United States had already successfully wooed most of Latin America (Argentina excepted) and acquired bases and support in Brazil, which a new map consciousness revealed to surprised Americans as remarkably close to the hump of Africa. More important, our successful contacts in Vichy helped keep the Germans from securing the North African colonies, although it also prevented our effective cooperation with the Free French forces in Britain. Finally, the British had helped keep Franco's Spain from joining the Axis, and thus Germany away from a critical Gibraltar. With war, the United States first tried a tough policy against a generally hated Franco, but soon reversed this in behalf of conciliation. We even shipped oil to Spain. Likewise, the conciliatory British policy in Portugal led first to Portuguese neutrality, and finally to open cooperation with the Allies, including the lease of naval bases in the Azores in 1943.

The actual invasion of Algeria and Morocco came on November 8. The Vichy French forces resisted, but only briefly. Admiral Jean Darlan, anti-British and a former Nazi collaborator, accepted an armistice in return for continued French political control (under him rather than the Vichy government). Our bargain with such a wily political opportunist seemed to belie the Atlantic Charter, and forced embarrassed apologies from Roosevelt. When Darlan fell to an assassin in December, we gladly replaced him with General Henri Giraud, a near incompetent but our lame substitute for General Charles de Gaulle. One of the main dramas of World War II involved the mutual distrust of Roosevelt and de Gaulle. Although the British wanted to recognize de Gaulle and his Free French forces, the United States (and particularly Hull) nourished lingering grievances over his high-handed occupation of St. Pierre (off Newfoundland) in 1941. We believed him to be incompetent, but he proved us wrong on that. In January 1943 he and Giraud agreed to a cooperative partnership of the Free French forces. Soon de Gaulle completely overwhelmed Giraud.

Just before the African invasion, General Bernard Montgomery launched a counterattack against Rommel. With the invasion, the Germans rushed into Tunisia ahead of the Allies. From February to May 1943, the Allies pursued Rommel from both east and west, and finally forced his surrender, but not before he gained their begrudging admiration. Already, in January, Roosevelt and Churchill met at Casablanca and planned an Italian invasion. This, again, was against the fervent advice of Marshall, who saw simply another British diversion from a cross-channel assault. Roosevelt and Churchill hoped to get Italy out of the war and gain complete control of the Mediterranean. Meanwhile, the Soviet Union held out in Stalingrad in late 1942 against a desperate and foolish German siege. In February 1943 the Russians either killed or captured the whole besieging army, in by far the most significant military victory of the war and one of the most significant battles of all history. With spring and summer the Soviet Union began the long drive to the west that would end at Berlin in the spring of 1945. We no longer had to fear a Soviet collapse.

At Casablanca, Roosevelt and Churchill met without Stalin, but his haunting shadow very much influenced the course of their deliberations. Stalin had received a steady stream of lend-lease supplies from the West. He wanted even more. He also sought a treaty that would guarantee the

Bob Hope's role as troop entertainer had its origins in World War II. In 1944, while entertaining U.S. troops in Tunis, Tunisia, singer Frances Langford and Hope load a 90 mm. gun. To the amusement of the men, Miss Langford fired the gun, probably becoming the first woman ever to do so. *United Press International*

Casablanca and Summit Diplomacy

Soviet Union major territorial gains in Eastern Europe. Most of all, he wanted a second front in Western Europe, a second front now pushed far into the indefinite future by the decision to invade Sicily. Churchill and the British were open to territorial concessions. They still believed in the idea of a balance of power, and either formal or informal spheres of influence. Foreseeing the preeminence of the Soviet Union after victory, wanting to avoid future conflict, the British were willing to concede reasonable Russian territorial ambitions and use these concessions to gain a better position for the West. Roosevelt often reflected a realistic or even cynical understanding of the necessary role of the Big Three Powers in determining and policing any postwar settlement. He later proved open to personal bargaining and even considered treaty concessions to Russia. But our traditional and official position permitted no such political deals over territory. Men like Hull sincerely hoped the war would end all such cynical bargaining of other people's lives, and looked to a world order that rested on independence, liberty, and self-determination. During 1942 the British pushed us to accept a treaty; we resisted, forcing Britain and the Soviet Union to bargain alone. Roosevelt preferred to use the commitment for an early second front as a consolation prize. We used persuasion with both the Soviet Union and Britain to get a completely innocuous British-Soviet treaty in May of 1942. It mentioned no territory, no frontiers, and thus allayed the growing fears of exiled Poles or former citizens of the Baltic republics. But we never fulfilled our side of the implied bargain—an early second front. An angry Stalin could not be appeased by a visit from Churchill in August 1942, even though Churchill then promised the cross-channel invasion for 1943.

This was the context for the Casablanca conference. Except for the shadow created by a distant Stalin, or far-off and faint cries of neglect from Chiang Kai-shek, the two leaders met in a period of unbounded hope. The war finally went well in all areas. Even the submarine threat had begun to subside. But how to appease the Russians, who, after all, still did the greatest share of the fighting? Some Americans even feared a separate Russo-German peace treaty, which would allow the Soviets all the portions of Eastern Europe that they wanted. The answer to all these problems was the acclaimed doctrine of "unconditional surrender." It scarcely committed anyone to a new policy, since complete defeat had been our objective all along. Now Roosevelt spelled it out in great detail: peace required the total elimination of German and Japanese warpower, a complete destruction of the philosophies, not the peoples, of these two systems. Implicit in the doctrine was a commitment that neither country of the grand alliance would lay down arms short of the enemy surrender (this, of course, did not apply to the Soviet Union and Japan, for they were at peace). The very concept of unconditional surrender, widely and early used for propaganda purposes, lessened the prospect for any negotiated peace, narrowed our options in any final peace settlements, neutralized peace groups in Japan and Germany, and required that we completely destroy the military capacity of both enemy states. It increased the likelihood of a military and diplomatic vacuum in Europe and Asia, and created the illusion that only Japan and Germany stood in the way of a blissful and peaceful world. Russia, although unappeased by mere promises, had no desire for a negotiated peace with Germany, and so loved such ideas as surrender and complete destruction.

Allied Military Successes

In the Pacific, the United States, Australia, and New Zealand fought a quite difficult war and, despite the major effort in Europe, consistently won. But not with ease. By 1943 the combined armies ground out slow gains in the jungles of New Guinea, while army and marine units moved north through the desperately defended Solomons (New Georgia in June, Bougainville in November). In late November our Marines jumped to the Gilberts, in a difficult but successful assault on Tarawa. More significant, by the end of 1943 our navy won complete ascendancy. But the beleaguered Japanese, short of resources and vital supplies, continued to dispute almost every foot of island territory. In China, Chiang Kai-shek held out despite chaotic internal dissent and a mere trickle of American aid. Roosevelt tried to appease China by massive loans ($500 million in one shot), which seemed to evaporate without any results, and by an unrealistic insistence on China's great power status (the British ridiculed, but had to indulge us this illusion). Conversely, the British insisted on great power status for France, against our better judgment and against determined Soviet opposition.

In May 1943 Churchill and Roosevelt met again in Washington. They completed plans for the invasion of Sicily, but only after the British agreed that future Mediterranean operations would not deplete the build-up for a cross-channel invasion. Roosevelt now insisted on this priority. The British, never really averse to a massive and successful invasion, finally agreed on a target date—May 1, 1944. This late date infuriated Stalin, who charged another act of bad faith. Meanwhile, the United States and Britain invaded Sicily on July 10, 1943. The ease of a successful, month-long campaign belied the treacherous obstacles awaiting Allied soldiers in Italy. On July 25, Italian insurgents, prompted by Allied propaganda and with the support of King Emmanuel II, arrested Mussolini, formed a new government, and sued for peace. But two problems loomed: the unconditional surrender policy and Russian cooperation.

With the excuse that Italy represented a separate issue, the Western Allies accepted her conditional surrender on September 8. Italy's opportunistic new government declared war on Germany on October 13, and thereby became a semi-ally. The Soviet Union did not participate in the negotiations nor in the occupation and reconstruction of the Italian government. Britain wanted very much to exclude Soviet influences in Italy, and above all avoid any Communist government. The Soviet Union received only a meaningless seat on the Allied Advisory Council in Italy. Not only did this Italian settlement further alienate the suspicious Russians, but the United States and Britain long wrangled over the type of government appropriate for Italy (Britain wanted a monarchy, the United States a republic). Even the early diplomatic victories soon turned sour. German troops quickly occupied Italy and soon controlled the whole peninsula. British and American troops first crossed from Sicily to the Italian boot on September 3. After capturing Naples and much of the southern part of the boot, the Allies bogged down in a bitter campaign that lasted until the war's end.

As a substitute for a cross-channel invasion, Britain and America tried to reduce Germany by aerial bombardment. After the 1940 Battle of Britain, and the brutal German bombardment of all major English cities, the British had reciprocated in kind. Using poorly armed Lancaster bombers, the British carried out nighttime raids on German industrial centers, particularly the Ruhr. After Pearl Harbor, the American Army Air Force

The invasion of Sicily on July 10, 1943, was the beginning of the long and difficult battle for Italy. Shortly after the invasion the Mussolini government collapsed and when the Allies reached the mainland in September, the new government, under Marshal Pietro Badoglio, surrendered. Despite the surrender, the occupying Germans doggedly defended Italy until the spring of 1945. *Courtesy of Daniel Handelsman*

thirsted for its chance to prove the effectiveness of pinpoint, strategic bombing of military targets. In our early idealism we rejected the idea of bombing civilian populations, or even imprecise nighttime bombing. In 1942 we supplied planes to the Royal Air Force but, because of so many worldwide demands on our air force, did not begin strategic bombing. In fact, our air force dropped its first bomb on Germany in January 1943. We followed this with a hopeful strategy of daylight bombing, aided by the secret Norden bombsight, and by the considerable guns carried on our prized B-17 bombers, the flying fortresses. But we quickly lost this game. Without armed fighter escort, even the B-17s could not overcome antiaircraft fire and effective Luftwaffe fighter squadrons. With an embarrassing loss of face, we joined the British in indiscriminate night bomb-

The colorful general, George S. Patton, Jr. (1885–1945), as he apologizes to the officers and men of the Seventh Army for striking a soldier during the Sicilian campaign (1943). After Patton graduated from West Point he served with General Pershing in Mexico during World War I. His long career in the army was marked by controversy, but he finally received his stars from General Eisenhower in 1945. *Wide World Photos*

ings after October 1943. Even this had minimal effect. Surprisingly, Germany had not fully mobilized even by 1943. She had excess plane capacity. By the end of 1943 the Allied bombings had not reduced her production by 10 percent and the bombs strengthened German morale. Only in 1944, with full air supremacy and long-range fighter escorts, would the bombing achieve devastating effects. By then it was too late to be decisive in the final outcome.

By August 1943 the most critical issue had to be Soviet relations, now at a wartime low. Roosevelt had tried, unsuccessfully, to gain Soviet trust. He felt that Stalin had some basis for his distrust of Britain, and foresaw possible Anglo-Soviet conflict in postwar Europe. Even though Britain was more open to direct territorial concessions to Moscow, she also had her own empire to defend, and in the postwar period might push her spheres of influence so far as to frighten Russia. Often, Britain had blocked an early second front, had competed for lend-lease aid directed to Russia, had tried to rebuild a powerful France, and now looked out for her interests in the Mediterranean and the Near East, or areas quite important also to the Soviet Union. In order to mediate a possible rivalry, Roosevelt first asked for a personal meeting with Stalin. He met not only Stalin's rebuff but Churchill's affected jealousy. This left only a possible three-way summit meeting, which Roosevelt eagerly awaited. He wanted to gain the personal respect of "Uncle Joe" and soften him up for continued cooperation, particularly in a postwar United Nations.

Teheran

The culmination of Anglo-American overtures to the Soviet Union came, first, in a foreign ministers conference in Moscow in October, and then in the Big Three meeting at Teheran in late November and early December. By this time, Poland was an added irritant. Clearly, the Soviet Union would never restore Poland's prewar boundaries. The Polish government in exile in London, which kept up a strident propaganda battle against boundary changes, soon gained the full contempt of Moscow and even caused a good bit of irritation for Roosevelt and Churchill. When the exiled government accepted German claims of having discovered the bodies of a group of missing Polish officers allegedly slaughtered by the Soviets, the Soviet Union broke diplomatic relations and began to organize a friendly Polish government from among Pro-Communist Poles in the Soviet Union.

Hull represented the United States at Moscow, meeting with Eden and Molotov. He again proved his brilliance at negotiating. Because of Roosevelt's dominance of big power diplomacy, this was the only time during the war that Hull led an American delegation. He came to Moscow with one main goal: to woo Soviet support for a strong postwar United Nations and finally redeem the tragic hopes of Woodrow Wilson. Already, the State Department had developed extensive plans for such an organization. Hull also successfully wooed bipartisan support in Congress. In September, both houses had voted overwhelmingly (on the House Fulbright resolution, 360–29; on the Connally resolution in the Senate, 85–5) in favor of United States support for an international organization with power to prevent aggression and preserve peace. If he could get similar support for collective security in the Soviet Union, then he believed the world could look forward to a virtual millennium of peace and good will.

In Moscow, Hull adhered to his one interest—agreement on the general principles to be embodied in a declaration on collective security. Eden wanted to open up the tangled and treacherous political problems that already loomed in the future, including detailed plans for Germany and for German-occupied areas of Eastern Europe. The British did not want to postpone these problems until war's end, when the Soviet Union would be strengthened and the Western Allies weakened by the expected early evacuation of American troops. The Soviet Union had only one main goal—to get sincere Western commitments to a second front. On this issue they received firm assurances. They willingly supported Hull's efforts to avoid or postpone divisive political issues. Hull secured an informal Soviet commitment to enter the Japanese war after Germany's defeat, and by tenacious bargaining forced the Soviet Union to accept China as at least a formal member of the big power club. But the main achievement was plans for Teheran, an agreement for a quite restricted European Advisory Commission to consider the problems of a liberated Europe, and finally the signing of Hull's Four Power Declaration. It committed all four powers to an international organization based on open membership and the sovereign equality of all peace-loving states, and committed to the maintenance of international peace and security. Back in Washington, to the thundering applause of a joint session of Congress, an elated Hull announced his glad tidings of a world forever peaceful, with no spheres of influence, no alliances, no balances of power.

Roosevelt traveled as far as Teheran reluctantly. Stalin refused to go further beyond the borders of Russia. On the way, at Cairo on November 11, Roosevelt met with Chiang Kai-shek, thus in part appeasing the generalissimo. The actual conferences at Teheran lasted only four busy days. The three leaders met jointly, and also paired off. Roosevelt particularly tried to cultivate Stalin in private sessions, rather recklessly exaggerating American disagreements with Britain in an effort to ingratiate himself. Even as Hull had done in Moscow, Roosevelt tried to be mediator and peacemaker. Churchill and Roosevelt at least persuaded Stalin of their sincerity in pursuing a second front. But on other issues the leaders divided. Britain pushed for big power status for France, and thus for de Gaulle. Russia vehemently opposed this and wanted if anything to punish the French. Roosevelt inclined toward the Soviet view, in part because of his contempt for de Gaulle, and in verbal exchanges with Stalin seemed committed to the exclusion of France from any postwar settlements. The British fear of a vacuum in Western Europe also influenced their plans for Germany. Churchill wanted to detach Prussia, block German militarism, but still leave intact the German state. Roosevelt again sided with Stalin in behalf of permanent destruction and the eventual division of Germany into five small states. Against Churchill's protest, Roosevelt even seemed to accede to Stalin's demand for the extermination of German officers. But all the discussion led to no agreements about Germany. As so many issues at Teheran, it had to be left for further study.

At Teheran Stalin made a firm commitment to enter the Japanese war, but for a price. Roosevelt, assuming the willingness of the Chinese, offered to pay it—the Kuriles, southern Sakhalin, and restored bases and privileges in Manchuria. The three leaders only touched on the later, critical issue of Eastern Europe. Churchill argued for a strong, independent Poland. Stalin would not commit himself. Roosevelt refused any private concessions to Stalin about Poland, but lessened the force of his stand by reference to the American Polish vote and his inability to make any decisions until after the election of 1944.

Despite the absence of firm decisions, the Teheran conference had nonetheless clarified many of the contours of a postwar world. Now, quite clearly, there would be a United Nations. Germany would be crushed and divided. Britain would have to struggle against the United States and Russia in order to secure any restored role for France. The United States secured formal big power status for China, but as a result of U. S. pressure rather than of Chinese realities. Finally, by sloughing over or postponing almost all potentially divisive issues, the conference helped to foster several illusions. For Stalin, it seemed a great victory, for he had rejected none of his long-term territorial and political goals for Eastern Europe. Behind the ambiguities of Roosevelt's smiles and seeming agreements, Stalin sensed much more of a blank check than really existed. Roosevelt, basking in the surface harmony of Teheran, came home to create illusions on our part—of a distrustful and suspicious Soviet Union finally won over by our good will and sympathy to collective security and continued cooperation. At the end of 1943, in the shadow of Teheran, he actually worried more over possible British and French threats to our ideals of collective security and self-determination (would they liquidate their empires? If not, then Western imperialism might provide the source of future conflict. Even our unbounded hopes for China depended on Western generosity and reticence).

Even as diplomats maneuvered around the grand issues of policy, arms still clashed throughout 1944. In the Pacific, the United States slowly drove Japan back toward its island fortress. American and Australian armies cleared most of New Guinea by February of 1944, and also captured the Admiralty Islands just to the north. These victories, plus success in the Solomons, isolated Japan's major naval base on New Britain. In the central Pacific a now completely dominant American navy carried our marines to the Marianas (Saipan, Tinian, and our own Guam), then to the Carolines. This, coupled with a decisive naval victory in June, left the Japanese vulnerable in the Philippines and their home islands finally open to massive bombing, which began in earnest in the fall of 1944. On October 20, MacArthur, finally honoring his commitment to return, led American troops to a landing on Leyte Island in the central Philippines. In the final decisive naval battle of the war, the Americans completely overwhelmed the Japanese fleet in Leyte Gulf, insuring only token naval resistance from that point on. Although it would take eight months to complete the Philippine campaign, we had now effectively cut Japan off from the valuable resources of the Indies and Malaya. The unbroken victories, the relentless push of American forces, and the clear superiority on our side, already presaged the eventual victory of our forces. But the victories came hard. The Japanese showed fanatical courage and fought tenaciously even in hopeless situations.

Just after Teheran, Roosevelt selected Eisenhower as supreme commander of the Allied forces now gathering in England for the oft-postponed cross-channel invasion. Eisenhower established headquarters in London, and there coordinated an unprecedented buildup of men and equipment. On the eastern front, Germany was unable to launch its customary spring offensive. Instead, Soviet forces advanced along most of the huge front, and by such pressure prevented any shift of German forces to the French coast. In Italy British and American forces advanced only with great difficulty. A January landing at Anzio beach proved almost disastrous for United States forces. But on June 4, just before D day, Rome fell. Finally, the Western Allies had gained nearly complete air supremacy, and used much of their bombing fleet to soften possible landing areas in France.

The long-awaited invasion came on June 6, D day. Contrary to German expectations (and by way of some brilliant Allied intelligence operations), Eisenhower selected the northern coast of Normandy, far to the south and west of the shores closest to England, or the ones most heavily defended by the Germans. Except for one sector, the Allied troops landed without heavy resistance. Mistakenly interpreting the Normandy attack as a diversion before the main onslaught, the Germans only slowly engaged the invaders. Within two weeks the Allies had one million troops in France and by July 25 began a major offensive. In August a second invasion, from Italy, created a pincerlike offensive. Paris fell on August 25. By September 15, Allied forces were in Germany. By December they were able to liberate almost all of France and much of the Low Countries.

In the winter of 1944–45 Germany made its last effective stand. During the summer Hitler barely escaped death from a bomb planted by predominantly military conspirators. This failure removed likelihood of early German surrender and condemned the German people to a horrible siege. Through the late summer of 1944, Soviet troops recaptured the Baltic states; in the fall they marched through eastern Poland. To the south, they entered Rumania in August, Bulgaria in October, and Hungary at year's end. In early 1945 Russian troops captured Warsaw, and by February were within forty-five miles of Berlin. In the west, the Allies temporarily reeled under the last major German effort, or what became known as the Battle of the Bulge. Concentrating their last airplanes and troop reserves, the Germans in December of 1944 attacked the center of the Allied line near the Belgian-German border. Secured from air attack by heavy clouds, the Germans pushed deep into southern Belgium, but failed in their objective of breaking through toward the coast and completely dividing the Allied armies. By February the Allies resumed their offensive and this time directed it at the heart of industrial Germany, the Rhineland.

At the end of 1944 Americans could only rejoice in their achievements. In three brief but hectic years they had moved from embarrassing defeats to sure victory. And the sacrifice had not been in vain. Our oldest and most revered ideals in foreign policy now seemed close to realization. This time we would win the peace as well as the war. We would soon excise the cancer of overt aggression, the tyranny of brutal conquest and subjugation. By our example and influence (as in the Philippines), we would eliminate the curse of Western colonialism. Finally, by our continued good will and generosity, we would finally secure the permanent friendship of the Soviet Union, and thus soften its expansive demands for territory or for subservient neighbors, and lessen worldwide insecurities that led to internal repression and external aggression.

20

With victory approaching in Europe, the United States could no longer postpone pressing political questions whose answers would determine the shape of the postwar world. Our continued insistence on limited strategic goals, and on Big Three agreements only at the level of vague and ambiguous principles, had too often postponed problems that had to be faced. These involved not only a critical divergence of postwar goals between the Western Allies and the Soviet Union, but also unresolved conflicts between Britain and the United States over the fate of Europe and of the Middle East. These issues dominated the Big Three conference at Yalta in February of 1945, or what turned out to be one of the most critical and controversial diplomatic conferences in history.

By Soviet insistence, this last conference attended by Roosevelt took place in the Soviet Union. Despite the controversy that later swirled around it, the Yalta Conference began and ended on a note of harmony and friendship. Since Teheran problems had certainly multiplied; so had suspicion and doubts. Unlike Teheran, the atmosphere of Yalta was often tense. It now seemed much less certain that the Big Three could pull it off, that they could find the secret of an enduring peace. Troublesome issues and nagging doubts intruded too often. At Teheran, Roosevelt had treated Stalin like a bad boy who might be won over by decency and generosity. Roosevelt had conceded little but had stood firm on nothing. He simply postponed divisive issues or left them enveloped in bland ambiguity. Now he had to face them. But even at Yalta, ambiguous words often concealed rather than solved difficulties. On the last day of the conference the three leaders offered sincere and glowing toasts. They had been through a lot. Like impatient boys at play, they had just divided up the whole world. But at the end they were tired. They were also old. In this atmosphere even Stalin softened a bit, and indulged in a bit of sentimentality.

When Roosevelt left for Yalta he was tired, if not ill. In November he had fought a strenuous campaign in order to win a fourth term against a formidable opponent, Thomas E. Dewey of New York. The campaign occasionally revealed him off guard, haggard in appearance, halting in speech, less patient with issues and subordinates. On the boat trip to the

Yalta

The Agonies of Success

Crimea he relaxed, without assimilating the detailed briefing papers prepared for him by the State Department. At Yalta he often seemed anxious to dispose of aggravating problems. But a distaste for prolonged controversy, a disinclination for prolonged intellectual effort, a desire for at least a surface harmony, had always typified Roosevelt, and if anything was only slightly more marked at Yalta. In no sense was Roosevelt incapacitated at the conference. His positions remained consistent with past commitments. He adjusted his views in response both to Churchill and Stalin, and did more than either to maintain harmony and at least a vague agreement on issues. In many ways he faced even greater pressure from Churchill than from Stalin, for Britain and the United States remained far apart on the German issue, and the United States remained as suspicious of postwar British imperial designs as of Russian threats in Eastern Europe. Thus, Yalta was to be no turning point in American policies even if it was a critical step in their achievement. The critical shift in those policies came later, and not because of anything conceded at Yalta.

Yalta would determine the disposition of Germany, the final shape of the United Nations, the status of France, the fate of Poland and of other Eastern European states, and the exact terms of Soviet participation in the Japanese war. At Yalta the Big Three agreed on the final details of an international organization. In August 1944 delegates from the Allied countries had already met at Dumbarton Oaks, in Washington, D.C., to plan a United Nations. On most issues, harmony prevailed. But Andrei Gromyko, the head of the Soviet delegation, then shocked the United States by a suggestion that all sixteen Soviet republics receive a vote in the UN Assembly. Even more divisive was the extent of veto powers by the Big Three (or Big Five if China and France should join the club). The Soviet Union already sensed their impending minority status in any world organization, and the domination of such a body by the United States, Britain, and their friendly allies (the United States had maneuvered most Latin

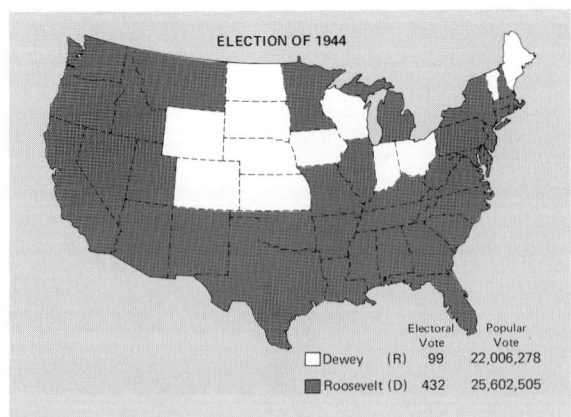

American states into a declaration of war against the Axis and thus into automatic seats in the UN). Soviet adherence depended upon a protective veto in the Security Council, or the action branch of the planned UN. Hardly less compelling, Roosevelt doubted congressional approval of the UN unless we reserved some unilateral control over the commitment of American troops. But we wanted a veto only on the ultimate use of force; the Soviets wanted an absolute veto even on agenda items in the Security Council. This issue awaited partial resolution at Yalta, and final resolution at San Francisco.

At Yalta, to the gratification of Roosevelt, the Soviet Union agreed to send delegates to the UN Conference in San Francisco in April of 1945. Also, the Soviet Union accepted a compromise veto proposal of the United States—a big power veto over all Security Council action but not over procedure, mere discussion, or seemingly over peaceful settlements of issues to which a big power was a party in the dispute. Finally, the Soviet Union lowered its demands for membership of all sixteen republics to membership only for the Ukraine and White Russia, a position

The Yalta Conference was held in February 1945, to allow the Big Three—England, the U.S., and the USSR—to determine the shape of the postwar world. Seated, left to right: Marshal Joseph Stalin (1879–1953), President Roosevelt, and Prime Minister Winston Churchill (1874–1965). Standing behind Stalin is Foreign Minister Molotov (1890–   ) and behind Churchill is Foreign Secretary Anthony Eden (1897–   ). *Wide World Photos*

acceptable to the United States. Britain secured membership for her do- minions and for India. The United States secured the right to ask for three votes in the Assembly, a right we did not exercise at San Francisco. Since Soviet cooperation in the UN, along with its participation in the Japanese war, were the prime goals of the United States delegation, the unexpectedly easy solution to the UN problem reinforced Roosevelt's normal inclination toward conciliatory gestures, and considerably eased Stalin's task in winning concessions on such sensitive issues as Poland. Clearly, Stalin never placed as much trust in the UN as did Roosevelt, and would never, as Roosevelt hoped, see it as a sufficient guarantee of Soviet security. He would press, even at Yalta, for much more tangible returns.

Much more important than the details of the UN were vital, unsettled is- sues about Germany. At Teheran Roosevelt had casually acceded to Sta- lin's desire to dismember the German state. But they then referred all de- tailed plans to a European Advisory Commission, located in London. During 1944 the commission worked out an instrument of surrender, zones of occupation, and plans for an Allied Control Commission. In Washington, Roosevelt received quite conflicting advice. The State and War Departments wanted a moderate policy in Germany, with continued national existence and minimal economic dislocation. A forgiving settle- ment would allow economic recovery, self-sufficiency, and a minimum of bitterness. Even the early guide for army occupation looked toward re- form rather than vicious punishment. But neither an embittered public nor Roosevelt accepted these moderate schemes, although they clearly paralleled Churchill's thinking.

**The German
Question**

One persuasive Roosevelt adviser, Secretary of the Treasury Henry A. Morgenthau, Jr., hated Germans and quite understandably so in the wake of unfathomable Nazi atrocities against European Jews. Morgenthau, himself a German Jew, reacted in horror to the mild occupation hand- books, and urged upon Roosevelt an extreme solution to the German problem: heavy reparations in kind and in forced labor, slices of territory to neighboring states, and the remnant core of Germany stripped of all industry and divided into rural states. To the horror of Hull and Stimson, Roosevelt welcomed the Morgenthau plan. In September Roosevelt took Morgenthau (and not Hull) with him to a second Quebec conference with Churchill. There, despite strong reservations, Churchill reluctantly agreed to an agricultural and pastoral Germany, consoled only by prom- ises of postwar American aid to Britain. Press leaks back home provoked considerable criticism; apparently most Americans hardly envisioned or desired such extreme retribution. Hitler quickly turned the plan into a Satanic, Jewish plot. Before the election of 1944 Roosevelt seemed to back away from such an extreme solution, but he offered no substitute. He came to Yalta seemingly still happy to join Stalin in dividing and dismembering a hated Germany.

The status of France interacted with postwar plans for Germany. Churchill, sensitive to the European balance of power, saw the clear import of American policies. If, as Roosevelt always assumed, Congress insisted upon our withdrawing all troops at war's end, if Germany lay desolate, and if we continued to refuse big power status to France, then the Soviet Union and its army would be sovereign on the continent. Perhaps

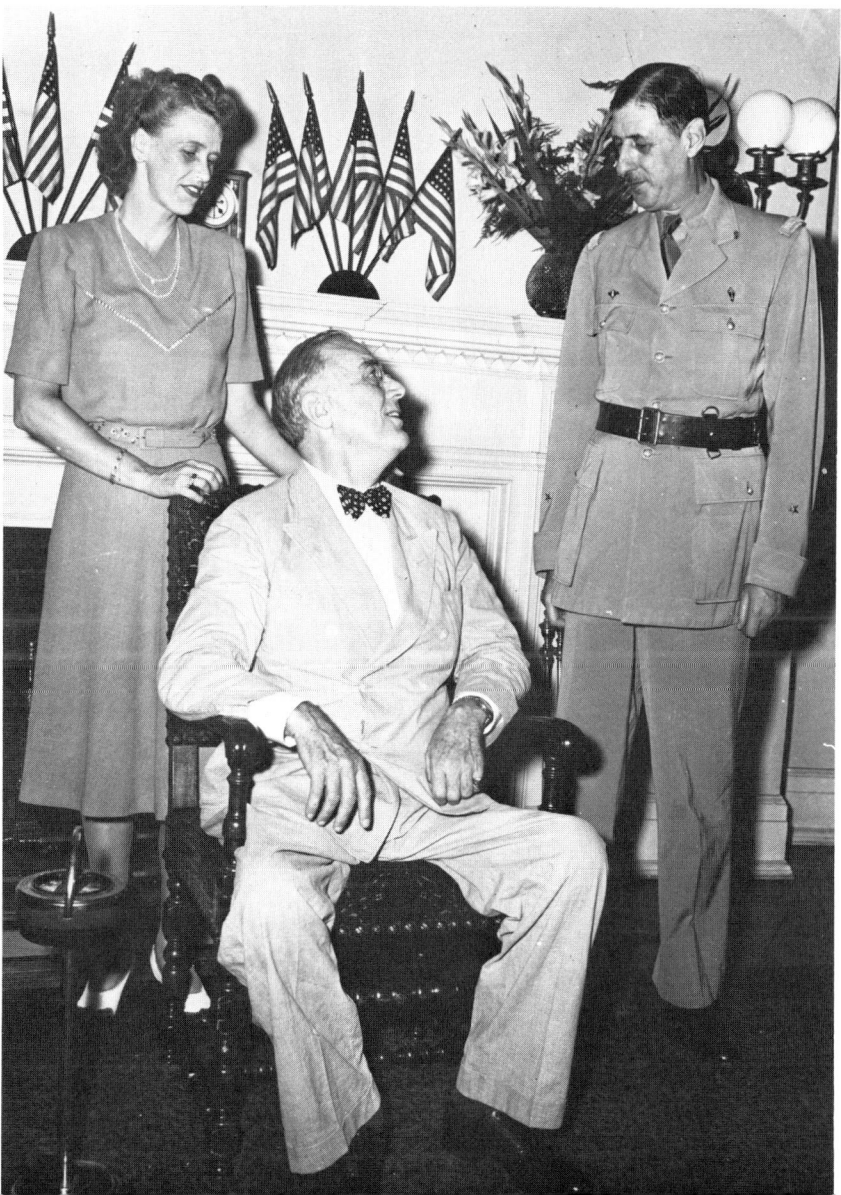

The constant tension between FDR and French General Charles de Gaulle (1890–1970) finally came to a head at the Yalta Conference over the issue of dividing Germany. De Gaulle, supported by Churchill, wanted big power status for France, but was blocked by FDR. At Yalta, Roosevelt gave in to Churchill, who hoped that France would act as a check against Soviet power. Anna Boettiger is standing with her father and General De Gaulle in the White House. *Wide World Photos*

Roosevelt accepted this as desirable. In any case, he hoped for a cooperative Soviet Union, disarmed of past fears, and protected from any future
insecurity by a successful UN. But Churchill saw such Soviet aggrandizement as a possible disaster for Europe and a dire threat to England. Thus,
even as he temporarily retreated on the German issue, he tried to bargain
in behalf of a revived France. Soon he used his France in about the same
way that Roosevelt used China. Stalin saw no operative power to justify
big power status for either country. But France, under de Gaulle, came to
life after the liberation. Even the United States had to recognize de
Gaulle's government, which had taken over the effective administration
of France. Roosevelt still hesitated. He saw a Gaullist dictatorship in the
offing, most likely to be followed by a leftist revolution and typical cycles of instability. But Churchill came to Yalta as an advocate for France,
demanding not only big power status but a French zone of occupation.
France, at least, represented a possible check on Soviet power and an answer to the vacuum threatened by the destruction of Germany. By Yalta,
Roosevelt, if not a believer, had at least decided to yield to Churchill and
to administrative advisers of the same mind (by 1945 Roosevelt's anti-
French position had few supporters in Washington).

Because of this backdrop, the Yalta decisions on Germany had to be
vague in detail. The big powers agreed to exercise supreme power over
Germany, and to take such steps toward complete disarmament, demili-
tarization, and dismemberment as they deemed requisite for future peace
and security. This blank check kept open measures as extreme as the

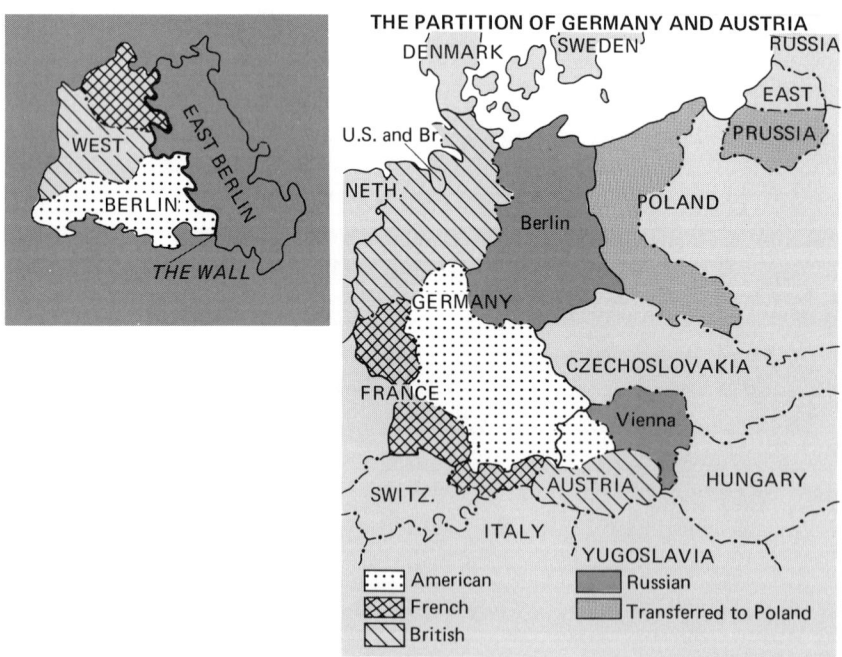

THE PARTITION OF GERMANY AND AUSTRIA

Morgenthau plan, but at the same time left Britain with some hopes for a more moderate settlement, a hope later vindicated by changed American priorities. The conference confirmed occupation zones worked out by the European Control Commission. Reluctantly, Stalin agreed to a French zone of occupation to be taken from the British and American sectors, and to French membership on the Allied Control Commission. The Soviets pushed for firm and specific guarantees of reparations. The delegates agreed that Germany should pay in kind for war losses of the Allies, with priority to those countries that bore the main brunt of the war, suffered the most, and yet helped organize the final victory over the enemy (e.g., the Soviet Union). These reparations would include much of the accumulated wealth of Germany, or industrial equipment, gold, and securities, a share of German production for unspecified numbers of years beyond the war, and finally the use of German labor. But the delegates referred all details on reparations to an Allied reparations commission to be located in Moscow. Stalin insisted on a fixed amount of $20 billion. Churchill vehemently opposed such a radical stripping of Germany and insisted on leaving the amount open. Roosevelt secured a seeming compromise: $20 billion would be the basis of discussion. One half of all reparations would go to the Soviet Union. Since Roosevelt had long supported extreme retaliation against Germany—he opened the discussion with a jocular but macabre reference to Stalin's earlier proposal to exterminate 50,000 German officers—the Yalta decisions seemed, in vagueness and in deference to future elaboration, a decided victory for Churchill.

Eastern Europe

The most pressing issue at Yalta was the fate of Eastern Europe, and most particularly the fate of Poland. Soviet troops had occupied much of Poland and a pro-Soviet government functioned on Polish territory at Lublin. The Soviets obviously planned to keep all the territory lost in 1919 and regained in 1939, compensating the Poles by a large slice of Germany. The western Polish government remained emphatically anti-Soviet and blocked any remote prospects of a compromise agreement. Roosevelt was in a typical bind. At Teheran he had seemed sympathetic to Stalin's plans for Poland. In Washington he had implied complete support for the Polish government in London. The western Polish government believed, apparently correctly, that the Soviets had deliberately refused to provide military aid for the Warsaw uprising from July to September 1944. While Soviet troops rested twelve miles outside the city, the German army slaughtered thousands of underground fighters, and thereby allowed the strength of the anti-Soviet resistance movement to ebb away. Churchill had then wanted to succor the Warsaw forces, even to the extent of sending air relief and then landing planes on Soviet territory. If rebuffed by the Soviet Union, he had proposed an immediate suspension of aid. Roosevelt rejected such a threatening gesture. He did not want to bristle Stalin and possibly undermine the Soviet commitment to the Japanese war. The West did nothing as the Warsaw uprising ended in a complete disaster. In its wake the delegates at Yalta had to find some possible Polish solution, now by far the most divisive issue facing the Big Three.

Churchill was sorely afraid of the long-term consequences of American policies toward the Soviet Union. Throughout 1944 he tried to reverse our insistence on purely strategic priorities, and upon what he now interpreted as a policy of continuous appeasement of Stalin, all in the vain hopes of turning him into a nice fellow and a good club member in the years ahead. Roosevelt's reliance on a future UN, his seeming refusal to accept the harsh realities of power, his naïve desire to do away with all colonial possessions, seemed to Churchill a license for a chaotic, unstable postwar world open not only to direct Soviet aggrandizement in contiguous areas of Eastern Europe, but to Soviet sponsored anti-Western revolutions in the colonial world. In 1941 a beleaguered Churchill, out to save Britain, had urged the United States to accept the Soviet Union as an ally, for him a matter of expediency. He also helped devise, and get Soviet adherence to, such principled statements as the Atlantic Charter and the Declaration of the UN. But in a crunch he knew such documents had no force; in fact, Churchill himself never showed any real scruples about ignoring them when British interests demanded it. Clearly, neither would Stalin, who was out to cash in all possible benefits from a hard-earned victory. Stalin had no gratitude toward the West, and would determine his own policies not by abstract principles but by Soviet interests. He would get what he could. Churchill would fight to limit his gains. He understood Stalin and talked his language.

In Eastern Europe diplomacy had clear limits. In areas they occupied, the Soviets could do very much as they wished. They wanted one-party socialist governments, allied economically and militarily with Moscow. From their perspective, this alone offered security. It also compared with what they perceived in the West—states with roughly similar political and economic institutions and a common ideological heritage. A Soviet-dominated Eastern Europe meant single-party "democracies," the elimination of the older owning and ruling classes, a vast reduction in the power of the Roman Catholic Church, a nationalization of major industries, major land reform, and Soviet trade priorities. When the war ended, Western economic aid would have little bargaining power in Moscow. Short of direct confrontation, or even a threat of military force, Stalin could not be forced to bargain away what he had and wanted to keep.

An early recognition of this influenced both Churchill's military and diplomatic priorities. Strategically, he successfully tried to win American support for an invasion of central Europe from the northern Adriatic. Later he tried in vain to get Eisenhower to push further into Germany, occupy Berlin and Vienna, and limit the area of Soviet conquest. Finally, in the summer of 1944, Churchill traveled to Moscow to bargain with Stalin over spheres of influence, strictly against Hull's firmest ideals and with only the vague approval of Roosevelt. There, in a now-famous conversation, Churchill traded a 90 percent Soviet dominance in Rumania, and 75 percent in Bulgaria, for a 90 percent British dominance in Greece. In Yugoslavia and Hungary it was to be 50 percent. And, up to Yalta, both sides had adhered to this bargain, as the USSR organized Rumania and Britain helped crush pro-Soviet resistance forces in Greece.

At Yalta the three heads of state resorted to the old and very American tactic of stating principles. Except for informal discussions of problems in the Balkans, the Declaration on Liberated Europe had to provide the only postwar guidelines in Eastern Europe. It was, quite simply, a bundle of pious ambiguities, inevitably understood differently by each of the three leaders. Roosevelt had rejected more detailed and concrete implementing machinery worked out by our State Department, and by this rejection came close to accepting Soviet predominance in Eastern Europe. The Big Three were to assist former Axis satellites "to solve by democratic means their pressing political and economic problems." The liberated people were to "destroy the last vestiges of Nazism and fascism and to create democratic institutions. . . ." In the terms of the Atlantic Charter, they would each "choose the form of government under which they will live." In the immediate aftermath of war, the three Allies promised to help bring internal peace, to provide relief supplies, and to form interim governments "broadly representative of all democratic elements in the population and pledged to the earliest possible establishment through free elections of governments responsive to the will of the people." They then reaffirmed their determination to "build in cooperation with other peace loving nations world order under law, dedicated to peace, security, freedom and general well-being of all mankind." Since the Soviets defined democracy primarily in class terms, and viewed almost any privately owned economy as fascist, they could use this declaration as an excuse for overthrowing older ruling classes and for transforming either peasant or capitalist economies into some form of state socialism. Britain could use this declaration as an excuse to restore the old order in Greece. Moreover, since the war produced a series of abstract statements, each subtly keyed to the evident interest of the originator, Stalin probably had an appropriately cynical view of all such, and indulged Roosevelt the possible political uses such declarations might have in the United States. It is doubtful that he understood the Declaration of Liberated Europe as a commitment to any specific policies in Soviet occupied areas, except for some type of referendum or election. And, as he well knew, specially planned elections are an excellent tactic for social control, for winning assent to policies already determined.

Poland could not be subsumed under generalities. For Churchill, Poland was the critical issue. In Parliament he faced possible censure if he sacrificed the London-based or "free" Polish government. Already, the Soviet-backed Lublin government had begun to intimidate or eliminate its political enemies. Earlier possibilities of compromise now seemed doomed. Stalin was probably open for some form of coalition government, friendly to Moscow but otherwise quite autonomous. He might have accepted a solution similar to that in Finland, where he allowed even a former enemy state to maintain political and economic institutions quite different from those in the Soviet Union. But the extremely anti-Soviet London government permitted no such arrangement. It adamantly refused to accept the Curzon Line (the boundary in 1919, before Poland seized Russian territory to the east) as Poland's eastern boundary, despite promised territory to the west. Churchill continually pushed them toward this minimal concession, but an evasive Roosevelt too long left the western Poles with a vain hope that the United States would support the 1939 boundaries. By Yalta, Stalin felt that almost no members of the London government would be acceptable to the Soviet Union and, quite clearly, the Western Allies had already agreed to a Polish government friendly to the Soviet Union. The historical antagonisms, the grating episodes of the war years, Stalin's earlier complicity with Hitler, the treatment of captured Poles, the accusations about Polish officers, and the purported betrayal of the Warsaw resistance forces all left grating issues and made any reconciliation almost impossible. Almost any non-Communist government in Poland would be anti-Soviet.

The Yalta agreement on Poland pleased no one. Roosevelt and Churchill largely conceded a *fait accompli*, bargaining for what few crumbs they might salvage. They accepted a slightly modified Curzon Line, but left western Polish boundaries for future determination. The special Declaration on Poland sanctioned a reorganized provisional government, with inclusion of "democratic" leaders from among the exiled Poles. This government of national unity had an obligation to hold free, unfettered, and secret elections as soon as possible, with all democratic and anti-Nazi parties offering candidates. The United States and Britain promised to recognize and exchange ambassadors with the new government. Stalin only reluctantly accepted these Western demands, and would soon so interpret them so as to nullify many of the seeming concessions. And few were the concessions. The existing, pro-Soviet government remained in power, able to determine what token "democratic" leaders to absorb, and when and how to conduct elections. The Western Allies could not even secure clear rights to supervise or observe the elections. Surely neither Churchill nor Roosevelt had any illusions about the Polish settlement. They had bargained a face-saving surrender; they could only hope for the best. They gave Stalin control in Poland, even as they had earlier taken full control over an Italy occupied by their own armies.

The Aftermath of Yalta

Roosevelt and Stalin, secreted even from their closest advisers, negotiated the final major agreement at Yalta. Consistent with informal agreements at Teheran, Stalin stated his price for entering the Japanese war (within three months of Germany's defeat). Roosevelt bought, and quite gladly. Stalin received the following promises: a continuation of the Mongolian Peoples' Republic (in an area still subject to traditional Chinese claims), a return from Japan of southern Sakhalin and the Kurile Islands (lost in 1905), a recognition of Soviet preeminence at an internationalized port of Darien, the lease of Port Arthur as a Soviet naval base, and despite the full sovereignty of China in Manchuria, the restoration of special Russian rail rights. The concessions by China would be contingent upon its concurrence, but Roosevelt clearly had the influence to insure this. For these gifts the Soviet Union promised to conclude a pact of friendship with Nationalist China. For Roosevelt this bargain promised a much earlier end to the Japanese war and a reduction in American casualties. The Soviet Union would most likely have joined the Japanese war in any case in order to pick up these plums, but the agreement assured their earlier entrance, placed limits on their demands from Nationalist China, and precluded an overt Soviet alliance with Chinese Communist forces. This agreement, more than any other, helped create the sense of exhilaration that accompanied the American delegation on its return voyage.

The Yalta Conference, greeted at the time even in the United States as a great achievement, became the object of a bitter controversy within six months. In part, this sprang from rapidly altered circumstances. At Yalta, the Soviet Union had an army almost within firing range of Berlin. The Western Allies had not broached the Rhine, and had barely recovered from the Battle of the Bulge. In Asia the United States still contemplated the difficult invasion of Japan. In only a few months the strategic situation so altered as to minimize the importance of the preeminent American goals at Yalta—maintaining the cooperative alliance against both Germany and Japan and securing Soviet adherence to a postwar United Nations. Victory in Europe, a reeling Japan, the atomic bomb and preeminent American military strength, a surprising willingness by Americans to assume postwar responsibilities around the globe, and a fuller revelation of the Soviet understanding of the Yalta agreements all so changed the perspective on Yalta as to invite bitter denunciation of the German, Polish, and Asian settlements. Roosevelt's death shifted more power to individuals who were suspicious and hostile toward either the Soviet Union or toward an abstraction called communism. Even the bipartisan support for collective security and the United Nations, symbolized by Senator Arthur Vandenberg of Michigan, increased anti-Soviet views and narrowed the range of possible agreements and compromises. In sum, the United States' position slowly became tougher and more unyielding after Yalta.

Yalta afterward seemed a diplomatic disaster, not because of the actual provisions (in many cases alternatives hardly existed), but because of the illusions or false expectations created by the conference. Roosevelt changed no major policies at Yalta. If anything, after Teheran he moved a bit toward the British position and away from the Soviet Union, reacting in part to the persuasiveness of Churchill. But Yalta prepared neither the United States nor the Soviet Union for the postwar scene. Disillusionment on both sides led to heightened tension, suspicion, and eventually to such a clash of policies as to deserve the vague appellation of "cold war."

Roosevelt never charmed Stalin into friendship or appreciably lowered his suspicions of endemic Western hostility toward Soviet institutions. But over and over again Roosevelt tried to see issues from a Soviet perspective. On the primary Soviet concern—security on its western borders—Roosevelt had proved a surprising ally. He at one time pushed an even more devastating fate for Germany than had Stalin. He always gleefully looked forward to a France stripped of big power status and even of its former colonies. Probably without detailed attention to all the implications, Roosevelt also wanted friendly or pro-Soviet governments in the states of Eastern Europe. He may not have expected that this would mean one-party governments or a loss of trade opportunities for the West. And only the developing conflict between East and West, launched more at Potsdam than at Yalta, insured the degree to which the Soviet Union would control and isolate its satellites. Finally, Roosevelt believed the UN was an instrument for guaranteeing Soviet security, for preventing the type of revisionist aggression that followed World War I.

Beyond a consensus of policy, Roosevelt easily fell into a gentlemanly paternalism—he and Stalin could run the world behind the rhetoric, the abstractions, and the UN paraphernalia that would be necessary at least for an American constituency. He never quite replaced his belief in four policemen. Often Roosevelt excused his more pressing demands by reference to public opinion, or to the imperatives of electoral politics. This led the Soviets to expect his continual winking at their departure from the ambiguous rhetoric of such declarations as those signed at Yalta. Even at ideological levels, Roosevelt's hostility to colonialism, his paternal concern for the masses, and his evident distaste for the entrenched and rigid class systems of Eastern European states, made him much less apprehensive about the results of pro-Soviet regimes than a nervous Churchill who feared incipient revolts in wide areas of the British Empire. Roosevelt preferred agrarian but constitutional democracies; the Soviet-style governments were closer to this than the old, "rightist" regimes. All this is not to argue that Roosevelt was a devotee of the Soviet system. Nothing in his own basic commitments allowed him fully to understand Marxism, let alone accept it. Nothing that he observed lessened his distaste for such a repressive and totalitarian government as that directed by Stalin. Rather, Roosevelt did not have any overwhelming fears either of ideological subversion or Soviet expansion, fears ever present in the State Department and by now constantly reflected in reports from Moscow by Averell Harriman. Roosevelt retained an almost unbounded confidence in his ability to continue harmonious relations with Stalin, and apparently believed that their continued friendship would render meaningless all the old, ideological and national fears. Typically, Roosevelt relied on personality and good faith to cut through what he never attended to with any rigor anyway—differences of ideology, of purposes and goals.

The effect of all this, at least on the part of the Soviets, was an expectation of continued American generosity, American willingness to continue to tolerate if not applaud Soviet actions in conflict with American ideals or sensibilities, and thus acceptance of a type of "peaceful coexistence" between what they called communism and capitalism. It seemed to them that the United States, by its unilateral policies in Italy, by an implicit acceptance of Churchill's and Stalin's agreements on spheres of influence, by Roosevelt's continued emphasis upon the four policemen as well as on the UN, had in effect accepted the realities of the situation and had therefore granted the Soviet Union a free hand in Eastern Europe, despite all the rhetoric of the Yalta agreements. All this meant that the Soviet Union was unprepared for later American toughness, as the actual power relations shifted toward the West after Yalta, particularly with victory and our successful atomic bomb. Even our insistence upon rigid adherence to abstractions, or our increasing demands for political payments for any American aid or concessions, seemed a reversal of American policy and clear evidence of a renewed Western offensive against the Soviet Union.

Neither did the Yalta accords prepare the American people for the inevitable strains and stresses of the postwar world. Already, wartime propaganda had either muted the profound differences between the United States and Soviet beliefs, interests, and institutions, or created the illusion that the Soviet Union had become almost like the United States. The glowing language of the Declaration on Liberated Europe joined with an exuberant Roosevelt's prediction that Yalta "ought to spell the end of a system of unilateral action, exclusive alliances, spheres of influence, balances of power, and all the other expedients that have been tried for centuries and have always failed." The crises came hard on Yalta. They came in part because of realistic reassessments of policies in both the Soviet Union and the United States, but even more because of inherent conflicts only camouflaged by the convergent military goals of the war, by endlessly postponed attention to divisive issues, and by the ambiguous abstractions of so-called agreements. When the disillusionment came, it had an even more devastating effect than that which followed World War I. In fact, we still live in the shadow of the deep divisions and bitterness that grew apace in the decade after the war.

Roosevelt died before the disillusionment became widespread. His death sparked a great debate, a debate marked by three often fervent positions. A small number of Roosevelt's disciples sincerely desired continued collaboration with the Soviet Union (later symbolized by Henry A. Wallace), and believed bad faith in American policies under Truman had sabotaged such cooperation. If only Roosevelt had lived all would have been as he planned it, and the world would have avoided all the horrors of the cold war. A bellicose and provincial Truman thus betrayed the wartime alliance.

On the other hand, those loyal followers of Roosevelt who embraced Truman's foreign policy decisions thought them a consistent extension of Roosevelt's own position. By 1947 they made up the dominant element in the Democratic party. Even Roosevelt, they insisted, had begun to get tough with the Soviet Union just before his death, reflecting a growing insight into the potential threat of Soviet aggression. Roosevelt's policies at Yalta had been not only realistic, but had also been generous and magnanimous to the Soviet Union. Stalin, not Truman, betrayed these bargains and plunged the world into near disaster. These critics attached almost all the blame for the cold war to the Soviet Union, exempted Roosevelt of any but peripheral blame, and applauded the pugnacious courage of a Truman. The vulnerability of their position in domestic politics often added to the vindictiveness of their cold war rhetoric, to their avowed hatred of Soviet calumny.

Finally, the long-time opponents of Roosevelt, and most particularly those with a bitter hostility to socialism, to the American Communist

When FDR died suddenly on April 12, 1945, no one was more shocked than his successor, Vice-President Harry S. Truman (1884–1972). Truman was untrained and unknowledgeable in foreign policy, not an auspicious beginning for a man who would soon have to take responsibility for some of the most ominous decisions ever made. He is shown here taking the oath of office with his wife, Bess, and his daughter, Margaret. *Wide World Photos*

party, to Marxist thought (including many who resented its hostility to Christianity), blamed Roosevelt, and particularly the Yalta decisions, for what they saw as a lost peace and a postwar world close to Armageddon. Either a conspiratorial Roosevelt betrayed our national interests and gave everything away to Stalin, or an ill Roosevelt allowed his pro-Soviet and traitorous advisers to give it all away. Strangely, considering the long-time State Department reservations against Roosevelt's collaborative efforts with Stalin, the cry of "treason" often pointed to the department or to individuals in it. But above all, those who so perceived Yalta saw a terrible consistency in Soviet policies. Nothing changed after Yalta, except particular new Soviet strategies directed, as ever, toward a Communist-dominated world. The cold war thus represented a belated, and always insufficient, American response to world "communism." Each of these three positions about Yalta contained an element of truth; each rested in part on questionable assumptions or pure fantasy.

Victory and Conflict—Europe

The apparent harmony of Yalta soon dissipated on the issue of Poland and the organization of governments in other Eastern European countries, and on Soviet suspicions of separate Allied negotiations with the Germans. Even as the delegates talked at Yalta, the Western Allies prepared to broach the Rhine in the west. By sheer luck, the Americans captured an intact bridge at Remagen on March 7, and thus opened their attack on central Germany, just as the Soviet forces gathered on the Oder River east of Berlin. At this moment Britain and the United States again disagreed on strategy. In March Eisenhower had decided on an overall strategy, and had communicated it to General Zhukov, commander of the Soviet forces. The Western forces would push to the Elbe and there await the Russians. We would also push into Bavaria, and try to penetrate the final alpine bastions of Hitler, which we incorrectly expected to contain a final, fanatical body of Nazi resistance. Churchill opposed this strategy and urged the Western armies to push as far east as possible, capturing Berlin and even Prague if at all possible. His reasons were political, and clearly anti-Soviet. Eisenhower, in full command of the Allied forces, rejected such political motives and adhered rigidly to his earlier strategy. From a military standpoint it was least costly in lives lost. It was also honorable. Churchill's strategy, among other things, would have amounted to a major act of bad faith against the Soviet Union. Thus, our armies waited before both Berlin and Prague.

Along with the ground offensive, Britain and America unleashed an unprecedented air war on Germany. Strategic bombing, of only marginal significance before 1944, had contributed decisively to the Normandy in-

vasion. After years of interservice rivalry, a nearly autonomous army air force finally developed effective liaison with ground forces. But only in September 1944 were the Allies finally in a position to direct massive raids on German cities. Until then neither German production nor morale had suffered enough to justify our air losses. And in technical areas, the Germans had easily outstripped the Allies, both in the development of rather sophisticated rocketry and jet airplanes. These innovations came too late to aid Germany. From September 1944 to April 1945 our bombers encountered increasing successes. They first devastated the industrial Ruhr, and then penetrated to Berlin and to central and eastern Germany. Finally, as the war came to an end, the Americans gave up on selected military targets and joined the British in nonselective but massive drops over cities, directed at personnel and morale as much as war production.

A real-life model for cartoonist Bill Mauldin's wartime creation, G.I. Joe, fighting in Geich, Germany, 1944. Mauldin's Joe, with his unshaven face, damp, soggy fatigues, and shoulders sagging under rain-soaked packs *were* our real fighting men. *Acme Photo*

A 1,000-plane raid on Berlin in February 1945 killed 25,000 people. Worse was to come. In what became, to the Germans, the very symbol of Allied atrocities, the British hit Dresden on the night of February 13–14. The streets were crowded with refugees from the Russian front. Bombs killed unknown and uncounted thousands, and almost demolished the defenseless and historic city. As the smoke rose 15,000 feet above the city, as survivors tried to escape in the eerie light of a new day, American daylight bombers again hit Dresden. By spring the bombers had finally destroyed most oil and other strategic materials, had completely disrupted communication, and had halted most heavy production.

On April 2 Roosevelt died, only two weeks before the convening of the UN conference at San Francisco, and less than a month before victory in Europe (May 8). In his last two months Roosevelt successfully worked to maintain Allied harmony. First in Rumania, then in Bulgaria and Hungary, the Soviet Union moved rapidly toward coalition governments strongly influenced by Communist parties. American representatives looked on helplessly at the formation of a pro-Soviet bloc, foreclosed to our influence and trade. More critical, the Soviet Union accused the Western Allies of bad faith because of some preliminary bargaining for a German surrender in Italy. The seeming collapse of German resistance to the West and the evident desire of Germans to surrender to the Western Allies and avoid Russian retribution fanned his suspicions. The unwarranted distrust hurt Roosevelt and revealed anew the difficulty of dealing with Stalin.

Poland caused the most extreme rupture. In Moscow, representatives of the Big Three could not settle on the exact composition of the reorganized provisional government. American and British representatives, denied access to Poland, could not even evaluate the situation. The Polish discord, combined with the Italian surrender incident, caused Stalin to withdraw Molotov from the San Francisco delegation, and thus threaten the emergent UN. Roosevelt again appealed successfully to Stalin, and died confident that there would be a UN. In his last communications he advocated firmness but otherwise minimized the Soviet problem to Churchill, and asked Stalin for an end to mutual distrust. However tempered his hopes, Roosevelt did not die in disillusionment over future prospects for American-Soviet cooperation.

An ill-informed Harry Truman presided over the final victory in Europe. In late April the German armies collapsed on all fronts. On April 27 the American and Russian armies met at the Elbe. On April 29 Hitler retired to his Berlin bunker, married Eva Braun, and joined her in mutual suicide the next day. Admiral Karl Doenitz negotiated the final surrender. Himmler and other German officials tried to arrange a unilateral surrender with the Western Allies, but Truman—committed to Roosevelt's pledges—would not countenance it. Truman also supported Eisenhower's strategic decisions, which allowed the Soviets to occupy Berlin. In Italy, Western Allies invited a Russian officer to participate in the final surrender in order to disarm all Soviet suspicions there. The Western Allies announced the German surrender on May 8. Hostilities ceased at midnight. Wild rejoicing occurred in all Allied countries, punctuated by exultant toasts to continued Allied unity.

Victory over Japan

With victory in Europe, the United States could turn its full might against Japan, and with devastating results. In February, in one of the most desperate battles of the war, our marines slowly conquered Iwo Jima, only 750 miles from Japan. In April we invaded Okinawa, a Japanese island only 350 miles from the main island chain. We slowly won major land battles but the fanatic resistance built up horrendous images of possible losses in the final, expected assaults on the home islands. Since the fall of 1944 our heavy bombers had pounded Japanese cities. At first, as in Europe, we tried precision bombing of military targets, with both heavy losses and unexpected inaccuracy. In March, by a decision fully as significant as that to use an atomic bomb on Hiroshima, we switched to low-level, nighttime terror raids on civilian populations. The Japanese cities, crowded with closely packed wooden buildings, represented perfect targets for our napalm bombs. In the first such raid on Tokyo, on March 9–10, the fires burned over fifteen square miles, reached the intensity of a fire storm, and killed 83,000 people. From then until August our superfortresses devastated 66 cities, destroyed over 8,000,000 homes, and killed over 300,000 people. The horror was beyond imagination. The air war forced Japanese officials to seek peace. Both in Switzerland, and then in Moscow, they tried to arrange contacts and to find some formula for capitulation short of unconditional surrender. They wanted to keep their national existence and to retain their emperor.

On July 16 the United States successfully exploded a fission bomb in New Mexico. Truman received the news on the eve of the Big Three conference at Potsdam. The success of the bomb assured an earlier victory over Japan than previously supposed and removed any pressing need for early Soviet intervention. But this was far from obvious even at Potsdam, since military planners still contemplated an invasion of the Japanese mainland. At the conference Truman vaguely informed Stalin of our new weapon, but gave no details. Whether gladly or reluctantly (the answer here depends largely on mind reading, which several historians have attempted) Truman helped arrange for the Soviet entry into the Japanese war, and later argued that this was a prime objective of his trip to Potsdam. Yet, as early as May, State Department officials had discussed possible ways to undo the Yalta agreements on Asia.

Even as the Allies met in Potsdam, the Japanese desperately sought an end to the hostilities. A growing number of cabinet officials, and quite clearly also the emperor, wanted to capitulate to the United States. We were aware of their peace moves. But Japanese diplomacy proved to be as inept as it was before the war. After unsuccessful feelers in Switzerland, they decided to make contacts through Moscow. At Potsdam, Stalin informed the United States of the overtures but joined us in discounting them. The Soviets, intent on entering the war in time to cash in on their Yalta bargain, successfully delayed and deceived the Japanese envoy. We now had a bomb almost ready for military use. Either it, or a Soviet invasion, would surely bring surrender. But as a prelude we issued a final warning to Japan (called the Potsdam Declaration even though Stalin did not help draft it). It warned of the impending disaster awaiting Japan, demanded the end to Japanese resistance, promised partial occupation and a loss of her empire, but did not mention the fate of the emperor, by now the most sensitive issue to the Japanese. They gave a guarded and ambiguous reply. Hiroshima was next.

In the aftermath of World War II, the United States' decision to use an atomic bomb, without clear warning, on massed civilian populations, and with the full knowledge that the war might be ended without its use, has seemed one of the most critical decisions ever made by a president of the United States. The debate over his decision still rages, but, as so often, the decision never secured nearly the amount of agonizing deliberation, the full evaluation of long-term consequences, that it merited. The built-in momentum of earlier decisions made its use seem almost routine. Only a decision not to use the bomb would have elicited a full-blown policy debate. This debate came afterward, too late to influence events. Truman, beleaguered later by requests for reasons, tried to produce some. He used the bomb, he said, for purely military reasons, to end the war more quickly, to save lives. But behind the rationalization lay the history of the bomb and of our air warfare on Japan. We built the bomb to use against our enemies. Many of those connected with its development, at all levels, wanted to see its effectiveness in an actual battlefield situation. We had already established the use of terror raids to erode Japanese morale; thus its use against Hiroshima amounted to little more than replacing a fleet of bombers with one bomber. The actual loss of life and property at Hiroshima roughly equaled that caused by our first night bombing of Tokyo. The horrible effects of radiation, in part unanticipated, did not seem more inhuman than the effects of napalm.

A U.S. army colonel stands amid the bodies of hundreds of Jewish prisoners burned alive by S.S. guards at Landsberg Camp, near Munich, in May 1945. When the U.S. army arrived, they forced 200 German civilians to tour the camp and view the atrocities. *Acme Photo*

In one sense, Truman could have made a much more deliberate and studied decision. That is, nothing prevented such a decision, save perhaps the pressure of events and Truman's usual lack of zest for far-ranging theoretical considerations in the midst of pressing political issues. Nonetheless, some Truman critics have seen far-ranging political considerations in the decision. Truman, they alleged, used the bomb as a means of either preventing Soviet entry into the Japanese war or, at a minimum, as a new bargaining tool to win our way in our negotiations with the Soviet Union. This is why the bomb had to be used quickly and with greatest impact, precluding any staged demonstration in the Pacific that might also have brought a surrender. In this perspective, Truman's decision was almost conspiratorial in its cleverness or deviousness. The only problem with this view: it involves a good deal of mind reading. The available evidence as yet cannot prove it or even make it seem very plausible. Of course, after the bomb's use, it became a vitally important ingredient in the calculation of foreign policy. But to note this is to note the obvious. No country ever calculates policy decisions in a vacuum.

Another group of critics offer some hard evidence to support its charges. Truman did have available penetrating policy considerations, offered in moral apprehension by scientists connected with the Manhattan Project. At the University of Chicago a committee of scientists, headed by James Franck, sent a carefully drafted report to Stimson (who possibly never read it). In it they warned that Soviet scientists could, in a few years, have an atomic bomb, and that a nuclear arms race might result. They wanted to end our strict secrecy, to use the bomb first in a demonstration on a barren island before all the UN, and to work for international control. Only such a procedure could alleviate the suspicions of the Soviet Union, the inevitable shock and disgust of neutral states, and what they expected to be an outpouring of American public opinion against our being the first country to introduce and use such a horrible weapon. An interim committee appointed by the president to advise him on the bomb included several leading scientists. The committee recommended use without prior demonstration, but on a strictly military target. After all, we had only two bombs available for use. An isolated demonstration, if a dud, would leave us no room for maneuvering. Even after this individual scientists offered protests, most notably physicist Leo Szilard, who desperately tried to get an interview with Truman. His petition against use before adequate warning and time to surrender gained the signature of sixty-seven scientists, but reached Truman only at Potsdam. There is much more to the complex story, but little to indicate that Truman ever reacted, intellectually or morally, to the broad range of policy issues presented by scientists remote from his immediate advisers. Scientists closer

In September 1945 the United States dropped two atomic bombs over Japan, and became the first and so far the only nation to so use atomic power. This picture shows the billowing smoke that resulted from the Nagasaki bomb. *Acme Photo*

to the president, and most directly concerned with the Manhattan Project, such as Karl Compton, James Conant, and Vannevar Bush, all concurred in its use over Hiroshima.

The atomic attack on Hiroshima came on August 6. On August 9 the Soviet Union entered the war. In Tokyo these crushing blows gave new urgency to the Japanese efforts to negotiate an end to the war. Even as we blindly dropped a second bomb on Nagasaki, a cloud-obscured secondary target (mercifully, the bomb missed the intended target and thus spared thousands of lives), the Japanese cabinet endlessly wrangled over the final offer to the United States. Against still militant opposition from the army, and largely through two crucial interventions by the emperor, the Japanese, on August 10, accepted the Potsdam Declaration, provided it did not change the status of the emperor. Our carefully phrased reply, itself a product of contending views in Washington, required that the emperor be subject to the Supreme Allied Commander Douglas MacArthur. The Japanese accepted these terms on August 14, thereby ending World War II. The rapid pace and magnitude of events after August 6 left Americans incredulous as well as jubilant, apprehensive as well as relieved. As so often when man struggles toward a difficult goal, the final achievement brings with it a sense of emptiness and loneliness.

In this photo of Nagasaki, charred bodies are scattered amidst the debris and wreckage of shattered buildings, flattened by the force of the atomic bomb. *Acme Photo*

21

Just as the depression dominated the thought and policy choices of the thirties, so Soviet-American relations dominated the decade from 1945 to 1955. Friction between the two giant world powers soon gained an imprecise and by now quite inescapable label, the "cold war." No one can say for sure when the cold war began or when it ended, if indeed it has ended. Events alone can be charted. Beyond that the cold war remains a battleground of competing ideological and historical interpretations.

The cold war led to extreme disillusionment in both Russia and the United States. The hopes of World War II seemed so quickly dashed as both sides felt obliged to maintain large military forces and endure the tension. The unexpected conflict created, in both countries, an intense desire for understanding. What went wrong? How did it happen? What caused it? Who was responsible? Both Soviet and American historians have sought answers to these questions, but usually from quite different perspectives. By persuasive arguments, either side can produce elaborate justifications for its suspicions of the other, vindicating its own policies as a necessary reaction to the aims of the other. In America we now have a lively controversy between those who still see a necessary logic in most of our policies, or who place the major responsibility for the cold war on the Soviet Union, and others who find the United States more often than not the culprit, pursuing either in ignorance or malice policies that practically forced Soviet aggression.

The historian faces almost insurmountable difficulties if he tries to deal causally with something as complex as the cold war. He faces additional perils if he tries to turn causes into moral judgments. Too often the question "What caused the cold war?" has really been a thinly disguised substitute for "Whose fault was it?" The varied conditions, proximate and remote, necessary for a cold war can never be fully enumerated. To select for special emphasis one condition, such as a policy decision in America or in the Soviet Union, much less to call this *the* cause, or even the most important cause, is inevitably arbitrary. The causes most likely cited in cold war analyses are deliberate policy decisions, which always interact with numerous other conditions and with earlier decisions that are not as subject to human control. The most elusive ingredients of all human behavior are motives and mental processes. When the attempt to "explain"

Origins
of the
Cold War

the cold war devolves into speculative estimates of what Stalin really believed or what Truman really sought, then varying judgments and endless controversies submit, at best, to merely suggestive evidence. By a more favorable attribution of intent, by a happier interpretation of motive, either side can be vindicated, the other damned. National and ideological loyalties easily and safely condition such mind reading.

The war against Germany had insured at least a minimal convergence of American and Soviet interests. Once victory came and the ambiguities of Yalta had to be reduced to concrete settlements, old differences and distrusts revived. The cold war in all its early phases centered on Europe, a near vacuum of power in which both the Soviet Union and the United States contended for the maximum returns from victory, and in which both had to accept considerably less than expected.

At war's end the Allies had no clear policy agreement on German reparations or the shape of the postwar German economy or the exact settlements in the other Axis states. The British already sensed the dangers of Soviet influences in the West, and did everything possible to contain the Soviets on all fronts. Churchill also wanted to stop the cruel Soviet retributions against Germans. In Austria the Western Allies practically had to fight to gain entrance to Vienna, to get a fair zonal agreement, and to prevent a Soviet-sponsored provisional government from assuming power. In Italy the United States delayed proposed British troop movements long enough to permit Tito's Yugoslav partisans to occupy Trieste (on the north Adriatic, and formerly part of Italy) and most of its surrounding district, leaving a nagging dispute not solved until long after the war. But in all these matters of occupation, the United States succeeded in gaining at least begrudging and temporary agreements with the Soviets. Each small crisis made Truman more aware of wide differences between the Soviet Union and the West. Continuously, he found Soviet diplomats discourteous and stubborn. His temperamental urge was to respond in kind, to fight back.

Throughout May of 1945 Truman had to contend with another aggravating policy decision—continued aid to the Soviet Union. Both he and the State Department wanted to use aid as a bargaining tool. But they turned it into too blunt a weapon, and soon lost all its utility. Apparently without careful review, Truman allowed all lend-lease to lapse at war's end in Europe. The Soviet Union interpreted this as a deliberate affront, although Truman quickly reversed the decision and resumed shipments. Indeed, as part of the bargain to get the Soviet Union into the Japanese war, we had agreed to continued aid. But the larger issue went way back to 1943, or even earlier. In several contexts, American and Soviet officials had talked of postwar loans or grants to the Soviet Union. American businessmen in Moscow had also talked of American loans; they looked forward to major Soviet markets for our expected postwar surpluses. Stalin apparently assumed that a capitalist society would have to find outlets for its surpluses. We assumed such a dire Soviet need that they would gladly cooperate with us on political issues in order to get our economic help. Both assumptions proved wrong. And in the aftermath of European victory, Soviet intransigence made us less generous. We would not yet join Churchill in bitter confrontation of Stalin, but we would no longer offer gifts with no strings attached. Even before Potsdam the idea of generous loans had become a memory.

The San Francisco Conference

The United Nations Conference in San Francisco symbolized hope but intensified American-Soviet discord. The conference culminated the careful American planning that led, by way of Moscow, Teheran, Dumbarton Oaks, and Yalta, to a new international organization, one modeled in most respects on American desires and already accepted, in broad outline, by the Big Three. During the war our desire for a successful instrument of collective security had always remained the very core of our foreign policy. Ironically, by the climactic conference at San Francisco, it had already become a secondary concern for many of our policy makers, although nothing in the concerted and successful propaganda campaign in behalf of the UN revealed the growing doubt. By effective appeals to the "lost peace" of 1919, by an idealistic emphasis upon the panacea of collective security, the Roosevelt administration succeeded beyond any expectation. By San Francisco over 90 percent of the American public favored our participation in an international organization; millions of Americans long cherished vague but idealistic hopes for a United Nations organization. In many ways, the Roosevelt administration oversold both the idea and the institution.

Hull officially headed our San Francisco delegation, but he was in fact too ill to provide leadership. Already, in November 1944, his illness, and his disappointment over Roosevelt's failure to include him in major conferences, led to his resignation as secretary of state. Edward R. Stettinius replaced him, and would continue in the office until the end of the San Francisco conference. Far less knowledgeable than Hull, in no way brilliant, Stettinius had the needed administrative skills and the rare ability to produce harmony out of many contending views. He continued to emphasize collective security, but without Hull's single-minded and uncompromising zeal. In a badly needed reorganization of the State Department he established clear liaison with the War and Navy Departments and their secretaries, Stimson and Forrestal. Neither of these men had any of

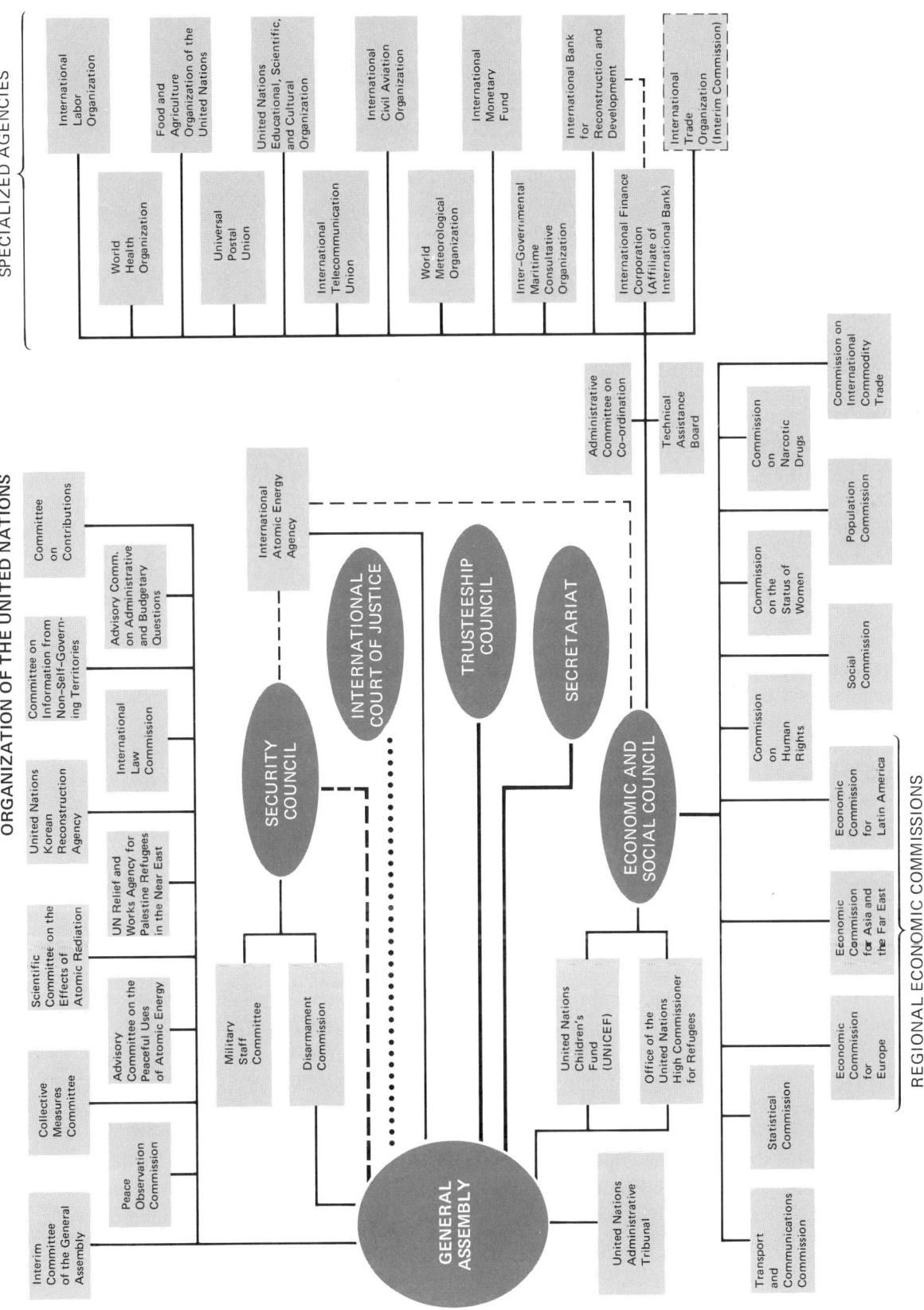

SPECIALIZED AGENCIES

ORGANIZATION OF THE UNITED NATIONS

REGIONAL ECONOMIC COMMISSIONS

Hull's enthusiasm for the UN; neither repudiated national policies or regional defensive pacts against the Soviet Union. Their views would soon
come to the fore in the Truman administration.

At San Francisco the one issue that almost disrupted the conference
was the old veto problem. The issue most disturbed the small states, who
saw in the Security Council a vehicle for Big Power domination. They
asked for a careful definition and delimitation of the veto provision. The
Soviet delegation had already made several concessions, including acceptance at Yalta of the existing veto provision, which the United States supported. But the Yalta scheme proved, as usual, ambiguous. Stettinius and
the Soviet delegate, Andrei Gromyko, interpreted a key section quite differently; we argued, against the Soviets, that the veto did not apply to
original Security Council consideration of a dispute, since rules of procedure (not subject to veto) could always permit such consideration. Gromyko insisted upon a veto over even the discussion of issues, and on this
refused to back down even an inch. The veto impasse received broad
newspaper coverage, and created extreme pessimism in America. In Moscow, Harry Hopkins appealed on June 6 directly to Stalin, and finally
won him over to our position. The jubilation was great in San Francisco.

After this flirtation with disaster, and in the face of a now unified stand
by the Big Five, the small countries finally had to drop their active opposition. They also failed in an attempt to increase the power of the General
Assembly over problems of security, at least beyond rights of discussion
and recommendation (this became significant during the Korean War).
Except for liberalized powers for the Economic and Social Council, the
smaller countries had been unable to change the basic agreement at Yalta,
but still joined in signing the Charter on June 25. The following day
President Truman praised the conference and joined his words to the
well-established litany of remorse over past sins: "If we had had this
Charter a few years ago—and above all the will to use it—millions
now dead would be alive."

Potsdam

To shore up a friendship sullied by conflict over Poland and the veto,
Truman sent a dying Hopkins to Moscow in late May. Hopkins repudiated Churchill's hard line, won Stalin's confidence, and secured from
him not only the surrender on the veto but a slight concession on Poland
(more Western representatives on the provisional government), a renewed
pledge to recognize and support the Chiang Kai-shek government and an
open-door policy in China, and support for another Big Three meeting
(what became the Potsdam Conference). Hopkins's discussions represented the high-water mark of postwar unity.

Truman did not go gladly to Potsdam in July. He postponed the conference as long as possible and when he arrived seemed to hate every moment of it. He proved a poor negotiator: impatient, tactless, inflexible, intolerant of ritual posturing and talking. When unable to achieve early agreement, he gladly postponed issues or left them for later disposition by the newly formed Council of Foreign Ministers of the Great Powers. He delegated concrete negotiations as much as possible, while maintaining outward harmony in his talks with an ailing Stalin. Truman resented Soviet intransigence. He left the conference at the earliest possible moment, and with a sense of relief. Never again would he join in a summit conference. The United States came to Potsdam in a strong bargaining position —our troops were still in Europe, we now had a proven new weapon of unprecedented power (the atomic test in New Mexico took place the day before the conference opened), and our economy, undamaged by war, gave us a near monopoly of persuasive monetary gifts. Two issues caused the most intense disagreement: the final disposition of the countries of Southeastern Europe and an economic settlement for Germany. In both, a confident United States tried either to revise the spirit and tenor, if not the words, of the Yalta agreements, or else interpret them in a way that seemed a reversal to the Soviet Union.

After many postponements, the Potsdam Conference finally got underway in July 1945. Truman disliked every moment of the negotiations and was never able to establish the rapport Roosevelt had with the other leaders. From left to right: newly elected Prime Minister Clement Attlee of Great Britain (1883–1967), President Truman, and Marshal Stalin. *Library of Congress*

Rumania, Bulgaria, and Hungary remained under Soviet occupation, and therefore under the de facto control of the Soviet military commanders. The future was not yet clear in these countries. In no case were Communist parties in full control or even clearly dominant in their provisional governments. But left-leaning parties did prevail, and the Soviets had already crushed right-wing parties except in Hungary. Elections were still to come. The United States, irked at Soviet expropriation of American oil properties in Rumania, solicitous of minority parties threatened by sure defeat, asked for reorganized governments in Bulgaria and Rumania as well as for carefully supervised elections. Russia refused to grant government reorganization, but did permit an American veto on the Control Commission for each country, and at the last moment postponed a Rumanian election. For the Soviet Union, our belated efforts to achieve almost equal influence in Eastern European settlements came as a shock, a seeming repudiation of Churchill's and Stalin's agreements on spheres of influence (which Roosevelt had tolerated by silence), and a betrayal of a Soviet Union that had honored that agreement by permitting the harsh defeat of pro-Soviet forces in Greece and acquiesced in British-American control over Italy. In retaliation for American criticism, Russia now protested the Greek settlement, leaving an embittered stalemate. Our stand for political pluralism and free elections gave new hopes to pro-Western parties in Eastern Europe, and thus helped create more bitter internal conflict later. This in turn may have assured harsher Soviet domination and more dependent satellite states.

The three Allies agreed at Potsdam on a political settlement for Germany, with an Allied Control Commission and zones of occupation. They did not agree on reparations. On this issue, for both humanitarian and economic reasons, the United States would not adhere to the clear intent of the Yalta agreement. There Roosevelt, against determined British opposition, accepted a reparations figure of $20 billion, not as a fixed amount but as a talking point; the Soviet Union expected reparations at or near this sum. By Potsdam we still accepted the destruction of German war industries and the removal of any excess German resources or income; but we defined excess as only the wealth beyond that needed to assure German living standards on par with neighboring countries (and thus possibly above Soviet standards). In part we had regained a sympathy for the suffering German people, and could react in horror to the cruel Soviet scavenging in East Germany. In part we realized that the United States would end up replacing any severe economic losses in the Western zones, and that reparations would be a concealed form of American aid to the Soviet Union, without attached bargaining power.

The Russians had an intense hatred of the Germans; they also acted in behalf of a victorious but devastated country, in dire need of industrial equipment and labor (the Soviet Union would keep German prisoners of war for over a decade). To the despair of the Soviet delegates, Britain and the United States now refused not only to accept the $20 billion figure but to accept any fixed amount at all. In spite of the earlier principle of "compensation," we now tried to revert to what amounted to an "ability to pay" formula. The final agreement, reluctantly accepted by the Soviet Union, in large part because there was no alternative, provided that reparations come directly from each country's zone of occupation. Since the Soviet zone had only 40 percent of German manufacturing, and the earlier agreements had assigned 50 percent of all reparations to Russia, the Western Allies agreed to permit Russia to get 10 percent of a still undetermined amount of industrial goods from the Western zones. This decision spared Western Germany from much potential devastation, but forced a nearly complete dismantling of East Germany.

**Escalating
Tensions after
Potsdam**

From Potsdam until a series of critical American policy decisions in 1947 (the Truman Doctrine and the Marshall Plan), American-Soviet relations worsened. Each new conference, each tense incident, helped consolidate a pervasive American belief that the Soviet Union did not want any real cooperation, and that their obstructionism reflected their perverse desire to gain some type of world dominance. Of course, our policies created just the opposite impression in the Soviet Union and, given the wide disparity of military strength, a somewhat more realistic one. At present, no compelling evidence supports either suspicion. Obviously, both powers pursued their own interests. Our dashed hopes for peace, combined with what seemed such obviously benevolent American policies, made the frustrations of foreign policy all the more unbearable, and even by Potsdam helped create at least a competitive if not completely hostile posture toward the Soviet Union. Increasingly, every conference became the occasion for scoring points and not for reaching compromise. Appeasement, already a word both derogatory and vague, seemed to apply to almost any American concession on any issue.

Immediately after Potsdam the most divisive issue remained the settlements in Eastern Europe. Truman insisted that these states not become spheres of influence for any major power, an idealistic position that could be reconciled with neither the implied concessions at Yalta nor the widespread American spheres, not only in Latin America but also in Japan and in several areas of the Pacific. On August 18 an American note to Bulgaria protested the exclusion of important "democratic" elements from its provisional government, and alleged that arrangements for a forthcoming election threatened force and intimidation. To the Soviet Union all this revealed a hostile Western diplomatic offensive. Bulgaria first postponed its elections, but then held them in November. By careful control over the voting lists, it secured 85 percent approval for a pro-Soviet government. Similar Western protests to Hungary possibly helped postpone an election and then secure a much fairer one, in which the Communist party won only a minority of votes and candidates. We granted diplomatic recognition to Hungary. In Rumania the Soviet Union exerted enough pressure to keep a pro-Communist government in power, and never allowed anything close to "free" elections. In Yugoslavia, Tito's partisans easily controlled the government, abolished the monarchy, and won an overwhelming majority in a November 11 election. Here, at least, the election, although not free by Western standards, probably reflected popular sentiment. Eventually, and begrudgingly, the United States would recognize all these governments.

The new Council of Foreign Ministers met first in London in September 1945, and again in Moscow in December. The first meeting ended in unresolved controversies and personal bitterness. The United States fought for new governments in Eastern Europe; the Soviet Union for control over the Dardanelles. Molotov in effect ended the conference by refusing to allow French and Chinese delegates to participate in all the sessions. In Moscow tensions eased. Secretary of State James Byrnes talked directly to Stalin. The Western Allies relented on details for the treaties with Nazi satellite states. Stalin allowed additional Allied representation in Rumania and Bulgaria. The United States and the Soviet Union agreed on a joint commission to form a provisional government in Korea, and both countries agreed to remove troops from China. The council approved a United Nations Atomic Energy Commission, broaching what would soon become one of the most aggravating issues of the early cold war—an acceptable form of international control over atomic energy. Molotov already feared any inspection plans, and wanted a firm Soviet veto over any atomic agreement. For all his success in Moscow, Byrnes suffered charges of appeasement in Congress, and received a rebuke from Truman for making too many concessions without presidential approval.

Iran posed the next problem. During the war the Soviet Union and Britain jointly occupied Iran. As Allies they temporarily dropped an ancient rivalry over this oil-rich country. At war's end Britain, quite secure with her valuable oil concessions and a friendly Iranian government, demanded that both countries honor their wartime agreement to withdraw all troops by March 2, 1946. As this date approached, the Soviet Union gave clear evidence that it would not comply. It formed a puppet government in Iranian Azerbaijan, began revamping the neofeudal society of northern Iran, and even refused admission to Iranian troops. Frustrated by the West in its attempt to gain control over the Dardanelles, the Soviet Union now seemed intent on encircling Turkey to the east, and possibly also sought oil concessions or access to warm-water ports. Whatever the relative merits of Soviet versus Iranian rule—neither was democratic in any Western sense—and quite apart from the exploitative nature of British interests in Iran, the continued Soviet occupation represented a clear violation of treaty agreements.

At the first meeting of the United Nations Assembly and Security Council in London in January 1946, Iran filed a formal charge of Soviet intervention in its internal affairs. In retaliation the Soviet Union filed similar but less clear-cut charges against Britain in both Greece and the East Indies. Then Lebanon, without Soviet complicity, filed much more serious charges against French and British troops remaining in both Lebanon and Syria. The West, with a clear majority in the Security Council, blocked even an investigation of these countercharges. The Soviet Union used the veto to defeat what it considered an overly conciliatory motion against the French and British. In doing this, the Soviet Union suffered the odium of first using the veto. They kept on using it, since on every vital issue they had a minority of votes.

The Security Council kept the Iranian protest on its agenda but awaited direct negotiations between the two countries. On March 25 the Security Council met in its permanent home, New York City, and placed the Iranian issue on the agenda for discussion (not a decision subject to veto because of Soviet concessions at Yalta and San Francisco). Because of pending negotiations, the Soviet delegate sought to postpone the issue till April. Refused this, he walked out of the Security Council. On April 3 the Soviet Union announced an agreement with Iran. On April 15 Iran withdrew its earlier charges, but the United States and Britain refused to drop the item from the agenda. On May 6 the last Soviet troops withdrew. Throughout the West this all seemed a great victory for the fledgling United Nations. But it was scarcely an auspicious beginning for a world organization that depended for success upon the cooperation of the major powers. It also seemed to make the United Nations a tool of Western diplomacy, posing a distinct threat to the small minority of Marxist states. The United States, formerly the mediator, now served as prosecutor. Only the veto provided any security for the Soviet Union and the minimal condition of its remaining in the United Nations. And Soviet use of the veto soon persuaded many Americans that the United Nations had a serious flaw. (It would be two decades before shifts in power alliances would make the veto appear a crucial protection for the United States.)

When the Council of Foreign Ministers again convened, this time in

Paris on April 26, the Iranian conflict still rankled. Even more, the mood on both sides had become more belligerent. In February 1946, Stalin had indicted capitalism and predicted the future economic superiority of socialist states. On March 5, Churchill traveled to Fulton, Missouri, to deliver an urgent call for Western unity against the barbarism that lurked behind an "Iron Curtain," ever threatening in its clandestine and subversive proselytizing in the West. His warning of a new "challenge and peril to civilization," another Armageddon, reinforced widespread fears in America of both Russia and communism. In this atmosphere the foreign ministers failed to agree on a treaty for Germany and Austria. The Soviet Union rejected a Western disarmament proposal for Germany. But Byrnes won domestic plaudits for the very failure. He had stood firm. Meanwhile, the United States tried to tighten its defensive alliance in the Western Hemisphere, and gained closer relations with Franco's Spain. Yet, as so often, confrontation gave way to some mutual concessions. Again at Paris, in June, the Soviet Union renounced any claims to trustee rights over former Italian colonies, and in return received $100 million in reparations from Italy. Both sides agreed to a free state in Trieste, and thus finally disposed of this nagging issue.

For most Americans still anxious to achieve some settlement with the Soviet Union, the greatest disillusionment came with its rejection of what seemed, at least to Americans and to many smaller nations, a most generous American proposal on atomic energy. After the Big Powers agreed, in December 1945, to seek United Nations control over atomic energy, the United States began work on a plan that would protect our security and yet eventually offer complete atomic security to all countries. We had the bomb. No one else had it, although Britain had the needed knowledge and, as we later learned, the Soviet Union was already at work on it. Despite some degree of guilt over Hiroshima, few Americans saw any real threat in our unilateral possession. As a peaceful nation we would use it only for defensive purposes. Of course we would not grant the same high purposes to the Soviet Union. Many Americans believed that, given an atomic advantage, the Soviet Union would surely use it against capitalist states. This fear fanned the extreme secrecy we tried to maintain around our atomic projects, and was a major cause for the frenzied efforts to screen subversives and to set up an elaborate loyalty program. But we could see the problem of a continued American atomic monopoly—inevitable resentment and fear of the United States. And we could also glimpse the future—the fear and tension when other countries secured the bomb and competed with us in an arms race. The American mandate

Atomic Energy and International Controls

seemed clear: preserve our atomic monopoly or clear superiority so long as any other country had any capacity to develop and use atomic weapons, but work for such an ironclad international control that we could, eventually, surrender our own atomic stockpiles. Surely, no one could expect American atomic disarmament without such safeguards. Surely, America was generous even to contemplate giving up such military superiority. Had any country ever done that before?

Our proposal to the United Nations came from an Atomic Advisory Committee (including such prominent men as Bernard Baruch, Dean Acheson, and James Conant), advised by a Board of Consultants (headed by David Lilienthal, and including physicist J. Robert Oppenheimer and three leading businessmen). The two groups recommended the creation of a United Nations Atomic Development Authority (ADA), which would hold a worldwide monopoly on atomic energy, from uranium mines to plants producing reactors. The productive plants would be distributed fairly in all parts of the world. The ADA would release atomic energy to national or private agencies only for power or health uses, and this under strict licensing controls. It would have access to all countries in order to maintain its rigorous controls. In effect, the ADA would be tantamount to a small world government. When the ADA finally assumed full control, after several stages of implementation, the United States would surrender to it its stock of bombs as well as its bomb-making capacity. After the Soviet Union presented a counterproposal, Bernard Baruch (in what became known as the "Baruch Report") further clarified our proposal, and for domestic consumption stressed the monitoring and enforcement mechanisms. We had to have ironclad guarantees in order to give up our bomb; among other things, this had to mean a surrender of Big Power veto rights over the ADA. The scope and daring of the United States's proposal made it seem much too generous to the more extreme critics of the Soviet Union. Had a final UN proposal ever been accepted by the Soviet Union, it might well have been rejected in the United States Senate.

The Soviet Union, not persuaded as to our generosity, would not accept our plan. It allowed the United States to keep its atomic bombs for an indefinite period, or until full implementation of a scheme that opened Soviet borders to any number of outside observers. The Russians still feared any outside intrusion and almost fanatically guarded their secrets. Quite consistent with its wildest hopes, the Soviet Union proposed an immediate outlawing of all atomic weapons, with no clear techniques for inspection and enforcement. Through the summer of 1946 the debates went on. Molotov eventually accepted some type of inspection. But he refused to concede veto rights over the form and the rules of an ADA. In

December 1946, the United Nations Atomic Energy Committee accepted the United States proposal, a meaningless gesture since Poland and the Soviet Union abstained. The veto remained the final obstacle, a symbol of ever sharper American-Soviet antagonisms. The debate continued throughout 1947, with few shifts in either position. The United Nations committee gave its final report in 1948. By then the cold war was at its climax; American air bases surrounded the Soviet Union. In the tense atmosphere of that year reckless Americans almost daily suggested a preventive use of the bomb against Russia, before it acquired the bomb and used it on the West. By then the Soviet Union had its own bomb almost ready for testing, and preferred to join the atomic club at a disadvantage rather than to surrender any full and irreversible control to an international agency, and one sure to be dominated by anti-Communist states. The atomic arms race was on.

Domestic Priorities and the Truman Doctrine

In the United States the disillusionment over atomic energy heightened critical policy debates over the cold war. In the midst of a congressional election campaign, Secretary of Commerce Henry A. Wallace challenged what he conceived as a mistaken diplomatic offensive against the USSR. He called for a Soviet Monroe Doctrine in Eastern Europe, decried our

Henry A. Wallace (1888–1965) was secretary of agriculture during Roosevelt's first two terms, then vice-president during his third term. In 1946, after a brief stint as secretary of commerce, Wallace became the editor of *New Republic*. Wallace, a political leftist and frequent critic of the government, was ultimately asked to resign his cabinet post by Truman. *Library of Congress*

support for British and French "imperialism," and denounced the results of diplomatic bipartisanship. He also acknowledged the inevitable sense of encirclement created in the Soviet Union by our Bikini atomic tests, our growing repertoire of air bases, our arms sales to Latin America, and our unchallenged economic power. Speaking as a member of the administration, Wallace seemed to undercut the tough bargaining position of the State Department. Byrnes offered his resignation after a Wallace speech, and forced Truman in effect to reprimand Wallace and, shortly, ask for his resignation.

The Republicans won control of Congress in 1946, their first such victory since 1930. This meant that Truman had to rely even more on bipartisan support for his foreign policy. He also needed to adopt both domestic and foreign policies calculated to win back support for the Democratic party. He combined new welfare proposals with a tougher anti-Communist foreign policy. Both had to be defended as anti-Communist. Large segments of the Republican party had already suggested links between governmental economic intervention at home and Marxist socialism abroad. Thus, the outcry against Soviet expansion paralleled the growing domestic campaign against any "leftist" policies. An internal, anti-Communist crusade lay just ahead. Politically, Truman needed to dis-

Long fingers of light focus on Communist party leader Earl Browder, as he speaks to thousands of his followers at a Lenin Memorial meeting in New York's Madison Square Garden in January 1940. In pre-cold war America communism still beguiled many intellectuals on college campuses; few saw it as a great threat. The end of the war, however, was the beginning of the ideological rift that was totally to divide this country in the fifties. *Associated Press Photo*

sociate himself and his administration from any "softness" toward communism, whatever the emotional meanings attached to the ambiguous word. After managed elections in Poland, a hostile congressional committee practically forced Dean Acheson, then assistant secretary of state, to describe the Soviet Union as an aggressive state, which brought Soviet protests. On March 6, at Baylor University, Truman unleashed his strongest cold-war language thus far. He defended the American economic system, defined freedom as a greater good than peace, and pointedly denounced the Soviet system for its denial of free speech, religion, and enterprise. Its closed economy, its control over private trade, made it an economic island, foreclosed to normal intercourse with other countries. Thus, the Soviet Union frustrated our efforts for more international trade and lower tariffs. This speech preceded by six days a turning point in our post-World War II foreign policy, or what came to be called the Truman Doctrine.

Greece provided the occasion for a new policy. In Greece, as in most of Nazi-occupied Europe, the wartime resistance helped create lasting divisions between Marxist-inspired insurgents and more traditional but equally nationalistic forces. With the tacit consent of Russia, Britain made postwar Greece a virtual protectorate. Despite some American apprehensions, Churchill insisted upon a restored and pro-Western monarchy. By vote, the Greeks approved the restoration, but at least a large minority continued in opposition, leading to civil war by early 1947. And, as would happen so often later, the war invited extensive outside involvement. By direct monetary and military aid, the British supported the Greek government against the insurgents. The countries to the north of Greece—Albania, Yugoslavia, Bulgaria—could not provide nearly as extensive aid to the insurgents, but offered supplies and a convenient sanctuary. Certainly the Soviet Union sympathized with the insurgent cause, led as it was by Greek Marxists, but apparently did not render direct assistance. Striving to meet a deteriorating situation in Greece, Britain came close to economic disaster at home. She had to give up many of her extensive overseas commitments, and announced a complete withdrawal from Greece by March 31, 1947. This meant an almost certain insurgent victory in the civil war, a major social revolution, and the probable absorption of Greece into the Soviet orbit. By a pro-Communist victory in Greece, the Soviet Union could finally extend its influence to the Mediterranean and threaten Turkish and Western control over the vital entrance to the Black Sea. The international stakes seemed high indeed, much too high for any great concern over the relative merits of either side in the Greek civil war.

On March 12, before a solemn gathering of both houses of Congress, Truman asked for a $400 million aid program for Greece and Turkey, but primarily for Greece. Unlike earlier relief efforts, this aid would be primarily military, and would require the use of American civilian and military advisers in Greece as well as training programs in the United States. Truman painted a dark picture of events in Greece, and stressed that a "self-respecting democracy" required our aid in order to survive indirect aggression from totalitarian states, aggression that endangered international peace and the security of the United States. If Greece fell, Turkey would be next, and confusion and disorder would reign in the Middle East. Also, Greek capitulation might help promote the "collapse of free institutions" in Western Europe. Beyond the specific problem of Greece, Truman cast his request in the form of a major departure in foreign policy. The swift course of events placed grave responsibilities on the United States. The long-run welfare of our country required a hard choice; we would have to maintain freedom in the world and insure for "free peoples" everywhere a chance to work out their own destinies in their own way, uncoerced by subversive and totalitarian minorities.

The aid program was not as significant as the justification for it. If Congress had approved, the United States might have assumed the British role in Greece without headlines or any obvious shift in policy. But Congress might not have approved. Also, Truman needed the political returns of a highly publicized and tough anti-Communist stand. Thus, he placed aid in the context of a vast Communist threat that might have to be contained in several areas of the world. The new policy reflected careful State Department preparation, particularly by Assistant Secretary Dean Acheson, who also ably solicited bipartisan support from Congress. When Congress approved the first aid bill on May 22, and on bipartisan lines, it approved in effect a broad, positive American program to counteract, possibly even reverse, Soviet or Communist expansion. Our postwar policy had been defensive; we kept our troops in Europe and Asia while awaiting final peace treaties. Now we decided to expand our diplomatic and military power in any area of the world necessary to contain communism. Further impetus to such a commitment came from our seeming success in Greece during the next two years. Our military and economic aid helped the Greek government defeat, and in some cases brutally massacre, the insurgents, although a 1948 Yugoslav defection from the Soviet bloc probably helped as much as our aid.

There is a footnote to the Truman Doctrine. In July 1947, *Foreign Affairs* published an article by Mr. "X" entitled "The Sources of Soviet Conduct." The author was George F. Kennan, Princeton graduate, a student of Russian history, and an embassy official in Moscow both in the thirties and during the war. He knew the Stalin regime first hand, its repressions and its cruelty. He remarked its immense departure from Marxist theory. Yet, he never believed that the Soviet Union would indulge in any madness in foreign policy; it would push its own interests as far as circumstances permitted, just as any other state. It would not respond to Western pieties but only to the realities of power. Kennan believed the United States had erred in making unnecessary concessions to the Soviet Union in behalf of a cooperation that was never forthcoming and should never have been expected. In 1947 the Soviet Union had limited power. Only Western mistakes or complaisance would allow her further expansion. Thus, in the famous article he asked for a long-term policy "of firmness, patience and understanding, designed to keep the Russians confronted with superior strength at every juncture where they might otherwise be inclined to encroach upon the vital interests of a stable and peaceful world. . . ." Elsewhere he also referred to this policy as "containment."

Kennan's article originated in a briefing he prepared for Secretary of the Navy James Forrestal, and in subsequent public speeches delivered across the United States. Because of his official role he cleared its publication with the State Department, where his main points had formed the basis of many discussions. Both governmental officials and private businessmen circulated his semiofficial article among employees. *Life* and *Reader's Digest* published excerpts. Soon the whole new orientation in American policy had a label, "containment"—a label loosely bandied about by people who never heard of Kennan much less read his famous article. Kennan himself deplored the sharp tenor of Truman's speech and the overt military nature of our involvement in Greece. Much later he also deplored some of his own language in the article, and what he considered the mistaken interpretation of his meaning. Yet, none of his clarifications erased his name from our most enduring cold war policy.

22

With the Truman Doctrine the United States finally and officially gave up on its great dream of a peaceful, American-hued world community. We now accepted an older, less illusioned foreign policy. As a nation-state we would avowedly use our power in behalf of our own national goals. We now openly sought a coalition of states to oppose the Soviet Union. Even the United Nations became an instrument of our policy and in no sense an end of policy. Political goals would justify our aid and military support programs. Maybe, in the future, the dream would be revived. Maybe the Soviet Union would alter its behavior and join us in our goals. Until such time we would play the game of power, and play it to win. What we interpreted as a Soviet or Communist threat, joined with the vacuum of power in Europe, achieved what Wilsonian aspirations could never inspire—an open-ended and extensive commitment of American power around the world.

With a hold on Communist expansion in Greece, the United States turned to Western Europe. There it had to lead a coalition of strong states against Russia and so rebuild the Western European economy as to assure political stability and a significant military contribution. A restored nucleus of power in Western Europe suggested, perhaps required, a revived Germany. This in turn threatened the whole security syndrome of the Soviet Union, the paramount goals of their postwar diplomacy. The quarrel of two self-affirming and powerful states over the spoils of war would now reach its most intense stage. For the next three years the United States and the Soviet Union would grab for all they could get, and desperately seek security for what they already had. By 1950 each had exhausted its possibilities. Although still wary of each other, still angry and bitter over chances lost, both accepted the final tally, a tally still essentially unchanged. By 1950 Europe was again stable, and stable it would remain. It was also divided, and divided it would remain. Both the Soviet Union and the United States would soon have enough problems in their own spheres to lessen their morbid fascination with each other and with what might have been. Both would become increasingly involved in other parts of the world. The cold war competition in Europe seemed harsh and disillusioning. What a vulgar way to work out the results of war!

Confrontation
and
Consolidation

But out of the tense and costly stalemate came a type of peace, much more enduring than that which followed World War I.

Both the Soviet Union and the United States behaved predictably. Each wanted as much of Europe as possible to be compatible in ideology and institutions, and open to profitable economic exchange. The exigencies of the competition required a great deal more direct economic and political intervention than either power had contemplated. The competition also narrowed the options for individual European states. Many, either because of economic need or overt military pressures, had to join one side or the other and accept the often stringent rules of the game. The United States began its offensive moves with the Marshall Plan of economic aid. It followed with its two strongest plays—the North Atlantic Treaty Organization (NATO) and a restored, dynamic West German Republic. In its countermoves a less powerful and often less adept Soviet Union gained control over Czechoslovakia, formed a competing military and economic alliance in Eastern Europe, and created a separate state in East Germany. But such a neat summary conceals all the doubts, the anxieties, the recriminations of those three horribly depressing years.

The Marshall Plan

By 1947 economic conditions remained perilous in most of Western Europe. The near famine of 1945–46 had yielded to American aid and to rapidly reviving agricultural production. But the war left shattered factories, exhausted credit, and at least in Italy and France very unstable coalition governments. Britain and France had large trade deficits, lacked hard currency, and retained expensive overseas commitments. Large Communist parties in France and Italy competed effectively for votes, and gained strength at the polls because of the economic hardship. While Europe had exhausted herself in war, the United States had gained economic strength —a doubled national product, an upgraded industrial plant, new technological innovations, and a near monopoly on gold supplies. But even as our economy boomed in meeting pent-up domestic demands, we too faced the dismal economic cost, as well as the political loss, of a European economic collapse. We needed markets and areas for investment. Europe remained the most likely source of both. In the 1920's we had loaned private capital to Europe, indirectly subsidized our own growth, but then reaped a whirlwind in the Great Depression. This time we had to do it better, and stimulate real, nondependent recovery. In the Communist threat the Truman administration had the excuse for early and massive aid, and for direct subsidies rather than loans. The State Department had a plan ready by early 1947.

In a speech on June 5, 1947, Secretary of State George C. Marshall first outlined the State Department scheme. This speech gave his name to the subsequent program. Marshall suggested that the countries of Europe plan their economic recovery in common. The United States would help all countries willing to join in such a cooperative effort. In a tone quite the opposite of the Truman Doctrine, Marshall stressed that we directed our promise of aid against no country or doctrine, but only against "hunger, poverty, desperation, and chaos." The closest thing to an ideological appeal was in his expressed hope that a revival of a working economy would permit "political and social conditions in which free institutions" could exist, and in his repudiation of countries that blocked the recovery of others or tried to profit from human misery. But behind the carefully articulated proposal lay a necessary consideration—neither Congress nor the American people would accept an economic task of such magnitude without the felt apprehension over Soviet expansion. Marshall's proposal bypassed the United Nations and was clearly unilateral in its goals. On the other hand, few European countries would have welcomed the aid if it had required an anti-Soviet alliance on their part, for with the possible exception of Britain the European countries were still anxious to achieve closer political and economic ties with the Soviet Union and did not yet share the intense American fears of either Soviet expansion or of Marxist thought.

Marshall proposed that the European countries take the first initiative in an aid program. He excluded no country. He realized that if the Soviet Union or its satellites joined in a cooperative recovery plan they would, by almost any conceivable rules, have to make many of the political concessions (such as opening Eastern Europe to Western trade) we had long sought. If the Soviet Union refused cooperation, or set such impossible terms as to lose Western European support, then she suffered the odium of rejection. We would win either way. The conception was brilliant. It worked. Russia played the game much as we anticipated. If the Soviet Union had asked for our economic aid, the game would have required much greater finesse on our part.

In Europe, France and Britain called the first preliminary economic conference and included the Soviet Union in the invitations. Britain wanted a Soviet rejection, and made it clear that the Western states would proceed with or without Soviet cooperation. Russia seemed seriously interested. Molotov led a large economic delegation to Paris. Both Poland and Czechoslovakia prepared aid proposals. In Paris Molotov bristled at a preliminary British-French plan, which called for a complete European balance sheet of resources and needs and which seemed to leave room for German participation. Molotov was unwilling to bare Soviet economic secrets, or in any way lose the preferred position it had over

Germany. He asked that each country submit its own requests. When he lost on this, he withdrew from the conference and denounced any economic organization that would stand above the countries of Europe and interfere in their internal affairs. Participating countries would lose their economic independence to "certain strong powers." Molotov reflected his old fear of conditioned gifts or economic bribery. Britain, in countering the Soviet plan, and in undercutting French efforts to find a basis of compromise, effectively carried out a critical step in our Marshall Plan diplomacy. In July, Russia and all her satellites rejected bids to a formal economic conference. Soviet pressure even prevented Finnish participation. Czechoslovakia's early willingness to participate possibly led to renewed Soviet pressure, and to the final collapse of its multiparty government early in 1948.

On July 12 fourteen European countries began to draw up their economic balance sheet. By August they completed a four-year, cooperative aid program which required $29 billion in aid from the United States. Our intercession reduced the total sum to $22 billion. At our insistence, much of the plan involved inter-European cooperation and even token amounts of reverse aid to the United States. In the United States three separate committees studied our possible response. With Russia out, and congressional votes at stake, we no longer camouflaged the clear, cold-war implications of such aid. In November 1947 Congress approved an interim aid bill of $540 million. An abortive Foreign Ministers meeting in November, the "fall" of Czechoslovakia in February, both helped sway congressional support. The House vote on March 31, 1948, on the first full aid appropriation ($4,300 million plus loan authorizations) was overwhelming—329 to 74. A delay in conference committee over aid to Spain (rejected then but revived in July) postponed final passage.

Europe responded with a group of new organizations. In April, France, Britain, and the Benelux countries joined in an economic and defensive pact (the Brussels Pact), or what was to be the embryonic origin of both NATO and the common market. To administer the American aid, sixteen countries formed the Organization for European Cooperation Administration. On the American side the Economic Cooperation Administration monitored the aid, and used it to force cooperation between recipient states, to strengthen "free enterprise" at the expense of governmental ownership, and to stimulate trade expansion. The aid usually took the form of American goods or technical help. European consumers purchased American products at competitive prices, but in national currencies. The pool of currency did not come to America (we hardly needed such foreign exchange anyway), but remained in the issuing country as counterpart funds available for economic development (transportation, education, utilities) or to pay for exports to other aid countries.

The Marshall Plan successfully furthered American policy objectives. The aid covered a four-year period, and in total amounted to over $12 billion. In 1951 this aid program gave way to a more overtly military Mutual Security Program, closely tied to the new NATO. During the Marshall Plan years most West European economies grew to surpass pre-war levels. The aid permitted Europeans to gain needed dollars to purchase American products. Our sales to Europe vastly exceeded purchases, but the Marshall Plan and continued military expenditures assured a near balance of payments. The aid was a necessary stimulus for an expanding trans-Atlantic trade, and a vital subsidy to our own domestic economy, especially to export industries or corporations with European affiliates. Both businessmen and labor leaders supported the aid program. Finally, the economic recovery in Europe lessened the appeal of Communist parties, and helped preserve private ownership, open avenues of investment, and receptive trade policies, all vital to American interests.

Czechoslovakia and Berlin—The Climax of the Cold War

The Truman Doctrine and the Marshall Plan forced the Soviet Union to develop effective counterpolicies. Germany remained the touchstone. Every hint of a revitalized Western Germany provoked strong Soviet retaliation. The first such came in Czechoslovakia; the second in Berlin.

At the end of the war Czechoslovakia remained perilously balanced between East and West, sure to suffer from any confrontation between the two. In 1943 President Eduard Beneš signed a treaty with the Soviet Union which preserved Czech autonomy. Czechoslovakia had a Western-type, multiparty parliamentary system, and unlike other Eastern European countries had a large industrial base and a wide distribution of property. It also had a strong socialist tradition. At war's end the Czechoslovakian government nationalized many basic industries. The Communist party remained a strong but minority party, abetted but not created by the Soviet occupation. The postwar Czech cabinet reflected a coalition of parties, including a slight majority for the combined Socialists and Communists. The Communist party held only a few key ministries, such as Interior. The government remained liberal in the sense of having well-protected individual freedoms.

The Marshall Plan provoked a Czech crisis. Czechoslovakia badly needed American aid, and drew up an economic proposal. Western newspapers, already inclined to treat foreign policy like a football game, hailed the Czech action as a major break from the Soviet Union, which had to block such cooperation with the West or lose control. Also, as the 1948 elections approached in Czechoslovakia, the Communist party faced declining popular support. Other parties even contemplated a non-Communist coalition after the election. In this threatening context, the Communist party created a major labor and cabinet crisis in early 1948. It tightened its control over labor unions, effectively dominated the police forces, and instigated a divisive political movement in nationalist Slovakia. Socialist members of the cabinet would not cooperate with other non-Communist members to block a Communist purge of the police. Twelve members of the cabinet resigned in protest, leaving a bare quorum of thirteen Socialists and Communists.

In the midst of this cabinet crisis, a large Communist labor congress filled Prague with workers. The Soviet deputy foreign minister arrived, ostensibly for talks but possibly to influence subsequent events. The labor unions called a massive strike to force President Beneš to accept the twelve cabinet resignations. The Communist party controlled most news-

Yugoslavian premier Marshal Tito (1892–) gets a light from Jan Masaryk (1886–1948), Czech foreign minister, at a reception held after the signing of the Yugoslav-Czechoslovak nonaggression pact, May 9, 1946. *Wide World Photos*

papers and radio stations, and continuously disrupted Prague by staged demonstrations. Under this pressure, Beneš, on February 25, sadly accepted the resignations, clearing the way for a new cabinet controlled by the Communists. The Czech people passively accepted the change. There had been no revolution, no illegal coup, only a cabinet crisis. A saddened, pathetic Jan Masaryk, foreign minister and son of the father of the Czechoslovakian Republic, remained in office and even led a group of workers in one of the strikes. On March 20 he plunged to his death from his apartment window, an apparent suicide. The West could bemoan the "fall" of Czechoslovakia, yet had no specific excuse for active intervention. The Soviet Union had used neither troops nor overt pressure.

The Berlin crisis of 1948 dramatized the one overwhelming failure of Big Power diplomacy—agreement on Germany. Conflicting interests made such an agreement unlikely. Hardening cold-war postures made it impossible. Germany became the balance in a divided Europe. Control would give clear superiority to one side or the other. Neither dared concede its existing position. Thus, the zonal boundaries eventually hardened into two Germanies. By 1947 the occupation zones were economic liabilities, but vital military and political assets. After its early ravages, the Soviet Union tried to turn its zone into a socialist state; the West retained a private economy and only temporarily tried to reduce West Germany's industrial capacity. But they did restore a strong federal system, with a large degree of autonomy in the individual states, and thus hoped to prevent a unified military nation. Because of German economic hardships, Britain and the United States unified their zones in June 1947, and France finally concurred in three-zonal unity in 1948. In June the Brussels Pact countries agreed to a restored West German government, a move that seemed particularly threatening to the Soviet Union.

The Berlin crisis grew directly out of a dispute over currency. The Western powers wanted to rebuild a strong German economy; monetary inflation threatened this goal. After several frustrating attempts to win Soviet support for a new currency, the Western powers announced unilateral currency changes for West Germany. In retaliation, the Soviet Union on March 30 began demanding special clearance for Western military trains into an isolated West Berlin; in none of the wartime agreements had anyone thought to clarify Western access rights, since the occupation zones had been viewed as interim agreements. When the West refused to allow inspection of trains, the Soviet Union blocked all Allied railroad and river traffic. On May 20 the United States closed its zone to all Soviet traffic.

When the new currency reached Berlin on June 23, the Soviet Union halted all overland traffic into Berlin, including even food trains. On June

28 the United States began airlifting food supplies as a temporary expedient. The Western powers began negotiations even as they seriously debated military action. Protests to Moscow led only to unacceptable Russian promises to feed West Berlin. In August a Western delegation in Moscow came close to an agreement, but finally saw it flounder on the currency issue. In October a group of small countries in the UN offered a compromise solution that the Soviet Union rejected. Meanwhile, the airlift worked much better than anticipated. By winter the growing stream of transport planes (this was before large jets) could carry all needed supplies to Berlin, including such bulky items as coal. The tactical and psychological success of the airlift destroyed almost all Soviet bargaining power and made Stalin receptive to a compromise. In conferences at the UN, the Soviet Union finally agreed to an ending of the blockade on May 12, 1949, in return for a meeting of foreign ministers in Paris. The meeting solved nothing, but helped ease tensions. And the tension had been great. In the fall of 1948 many Americans believed war imminent. American military intelligence agents, strung out along the borders of East Germany and Czechoslovakia, apprehensively watched Soviet military maneuvers just across the borders. Maybe next time the Soviet tanks would not turn back from the border.

NATO

The Berlin blockade hastened the formation of a Western European defensive pact. The idea predated the crisis. In the aftermath of Czechoslovakia, Truman met in conference with State Department officials and congressmen to consider the Soviet threat and the possibility of a war in Europe. The conferees agreed that the United States should seek a regional pact. Senator Vandenberg, now the very symbol of bipartisanship, not only agreed to the idea but supported a Senate resolution approving our participation, which passed on June 11, 1948 (by 64 to 4). It cleared the way for the United States to push containment beyond economic techniques to overt military alliances. Talks with Canada and ten European governments began in July. The first treaty draft was ready by April 1949, or near the end of the Berlin crisis. The final treaty obligated each party to come to the aid of the others in case of an attack on any one. The treaty also provided a possible future vehicle for incorporating West Germany into a Western defensive system. Senatorial objections centered on the permanent stationing of American troops abroad, on our open-ended obligation to supply even atomic arms for the defense of Europe, and on our clear shift away from the UN and collective security toward a narrow, defensive alliance. Easily approved by the Senate, however, the new treaty took effect in August 1949. The North Atlantic

Treaty Organization (NATO) became the permanent agency to carry out the treaty mandate of economic cooperation and an integrated defensive system.

As a corollary to NATO, Congress approved a Mutual Defense Assistance Act and appropriated an original $1 billion for military assistance in 1949. Our shift to a military alliance against the USSR considerably lessened the role of the UN, and forced neutral, non-Western states to form a third force in the world. Our commitment to military treaties (later we would organize others in the Middle East and in Southeastern Asia) reversed a traditional American antipathy to entangling alliances, particularly outside the Western Hemisphere. Our military assistance testified to European dependence on America, and made NATO something less than a multilateral pact. Congress insisted upon political cooperation as a basis of aid. Finally, only the threat of the Soviet Union broke down the barriers to a common military effort and to vastly increased economic cooperation between jealous European states.

West Germany was not part of the original NATO. Because of the intense opposition of France, the United States had to go slowly in its plan to make a restored German Republic a part of the Western anti-Soviet alliance. American memories were not as long as those of the French. In

Senator Arthur Vandenberg (1884–1951) was the symbol of bipartisanship in a GOP Congress. The Republicans came to depend on Vandenberg for leadership. *Library of Congress*

1948 our State Department took over control of our occupation government in Germany. A conference of concerned states in March agreed to international control of the Ruhr, a concession to France. In turn, France finally agreed to a restored federal government for West Germany. This decision, so frightening to the Soviet Union, finally ended the fiction of four-power cooperation in Germany and made very unlikely any early German peace treaty. On May 12, 1949, the day the Berlin airlift ended, the three Western powers approved a basic law for a new Federal Republic of Germany. At the Council of Foreign Ministers meeting in Paris the Soviet Union vainly fought for a common, dependent German government, under four-power control. We offered to incorporate the Soviet zone into the Federal Republic. The impasse was complete. In September the Federal Republic became a reality; in due time it would assume an equal role in the defensive alliance against the Soviet Union. Thus, by September 1949, our grand strategy in Europe seemed almost complete —a revived European economy, NATO, and a restored Germany.

In retaliation the Soviet Union formed the German Democratic Republic, strengthened its hold over its satellites, and increased its military forces. By now the United States had lost all influence in Eastern Europe, although as late as 1949 we still protested Soviet policies in its satellites. With a sense of futility, we finally resorted to propaganda campaigns (Radio Free Europe) directed from our bases in Germany at the countries of Eastern Europe. Soon we could only lament the fate of these countries, or talk vaguely of future "liberation." Two border states—Austria and Yugoslavia—alone marked ambiguous exceptions to the rigid division between East and West. The occupying powers in Austria argued interminably about terms for a possible peace treaty, but the stalemate there did not have any of the charged significance of Berlin or Germany. The occupation zones never became as rigid as in Germany, and zonal conflict remained minimal. Final Austrian unification awaited only a thaw in the cold war. Yugoslavia remained Communist but detached itself from the Soviet bloc in 1948. Tito simply refused to submit to Moscow's dictation and defied Soviet attempts to hold him in line. His defection, and subsequent wooing of Western aid, revealed the vulnerability of Soviet control over Communist parties in nonbordering states not immediately or potentially under Soviet military occupation. Tito also made Americans aware, often for the first time, of the significant differences that had always existed among national Communist parties.

In 1950 the Korean War changed the very complexion of the cold war and placed severe strains on our NATO policy in Europe. The war both diverted our attention from Europe and increased our apprehensions over Soviet military strength in Eastern Europe. Few of our European allies gave substantial help in Korea, and, genuinely frightened, tried to limit the scope of the war. Any all-out war threatened them first of all. Their reservations about Korea created a considerable congressional campaign to make continued aid and military support in Europe conditional on their reciprocal support in Asia. As the Korean War began, Truman asked Congress for $3,500 million for military assistance to NATO countries. We also pushed rearmament programs in Europe. But above all, we now felt impelled to rebuild West Germany as a military power.

The early NATO plans provided for the defense of West German territory but not for German rearmament. Germany only participated in the economic cooperation programs. France so opposed German militarism that she blocked early discussion of a new German role. By the Korean War the United States calculated that Western Europe would need thirty-six divisions by 1953 in order to provide a minimal defense against the Soviet Union. Korea had again demonstrated the importance of conventional ground forces. Such a defensive effort seemed impossible without a German contribution. Our aid, and our political pressure, slowly persuaded the French. In late 1950 France agreed to use German troops in NATO, provided they remained in small units, never exceeded 20 percent of the total, and used outside arms. Germany rejected such an unequal and imposed status. Finally, at Lisbon in 1952, the NATO Council approved a formula. Germany would enter a multinational European Defense Community, a separate unit of NATO and a correlate of a closer economic union between the same six countries (the Common Market countries of Germany, France, Italy, Belgium, the Netherlands, and Luxembourg). After complex negotiations, the EDC took effect in 1954. In 1955 the Federal Republic of Germany gained full sovereignty.

The successful American effort to contain the Soviet Union in Europe paralleled a growing arms race between the two countries and their dependent allies. The successful test of a Soviet fission bomb in 1949 symbolized an almost restored balance of military power between East and West, although Soviet strength would never match that of the United States. In a frightening announcement on February 1, 1950, Truman revealed his decision to push ahead with work on a fusion bomb (the power potential of fusion, the energy process of the sun, is many times over greater than fission). A vast majority of atomic scientists opposed the H-bomb program and helped touch off a policy debate that still goes on. Both the Soviet Union and the United States continued major atomic testing programs, much to the despair of small countries who suffered not only some of the fallout (its deadly potential was not yet fully appreciated), but also a growing impotence in a world shaped by the competition of two giants. We blamed the arms race, and the tension, on the Soviet Union. In 1950 Acheson summarized our position. We would gladly cooperate with the Soviet Union if it would withdraw from the satellites of Eastern Europe, end its obstructionism in the UN, stop all subversive activities in other countries, and accept our plan for international control of atomic energy. Such a request for virtual surrender hardly invited fruitful negotiations.

Cold war imperatives influenced our policies in areas other than Europe. The Truman Doctrine gave us a vital role in the Eastern Mediterranean and in the explosive Near East. Here, in an oil-rich area, we began, slowly, to replace the British, but not without intramural conflict with our closest ally. At war's end we favored a peaceful end to European colonialism. We hoped to preserve the friendship and the vital trade of former colonies; later, with mixed success, we tried to enlist them on our side in the cold war. In the Near East we eventually lost Egypt, retained an independent Turkey in our alliance system, and claimed a special friendship with Israel. But the very creation of Israel revealed lasting ambivalences in our policy.

In 1946 the United States pushed the British toward vastly increased Jewish immigration to Palestine (a humane as well as domestically a politically astute position). Pressed between competing Arab and Jewish claims, the British vainly sought some settlement that would allow both groups to live together in Palestine. A beleaguered Britain finally turned the problem of Palestine over to the UN, which advocated partition and the end of British control. This infuriated the Arab countries, which prepared for war. The United States, anxious to maintain friendship with both sides, tried to get a temporary UN trusteeship and a type of international policing.

In May 1948, when Britain withdrew its troops, the Palestinian Jews immediately proclaimed a new State of Israel. Arab armies massed on all sides and forced Israel to defend its newly proclaimed independence. An informal but often intense war ended in a UN truce in 1949, with a division of Palestine between Jews and Arabs. The truce would not last, as three later wars would prove. Jewish refugees now flocked to Israel to help build a modern, industrialized, and intensely nationalistic state. Bitter Arab refugees vowed their return, and helped create an intense nationalism among almost all Arabs. The United States had worked indirectly for the partition, and almost immediately recognized the new Israeli state. Great Britain had favored the Arab cause. But the situation was much more complex than any such simple summary can indicate. By 1956 the sympathies of the United States and Britain would seemingly shift, with the United States then favoring the Arab position in a resumed war. Even today, no permanent settlement seems close in this tense area.

The cold war at first diverted American attention from Latin America. In World War II the Atlantic had been a battlefield, Latin American countries possible pawns in a world conflict. But few early cold war conflicts involved Latin America. In the aftermath of war the most nagging problem remained a neofascist regime in Argentina. In 1947 we helped sponsor closer inter-American cooperation by the Treaty of Rio, which provided for collective hemispheric action against aggressors (and a precedent for NATO). At Bogotá in 1948 we supported the formation of a new inter-American union, the Organization of American States, dedicated to the mutual settlement of inter-American conflicts and to cooperative social and economic development. In a limited way, this regional alliance formed part of our growing coalition against the Soviet Union. The organization provided a mechanism for resisting internal Communist governments; in the UN the Latin American countries helped insure an overwhelming Western majority on most issues. But Latin America was much more a source of problems than a major help in the cold war. Many countries remained vulnerable to social upheaval and, therefore, to Marxist solutions. In the Caribbean and in Central America most states were politically unstable, economically undeveloped, and socially divided. A few were still economic pawns of American importers. In the early cold war the United States poured most of its foreign aid into Europe, limiting its Latin American assistance to small loans, technical assistance, and outdated and unneeded arms. Only in the fifties, when Latin countries finally succumbed to Communist lures, would we begin new aid programs and once again contemplate direct political and military intervention.

The end of World War II invited either immediate or eventual conflict in almost every area of European colonization, and particularly in Africa and Southeast Asia. The United States had rather consistently opposed overt colonization, and at war's end welcomed independence movements, at least if they could come peacefully and gradually. Americans generally greeted the relaxation of French rule in Syria and British rule in India and Egypt. Only later would we perceive the disorder and instability that could come in the wake of independence. Such instability already punctuated the struggle for independence, especially in the East Indies and in Indochina. The Netherlands accepted a plan for an independent Indonesia in 1946, but a plan that left a large paternal role for the Dutch. When the agreement ran aground on interpretative problems, a civil war began, with the Dutch trying an extended "police action" to restore order. When brought before the UN, the Indonesia issue aligned the Soviet bloc against the colonial powers. The United States tried to hold a middle view. It needed Dutch support in Europe, but also, and more desperately,

wanted to gain the friendship of newly independent countries around the
world. Support for non-Communist, nationalist revolutions then seemed
most consistent with a containment policy. In effect, Indonesia won independence by its civil war, but direct American pressure helped persuade
the Dutch to accept a moderate settlement.

We followed different policies in Indochina. There, as in Indonesia, resistance forces set up independent states at the end of the war. (See pp.
593–618.) The most important was Vietnam, headed by the veteran Marxist, Ho Chi Minh. The French reoccupied, or tried to reoccupy, Indochina in 1946, but also began negotiations in behalf of some type of independence. By the end of the year a virtual civil war raged. Soviet concern
for improved French relations helped keep the issue out of the UN. The
civil strife seemed quite similar to that in Indonesia, except for one critical
difference—Ho Chi Minh was a Communist. This had major cold war
implications. Substantial American aid to France indirectly abetted the
war. We never used pressure against France to win an early compromise
settlement. We soon needed French cooperation in NATO and, much
more ticklish, her support for some type of German rearmament. The
civil war would continue until 1954, with increasing but never conclusive
American support for the French.

Our first general policy toward the underdeveloped world followed the
Marshall Plan. In his inaugural address of January 1949, Truman added a
new, or fourth, proposal to his foreign policy recommendations (and thus
the enduring name for a program—"Point Four"). He asked Congress
for funds for a major development program in "underdeveloped areas."
His proposal echoed unselfish concern and a humane sympathy for
former colonial peoples. Above all, Truman renounced any political
objectives behind our promise of financial and technical assistance. But his
reference to the possibilities of "democracy" in routing the ancient
enemies—hunger, misery, and despair—showed his political objective
of winning such people to a Western life-style and lowering their susceptibility to Soviet bribes and propaganda. In this sense, Point Four was
part of a containment policy. Also, we recognized the economic importance of such areas even for our own future. Expected access to their raw
materials influenced our policies. Yet, in 1949, Truman did not contemplate much more than a token program. In May 1950, Congress appropriated the first funds, and then only with stringent conditions about use:
recipient countries had to cooperate with each other and make full public
acknowledgment of the American source of aid. Only later would the
most critical confrontation of American and Soviet goals shift to the underdeveloped world. Before that, we became involved in an Asian war.

23

In Asia the end of World War II seemed to leave few explosive issues to divide the Soviet Union and the United States. The USSR received its full pay for entering the Japanese war, bargained for more, but seemed half-satisfied with the final returns. The United States insisted upon a unilateral role in Japan, a role carried out with greater ease and greater apparent success than anyone had dared hope. The Soviet Union protested its complete exclusion from the Japanese occupation, but as always seemed ready to accept the realities of operative power. In China the Soviet Union in most ways honored the Yalta Agreements and its subsequent treaty with Chiang Kai-shek. By the fact of its occupation in Manchuria, it secured arms and other booty for the Chinese Communists, who often alone had the means to collect these goods. But the Soviet Union did not recognize Mao's North China regime or directly aid it in an expanding civil war. Only in Korea did Soviet and American armies meet. Only there did the two powers resort to an arbitrary, temporary zonal division of territory, a division that soon conformed to the same logic as in Europe—two separate governments and two virtually autonomous countries.

We occupied Japan with the avowed intention of reducing it to a nonmilitary, "democratic," secondary power. We never intended to destroy its economic system. At war's end we tried Japanese war criminals, purged all military leaders, and dissolved the large cartels or holding companies. In late 1946 we forced a Western-style constitution on Japan, which provided for many individual freedoms and renounced war as an instrument of policy. But a reduced and demoralized Japan was not economically self-sufficient and required large American subsidies. By 1947 our goals changed. By then the cold war increased our fear of the Soviet Union in Asia. We helped restore the peculiar Japanese economy with its large-scale enterprise and helped stabilize its currency. After 1948 we dropped all further efforts to Americanize Japan, and welcomed a revived Japan as a self-sufficient base for American power in the Pacific. Japan entered a long period of economic growth, unhampered by military expenditures. After the fall of China in 1949 we sought a peace treaty, a stable government, and even a limited amount of Japanese rearmament. Each of these goals would be achieved in the fifties.

East Asia and the Korean War

The hopes and dreams of America centered on China. The hopes proved illusory. Perhaps our policies betrayed them. The dreams lay shattered within four years of V-J Day. We fought Japan to save China; in the end we "lost" China. And the possessive rhetoric reveals how much of an emotional investment Americans had in a stable, "democratic" China, open to friendly and mutually profitable intercourse with the United States, strong enough militarily to fill the vacuum created by the defeat of Japan. Such a China was an ideal, never a reality. Whether other American policies could have created the reality remains one of the controverted questions of our post-World War II diplomacy. Nothing in the wartime propaganda, or in our half-successful effort to invest China with big-power status, prepared the American public for the magnitude of the task or for the likely failure of even our best efforts.

In China we tried unsuccessfully to unify the contending forces. We hoped to get Chiang Kai-shek and the Chinese Communists into some type of coalition government. The American public hardly appreciated the size of the Communist forces or the weakness of the Nationalist regime. In retrospect, it seems that only a vast expenditure of economic aid and possibly direct military intervention could have saved Chiang's government. Perhaps even a massive aid program would have been wasted; most of our aid wound up in Communist hands. But in 1946 we did not have such a commitment. If the cold war had intensified much earlier, we might have committed ground troops to China. But in 1946 our policy was one of reconciliation, not of crusades against Communists.

Reconciliation failed. Our most elaborate effort began in 1945 under the effort of General George C. Marshall. He chaired a joint committee of Communist and Nationalist leaders and tried without success to get them to merge their armies. An interim cease-fire broke down under violations by both sides. The most bitter conflict occurred in Manchuria. Here the Soviet Union had turned Japanese weapons over to Communist cadres. They used them to resist feeble Nationalist efforts to regain sovereignty in Manchuria, where American planes had transported the first Nationalist troops. Marshall felt helpless. Caught in the middle of irreconcilable groups, he could only try to moderate each extreme. Neither side would make concessions. Despite early reverses, the Communists believed time was on their side. The Nationalists rejoiced in ephemeral victories and kept raising their demands. They expected complete victory. Marshall soon had contempt for both sides. A last hope for negotiation ended in August of 1946. From then on the civil war raged. Marshall believed his mission hopeless, and feared that the Chiang Kai-shek government could never win a military victory. Early in 1947 he ended his mission. When our last marines followed, the Chinese Nationalists were on their own except for a small trickle of American aid.

The Nationalist regime won military victories in 1947 but quite clearly lost popular support. Whole segments of the Nationalist forces defected. Manchuria seemed certain to fall. In July 1947, we sent General Wedemeyer on a fact-finding mission. He found little basis of hope, warned against direct American military intervention, but did support continued aid. He wanted UN action in Manchuria, and some American effort to get Chiang to agree to desperately needed economic and social reforms. He expected these efforts, at best, to preserve a part of China for the Nationalists. The Communists were winning in the North, and would no longer cooperate in any coalition. Thus, he advocated an open policy of support for Chiang but in behalf of very limited objectives. We would not embrace a containment policy as in Europe. The risk was too great, the costs too high. In Washington the State Department secreted the Wedemeyer reports, and tried to find a way out of a growing dilemma. Strong domestic pressures forced our aid to Chiang, however quickly he dissipated or wasted it. Yet, the clear choice of sides, the economic support, created the illusion of containment and of another Marshall Plan. The final collapse of the Nationalist regime in early 1949 seemed, to many Americans, a tragic failure in our policies. This assumed failure abetted a search for scapegoats in the State Department and in the Truman administration.

The Communist victory in China was not a direct Soviet victory, however much Russia rejoiced in the expansion of Marxist ideas and institutions. The Soviet Union had withdrawn its troops by agreement and had not directly supported the Communist forces. It did not have to. By way of the Nationalists, the United States provided quite enough tools of war. In no literal sense did China "fall." It did go through another major revolution. What fell were American dreams. "Our" China no longer existed. Our support for Chiang, the intense bitterness of Americans, the intensifying cold war, all helped push the new Chinese Republic into the category of an enemy state. After a few years, some rapprochement might have been possible. Korea postponed this until 1972.

Origins of the Korean War

In Korea the Soviet Union and the United States met face to face, much as in Germany. Both sides professed a desire for a unified and independent Korea. Both failed to secure it through negotiation. Both had to accept de facto division. An early people's government in the Russian zone became the Communist government of North Korea. In the South the United States supported a formerly exiled provisional government headed by Dr. Syngman Rhee. As the cold war developed, the two republics moved ever farther apart. Rhee cooperated with the traditional landlords and with private business in the more populous South. The Communist government carried out the typical Marxist "land reforms" and nationalized the considerable industry in the less agricultural North. Both governments wanted, and promised, reunification, a reunification badly needed because of the economic dependence of each section. Neither the United States nor the Soviet Union had a compelling interest in Korea. In 1947, in what later proved a very significant move, the United States submitted the Korean unification issue to the United Nations. The United Nations proposed national elections in 1948 for a Korean National Assembly, to be followed by a new, unified government. North Korea refused admission to an implementing United Nations commission. Thus, in 1948, it held elections only in the South, elections that produced an assembly loyal to Rhee. This gave him some claim to represent all the Korean people, a claim the United Nations rejected. After the election the United States withdrew its military government. At the end of 1949 both the United States and the Soviet Union agreed to withdraw the last of their occupying troops, thereby granting autonomy to the two antagonistic products of their mutual distrust.

With the fall of the Chiang Kai-shek regime, the United States faced the prospect, even the likelihood, that Formosa would also fall to the Communists. The State Department had to make another hard choice: Would it defend Chiang's remnant army on Formosa? The early decision was against any further support for a lost cause. After refusing to commit our forces in China, it seemed absurd to make a major commitment to defend Formosa, which had become Nationalist property only as a result of the war. On January 5, 1950, Truman refused military aid and advice to Chiang, who already planned an early return to the mainland. Some congressmen also talked of ending all aid to South Korea, feeling that it also would not be worth the cost and effort necessary to defend it against any Communist attack. Such a renunciation of responsibility for Formosa and possibly Korea incited intense political pressures in their behalf. Chiang Kai-shek had a large American constituency (the so-called China lobby, a group of congressmen, predominantly Republican and from the West, fervently committed to undoing past failures). Chiang wanted a Southeast Asia alliance comparable to NATO.

Syngman Rhee also failed to get a defensive alliance with the United States. He resented State Department efforts to "liberalize" his regime by free elections and a broader tolerance of dissent. In a May 1950 election, Rhee's party lost seats in the Assembly, portending future political instability. Rhee had strong support from General MacArthur and from the China lobby. By 1950 he had his own plans for unifying Korea, eventually through force if necessary. North Korea pursued the same goal. Although it did not match the South in population and wealth, it had a much more able and efficient army, in part because of Soviet aid. In a speech on January 12, 1950 (undoubtedly regretted later), Secretary of State Dean Acheson defined our Asian defensive perimeter to include Japan, but neither Formosa nor Korea. Beyond this perimeter, defense would be the responsibility of the country attacked, or secondarily of the United Nations. Such statements, at once indicative of the thinking in the State Department but often at odds with congressional and even public opinion, may have influenced the policies of both the Soviet Union and North Korea.

Hostilities Begin

On June 25, 1950 (Korean time), the American ambassador in Seoul sent an urgent message to Washington. At several points North Korean troops had crossed the 38th parallel into South Korea. The preceding events on the border remain hidden behind the opposing accounts of the two sides. North Korea announced by radio, and consistently argued thereafter, that South Korea had not only rejected all proposals for unification but had first launched a futile invasion across the border to the North. South Korea continued to insist that the North Korean attack was a complete surprise, and that their forces had neither the equipment nor the preparations necessary for an invasion of the North. There is no doubt that the successful North Korean invasion was a surprise to Washington. In fact, Truman was in Independence, Missouri, at the time. The Korean crisis forced the United States to adopt a clear and coherent Asian policy, and to take on many new commitments. These commitments all involved one almost unchallenged assumption—that the North Korean invasion had been planned in Moscow ("they pushed the button"). We now have compelling reasons to believe the assumption wrong, at least in part.

Truman decided almost immediately, perhaps on his air trip back to Washington, to counter the North Korean action. But the extent and magnitude of that task would not be clear for several days. Since the United Nations had already assumed responsibility for Korea, and had a commission in South Korea, Truman first asked for an emergency meeting of the Security Council in order to brand North Korea an aggressor, to demand a cease-fire and withdrawal, and to gain the assistance of members in attaining this goal. The Soviet delegate had walked out of the Security Council five months earlier because of a UN decision against replacing Nationalist China by a delegation from the new People's Republic. This left the United Nations a convenient, although in the long run hazardous, vehicle for American policy. On June 25 the Security Council voted a resolution that demanded an immediate cease-fire and the withdrawal of North Korean troops north of the 38th parallel. It had no effect. By June 27 the invasion had turned into a military disaster for the South. The United States pledged the use of its own troops in asking the Security Council to approve armed intervention by the United Nations. A Yugoslavian appeal for a mere cease-fire failed. The American resolution passed overwhelmingly (only one Soviet bloc state held a Security Council seat). The Soviet delegate refused an invitation to attend the crucial voting session, but subsequently denounced the action as illegal with-

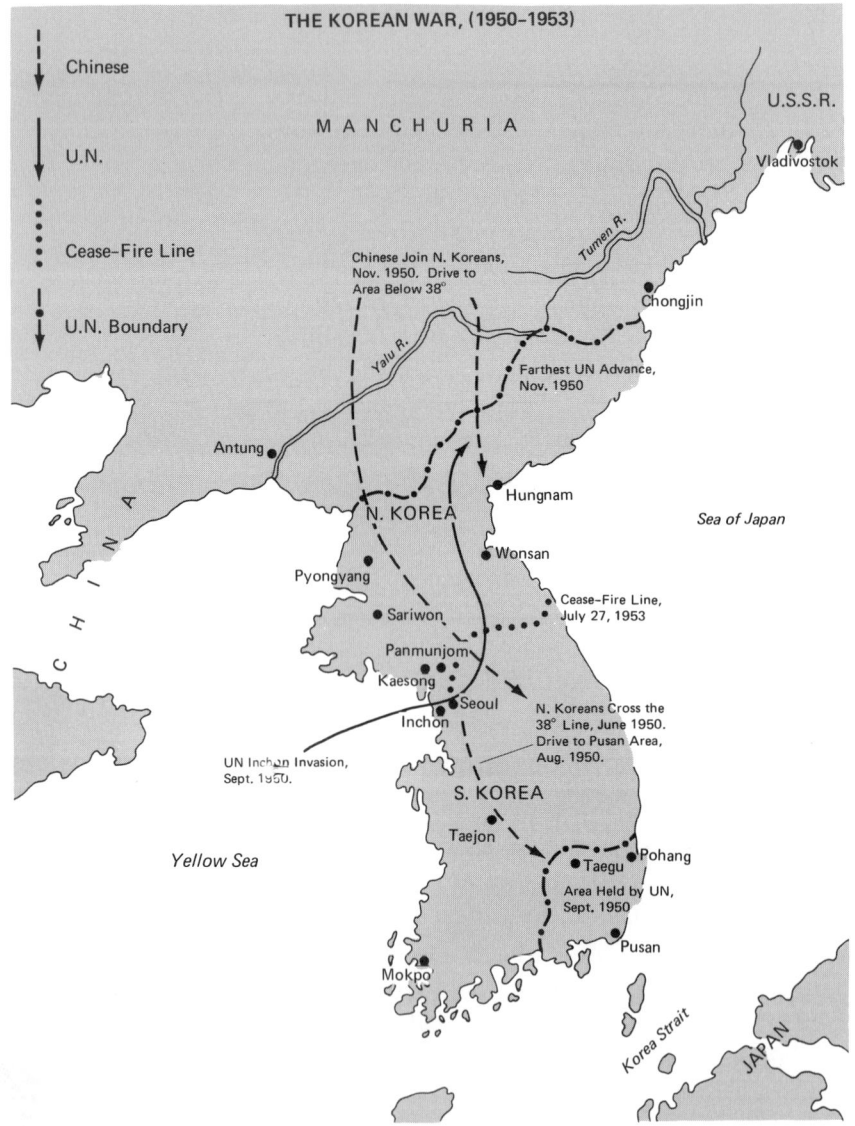

THE KOREAN WAR, (1950–1953)

out Soviet concurrence. The Security Council resolution approved armed intervention and amounted to a declaration of war. It gave the only legal justification for a largely American "police action" in Korea.

Even as the Security Council debated, South Korea seemed close to surrender. The United States was almost helpless. With the outbreak of war we tried to evacuate civilians and lend air and naval support to the South Korean army. After the June 27 United Nations resolution we decided to defend a small perimeter around the port city of Pusan in the extreme South. On June 29 MacArthur asked for a major task force and direct American tactical support for South Korean troops. Truman gave the critical order on June 30. In less than a week we had become involved in a major war. And for the next three weeks green American troops could do little but retreat, eventually falling back on Pusan. There, our air power and an increasing number of troops finally turned the tide. By August 6 the lines stabilized. On September 15 we launched a massive offensive.

With the Korean War we broadened our whole Asian military strategy. Since American officials saw the invasion as part of a Communist world offensive, and possibly only a diversionary maneuver, we anticipated new moves both in Europe and in Asia, and particularly in Formosa. Just after the original invasion of South Korea, Truman ordered the American Seventh Fleet into the China Sea to protect Formosa. We did request that Chiang end air and sea operations against the mainland. Shortly thereafter we increased our aid for the French in Indochina. Our new initiatives reflected what would later be called the domino theory—successful Communist expansion in one area would only lead to new demands and new expansion. Thus, Korea began a containment policy for all of eastern Asia.

The fast pace of events hardly allowed Truman time to work out a clear Korean strategy. In the leisure of hindsight, it is tempting to read clear policies back into adventitious acts, and particularly into two critical decisions: to intervene directly in Korea and to use the United Nations as a vehicle of our policy. As Republican critics pointed out, the decision to defend South Korea just after allowing all of China to fall to Communist forces seemed an abrupt turnabout in administration policies. Perhaps the Korean invasion was not part of any global Communist strategy, but only an understandable attempt to move into an area that we had avowedly dropped from our sphere of influence. In another perspective, the war was a civil war between two "nondemocratic" governments, each contending for the whole country. A victory for Rhee might not be

**Our Korean
Strategy**

worth the cost to us, and might weaken us in such strategically vital areas as Europe or the Near East. As Truman officials later argued, these reservations all ignored the overt form of the aggression, the loss of face that would be involved in our submission, the likely domino effect, the prospective harm to the United Nations, and the loss of a good opportunity to establish a lesson for any future aggressive plans of the Soviet Union. In Korea the idea of collective security, they believed, met its first real challenge. From the official perspective, much more was at stake than Korea itself.

The emphasis upon collective security, or upon lessons for the future, apparently justified our use of the United Nations. But there were risks. As events proved, we still did almost all the fighting. Our troops alone gave the Security Council a military arm. At first most Western states applauded our stand in Korea. Without much cost to them, we had supported the integrity of the United Nations and the principles of collective security. But the United Nations label was always in part a false label. We could use it to sanction our own policies, but by linking our action with majority votes in the United Nations we always risked a loss of full control over the Korean War. The Soviet delegate could, and would, return to the Security Council, and there use his veto to prevent subsequent votes favorable to the United States. As time passed, a majority of our allies might adopt more conciliatory policies, exerting an undue influence over events in Korea without contributing very much to the war effort. We might fight a war and have others dictate a peace, or else have to break from the United Nations and then lose all the propaganda benefits.

The early Korean decisions were popular in America. It seemed that Truman had regained the unity of World War II. But soon events, and important policy controversies, made the Korean War a point of bitter contention and an albatross for the Truman administration. Senator Robert A. Taft of Ohio, the acknowledged leader of the traditional wing of the Republican party, had to support our military role. He had long argued for a tough stand against communism. But he indulged in a bit of ridicule. The Truman administration had finally reversed policy. After Acheson eliminated Korea from our defensive zone we now went to war to defend it. Since we had repudiated his policy, he should resign. But more significantly, Taft condemned a new departure in the making of foreign policy. Truman went to war in Korea without consulting Congress. Yet, the American Constitution gave to Congress the exclusive right to declare war. Our adherence to the United Nations Charter did not change that fact. Such unprecedented executive action therefore threatened the Constitution and our traditional separation of powers.

In September our Korean forces began a long march to the North. An amphibious assault at Inchon helped break the North Korean lines. By the end of September we had recaptured Seoul and almost fulfilled the United Nations mandate—to repel an armed attack from the North. Would our troops stop at the 38th parallel? MacArthur, quite correctly from a purely military perspective, believed we should invade the North, destroy the North Korean army, and unite Korea under a friendly Rhee. Unless we took such an extreme course the North Koreans could regroup behind the 38th parallel and later resume the war. The risks were political, and quite apparent to policy makers in Washington. North Korea bordered both China and Russia. The apprehensive and reckless Chinese, already angry over our Formosan policy, might enter the war for defensive reasons. The Soviet Union, heretofore long on rhetoric but short on active support of North Korea, might feel impelled to give closer tactical support or even commit its own troops. Korea might spark a major war. The solid non-Communist front in the United Nations began to break before these possibilities. India led a group of neutral states in opposition to invasion of the North, and only lost 24 to 32 on a resolution to that effect.

Senator Robert A. Taft (1889–1953) was a brilliant but undramatic leader of the Republican "loyal opposition" in the Senate. *Library of Congress*

In August the Soviet Union had rejoined the Security Council. Its veto prevented any further enabling resolutions on Korea, precluding any Security Council sanction for crossing the 38th parallel. In late September our Joint Chiefs approved crossing. Then, on October 7, a joint British-American resolution in the UN General Assembly (the Assembly could only recommend, not authorize, action) directed MacArthur to take necessary steps to insure stability throughout Korea, and then to hold elections and to establish a unified, independent, and democratic government. When he achieved these goals he was to withdraw all United Nations forces. The resolution carried 47 to 5, with 8 abstentions. We interpreted it as authority to continue the offensive. MacArthur promptly invaded the North (his bombers had already attacked northern bases). China vehemently protested. Later, critics of MacArthur would hold him responsible for this crucial decision, noting that it led to almost disastrous results. Such criticism was unfair. MacArthur wanted authority to do what he believed desirable; he certainly never repudiated the decision. But the choice was not his. Ultimately it was Truman's. And most officials in both the State and Defense Departments supported it. Further, our Western allies, whatever their reservations, concurred by their United Nations vote. Even Trygve Lie, Secretary General of the United Nations, endorsed the move, which in effect transformed the earlier United Nations challenge to aggression into a new effort to impose a final settlement on Korea.

The war seemed about over by the end of October. Our armies pushed north against the remnants of a demoralized North Korean army. But how far north should we go? And what should we do about the increasing Chinese threats and, unmentioned as yet, the first Chinese volunteers already in Korea? Truman conferred with MacArthur on Wake Island on October 15. A haughty MacArthur, reluctant to go to such a conference at all, treated Truman as an inferior. He insisted upon a continued offensive and predicted a near victory by Thanksgiving. MacArthur discounted the possibilities of a Chinese intervention and minimized Chinese capabilities. Truman already resented MacArthur's informal diplomatic efforts in Formosa and policy statements he kept releasing in Tokyo. But Truman conceded the main issue—we would move on toward the Yalu River, and thus toward the borders of China and Russia. In that effort MacArthur would twice deviate from instructions. Despite United Nations statements that the Rhee government had no legal authority north of the 38th parallel, and that a separate United Nations civil administration would have to be established, MacArthur allowed the Rhee government to take over as the troops advanced. Also, against the advice of his chiefs of staff, MacArthur did not use only Korean soldiers in the border areas, citing pressing military reasons as justification. By November a growing rift existed between Truman and MacArthur. At home, sharp divisions of opinion developed around our Korean strategy.

Early in November American troops met large forces of Chinese. The Peking government called upon the people of China to stop the imperialistic Americans, who in the past had tried to dominate China, and who now followed the path of the Japanese—through Korea to get at China. After the first massive evidence of Chinese intervention, our European allies tried to moderate American policies. They now wanted to stabilize the front, establish a buffer zone along the border, and seek a negotiated settlement. The Chinese seemed open to such an agreement if assured a path to Formosa and membership in the United Nations. Instead of restraint, MacArthur launched a two-pronged, pincerlike offensive toward the Yalu, an effort to end the war by Christmas and a direct challenge to the Chinese. The strategy led to disaster. On November 26 the Chinese moved in large numbers across the Yalu (we knew that they had been massing north of the river), and moved between MacArthur's separated forces. Our troops began a long, winter retreat back down the Korean peninsula. Disorganized, disappointed, they suffered terrible casualties. Bitter soldiers joined MacArthur in requests for more extreme American action—the bombing of Chinese bases across the Yalu, or even the use of atomic weapons. By year's end the Chinese had pushed south of the 38th parallel and had retaken Seoul.

The Long Path to an Armistice

In early 1951 the United States halted the Chinese advance, and by February pushed back near the 38th parallel. Here the battle lines stabilized, and would remain basically unchanged for the next two years. The fighting remained intense and costly to both sides. MacArthur was unhappy with the stalemate, and futilely requested additional troops, air attacks on China, and diversionary attacks from Formosa. The lack of added support convinced MacArthur that he fought from an untenable military position and that his troops died as a sacrifice to mistaken political decisions in Washington. He gained considerable support for his position in Congress, especially from Republicans. Victory is always an appealing goal in war; now, it seemed, we had other goals. MacArthur came to symbolize a "win" posture. His extreme nationalist supporters believed that Stalin used peripheral wars such as Korea to wear down American strength. He pushed a button in the Kremlin and satellite states did his bidding. This position ignored the particularities of Korea, the quite local issues that helped cause a civil war, and the intense nationalist sentiments on both sides. But this view of the war created a consistent policy proposal—

that we move from a passive response to Communist aggression to antici-
patory thrusts of our own. We should fight the enemy at its source, and
thus in China and, if necessary, in the Soviet Union. Even congressmen
proposed severing relations with the Soviet Union and moving to exclude
all Communist states from the United Nations. Such extreme positions
paralleled an intense anti-Communist crusade at home, and fed on the
frustrations of a war that seemed to offer no prospect of eventual victory.

Despite the political pressures, Truman rejected the more extreme and
militant proposals. He committed himself to a limited war. This position
had strong support at home. It alone appeased our allies in the United
Nations. Even a veiled reference by Truman to atomic weapons in November 1950 had triggered a horrified reaction in Europe. MacArthur's
militancy had only increased their apprehension. Small countries resented
the American use of the United Nations for what seemed an increasingly
unilateral strategy, and one carried out with a minimum of consultation
with other countries. In January 1951 strong Senate pressure almost
forced the State Department to go back to the UN and press for a resolution that condemned Chinese aggression in Korea and called for new
economic sanctions. We pressured a majority in the General Assembly,
but won new resentment. It was now clear that if we expanded the war
we might lose UN support. Indirectly, we made clear our openness to negotiation as early as January. But before such a policy could be effective,
Truman had to get rid of MacArthur.

MacArthur was a brilliant man, eloquent, strong-willed, egotistic. His
almost unlimited power in occupied Japan, his friendship with Chiang
Kai-shek and Rhee, his extensive political following in America, made it
almost impossible for him to accept and adhere to the moderate administration policies on Korea. He would not be part of a "no-win" strategy.
Perhaps without quite intending it, he flirted with insubordination. In
March 1951 Truman prepared a speech in which he planned to announce
his support for UN negotiations with the Chinese, negotiations directed
at an armistice but that might well have led either to Communist Chinese
control over Formosa or to their membership in the UN. Either possibility horrified MacArthur. He learned of the forthcoming speech on March
20 when the Joint Chiefs asked him to limit all military operations north
of the 38th parallel. Four days later, and on his own, MacArthur proposed a harsh truce agreement to the Chinese, gained their emphatic
rejection, frightened our allies, and forced Truman to give up on his
speech. On March 26, fearful of other such unilateral proposals, Truman
requested MacArthur to clear all speeches with Washington. On April 5,
Representative Joseph Martin, Jr., a Republican supporter of MacArthur's
views, quoted from a MacArthur letter that urged the United States to

expand the war in Asia, where the Communists were making their bid for world conquest. In one slighting remark, MacArthur suggested that we were fighting Europe's war while Europeans fought only with words (a reference to the paucity of European military support in Korea). In reaction to the letter Truman removed MacArthur from his command on April 11, a decision that, quite unfairly, first reached MacArthur through the press.

The dismissal led to a wave of hostile popular reaction. Polls showed that up to 70 percent of Americans supported MacArthur and condemned Truman. Truman's popularity sank to an all-time low in the weekly polls; only 26 percent approved of his performance as president. Millions of people flocked to cheer MacArthur at San Francisco, in New York, and finally in Washington. Many Republicans sensed that they finally had a winning presidential candidate. In an emotional address before a joint session of Congress on April 19, heard by possibly a majority of

General of the Army Douglas MacArthur surveying damage done by retreating Japanese troops. After dismissing MacArthur, Truman's popularity dropped to an all-time low for any president, not to be rivaled until Nixon suffered the fallout from the Watergate scandal. *Acme Photo*

Americans via radio, MacArthur defended his policies, denied insubordination, and played on popular sympathies for an "old soldier" who had done his duty and now "faded away." But popular passion proved as ephemeral as ever. A Senate committee investigated the whole MacArthur case, found MacArthur sincere but often extremely naïve politically, and so extreme in some of his strategic views as to frighten even former Republican admirers. As emotions settled, a growing number saw his dismissal as a clear affirmation of civilian control over the military. More was involved than a correct policy in Korea.

Fulfilling a campaign promise, President-elect Eisenhower begins his tour of the Korean War fronts and training areas. Behind him is General Mark Clark, Far East supreme commander.
Wide World Photos

With General Matthew B. Ridgway as the new UN commander in Korea the way was now open for negotiations. Few realized how long and difficult would be the road to any armistice. Finally, in June, and after numerous appeals, the Soviet Union urged North Korea and China to negotiate. On June 25 China endorsed talks, but still insisted upon tying them to her demands on Formosa and for Chiang's United Nations seat. On June 30 both sides agreed to meet in order to arrange an armistice. The actual talks began on July 8. They lasted for two years. The fighting continued. By the end of 1951 both sides had agreed on the existing battle line, and not the 38th parallel, as the new demarcation line, and almost agreed on the supervision of an armistice line. But all through 1952 they battled over terms for the exchange of prisoners. The United Nations insisted upon voluntary repatriation. In 1952 the Chinese muddied the waters by a charge that the United States had used germ warfare. They also carried out an intense and often successful program of political "education" for American prisoners, securing an unusual degree of cooperation from many, a shift of allegiance from a few.

The presidential election of 1952 helped end the impasse. Americans were by now weary of a protracted and seemingly pointless war. They responded to Dwight D. Eisenhower's promise to go to Korea and to end the fighting. After the election he did go to Korea, but even he could not quickly secure a compromise settlement. We finally accepted a Chinese offer to turn reluctant prisoners over to a neutral state. In April both sides agreed to an exchange of ill prisoners. Rhee, bitterly opposed to any truce, sabotaged the final, detailed negotiations. He arbitrarily released a group of anti-Communist prisoners of war, and put the United Nations in the absurd position of trying to recapture them. The Eisenhower administration had to use direct pressure to bring Rhee into line, and then only by a promise of extensive economic aid and continued military support. Both in pressuring Rhee and in softening our bargaining position on repatriation, Eisenhower alienated some of the most determined anti-Communists in his own party. An unpopular Truman could never have conceded as much. The final armistice agreement was signed on July 27, 1953. It ended the fighting, but was not a peace settlement. That still remains unachieved. Since it was only an armistice, China could not bargain for her desired goals—access to Formosa and to the United Nations.

Even as negotiations stalled at Panmunjom, the United States completed a defensive alliance in Asia. Against Russian protests, we negotiated a final peace treaty with Japan. Signed on September 8, 1951, it restored full sovereignty, permanently stripped the Japanese of their empire, and granted limited rights of rearmament. A simultaneous Japanese-American Security Treaty gave the United States the right to maintain land, sea, and air forces in Japan, a point of bitter controversy later. On August 30, 1951, we signed a mutual defense treaty with the Philippines, and in September a tripartite security treaty with Australia and New Zealand. Combined with our less orthodox ties with Formosa and Korea, these agreements gave us a string of allies around the entire eastern perimeter of Asia. The British and French still held Southeast Asia, although the French were increasingly beleaguered in Indochina and increasingly dependent on our aid.

The election of Eisenhower, the death of Stalin in March 1953, the Korean truce in July, all provided the opening for a degree of reconciliation with the Soviet Union. The new Soviet leaders desired a détente with the West. In the more relaxed atmosphere the dual alliance system weakened. China would soon break from the Soviet Union. France and Britain reasserted their autonomy in Europe. Problems in their colonies or former colonies (Egypt, Indochina, Burma, North Africa) soon diverted attention from the first cold war arena—the areas of Allied occupation. In the changed perspectives of 1953, Eisenhower gladly moved toward another Big Power conference, and back to the problem of negotiating European settlements (an Austrian agreement would come from these renewed efforts). The thaw climaxed in a Foreign Ministers Conference in Berlin in 1954, and in a "summit" Conference in Geneva in 1955. The new era of good feelings would not last long (Suez, Hungary, and the U-2 overflight lay just ahead), but to the extent that one could date the cold war from the Truman Doctrine of 1947, one could just as plausibly argue that it ended at Geneva in 1955.

24

Victory in World War II posed anew an unanswered question of the thirties: could the United States ever again attain either a prosperous peacetime economy or a stable and harmonious social order? The boom psychology of the war never fully suppressed the widespread apprehensions about its aftermath. Just as the past, or an official interpretation of the past, spoke so eloquently to Americans of their need to undo the failures of Versailles, so the depression of 1920–1922 warned of the economic hazards of reconversion. The dislocations of the First World War also spawned Communist revolutions abroad and all manner of discontent and youthful rebellion at home. Should we not expect the same social tensions after 1945?

Roosevelt died just as the new era of peace dawned. He left all the fulfillment, all the hazards, to Harry S. Truman. Roosevelt could anticipate neither how much international tensions would continue to dominate domestic life nor that within five brief years we would be at war again. As usual, the past did not repeat itself. We had nourished all the wrong apprehensions. The cold war shaped our postwar priorities in economic policy and helped stimulate continued economic growth, but only at the cost of a vast diversion of unreplenishable resources into military uses. It also diverted national attention from domestic problems and channeled a plethora of emotional energies into a continued, often bitter debate over foreign policy or into an almost frantic effort to insure internal security.

Truman became president through a series of improbable choices and at least occasional good luck. He was born in 1884, and grew up on farms, first in western Missouri then on the outskirts of Independence, a small town just east of growing Kansas City. He always retained the simple tastes and habits of the small town. He entered politics in the very midst of business failure. After World War I he and a friend used most of their savings and several loans to stock a men's clothing store which at first thrived, but then floundered in the depression of 1921. By 1922 the two owners had to default on debts and sell their store (Truman would later repay his debts in full). In that year Truman ran for the office of county judge (an administrative rather than a judicial position) at the behest of

The Man from Missouri

The Truman Years

the Pendergast machine of nearby Kansas City. He won and began his climb in Jackson County politics, also gaining prominence in his Army Reserve Officers group, in the Masonic Order, and in the American Legion. As a straightforward and honest public servant, Truman was a needed asset for the Pendergasts, whose dynasty was later destroyed by scandals.

Truman's big chance came in 1934. Tom Pendergast pushed him as a candidate for the United States Senate. In an arduous campaign he won a narrow victory in the Democratic primary and then an easy one in the general election, as did so many Democratic candidates in that depression year. As a junior senator he was one of the Young Turks of 1934, completely loyal to Roosevelt and administration policies. Not a highly vocal or visible senator, he worked faithfully on committee assignments. In 1940, embarrassed by the Pendergast scandals (Tom Pendergast was then in prison for income tax evasion), he barely won against a primary challenger. A degree of fame finally came his way during World War II when he chaired a vital committee to investigate the national defense program. Throughout the war his committee remained the overworked watchdog of contracts granted to private corporations, preventing some of the overcharges and graft endemic to hasty mobilization.

Truman became vice-president because of his low-keyed loyalty, his successful committee work, and the varied liabilities of much better known candidates. Because Henry Wallace had so many enemies within the party, Roosevelt agreed to drop him in 1944, in part to appease older party leaders who resented Roosevelt's domestic policies, his multiple terms, and his grip on the party machinery. For Roosevelt the fourth term decision came easily. He wanted to preside over the coming victory and supervise the settlements that followed. He felt no one else could take over at such a critical point. And he parlayed this sentiment into victory, even in a time of rising Republican fortunes and of a decided shift away from New Deal policies. But victory, although likely, was not assured. He could not risk a divided party. Also, Roosevelt knew that his health had deteriorated, and that the vice-president might well be president before four years were over. The vice-presidency, up for grabs for the first time during Roosevelt's presidency, pitted rival factions of the party against each other. The party traditionalists blocked Wallace; organized labor vetoed Roosevelt's first choice, James F. Byrnes of South Carolina. Only then did Roosevelt agree either to William O. Douglas or Truman, who had heretofore supported Byrnes. Truman was nominated on the third ballot. Less than a year later he would be president.

Truman had few of the personal and social assets of Roosevelt. He also had the disadvantage of following a powerful man. Inevitably, some peo-

ple hated him for not being another Roosevelt, even as others hated him for not being the very opposite of Roosevelt. Yet, Truman had considerable talents of his own. He had a more tenacious mind, more consistent and matured convictions than Roosevelt. He read more extensively, particularly in biography and popular history, and had the ability for prolonged intellectual efforts. But he was no more an intellectual than Roosevelt. His commitments were conventional, direct, and visceral. He remained a simple moralist, a small-town booster who idealized women, venerated patriotism, and reflected a sincere regard for the welfare of farmers, small businessmen, and laborers—or people just like himself. For men of power, for big businessmen, for successful generals, even for brilliant academics, he mixed resentment with awe, a sense of inferiority with a desire to control or put down.

Truman never had Roosevelt's sense of social mastery. At times he seemed to be lacking in style or finesse, and even tried to establish an

Senator Harry Truman with his mother, Martha, at the polling place in Grandview, Missouri, November 7, 1944. Mrs. Truman, at ninety-one, is about to vote in the election that made her son a vice-president. *Wide World Photos*

image of artlessness joined with great tenacity and courage. He venerated the office of the presidency and tried to increase its prerogatives. In gesture and rhetoric he was bold and even defiant; in policies usually circumspect or even timid. Truman completely identified with the New Deal but defined it largely in welfare terms. His goals were to extend the fledgling welfare state and to retain the varied political support attracted to Roosevelt.

Apart from the overwhelming problems of foreign policy, Truman's first great task was the reconversion from a wartime to a peacetime economy. In dealing with this problem Truman had to face one unending domestic crisis after another without a cooperative Congress and without the prestige so essential for public support. The popular demand was quite clear: bring the boys home (in Europe impatient soldiers came close to insubordination), end the wartime rationing and controls, and fulfill the long postponed promise of a good life for all. Truman accepted all these goals, but had to face the hard realities and the inevitable frustrations that impeded their achievement. Growing tension with the Soviet Union required continued military readiness. The prospect of unbearable inflation required a gradual relaxation of controls, and scarcities in consumer goods forced a postponement of any immediate cornucopia. No one was satisfied.

Wartime policies assured a continued postwar market for capital, labor, and durable consumer goods. The wartime savings, the continued low interest rates, and the accumulated scarcities created a demand for goods

The Pitfalls of Reconversion

COLLEGES AND COLLEGE ENROLLMENTS, 1930–1970

Year	ALL INSTITUTIONS			JUNIOR COLLEGES	
	Number	Enrollment (1,000)	Percentage of Population 18–21	Number	Enrollment (1,000)
1930	1,409	1,101	12.42	277	56
1936	1,628	1,208	12.50	415	102
1940	1,708	1,494	15.68	456	150
1946	1,768	1,677	20.84	464	156
1950	1,851	2,659	29.88	483	243
1956	1,850	2,637	N.A.*	N.A.	N.A.
1960 †	2,008	3,216	34.86	509	403
1966	2,230	5,526	N.A.	N.A.	N.A.
1970	2,556	7,136	N.A.	827	1,630

* Indicates figures not available.
† First year for which figures for Alaska and Hawaii are included.
Source: *Historical Statistics of the United States: Colonial Times to 1957; Statistical Abstract of the United States, 1971.*

not satisfied until 1948 and 1949. Except for some temporary lay-offs during factory reconversion, or the time required to relocate discharged soldiers, there were enough jobs for all. The new spurt of civilian production helped absorb the 15,000,000 veterans. The end of most overtime work and continued plant expansion allowed an expansion of the civilian work force. Late in the war Congress approved a Serviceman's Readjustment Act (the GI Bill) which, in addition to insurance and medical benefits, offered special credit guarantees for home purchases and funds for a vast retraining program. Approximately 8,000,000 veterans would eventually collect over $15 billion for attending colleges or technical schools. The GI Bill tremendously increased college enrollments, brought into higher education a new type of student (married, serious, career-oriented), transformed college life, and quickly raised the national norm in educational attainment. Not incidentally, the retraining programs also released veterans slowly into the job market, and thus helped cushion the expected chaos in employment. Also, the Veterans Administration loans for new homes and farms added to the total demand for goods and services.

Controversy punctuated the ending of wartime controls. At first Truman tried to relax the restrictions as quickly as possible by ending most rationing in late 1945, even though domestic prices rose only 7 percent during the first six months after V-J Day. After he disbanded the Office of Economic Stabilization he had to revive it in 1946 as prices pushed upward at alarming rates. Since most of his special executive powers over the economy lapsed on June 30, 1946, Truman appealed to a power jealous Congress for authority to continue the Office of Price Administration (OPA). Pressured from all sides by the various interests anxious to cash in on the huge profits insured by insatiable consumer demands, Congress passed a weak bill permitting only an attenuated OPA, which an angry Truman vetoed. Chester Bowles also resigned as Director of Economic Stabilization. In less than a month, unchecked prices rose by as much as 35 percent—the most rapid inflation in our history. A chastened Congress passed a new, yet still weak, control bill in July, which authorized price controls on many items until mid-1947. But the restored controls had their pitfalls. The black market flourished for many scarce items and the new ceilings on meat led to farmer withholding, to all types of retail favoritism, and to shortages in many cities. After a Republican election victory in November (ironically, in part a result of citizen resentment of inflation and scarcities), Truman removed most price and wage (not rent) controls.

Inflation remained a controversial issue throughout 1947. Through later economic analysis, we now know that the inflationary pressures were largely of a temporary nature, and self-correcting as soon as supplies caught up with demand. But no one could know this at the time. Truman appealed to Americans for economic restraint without success. In January 1947, he appealed again to Congress for special authority to extend his few remaining controls over critical food supplies, and to continue his authority to allocate scarce materials. Congress passed short-term control authorizations which ended in the fall, although prices continued to rise. Then, Truman called Congress into special session to consider anti-inflation measures. In a clearly political move, he proposed a bill he surely knew Congress would not pass. It included curbs on speculation in the commodity exchanges, new allocation powers over scarce materials and transportation facilities, new export controls, extended rent controls, and new price ceilings on products in scarce supply. Congress, in rejecting the more stringent proposals, gave Truman a bit of ammunition for the 1948 elections. From the end of 1945 to the end of 1947, consumer retail prices rose by about 35 percent, and would climb a bit higher before climaxing in mid-1948.

Labor Strife

The rise in prices outpaced wage gains, and in conjunction with the loss of overtime hours set back the living standards of workers. They fought back, and in so doing put Truman in a bind. He had long been a partisan of organized labor; the Democratic party depended on its support. He heralded the Employment Act of 1946, which committed the resources of the government to full employment in a privately owned and free economy, and which established the Council of Economic Advisers to help the president develop policies to this end. Yet, as president, Truman saw excessive wage demands and severe labor unrest as a threat to both his foreign and domestic policies. In a series of confrontations he became an antagonist of organized labor.

The war hardly ended before a wave of strikes hit the largest industries. The workers sought wage increases sufficient to maintain income levels and to match the effects of price inflation. In the winter of 1945–1946 over 175,000 General Motors employees struck for 113 days, retarding the production of badly wanted new automobiles. In early 1946 a general steel strike threatened all areas of heavy production; only anxious mediation efforts and threats of government operation ended the strike. In May 1946, a number of national railroad unions threatened to strike for wage increases and improved work rules. Despite mediation efforts, two unions called the strike for May 18. On May 17 Truman seized the railroads and persuaded union leaders to delay a strike for five days. At that point the unions struck in defiance of the government.

In the midst of an unprecedented transportation crisis, Truman fought back angrily and deviously. In a speech to the nation on May 24 he castigated the selfishness of the union leaders, dramatized the economic effects of the strike, particularly on food and housing, and made the issue one between selfish private interests and the American public. He asked individual strikers to return to work within twenty-four hours; if they refused he promised to use the army to operate the trains and to protect loyal workers. On the next day, just before Truman delivered a speech to a joint session of Congress, the unions finally capitulated. Perhaps intentionally and for dramatic effect, Truman delayed the announcement until the end of his speech. In this speech he asked Congress for extraordinary powers he felt necessary to protect the public interest. He wanted authority to use court injunctions for the next six months to keep workers on the job in government-operated industries, and to punish by loss of seniority, union leaders or employees who refused to comply. Finally, as a last resort, Truman asked for the authority to draft into the armed forces such recalcitrant workers, in effect making them subject to military discipline. No president in the twentieth century had ever requested such an extreme weapon against organized labor.

Congress never granted Truman all that he asked, for however antilabor their sentiments, Republicans were not about to grant such extreme power to the chief executive. Robert A. Taft rather gleefully condemned the drafting of workers as an abuse of civil liberties. But both houses approved the temporary injunctive power. Truman vainly defended his request as a necessary defense of governmental authority, and in no way an antiunion crusade. He blamed irresponsible labor leaders, not the rank and file of workers.

Truman quickly used the new injunctive authority against the bellicose John L. Lewis, who had led his workers out in April 1946. After forty-five days Truman took over the mines and ended the strike. Then in November, as a coal shortage became more threatening, a defiant Lewis resumed the strike, this time against the government. Truman secured an injunction. A federal court fined the still defiant union $3,500,000, forcing even Lewis to back down. In 1947, in a politically imperative retreat from antiunionism, Truman voiced his opposition to many pending labor bills in the Republican controlled Congress. He asked for special committee study of such alleged abuses as the secondary boycott and jurisdictional strikes (strikes over which union would represent a given body of workers). He also wanted better mediation machinery, but balanced these proposals by reiterating pleas for welfare legislation that would improve the position of laborers. Instead of a mild labor bill, he got a political hot potato—the Taft-Hartley Act of 1947.

After the fall elections of 1946, some new labor legislation was inevitable. By capitalizing on inflation, labor unrest, and international tension, the Republicans had captured both houses of Congress. They expected to win the presidency in 1948. Truman carefully began to calculate his strategy in such a way as to embarrass the Republicans. The two first clashed on the Taft-Hartley Labor Management Relations Act of June 1947, a measure that actually secured broad enough support in Congress to deserve the label "bipartisan." The architect of the Senate version, Robert A. Taft, was a likely Republican candidate in 1948 and a convenient symbol of antiunion feelings among Republicans. The act was a revision of the Wagner Act of 1935, the very symbol of Democratic solicitude for labor. Its main provisions curtailed the power of unions, although its proponents stressed its intent to bring a new balance and fairness to labor-management relations and to protect the public interest against major, national strikes. In many ways it even fulfilled Truman's own earlier requests for federal power over irresponsible unions.

As later events proved, the most important provision of the Taft-Hartley Act was a cooling off provision for prospective strikes that threatened the national safety or health. The president could use an injunction to postpone such strikes for eighty days, and during this period use government mediation to seek a settlement. At the end of the eighty days the strike could take place unless the president sought additional legislation from Congress. The act established a list of unfair labor practices for unions that outlawed jurisdictional strikes and secondary boycotts (as Truman had urged), but that also included restrictions on exaction of pay for work not performed, on union refusal to bargain in good faith, and on union contributions to political campaigns (the last a pointed threat to many Democratic politicians). Other provisions seemed even more antiunion, at least to unions. One, aimed at graft and cheating, required unions to register with the secretary of labor and submit annual financial reports. Another required officers of unions to file affidavits that they were not Communists before their union could be certified as a bargaining agent. The act gave employers the right to publicize their side in a labor dispute, to petition the National Labor Relations Board for elections to determine bargaining agents, and to sue unions for breach of contract. Finally, it outlawed the closed shop (union membership as a condition of employment), but allowed a union shop (if the contract so provided, one had to join the union in order to retain employment).

Truman vetoed the act on June 20. His decision was a political one, made after extensive consultation with his cabinet and with such close political advisers as Clark Clifford, and after a poll of party leaders across the country. In his veto message, and in a radio address, Truman departed from his usual, meticulous examination of the details of a bill, and instead launched a highly emotional campaign against Taft-Hartley, which he pictured as "unfair to the working people of this country," and a threat to the rights of collective bargaining. Perhaps as he expected, Congress quickly overrode his veto, and thereby projected the Taft-Hartley Act into the forefront of Truman's gathering campaign strategy. By continued appeals for modification or repeal, he helped regain much of the labor support lost during the strikes of 1946, and by so doing gained one margin he needed for his victory in 1948. On labor issues, as on inflation, Truman seemed to go in two directions at alternative times, and to take the stronger positions when he knew he could not win congressional support.

Frustrated on many economic issues, Truman gained congressional approval for his foreign policy and for governmental and military reorganization. He reshuffled government agencies in 1946, and then in 1948 appointed the Hoover Commission, which studied the total federal bureaucracy and made extensive proposals in behalf of efficiency and economy. Truman eventually won approval for thirty-five administrative revisions, losing only in his effort to create a new Department of Welfare. He first proposed a unification of the armed forces in 1945, but it took two years of struggling against interservice jealousy and resentment to win begrudging support for a major legislative proposal. The National Security Act of 1947 provided for a Department of Defense, established the air force as a separate military wing, gave legal status to the Joint Chiefs of Staff, and created the National Security Council as the highest executive agency dealing with national security. The act also provided for a Central Intelligence Agency to coordinate the confusing and expanding civilian and military intelligence operations. In 1946 Truman also defeated military efforts to control atomic energy. He supported instead the 1946 McMahon Bill, which established the present Atomic Energy Commission (AEC). The AEC is under civilian control, and has a monopoly over all atomic energy.

On one military priority Truman lost. From the very beginning of his administration he fought for universal military training but received from Congress only a new Selective Service Act. Truman had an almost romantic image of the military. He believed that a period of military training for every male (one proposal was six months at age eighteen) would enhance physical health, bring a needed disciplinary approach to life, induce a sense of responsibility, and increase patriotism. He lamented the number of physical rejects during World War II and feared an increasingly flabby society. His scheme was never well understood; many incorrectly viewed it as an extension of the draft. Truman loved the Swiss system, with every person trained, a large ready reserve, and a vast inactive reserve of potential soldiers, all without a large, permanent army or navy. In many ways he saw universal training as a safeguard against a powerful military establishment, which he increasingly feared.

Governmental Reorganization

As soon as he could escape the immediate problems of reconversion, Truman made welfare extension the crux of his domestic program. He soon dubbed his proposals in behalf of the "great precepts of social welfare" a "Fair Deal," and tried thereby to recapture the political appeal of Roosevelt. In 1945 he stressed veterans benefits, government funding for public works and scientific research, increased social security benefits and broadened coverage (especially for unemployment compensation), higher minimum wages for a broader number of workers, increased farm subsidies, increased support for private housing and new funding for public housing, a continued Fair Employment Practices Committee, and a broad health-care system. He would later add and delete individual proposals. In most areas friendly congressmen, or executive bureaucrats, would develop the implementing legislation. Some of this legislation, such as the Brannon Plan for agriculture, surfaced only after the 1948 election. Truman's most zealous advocacy of welfare legislation came in the wake of what he saw as the disastrous elections of 1946, and thus as a calculated political strategy for 1948. But however politically motivated or conditioned, however circumstance or strategy shaped the details or the timing, such an expanded welfare state reflected Truman's own personal commitments. Politics might force compromise, but conviction underlay the goals.

It is significant that the political controversies of the Truman administration revolved around welfare extension, not repeal. Expansion of welfare benefits now came slowly, by degrees, unlike during the depression thirties. Most of the more daring Truman proposals—Negro rights, health care, an income-oriented policy for farmers—failed in Congress, and most by large margins. But this should not conceal the less controversial expansion of Social Security benefits, the higher minimum wages, and the wide array of housing subsidies. Even as debates intensified on details the principle of welfare became more secure. The most concerted opposition to individual welfare proposals came from affected interest groups —those who would pay, or suffer losses, or feel threatened. Their appeal to principle could not always be taken at face value.

The growing acceptance of welfare measures accorded with reality— a highly collectivized but private economy increased individual vulnerability, and made increasing demands upon ability and skills. More and more people faced the loss of significant or fulfilling economic roles, particularly the unskilled, the young, and the elderly. More and more they would have to adjust either to poorly rewarded or socially stigmatized types of labor that would not provide humanely acceptable levels of subsistence.

The acceptance of welfare also accorded with ideology. Unlike during the thirties, there was only minuscule political support in the Truman era

476

for major changes in the private economy, such as decentralization, redistribution of wealth or managerial rights, dissolution of large corporations, or the nationalization of major industries. Given private management, large industrial units, specialization, and impersonality in production, and a continued emphasis upon rapid economic growth, radical proposals had no standing and welfare efforts seemed the only convenient and humane answer to growing social problems—problems that seemed to grow as fast as the overall living standards. Critics could protest. Surely the vision of ever more welfare, so congenial to a Truman, was not as humane as a larger vision that looked to major structural changes in the economy, or even to an entirely different economic system —for example, to restored entrepreneurial opportunity, to broader individual participation in industrial processes, to cooperative production, to a new emphasis upon artistry rather than mere growth. But a conventional Truman hardly understood such possible but difficult alternatives, and rarely saw issues in such a broad perspective. To him welfare was virtue. And thus he brought a simple and appealing moral fervor to his campaign for a fair deal—at least as soon as he was convinced that his political future might best lie in that direction.

However one feels about a welfare state, there remain wide options for welfare measures. The larger policy issue—Is the welfare approach the best one for dealing with modern problems?—should not conceal the proximate areas of often bitter controversy about the exact form the welfare should take. Behind the detailed legislative proposals of the Fair Deal were dedicated agency heads and idealistic research staffs. They conceived imaginative new programs worthy of study in their own right, even though they contributed, in the larger perspective, only to more welfare benefits. Particularly in his health care proposals and in civil rights, Truman effectively conveyed some of their underlying idealism, an idealism unalloyed by the foreground problems of practical politics.

But politics had to be a constant focus. Truman had to win in 1948 both to vindicate his first administration and also to show that he could win an election on his own. The harassed Democratic party needed to retain power in behalf of extensive patronage. After the election of 1946 Truman's personal advisers began work on a winning political strategy. Clark Clifford, Truman's friend and special counsel, argued successfully for a welfare, labor, and civil rights posture, or to what in the peculiar rhetoric of 1947 passed as a "liberal" stance. This emphasis in domestic affairs balanced his increasingly tough anti-Communist foreign policy. It ran counter to the advice of several probusiness members of his official family, and risked the loss of support from many southern congressmen. But such a domestic posture had the best chance of holding labor and

Negro support, and would also appease the remnants of western Progressivism (conservation, public power, agricultural interests). Thus, in both 1947 and 1948 Truman presented Congress with a detailed Fair Deal program, and in effect challenged the Republican leadership to defeat it. In most cases they did just that.

Legislative Goals

In his legislative proposals of 1947 Truman tried to appeal to as many groups as possible, save only the South. He muted earlier proposals for national health insurance, but placed new emphasis on civil rights and added an appealing proposal for an essentially progressive tax cut. In addition to his earlier attempt to rescue the expiring Fair Employment Practices Committee, he now used a special speech to request poll tax repeal, legislation against lynching and racial discrimination in interstate travel, and laws to protect voting rights. Personally appalled by the legal and economic inequities faced by blacks, he responded to growing pressure from organized blacks for new federal legislation. In 1946 he had appointed a distinguished Civil Rights Committee, whose report would remain the basis of most of his legislative proposals. Politically, he feared that the Republican party might capture civil rights leadership and regain the black voters won over by New Deal economic policies. In large northern cities the swing vote might be either black or the small white minorities actively committed to equal rights. In any case, he did not expect the South to go Republican.

The civil rights speech, joined with active administration efforts in Congress (it was not just words), caused a revolt among Deep South Democrats, a revolt that ended in the Dixiecrat party in 1948. Typically, Truman vacillated. In an attempt to mute the revolt he dropped his civil rights emphasis in 1948, and even helped exclude a strong civil rights plank from the original draft of the Democratic platform. But at the convention a group of northern delegates successfully amended the platform on the floor, and thus committed the party to Truman's earlier, ambitious program. This occasioned the withdrawal of Southern delegates and freed Truman to take unilateral action in behalf of blacks. On July 26, even as he called Congress into special session, he issued executive orders requiring nondiscrimination in federal agencies and in the armed forces. The ambiguous military order invited varied interpretations. It stressed that it was the policy of the commander in chief that there be "equality of treatment and opportunity for all persons in the armed services. . . ." Such a policy was to be effected as rapidly as possible, but with due regard for efficiency and morale. In a subsequent press conference Truman said he intended it to end all segregation, which in fact it did not. Only in 1950

Among Truman's legislative proposals of 1947 were several civil rights initiatives. To a war-weary country, however, civil rights was not yet the issue it was to become. Most whites preferred to ignore the problem, and to think of blacks "stomping at the Savoy," a New York ballroom in Harlem, where blacks went to dance and whites went to gape. *Wide World Photos*

would the army require integration in areas of special skills (such as medicine). Although in the early days of the Korean War most infantry units remained segregated, most units finally tried integration, often as much for practical reasons as because of official policy. Yet even at war's end, in 1953, de facto segregation remained the rule in the navy and in some army units.

The Eightieth Congress rejected all civil rights proposals and most of Truman's welfare bills. Politically, this may have helped him in the subsequent campaign. Truman sharpened the differences between himself and Congress and soon ridiculed its do-nothing record. He became a master of the veto, even using it against two tax bills in 1948 because of their inflationary and regressive features. Congress passed a slightly less regressive bill over Truman's veto, in part out of resentment for his intrusion into such fiscal matters. Congress also refused to reward labor with new social security or minimum wage benefits, or to provide adequate storage facilities for growing agricultural surpluses. This gave Truman the class appeal he wanted in the campaign. But as Congress adjourned for the summer conventions, it seemed that Truman might not be able to exploit any popular dissatisfaction with Congress. Many despairing Democrats sought the means, and the candidate, to displace Truman. If one thing was clear in the summer of 1948, it was that Truman could never win an election. A short-lived Truman administration seemed to be drawing to an anticlimactic and bitter end. Few seemed ready to mourn its unhappy passing.

Reprieve in 1948

The Democrats had few alternatives to Truman in 1948. To repudiate an incumbent is to take a desperate gamble. A northern delegation tried unsuccessfully to woo General Dwight D. Eisenhower as a candidate, feeling that he was the only person who might have stolen a majority of delegates from Truman. The Democrats met in Philadelphia in July and

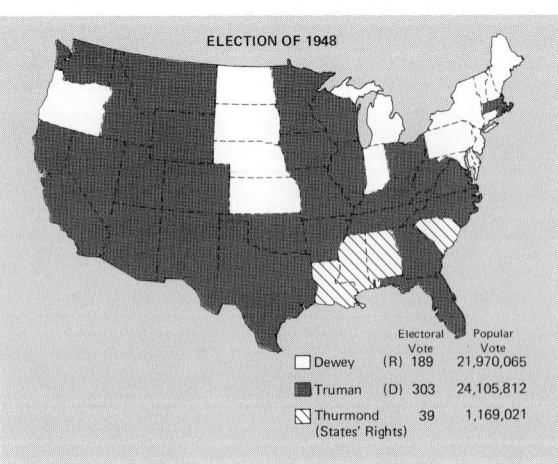

ELECTION OF 1948

		Electoral Vote	Popular Vote
☐ Dewey	(R)	189	21,970,065
■ Truman	(D)	303	24,105,812
▨ Thurmond (States' Rights)		39	1,169,021

nominated Truman without enthusiasm; Southern dissidents prevented unanimous endorsement. An earlier Republican convention had made Truman's prospects even dimmer by nominating not Taft, but a moderate Easterner, Thomas E. Dewey. In this, his second campaign, Dewey seemed sure to redeem his strong but losing effort of 1944, and by his moderation seemed well equipped to win critical, industrial states to the Republican party. Although Southerners found no consolation in either Truman or Dewey, they did respect the Democratic vice-presidential candidate—moderate, likeable, eloquent Alben W. Barkley of Kentucky. Truman accepted him but did not choose him. He had preferred Justice William O. Douglas, who had declined the honor.

Truman's policies and platform split the Democratic party. In Birmingham, Alabama, on July 17, Deep South Democrats gathered for their own convention, at which they nominated Strom Thurmond of South Carolina. When they were unable to gain a place on Southern ballots as Democrats, they campaigned as a third party. Staunchly sectional, they threatened a Democratic victory in a close election. Their platform condemned civil rights legislation as a "totalitarian" extension of federal power. They stressed state rights and constitutional government, but this only to embellish their one overweening devil—Negro rights. The platform actually affirmed a belief in racial segregation.

In late July a quite different and less homogeneous group gathered in Philadelphia to form a new Progressive party and to nominate Henry A. Wallace for the presidency. The delegates were unprofessional, youthful, enthusiastic, militant. In this convention alone blacks and women participated in more than token numbers. The new party primarily reflected disillusionment with Truman's cold war diplomacy and with the rising tide of domestic anticommunism. Wallace symbolized opposition to our tough stand against the Soviet Union and to the vast expansion of American military power around the world. The domestic concerns of the new party—suppression of the military and of related industries, a truly militant effort in behalf of black equality, an end to monopolies, and an even more aggressive welfare program than the Fair Deal—took second place to its foreign planks. The Communist party not only supported Wallace but quickly achieved a leading role in his hectic campaign (he faced eggs, rocks, and physical attack). Wallace, in so many ways a political innocent, could never dissociate his policies from those of his supporters. By the time of the election he was such a clear loser that his low popular vote did not fairly reflect the appeal of his policies.

Against all the predictions and all the polls (discontinued too soon before the election), an underdog Truman won, making the 1948 election the classic upset in our political history. After it was over chastened experts could retrace the campaign and point out some of the reasons for his success. Dewey's low-keyed, noncontroversial, but confident campaign had either lulled his potential supporters into staying home (it was a low turnout election), or provoked many to vote for Truman out of sympathy or admiration. During the campaign the trials and tribulations of Truman had concealed the strength of the Democratic party (still the majority party by a large margin). In a time of trial the party organization worked hard, and brought out needed but wavering voters. Even the two splinter parties on each ideological flank hurt less than anticipated—the Dixiecrats won for Truman Negro and northern support; the embarrassing Communist ties of Wallace helped disarm charges of radicalism against Truman.

Truman's campaign strategy—an all-out attack on the Republicans —gained votes in the last weeks of the campaign. Even the polls showed this. As a political gamble he called the berated Eightieth Congress back into session after the conventions, and let it reject his Fair Deal all over again. Then, in a strenuous (over 290 speeches) whistlestop campaign, he lambasted the Republicans. Truman wanted to talk directly to the people and bypass the generally adverse newspaper coverage. He defended his own policies in a general and simple way by using an impromptu, direct, even abrasive but somehow effective style. Everywhere he fought against the in-part mythical "special interests" and in behalf of "the people," with special speeches for farmers, laborers, and, finally, even for blacks. His campaign peaked late. His victory margin was ample with 304 electoral votes to Dewey's 189 and Thurmond's 38; 24,105,695 popular votes to Dewey's 21,969,170, Thurmond's 1,169,021, and Wallace's 1,156,103.

The Last Chance for a Fair Deal

Truman carried with him a Democratic Congress. The election results seemed to be a mandate for his Fair Deal legislation. Not so. Most of his more daring proposals floundered in an ideologically divided Congress. Only on foreign policy could Truman depend upon a clear majority. By a varying coalition of administration Democrats and a fluctuating minority of Republicans willing to support certain welfare measures on their merits, or because of constituent pressure, Truman finally won a new housing bill, an increase in minimum wages (40 to 75 cents), broadened Social Security coverage (10,000,000 additional nonagricultural workers), and higher retirement benefits. But he lost on more original proposals in agriculture, health care, civil rights, and federal aid to education. The latter failed not so much on its merits as on the intensely emotional issue of aid to parochial schools. The problems of church and state came to the fore just after World War II, in part because of secularist resentment of all favoritism to religion, in part because of a new upsurge of anti-Catholic fears.

Of Truman's 1949 legislative proposals, those in three areas—housing, agriculture, and health care—deserve additional analysis. By the end of World War II almost everyone agreed that the country had a housing problem. The slack in building throughout the thirties, the prohibitive scarcities of the war, and an exploding postwar population all contributed to the scarcity and to a plethora of substandard units. As early as 1945, Truman advocated expanded aid to the private housing industry and new federal spending to add to the existing public housing units. In each session of Congress before 1948 he tried unsuccessfully to get new public housing authorization. Thus, public housing became the controversial issue as well as the one that seemed closest to other welfare proposals. Less controversial were techniques for aiding private construction. Both home builders and prospective purchasers pushed for expanded FHA and VA mortgage insurance. In the immediate aftermath of the war, Congress also approved more direct boons for builders—early relaxation of controls, premium payments, and special loans.

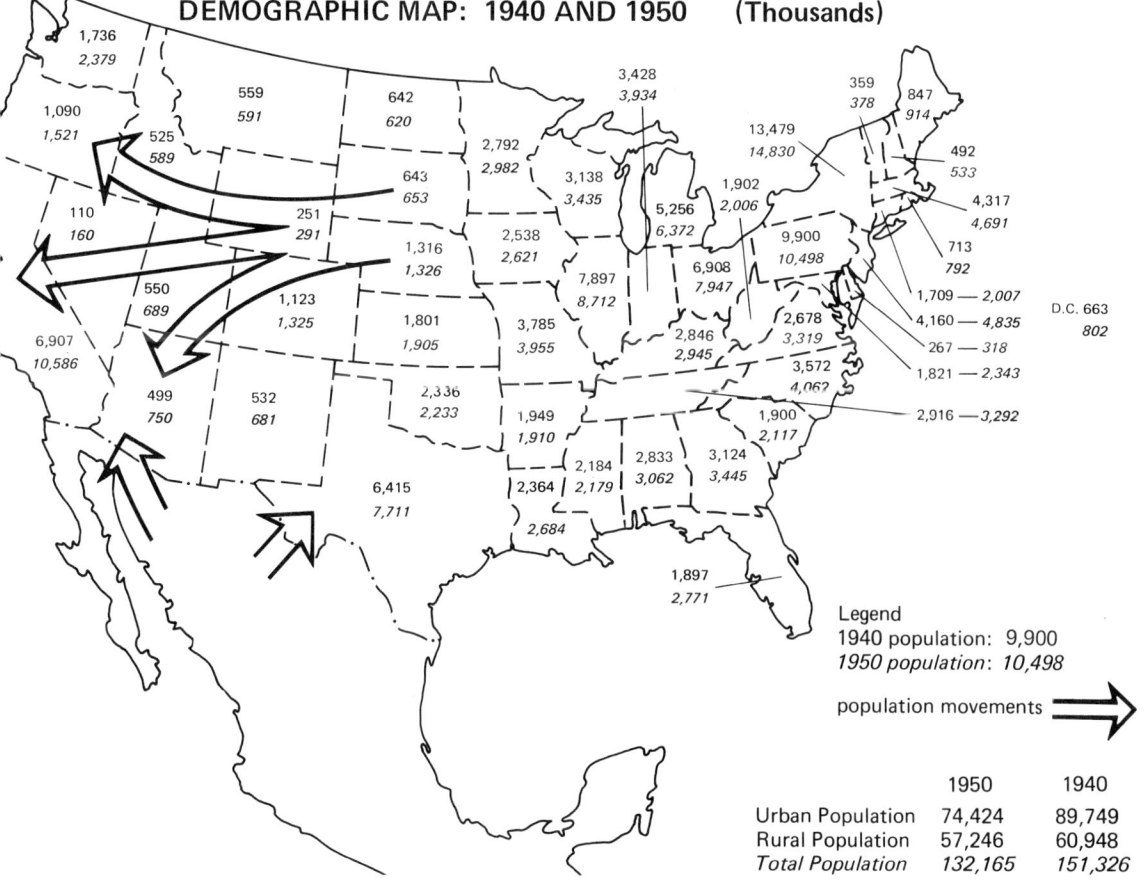

DEMOGRAPHIC MAP: 1940 AND 1950   (Thousands)

Legend
1940 population: 9,900
1950 population: 10,498

population movements ⟹

	1950	1940
Urban Population	74,424	89,749
Rural Population	57,246	60,948
Total Population	132,165	151,326

But the big impetus was easy mortgage money, facilitated not only by government insurance, low down payments, and long repayment schedules, but also by government monetary policies which preserved low interest rates in a period of inflation. Even in 1946 housing starts exceeded the peak year of 1929. By 1949 the starts exceeded 1,000,000 a year, and would continue to grow on into the fifties. By 1951 over half of the new housing units would be financed by VA or FHA insured loans. Access to mortgage liability by families with almost no savings and only average incomes finally pushed home ownership in America up to 55 percent. This boom in private home construction had long-run social implications. It facilitated a growing exodus of those whites with stable employment from center cities to outlying suburbs, only to be replaced by less stable, less skilled, and often nonwhite immigrants from the rural South or the Appalachian highlands. Urban problems mounted. The federal loan programs provided some control over construction standards, almost none over local planning or design. The spiraling new subdivisions so often lacked esthetic appeal that, by the fifties, a growing body of literature would stereotype and castigate the shabby uniformity, as well as the alleged social conformity, of suburbia.

Public housing (or government subsidized, low-rent housing) began in 1932, but became an accepted and permanent welfare policy only in 1937. The limited public housing program of the New Deal seemed an inadequate precedent for the scarcities of the postwar period. Thus Truman and a large block of congressmen in both parties sought new programs and a higher level of financing. This they finally achieved in the Housing Act of 1949, which passed in part because of the continuous support of Robert A. Taft. The act provided funds to cities for slum clearance and for 810,000 units of low-rent housing. Such an expanded program then seemed, at least to welfare advocates, a brilliant achievement of the Truman administration. Despite some imaginative planning by the new Housing and Home Finance Agency, and some excellent uses of funds by a few cities, the program soon seemed either hopelessly inadequate (the optimistic appraisal) or essentially misdirected. The decay of center cities continued, with slum conditions developing not only faster than public housing but all too often in the projects themselves. These urban problems reflected grave social and economic ills well beyond the curative action of any government housing program—problems that soon swamped all the resources of the housing agencies.

The Social Security Act of 1935, in addition to all its other exceptions and limitations, ignored health insurance. Orthodox proponents of a broad system of social insurance viewed this as its greatest deficiency. From 1936 on Senator Robert Wagner of New York, as well as other congressmen, annually confronted an uninterested Congress with various plans for compulsory medical insurance or public health care systems. In 1945 a hopeful Truman devoted an entire speech to a complex plan for a broad health care program. This included not only federal aid for hospital construction, more funding for the United States Public Health Service, and federal aid for medical research (each eventually funded by Congress), but a compulsory, prepayment type of medical insurance. This scheme, and various modifications of it, gained the vague label of "socialized medicine." Truman, however, vainly insisted on its variance from European plans, and defended it as a necessary extension of Social Security into a new area and as a fair and just technique for sharing risks. His plans did not require physicians to participate, left most fees open for local determination, and gave patients the freedom to choose their own physician (provided, of course, that they chose one who would cooperate with the plan). The overall proposal came close to a universal Medicare.

In the postwar period the American Medical Association (the main professional organization for physicians) hardened its opposition to compulsory government insurance programs, private prepayment plans, and any type of cooperative or group medicine. It insisted on retention of the private fee system and what it described as a personal relationship between physician and patient. When Truman launched his last real campaign for medical insurance (in 1949), the AMA countered with intensive lobbying and an effective public "educational" effort, and helped persuade a majority of congressmen to vote against any plan, including even the mildest one possible. The debate often strayed far beyond the merits of individual proposals and into abstract considerations of socialism, the dangers of government bureaucracy, and even the virtues of free enterprise. Later experience with Medicare would vindicate at least one contention of the AMA. Many of the voluntary and local features would have to yield to national standards and, eventually, even a national fee schedule. Many prepaid systems might succumb to the rigidity of a national health service and still fail to provide vital preventive services. But failure to adopt some universal program meant, on the one hand, that private medicine in America would excel in most areas of research and technique, but fail in attaining an overall high level of clinical services. For geographically well located and financially secure families, the United States often had the best medical care in the world. For others, in isolated areas, or without financial resources or private health insurance, we had close to the worst medical care of any advanced country.

Truman's efforts to reorient our agricultural programs also failed in Congress (his one major bill never got through committee). Soon called the Brannon Plan after his secretary of agriculture, the main proposal harked back to 1933 and the income-maintenance proposals of the Farmer's Union (the one major farm organization to support the Brannon Plan). After the war, Truman continued the New Deal program of production controls and price supports and Congress fulfilled its wartime pledge—to support prices of basic commodities at 90 percent of parity. Even in 1949 Congress approved a farm bill quite generous to farmers. With the waning of wartime scarcities after 1947, American farmers again had to deal with mounting surpluses, and the Commodity Credit Corporation (CCC) soon faced a severe shortage of storage facilities for wheat and feed grains. Under the existing price support scheme, the consumer continued to pay most of the subsidy to the farmer through higher-than-world prices.

Brannon urged the abolition of the CCC and all government purchase, storage, and sale of farm products. Instead of propping prices, he wanted to pay direct subsidies to farmers, allowing agricultural prices to find their own level in the marketplace. When surpluses developed, they would aid consumers through lower prices and help correct the surplus by increasing the demand. The farmer would not have to suffer from the vagaries of the market, for he would now receive payments sufficient to raise his total income to parity level, or to what he would have received through supported and higher prices. This device still tied income to production and not to costs or to need. It was no scheme to redistribute income, and despite critics' charges in no sense socialistic. Neither would it anchor inefficient farmers to the land. But it was a direct subsidy and a further extension of governmental paternalism (it did not abolish acreage controls). The most powerful farm organization, the Farm Bureau, had shifted from its support of the AAA in the thirties to a belief in free agricultural markets, and so vehemently opposed the Brannon Plan. Suggestive at least in its implications (but not a major issue in the debate), the plan placed an upper limit on the amount of production eligible for subsidy payments ($20,000 for any one farm). The plan clearly offered the prospect of more direct tax funding of the farm program while promising overall savings in storage and marketing. As the problems of commodity management almost overwhelmed the CCC in subsequent years, Congress finally accepted direct payments to farmers, not as income supplements but as grants to induce acreage retirement. Since the Brannon Plan there has been plenty of support for a free agricultural market, but no effort to tie this idea to any form of direct subsidy to farmers, whether large or small.

Truman was no more adept in economics than his predecessor. His fiscal and monetary policies followed no clear pattern, and varied not only because of circumstances but also because of political priorities. In spite of the Employment Act of 1946 (in so much of its rhetoric a commitment to Keynesian views), and in spite of his willingness to subordinate budgetary goals to priorities of defense and welfare, Truman retained the commitments of a cautious merchant. Budgets should balance, debts should be paid off, and prices should remain stable—even if these orthodox commitments often warred with each other.

From 1945 to early in 1949, Truman more than attained his goal of a balanced budget. By the end of fiscal 1946, the national debt reached $269 billion, or what seemed an astronomical figure to most Americans. In the next year it declined by $11 billion, in large part through a shift of balances. Yet, in fiscal years 1947 and 1948, Truman achieved a budgetary surplus of over $9 billion, and thus a small but symbolically significant lowering of the national debt. The added spending during the mild recession of 1948–1949, and then during the Korean War, once again required small deficits. But the national debt remained remarkably stable for over a decade (as late as 1958 it amounted to only $276 billion, or only $7 billion more than in 1946). The surpluses and repayments abetted Truman's efforts to limit inflation and were immensely popular with the public. He wanted even more savings during those years, and so vetoed

GROSS NATIONAL PRODUCT

Year	Current Dollars (Billions)	Constant (1958) Dollars (Billions)	Implicit Price Deflators (1958 = 100)
1900	18.7	76.9	24.3
1905	25.1	96.3	26.1
1910	35.3	120.1	29.4
1915	40.0	124.5	32.1
1920	91.5	140.0	65.4
1925	93.1	179.4	51.9
1930	90.4	183.5	49.3
1935	72.2	169.5	42.6
1940	99.7	227.2	43.9
1945	211.9	355.2	59.7
1950	284.8	355.3	80.2
1955	398.0	438.0	90.9
1960	503.7	487.7	103.3
1965	684.9	617.8	110.9
1970	977.1	722.5	135.2
1972	1155.2	790.7	146.1

Source: United States Department of Commerce, Bureau of Economic Analysis.

congressional tax cuts in 1948. The government debt declined even in current dollars. But such dollar amounts still drastically distorted the magnitude of the decline. From 1945 to 1948 the wholesale price index climbed by almost 50 percent; the retail price index by about 35 percent. By a reasonable calculation, the 1948 dollar was worth 40 percent less than in 1945. This inflation effectively cancelled over a third of the national debt (just as it took away a third of the purchasing power of people who held that debt in the form of bonds). In these same three years the gross national product, in current dollars, rose from $213 billion to $259 billion. Thus the debt also declined as a percentage of the gross national product. Finally, the rapid population growth caused the per capita debt to decline. The added spending in the mild recession of 1949, and then in the Korean War, once again required small budget deficits. But as a percentage of gross national product, and in per capita amounts, the national debt continued to decline until the sixties.

The rapid inflation of prices in 1946 and 1947 reflected the heavy demands for goods but few other inflationary pressures. Most Americans still looked ahead to a depression, maintained high levels of savings, and despite low interest rates kept a higher than usual proportion of their assets in liquid form. This kept money from turning over rapidly. Even the total supplies of money (currency and demand deposits) grew only slowly after 1946 (about 4 percent a year). Even had it so desired, the Federal Reserve System had few means to control credit or curtail postwar price increases. Despite high reserve requirements, most banks had plenty of money to loan and rarely had to rediscount with Reserve banks. More important, Truman insisted upon keeping the Federal Reserve Sys-

UNEMPLOYMENT, 1900–1970

Year	Percent of Work Force	Number (1,000)
1900	5.0	1,420
1905	3.1	1,000
1910	5.9	2,150
1915	9.7	3,840
1920	4.0	1,670
1925	4.0	1,800
1930	8.7	4,340
1935	20.1	10,610
1940	14.6	8,120
1945	1.9	1,040
1950	5.0	3,142
1955	4.0	2,654
1960	5.5	3,852
1965	4.5	3,366
1970	4.9	4,088

Source: *Historical Statistics of the United States: Colonial Times to 1957; Statistical Abstract of the United States, 1971.*

tem chained to the government security market, and therefore to a low-interest policy. Perhaps this decision had more wisdom than he knew. The soaring prices exaggerated the economic dislocation. They would stabilize and come down in 1949. Considering the long drought on durable goods, consumer demands remained unexpectedly moderate. There was never the self-perpetuating inflation of the late sixties and early seventies, when prices failed to respond to almost any monetary restraints. Additional monetary weapons in 1946 or 1947 might have fanned the widespread fears of depression and pushed the country into a severe recession. Recession came in 1949 not as an aftermath of runaway inflation, but with the fulfillment of the modest backlog of consumer demands. A seller's market quickly became a buyer's market. This helped clear out fly-by-night retailers, bankrupted a few corporations that cashed in on the artificial and not very discriminate demand for goods (remember the Kaiser and Fraser cars?), but also led to the first severe unemployment of the postwar era.

The American economy grew slowly during the reconversion period, not at all during the 1949 recession, and more rapidly during the Korean War. In light of widespread expectations of a postwar depression, the modest growth rate did not seem disappointing. Truman always referred back to the levels of the thirties, taking keen satisfaction in his economic achievement. Both production efficiency and profits increased, which justified labor's demands for higher wages. The major shift in the work force continued to be away from farms. During the Truman administration the total number of American farms dropped by over 600,000, a rate of decline that increased during the Eisenhower administration.

By the end of 1949 the economic indices indicated a recession. The facts combined with all the fears suggested profound psychological implications. If the recession were quickly mastered, investors and consumers would be less apprehensive than before, but if it worsened, a wave of pessimism might make it almost impossible to reverse. By the early months of 1949 wholesale prices declined by about 5 percent; retail prices by considerably less. The rate of production declined by only 2 percent. But unemployment rose from a 1945 low of about 1,000,000 to a postwar high of 4,600,000 in 1949. The recession proved so mild and short as to seem ephemeral to those with memories of the thirties, for recovery began in the fall of 1949. By June 1950, and the beginning of the Korean War, the economy was already growing and unemployment was declining. Contrary to later criticism, the war did not rescue the Truman administration from economic disaster; however it did accelerate the growth rate and lead to a new concern over inflation.

With the Korean War, inflation again became the key economic concern. Despite wide discretionary powers granted by Congress, Truman resisted all pressures for unpopular economic controls. He chose to use indirect tools to cool a wartime economy. Congress helped with a hefty tax increase in 1951 ($4.5 billion added to annual revenue) which helped inhibit private spending. But consumers still behaved normally—they borrowed and spent at unprecedented rates, forcing dramatic price increases in scarce areas. It was in these circumstances that a reluctant Truman consented to new credit controls, and thus to a major shift in federal economic policy.

Until 1950 Truman backed the easy money policies which Roosevelt had maintained throughout World War II. The Open Market Committee of the Federal Reserve System continued to buy at set prices all securities offered, thus keeping credit supplies abundant and maintaining stable but low interest rates. This policy abetted price inflation by stimulating private demand, but it also kept federal debt payments low, made home financing easy even for working people, and generally appealed to low-income groups. But by 1951 an increasingly independent Federal Reserve Board responded to demands from Congress and from businessmen in behalf of new credit restraints. Truman risked criticism if he applied more political pressure on a supposedly independent agency. In March 1951, the Federal Reserve Board stopped supporting the prices of government securities and began using discriminatory Open Market operations to regulate the supply of money. There was no immediate, dramatic change in credit costs, but interest rates began a steady rise that continued for over a decade. Never again would Americans finance home purchases with 4 percent mortgages. From 1951 on Federal Reserve restraints vied with budgetary and taxing policies as a means of economic management. During the Korean War, at least, these monetary and fiscal tools allowed steady economic growth without runaway inflation, and without rationing or price controls. This was, of course, also testimony to the productiveness of an economy that could provision a war of the magnitude of Korea and still allow a continuous growth in private consumption.

Truman in Eclipse

Prosperity did not mean happiness, nor did it insure an equitable distribution of income and wealth. The last two Truman years were contentious and angry years. Most of the anger reflected competing priorities in foreign policy and the growing frustration of the peace negotiations in Korea. It also reflected the domestic standoff between Truman and an unresponsive Congress. He kept up a futile fight for the Fair Deal even in the midst of war, and continuously quarreled with Congress (in 1950 the Republicans regained a majority). For example, in 1952 he vetoed what he perceived as a congressional sellout to local and largely private interests—a bill that gave to individual coastal states all oil rights in the first three miles off shore (for Texas, the first ten). Congress pressed the bill over his veto, to the glee of a few coastal states and the oil companies. But, as Truman now so well knew, charges of political sellouts respect no parties and no branch of government.

After his unexpected victory in 1948, and then again just after our first involvement in Korea, Truman basked in temporary vindication and popularity. He had few such moments. Late in his administration he faced a final political embarrassment—well-supported charges of scandal in his own official family. Truman suffered fawning fools and cronies all too gladly. His administration gained luster for the brilliance of some of his advisers, the mediocrity of others. Top officials in both the Bureau of Internal Revenue and the Reconstruction Finance Corporation accepted bribes for influence peddling (a deep freeze and a mink coat became the symbols of federal corruption). The Justice Department obstructed congressional investigations. Truman only reluctantly fired the guilty. And he gained little popular sympathy by contrasting the giveaway of billions of oil rights with the minuscule value of a deep freeze.

The governmental scandals combined with widespread stories of corruption in many spheres of American life, including sports scandals at the City College of New York, the University of Kentucky, and even among football players at West Point. National attention centered on juvenile delinquency, and on the widespread political influence of organized crime (revealed in sensational television hearings conducted by Senator Estes Kefauver of Tennessee). The hearings implicated many political machines, mostly Democratic, and helped vaguely focus all the apprehensions about moral decay on Truman and on his party. The tinge of scandal, the unpopularity of the Korean War, and widespread doubts about internal security, all helped defeat the Democratic candidate in 1952 and end a twenty-year period of Democratic ascendancy. The concern over internal security, so omnipresent in the early fifties, so perplexing and so full of possible meaning in retrospect, deserves extended treatment.

25

In the insecure years between 1947 and 1953 millions of Americans joined their fear of Soviet military aggression with an equally intense, at times almost hysterical, fear of Soviet or "Communist" subversion at home. The issues of internal security and of loyalty to "our side" or to a vague "Americanism" proved irresistible to politicians at both the national and local level. For many Republicans, who had long suffered from veiled Democratic charges of "softness" toward fascism or toward neofascist industrialists (a minor theme of Roosevelt's 1944 campaign against Dewey), the abrupt postwar shift in ideological devils proved a godsend. Many Republicans seized the opportunity, and with some political success tried to prove Democratic "softness" toward communism and to establish some identity between communism abroad and New Deal, or "liberal," or "socialist" programs at home. In defense, the Truman administration took a tougher stand toward the Soviet Union in its foreign policy and inaugurated stringent loyalty programs for federal employees. Defensive Democrats, particularly those who had been in the forefront of New Deal fiscal and welfare innovations, had to spend much time and energy in anti-Communist avowals or in cold war posturing.

What realities lay behind the security and loyalty issues? This is not easy to answer because of all the conceptual subtleties that haunt such emotional issues. One problem was security. Governmental employees charged with important duties, or trusted with information the government deems secret, have to be reliable. An employee in a responsible position who is vulnerable to monetary bribes, mental illness, alcoholism, drugs, compromising sexual liaisons (or other blackmail susceptibilities), would constitute a security risk. "Disloyalty" or susceptibility to the philosophical or moral enticements of an enemy state or a competing ideology is yet another facet of the larger problem of security.

By simple definition, a "loyal" person gives his highest political allegiance to his own country, however much he wants to change its beliefs or institutions. Loyalty does not require the acceptance of the status quo. A completely loyal person may even sympathize with the beliefs or institutions of an enemy state. Presumably, many Americans throughout

The Problem of Loyalty

492

Loyalty and Scapegoats

World War II sympathized with certain Nazi tenets, including an extreme anti-Semitism, yet supported the American war effort. However, ethnic or ideological areas of commonality with an enemy state do give rise to warranted suspicions of disloyalty, as evidenced by the World War II treatment of American citizens of Japanese ancestry. However blameworthy he was for that treatment, one could scarcely condemn Roosevelt for denying positions of trust to avowed fascists, although one might question his efforts to stigmatize someone like Lindbergh. Likewise, during the cold war years one could hardly expect the government to place avowed Marxists or Communists in sensitive positions, although such individuals need not be disloyal, unless loyalty be so narrowly defined as to require commitments not only to country but also to some of its existing institutions or, even, to its existing government and policies. If so narrowly defined, loyalty in itself precludes basic and fundamental disagreement with the existing order and any radical efforts to gain changes in the form of government or the economic system. The more zealous advocates of "Americanism" usually pushed the meaning of "loyalty" to such extremes.

By its very purpose, any governmental effort to guarantee the security or, even more, the loyalty of its employees has to involve predictive judgments—what will a person do in a hypothetical situation? What crimes will he commit? The evidence for such judgments may well be past behavior, but this behavior is not itself on trial. Thus past criminal activity, long since paid for by fine or imprisonment, may preclude security clearance for certain positions in government. Past beliefs or associations may likewise determine the decision, and in a major way help or hinder one's whole career. Thus a security decision, which may blight a person's entire life, does not permit the procedural safeguards of a criminal indictment, however careful and conscientious the clearance process. This means that the problems of security and loyalty relate closely to the problem of individual rights. When disloyalty, with all its ambiguities, its emotional overtones, its susceptibility to subjective judgments and parochial prejudices, becomes the prime criteria of security, then even more does it threaten civil liberties long celebrated by Americans as the highest end of government. In other words, an inordinate concern over loyalty may be a backdoor to tyranny. At the very least, loyalty checks and oaths raise quite profound policy and constitutional issues, issues that have endlessly occupied both Congress and the courts since World War II.

The cold war provided a perfect environment for renewed concern over security and loyalty, as well as for demagogic exploitation of these issues. The disillusionment over lost causes and blighted hopes, the complexities of foreign events, invited easy, comprehensive explanations and a search for scapegoats. Perhaps more important, the cold war policies of Truman reflected an uneasy compromise between contending and highly vocal minorities. There was no such consensus as in World War II. One large, incohesive group of Americans wanted a much harsher anti-Soviet and anti-Communist posture, including a preventive war against "world communism." A smaller and equally incohesive group, including many academicians, clearly opposed our inflexible cold war stance, retained some degree of sympathy both for the Soviet Union and for Marxism, and desired a more conciliatory American policy. They provided targets for the other side. Finally, the "enemy" in the cold war was more than a foreign state, threatening us by its military or economic expansion—it was also a creed, an ideology, a quite different life-style, with the lingering evangelism of a recent revolution.

Fear of communism and other types of radicalism went back to the nineteenth century. The Soviet Revolution added fuel to frenzied efforts to suppress "radicals." In the loyalty crusades of World War I and its immediate aftermath Americans revealed their inability to deal intelligently with ideological differences. They indiscriminately merged anarchists, syndicalists, Marxists of various hues, mild American socialists, and even militant labor organizers, often under the loose label of "bolsheviks." But the most hysterical fears subsided in the twenties, leaving only a generalized anti-Communist feeling. During the thirties ideological labels became fuzzy, while policy issues generated the most intense controversy. Different "radicalisms" rose and fell. The thousands of writers, students, and labor leaders who openly joined the American Communist party faced intense resentment but few legal disabilities. Many held high government positions; the civil service did not screen on ideological grounds. The Communist Popular Front of the mid-thirties made such "radicalism" even more respectable. The tolerance quickly evaporated in 1939 and 1940, with the Soviet-Nazi pact and the Russo-Finnish war. The first legal restraints date from this period. But then our wartime alliance with the Soviet Union once again muted the heretical content of "communism" or of Marxist economic systems.

There was another, somewhat hidden side to the thirties. The political success of Roosevelt, the frightening reality of New Deal programs, created an intensely bitter and horrified minority, sure by World War II that the very soul of the country had been sold out to a foreign type of radicalism of a liberal, or socialist, or communist variety (the labels are too imprecise for exact interpretation, and often blended together as if synonymous). Roosevelt was their devil; the New Deal a form of hell. A quite vague but vocal coterie of Roosevelt haters, of people fearful of any major social change, clung almost desperately to the loyalty issue after 1947, and gladly joined in a highly emotional crusade, not only against the somewhat elusive Communists but also against the still-powerful image of Roosevelt, the new welfare policies, "liberals" of all stripes, the sophistries of academics, and anyone still anxious to make basic changes in America—from striking labor unions to "uppity" Negroes.

Slowly, even during the unifying crusade of World War II, this vague minority (call it the Right) regained some degree of political power and respectability through the emergence of the Republican party, through the continued power of Deep South Democrats, through Roosevelt's sacrifice of earlier social goals in behalf of wartime unity. By war's end the very labels "New Deal" and "liberal," imprecise as they remained, symbolized for many a type of radicalism, or socialism, or things vaguely "un-American." This minority of the Right had justice on their side. They resented the unfair political tactics of Roosevelt, his successful prostitution of traditional moral and political icons for his own political uses, his masterful use of power and persuasion to gain partisan victories, his dramatic use of class rhetoric to win votes, his continuous insinuations that opponents of the New Deal were somehow unprincipled, selfish, or even un-American. The New Deal created enduring political cleavages which, through time, took on more ideological meaning. The losers now rejoiced at the opportunity to reverse the odds, to use the same tactics on the other side, to put down all the smug and pompous New Dealers.

The earliest concrete effort to contain "communism" and other foreign ideologies came just before World War II. Through the alliance of both antifascist and anti-Communist factions, the House of Representatives in 1938 established a seven-member House Committee on Un-American Activities (HCUA) to investigate foreign propaganda and attacks on our basic form of government. Under the leadership of Martin Dies of Texas, HCUA followed the pattern of so many other congressional committees of the thirties by directing its intimidating and well-advertised inquiry at the German Bund and, much more assiduously, at Communist influences in labor unions, strikes, the American Civil Liberties Union, and in New Deal agencies.

The Hatch Act of 1939 not only regulated the political activities of government employees, but for the first time made loyalty to the United States a condition of employment, and prohibited employees from belonging to any party or organization committed to the overthrow of our constitutional form of government. In a few cases such "loyalty" screening probably determined the employment decision, but such screening was quite cursory compared to that instituted after World War II. After 1940 the military services had congressional authority to dismiss "security risks," a category much broader than belief of loyalty. Finally, in 1940 Congress approved the Smith Act, which for the first time made not only revolutionary or seditious activity illegal, but also the advocacy of such or, in what eventually became a pat phrase, advocacy of the forceful overthrow of the government of the United States. The first significant prosecution under the act came after the end of the war, when, in a 5 to 4 decision the Supreme Court upheld the conviction of a group of Communist party members (the Dennis case). During the Truman years the Court adhered rather consistently to the favorite New Deal tactic—judicial restraint—and thus did not readily or often overturn congressional acts, even in areas related to civil liberties. The Warren Court, under Eisenhower, would reverse this restraint, and either disallow a large proportion of the anti-Communist legislation or neutralize its effectiveness.

In its broadest sense, "security" was a vital issue in World War II; loyalty was not. Except for a few efforts to suppress a handful of known Nazi sympathizers (and most of these efforts ran aground in the courts), the concern during World War II was overt Axis espionage, directly controlled from abroad. But the war did lay the groundwork for many postwar fears. Intelligence operations reached a new level of importance and sophistication. The Manhattan Project, and therefore atomic energy, invited the most rigorous secrecy in our history and thus helped create much of our security program. When American-Soviet relations deteriorated in 1946, and the Soviet Union rejected our plans for international control of atomic energy, we developed a near phobia about the bomb. What if the Soviet Union stole our secrets? Useless was the continued warning by scientists that the Soviet Union could have the bomb in a matter of years—without stealing any secrets.

The cold war, on one level, was an unending battle between American and Soviet intelligence organizations. The Soviet Union, secretive and suspicious, used cooperative Communist party members in the West as intelligence agents throughout the war and beyond. We undoubtedly sought secret information about Russia. In the cold war years the Soviet Union seemed to enjoy the espionage game, particularly the small but necessarily clandestine side of it. The refugee camps in Germany became recruiting grounds for both American and Soviet agents. Our CIA joined its underground operations with those of the military intelligence units. We flooded Eastern Europe with agents, controlled and directed from the safety of our German and Austrian zones, and tied this espionage or positive intelligence with such major propaganda organs as Radio Free Europe, a CIA front. By every indication, the Soviet Union tried to reciprocate in kind, but they never had our sophistication. We won the intelligence war. To what advantage? Perhaps none at all. A no-secrets policy might have risked nothing and changed very little. But it would have spoiled all the fun. It would also have removed one of the few substantial reasons for our internal security effort—the occasionally realistic fear that disloyal employees would cooperate with Soviet intelligence gathering operations.

The first major revelation of Soviet espionage in the United States came in the spring of 1945. Two well-placed State Department employees and a naval intelligence officer apparently helped pass secret documents to a pro-Communist periodical (the *Amerasis* case), although possibly without any harmful intent. In part out of deference to Soviet wartime sensibilities, the Roosevelt administration delayed both arrests and prosecution, which later gave to the case magnified implications. The first publicity came in 1946. In that year the Canadian government gained knowledge of a major atomic espionage ring from a code clerk in the Soviet Embassy at Ottawa. This information eventually led to the arrest of Klaus Fuchs in England, Julius and Ethel Rosenberg and several associates in the United States. The federal courts convicted the Rosenbergs and, after appeals to the Supreme Court and well-organized and humane appeals from around the world, finally secured their execution in 1953. This espionage ring shocked Americans, created the first major demands for improved internal security, and fanned growing fantasies about a major Communist fifth column in the United States.

In 1946 and 1947 Congress considered several internal security bills, which forced a response from Truman. His new loyalty program grew out of extensive hearings by a temporary presidential commission. The commission tried to estimate the severity of the loyalty problem, but found that witnesses varied in their judgments in almost exact proportion to their political and ideological commitments. Representatives of the military intelligence agencies revealed unbelievable political naïveté and seemed to define disloyalty as some type of "liberalism." Even the FBI, which had already mounted a thorough surveillance of potentially "disloyal" employees, seemed to confuse disloyalty with leftist political commitments. It asked for a more rigorous screening. Under existing civil service regulations, over 700 employees had suffered loyalty investigations; only 24 lost their positions, and apparently many of these on "security" rather than "loyalty" grounds.

The growing concern with loyalty contributed to the rapid decline of the American Communist party, particularly as an open organization. In fact, left-wing movements as a whole had their last great stand in the

Wallace candidacy of 1948. Internal purges and the provisions of the Taft-Hartley Act drove most Communists from their major power base in unions. Few respected writers or academics remained in the party beyond the war, or even maintained contact with related organizations or publications. In the thirties, and even during the war, both Communist party members and sympathetic Marxists held important government positions. Some of the most able and dedicated officials in the Department of Agriculture had been party members. But not by 1947, for by then no avowed party member held a high government office; some may still have held low-level and nonsensitive civil service positions. The FBI surely had detailed knowledge about even these. Thus, in some ways, the new loyalty program came at the very time it seemed least justified. Political motives, a misinformed public opinion, and the myopic zeal of investigative agencies produced it.

Truman established the Loyalty Review Boards by Executive Order on March 12, 1947. The program remains in effect today. Its avowed purpose was the elimination of all disloyal employees in order to protect all loyal employees from unfounded accusations. The order provided for an elaborate loyalty check of all new government employees to be carried out by the Civil Service Commission with the needed assistance of the FBI. In addition, the head of each agency or department was responsible for determining and certifying the loyalty of all existing employees, again through civil service and FBI record checks. Each agency had to establish a loyalty review board to hold hearings for any employee charged with disloyalty. The accused could have counsel and invite witnesses, but could not face accusers or force investigators to reveal the source of their information. Finally, the accused had the right to appeal any final verdict to a National Loyalty Review Board in the Civil Service Commission, but it could only render an advisory decision. The final arbiter of loyalty was the agency itself, which in effect meant small, local branches of the federal bureaucracy. The decentralization later invited parochial and extremely arbitrary standards in some agencies and in some areas of the country. Quite frequently, involvement in civil rights activities made one "disloyal" in the eyes of some regional boards.

Truman's order contained a definition of "disloyalty," and thus should have lessened the arbitrariness of local boards. Yet, the definition failed to meet the criteria of most civil libertarians. The basis of dismissal was "reasonable grounds for belief," not proof, which admittedly would be almost impossible to obtain in such an intangible area as loyalty. Indicative activities and associations included such obvious and usually criminal acts as treason, sabotage, and espionage. But the order also listed "advocacy of revolution or force or violence to alter the constitutional form of government of the United States," a quite ambiguous and sweeping criteria. Finally, and eventually most significant, disloyalty included "membership in, affiliation with or sympathetic association with any foreign or domestic organization, association, movement, group or combination of persons, designated by the Attorney General as totalitarian, Communist, or subversive, or as having adopted a policy of advocating or approving the commission of acts or force or violence to deny other persons their rights under the Constitution of the United States, or as seeking to alter the form of government of the United States by unconstitutional means." The order did not prescribe a loyalty oath. But most states soon enacted their own junior loyalty programs, often with even fewer safeguards, more sweeping language, and mandatory loyalty oaths. For these local boards, and for a growing number of loyalty sleuths, each with a card file and vague and mysterious hints of momentous conspiracies, the attorney general's list of "subversive" organizations became a bible, an infallible authority. Membership in a "listed" organization, even in the distant past, not only precluded state employment but often made one subject to numerous private "blacklists." And here there was no appeal.

The Congressional Role

The shape of the future appeared in the congressional investigations of 1948. A large spectrum of congressmen either sincerely believed in a domestic Communist threat, or exploited the issue for its political appeal. In early 1948 a large minority in the Senate held up, and almost blocked, David Lilienthal's appointment as chairman of the new Atomic Energy Commission, turning their antipathy for a "socialistic" TVA into emotional charges of "softness" toward communism. The HCUA, still the acknowledged leader in a growing Communist hunt, directed its hearings away from government employees and into the extent of Communist influence in the whole society, particularly in labor unions and in Hollywood. Here it found some authentic devils. It soon acquired a stable of ex-Communists willing and even anxious to perform in its well-publicized hearings. Of these, by far the most articulate, and possibly the most ethical, was Whittaker Chambers. At war's end he had accused a former State Department officer, Alger Hiss, of passing secret documents to Soviet agents during the Popular Front thirties. Few had believed his charge. But in the summer of 1948 he gave the fullest details to HCUA. In the midst of the campaign Truman denounced the House committee and referred to Chambers's charge as a "red herring." For a time the charge remained just that—an unsubstantiated accusation by an ex-Communist against a former cell member (the force of his charge against Hiss was espionage, a criminal offense, and not membership in the party).

After the election the Hiss case regained national headlines. A young California congressman, Richard Nixon, came to believe Chambers, and assumed a prosecutor's role in the committee. Before HCUA Hiss completely denied Chambers's accusations, and even sued for slander. But Chambers produced microfilm documents from a pumpkin on his Maryland farm that purportedly proved his espionage charges. In December 1948, Hiss was indicted for perjury (the statute of limitations prevented an espionage indictment). In his defense, Hiss produced such prominent character witnesses as Justice Felix Frankfurter and Adlai Stevenson of Illinois. The first jury hung. A second, impressed by compelling evidence involving a typewriter, convicted Hiss in January 1950.

Although the Hiss conviction reflected its only tangible vindication, HCUA did not relent in its investigations. The Hiss case did not involve a government employee (only a past one), but the long trial paralleled the dark days in which China "fell" and the Soviet Union exploded its first bomb. Surely, somewhere in the interstices of a newly conspiratorial State Department there were other Hisses, traitors who had cleverly guided

Young Representative Richard M. Nixon (1913–) reading to reporters Whittaker Chambers's testimony that Alger Hiss, former State Department official, gave him "restricted" government documents that were relayed to Russia. The case became known as the "Pumpkin Papers" case because of the microfilm Chambers produced from a pumpkin from his Maryland farm. *Wide World Photos*

policies so as to aid the Communists. Surely Russia stole the bomb secrets through the aid of its American cadres. Ironically, a State Department that had pushed a harsh policy toward the Soviet Union, and a Dean Acheson who had, more than anyone else, matured the containment policy and won support for it in Congress, became the devils in a new morality play. The climactic act was just ahead. McCarthy was in the wings.

Joseph McCarthy

However minimal the justification, however callous the political exploitation, the congressional fears of an ill-defined communism had been sincere. With Joseph McCarthy, a first-term senator from Wisconsin, the search for domestic Communists seemed to become a deliberate political

Grim-visaged Alger Hiss, homeward bound on a New York City subway train, ignores headlines telling of the latest developments in his court case. On January 25, 1950, Hiss was sentenced to five years in prison for perjury, the statute of limitations on espionage having already run out. *Wide World Photos*

game played with a degree of detachment that matched its careful calculation. But possibly even this judgment presumes too much about a tremendously strange and troubled man. McCarthy, a youth of average ability, grew up in rural Wisconsin, with great effort won a law degree from Marquette University, and then opportunistically switched his political allegiance from the Democratic to the Republican party, serving before the war as an elected circuit judge. He had an undistinguished war record in the Marine Corps, but came back to Wisconsin ready and willing to magnify his wartime exploits. As "Tail-Gunner Joe," he took on a favored Robert La Follette, Jr., in the 1946 Senate race, and won in the heavy swing toward the Republicans. As senator he seemed retiring, and voted as a moderate Republican, sensitive to the economic intersts of his own state. He first gained at least a smattering of information about alleged Communist subversion in America from a professor at Georgetown University. Whatever his exact motives, he decided to do something about it.

On February 9, 1950, McCarthy addressed a Lincoln Day dinner in Wheeling, West Virginia. During the address he claimed to have in his hand a list of 205 State Department employees known by the secretary of state (he apparently used information from former Secretary Byrnes and not existing Secretary Acheson) to be members of the Communist party. In subsequent speeches he reduced the number to fifty-seven, and hedged on whether they were "card-carrying" Communists or simply loyal to the party. His shocking allegation at first received little national publicity. Before the Senate he again tried to make good his claim, but actually identified several people never in the State Department, some long-since departed, and some who in no sense qualified as Communists. He ended with charges against no more than eight employees. But all his pleading gained him immense publicity. His reckless charges frightened even certified "anti-Communists" by their very exaggeration. But apparently millions of Americans wanted to be persuaded, to find an answer to all the seemingly disastrous reversals in foreign policy. They rallied to McCarthy. He loved their adulation and all the headlines. For his fans, all queries about facts, all challenges to his exaggerations, only proved his emerging point—the Communists were out to get him. Soon he seemed to believe his most paranoiac attacks on critics, and recklessly and often viciously attacked men of prominence, regardless of their political position or party identification (yet, in private contexts, he remained genial and seemed to have no personal animosities to match his public vitriol).

To stop McCarthy, Democrats in the Senate launched an investigation of his charges, hoping full exposure would destroy his appeal. Senator Millard E. Tydings of Maryland, a "conservative" whom Roosevelt tried

Senator Joseph McCarthy (1908–1957) cross-examining a witness during the army-McCarthy hearings. The hearings were an outgrowth of aide Roy Cohn's (left) attempt to secure special treatment in the army for his friend David Schine. *Wide World Photos*

c em-
vatch-
s. The

he table
on rally,
who is
f the oil

ver. The
or good
ks of oil
mpanies
e's blue-

the cor-
pension
y before

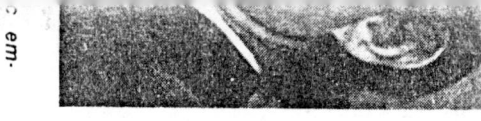

'60 Minutes' Dusts Off McCarthy Myth

By WILLIAM A. RUSHER

Some stories are just too good to stop telling, even when we find out they aren't true. Parson Weems' tale of young George Washington and the cherry tree is one such favorite; another is that old chestnut about Sen. Joe McCarthy and Annie Lee Moss. CBS' "60 Minutes" dusted off the latter recently and treated a fresh generation to this edifying tale. As told by CBS, through the simple device of replaying Edward R. Murrow's famous 1954 television broadcast on the subject, it goes like this:

Once upon a time there lived, in the faraway city of Washington, a fire-breathing dragon named Sen. Joseph McCarthy. One day, having nothing better to do, he hauled before a committee of which he was chairman an elderly black lady named Annie Lee Moss, who eked out a slender living by emptying wastebaskets in the Code Room at the Pentagon. McCarthy recklessly accused this good woman of being a Communist!

Her voice quavered as she responded to Sen. Symington, another member of

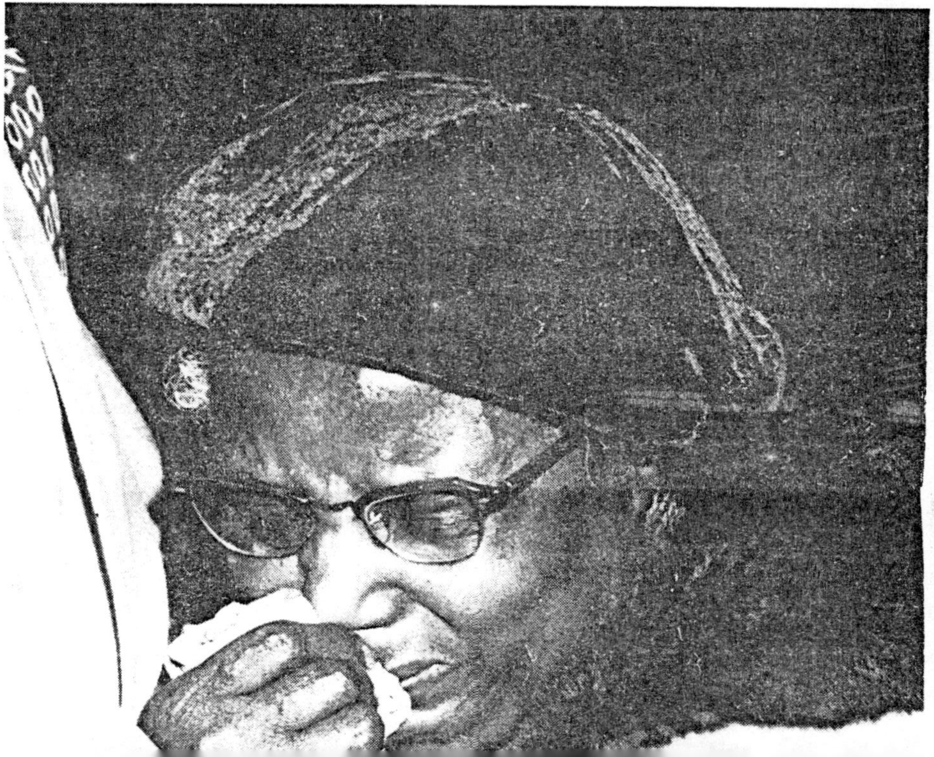

It seemed all too clear that the poor old soul was out of her depth; there had been, at the very least, some awful case of mistaken identity. It was the sort of casually ruthless thing McCarthy did all the time.

Mrs. Moss was temporarily excused by Sen. McCarthy when she broke down during her testimony on Feb. 25, 1954.

There, children! Now go upstairs to bed, shivering perhaps just a little, as your parents did a quarter of a century ago, at man's inhumanity to man.

Unfortunately for Parson Weems and Edward R. Murrow, however, the Muse of History has a way of doubling back and casting ugly doubts on these lovely old stories. In the case of Annie Lee Moss, dawn began to break in the late 1950s, when an FBI informant in the Communist party provided the authorities with a list of party members filched from the party's own records. On that list, clearly recorded as a Communist party member in the 1940s, was the name "Annie Lee Moss."

Well! Great was the uproar in anti-McCarthy circles. For, although the dragon had been dead for over a year, guards were posted over his grave 24 hours a day to make sure he didn't emerge to ravage the earth again.

Luckily the Washington phone books for September 1953 and September 1954, covering the period of Mrs. Moss' testimony, listed an "Anna Lee Moss," and an "Annie L. Moss." And by late 1958, when McCarthy's tireless critics got around to muddying the waters, there was even a third, listed simply as "Annie Moss." Here, surely, was ambiguity enough to perpetuate the exculpation of that old black dustwoman Ed Murrow had all but wept over back in 1954. It probably was—it must have been—just a case of mistaken identity.

Ah, but it wasn't. On March 11, 1954, Roy Cohn, counsel to McCarthy's committee, had asked Mrs. Moss: "...isn't it a fact that you regularly received the *Daily Worker*...?" To which the witness had replied, "[not] until after we had moved Southwest, at 72 R Street."

From Subversive Activities Control Board Docket No. 51-101, Recom-mended Decision of Board Member Francis A. Cherry on Second Remand Proceeding, Issued Sept. 19, 1958, Page 5, Footnote 6: "The situation that has resulted on the Moss question is that the [Communist] party's own records, copies of which are now in evidence, and the authenticity of which it does not dispute (A. G. Exs. 499-511, inc.), show an Annie Lee Moss, 72 R Street, S.W., Washington, D.C., was a party member in the mid-1940s."

The really frightening thing about all this is what it tells us about the quality of the information being shoveled at our young people, who cannot possibly remember the 1950s because they simply weren't around then. The Moss myth has been inscribed upon the tablets of American liberalism, and it will echo down time's corridors as indifferent to mere veracity as any random page of the Soviet Encyclopedia.

Pass the word, and guard the truth.

Universal Press Syndicate

to purge in 1938, chaired the committee. The investigation succeeded in one level—it almost completely dissipated his charges. In fact, every single State Department employee met the now stringent loyalty criteria. None could be legally dismissed. But in another sense the hearings gave added support to McCarthy. He was able to indict those in or out of the State Department who were responsible for our China policy. He rested his case on two men. One, Philip C. Jessup, was ambassador-at-large, a long-time State Department official, and an expert on Far Eastern affairs. He had testified for Hiss and, even more critical for McCarthy, had connections with the Institute of Pacific Relations, a private, academic organization that had sponsored a wide spectrum of research and publication on the Far East, some of it, consistent with the political views of more "leftist" members, quite sympathetic to the Chinese Communists.

After Jessup defended himself before the committee (he could not undo the harm to his career, or the increasing anxiety of other career diplomats), McCarthy turned on Owen Lattimore of the Johns Hopkins University. For McCarthy's purposes, Lattimore was an excellent target. A renowned Mongolian scholar, he had never worked for the State Department but had served in the Office of War Information during the war, and had advised the Wallace mission to China in 1944. No one produced evidence that Lattimore was ever a member of the Communist party, but he admitted his own sympathies with some of the Chinese Communist policies, and acknowledged his past friendship with prominent Communists. He had clearly sympathized with revolutionary movements in Asia in his academic work, a stance not unfamiliar or in any way suspect among a small group of scholars in his highly specialized field. Even McCarthy withdrew charges of overt espionage by Lattimore, but still managed to leave an impression that Lattimore, almost singlehandedly, had been the architect of a disaster in China, working through Hiss and uncounted other Communist accessories in the State Department, and abetted by such "soft" officials as Jessup and Secretary Acheson.

By the election of 1950 McCarthy was a divisive national issue. His obvious popularity made him an embarrassment for the Truman administration. He seemed an enticing even if treacherous asset to aspiring candidates looking for campaign issues. Truman seriously contemplated a new commission to investigate the government loyalty program. Cautious Republican congressmen, formerly frightened by McCarthy's excesses, began to hedge their remarks and at least applaud his purposes if not his tactics. A coterie of congressmen from both parties tried to capitalize on McCarthy's success; some almost outdid McCarthy (in particular William E. Jenner of Indiana, Karl Mundt of South Dakota, Francis P. Walter of Pennsylvania, Pat McCarran of Nevada, and Richard Nixon of

California). It was Jenner who first led a vicious attack on General George C. Marshall, whom Truman appointed as secretary of defense in September 1950. In the fall elections McCarthy helped fake photographs of Senator Tydings and Communist party leader Earl Browder; Tydings lost to an undistinguished Republican opponent. Carefully exploiting the Communist issue, Everett Dirksen of Illinois ousted a leading Truman Democrat from the Senate. In California, Richard Nixon successfully used charges of "leftist" sympathies to defeat the "Pink Lady," Helen G. Douglas. It is, of course, impossible to know the degree to which the Communist issue, or support for McCarthy, influenced the vote in such critical elections. But clearly, on the surface, it seemed profitable to be on McCarthy's side.

The Legislative Climax

Even before the election Congress presented Truman with unwanted internal security legislation (the McCarran Act). As early as 1947 the Justice Department had recommended tighter antisubversive legislation, but its drastic proposals (blanket wire-tapping authority for the FBI and the military services, the use of such evidence in courts, and espionage liability for the innocent passing to another of national defense information) ran aground on the opposition of civil libertarians in other government departments. Truman did not oppose antisubversion laws, but showed consistent concern over blatant violations of civil liberties.

In 1949 administration leaders introduced a modified Justice Department bill, still stringent but with enough safeguards to meet Truman's objections. Already in 1948 the House had passed the Mundt-Nixon bill, which stiffened existing espionage legislation, required all Communist organizations to register with the attorney general, provided for a Subversive Activities Control Board to designate such organizations, and denied to members of subversive organizations such traditional privileges as passports, the use of the United States mail for any material not labeled "Communist Propaganda," and, most important, any type of federal or private defense employment. By 1950 a version of this bill seemed sure to pass. The administration failed in its attempt to get a milder substitute. Even Truman's own Justice Department supported features of the stronger bill. By introducing the bill in the Senate, Pat McCarran of Nevada gave his name to the final product.

The McCarran Act represented the legislative peak of our domestic anti-Communist campaign. After careful study, Truman vetoed it. Congress, sensitive to voter opinion in an election year, almost immediately overrode his veto (in the House by 286 to 48; in the Senate by 57 to 10). Truman wrote one of his most extensive and carefully argued veto messages, and then failed to get Congress to give it the attention it deserved. In part, he objected to the practical damage the bill could do to existing security programs, and thus argued, a bit sophistically, that the legislation really aided the Communists. The registration requirement, and the exclusion from defense work, would only drive Communists underground. Enforcement would require immense time and effort by the Department of Justice and force an open identification of defense industries.

But Truman made his most eloquent appeal on libertarian grounds. He argued that the language requiring registration was so broad and vague as to penalize legitimate activities by loyal citizens (later the Supreme Court would agree with this judgment), and would be so difficult to enforce that only years of legal action could lead to the definition of a single organization as either Communist or a Communist front (again, he was correct), and that even then such an organization would not register (none ever did). The whole attempt to control such unwanted organizations would mark the greatest threat to speech, press, and assembly since the Alien and Sedition Acts. It meant the imposition of thought control, of official efforts to control political expression. He believed stringent new rules for the admission of aliens would exclude people badly needed for defense and for intelligence purposes, including businessmen and officials from "totalitarian" countries friendly to the United States. Finally, the act gave the federal government power, in time of invasion or insurrection, to seize and hold innocent persons *expected* to attempt espionage or sabotage, a power that any government would probably exercise in fact, but a license for action that violated several hallowed traditions.

The hunt for subversives continued in Truman's last two years of office. Both the HCUA and the Internal Security Subcommittee of the Senate Judiciary Committee (McCarthy's Committee) investigated almost continuously. McCarthy, at times peeved by the ability of others to exploit the Communist issue, sought ever more newsworthy targets. In June 1951, he openly and violently attacked General Marshall, and then moved to other people close to Truman. Truman's 1951 removal of General Douglas MacArthur proved a new stimulant to the connoisseurs of chaos. MacArthur seemed to insure a domestic leader of the anti-Communist crusade, and to provide the Republicans with a perfect candidate in 1952. Public airing, and time, diminished his appeal. Truman tried to coopt the whole issue by a major public investigation. He appointed a high-level Commission on Internal Security and Individual Rights (headed by Admiral Chester Nimitz) in 1951, only to have Congress sabotage it by refusing legislation to exempt members from the conflict-of-interest rules for federal employees (this is a normal courtesy for such commissions, and a necessary one for attracting the best private talent).

The State Department remained the focus of dissatisfaction—especially Dean Acheson, the worst devil in the Truman administration. In late 1951 the Senate blocked the appointment of Philip Jessup to a United Nations post. The Senate, behind its immunity, aired charges that another State Department official, John Carter Vincent, was a Communist. Pressed because of memories of the old *Amerasia* case, the State Department Loyalty Review Board finally ruled against John S. Service (he won reinstatement from the courts). Almost everyone in the State Department connected with Far Eastern affairs seemed vulnerable to attack in Congress. Morale remained low; many long-time employees sought other careers.

Congress enacted the last major security legislation—the McCarran-Walters Immigration Act—in the summer of 1952. It retained the national origins quotas (despite Truman's recommendations), and immensely stiffened the ideological requirements for entry into the country (it later posed severe restrictions on the humane refugee program of the Eisenhower administration). On the same grounds it made naturalized citizens vulnerable to denaturalization; resident aliens subject to deportation. Finally, it permitted a detailed search and interrogation of returning American citizens. The State Department had already stiffened the rules for securing passports and visas. Truman vetoed the new immigration act; Congress gleefully overrode.

Loyalty and the 1952 Election

Loyalty was an issue in the 1952 campaign, particularly in many congressional races and also in muted form at the presidential level. But loyalty issues hardly determined the outcome. Truman left a hard legacy—scandals, an interminable war, domestic bitterness—for his would-be successor, Adlai Stevenson of Illinois. Even the urbanity of Stevenson, as that of Acheson, fed the know-nothing and nativistic elements that made up such a large part of the anti-Communist crusade. Eisenhower did not need demagoguery or highly emotional issues. He preferred milder platitudes, less controversial generalities. He neither claimed nor repudiated the McCarthy wing of the party. He rarely attacked Truman's foreign policy or his loyalty program. In a loose way he gave support to party slogans that condemned "socialism" or chanted "Korea, communism, and corruption." And, of course, his vice-presidential candidate, Richard Nixon, was a symbol of anticommunism. But Ike's smile, his record, and his popularity won the election.

At a national level, Eisenhower's election undercut the loyalty issue. Many of the wildest accusations had reflected the freedom, and often the irresponsibility, of those out of power. When, in a sense, their side won, their issue both won and evaporated. Vaguely, Republicans could still talk of past Democratic lapses, or still seek Communists well outside the federal bureaucracy, but they could hardly condemn Eisenhower's State Department. Also, the loyalty issue had been bipartisan, as names such as McCarran and Walters testify. The congressional investigations would continue throughout the fifties. In 1954 Democrats would take the lead in enacting a new Communist Control Act, which practically outlawed the Communist party. The federal and state loyalty boards would continue to function, although soon under closer court supervision.

Only McCarthy refused to bow to political changes. He tried the near impossible—to convince Americans that Eisenhower's bureaucracy still harbored Communists. He even took on the army, accusing it of softness toward communism for giving an honorable discharge to a dentist with past Communist connections. The general in charge refused to give full details before McCarthy's Senate Subcommittee, and the army in turn charged McCarthy with seeking preferential treatment for one of his young assistants. National television carried the army hearings and saw McCarthy in his crudest and cruelest moments. In December 1954, the Senate censured McCarthy. He faded from the headlines, crushed and ill, and died in 1957.

The Decline of Anticommunism

In the perspective of twenty years, the McCarthy era (for such it has become, and in this perverse way a publicity-seeking McCarthy gained a quite unintended type of immortality) still awaits our full understanding. The swift shift in ideological alignments after the war created an intimidating atmosphere. The repeated charges and accusations established a climate of opinion quite hostile to anyone who was, or ever had been, a Marxist, a Communist party member, or even unduly sympathetic with the Soviet Union. Ideological politics did not originate in the Truman administration. Neither did the political exploitation of disloyalty and un-Americanism. But the ideological component in American politics, the emphasis upon foreign creeds, was greater from 1947 to 1953 than at any time since the election of 1800.

Even yet it is impossible to find the exact lay of meaning in the word "communism" as used in the postwar years. It carried intense emotional connotations but varied denotations, some scarcely related either to Marxism or to Soviet policies. The very public concern helped camouflage the most critical issues at stake. Rarely did even the accused escape the atmosphere of guilt. Part of the atmosphere came from the role of "self-confessed" (note the words) former Communists. Being a Communist of any variety or at any time in the past, seemed to call for confession and repentance. Thus those who were indeed "innocent" (note the word) tried desperately to prove their innocence. Their jobs, their public reputations, were at stake. They had no compelling reason to say "so what," and every reason to say "no, no," and by the intensity of their denial further reinforce the prevailing, rhetorical orthodoxy. Actual, unrepentant, identified Communist party members rarely came before either loyalty boards or congressional committees. They had long since operated far from government agencies or even defense industries. But when the "guilty" (note the word) came before the committees, they faced self-incrimination under the Smith Act and, for this reason or out of principle, took the Fifth Amendment (refused to testify against themselves). Former party members, or many others who had joined front organizations, wanted to put this past behind them. They were often evasive, cringing, and ready to exploit legal technicalities. Thus, almost no witnesses rejected the atmosphere of guilt, or defended the right of an American to believe what he wanted or to join any political party he wished.

Back of this failure to confront the one vital issue at stake lay some of the realities of what could vaguely be called the American Left. There had been a considerable Communist party establishment in America, perhaps even more than many congressmen believed. Beyond the party there had been literally hundreds of small publications and small organizations closely related to the party and often used by it. The large list of front organizations assembled by the attorney general was essentially correct, at least when qualified by time designations. In their rough way, congressmen, through frustrating hearings, tried to bare this past or present reality, and in the voluminous records of the Senate and House Committees did record a wealth of accurate data on, as well as numerous fantasies about, Communist activities. In New York City, in labor unions, among literary groups, among students there had been a large apparatus. Surely it did not evaporate in 1947 or 1948. The legislators knew better; they saw its continued effectiveness in the Wallace campaign.

And to an extent that no one will ever be able to judge, this native Communist movement (if such it can be termed) had multiple and direct ties with the Soviet Union. The Communist party, for example, was never just a political party. To an extent it was always subservient to Moscow (but not all its members); at times its most dutiful functionaries acted as "agents" of a foreign power and directed espionage operations. This tie to the Soviet Union made everyone connected with the party peculiarly vulnerable. It helped blur two issues—belief and criminal activity. The very willingness of the American party to follow Moscow's bidding had compromised its "radical" edge, and betrayed the moral investment of many of its most idealistic members. The real "dupes," to use a word so prevalent in the hearings, had been those who allowed the party to channel their energies away from revolutionary politics, as in the Popular Front. The followers of Trotsky, for example, had often been much more consistent, and much more critical of American institutions, but in no sense Moscow-directed. These subtle issues escaped the congressmen, and left the issue of foreign espionage, or internal subversion at the command of a foreign power, mixed with the issue of extreme dissent, of unpopular belief, of efforts to achieve major economic and social change.

In one goal the crusade against Communists won. It effectively crushed the American Communist party and demoralized most of its fronts. But the crusading scythe was blunt. It cut down leftists of all types. In extreme cases, cruelty and suffering followed in its wake. The human costs remain beyond accounting. The absurdities stagger belief. One Hollywood writer went on the blacklist for taking a stand against fascism too early in the thirties. Loyalty boards in the South linked militant civil rights activities with subversion.

But change did come. In a drastically new environment, in a more accommodating atmosphere, a varied, youthful, and quite native Left would revive, with all its contradictions, its internal quarrels, its romantic dreams, and its persuasive criticism. It did not have the one critical vulnerability of the old; it had no foreign ties or dependency, although it often welcomed support from all quarters. This "new Left" made no sense to the old crusaders against communism. As congressional committees tried to cope with it, the congressmen looked as pathetic as the cringing witnesses of the fifties. The atmosphere of guilt could not be fabricated. When pulled before the House Un-American Activities Committee in the sixties, a group of college students seemed to have more fun than anything else. Charged with ideological sins, they neither took the Fifth Amendment nor looked guilty. Instead, they rejoiced in the political exposure and gleefully admitted any and every heresy. When to the query, "Are you a Communist?" a youthful, long-haired boy could reply, "Yeah, man!" and to the almost unanimous cheers of a friendly audience, the McCarthy era was finally over, doomed not by political opposition but by ridicule.

Bibliography

The literature on American foreign relations from 1933 to 1955 rivals in volume that on the New Deal. It seems to grow exponentially. It has also become sharply controversial, divided between defenders and critics of American policies. The most bitter debates involve an amorphous cold war, but others encompass the policies that preceded World War II and the strategies and diplomatic choices made during that war. The differences are primarily evaluative, and thus reflect variant beliefs and ideological assumptions on the part of historians, divergent sympathies for foreign countries or creeds, and quite different conceptions of what American goals should be, or what principles America should stand for in the world. Such differences insure all manner of confusion over standards of wisdom and morality, and invite easy semantic pitfalls. Almost always, disagreements over causes and consequences, which at least submit to difficult empirical resolution, intermingle with moral issues that remain unresolvable. The following reading suggestions thus require a special warning for students—be cautious, and be very, very suspicious.

Neutrality in the Thirties

The most careful, analytical study of American neutrality and noninterventionist thought is Selig Adler's *Isolationist Impulse: Its Twentieth Century Reaction* (New York: Collier, 1957). The most entertaining and readable account of the neutrality legislation of the thirties is in Robert A. Divine's *The Illusion of Neutrality* (Chicago: University of Chicago, 1962). His title reveals his lack of sympathy for noninterventionists or isolationists. A more restricted survey is Manfred Jones, *Isolationism in America, 1935–1941* (Ithaca: Cornell University Press, 1966). Dexter Perkins, in *America's Quest for Peace* (Bloomington: Indiana University Press, 1962) considers the broader goals of American diplomacy. So far, the noninterventionists have not received a very sympathetic treatment. But Wayne S. Cole at least presents a scrupulous, accurate account in *America First: The Battle Against Intervention, 1940–1941* (Madison: University of Wisconsin Press, 1953), and in *Senator Gerald P. Nye and American Foreign Relations* (Minneapolis: University of Minnesota Press, 1962). For a detailed account of the Nye Committee, see John E. Wiltz, *In Search of Peace: The Senate Munitions Inquiry, 1934–1936* (Baton Rouge: Louisiana State University Press, 1963). For two key tests of American neutrality, see Brice Harris, Jr., *The United States and the Italo-Ethiopian Crisis* (Stanford, Calif.: Stanford University Press, 1964) and Allen Guttman, *The Wound in the Heart: America and the Spanish Civil War* (New York: The Free Press, 1962).

The best account of the American involvement in the London Monetary Conference of 1933 is in Herbert Feis, *1933: Characters in Crisis* (Boston: Little, Brown, 1966); Raymond Moley gives his version in *After Seven Years* (New York: Harper and Brothers, 1939). An excellent account of the recognition of the Soviet Union is Edward Bennett, *Recognition of Russia: An American Foreign Policy Dilemma* (Waltham, Mass.: Blaisdale, 1970). For

511

early trade policies, see Edward Guerrant, *Roosevelt's Good Neighbor Policy* (Albuquerque: University of New Mexico Press, 1950).

For the broadest background, Foster Rhea Dulles's *America's Rise to World Power* (Boston: Houghton Mifflin, 1954) remains the classic. Equally balanced and meticulous is Selig Adler, *The Uncertain Giant: American Foreign Policy Between the Wars* (New York: Macmillan, 1965). By far the most detailed and useful survey of American foreign policy in the thirties is the semiofficial study by William L. Langer and S. Everett Gleason, *The World Crisis and American Foreign Affairs*, 2 vols. [I, *The Challenge to Isolation*; II, *The Undeclared War, 1940–1941* (New York: Harper and Row, 1952 and 1953)]. Their account is proadministration, but provides such a wealth of detail that a student can easily make his own evaluation. Less detailed, but equally approving of Roosevelt's policies is Herbert Feis, *The Road to Pearl Harbor* (Princeton, N.J.: Princeton University Press, 1950). Other sympathetic accounts are Robert A. Divine, *The Reluctant Belligerent: American Entry into World War II* (New York: Wiley, 1965); Allan Nevins, *The New Deal and World Affairs: A Chronicle of International Affairs* (New Haven, Conn.: Yale University Press, 1950); and Donald F. Drummond, *The Passing of American Neutrality* (Ann Arbor: University of Michigan Press, 1955). John E. Wiltz, *From Isolation to War, 1931–1941* (New York: Thomas Y. Crowell, 1968) offers the best brief survey of both issues and literature. Basil Rauch, in *Roosevelt: From Munich to Pearl Harbor* (New York: Creative Age Press, 1950) is almost an apologist for American policies.

There are many detailed, monographic studies of American diplomacy before the war. Only one, Lloyd C. Gardner, *Economic Aspects of New Deal Diplomacy* (Madison: University of Wisconsin Press, 1964), treats economic issues in detail, but it has a very critical, almost conspiratorial thesis. Two studies trace our relationship with Germany just before the war: Saul Friedlander, *Prelude to Downfall: Hitler and the United States, 1939–1941* (London: Chatto and Windus, 1967), and Hans L. Trefousse, *Germany and American Neutrality 1939–1941* (New York: Bookman Associates, 1951). Other topical studies are Dorothy Borg, *The United States and the Far Eastern Crisis of 1933–1938* (Cambridge, Mass.: Harvard University Press, 1964); Andrew J. Schwartz, *America and the Russo-Finnish War* (Washington: Public Affairs Press, 1960); and Warren F. Kimball, *The Most Unsordid Act: Lend-Lease, 1939–1941* (Baltimore: Johns Hopkins University Press, 1969).

Another approach to the events is through biography and memoirs. Cordell Hull presented his perspective on events in his *Memoirs of Cordell Hull*, 2 vols. (New York: Macmillan, 1948); matching this in size is Julius W. Pratt's two-volume biography, *Cordell Hull* (New York: Cooper Square, 1963). William E. Dodd gave a running commentary on European events in *Ambassador Dodd's Diary, 1933–1938* (New York: Harcourt, Brace, 1941). A central figure in our Asia policy was our ambassador to Japan, Joseph C. Grew. He published his own, often critical commentary on our Japanese policy in *Ten Years in Japan* (New York: Simon and Schuster, 1944). More revealing still are his papers, published by Walter Johnson as *Turbulent Era: A Diplomatic Record of Forty Years*, 2 vols. (Boston: Houghton Mifflin, 1952). His biographer is Waldo H. Heinrichs, *American Ambassador: Joseph C. Grew and the Development of the U.S. Diplomatic Tradition* (Boston: Little, Brown, 1966).

Very early, our entry into World War II provoked a body of revisionist or highly critical literature. Some of it was overtly conspiratorial: Roosevelt deceptively planned and plotted ways of getting us into an unnecessary or even disastrous war. Of the conspiratorial accounts, the following two, by eminent historians, have a continuing interest to historians; however unbelievable in their indictment, they still adhere to canons of evidence and scholarly integrity: Charles A. Beard, *American Foreign Policy in the Making, 1932–1940* (New Haven, Conn.: Yale University Press, 1946), and Charles C. Tansill, *Back Door to War: Roosevelt's Foreign Policy, 1933–1941* (Chicago: Henry Regnery, 1952). Without seeing any conspiracy, several historians have questioned the assumptions behind American policy toward both Germany and Japan. Two detailed analyses of German intentions help dissipate some of the theories of world conquest associated with Hitler: Alton Frye, *Nazi Germany and the American Hemisphere* (New Haven, Conn.: Yale University Press, 1967), and James Compton, *The Swastika and the Eagle: Hitler, the United States, and the Origins of World War II* (Boston: Houghton Mifflin, 1967). Bruce Russett defends a much more extreme view—that Hitler offered no threat at all to American security. See his *No Clear and Present Danger: A Skeptical View of U.S. Entry into World War II* (New York: Harper and Row, 1972). Even Grew felt the United States was overly inflexible in refusing opportunities for negotiation with Japan. This mildly revisionist judgment has probably become the prevailing position among recent historians. Representative of a more critical evaluation are Robert J. C. Botow, *Tojo and the Coming of the War* (Princeton, N.J.: Princeton University Press, 1962); Francis C. Jones, *Japan's New Order in East Asia: Its Rise and Fall, 1937–1945* (New York: Oxford University Press, 1954); and Paul W. Schroeder, *The Axis Alliance and Japanese-American Relations, 1941* (Ithaca, N.Y.: Cornell University Press, 1958).

A final issue was the Pearl Harbor attack, surrounded by controversy almost from its occurrence. A dramatic account is Walter Lord, *Day of Infamy* (New York: Holt, Rinehart and Winston, 1957). More detailed studies include Roberta Wohlstetter, *Pearl Harbor: Warning and Decision* (Stanford, Calif.: Stanford University Press, 1962), and Adolph A. Hoehling, *The Week Before Pearl Harbor* (New York: W. W. Norton, 1963). A provocative but dated anthology is George M. Waller, ed., *Pearl Harbor: Roosevelt and the Coming of the War* (Boston: D. C. Heath, 1965).

There are few comprehensive books on domestic policy during World War II. The best survey is Richard Polenburg's *War and Society, 1941–1945* (Philadelphia: Lippincott, 1972). Donald Nelson, head of the War Production Board, gave his side of the story in a very readable *Arsenal of Democracy: The Story of American War Production* (New York: Harcourt, Brace, 1946). Beyond these general accounts there are only topical studies. The best of these are Roland Young, *Congressional Politics in the Second World War* (New York: Columbia University Press, 1956); Walter W. Wilcox, *The Farmer in the Second World War* (Ames: Iowa State College Press, 1947); and Joel Seidman, *American Labor from Defense to Reconversion* (Chicago: University of Chicago Press, 1953).

The history of American military strategy has been recorded in almost infinite detail, but in too much detail for any but the specialist. The magnificent *History of United States Naval Operations in World War II*, under the general authorship of Samuel E. Morison, runs to fourteen volumes. In an ongoing project, the United States Army historians have already published ninety-one volumes. There are also shorter official histories of the air force and the marines. Fortunately, Morison has an abridged overview of his naval histories, *The Two-Ocean War* (Boston: Little, Brown, 1963), and a leading military historian, Basil H. Liddell Hart, has completed a detailed synthesis of the strictly military aspects in his *History of the Second World War* (London: Cassell, 1970). More likely sources for beginning students are two readable, brief accounts: Samuel E. Morison, *Strategy and Compromise* (Boston: Little, Brown, 1958); and Fletcher Pratt, *War for the World* (New Haven, Conn.: Yale University Press, 1950). A. Russell Buchanan provides a more detailed summary in *The United States in World War II*, 2 vols. (New York: Harper, 1964). The accounts of wartime commanders include Dwight D. Eisenhower's *Crusade in Europe* (Garden City, N.Y.: Doubleday, 1948), and Omar N. Bradley's *A Soldier's Story* (New York: Holt, Rinehart and Winston, 1951). On strategic decisions, see K. R. Greenfield, *American Strategy in World War II* (Baltimore: Johns Hopkins University Press, 1963), and H. Janson W. Baldwin, *Great Mistakes of the War* (New York: Harper and Row, 1950).

Wartime diplomacy has received detailed historical attention, although often in connection with the later cold war. The best brief account is Gaddis Smith, *American Diplomacy During the Second World War, 1941–1945* (New York: Wiley, 1965). As for so much of our diplomacy, Herbert Feis, himself formerly in the State Department, has surveyed World War II in *Churchill, Roosevelt, and Stalin: The War They Waged and the Peace They Sought* (Princeton, N.J.: Princeton University Press, 1957). John L. Snell has written a synthesis from an international perspective: *Illusion and Necessity: the Diplomacy of Global War, 1939–1945* (Boston: Houghton Mifflin, 1963). For Roosevelt's role, see James MacGregor Burns, *Roosevelt: The Soldier of Freedom* (New York: Harcourt, Brace, 1970); and Robert A. Divine, ed., *Roosevelt and World War II* (Baltimore: Johns Hopkins Press, 1969). George F. Kennan provides his provocative evaluation in *Russia and the West under Lenin and Stalin* (Boston: Little, Brown, 1969).

Yalta was the most decisive conference of the war, and one of the most controversial events in the history of American diplomacy. An anthology introduces the issues: Richard F. Fenno, Jr., ed., *The Yalta Conference* (Boston: D. C. Heath, 1955). More critical accounts appear in Athan Theoharis, *The Yalta Myths* (Columbia: University of Missouri, 1971); and Diane Shover Clemens, *Yalta* (New York: Oxford University Press, 1970). Gabriel Kolko, perhaps the most vehement critic of American cold war policies, considers Yalta in his heavily loaded *The Politics of War: The World and United States Foreign Policy, 1943–1945* (New York: Random House, 1968).

The Cold War

It is difficult to talk about the cold war without distinguishing pro-American position from a revisionist and in some sense anti-American stance. The divergence of perspective existed from the beginning, but most of the earliest books on American-Russian relations at least accepted the overall rightness of American policies. By the 1960's the weight of historical opinion shifted; in the last decade the majority of books on the cold war have been revisionist.

There is no official history of American cold war policies, but many early accounts came close to this. A few examples are Thomas A. Bailey, *America Faces Russia* (Ithaca, N.Y.: Cornell University Press, 1950); William C. Carleton, *The Revolution in American Foreign Policy, 1945–1954* (Garden City, N.Y.: Doubleday, 1954); William H. McNeil, *America, Britain, and Russia: Their Cooperation and Conflict, 1941–46* (London: Oxford University Press, 1953), and John Lukacs, *History of the Cold War* (Garden City, N.Y.: Doubleday, 1961). More recent, yet nonrevisionist books include John W. Spanier, *American Foreign Policy Since World War II* (New York: Praeger, 1965); and Stephen E. Ambrose, *The Rise to Globalism: American Foreign Policy since 1938* (London: The Penguin Press, 1971). Dean Acheson, the major architect of American cold war policies, provides a very literate and persuasive defense of his policies in *Present at the Creation: My Years in the State Department* (New York: W. W. Norton, 1969). Second only in importance to Acheson was George F. Kennan, whose perspectives appear in his *Memoirs, 1925–1950* (Chicago: University of Chicago, 1951). Herbert Feis, as always, has his say in *From Trust to Terror: The Onset of the Cold War, 1945–1950* (New York: W. W. Norton, 1970).

Revisionist literature is vast, but not of one persuasion. William A. Williams first gained wide attention for a searching new look at American foreign policy, and for what he saw as a long developing, widely supported policy of economic expansion. Young scholars were much influenced by his *The Tragedy of American Diplomacy* (New York: Dell, 1962) and *American-Russian Relations, 1781–1947* (New York: Holt, Rinehart and Winston, 1952). One of the earliest, most detailed attacks upon American policies was D. F. Fleming, *The Cold War and Its Origins, 1917–1960*, 2 vols. (London: Allen and Unwin, 1961). Fleming was an earlier disciple of Wilson, but tried to view the cold war from the other side, to see it as Europeans and even Russians viewed it.

Among recent, revisionist books, Walter LaFeber, *America, Russia, and the Cold War, 1945–1966* (New York: Wiley, 1967) is not only the most moderate in judgment, but also the best overall survey, with a detailed bibliography. Lloyd C. Gardner has written a restrained although critical biography of leading cold warriors in *Architects of Illusion: Men and Ideas in American Foreign Policy, 1941–1949* (Chicago: Quadrangle, 1970). Much more vindictive and harsh in judgment are two books by David Horowitz: *The Free World Colossus* (New York: Hill and Wang, 1965), and *Empire and Revolution* (New York: Random House, 1969). Gar Alperowitz, in addition to his conspiratorial book on atomic diplomacy, *Atomic Diplomacy: Hiroshima and Potsdam* (New York: Simon and Schuster, 1965), has written *Cold War Essays* (Garden City, N.Y.: Doubleday, 1970). Richard J. Barnet, in *Intervention and Revolution* (New York: Meridian, 1969), offers a popular indictment of American policies in the third world. Two of the more extreme, and certainly among the most controversial, revisionist books come from one family: Gabriel Kolko, *The Roots of American Foreign Policy* (Boston: Beacon, 1969) and Gabriel and Joyce Kolko, *The Limits of Power: The World and United States Foreign Policy* (New York: Harper and Row, 1972). For a review of revisionist positions, and a thorough attack against them, see Robert Tucker, *The Radical Left and American Foreign Policy* (Baltimore: Johns Hopkins Press, 1971). Thomas G. Paterson, ed., *Cold War Critics: Alternatives to American Foreign Policy in the Truman Years* (Chicago: Quadrangle, 1971) offers a good sample of revisionist arguments. The clash of argument is well represented in Lloyd C. Gardner, Arthur Schlesinger, Jr., and Hans Morgenthau, *The Origins of the Cold War* (Waltham, Mass.: Blaisdale, 1970) and in Thomas G. Paterson, ed., *The Origins of the Cold War* (Boston: D. C. Heath, 1970).

Several topical histories supplement the above interpretations. Ruth B. Russell has written a *History of the United Nations Charter* (Washington, D.C.: Brookings Institution, 1958). For the transition from Yalta to Potsdam, see Martin Herz, *Beginnings of the Cold War* (Bloomington: Indiana University Press, 1966). Joseph M. Jones, *The Fifteen Weeks* (New York: Viking Press, 1955) details the development of the Truman Doctrine. For an analysis of our greatest foreign aid program, see Harry B. Price, *The Marshall Plan and Its Meaning* (Ithaca, N.Y.: Cornell University Press, 1955). Two titles are self-explanatory: Joseph Lieberman, *The Scorpion and the Tarantula: The Struggle to Control Atomic Weapons, 1945–1949* (Boston: Houghton Mifflin, 1970) and Joseph Korbel, *The Communist Subversion of Czechoslovakia, 1938–1948* (Princeton, N.J.: Princeton University Press, 1959).

Most interpretations of the cold war embrace the Korean War. Additional books on that war include Leland M. Goodrich, *Korea: A Study of U.S. Policy in the United Nations* (New York: Council of Foreign Relations, 1956); David Rees, *Korea, the Limited War* (New York: St. Martins Press, 1964); John W. Spanier, *The Truman-MacArthur Controversy and the Korean War* (Cambridge, Mass.: Harvard University Press, 1959); and Allen Whiting,

China Crosses the Yalu (New York: Macmillan, 1960). For MacArthur's perspective, see his *Reminiscences* (New York: McGraw-Hill, 1964).

As yet, there is no competent, scholarly biography of Truman, and no comprehensive history of his administration. Eulogistic biographies, such as Jonathan Daniels, *The Man of Independence* (Philadelphia: Lippincott, 1950) hardly add anything to our understanding. Truman's two-volume *Memoirs* (Garden City, N.Y.: Doubleday, 1955–56) give his own perspectives on his administration, and reveal several facets of his character. A favorable, journalistic account of Truman's presidency is Cabell Phillips's *The Truman Presidency: The History of a Triumphant Succession* (New York: Macmillan, 1966). A provocative anthology is Barton J. Bernstein and Allen J. Matusow, eds., *The Truman Administration: A Documentary History* (New York: Harper and Row, 1966). Bernstein most clearly espouses a sharp, critical revision of earlier, highly sympathetic treatments of Truman, a position that he best articulates in two edited volumes, *Toward a New Past* (New York: Random House, 1967), and *Politics and Policies of the Truman Administration* (Chicago: Quadrangle, 1970). The whole range of opinion on Truman appears in an excellent anthology edited by J. Joseph Huthmacher, *The Truman Years* (Hinsdale, Ill.: The Dryden Press, 1972).

There is a growing volume of books on Truman's domestic program. On his economic policies, see A. E. Holmans, *United States Fiscal Policy, 1945–1959* (London: Oxford University Press, 1961) and Edward S. Flash, Jr., *Economic Advice and Presidential Leadership: The Council of Economic Advisers* (New York: Columbia University Press, 1965). Other topical studies include R. Alton Lee, *Truman and Taft-Hartley: A Question of Mandate* (Lexington: University of Kentucky Press, 1966); Richard O. Davies, *Housing Reform during the Truman Administration* (Columbia: University of Missouri Press, 1966); William C. Berman, *The Politics of Civil Rights in the Truman Administration* (Columbus: Ohio State University Press, 1971); and Richard M. Dalfiume, *Desegregation of the United States Armed Forces: Fighting on Two Fronts, 1939–1953* (Columbia: University of Missouri Press, 1969). The report of the President's Committee on Civil Rights, *To Secure These Rights* (Washington, D.C.: Government Printing Office, 1947) had an immense impact on subsequent legislation and Negro agitation. On Truman's unexpected victory of 1948, see Irwin Ross, *The Loneliest Campaign: The Truman Victory of 1948* (New York: New American Library, 1968).

The issues of security and loyalty during the Truman years provoked a virtual deluge of books on civil liberties, on communism, on the Hiss case, and on the role of congressional committees. Two excellent studies are only samples of the massive literature: Earl Latham, *The Communist Controversy in Washington* (Cambridge, Mass.: Harvard University Press, 1966) and Walter Goodman, *The Committee: The Extraordinary Career of the House Committee on Un-American Activities* (New York: Farrar, Straus, and Giroux, 1968).

Alan D. Harper provides a balanced, reasonable explanation of Truman's loyalty program in *The Politics of Loyalty: The White House and the Communist Issue, 1946–1952* (Westport, Conn.: Greenwood, 1970). Athan Theoharis offers a much more critical evaluation in *Seeds of Repression: Harry S. Truman and the Origins of McCarthyism* (Chicago: Quadrangle, 1971). A provocative, even brilliant work on McCarthy is Michael Rogin, *The Intellectuals and McCarthy* (Cambridge, Mass.: Harvard University Press, 1967). A standard biography is by journalist Richard Rovere, *Senator Joe McCarthy* (New York: Harcourt, Brace, 1959). An excellent analysis of McCarthy as a politician appears in Robert Griffith, *The Politics of Fear: Joseph R. McCarthy and the Senate* (Lexington: University of Kentucky Press, 1970). For a defense of McCarthy, see William F. Buckley, Jr., and L. Brent Bozell, *McCarthy and His Enemies* (Chicago: Henry Regnery, 1954).

PART FOUR

America
since
1953

26

The 1950's became stereotyped even before the decade ended. Placid, sterile, anti-intellectual were words used by many to define the times and the president. But perhaps the portrait was too simple. Even in the seventies historians are not at all certain what lay beneath the surface of the Eisenhower decade. Born in 1890 in Denison, Texas, and reared in the modest surroundings of Abilene, Kansas, Dwight D. Eisenhower was a product of the American frontier town. The young Eisenhower possessed the quick mind of one accustomed to making his own way. He secured entrance to West Point and despite a mediocre academic record, distinguished himself in campus leadership. At Command and General Staff School in Fort Leavenworth, Kansas, he graduated first in his class after a year's study in 1925–1926. As a soldier Eisenhower did not affect the bluff arrogance and the disdain for civilian direction that can go with the military temperament; in 1932 he participated in dispersing the makeshift camp of unemployed veterans—the bonus marchers—on Anacostia Flats in Maryland. But he later faulted the haughty chief of staff, Douglas MacArthur, for disobeying President Hoover by marching on Anacostia with bayonets and destroying the shacks. Eisenhower's military and strategic skill was perhaps best demonstrated during the Second World War by his conduct during the 1942 North African invasion and later as supreme commander of Allied forces in Europe. He owed thanks for his rapid promotions to Chief of Staff General George C. Marshall, who perceived him as both an excellent administrator and strategist.

After the war Eisenhower served as army chief of staff and then for two-and-one-half years as president of Columbia University. There he instituted the American Assembly, a forum for discussion of major national problems, and, as he later recollected with some pride, an academic "Chair of Peace." Late in 1950 President Truman appointed him military commander of NATO. Two years later, from this post in Paris Eisenhower allowed a group of eastern internationalist Republicans, led by Governor Thomas E. Dewey of New York and Senator Henry Cabot Lodge, Jr., of Massachusetts, to draft him for the presidency. Pursued by both parties since Germany's defeat, the likeable and glamorous "Ike" seemed an ideal presidential candidate.

Eisenhower was of two minds about seeking the presidency. After a

The Eisenhower Fifties

long and busy career he looked forward to neighborly encounters with card-playing friends and hours alone on a farm in the country. Since his youth Eisenhower had believed in concentrating power and decision making at the local level of government, in balancing the federal budget rather than in expanding welfare programs. His European command during World War II gave him an education in international affairs superior to any university training; broadened by this experience he rejected middle American distrust of foreign involvements. The general at first resisted those who urged him to provide leadership at home; he believed that a military man was unsuited for national politics. Ultimately, Eisenhower's decision in 1952 to resign as NATO commander and seek the presidency —so his *Memoirs* assert—came from a fear that the foreign policy commitments of Senator Robert A. Taft of Ohio might otherwise prevail.

Within the Republican party a fierce battle raged between eastern and midwestern leaders. Since Willkie's nomination in 1940, the financial and industrial East had twice forced its candidates on the party. But after Governor Thomas E. Dewey's successive defeats the supporters of Robert Taft, majority leader of the Senate, demanded a chance for their candidate. The son of William Howard Taft, the brilliant but drab senator, espoused a variety of causes. He warned against government spending and "socialistic" government, yet supported federal aid for education, health, and housing; a higher minimum wage; and expanded social security. Like Eisenhower, he believed local government to be more democratic and closer to the people than federal bureaucracy. The two candidates differed principally in their views on foreign policy. Taft denied that America had a duty to extend its institutions abroad; conscious of the limits of American power, he shied away from foreign commitments, asserting that America could sustain itself on its own domestic markets, which should be protected by high tariffs.

Eisenhower, whose background and personality best suited the Republicans in 1952, easily defeated Taft in the early New Hampshire primary, and later in New Jersey, Massachusetts, and Oregon; Taft won in his native Ohio and, narrowly, in South Dakota. Deprived of the White House for so long, the Republicans dared not risk the dour Taft (who probably better represented the personal views of the delegates); they nominated instead the easygoing and politically promising Ike. Eisenhower's record equaled Taft's for high seriousness and more than matched it for drama; and Ike's personality was by far the more attractive. For vice-president Governor Dewey successfully recommended California Senator Richard M. Nixon, whose success in prosecuting Alger Hiss had won him national fame.

The plight of the Democrats under President Truman weakened their political chances. Truman's slim popularity had visibly eroded during four years of war, high taxes, inflation, and the exposure of corruption and espionage in the federal government. Because Truman had not asked for a congressional declaration of war in Korea, the Republicans were free to criticize his decision to intervene. And when the president fired General Douglas MacArthur, the supreme allied commander in the Pacific, the whole nation seemed to rise in protest against the conduct of the war. Finally, after twenty years of Democratic rule, polls showed that the nation was ready for a Republican in the White House.

The Democrats settled on a presidential candidate at least as cerebral as Taft: Governor Adlai E. Stevenson of Illinois, a man of colonial ancestry and fastidious intellect. As governor he increased funds for schools and roads, wiped out downstate gambling operations, and modernized the state bureaucracy. Other candidates had presented themselves, most notably Senator Estes Kefauver of Tennessee, whose face had become familiar through daily television appearances as head of the Senate Crime Investigating Committee. President Truman, in firm control of the convention, wanted Stevenson, even though the governor possessed an introspective and self-deprecating manner that bordered on indecision. Stevenson never quite sought the nomination, describing himself as unfit for the presidency, and indeed was not a candidate until the moment he was nominated on the third ballot in Chicago.

The 1952 campaign sparkled with Stevenson's cultivated, witty speeches that he wrote himself; but his manner and bearing were both an asset and a liability. To Republicans and many independents, the speeches conveyed an impression that he did not take seriously the charges against the Truman administration. Many Democrats, on the other hand, found him an exciting leader for a party demoralized and in retreat. "Volunteers for Stevenson" groups sprang up all over the country, stressing their candidate's humility, intelligence, and rectitude. But though the governor campaigned honestly, he could not hope to overcome Eisenhower's popularity.

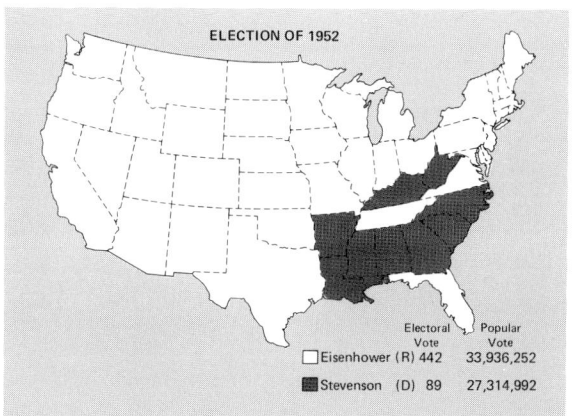

ELECTION OF 1952

	Electoral Vote	Popular Vote
Eisenhower (R)	442	33,936,252
Stevenson (D)	89	27,314,992

Yet Stevenson actually had wanted Eisenhower to win the Republican nomination, fearing the effect of Taft's foreign policy ideas on the western alliance. For Stevenson, like Eisenhower, represented an internationalist position the Truman administration had itself sustained and that contrasted with Taft's beliefs. The language of this internationalism may sound belligerent today, for its proponents looked toward American leadership on a worldwide scene. Speaking standard foreign policy to a Kansas audience, for example, Stevenson explained that we were fighting in Korea "so we wouldn't have to fight in Wichita"; Korea was "a crucial test in the struggle between the free world and communism."

Eisenhower, meanwhile, worked to heal wounds in the Republican party. He welcomed Taft to a breakfast at Morningside Heights, Columbia University, after which they agreed on the essentials of domestic policy. Easily projecting his folksy style across the land, the general spent more time campaigning in the South than had any previous Republican candidate. And he deleted from an important speech a remark criticizing the redhunters like Senators Joe McCarthy and William Jenner; Eisenhower did little to support his old boss, General Marshall, against their attacks. A storm broke when the *New York Post* charged Nixon with accepting money from friendly businessmen for personal expenses. Nixon rebutted the claim—Stevenson had a similar fund to supplement the salaries of public officials—and also demonstrated a command of "television politics" in a highly sentimental and effective speech. Both major candidates seemed ready to accept the accomplishments of the New and Fair Deals, though neither was anxious to promote civil rights in the spirit of the 1948 Democratic convention.

The results on election day shocked no one. After October 24, when Eisenhower promised, in the event that he won, to "go to Korea," the polls showed his margin to be widening. On November 7 Eisenhower won 55 percent of the vote and even carried the southern states of Virginia, Florida, and Texas. He received a majority vote from all income groups and drew unexpected support from normally Democratic Roman Catholics. What Eisenhower offered in the 1952 campaign and would consummate in the first term of his presidency was something the country needed rather desperately: an easing of tensions after the hectic recriminations of the Truman years.

The early fifties, the time of Joe McCarthy and the Korean War, had reflected political and social turmoil. The breakdown of the wartime Russian-American alliance, the "fall" of China to the Communists, the Russian nuclear threat, the fear of internal subversion, and the emerging tensions over race relations marked by a split in the Democratic party—all contributed to the irritable and sour malaise. Soon after the new president

An exuberant Eisenhower ushers in the first Republican administration in twenty years. Eisenhower's folksy campaign style and war hero image won him the wide base of support that netted him 55 percent of the popular vote in 1952. *Magnum*

took office the Eisenhower "decade" opened: the time of political calm began with the Korean armistice in mid-summer 1953 and the Senate censure of McCarthy in January 1954.

Eisenhower continued most of the policies of economic regulation, social welfare, and internationalism associated with his Democratic predecessors. But by removing these policies from partisan debate, first in the campaign and then later in handling congressional Democrats (who often supported him more strongly than did his own party), Eisenhower shaped them into a national consensus that reached its greatest appeal after the end of the Korean War. Unfortunately, the political tranquillity of the Eisenhower era was short-lived, ending in October 1957 with the strange beeps from space of the Russian earth satellite, Sputnik, and ensuing criticisms of economic and cultural trends. Four years in which people feel a bit more placid hardly make a dominant trend.

Eisenhower Diplomacy

Eisenhower's good fortune in foreign policy was more impressive than his work at home. A peace-loving man, Eisenhower quickly ended the Korean War and began his self-appointed task of resolving the victors' clash over the spoils of World War II. At the same time, the Soviet Union moved toward improved relations with the West. Freed of Stalin's arbitrary cruelty by his death on March 5, 1953, and perhaps sobered by Truman's determined containment politics and the unexpected strength of decadent capitalism, Georgi Malenkov, Stalin's nominal successor, sought détente. He received support from Foreign Minister Vyacheslav Molotov, Defense Minister Nikolai A. Bulganin, and Nikita Khrushchev, first secretary of the Communist party. Although a three-year struggle for dominance ensued among Stalin's successors—a contest Khrushchev won largely because of timely support from Marshal Zhukov, a war hero who controlled the Red Army—the dispute nevertheless increased hopes for a more stable world order. So far did the so-called "thaw" go that Khrushchev later announced the doctrine of peaceful coexistence and economic competition, both direct repudiations of Marxist militancy. Old habits and problems did not magically disappear, but given an atomic standoff (in 1953 the Soviet Union exploded its first hydrogen bomb), the decline of McCarthyism in America, and new faces on both sides of the Iron Curtain, the world appeared headed toward a more peaceful future.

In Washington, a new tenor and even a new substance entered the making of foreign policy. The president's caution and his immense following prevented the public furor and congressional alarms that had plagued the Democrats. His word on military matters was definitive. And Dwight Eisenhower knew the horrors of war: in *Crusade in Europe*

(1948) he recalled the harrowing experience of entering the Falaise Gap zone in Normandy in 1944. "It was literally possible," he wrote, "to walk for hundreds of yards at a time, stepping on nothing but dead and decayed flesh." Eisenhower turned the day-to-day control of foreign affairs over to John Foster Dulles, a somber, able man who espoused an unbending anticommunism. Soon famous for his willingness, at least rhetorically, to "go to the brink" of nuclear war in order to contain communism, the new secretary of state's caution occasioned less comment and recognition. Though "brinkmanship" implied militancy, perhaps it no less forcefully evoked pacifism: to the brink, not into the abyss.

The most dramatic break with Democratic foreign policy concerned Korea. Although Ike's threat to use atomic weaponry there echoed Truman's belligerency, America's most successful recent general became the nation's first president in over a century to halt a war short of victory. Soon afterward Eisenhower managed to stabilize the postwar disputes that

With grim looks on their faces, U.S. delegates to the United Nations John Foster Dulles and Eleanor Roosevelt listen to Russian Foreign Minister Andrei Vishinsky call Dulles one of the nine leading "warmongers" in the U.S., September 9, 1947. The speech by Vishinsky symbolized the growing rift between the U.S. and Russia. *Acme Photo*

had long divided the European continent. Dulles negotiated the Paris Accords, which guaranteed French security and at the same time brought West Germany into the NATO alliance. Although this move provoked the Soviets into the Warsaw Pact, an alliance system in Eastern Europe, the continent seemed more stable when organized into two blocs.

The Republicans also fashioned a new approach to the Soviet Union. Both Eisenhower and Dulles relied heavily on the deterrent power of nuclear weapons as opposed to conventional forces. This strategy produced "more bang for the buck" in the colorful words of economy-minded Charles Wilson, the secretary of defense. Yet the nuclear approach generally restricted the United States either to doing nothing or to threatening catastrophe, and Russia's acquisition of nuclear weapons blunted the device. Dulles believed that the best way to maintain peace was for America to make known what it would do in a given situation; in this way we might have avoided Korea. Eisenhower himself probably never thought nuclear war to be an option. Surely his diplomatic initiatives—forging new alliances, holding summit meetings, supporting the United Nations, and offering the open skies disarmament proposal—were all calculated to avoid confrontation.

In the most dramatic departure from the techniques of the Truman and Acheson years, Eisenhower sought direct meetings with Soviet leaders —a diplomatic device unused since 1946. In the afterglow of the Korean settlement, Winston Churchill proposed a "summit meeting" to resolve outstanding European problems. But by the time the four heads of government reached Geneva, their goals had become less ambitious. Eisenhower; Bulganin and Khrushchev for the Soviets; the new British prime minister, Anthony Eden; and Premier Edgar Faure of France attempted only to list problems and outline procedures for their solution. Meeting from July 18 until July 23, 1955, the statesmen discussed three principal topics: German unification and the closely allied issue of European security, disarmament, and increased communication between East and West. Although considered the least important at the time, the third objective alone achieved realization. Since 1955 a small but sustained series of mutual concessions has reduced the barriers to the exchange of "people, ideas, and goods" between the formerly almost isolated blocs.

When the foreign ministers met in the fall to work out concrete proposals for solving the remaining problems—a united Germany and disarmament—they failed to reach any agreement. The West's NATO and the East's Warsaw Pact had already divided the continent. Not just the Soviet Union, but every nation in Europe feared a revival of German militarism. Many West Germans, particularly in the Rhineland and Bavaria, questioned whether the prosperous West should bail out the depressed East.

Premier Nikita Khrushchev (1894–1971) and his wife on the steps of Camp David with President Eisenhower. Khrushchev visited the United States in 1959 for a series of talks with President Eisenhower. The "spirit of Camp David" that resulted was short-lived, however, for shortly before a summit conference scheduled for May 1960, the Soviet Union shot down a U-2 airplane, whose pilot, Gary Powers, was conducting photo-reconnaisance. *Magnum*

But though Germany remained divided, the greatest disappointment was the failure on disarmament. At Geneva Eisenhower had outlined his famous "open skies" proposal: mutual aerial surveillance and an exchange of military blueprints. The Russians politely scuttled the idea, preventing a test of congressional sentiment on "spy flights" over the United States. Despite this setback, the first summit meeting had positive results: both sides moved away from the cold war rhetoric of accusation and threat; everyone understood that nuclear war would be, in Eisenhower's words, "race suicide." The Russians apparently accepted the president's protestations of America's peaceful intent. The summit launched the "spirit of Geneva": fundamental tensions remained, but peace—defined as the absence of war—seemed possible.

Throughout 1956 and 1957 caution dominated American foreign policy as lightning changes left the administration bewildered. Both the Communist and the Western blocs suffered internal rebellions during the summer and fall of 1956. First, the Soviet empire in Eastern Europe nearly collapsed. Some 15,000 impoverished Polish factory workers revolted in Poznan on June 28. While the Kremlin hesitated, the Poles demanded that Wladyslaw Gomulka take over the government. A national Communist who opposed "hasty" collectivization, Gomulka refused to compromise with Soviet leaders clearly caught off guard. After a bewildering series of Byzantine maneuvers, he forced Moscow to accept a revisionist politburo under his leadership.

Gomulka's success triggered the much more devastating Hungarian rebellion of October and November, which sought political independence as well as economic reform. On October 23, a demonstration supporting Polish liberation quickly changed into a huge mob of workers, soldiers, and students who demanded the return of Imre Nagy, a former Communist minister. Nagy, who opposed Soviet economic methods and Moscow's political domination, formed a new government on the Polish model. But demonstrations turned into armed rebellion; the provinces almost immediately went over to the rebel cause and Budapest soon followed. Encouraged by signs of support from the West, the revolutionaries opted for complete independence. Although Moscow offered a remarkable and often overlooked compromise solution—Hungarian membership in a "commonwealth of socialist countries"—Nagy and his cabinet could no longer control events. When the Hungarians persisted in trying to escape its orbit, Moscow brought in a heavy military force to forestall piecemeal breakdown of the Warsaw bloc.

Worried about nuclear confrontation and tacitly recognizing Soviet dominance in Eastern Europe, the West never considered intervention. In any case, events elsewhere had dissolved Western unity into barely disguised animosity. On November 5 England, France, and Israel launched a joint attack on Egypt, ostensibly to reopen the Suez Canal which President Gamal Abdel Nasser had nationalized in July. But the canal issue was only a pretext. For the Israelis, the operation had all the trappings of preventive war. In Paris the moribund Fourth Republic hoped to recoup its prestige after frustrations in Vietnam and Algeria; Premier Guy Mollet belligerently overreacted to Nasser's act. Only Britain hesitated. If anxious to topple Nasser, whose action against British interests in the Suez created a dangerous example to other Arab states, London understood the enormous military risks. British officials misread Eisenhower's mild warnings—the election campaign was just peaking in the United States—and concluded that he would not object. Given Soviet preoccupations in Hungary, Washington's response determined the outcome of the tripartite maneuver; the United States, anxious to avoid identifying itself with European colonialism, abruptly condemned the attack. Eisenhower even threatened to bankrupt the British pound unless Eden withdrew British troops. Beset on all sides—the entire Arab world had broken off diplomatic relations—the prime minister accepted a Canadian-American proposal for a United Nations peacekeeping force in the Sinai peninsula. If this solved a diplomatic dilemma for the West, Egypt did not forget that troops were stationed only on its soil, not on Israel's.

The next jolt occurred outside the field of politics. On October 4, 1957, the first Sputnik beeped the beginning of the space age and seemed to tip the tactical balance in favor of the Soviet Union. Economies in the Defense Department, together with an exaggerated reliance upon manned bombers, had limited America's missile development program. Despite the quiver that ran through the Western world, the new earth satellite had little strategic significance; America's military technology and gross national product far surpassed those of the Russians. Yet in less than fourteen months, both the Communist and Western blocs had suffered severe internal divisions, the cold war had moved into the third world, and Soviet rocket engineers had given their government a strong propaganda weapon.

Eisenhower responded characteristically to these events: the former general decided to "wage peace." He envisioned a prudent defense against Soviet power, executed less belligerently and less myopically than under Dulles, who left office in 1958 and died of cancer in 1959. At the same time, Soviet policy became less aggressive. Khrushchev's colleagues rebuked him severely for the disastrous effects of Soviet intervention in Hungary, particularly the damage to Russian prestige in the third world. Yet with the decisive help of the army, the skillful Ukrainian solidified his control over the Soviet state. Growing Russian power and Western division tempted Khrushchev; memories of Hungary and the devastation of his homeland in World War II held him back. A balance of sorts developed unintentionally, creating a pushing and pulling, a minute-by-minute policy. Until John Kennedy raised the specter of a "missile gap" the two superpowers moved, if not toward reconciliation, at least toward a mutual determination to avoid nuclear war.

Despite his restrained reaction to potentially explosive situations, Eisenhower never believed in making a virtue of weakness. With his encouragement Secretary Dulles strengthened collective security in Europe by granting Germany a nonnuclear role in NATO. In 1957 Dulles also enunciated the Eisenhower doctrine for the Middle East, offering not only economic assistance but also American soldiers, if requested, to governments protecting their territorial integrity against Communist advances. The new policy resulted from the rapid erosion of the West's position throughout the strategically significant Near East. Nasser's attempt to unify the region politically, together with general Arab confidence that their oil reserves would fend off reprisals and gain concessions, accelerated the trend toward nationalism. Prospects of an independent role outside the bipolar, Soviet-American world undercut the pro-West Baghdad Pact, a military alliance composed of Iraq, Turkey, Iran, Pakistan, and Great Britain. For many reasons, its viability depended primarily upon Iraq. But Nasserism had permeated the Iraqi army, and in July 1948 its leaders ousted Premier Nuri es-Said, killing him later along with King Faisal and the crown prince. The new regime immediately realigned Iraq's foreign policy with Nasser's increasingly successful drive for Arab unity.

In Lebanon during 1958, a confused, intricate civil war erupted between Christians and Arabs, pro-Nasser and anti-Nasser factions, and Western-oriented, urban Beirut against the native impulses of the hill areas. Shortly after the Iraqi coup, the pro-Western president of Lebanon asked the United States for military support to end the civil war. Eisenhower invoked his new doctrine and dispatched 3,500 marines, a force that eventually grew to 14,000. The intervention, so brief, bloodless, and well-executed, deserved commendation at least for its technical skill. But the larger purpose of the landing failed; the attempt to set up an alternative to Nasser in the Middle East collapsed around regional fears of renewed colonialism and the Arab countries' reluctance to combine with outside powers against one another.

Eisenhower deftly handled another crisis, potentially the most serious of the decade, when Russia sealed off East Berlin in the late summer of 1958 to thwart black market currency operations by West Berliners and to halt an embarrassing efflux from East Germany. His determination to stand firm without overreacting quickly diminished tension. As if to reiterate the common resolve to avoid war, Khrushchev paid a successful visit to the United States in 1959, and met a cordial Eisenhower at Camp David, Maryland. Observers spoke of the "spirit of Camp David," the dissipation of mistrust. The Eisenhower peace offensive was to culminate in a summit conference planned for Geneva on May 14, 1960. But on May 1, deep inside the Soviet Union, Russian artillery shot down an American U-2 spy plane; Khrushchev used the incident, following contradictory White House statements, as an occasion for jettisoning the conference.

If Eisenhower oversaw a sophisticated and for the most part successful relationship with the Soviet Union, his administration never satisfactorily solved another dilemma. As illustrated in the inconclusiveness of the Lebanon intervention, America seemed unable to deal with the challenge of the so-called underdeveloped world. Although the lack of urban-industrial areas, the existence of fragmented social structures, and native hostility to notions of materialistic progress seemed unpromising ground for Marxist ideas, the Republican administration, like its predecessor, seemed to equate neutralism with procommunism. The breakup of Europe's empires promoted political and economic revolution as nationalists sought to destroy the remnants of colonialism, particularly its class structure. Superimposed over this struggle was the necessity to restore economic balance after years of European "warping." Throughout Africa and much of Asia, imperial emphasis upon extractive wealth and protected colonial markets had inhibited native manufactures, weakened agriculture, and created parasitic cities that functioned principally as administrative capitals and pleasure domes. The struggle to break these colonial legacies, occurring within the context of cold war, guaranteed years of violent change and frustrating complexity. Eisenhower himself was so disillusioned that he frankly admitted to John Kennedy in 1961 that foreign affairs were "in a mess."

In 1959 a revolutionary leader, Fidel Castro, overthrew the heavy-handed Cuban dictator, Fulgencio Batista. At first the administration easily adapted to the change; only six days after Batista fled Cuba, Washington recognized his bearded, thirty-two-year-old successor. Worried about their large investments, several American corporations paid their Cuban taxes a year in advance, a transparent and ineffective attempt to change Castro's goals. In March the new premier declared 1959 the Year of Revolution; even more than executions in Cuba, Castro's propaganda appeals to American minorities shocked domestic public opinion. If Cuban-American relations faltered in 1959, in the next year—the so-called Year of the Agrarian Reform—they collapsed. After Castro nationalized one billion dollars of American property in Cuba and publicly consorted with Khrushchev at the 1960 United Nations General Assembly meeting, Eisenhower tried to isolate Cuba by cutting first its economic lifeline, the all-important sugar quotas, and then its political connections with the Organization of American States. That Castro subsequently turned to the Communist bloc surprised no one except a few Americans. Eisenhower himself had already authorized a possible attack on Cuba, which would ultimately materialize as the Bay of Pigs fiasco under Kennedy.

The domestic economy, like foreign policy, underwent a transition during the 1950's. Within the Republican party three major economic strategies contended for predominance: a remnant of classical theory decrying government involvement and urging free competition existed almost wholly in rhetoric; a belief in the possibility of economic stability and steady growth by means of monetary policy, primarily developed by the federal reserve system; and a third position which few Republicans acknowledged but which actually prevailed—the academically orthodox Keynesian emphasis upon fiscal policy and carefully defined policies for government spending and taxing. Overt Keynesianism awaited the Kennedy-Johnson years. Yet under Eisenhower even Arthur F. Burns, the cautious chairman of the Council of Economic Advisers, remarked that "it is no longer a matter of serious controversy whether the Government should play a positive role in helping to maintain a high level of economic activity."

A Dormant Economy

During the recession of 1953–1954, Eisenhower used both fiscal and monetary policies to reinvigorate the economy; he remarked at this time that controls practically guaranteed no depression would occur. Especially from 1954 on, monetary policy gained popularity with the administration, notably manipulation of the rediscount rate and extensive open market operations. The problem was that the reserve policies came in response to various economic problems rather than in anticipation of them.

Unemployment was the central economic issue of the decade. The three recessions of the 1950's, each one worse than the last, were puzzling phenomena. The end of the Korean War and a sharp cut in military expenditures brought on the first recession in 1953–1954. An easy money policy adopted by both the Treasury and the Federal Reserve Board, combined with a tax cut and an increase in old age and unemployment payments, eventually managed to offset the economic decline resulting from postwar layoffs. But the administration, worried over inflation, reacted slowly to another recession in 1957–1958; with unemployment rates remaining at 7 percent during the congressional elections, Republi-

cans suffered disastrous consequences. Even in 1960, though a presidential campaign hung in the balance, inflation troubled Eisenhower more than unemployment or the slow rate of economic growth.

The president's advisers, though they prevented a weak economy from slipping into depression, were unable to avoid repeated economic declines and an unemployment rate of up to 7.7 percent. They failed to stem inflationary price increases even as the national economic growth rate remained below levels then prevailing in Western Europe and apparently in the Soviet Union. Russian annual growth averaged 7.1 percent between 1950 and 1958, nearly 50 percent above that of the United States. In America greater productivity per man hour required an economy expansive enough to supply new jobs; the postwar rise in the birth rate further increased the demand. Neglect of what John Kenneth Galbraith termed the public sector of the economy, of needs in health, welfare, and education, also suggested a need for a more active economy yielding larger tax receipts.

The Eisenhower administration no doubt wanted to curb rising prices, but it could not do it with voluntary restraints, especially when the steel industry resisted. Large firms aimed not for competition at home and abroad, but for secure growth based on rising prices in a carefully planned market, or for an "administered price." The elites of organized labor pressed for higher wages, passing the resulting higher price on to the consumer. Even in agriculture ever higher payments to keep land out of production balanced lower farm support prices. In the 1950's business-oriented Republicans appeared fearful of stimulating more rapid economic growth, while at the end of the decade, Democrats, less frightened by inflation, made growth their major objective.

During the 1950's investments in new plants and equipment shrank far below any comparable European figures. As usual, the poor suffered most during the economic doldrums. Blacks, Indians, Mexican Americans, and growing numbers of the elderly were, in Michael Harrington's apt word, "invisible"—physically shut away and forgotten in slums, on reservations, in migrant workers' camps, and in filthy nursing homes as medical indigents. Mass-produced clothing masked their true economic condition. These same groups were also politically invisible, lacking a voice even in the Democratic party, which had its institutional base in the unions.

Eisenhower's Social Policy

On social issues, much activity resulted in little action. Aid to public education was so popular, and the need for classrooms so great, that most people expected Eisenhower to implement his campaign pledge for direct federal aid as "the American answer." Yet he failed to do so. Perhaps the president had expressed his true sentiments in 1949 when he testified while president of Columbia University in opposition to a school-aid bill, calling it socialistic and paternalistic, even though Senator Taft sponsored it. Or perhaps his advisers, particularly Secretary of Health, Education and Welfare Oveta Culp Hobby, influenced him in their opposition to immediate action in the field. In either event, Eisenhower did nothing to speed up time-consuming "conferences" which Hobby insisted upon. For three years a parade of witnesses argued over the extent of the "education crisis," particularly the lack of school buildings. Congress would probably have passed its own measure, but bills to finance construction foundered on tangled controversies over race. An amendment proposed by Congressman Adam Clayton Powell of New York to withhold funds from segregated districts produced almost solid southern opposition. Despite the replacement of Mrs. Hobby by the more activist Marion Folsom, and despite another campaign pledge for massive aid to schools crowded by postwar babies, Eisenhower's post-election silence once again helped sabotage immediate action.

Congress did pass one important education measure, the National Defense Education Act of 1958. Yet both the act's provisions and Congress's motivation seemed far removed from concern over the quality of local education. During the near-hysterical period following the 1957 Russian launching of Sputnik I, the national government had quickly decided to improve college-level education, primarily in the applied sciences and engineering. Implementing this decision, NDEA provided loans, scholarships, and fellowships directly to students and a lesser amount in grants to the colleges themselves. Yet perhaps more important than these provisions of NDEA was its psychological impact: for better or for worse, education had become a concern of the federal government. For the remainder of Eisenhower's term, however, the president's inaction and congressional friction over race prevented further subsidies.

Caution also marked the concern over health care. Skyrocketing medical costs had troubled some congressmen since the 1930's when Congress first debated a program for universal health insurance under social security. Truman had revived the issue, but Eisenhower and the American Medical Association denounced such projects as "socialized medicine." (Mrs. Hobby even opposed the free distribution of the Salk polio vaccine.) Although the AMA grudgingly advanced broad-based private health plans financed in part by government, Eisenhower kept silent and Congress ignored his requests for aid to hospitals. Yet the issue would not go away, despite presidential opposition.

By the mid-fifties, health care became linked with another issue, the plight of the elderly. Prodded by organized labor, Congress took up the

Forand Bill, a modest proposal including limited hospital benefits for those over 65. The AFL-CIO and most northern Democrats actively supported the legislation. Strident AMA protests suggested ulterior motives and its extensive propaganda campaign against the measure actually made people more aware of the problem. The Eisenhower administration initially opposed the Forand Bill, preferring voluntary health insurance plans. Most Republicans, the medical lobby, and the insurance industry opposed any government scheme, even one by the new HEW secretary, Arthur Flemming, for voluntary social security taxes. Together with southern congressmen, the Republicans passed the Kerr-Mills Act, providing limited aid to the indigent. This returned the issue to where it had started—an attempt to prevent medical catastrophe from pauperizing the elderly; thereafter frustrated Democrats as well as several Republicans found ready allies among senior citizens for a more comprehensive program.

Eisenhower's determination not to expand federal patronage or the federal budget surfaced emphatically in the struggles over environmental bills. In 1960 the president vetoed a water pollution bill which would have established federal grants to build sewage treatment plants. He argued that pollution was "a uniquely local blight," and that responsibility rested with state and local governments. This theme pervaded his statements concerning natural resources and conservation. Half-convinced that the Tennessee Valley Authority represented "creeping socialism," he backed the Dixon-Yates utility proposal to sell private power in the area to the Atomic Energy Commission. This plan ended in scandal and failure, but the Submerged Lands Act of 1953 assigned lucrative offshore oil and natural gas interests to the coastal states. Although the few bills providing new programs for clean air, recreation areas, wilderness preservation, and highway beautification ran afoul of Eisenhower's states' rights philosophy and budgetary concerns, the president did not hesitate to improve areas already under federal jurisdiction. In 1956, he inaugurated a ten-year program to modernize facilities in the national parks; in contrast, he delayed efforts to purchase private seashore for public use.

If caution and philosophical objections guided Eisenhower's approach to social and ecological issues, the Republican president was curiously ambivalent about federal spending on "internal improvements." Public works projects that promoted the economic development of the country —what economists call the "capital infrastructure"—received quick, almost enthusiastic approval despite often costly drains on government funds. The Middle West welcomed plans for joint United States-Canadian construction of the Saint Lawrence Seaway, a dream of Herbert Hoover's brought to fruition in 1959, thirty years after he recommended it to Congress. Massive highway building programs, justified to a frugal Congress as an aid to "national defense," gained support from local businessmen and commuters, as well as construction companies and unions. But in 1959 Eisenhower rejected a bill providing for low-income housing as too inflationary. During his last term, Congress passed two area redevelopment bills that called for federally guaranteed loans to "depressed" or chronically poor areas, but Eisenhower vetoed both, primarily because they would "greatly diminish local responsibility."

Negro Rights and the Warren Court

Yet in spite of his cautious attitude on domestic issues, Eisenhower had appointed one of the most activist of Supreme Court chief justices. The Court under Earl Warren spanned the years 1953–1969, a time of increasingly militant confrontations over civil rights and race relations and of unprecedented dissent from American foreign policy. The Court majority headed by Warren repeatedly intervened in American social life with a series of dramatic decisions, prompting critics to claim that the Court was usurping legislative power and willfully imposing its own blueprints of reform. The energy displayed by the Warren Court was hardly unique: the great chief justices beginning with John Marshall gained renown not for the elegance of their constitutional arguments but for their involvement in social transformation. Surely the Court's enunciation of the doctrine of "separate but equal" in *Plessy* v. *Ferguson* (1896) savored as much of political motivation as the rejection of that position in *Brown* v. *Board of Education* (1954). The defenders and critics of the Warren Court divided ultimately not over the Court's methods but over the wisdom of its decisions.

The personnel of the Warren Court created the most intriguing puzzle. In all, sixteen associate justices served during the Warren years, but the central figures were only three: Warren himself, and Justices Black and Douglas. Warren came to the bench from the moderate wing of the Republican party after two terms as governor of California and an unsuccessful vice-presidential bid as Dewey's 1948 running mate. His appointment by President Eisenhower in 1953 was scarcely taken as a green light for social engineering. Hugo Black, a Democratic Senator from Alabama, had been an honorary Klansman when FDR appointed him to the Court in 1937, yet he staunchly and consistently defended civil liberties. William O. Douglas, the particular target of those who saw the Court as the embodiment of wickedness, worked as a young lawyer for a Wall Street firm and headed the Securities and Exchange Commission before his appointment; his nomination in 1939 aroused in Congress only the fear that he would be too subservient to corporate wealth. Yet these three men

gave the Court its distinct cast much more than the appointees of Presidents Kennedy and Johnson.

The impact of the Warren Court's first major decision is still sharply evident; the furor over school desegregation mounted as the focus of compliance moved from south to north. The NAACP, through a team of lawyers headed by Thurgood Marshall, had been hammering away at school segregation for fifteen years before 1954, but the Supreme Court under Chief Justice Vinson responded only by tightening the equality promised under "separate but equal." Then the Warren Court, overturning the "separate but equal" doctrine of *Plessy* v. *Ferguson* (1896), unan-

Earl Warren proved his social concern as chief justice, and his court made landmark and controversial decisions in many areas. Here, a group of John Birch Society members picket outside a session of the California State Bar Association, as Warren arrives to address that group. *United Press International*

imously held in *Brown* v. *Board of Education of Topeka* that "separate educational facilities are inherently unequal." In its unanimous decision the Court mentioned social and psychological factors. The basic constitutional issue, Chief Justice Earl Warren wrote, was whether segregation on the basis of race, even though all other factors were equal, deprived the minority group of equal educational opportunity. "We believe that it does," the nine judges asserted. Since the Fourteenth Amendment guaranteed the "equal protection of the laws," segregation was clearly unconstitutional. Aware that desegregation was not a simple matter, the Court further ordered that steps be taken to implement the decision "with all deliberate speed"; a loose phrase which allowed a further decade of inaction. Though surprising to laymen, the decision climaxed a long chain of Court action against discrimination. Although the Court did not invent the racial tensions that came to dominate American politics, the Brown decision served as a constant reference point and helped initiate the civil rights movement.

Eisenhower rarely put the moral prestige of his office clearly behind the Court's decision; he told a friend that it had set back progress in the South by at least fifteen years. He believed that the battle against intolerance had to be won in "the hearts of men," not in legislative chambers. Once again, the president resisted expansion of the powers or scope of federal government. A curious ambivalence marked Eisenhower's position on the rights of minorities. Soon after taking office he abolished most public segregation in the District of Columbia and completed desegregation in the armed forces. Yet when violent resistance to school desegregation erupted in Little Rock, Arkansas, in 1957, Eisenhower did not hesitate to enforce federal supremacy. A state court had blocked an integration plan approved by the Little Rock School Board on grounds that violence would break out if it went into operation. When a federal court countermanded this decision and ordered integration, Governor Orville Faubus mobilized the Arkansas National Guard to bar entrance to black students. Eisenhower quickly backed up the authority and supremacy of the federal court. At a private meeting with Faubus, he forced the governor to replace soldiers with policemen and on September 23 blacks entered the school. A violent mob gathered and school authorities sent the black students home. The next day, when the crowd refused to leave, Eisenhower placed the National Guard under federal authority and also ordered paratroops from the United States Army into Little Rock. With bayonets fixed, the troops broke up the mob and stood guard while the integration plan went into effect. Throughout the crisis, the president approached the problem as a constitutional one, a conflict between state and federal authority. He never commented on the *Brown* case—believing a president should not discuss Court decisions—and he did not personally aid desegregation efforts. But in the Little Rock crisis he placed the faith and power of the national government fully, if temporarily, behind the civil rights movement.

In 1956 Attorney General Herbert Brownell transmitted arguments for a strong civil rights bill to Congress, although Eisenhower himself approved only two sections—one calling for an investigatory commission, the other reorganizing the civil rights unit in the Justice Department. Republicans hoping to gain a high Negro vote in the 1956 election convinced the president in October to give lukewarm endorsement to the rest of the proposed legislation, which extended the injunctive powers of the federal government in protecting civil and voting rights. But in July 1957, as the bill was receiving serious consideration in Congress, the president withdrew his support from the critical Part III; at a news conference he answered "no" on whether the attorney general should be allowed to bring about school desegregation suits if local authorities did not request such action. In spite of pleas from prominent blacks to veto a weakened measure and demand something better, the president signed it. Nevertheless, the Civil Rights Act of 1957 was the first federal civil rights legislation in more than eighty years.

Still, the party of emancipation did not take the lead in implementing Negro rights. During the last three years of Eisenhower's administration only forty-nine school districts desegregated—a slowing down that must be attributed in part to the president's attitude. And the 1957 legislation added few southern blacks to the voting rolls by 1959. An attempt to pass Part III of the 1957 bill failed again in 1959 with the president flatly opposed. The Civil Rights Act of 1960 at last empowered federal courts to review state voting laws.

Despite the inactivity of the Eisenhower administration, black Americans were changing their perspective on their country more rapidly than any other group. World War II had cracked some of the old customs of segregation. The war economy and subsequent good times produced a new black middle class, more aggressive than its prewar predecessor and unequivocally committed to some type of integration. The Reverend Martin Luther King, Jr., became the foremost spokesman of the new civil rights movement. The bus boycott he directed in 1955 in Montgomery, Alabama, was its first great nonviolent triumph. The National Association for the Advancement of Colored People, founded in 1909, began to push with new force its goals of legal, political, and social equality—the classic aims of integration traditionally contrasted with the self-help methods of Booker T. Washington. Government and education, not business enterprise, would ease entry into the white world.

Both buoyant and fragile, the civil rights movement depended not

merely on the ability of concerned whites and blacks to cooperate politically, but also on the acquiescence of black and white Americans outside the coalition. Many northern whites seemed to tolerate the civil rights movement only so long as it was confined to the South; they themselves would not willingly become its targets. Most ghetto dwellers, on the other hand, lived below the economic and social level at which integration could help; for them the movement awakened a militancy without offering a program. By the end of the fifties the Black Muslims, a small but growing nationalistic sect, opposed integration. James Baldwin explained to a white upper-class audience in 1961 that the Muslims were the "rainbow sign": "No more water, the fire next time!"

Another group asserting its identity amidst the anomie of the fifties came to be known as the radical Right. Older members could recall a day when they had belonged to a political minority in opposition to the New Deal. But for a time, after the fall of China and during the years of Joe McCarthy, Americans on the right assumed that their values and goals

Martin Luther King, Jr. (1929–1968) and his wife Coretta, at the time of his first arrest in Montgomery, Alabama, 1955, while directing a bus boycott. *Black Star*

were respectable if not ascendant. When they realized that Eisenhower's administration meant a moderate politics and the continuation or even the extension of New Deal welfare legislation, hostility developed even toward the Republican party. This alienation became obvious after the cold war shifted from ideological to technological concerns. The more militant Rightists then created an enclave all their own, forming secret fraternities such as the John Birch Society and publishing apocalyptic journals like *American Opinion*. In some suburban areas they took over school and library boards, defending the young from communism and other subversive influences. They struck one prophetic note; tastes not unlike theirs—opposition to bureaucracy and a preference for smallness of scale—would become very important to the Left in the next decade.

The Campaign of 1956

Moderation in both major parties marked the 1956 campaign, which featured the same candidates as in 1952. Stevenson presented a vision of possible disengagement from the cold war; he recommended a unilateral halt to nuclear testing and an end to the draft. At the same time, however, he implied that Eisenhower had sacrificed our national security in exchange for a balanced budget and had failed to answer Russian ideology with an articulate program and philosophy. Early in 1956 Stevenson told a Los Angeles audience that the use of federal troops to enforce desegregation court orders would be "a fatal mistake." He explained: "That is exactly what brought on the Civil War. We must proceed gradually, not upsetting habits or traditions that are older than the Republic." Like his hero Abraham Lincoln, Stevenson put the issue of maintaining national unity before that of racial justice. Many Negro newspapers backed Eisenhower, who later ran well in black precincts. Senator Estes Kefauver of Tennessee, whom Stevenson defeated at the 1956 convention, had represented a reformist impulse of greater drive and tenacity, and might have provided a more distinctive program for the Democrats. Kefauver, for example, fa-

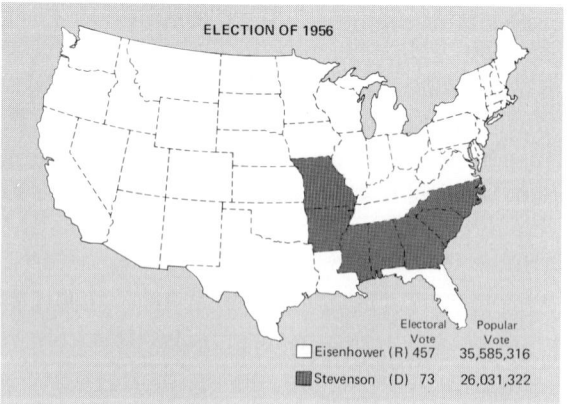

ELECTION OF 1956

	Electoral Vote	Popular Vote
Eisenhower (R)	457	35,585,316
Stevenson (D)	73	26,031,322

vored rapid conformity to the Supreme Court decisions on school desegregation, while Stevenson stuck to gradualism—and won an important
early primary in Florida. The luster of Stevenson's reputation has been
preserved as in amber, but he was a man far removed from the issues that
would prevail in the mid-sixties and it is questionable whether he provided much of an alternative to the middle ground of Republican moderates.

In the 1956 election Eisenhower faced the political disadvantages of a
serious heart attack suffered in September 1955 and of a major operation
for ileitis performed in June 1956. Stevenson, in a moment of bad taste on
the eve of the voting, reminded the electorate of the president's condition,
commenting on November 4 that an Eisenhower victory would make
Nixon president within four years. But Eisenhower occupied an unassail-
able position. He had ended the war in Korea and avoided others in Vietnam or China. He also had the good fortune to run while the economy
was healthy. Beyond that, Eisenhower stood for reducing tension; in a
decade of rapid social change the gentleness and strength of the man—
qualities he naturally projected—created an unbeatable appeal. In the
last days of the campaign the Middle East crisis further strengthened Eisenhower. His margin of victory did not reach the fabled triumph of
FDR twenty years before, but a tally of 457 to 73 electoral votes and a
nine million popular vote margin gave the Republicans much reason for
self-congratulation. It was a far more conclusive triumph than that of
1952. Even the Democratic Solid South crumbled; Stevenson lost Virginia, Florida, Louisiana, and Texas.

Had they read the congressional returns more carefully, however, the Republicans might have been somewhat less jubilant, for they had not built
a lasting national majority. In 1956 Eisenhower ran 6.5 million votes
ahead of the Republican congressional candidates. All through the fifties,
in fact, the Democrats gradually regained congressional seats they had
lost in 1952: in 1953, 48 percent of the House was Republican, in 1955, 47
percent, in 1957, 46 percent, and in 1959, 35 percent.

The congressional elections of 1958 produced a landslide for the Democrats: in the next Congress they would outnumber the Republicans by
283 to 153 in the House, and by 64 to 34 in the Senate. Important trends
reflected in the realignment of forces changed the politics of the era.
Older men such as William Knowland and John Bricker retired from national life, and many of the new faces of the sixties first came to Washington in the Congress that met the following year. The movement that
had first shown itself outside of Congress in the Supreme Court desegrega-

**Eisenhower's
Second Term**

tion decision of 1954 and the Montgomery bus boycott of 1955 began to trickle into national debate. Republicans like Nelson Rockefeller acquired prominence while some older leaders, adjusting to the times, pushed through the Negro rights act. These tendencies made it plain that the immense popularity of Eisenhower had not been translated into a general or lasting Republican resurgence.

The results of the 1958 elections reflected national concerns. First came the economy: the 1957 recession suggested that perhaps only under the Democrats could a stable prosperity be sustained. The Republicans unwisely chose 1958 to push "right to work" or open shop laws through state referenda. The national debt apparently had not leveled off as expected under Eisenhower; rising from $259 billion in 1952, it stood at $276 billion in 1958 and would reach $286 billion in 1960. (At level dollars, and as a percentage of the gross national product, it did decline.)

Eisenhower's secretary of agriculture, Ezra Taft Benson of Utah, possessed a Mormon zeal for self-reliance and despised federal subsidies. Replacing firm farm subsidy prices with flexible supports in 1954, the Eisenhower agricultural program favored large farms that employed the latest technology and indirectly forced more and more small farmers to sell their holdings and to become tenants or move into the cities. But the president restrained Benson from reverting to no government controls even as he vetoed a Democratic bill to restore high parity prices; he did, however, accept a billion-dollar soil bank that paid farmers to take land out of production. Here more than in any other area, the Republicans tried to reverse twenty years of Democratic rule, but they scarcely altered the agricultural structures erected by Roosevelt and Truman and actually increased total government payments to support farm prices.

Even new concerns in foreign policy hampered the Republicans. The Soviets had launched their two Sputniks in October 1957; the second one demonstrated that they had perfected the rocket fuel necessary for space exploration, and that the booster rocket could propel a nuclear weapon at high speed to a radius of 4,000 miles. These developments shocked those who presumed that under a military man, America would naturally hold its own in competition against the Russians. Questions about the administration had already appeared with the dismissal of Eisenhower's closest adviser, Sherman Adams, for accepting gifts. On a broader scale, sociological muckrakers like C. Wright Mills, and journalistic popularizers like Vance Packard, were exposing unsettling social problems. As public opinion polls indicated, attitudes were changing on the government's role in the economy and on a whole range of social issues.

The criticism by publicists probably had less influence on the 1958 election than it did on the Kennedy-Johnson programs of the 1960's. But even Eisenhower, upon leaving office in January 1961, warned of the "military-industrial complex" that Mills and others had described. Certainly the postwar era—the period defined by the problems World War II had created—was coming to an end. No one anticipated in the mid-fifties that the next decade would bring distinct generational shifts among the young. The sixties would also bring much progress, much discord, and much complexity. Even the horror of totalitarianism would lose its simple face. The trial in Israel of Adolf Eichmann revealed that Nazism was the product not only of a mad demagogue, but also of "sensible" bureaucrats. A society might evade madmen with luck, but there seemed no clear way to control the morality of those essential technocrats whose attitudes the culture had revered as a bar against the romantic, the irresponsible, and the sinister.

27

Millions of Americans remember the hope and energy that attended the presidency of John Kennedy. A third-generation American, Kennedy was well established socially. He sometimes displayed an aristocrat's aloofness that perhaps stemmed from inherited wealth and a father ambitious for his son. He possessed intelligence, good looks, a Harvard education, a war hero's record, and a beautiful wife. For all its overuse, the word "image" is inescapable in any discussion of the Kennedy years. Perhaps the clearest achievement of his administration was his communicating an image of dynamic youthfulness.

What Matter of Man?

The Massachusetts senator of the 1950's gave clues to the later man. A political figure notable for his independence, Kennedy was neither a member of the Senate's inner club nor one of a group of consistent dissenters. Earlier he had refused to join his Massachusetts Democratic House colleagues in a plea for the release from prison of the corrupt mayor of Boston, James Michael Curley. A war hero, he denounced the American Legion on the floor of Congress and supported President Eisenhower on the St. Lawrence Seaway though it was unpopular in Atlantic-oriented Massachusetts. In an obvious effort not to antagonize his Irish Catholic supporters, he kept silent on Joseph McCarthy in the early 1950's. When Eleanor Roosevelt asked him to go on record against the late senator at the end of the decade, Kennedy pointed out that doing it then would be hypocritical, though it would bring needed convention support. It was hard to comprehend an eager young senator who denounced the labor leader Jimmy Hoffa on grounds that he had "no discrimination or taste or style. . . ." In short, he was refreshing and unpredictable, commanding the resources of an immense fortune; yet because of his Roman Catholic religion he was a political underdog.

When he first entered national politics in 1956 as a candidate for the vice-presidency, Kennedy allowed his adviser Ted Sorenson to leak a memorandum arguing that a Catholic candidate would strengthen rather than harm a national ticket. Kennedy also let himself be cast as a Northerner friendly to the South and willing to let that section move slowly on the race issue. He thus lost in 1956 to Senator Estes Kefauver of Tennes-

548

The Kennedy Style

see. In 1958 he won reelection in Massachusetts by 875,000 votes, the largest majority in the state's history. He apparently sensed the changed priority in the electorate in the later 1950's, for he dwelt on national preparedness and the need for "moving ahead" in all areas of national life.

Thanks to shrewd political methods and an able staff, by 1960 Kennedy held a commanding lead in the race for the Democratic presidential nomination. But party leaders worried about his religion and his youthfulness —he would have to prove himself in the primaries. The first major test came in early April against Minnesota's Senator Hubert Humphrey in Wisconsin. But the results were inconclusive, for although Kennedy won a majority of the votes, the state's large Catholic population made it untypical of the nation at large. He would have to prove his vote-getting ability again in West Virginia on May 10. Humphrey campaigned strenuously in that state on economic and social issues. Kennedy obviously responded to what he saw of poverty, and he strongly emphasized the need for a more active economy. He repeatedly drew attention to his religion, asserting that it posed no threat to other Americans. He believed the

President John F. Kennedy (1917–1963) applauds as his children, John, Jr. and Caroline demonstrate their dancing ability, November 1962. The Kennedys were American heros in the Lindbergh tradition of youth and beauty. *United Press International*

Protestant Democrats of West Virginia would not consider religion a leading issue, for the nation had changed in the years that separated Kennedy from Al Smith, the Catholic Democratic presidential candidate in 1928. Also, the average West Virginian sensed that he was being tested and that his state's vote would be seen by the country at large as a repudiation or an endorsement of religious bigotry. Accordingly, Kennedy won 61 percent of the primary vote.

After West Virginia it was plain that Kennedy would be the nominee. The tumultuous greeting given him in mid-July outside the Biltmore Hotel in Los Angeles showed he had garnered an enthusiastic convention following. Senator Eugene McCarthy of Minnesota eloquently nominated Adlai Stevenson, who was willing to be drafted: "Do not reject this man who made us all proud to be called Democrats. . . ." Stevenson replied with some characteristically self-deprecatory humor—he seemed, so said his detractors, to want to be appointed president. Kennedy, who easily defeated all his challengers, hoped for a united party despite the platform's strong civil rights section. Many northern Democrats and labor leaders were chagrined at Kennedy's choice of Lyndon B. Johnson of Texas as his running mate, but they had nowhere to turn because the Republican party had nominated their old enemy, Vice-President Richard Nixon.

Nixon enjoyed a substantial lead in postconvention polls, but bad luck plagued him throughout the campaign. Midwestern Republicans, especially those on the platform committee, continued to resent a preconvention meeting between Nixon and Nelson Rockefeller in the governor's New York City apartment, which they wrongly regarded as a capitulation to Rockefeller's advanced social views. The purpose of the meeting was actually for Nixon to attempt to enlist Rockefeller's active support. Nixon suffered an infected knee in August which postponed the beginning of his campaign for two weeks and left him fatigued and an easy

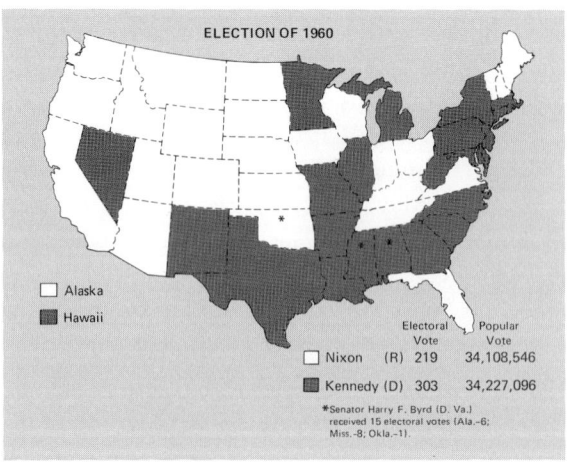

ELECTION OF 1960

☐ Alaska
■ Hawaii

	Electoral Vote	Popular Vote
☐ Nixon (R)	219	34,108,546
■ Kennedy (D)	303	34,227,096

*Senator Harry F. Byrd (D. Va.) received 15 electoral votes (Ala.-6; Miss.-8; Okla.-1).

prey to colds. Yet he held to his earlier promise to visit all fifty states, wasting valuable time in Alaska when he should have been in the critical areas of the Midwest. Nixon's running mate, Henry Cabot Lodge, Jr., was an inept and slow-paced campaigner. President Eisenhower's planned May summit meeting with Khrushchev collapsed after the Soviet Union shot down a U-2 reconnaissance plane deep in Russian territory. Later in the spring Ike canceled a visit to Japan because of anti-American sentiment. The president hardly helped Nixon by an offhand response to a reporter's question about what major administrative decisions Nixon had participated in: "If you give me a week I might think of one." And in the closing weeks of the campaign Nixon could not make use of Eisenhower, who was in fragile health. Finally, Norman Vincent Peale, Nixon's own pastor, condemned Kennedy on religious grounds, giving credence to the view that the Catholic candidate was indeed a victim of prejudice. Methodist leaders gave Kennedy a dramatic opportunity to prove to a skeptical audience of Houston ministers—by way of television to the nation at large—that they had no religious reasons to fear him. Here again Kennedy stood in sharp contrast to Al Smith. Smith had regarded as bigotry the mere questioning of his faith, while Kennedy welcomed queries and responded openly and at length.

In the course of the campaign Kennedy emerged as the more activist candidate, while Vice-President Nixon had to defend the Eisenhower administration. When Kennedy endlessly said it was time "to get moving again" he referred principally to the national economy. But economic expansion also had its foreign policy dimension. When Khrushchev threatened "We will bury you," he may have meant that the cold war had become a struggle for the underdeveloped countries, with the United States and Russia offering competing models of economy. Kennedy also repeatedly charged that the Russians held a lead over America in the development of missiles. He managed to link the issues of national prestige and economic growth, implying that Nixon, as a high official in the decent but ineffectual Eisenhower administration, could not solve these problems. Kennedy's charm and confident handling of the complexities of public problems cast him as a man with a more dashing and more effective response to the familiar problems of the 1950's. Nixon agreed to a series of television debates in which Kennedy appeared fresher and more vibrant, thus confirming in the minds of voters the contrast between him and the exhausted Republican candidate.

Still, the electorate expressed no clear preference for Kennedy over Nixon. Kennedy won the election with less than 51 percent of the two-party vote, and by 303 to 219 in the electoral college. The solid South, broken in the 1950's by Eisenhower, remained split in 1960: Nixon re-

ceived almost half its vote. Anti-Catholicism weighed against Kennedy in the South, though his losses in that section were partially balanced by gains in important urban areas in evenly contested states. At the same time Democrats won in the House 263 to 174 and in the Senate 64 to 36. Many voters in 1960 clearly preferred the tension-reducing style of Nixon to the vigorous thrusts of Kennedy. The new president—the youngest, at forty-three, in American history—seemed to sense that, for he immediately took steps to draw the nation together. He met with Nixon in Florida after the election. He retained such icons of government as J. Edgar Hoover of the FBI and Allen Dulles of the Central Intelligence Agency. This meant not only that he wanted continuity in government but also that he had patience with symbols of the past. In January he forced through a change in the size of the House Rules Committee, "packing" it with his supporters, but here the closeness of victory reinforced a cautious approach to the domestic scene.

Outgoing Vice-President Richard M. Nixon (right) congratulates President John F. Kennedy, January 20, 1961, after Kennedy was sworn in as the thirty-fifth president of the United States. The new vice-president, Lyndon B. Johnson (center), looks on. *United Press International*

It was in foreign affairs that Kennedy determined to leave his mark. Although remarkably bellicose, he foresaw the end of atomic confrontation and the coming of a new age of wars of national liberation. With problems like Cuba and Laos in mind, Kennedy joined Generals Maxwell Taylor and Matthew Ridgway in calling for a more mobile and technically skilled armed forces capable of fighting in limited wars. (Taylor, who had retired in 1959 protesting Eisenhower's policies, returned in 1961 as a prime adviser and in 1962 became chief of staff.) Kennedy's background made him especially receptive to the new brand of warfare: a naval hero, a reader of James Bond stories, the creator of the Green Berets, he combined a fascination for military technology with a sense of military dash and elitism. He welcomed the opportunity to build heroic new armed forces. Yet at the same time Kennedy seemed to believe that he could bring about an easing of international tension.

The main thrust of Kennedy's foreign policy was suggested by his cabinet selections. For secretary of state he passed over such independent minds as William Fulbright of Arkansas, chairman of the Senate Foreign Relations Committee, and Adlai Stevenson, who, as early as the middle fifties, called for an end to nuclear testing. Instead, following the advice of former Secretary of State Dean Acheson, Kennedy turned to the State Department bureaucracy for Dean Rusk, a strong-willed man who favored cold war policy goals if not traditional techniques. Robert McNamara brought a degree of efficiency to the Defense Department, but rarely disagreed on policy with the joint chiefs of staff.

Some of the foreign policy attitudes Kennedy brought to office quickly took concrete form in the Bay of Pigs fiasco. Under the Eisenhower administration, the Central Intelligence Agency had prepared an invasion force to spark a general uprising against Fidel Castro in Cuba. More than a thousand Cuban refugee guerrillas awaited orders on a coffee plantation in a mountainous region of Guatemala. To cancel the planned invasion, Kennedy reasoned, would make the new administration look weak. So in April of 1961 he gave the signal. The CIA chose a well-fortified landing spot, which allowed the rebels no opportunity to retreat to the mountains. The motley force put large quantities of radio equipment and munitions in a single boat, which was blown up; air cover was wholly inadequate. Castro easily destroyed the invaders.

Kennedy apparently thought that the well-entrenched Castro could be overthrown without the cooperation of the United States air force, army, and navy. Perhaps the anti-Communist traditions of his family and church, and the memory of congressional resolutions calling for the "liberation" of Eastern Europe, had engendered in Kennedy such naïveté. He may have entertained the fallacious premises that people who lived under any form of communism yearned for freedom and would revolt if given an opportunity, and that since communism was evil it could not succeed. Certainly the president braced himself for conflict. He believed that during his administration America would face the greatest crises of its history. His inaugural and state of the union addresses conveyed the need for austere self-discipline in order to prepare for an era of testing and danger.

One Kennedy response to the failure in Cuba—it was after all an act of aggression by one sovereign state against another—was to press for an Alliance for Progress, a $10 billion, decade-long program of economic aid to Latin America. Also in 1961 the Development Loan Fund provided over a billion American dollars in aid to underdeveloped nations. The Bay of Pigs, which ironically lifted his standing in public opinion polls, made Kennedy more rather than less belligerent. He pushed harder for greater military spending, and in 1961 Congress responded with a 15 percent increase. Kennedy discounted the argument that building up an arsenal of new weapons would provoke the Soviet Union into a like response. Nevertheless, the Russians did respond with a similar increase in their defense expenditures.

A Darkening Plain

In June 1961 Kennedy and Khrushchev met in Vienna, where they accomplished little except an exchange of polemics. As Kennedy judged his rhetoric, Khrushchev seemed intransigently committed to disrupting world order, for he threatened to sign a peace treaty with East Germany. At worst this could lead to a ban on entering Berlin, at best force us to negotiate with a government we had not recognized. Kennedy was disturbed at the confrontation over the nature of the status quo, which for him meant the existing international balance of power. He hoped that future changes in the world would take place without upsetting this balance between West and East. For Khrushchev, any sort of global freeze would disrupt the revolutionary process itself. At Vienna the Soviets sought to counter Western economic expansionism with an assertion of the right to rebel against reactionary governments.

The encounter discouraged Kennedy. Upon returning home he increased draft quotas, called up the reserves, demanded a crash civil defense program that led to a popular frenzy of bomb shelters, and asked for estimates on casualties in the event of nuclear war. Dean Acheson urged a hard line on Berlin, calling it a "simple contest of wills." He recommended sending a division of American troops on the autobahn through East Germany to Berlin, and urged Kennedy to make it clear that we would fight a nuclear war if necessary. Since there was nothing to negoti-

ate, a willingness to go to the conference table would be taken as a sign of weakness. Kennedy seemed momentarily to agree with Acheson; in an address on July 25, 1961, he said: "We do not want to fight, but we have fought before." He incorrectly regarded Russian belligerence as an audacious effort on their part to upset the one area of the world with a clear balance of power. When Khrushchev in August acceded to the construction of the Berlin Wall, sealing off East Berlin from the western sector, Kennedy remained distraught, remarking that there was one chance in five of a nuclear exchange. He sent 1,500 troops from West Germany to West Berlin, and Vice-President Johnson came to pledge American lives to the defense of the city. When it eventually became clear to Washington that the wall was only a defensive measure, some congressmen charged that the administration had overreacted on Berlin, that Kennedy had created a pseudo-crisis.

Apart from Berlin, world tension remained high. In September 1961 Russia began to detonate nuclear bombs of enormous power; America followed suit in the spring of 1962. The older Eisenhower-Dulles policy of

President Kennedy and West German chancellor Konrad Adenauer (1876–1967) at the start of Kennedy's twelve-day European tour of June 1963. The purpose of the trip was to stress the United States' determination to continue to defend Western Europe despite some skepticism from French president De Gaulle. United Press International

massive retaliation now existed perilously alongside a new Kennedy policy of conventional arms and a willingness to use them in any part of the world. On every continent ambitious third powers threatened to upset the world balance and precipitate the ultimate conflict between the Soviet Union and the United States.

In distant Southeast Asia, the existing regimes in both Laos and South Vietnam were endangered by indigenous Communist forces. In Laos the president, remembering the Bay of Pigs, voided direct intervention. He also sensed that America, as he uncharacteristically expressed it in a speech at the University of Washington in November 1961, "cannot impose [its] will upon the other 94 percent of mankind. . . . We cannot right every wrong or reverse each adversity. . . . There cannot be an American solution to every world problem." Kennedy eventually compromised by abandoning a right-wing faction in Laos and supporting a "neutral and independent" government. Here perhaps the president had made some headway with Khrushchev in Vienna: the Russians also exercised their influence in behalf of neutrality. Eventually, the parties agreed on a "troika" coalition government in 1962, which at least succeeded in approving a genuine cease-fire.

In October 1962 the world came close to nuclear war. The previous winter the United States stopped altogether the importing of Cuban sugar. In response, Castro decided in the late spring to allow the Russians to place intermediate-range missiles in Cuba; never before had the Soviet Union placed missiles outside its own national boundaries. Our air surveillance first revealed the sites as their construction neared completion. Kennedy quickly decided that we could not tolerate interference in an area so patently within America's sphere of influence. Although quite congruent to international law, and no real military threat to the United States, the placing of missiles was a blatant challenge to the balance of power dictum Kennedy had outlined in Vienna. Khrushchev had evidently decided to test American intentions. His justification was the protection of a sovereign Cuba against a United States invasion—a possibility Kennedy's Bay of Pigs fiasco made not unreasonable even in the opinion of our allies.

Both the president's military consultants and Dean Acheson recommended an immediate air strike, which would wipe out Russian advisers along with the missiles. But Robert McNamara and Robert Kennedy disagreed; the attorney general argued that it was not in the American grain to launch an air attack against a small island unable to retaliate. America would be faithless to its past if it attacked Cuba much as the Japanese had attacked Pearl Harbor.

The president decided on a less drastic course; he instituted a naval blockade against Russian ships bringing additional missile equipment to Cuba. Kennedy set the barrier as close to the Caribbean as he dared, hoping that Khrushchev would decide not to risk an incident. The US permitted a harmless tanker to penetrate the quarantine area, but then, as millions waited breathlessly, the first ship carrying technical equipment turned back. Some critics blamed Kennedy for bringing the world close to the brink of nuclear war—unnecessarily because he could have brought about an exchange; the Soviet Union evidently would have given up the missile sites if the United States had relinquished some useless Turkish bases on its borders. Khrushchev, they said, displayed the greater maturity by refusing to risk war. But Kennedy, too, had exercised some restraint in the face of a Soviet provocation, and did promise not to attempt further aggression against Cuba. Before his countrymen Kennedy appeared a courageous and mature statesman. Since the crisis occurred just before the mid-term elections, it probably helped the Democrats to gain four seats in the Senate and lose only two in the House—an excellent performance for a party in power at off-year.

The Great Thaw

After the missile crisis, antagonism between Russia and the United States shifted to the third world. There confrontation would continue but with less immediate risk of world-shaking consequences. Direct relations between the two superpowers, in fact, underwent a kind of thaw. A "hot line" insured instantaneous telephone communication in emergencies. Kennedy, in a speech at American University in June 1963, heralded a new era of cooperation between the two countries. In that year, too, the Soviets rejected Chinese militance, insisting on an era of peaceful coexistence and the avoidance of nuclear war. Finally, the Test Ban Treaty of 1963 outlawed atmospheric testing of nuclear weapons. This became the only enduring accomplishment of Kennedy's foreign policy, even though two powers close to a nuclear capacity, France and Communist China, refused to sign.

Until the missile crisis Kennedy had to direct his abundant energies largely toward foreign policy. In 1961 he made a beginning in the domestic area in the close vote to enlarge the size of the House Rules Committee, which had long stymied his programs. Then, Congress in 1961 passed several administration measures: a higher minimum wage law; a Housing Act, which granted almost $5 billion for urban renewal projects; an Area Redevelopment Act, which provided funds for retraining in areas of high unemployment; and money for water pollution control. Although some of his cabinet appointees, like Stewart L. Udall of the Interior Department, promoted conservation programs, the president did not press Congress for new welfare or social legislation. Udall, after speaking to the president about conservation in the summer of 1961, remarked: "He's imprisoned by Berlin." In 1962 and 1963 few Kennedy laws passed Congress. The president himself lacked the time or patience necessary to work on details of legislation. Whenever Secretary of Health, Education and Welfare Anthony Celebrezze tried to engage him in discussion about proposed laws, the president cut him off, saying, "You were the mayor of a large city. You know how to handle these problems. Now handle them."

On the major social issue of the era, that of civil rights, Kennedy brought to the presidency a record of compromise and expediency. He voted twice to weaken the 1957 Civil Rights Act: to return the bill to committee where Senator James Eastland of Mississippi might strip it to nothing; and in favor of a successful amendment guaranteeing jury trials in contempt cases (white southern juries could be relied upon not to convict civil rights violators). But Title III of the act, which promised decisive action in school desegregation, received his support. In both Kennedy's vice-presidential and presidential campaigns he sought support from the most truculent segregationist governors. He seemed scarcely aware of the moderate civil rights movement that crystallized after the Supreme Court desegregation decision of 1954.

The first massive direct action in the civil rights movement came in Montgomery, Alabama. There, in 1955, under the leadership of Martin Luther King, Jr., blacks refused to patronize the city's public transportation system, which required that they sit in the rear of buses. After months of unrelenting economic boycott, the city fathers agreed to end the demeaning practice, in the first great victory of the movement. In February 1960 four black college students in Greensboro, North Carolina, sat down at the local Woolworth's segregated lunch counter. They asked for cups of coffee but were summarily refused. They remained seated. The next day sixteen fellow students joined their sit-in and the group attracted attention in the national media. On the third day, more than fifty students came, joined by a few white girls from the prestigious Women's College of North Carolina.

The effect was electric. The sit-ins spread, first to other stores in Greensboro and later to more than a hundred other towns and cities. The white-led Congress of Racial Equality assumed leadership, offering a generation of experience with nonviolent direct action techniques. The legal defense fund of the National Association for the Advancement of Colored People, founded in 1911, aided students imprisoned by local authorities.

The Civil Rights Movement

The membership of the Southern Christian Leadership Conference expanded, and the Student Non-Violent Coordinating Committee—the guiding force of the student movement in the South—was born. Even the staid Urban League, under its new leader Whitney Young, Jr., supported the campaigns of Martin Luther King.

President Kennedy did not seem to care deeply about the fleeting dream of the early civil rights movement, a community of brotherhood bound by love. In January he omitted civil rights from a list of the "real issues of 1960." Along with Richard Nixon, Kennedy made promises during the presidential campaign, but he translated few of them into concrete proposals after he took office. His telephone message of sympathy to Mrs. Martin Luther King while her husband sat in an Atlanta jail was a symbolic gesture of great political value, but it ironically summed up his detachment—it was a gesture that led to no lasting achievement.

Genuinely fearful of losing support for other programs, Kennedy sent

Martin Luther King, Jr. (center) leading 250,000 people in a march on Washington in August 1963. Nonviolent tactics were at their peak during the Kennedy years with sit-ins, boycotts, and peaceful demonstrations winning blacks favorable legislation. *United Press International*

no new civil rights legislation to Congress in 1961 and 1962. During the campaign he had castigated President Eisenhower for tolerating segregation in federally financed housing. It took Kennedy two years to make good on his promise to eliminate it with "a stroke of the presidential pen" (he received thousands of pens through the mail), and even then he acted deviously, burying the order among more striking acts so that the presidential deed earned him little credit or blame. He did appoint Vice-President Johnson to head a new Committee on Equal Employment Opportunity, and Johnson, with some success, used his powers of persuasion to insure that blacks would be employed under all types of federal contracts. In addresses at Gettysburg and Detroit in 1963, Johnson spoke sincerely and strongly for full civil rights—and with a southern accent. Kennedy also appointed the prominent Negro Robert C. Weaver to be federal housing administrator. Yet the president generally followed the Eisenhower pattern and seemed not to realize the explosive potential of the race situation. Had he sensed it he would never have appointed his brother attorney general, for that office would bear the brunt of white resentments. Robert Kennedy, in fact, accomplished what little the government did for the Negro before 1963. He tried to enforce the weak laws of the fifties, especially those requiring the desegregation of transportation facilities, and he speeded voter registration of southern blacks. The freedom rides of 1961, designed to desegregate bus station waiting rooms, required Robert Kennedy to send federal marshals into Alabama to protect the young people, although he had tried to discourage the project. But RFK's efforts were canceled out when his brother appointed outspoken segregationists to lifetime positions on several southern district courts.

The civil rights movement proceeded without Kennedy, eventually forcing him to act. Coverage by the media sustained the conviction of coming success with television in particular dramatically transmitting the new tactics: confrontation, the threat of violence from the opposition, the posing of moral issues in absolute terms. The forward momentum continued in 1961 with the freedom rides and in the fall of 1962 with James Meredith's attempted enrollment at the University of Mississippi. The next year federal troops came to the university to enroll Meredith, and Vivian Malone entered the University of Alabama under similar conditions in the spring of 1963. The most incendiary situation, however, developed in Birmingham, Alabama, during May 1963. The only strategy that could work for the oppressed blacks in that city was the forcing of massive arrests. Vivid events transpired: police dogs, electric cattle prods, and fire hoses; rioting, bombing, and three small Negro children dead. And Kennedy, foreseeing the "fires of frustration and discord . . . burning in every city, North and South," responded. He asked Congress to

pass a civil rights bill ending segregation in most public places. At last the
national administration of the Democratic party drew its mantle about the civil rights movement.

In 1963 Kennedy, a majority of Congress, the churches, and much of the nation finally awakened to some of the inequities suffered by American blacks. The president requested a partial ban on discrimination in public places, asked for Justice Department powers to sue for school desegregation if requested to do so, and urged broader powers to withhold funds from federally assisted programs in which discrimination occurred. Congressional civil rights leaders pushed Kennedy further, persuading him to give the attorney general power to intervene in all civil rights cases. But Kennedy told a press conference that tax reform was more important than the rights bill; a stronger economy, he believed, would help blacks more than anything else. Before his death later that fall, he secured an agreement from congressional leaders that would probably have led to the passage of a civil rights act in 1964.

Martin Luther King complained in June 1963 that Kennedy might have done "a little more" for blacks than Eisenhower, but "the plight of the vast majority of Negroes remains the same." King himself was the hero of the early movement. When 250,000 people marched on Washington the next August to be counted for the proposed legislation, King addressed them: "I have a dream that one day on the red hills of Georgia the sons of former slaves and the sons of former slaveholders will be able to sit down together at the table of brotherhood. I have a dream that one day even the state of Mississippi, a desert state sweltering with the heat of injustice and oppression, will be transformed into an oasis of freedom and justice. . . . I have a dream that one day the state of Alabama . . . will be transformed into a situation where little black boys and black girls will be able to join hands with little white boys and white girls and walk together as sisters and brothers." Despite Kennedy's failure to share King's vision, in few places did the president's assassination that November arouse such an outpouring of grief as in black communities. Efforts to pass legislation gained strength by construing it as a memorial to Kennedy; Congress easily approved the first law in 1964, and others followed in 1965 and 1966.

The early, nonviolent civil rights movement died with Kennedy or soon afterward. It had always been a fragile coalition. Dependent on keeping the race problem confined to the South and on the acquiescence of lower-class blacks not able to profit from its goals, the movement broke apart in the era of ghetto riots, northern demonstrations, and growing black nationalism.

Kennedy's most successful domestic accomplishment came belatedly in his handling of economic problems. In the 1960 campaign he had charged the Eisenhower administration with failing to maintain as high a national growth rate as that of Western Europe or the Soviet Union. Kennedy, like almost everyone else at the time, assumed that economic growth was highly desirable. Once in office, though, Kennedy acted cautiously. To cure the recession that Nixon later claimed had cost him the presidency, Kennedy relied on piecemeal measures including the raising of social security payments and the minimum wage—techniques akin to those Eisenhower had employed. Increased military spending, too, helped alleviate unemployment. The new president faced problems that discouraged more forthright fiscal or monetary tactics, notably an adverse balance of payments. And until the third quarter of 1962 his prudent policies held the cost of living steady without causing either substantial new unemployment or inflation.

A severe drop in the stock market began in May 1962. It threatened the somewhat shaky prosperity and persuaded Kennedy to embark upon a venturesome new policy. Treasury Secretary Douglas Dillon, a Republican, had been convinced of the need for more federal action through the patient counsel of Kennedy's chief economic adviser, Walter Heller. For the first time during relatively prosperous times, an administration proposed a budget deficit through tax reduction, much more acceptable to business than new spending. The Senate concurred, a reversal of its earlier views. When Senator Paul Douglas had asked for a $6 billion tax cut in 1958 he was rebuffed by a vote of 65 to 23. Yet in February 1964, 77 senators favored a tax cut of over $10 billion—and at a time when the economy merely lagged. The economy responded; the tax cuts helped

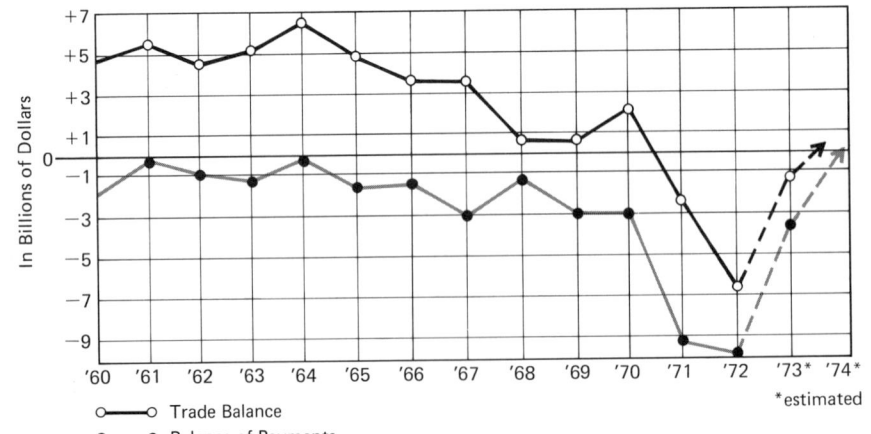

The Federal government expects surpluses in 1974 in America's balance of trade—exports vs. imports of merchandise—and balance of payments, the inflow and outflow of money for all reasons. Such surpluses are a prerequisite for a new monetary agreement.

In Billions of Dollars

'60 '61 '62 '63 '64 '65 '66 '67 '68 '69 '70 '71 '72 '73* '74*

*estimated

o———o Trade Balance

●———● Balance of Payments

spur a $30 billion yearly increase in stable dollars in the gross national product, and unemployment declined sharply.

Although businessmen profited enormously from the expansive economy, they never trusted John Kennedy. Kennedy signed tax credits and a generous depreciation allowance for business in 1962, and reduced corporate income taxes by 20 percent in 1963, gifts of unprecedented generosity. The Trade Expansion Act of 1962 won some business concessions from the European Common Market through a mutual reduction of tariffs. But in April 1962 Kennedy so confronted the steel industry that, for many businessmen, his name would join that of a despised Franklin Roosevelt.

On April 10, late in the afternoon, Roger Blough, chairman of United States Steel, appeared at the White House for an appointment with the president. He told Kennedy that even as they spoke press releases were announcing a steel price rise. The president was furious. Labor Secretary Arthur Goldberg had persuaded the unions to settle for a modest wage hike on the understanding that prices would remain steady. Blough seemed both to deceive and insult the president of the United States. Kennedy privately quoted his father's denunciation of businessmen as "sons of bitches" and launched an unprecedented government attack on the industry. The Defense Department threatened to shift steel contracts to the small companies that had not yet raised prices; the Justice Department and the Federal Trade Commission threatened antitrust action and the passage of new antitrust laws; the Treasury hinted at a tax investigation. Kennedy himself spoke on television: "In this serious hour in our nation's history, when we are confronted with grave crises in Berlin and Southeast Asia . . . , the American public will find it hard, as I do, to accept a situation in which a tiny handful of steel executives whose pursuit of private power and profit exceeds their sense of public responsibility can show such utter contempt of the interests of 185 million Americans." It was a spectacular display of presidential power (including an obscure role for the FBI) in the service of what he believed to be the public interest. Big steel, following the lead of some smaller companies, grudgingly rescinded the increase.

An Enigmatic Figure

Belatedly successful in managing the economy, Kennedy gave promise later in 1963 of responding to more domestic needs in the next years of his administration. Then he went to Dallas. Riding unprotected in an open car, Kennedy was an easy target for an assassin's bullet. Lee Harvey Oswald, a refugee of the political Left, evidently killed Kennedy. The presidential plane promptly flew his body home to Washington where

the next day, November 23, a Roman Catholic mass was held in the White House. Chief Justice Earl Warren directed a comprehensive but hurried report on the killing, which uncovered no evidence of conspiracy. Subsequent efforts to link Oswald with one or more additional marksmen or conspirators remained highly speculative.

The achievement of the Kennedy administration lay elsewhere than in a relatively meager legislative record. Kennedy occupied the office during a demanding time. His ultimate success with the economy and the fruitful negotiation of the Test Ban Treaty brightened only the end of his 1,000 days. But, as all presidents, he gave something intangible to the country. The Kennedy style, whatever the vague word means, had its trivial

A young girl helps a Peace Corps worker aboard a bus in Ghana. The Peace Corps was established in 1961, according to President Kennedy to, "help foreign countries meet their urgent needs for skilled manpower."
United Press International

side. Memory of him was colored by his youthful appearance and his vigor, by fashionable form more than by substance. Yet, President Kennedy created expectations as yet unfulfilled. The Kennedy name, quite apart from the president's acts or statements, rekindled hope. A people of growing affluence, still emerging from a restricting past, reacted in different ways to the inflated values the Kennedys represented. Most important was the president's effect on many of the young. By the end of his administration the life of business no longer held great appeal for college students; they increasingly desired something more personally rewarding and idealistic, such as the Peace Corps. He surely had some impact on their changing taste. Through the office of the attorney general, he gave some legitimacy to their new political involvements, and along with it to a more relaxed life-style, to passive nonviolence, and to the stirrings of a coming estrangement.

28

President Kennedy once told an off-the-record press conference that he did not have much hope for solving America's problems. Kennedy's pessimistic vision of what was possible for mankind—a side of his intellectual sophistication not sufficiently appreciated—inevitably narrowed his perspective and his goals. In sharp contrast to Kennedy, Lyndon Johnson's strength—and his weakness—lay in a faith that in America government could accomplish almost anything. Johnson's pride, daring, and technical skill reached their greatest effectiveness in attacking stubborn domestic ills. During his years in office Congress passed more laws for civil rights, health, and education, the arts and science, the eradication of poverty, and aid for the cities than in any earlier era.

The Shaping Influences

Johnson's confidence originated in the New Deal of Franklin Roosevelt. Raised in the hill country of central Texas, Johnson himself knew at first hand the brutalizing effects of poverty. His calculating ambition was evident at Southwest Texas State Teachers College: he dominated the student body and managed to influence the administration as well. Afterward he taught briefly in a rural school and learned something of the needs of poor Mexican Americans. In 1931 he moved to Washington, D.C., where he served as secretary to a Texas congressman and soon aspired to Congress himself. Securing the friendship of President Roosevelt helped: an appointment as Texas director of the National Youth Administration gave Johnson a base from which he campaigned successfully for a congressional seat in 1937. Roosevelt's efforts to raise Johnson to the Senate came to naught, but under the president's tutelage Johnson grew to appreciate both New Deal welfare programs and the art of political manipulation.

After the war Texas politics became more cautious, and Johnson seemed to bend with the times. He became closely identified with some of the natural gas and oil interests and took special care of the burgeoning aircraft industry. In 1947 he voted with the majority of Congress to override President Truman's veto of the moderately antilabor Taft-Hartley Act. He judged well in taking such a course; it helped him to win an extremely close, contested election to the United States Senate in 1948.

566

Johnson's Great Society

Though often an ally of southern segregationists, he remained sufficiently independent to earn the trust and respect of many Northerners, including Senator Hubert Humphrey of Minnesota.

With the coming of the Eisenhower era Johnson moved to the political center; in 1953, by virtue of his impressive legislative skill and bland ideology he won the post of Senate majority leader. Willing to work with the president on foreign policy and economic matters during his first term in the White House, Johnson by 1957 had abandoned the Republican pleas for thrift and called for greater public spending to offset the recession and to fill defense needs. Everything Johnson did portrayed him as a masterful politician. Many Democrats were delighted when in 1959 he led them in a stereotyped crusade against the appointment of Admiral Lewis Strauss as secretary of commerce.

Given his personal temperament, Johnson probably thought of running for the presidency at an early date, but was deterred by a major heart attack in 1955. In 1960, however, he became a presidential candidate although he entered no primaries, preferring to stick to Senate business in Washington. Johnson's southern origins hindered his efforts. While John Kennedy's Roman Catholicism was both a positive and a negative reference point in the nation at large, Johnson's presumed sectionalism, in a time when the civil rights movement was reaching its full strength, counted against him outside the South. After the Johnson candidacy failed, Kennedy thought it desirable to have the popular Southerner as a running mate. Analysts who wonder why Johnson was willing to "retire" to the vice-presidency perhaps fail to remember the obsessive fascination the highest office holds for inveterate politicians like Lyndon Johnson; though an isolated position, the vice-presidency brought him closer to the White House than he had been in the Senate. This may be an unfair attribution of motives, but it is one explanation that fits.

What made the new office lonely was the lack of power and status attached to it. Except for executive control over Texas patronage, Johnson had to search out positions of leadership. By 1961, if not before, he had become convinced of the civil rights movement's moral status and political appeal among many Northerners, and he gladly accepted an offer to head the President's Committee on Equal Employment. Here he learned the limits of persuasion as a means to accomplish fair employment practices. In 1963 he spoke courageously in favor of strong civil rights legislation. Johnson also became a spokesman for the exploration of space, heading up a committee for that end; he was always on hand for each new extraterrestrial encounter.

Johnson's best-known role as vice-president was that of a traveling emissary of the United States. In Berlin, during a tense weekend in 1961, he

magnificently reassured the people of the western sector who were an-
guished over the erection of the Berlin Wall. Always a hard-liner on the
cold war, Johnson had contemptuously rejected efforts to conciliate the
Soviet Union. In 1954, anxious to secure a strong position against Joe
McCarthy, he had said that Red China should never be admitted to the
United Nations; in that year he also helped Hubert Humphrey pass a bill
outlawing the American Communist party. In 1956 he disdained Adlai
Stevenson's suggestions to end nuclear testing or to abolish the draft.
Johnson's views seemed unchanged during his vice-presidency. In 1961 he
visited Premier Diem of South Vietnam and called him the "Churchill of
Asia," and recommended greater United States involvement in Southeast
Asia. Throughout the Kennedy years he supported the growing commitment in Vietnam. He attended meetings of the important National Security Council and rarely disagreed with Kennedy's own judgments. The
continuity between the Kennedy and Johnson administrations in foreign
policy will justify future historians in labeling the period the Kennedy-
Johnson years.

In the years following the assassination of Kennedy, Johnson behaved
with skill and tact. He publicly dedicated himself to fulfilling the Kennedy program and reassured the nation by persuading Chief Justice Earl
Warren and other notable figures to serve on a panel to investigate the
killing. He persuaded all of Kennedy's advisers to stay on, at least for a
time, and gave Jacqueline Kennedy ample time to leave the White
House. There is good reason to suppose that Kennedy would have expanded his social programs into something like Johnson's Great Society;
before his death his executive staff was working on antipoverty proposals
that became law in 1964 and 1965. The tax cut, already assured in October 1963, created an expansive economy in which his reelection would
have been likely. But Johnson's aggressive mastery carried such programs
to a greater intensity. He gathered into his policy much of what had
latently existed for a decade, and he completed and presided over a loose
coalition that had its origins in the elections of 1958.

Such coalitions as Johnson's are familiar in American history, accom-
plishing in a few years of intense activity what reformers had wanted
for many years. The Johnson coalition, or convergence of interest groups,
originated in the spring of 1963, drawing energy from the new economic
and civil rights proposals of Kennedy, whose death gave it added force.
The legislative deadlock of 1963 had begun to loosen even before Kennedy's death; the apparent ease with which Johnson and the Eighty-
eighth Congress produced dramatic social legislation owed much to
Kennedy's ground-breaking. The first landmark of the Great Society

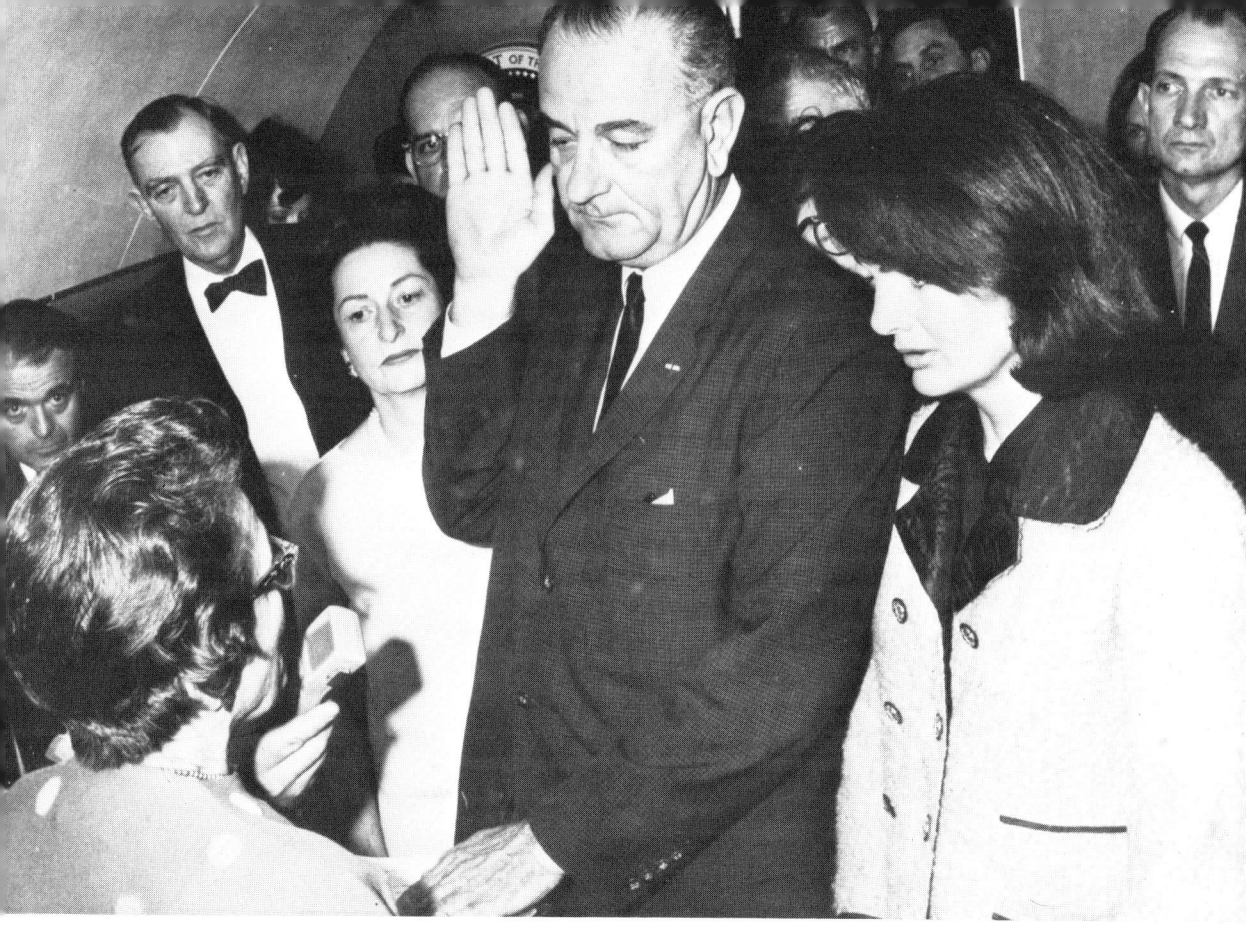

was the tax reduction bill of 1964, which had been in the works for some time. By reducing income tax rates a total of $11 billion, individuals and corporations would have increased spending power. This resulting increase in demand would then spur production, slacken unemployment, and ultimately swell federal revenues. Some economists who endorsed the idea doubted whether $11 billion was enough to produce the desired effect, while the prospect of bigger federal deficits alarmed fiscal conservatives. To pacify those who charged fiscal irresponsibility, Johnson promised to cut spending by $4 billion, beginning with the symbolic gesture of turning off the White House lights at night. But Congress defeated attempts to couple tax reduction to tax reform by closing some long-standing loopholes. The final bill cut personal income taxes by $9 billion and corporate taxes by $2 billion, with impressive results. Unemployment fell in 1965 to the lowest level in eight years, and federal revenues actually rose. On the other hand, the tax cut, along with other incentives to activate business and the pressures of massive spending for the war in Indochina, probably contributed to the inflationary economy of the late 1960's and early 1970's.

Vice-President Lyndon B. Johnson (1908–1973), flanked by his wife, Lady Bird, and by Jacqueline Kennedy, is sworn in as the thirty-sixth president of the United States by Federal District Judge Sarah T. Hughes of Dallas aboard the presidential plane prior to returning to Washington. *United Press International*

Negro rights was a main goal of Johnson. Here President Kennedy had made a slow start: no legislation at all passed Congress during his term in office. His great fear had always been to lose other important legislative goals by taking a strong stand in behalf of blacks. But in 1963 great peaceful demonstrations had a favorable effect on some legislators, and the violence in Birmingham during May frightened others. More important, the churches—a force behind the successful enactment of prohibition a generation before—influenced church-oriented senators in the direction of social justice. Churchmen, along with many Republicans and the president himself, besieged Senator Everett Dirksen, a key figure in his post as minority leader. Success came on a vote to end the sourthern filibuster, 71–29, in June 1964; it was the first time Congress invoked cloture on civil rights. Then a new civil rights law passed by an even wider margin. Only five Republicans from outside the South, including Barry Goldwater, and even fewer nonsouthern Democrats opposed the bill.

The new law covered a wide range of subjects, generally promising more than it could deliver. Title I of the act barred unequal application of voter registration requirements, but did not abolish literacy tests, a traditional device for disenfranchising both poor blacks and poor whites. The most controversial portion, Title II, outlawed discrimination in hotels, motels, restaurants, theaters, and all other public accommodations engaged in interstate commerce; this section exempted "private clubs" without defining "private," making evasion of the law fairly simple. Title III encouraged the desegregation of public schools and authorized the attorney general to file suits to compel desegregation, but explicitly stated that it did not authorize busing to overcome *de facto* residential segregation. Title IV authorized but did not require the withdrawal of federal funds from projects and programs which practiced discrimination. Title VII outlawed discrimination in employment in all businesses exceeding twenty-five people; it also created an Equal Employment Opportunity Commission with broad powers to investigate and review complaints but with little power to enforce compliance. In fact, a lack of power to enforce the various provisions weakened the entire act; the maximum penalty for violations was a $1,000 fine and six months in prison. Furthermore, the law placed responsibility for enforcement on aggrieved individuals, who were required to pursue costly and time-consuming legal action in order to gain satisfaction.

In spite of major weaknesses, the Civil Rights Act represented a signal victory for the activists and friends of the civil rights movement. The public accommodations provisions were generally obeyed. Those for equal employment worked no radical change on the composition of the labor force, but did facilitate opportunities for skilled blacks. The legal

This was the reaction of deep south Sheriff Lawrence Rainey (holding "Red Man" bag) and his friends upon hearing of the brutal murders of civil rights workers James Chaney, Andrew Goodman, and Michael Schwerner. The three men were part of the Mississippi Summer Project of 1964, whose primary aim was to register for voting as many blacks as possible. *Black Star*

570

commitment to racial equality embodied in the act provided another
weapon for organizations like the NAACP which could now argue simply for enforcement of the law. With the elimination of legal inequality,
both the civil rights movement and the Johnson administration shifted
their attention to the problems of social and economic inequality.

A veteran of the New Deal, Lyndon Johnson remembered that great social change tends to come rapidly in periods of intense activity before the
impulse slows. Instead of resting on his tax cut and civil rights victories,
he pushed ahead with another plan close to his heart. President Johnson

The War on Poverty

had seen much of poverty during his youth; its abolition became his next major goal. In the Eisenhower era urban renewal had simply aggravated the social conditions its advocates sought to improve. As with tax reform, Kennedy realized the potential political dividends and had prepared the way. His programs included the retraining and rehabilitation of the unemployed, area redevelopment, the eradication of illiteracy, youth employment, and accelerated public works in poverty regions. By 1963 coordinated efforts were underway in several large cities.

Johnson brought these programs and others together early in 1964 by declaring a "war on poverty"—a theme he found irresistible considering the impending presidential campaign. After hearing from the Council of Economic Advisers that 20 percent of all American families were "poor" (earned less than $3,000 annually), Congress passed the Economic Opportunity Act of 1964, appropriating $800 million for the first year. Johnson chose Sargent Shriver, John Kennedy's brother-in-law, as the first director of the new Office of Economic Opportunity.

Programs under OEO differed from past efforts in design as well as in size. Three hundred million dollars supported local community action

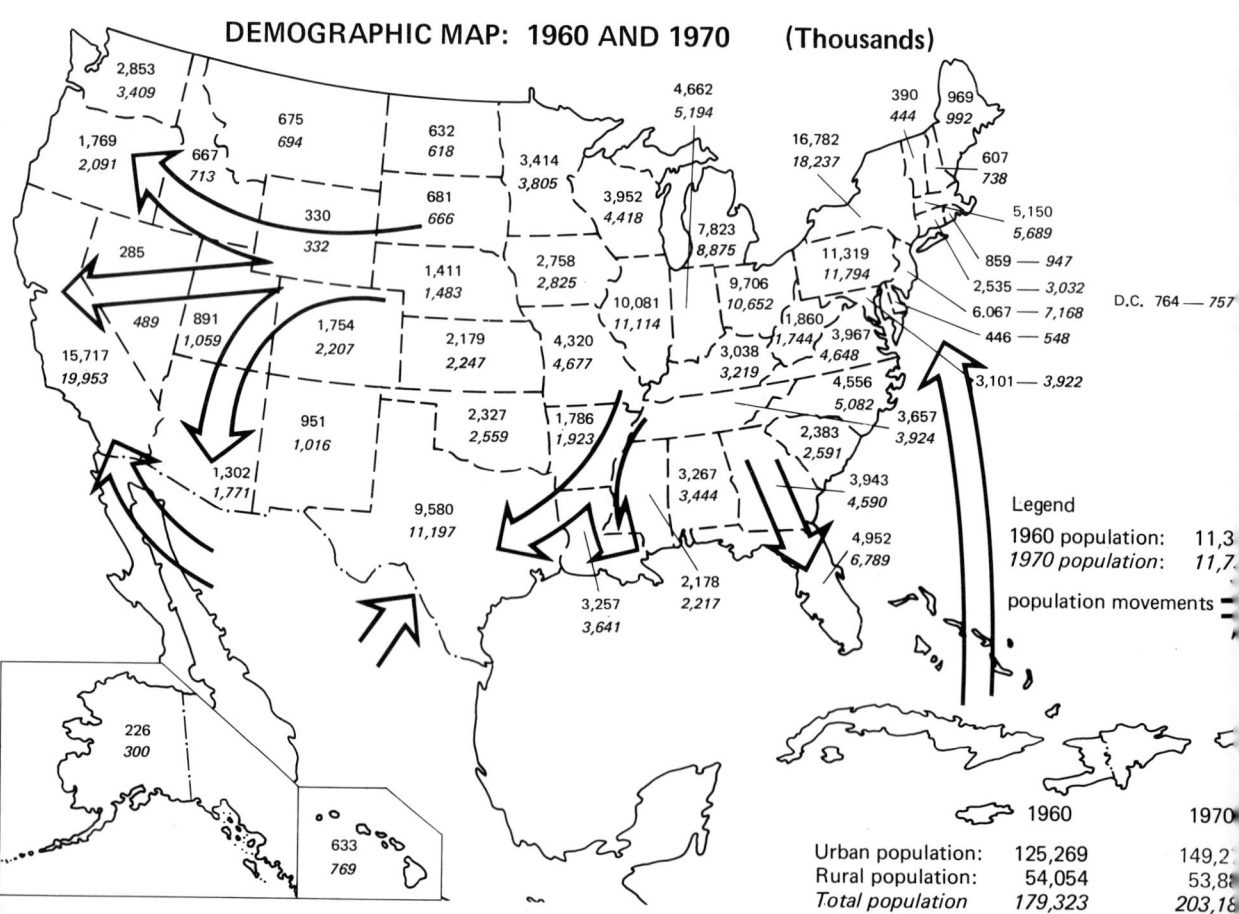

DEMOGRAPHIC MAP: 1960 AND 1970   (Thousands)

Legend

1960 population: 11,3
1970 population: 11,7.

population movements

	1960	1970
Urban population:	125,269	149,2
Rural population:	54,054	53,8
Total population	179,323	203,18

agencies, the central innovation of the program. In each community, advisory boards, comprised of local business and political interests and representatives of the poor themselves, administered the funds. Local control of antipoverty efforts produced varied results, ranging from the successful minority-group insurgencies to the disappearance of funds into emerging poverty bureaucracies. Another major emphasis of OEO programs was on the young. The Job Corps, an urban version of the New Deal's Civilian Conservation Corps, established remedial vocational and educational training facilities for young slum-dwellers. The Neighborhood Youth Corps provided summer jobs paying $50 a week for high school students, with an eye toward pacifying ghetto youth during the "long, hot summers." A work-study program assisted many college students. One of the most controversial programs, the Volunteers in Service to America (VISTA), a domestic equivalent of Kennedy's Peace Corps, sent teams of idealistic young people into communities across the country to assist in federal and local programs. Many VISTA volunteers, drawn from the student movement of the 1960's, took a more radical view of the fight against poverty than did officials in Washington or in most states. As a result, some governors exercised their right to veto VISTA activities, and legislation in 1965 required a stiff loyalty oath from VISTA workers. Still, appropriations for VISTA and other fronts of the war on poverty increased in 1965 and stayed high for several years. But the activities of the younger and poorer segments of the antipoverty coalition generated increasing opposition. OEO efforts, especially the more responsive local ones, inevitably raised demands for redistribution of income and resulted in confrontations with established interests.

In a single year Congress had passed more important domestic legislation than it had in a decade. In the spring of 1964 Walter Lippmann wrote that "the country is far more united and at peace with itself, except over the issue of Negro rights, than it has been in a long time. [Johnson has] done, I think, what President Kennedy could not have done had he lived." In fairness, Lippmann should have granted that some of Johnson's success was contingent on the mood of atonement generated by the death of Kennedy, as well as the economic means generated by the 1964 tax cut. Johnson took fuller advantage than Kennedy might have of the prevailing consensus on these welfare issues. During the fall campaign he spoke of a "Great Society" so warmly and expansively that no one doubted that another flood of legislation would be forthcoming if he were reelected.

The Democratic Convention in Atlantic City needed suspense, and this Johnson provided by holding back until the last moment the name of the vice-presidential nominee. He enjoyed dangling the prize before one likely candidate and then another, playing out the performance as far as it would go. Actually, only one candidate was uppermost in his mind: Senator Hubert Humphrey, a seasoned politician and a tireless campaigner. A statement that eliminated all of the cabinet rejected Attorney General Robert Kennedy, who grated on Johnson. Senator Eugene McCarthy of Minnesota, a definite possibility, removed himself in favor of Humphrey. Humphrey was a man the president could reason with and trust. As a final test, the loyal Humphrey put through a seating compromise that sent most of the Mississippi delegation home rather than sign an oath of loyalty; the maneuver left a counterdelegation of blacks angry that a moral issue had been disposed of so circuitously.

With the gross national product rising rapidly under Johnson, the Republicans needed to produce an unusual candidate to defeat him. Governor Nelson Rockefeller of New York had recently divorced his wife after twenty-four years of marriage. In May 1963 he married a divorcee whose young children remained with her former husband. Despite the anticipated political repercussions of his personal affairs, Rockefeller entered the March primary in New Hampshire. He faced a man he regarded as a dangerous threat to American institutions, Senator Barry Goldwater of Arizona. His own worst enemy, Goldwater ruined his chances among cautious New Englanders by an offhand comment about "defoliating" Vietnam with atomic weaponry—ruined them just as surely as Rockefeller's remarriage had destroyed his. The victor in the primary was not even on the ballot: Henry Cabot Lodge, ambassador to Vietnam and a write-in candidate.

But Goldwater's devoted followers had accumulated major delegate strength for him in states without popular primaries. He needed only one major primary victory to win. In May Rockefeller won in Oregon with

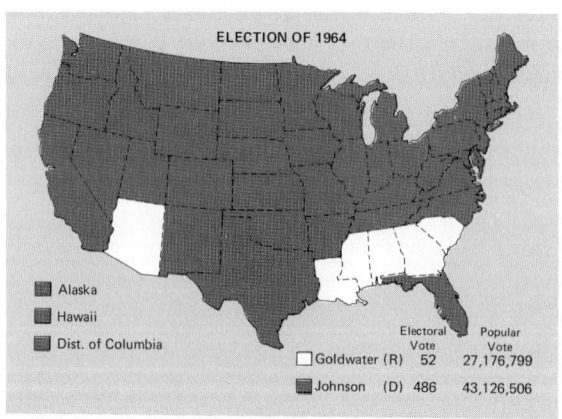

ELECTION OF 1964

Alaska
Hawaii
Dist. of Columbia

	Electoral Vote	Popular Vote
Goldwater (R)	52	27,176,799
Johnson (D)	486	43,126,506

574

Lodge second and Goldwater third. California was the Arizonan's last chance. Fate blessed him during the weekend before the June election when the second Mrs. Rockefeller gave birth to a son, and Dwight Eisenhower characteristically backtracked after making an implicitly anti-Goldwater remark earlier. Goldwater won the primary by a 1 percent margin. Before the Republican convention in San Francisco, last-minute support developed for Governors William Scranton of Pennsylvania and George Romney of Michigan, but it was too late. Goldwater won on the first ballot. To party pros his selection was a calculated risk. A year so bleak for the Republicans as 1964 could put to the test an old proposition that there was a large potential electorate made up of nonvoters and working-class Democrats that would awaken and come to the polls for the right candidate. Goldwater accepted the nomination in the spirit that would dominate his campaign: "Anyone who joins us in all sincerity we welcome. Those who do not care for our cause, we don't expect to enter our ranks. . . . Extremism in the defense of liberty is no vice. . . . Moderation in the pursuit of justice is no virtue." Unfairly attacked by the Democrats, the last statement won praise from the local chapter of the American Civil Liberties Union. For his vice-presidential running mate, Goldwater chose Congressman William Miller of Lockport, New York, but Miller's strength as a Roman Catholic was offset by his vitriolic tongue and stiff personality.

During the course of the campaign Goldwater retreated from some of his extreme positions expressed earlier in his books, *Why Not Victory?* and *The Conscience of a Conservative*. Although signed by Goldwater, ghost writers had composed them. In the campaign he still revealed a knack for making a handicap of honesty. In Appalachia he insisted on attacking the poverty program; in Knoxville, Tennessee, he declared in favor of selling part of the Tennessee Valley Authority; in St. Petersburg, Florida, a city filled with retired people, he criticized social security; in North Dakota he told farmers that a decline in price supports would be good for them. Vice-presidential candidate Miller on Labor Day criticized liberal immigration policies before an audience composed chiefly of first- and second-generation immigrants.

Many Republicans deserted Goldwater. Romney and Rockefeller along with Mayor John V. Lindsay of New York refused to mention his name in campaign appearances. The Democrats seized the opportunity to portray Goldwater as extreme and unpredictable: one television commercial showed a social security card being ripped in two; another vicious one (repudiated by Johnson) pictured a little girl counting petals plucked from a daisy until a mushroom cloud appeared, while a voice urged the prudent to vote for Johnson. One magazine had the audacity to poll psychiatrists by mail in an attempt to demonstrate Goldwater's psychic shortcomings; it was no credit to the profession that hundreds offered highly speculative responses.

Goldwater was a patriot; at his Arizona ranch an electronic gadget raised the American flag at dawn and lowered it at sunset. But since he occupied a seeming extreme in the political spectrum, Johnson could range across much of the rest of it. Johnson's use of two minor incidents in the Gulf of Tonkin to justify retaliatory bombing of North Vietnam made it impossible for him to be cast as an appeaser. Most of Johnson's attention went, in Richard Rovere's words, "to evangelistic and almost utopian views of the future." Bold and all-encompassing, the Johnson program remained in the tradition of the New Deal, and by the 1960's this was a moderate position. On the other hand, many voters perceived the Goldwater alternative as a dangerous departure from the status quo. Crop subsidies and social security were preferable to some ill-defined and risky adventure against international communism.

Still, two incidents threatened to make the campaign a close race. The first was summer rioting, beginning in Manhattan and Brooklyn ghettos just after the Republican convention. Blacks were part of the Democratic constituency, yet voters apparently perceived Goldwater as stimulating more rather than less social conflict. The second incident took place in October when an able Johnson assistant was arrested in Washington, D.C., for a homosexual act. Momentarily hopes arose in Republican headquarters for a voter reaction against the president, but the public, though aroused by the circumstances of the Rockefeller divorce, scarcely seemed to care. Perhaps this was because the incident came in the midst of a tense baseball world series, the downfall of Nikita Khrushchev in Russia, and the exploding of their first nuclear bomb by the Chinese Communists.

All the pollsters agreed that November 4 would be a cold day for Goldwater. He received only 38.9 percent of the two-party vote and 27 million popular votes compared to Johnson's 43 million. The election turned on the question of whether Goldwater should be president; the answer was a resounding no. He carried only his home state, plus Mississippi (where he won 87 percent of the vote), Louisiana, Alabama, South Carolina, and Georgia. The Democrats maintained their two-to-one Senate margin and picked up thirty-eight more seats in the House, enhancing prospects for Great Society legislation. Such were the results of the Republican candidate's "Southern strategy." In part its employment was simply premature; the candidacy may have marshaled opposition to bureaucratic reform with a substantial future impact. The race issue had not yet ripened to cause a backlash against the Democrats among whites in the North. The civil rights movement was still largely in its southern nonmilitant phase, and no one knew that the riots in northern ghettos would multiply in number and ferocity. Nor had black nationalism come into its own. It is not certain, then, that the rejection of Goldwater meant that his doctrines had little appeal for Americans—assuming that most of the votes he did earn were simply those of Republicans who could vote only a straight ticket. Probably the presidential election was too inclusive and murky on issues to provide such a test, but one outcome was certain: it would be a long time before a major party would risk nominating another figure of Goldwater's views. The same principle had kept the Democratic party from nominating another Roman Catholic for a generation after Al Smith's massive defeat in 1928. Yet Governor George Wallace of Alabama had run well in early Democratic primaries on a program similar to Goldwater's. And as the Warren Court continued on its activist course, the Right seemed to gain in strength.

The Warren Court under Johnson

The social disruptions of the 1960's inevitably directed judicial attention toward the system of law enforcement, and some of the most controversial decisions of the Warren Court concerned criminal procedure and the rights of the accused. In *Gideon* v. *Wainwright* (1963) the Court guaranteed the right to legal counsel in all felony cases. Clarence Earl Gideon, a white Southerner with a long criminal record, had been convicted of breaking and entering a Florida poolroom at a trial in which insolvency forced him to carry on his own defense. His handwritten appeal to the Supreme Court combined a moving personal history with imperfect legal terminology; the actual argumentation in the case before the Court was handled by Abe Fortas, a prestigious Democratic lawyer in Washington who later became an associate justice until he resigned over a conflict of interest. The guarantee in *Gideon* of courtroom counsel regardless of capacity to pay expanded to cover the police station three years later in *Miranda* v. *Arizona*, wherein the Court affirmed a prisoner's right to see an attorney before answering questions.

Concern for individual rights also shaped other decisions. With one notable exception the Court consistently refused to uphold obscenity convictions, protecting the sales of such cultural gems as the novel *Lustpool*. Only in *Ginzburg* v. *United States* did the Court depart from its norm to sustain Ralph Ginzburg's conviction for publishing some rather pretentious, high-art erotica. Even more shocking to conventional sensibilities than permissiveness toward pornography, a series of decisions in 1962–1963 outlawed compulsory Bible reading and similar religious practices in public schools. The Court rejected not only an apparent abridgment of the separation of church and state, but also the enforcement, however symbolic, of a particular morality on the individual student. The Warren Court's most notable dictum on political life also had an individualist ring: the principle of "one man, one vote." In a series of legislative apportionment cases beginning with *Baker* v. *Carr* (1962), the Court required that both houses of the legislature in each state reflect the actual distribution of population in that state. This ruling ended some of the more extreme cases of rural areas dominating big cities.

The increasing congressional hostility to Great Society programs reflected divisions in the larger society. Racial division intensified and grew uglier; the National Advisory Commission on Civil Disorders concluded that "Our nation is moving toward two societies, one black, one white —separate and unequal." Opposition to the Vietnam War grew to unprecedented heights, with larger and more militant demonstrations making concrete the increased dissatisfaction registered in public opinion polls. Each day Vietnam became more clearly the central political issue of the later 1960's.

More Great Society Legislation

What followed the 1964 election was an ingenious manipulation of Congress by the president, who continued to capitalize on the memory of Kennedy as well as on his own long-standing legislative skills. Knowing the opportunity would not soon return, Johnson showered Congress with Great Society proposals. The legislation had to pass in 1965, and aid to public education was the first on Johnson's list of priorities. Eisenhower had managed to secure passage in 1958 of the National Defense Education Act, which aided the nation's universities especially in science and engineering. Kennedy signed an important bill for vocational education, a federal responsibility of long standing, and increased loans and fellowships to college students came into being during his administration. But large-scale aid to elementary and secondary schools had not been realized. Johnson effectively steered the legislation through Congress between the threats of race and religion: antisegregation amendments had marked the downfall of good bills in the past, and loss of support from Roman Catholic congressmen had killed others. But now civil rights legislation had removed the need to attach racial provisos to school bills, and the president included just enough parochial school aid to satisfy the Catholics without alarming the Protestants. Private schools received funds for "special services" like transportation and medical care but not for pedagogy in standard fields. No one, moreover, wanted a religious squabble while the memory remained fresh of John Kennedy, who had done so much to quiet the objections of purists on the separation of church and state.

For the first time Congress passed substantial aid for elementary and secondary schools, concentrating on districts with pupils from low-income families. The award for each school district was computed by multiplying the number of low-income pupils in that district by one-half of the average annual expenditure per child on education in that state. Congressmen from states with low per-pupil education budgets argued for a system of flat grants, but the state-expenditure formula won adoption because of its simplicity. Although the sizes of the grants were determined on a school district basis, the actual funds went to the states for distribution and administration in order to quiet fears of a federal takeover of local schools. The billion-dollar measure sailed through the House by a vote of 263 to 153, and only 18 senators opposed it. Johnson flew to the small Texas schoolhouse where he had once taught to provide a dramatic context for signing the bill.

Another of Johnson's major legislative goals was Medicare, health care for the elderly funded through social security. Harry Truman had approached the question of medical care in a more comprehensive way through a national health care plan. Both political parties advanced limited medical insurance plans for the elderly during the 1950's, and John Kennedy proposed a broad Medicare plan in the 1960 campaign. The American Medical Association led the resistance to all of these plans; its members hung warnings in their waiting rooms against upsetting the "sacred" doctor-patient relationship. By so marshaling public opinion and with a multimillion dollar lobbying effort, the AMA influenced key congressmen and bottled up any significant legislation through 1964. Armed with a mandate from the 1964 elections, however, Johnson assigned the highest priority to a limited program of Medicare for the elderly. And despite continued opposition from the AMA, the legislation passed rather easily. The basic plan provided hospitalization, rest home, and home care benefits for people over sixty-five; a supplemental voluntary plan permitted individuals to enroll for a coverage of doctor's bills and laboratory fees for $3 a month. Within two years, 17 million Americans had taken advantage of this opportunity. Legislation in 1965 and 1966 extended federal medical care to other large categories of needy people—dependent children, the blind and disabled, and many low-income families—under the Medicaid program. Although Medicare and Medicaid laws set maximum amounts of coverage and required patients to assume responsibility for a deductible amount, they still constituted a major victory for the administration.

Many other social welfare programs with the Great Society stamp became law in 1965, many with generous initial funding. New legislation provided rent supplements for low-income families and increased appropriations for public housing and public works construction and for small business loans in poverty areas. The 1965 congressional appropriation for the programs under the Office of Economic Opportunity nearly doubled the previous year's grant. Head Start, perhaps the single antipoverty program with the greatest lasting effect, was initiated in the summer of 1965. Centers across the country prepared half a million disadvantaged children about to enter the public schools in the fall. With a budget of $85 million, employing 50,000 professionals and nearly 200,000 volunteers, Head Start gained popularity as an example of an effective antipoverty measure.

Environmental Programs

As early as 1948 the federal government had begun to conduct research on the problem of growing water pollution. Eisenhower recommended a strengthening of enforcement powers against polluters under the Public Health Service, and Representative John Blatnik of Minnesota was instrumental in forcing higher grants for new sewage treatment plants. But in 1957 the president proposed returning the responsibility to the states and, when that failed, he vetoed early in 1960 a stronger Blatnik bill, characterizing water pollution as a local problem. Kennedy spoke strongly in behalf of such environmental goals but resisted the bolder fiscal measures necessary to implement them. Senator Edmund S. Muskie had gained interest in the problem as governor of Maine when lobster fishermen had demanded clean coastal waters. Muskie at first moved cautiously, but after Johnson became president the senator pushed for an ambitious program. Not satisfied with the Water Quality Act of 1965, which provided demonstration grants for sewage control, he demanded $6 billion for a six-year national program with the federal government ultimately imposing water purifying standards. The Clean Water Restoration Act of 1966 authorized $3.5 billion to be spent over five years, but Presidents Johnson and Nixon used less than one-third of these funds.

The struggle against air pollution has a similar history. Eisenhower's Secretary of Health, Education and Welfare Arthur Flemming suggested in 1958 the need for comparable enforcement procedures to abate interstate air pollution. Nothing was accomplished, however, until the Clean Air Act of 1963, which allowed HEW, upon request of a state or local government and an advisory hearing, to compel enforcement of reasonable standards. Under Johnson legislation set standards for exhaust emission on combustion engines, but left the enforcement date to government discretion. Here was an example of cooperation between business and government: the deadline for nearly fume-free combustion engines was later advanced to 1976.

The Eisenhower administration made some efforts but accomplished little in the area of conservation. Even so staunch a friend of the natural environment as Senator Richard Neuberger of Oregon capitulated in 1955 on his amendment to restrict billboards when the entire national highway bill came into jeopardy. But in 1958 a modest federal incentive for billboard restriction by states became law. For his part President Kennedy favored federal land purchases financed through fees on users of recreation facilities; the bill passed in 1962. The next year an imperfect wilderness bill passed that allowed miners to work certain areas. It remained for Johnson to try to put teeth into the billboard control legislation of 1958. Thanks to efforts of the Outdoor Advertising Association of America, the administration compromised on a scheme whereby the despoilers gave up their interests in scenic areas in exchange for unrestricted access to business zones.

On most of these new programs, however, business interests kept silent or encouraged the government. A decade earlier all such schemes would have met sharp resistance from most business leaders. But during the Kennedy-Johnson era corporations especially began to appreciate the benefits of a vibrant economy and a government wanting such goals as retraining the unskilled and satisfying the manpower needs of industry. Particularly during the sixties, as business began to need very advanced technological skills, the concept of government retraining became extremely attractive. In Johnson's poverty program business even lent its personnel to training centers to increase their efficiency. Such government programs amounted to a giant subsidy for business. Government spending, moreover, sustained aerospace, publishing, and other major industries throughout the decade. Another instance of cooperation between business and government earlier in the sixties was support for a loosening of immigration laws, which provided a needed increase in the labor supply. Finally, throughout the period there was a fear of racial disturbance, harmful to local business, that enhanced chances of civil rights reform; particularly in the South racial unrest could reduce the chances of securing capital investment.

**The Johnson
Coalition
Comes Unglued**

In 1965 Congress strengthened the guarantee of voting rights which the 1964 Civil Rights Act had promised. The Voting Rights Act empowered the attorney general to appoint federal examiners to supervise voter registration in states and counties that had used such devices as literacy tests to maintain a low number of registered voters. By the end of 1965, examiners had been appointed in thirty-five counties, and within five months Negro registration in Deep South states increased 40 percent. The Voting Rights Act worked in tandem with the Twenty-fourth Amendment, ratified in 1964, which eliminated poll taxes in federal elections. Together

they provided a base of voters in many areas for the election of the first black officials since Reconstruction.

Johnson made his most controversial civil rights request in January 1966. He wanted laws prohibiting discrimination in the sale or rental of all housing and punishing interference with the rights of Americans in education, employment, jury service, and travel. Congress responded with legislation in these areas, although some whites had begun to resist such demands. When Martin Luther King led a group of followers into a white suburb of Chicago, a white mob met them filled with a rage King claimed never to have encountered before, even in Mississippi or Alabama. The popular image of the civil rights movement had changed from nonviolence to militant demands for black power.

By 1966 Johnson's support in domestic and foreign affairs was waning. Ghetto rebellions, most notably those in Los Angeles (1965) and Detroit (1967), frightened even those voters who lived far from black neighborhoods. Once they touched the delicate matter of housing, civil rights programs became considerably less popular. Although spending for the war in Indochina seemed to be contributing to an apparently healthy econ-

Muhammad Ali and Sonny Liston exchange lefts in the first round of the 1964 Heavyweight Championship fight in Miami Beach, Florida. Ali unseated champion Liston with a knockout in the seventh round. Ali is a member of the Black Muslims, a group that espouses racial purity and pride, self-help, hard work, and sobriety. *United Press International*

omy, antiwar opinion was mounting. The off-term elections in November registered a general although not total dissatisfaction with the president's policies: the Republicans gained three seats in the Senate, forty-seven in the House, and eight governorships, but remained decidedly the minority party in Congress. Regardless of party affiliation, the members of the new Congress would go much slower with social legislation than in the preceding two years.

A political stalemate characterized the final two years of the Johnson administration. Appropriations for the war on poverty remained fairly constant, but no new programs were initiated. Congress slashed the administration's foreign aid requests. To decrease the deficits caused by Vietnam spending, the president asked for a 10 percent tax surcharge in 1967, claiming that the surcharge was necessary if the federal government was to provide both guns and butter. Congress grudgingly passed the measure in 1968, but also forced budget reductions that began to cut into the butter. Symbolic of the new congressional mood was the defeat of an appropriation for a ghetto rat-control program; the debate centered not on the amount of money, a relatively small $100 million, but on the extent of the federal government's interest in social welfare. In 1968 Congress enacted the Omnibus Crime Bill, allocating funds to upgrade local police forces, broadening the wire-tapping authority of law enforcement agencies, and attempting to restrict some of the Supreme Court's guarantees of the rights of the accused.

1968

The most important political event in these years took place not at home but in Vietnam. The successful Vietcong "Tet" offensive of January–February 1968 further challenged the credibility of the president. For too many years both cabinet members and the president had been promising that the war would soon begin to wane. The antiwar movement, initially a product of young activists, began to attract all elements of society.

For some time the peace movement had been served devotedly in Congress by such senators as Wayne Morse, Ernest Gruening, and, for a lesser period, William Fulbright. Later in the decade Allard Lowenstein, a New York lawyer who had organized antiwar protests on a national level, approached Robert Kennedy, who had won election to the Senate from New York in 1966. Johnson's natural political antagonist, Robert Kennedy had come to believe that the war was a calamity. Yet Kennedy, who was only an oblique critic of the Johnson policies, worried that a peace candidacy would identify him with radicals who carried the Vietcong flag and forced confrontations in front of the Pentagon.

Another senator, scarcely known outside his native state of Minnesota, took the step that Kennedy contemplated. Eugene McCarthy, a handsome gray-haired man of fifty-one, seemed a study in political detachment and nonchalance. But when Attorney General Nicholas Katzenbach told the Senate Foreign Relations Committee in August 1967 that a president could no longer lose time by consulting the Congress on whether to involve the country in war, McCarthy lost his customary composure. Angrily he told Katzenbach that such extensive executive authority deprived the Senate of any decision-making role in foreign policy. In the thinking of McCarthy, who had written a book on the American political process, the Katzenbach interpretation was unconstitutional.

Late in November McCarthy decided to oppose the president in the coming spring primaries. The first contest came in New Hampshire on March 12 when snow still covered the ground. An energetic band of young students carried the antiwar message across the state. The Democratic governor and senator mismanaged the Johnson campaign, employing heavy-handed tactics such as a signed postcard pledge to support the president. Gene McCarthy exerted a positive appeal on New Englanders; he was, in his dry and self-contained manner, almost a New Englander himself. His arguments against the war were low key and highly factual. Beyond that, however, he stood for an end to conflict between generations and a renewing of traditional political institutions. In the vote itself, McCarthy's Roman Catholicism must have counted, for about two-thirds of the state's Democrats shared his faith. The senator won 42 percent of the two-party vote, almost as much as Johnson's write-in total of 49 percent. It was unprecedented to come so close to winning against an incumbent president during a war.

Three days later, in what appeared to some the quintessence of opportunism, Kennedy announced that he, too, would oppose the president in those primaries he could still enter. Actually, he had been reconsidering his earlier decision for some weeks. The timing of the entry reflected his ego and political practicality: only a Kennedy, so he believed, could unseat Johnson. Yet Kennedy's campaign lost its initial momentum when Lyndon Johnson delivered a television speech on March 31, just two days before the Wisconsin primary. The president declared that the time had come to deescalate the war. He would cut back bombing of the North and would turn down army requests for more troops. Then in a surprising coda he remarked that since he wanted to devote full time to the search for peace, he would not seek reelection in November. Johnson's decision not to run was a response in part to peace activists at home and the Tet offensive abroad.

Johnson's major advisers had gradually drifted away from an aggressive stand on the war. First to go (after George Ball) was Robert Strange McNamara, who, as early as May 1966, had begun to express doubts after having been certain of rapid victory just a year or two before. Clark Clifford replaced McNamara as secretary of defense on March 1, 1968; he was an honest observer and soon expressed reservations of his own. Former Secretary of State Dean Acheson added his voice of caution, and Dean Rusk ceased his opposition to the idea of a partial bombing halt. Johnson reluctantly gave in (and soon wished he had not). In response to the limited bombing halt announced in Johnson's speech, Hanoi agreed to talk. The talks dragged on for months and then for years.

Deprived of their most effective campaign issue—the president himself—Kennedy and McCarthy then had to campaign, to a great extent, against each other. Because they were thoroughly different in temperament, the rivalry between the two men became highly personal. In the process of their bickering the peace movement fragmented. McCarthy, never an admirer of the Kennedy clan, found offensive RFK's fascination with power. Kennedy thought McCarthy lazy, snobbish, and politically ineffectual. The two competed for the support of the young, who could be of assistance in the remaining primaries. McCarthy, after winning decisively against Johnson in Wisconsin, lost to Kennedy in Indiana and Nebraska. Then McCarthy made an unexpected comeback by winning easily in Oregon. One final primary would in large part determine the winner; Kennedy promised to drop out of the race should McCarthy defeat him in California on June 4. Kennedy won by a few percentage points, but on the very night of the election he was shot down by a Jordanian immigrant, Sirhan Bishara Sirhan. Six weeks before, on April 24, a criminal had shot and killed Martin Luther King, Jr., an event that sparked riots in the nation's capital and other major cities.

Curiously, McCarthy scarcely attempted to unite the antiwar forces after California. He ran very well in the mid-June New York primary, but instead of building support for the convention, he set aside part of each day to write poetry and finally withdrew for a period to a Benedictine retreat. When polls showed him to be only slightly ahead of Vice-President Hubert Humphrey, McCarthy appeared uninterested in politics. His virtual neglect of the Soviet injuries to Czechoslovakia during the summer called his judgment seriously into question.

But if the McCarthy candidacy petered out in the weeks before the convention, the peace movement itself was still quite strong. The Humphrey forces had no wish to alienate the peace Democrats and quietly agreed to sweeping reforms in the Democratic party. In Chicago, a broad

democratization of delegate selection through the primaries was instituted for 1972. McCarthy had won 75 percent of the vote in Pennsylvania, for example, but collected only 25 percent of the delegates. In retrospect it appears that McCarthy never believed he would win the nomination. Though his wit, intellect, and uncompromising virtue had its attraction for college campuses, he willfully resisted using pat formulas for political success.

On at least one occasion McCarthy recognized political practicality. At the Chicago convention Richard Daley encouraged an effort to draft the surviving Kennedy brother, Edward, a Massachusetts senator, and McCarthy offered to withdraw in his favor. It was the last hope of the amorphous peace movement. Edward Kennedy might well have denied the nomination to Vice-President Humphrey, who was so closely identified with an unpopular Johnson. Thousands of young people demonstrating outdoors reminded the delegates of their passionate dislike for the administration and for its policy in Vietnam. Several large states would have supported Kennedy, and in the psychology of a national convention enthusiasm for him as a potential winner might have put him across. But Kennedy refused to run.

During the Democratic convention in August 1968, antiwar demonstrators riot near the Conrad Hilton Hotel in Chicago. The violence occurred when demonstrators, determined to enter the convention site, broke through the police and national guard lines. Police used rifle butts, tear gas, and clubs to battle the demonstrators. *United Press International*

Inside the convention site a battle raged for control of the Georgia delegation. An August 27 compromise gave half the state's votes to the regulars and half to a biracial group headed by Julian Bond. In this picture regular Georgia delegate Carling J. Dinkler votes while rebel delegate Bond awaits his turn. *United Press International*

587

Without effective leadership the peace forces broke into anarchic fragments at the convention. A platform provision calling for a halt to all bombing in Vietnam failed by a 3 to 2 vote. Outside the convention hall in Grant Park the Chicago police battled with the young, engaging in what a government report later termed a "police riot." Inside, Senator Abraham Ribicoff of Connecticut told the delegates about the outside skirmishes and lashed out at the "Gestapo tactics of the police." After the riots Humphrey's nomination by a 2 to 1 margin over McCarthy and another peace candidate, Senator George McGovern of South Dakota, seemed anticlimactic. The drama of the convention centered on the confrontation between police and students, which included both harassment of young people by the police and the goading of authorities by the youths. Late in the evening the police invaded hotel suites used by McCarthy supporters, who had allegedly showered the police with debris. The violence was an enduring monument to the nation's temper in 1968. And the events in Chicago cast a pall over the coming Democratic campaign.

The Campaign and Election of 1968

Vice-President Hubert Humphrey was a particularly enigmatic figure. Just two decades before he had forced a split in the Democratic party on the issue of civil rights. He had also symbolized support for various welfare programs. But when asked as vice-president what happened to the program he once had battled for, he answered simply and correctly: "We passed it." The voluble Humphrey welcomed opportunities to explain our intervention in Vietnam. He informed University of Pittsburgh students about Vietcong atrocities. Before an AFL-CIO convention he associated the critics of the war with appeasers of Hitler. He compared the corruption of South Vietnam's government with that of American cities. The Chinese Communists, he said, prolonged the war.

Understandably, the Humphrey presidential candidacy dismayed antiwar Democrats. Any skillful Republican candidate could hope to draw their support in the November election. The first active Republican candidate was Governor George Romney of Michigan, a strong civil rights advocate. But Romney's casual and contradictory remarks on the Vietnam War worried the voters, and his reference to a "brainwashing" given him by briefing officers proved a catastrophe. After poor showings in early national polls he withdrew from the race. At the end of April Governor Nelson Rockefeller of New York, who favored the war, declared his candidacy. But even a $5 million media campaign did not compensate for his late start. Governor Ronald Reagan of California, the only right-wing candidate, stayed publicly out of the race, but he was privately available and friends paid for a low-pressure television campaign. The strongest contestant was the vintage Republican, former Vice-President Richard Nixon. He hewed to the political center and won victories in the spring primaries. Reagan tried to whittle away Nixon's southern support. Rockefeller hoped that preconvention polls would show him as the strongest candidate. But neither strategy succeeded. Nixon needed only 667 votes to win—and on the first ballot he received 691.

Richard Nixon was real Americana: Protestant, Anglo-Saxon, clean-cut, ambitious. As a boy he had cranked homemade ice cream at parties, played the piano at church, and led his high school debating team. While serving in the navy in the South Pacific, he set up a hamburger stand. He worked his way through Whittier College and Duke University Law School. Legal training, as well as skills in debate and card playing, constituted good preparation for a career in politics.

Nixon conducted the public investigation of Alger Hiss, accused of having been a Communist agent in the 1930's. But he was quite scrupulous about procedural rights, as some other members of the House Committee on Un-American Activities were not. Of course, he won votes by portraying his congressional opponent in 1946, Jerry Voorhis, as indifferent to communism, and he also pursued the theme in 1950. But the successful Senate campaign of that year against Helen Gahagan Douglas was a crude spectacle on both sides; the incumbent's lieutenants charged Nixon with both anti-Semitism and fascism—and he tried to link Douglas with radical congressmen who voted similarly. Nixon's voting record in the House and Senate is hard to characterize. In 1952 he certainly found no difficulty in supporting President Dwight Eisenhower over Robert Taft, whom he regarded as the weaker candidate politically. Nixon's fame in the Hiss case, his prestige as a California senator and influence with the state's convention delegates, his service and uncontroversial voting record in both houses of Congress all cast him as a strong vice-presidential candi-

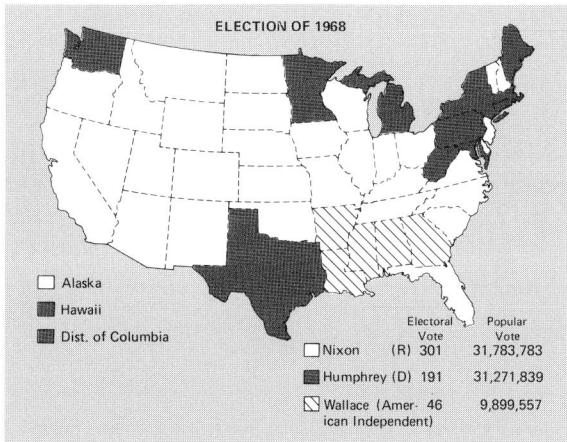

ELECTION OF 1968

Alaska
Hawaii
Dist. of Columbia

	Electoral Vote	Popular Vote
Nixon (R)	301	31,783,783
Humphrey (D)	191	31,271,839
Wallace (American Independent)	46	9,899,557

date. Governor Thomas E. Dewey of New York persuaded Eisenhower to accept Nixon as his running mate.

After effectively meeting an ill-supported charge of corruption made during the 1952 campaign, Nixon went on to become an active vice-president, although Eisenhower never liked Nixon very well and failed to appreciate his political talent. The president's Quaker running mate outdistanced him on the issue of civil rights. A member of the NAACP after 1950, Nixon received Eleanor Roosevelt's approval for his work promoting nondiscriminatory hiring as chairman of the Committee on Government Contracts. The vice-president's trip to Russia in 1959, and his famous debate there in the kitchen of a model house, was but one of a long series of world journeys as emissary of the United States. After losing to Kennedy in 1960, Nixon moved to California and two years later failed in his bid for the governorship. During the 1964 presidential campaign he supported Barry Goldwater and thereby survived the year with political currency among party regulars. In mid-decade he practiced law in New York City, defending the right to privacy in *Time Inc.* v. *Hill* (1966). The case, however, followed by a year Nixon's intemperate denunciation of a Rutgers University assistant professor who had said he would welcome an enemy victory in Vietnam. Nixon thereafter avoided a clear position on Vietnam. By 1968 he seemed more relaxed and confidently in command of himself and his career than ever before. In the presidential campaign Nixon spoke in generalities, intent on keeping his large lead over Humphrey in the public opinion polls.

The Humphrey campaign, inaugurated so dismally in Chicago, got off to an unpromising start. Repeatedly the candidate misspent his energies in answering antiwar hecklers, who may have had some impact on forcing him to reconsider his position on Vietnam. For some months Humphrey had had growing doubts about the war, but the president was so hypersensitive and Dean Rusk so dogged about it that the candidate dared not speak his own thoughts. When Humphrey did promise an early end to the war, Rusk said that no one could predict when it might let up. Not until a nationwide television speech on September 30 did Humphrey dissociate himself from Johnson, calling for an immediate and unconditional halt to all bombing of North Vietnam. At once the gap in the polls between him and Nixon began to narrow.

A special dimension to the 1968 campaign was added by the candidacy of Alabama's Governor George Wallace, whose American Independent supporters listed him on the ballot in all fifty states and launched the most ambitious third party candidacy since Robert La Follette's in 1924. Wallace had become the candidate of the South on the strength of a single slogan: "Segregation now—Segregation tomorrow—Segregation forever." But now he reached out for a broader and more generalized campaign theme and insisted he was no racist. He blasted "bearded bureaucrats," "pointy-headed professors," and "poor-folks haters"—his campaign resembled a class movement, fueled by the divisions in taste, style, values, and education that have eclipsed wealth as social differentia. The Wallace campaign employed the slogan "law and order," which took on a menacing tone in the context. Above all, Wallace took as his target the Supreme Court under Chief Justice Earl Warren. Wallace denounced a long series of decisions, beginning with the school desegregation case of 1954 but also including those that outlawed school prayers, protected the rights of accused criminals, and strengthened the civil rights of minorities.

As late as the second half of September the Gallup poll credited Wallace with about 20 percent of the vote, most of it formerly Democratic. But the Alabamian's popularity declined steadily throughout the last weeks of the campaign, with Humphrey the beneficiary. Labor unions used scare tactics, portraying Alabama as a low-wage, open-shop state. In California, long-haired boys and girls confused the candidate's audiences by pretending to be on his side, sometimes shouting "Sieg Heil, y'all!" Wallace's vice-presidential candidate, General Curtis LeMay, proved a liability. In a moment worthy of Barry Goldwater he said: "We seem to have a phobia about nuclear weapons. . . . I don't believe the world would end if we exploded a nuclear weapon."

Wallace's presence in the campaign permitted Nixon to portray himself as a middle-of-the-road candidate, even though he pursued "Southern strategy" on civil rights and civil disorder. Spiro Agnew, the Republican vice-presidential candidate, provided a more direct appeal to the South and to middle-class whites uneasy over racial troubles. In 1966 Agnew had won the governorship of Maryland on an open-housing platform, but he had acted forcefully to maintain order during the race riots of 1968. His addition to the national ticket was a gesture to the South. In the course of the campaign, Agnew made numerous blunders. Vernacular gibes about "Polacks" and "that fat Jap," while not delivered in an intentionally mean spirit, made no friends. He charged Humphrey with being "soft on communism" and then retracted the phrase, pleading unfamiliarity with its "political history." Democrats bought a television ad that showed his face and played the sound of a beating heart, suggesting the possibility of President Agnew. The running mate on the Democratic ticket, Senator Edmund Muskie of Maine, conducted an effective campaign, quietly gaining the loyalty of traditionally Democratic supporters among labor and the foreign born.

Nixon almost lost the 1968 election. At the end of October peace talks began in Paris and the bombing of North Vietnam ceased; had these signs of the war's diminution come a bit sooner, Humphrey might have won. But Nixon was lucky in 1968 as he had been unlucky in 1960. Drew Pearson held back a syndicated story about Nixon's allegedly having received psychological counseling in the late 1950's. And Humphrey himself refused to publicize the efforts of Mrs. Anna Chenault, a cochairman with Mrs. Dwight Eisenhower of the Republican campaign, to hold up South Vietnamese acceptance of the peace talks. As it was, Nixon won by almost as close a margin as he lost eight years before. Humphrey took some 88 percent of the black vote and even more of the Mexican American. Not one large city went Republican, and that party gained only four House seats along with five in the Senate. The Democratic coalition had held together remarkably well under the pressures of Vietnam.

29

Since the middle of the nineteenth century, Southeast Asia's vast deposits of raw materials and its relative accessibility have attracted rival empires and ideologies. In Indochina (Vietnam, Laos, and Cambodia) France established itself in two spurts, first during the 1850's under the Second Empire of Louis Napoleon, and later in the 1870's, after a humiliating defeat in the Franco-German War. Local Frenchmen in Vietnam almost immediately seized *de facto* control of the new colony and, together with native mandarins, ruled Indochina largely for private gain. The two groups set up a Grand Council which taxed the Vietnamese, protected monopolies, and enclosed vast estates—mostly for the benefit of a few hundred Frenchmen. This oligarchy thwarted reforms proposed by a few capable governors.

Economic exploitation and Vietnamese fears about French cultural aggression prompted resistance almost from the beginning. Until after World War I, urban radicals under the leadership of Phan Boi Chau called for a revolutionary cadre to oust the French, with Japanese support if necessary. But those Vietnamese identified with the colonial regime advocated cooperation and hoped for eventual independence; unfortunately, French intransigence discouraged such optimists. Neither course of action attracted discontented intellectuals nor the small, thoroughly disillusioned middle class, and when Paris vetoed moderate reforms during the early 1920's, nationalists adopted more militant tactics. In 1925 leftists set up the Thanh Nien, which Ho Chi Minh—who had earlier studied Marxism in France—reorganized in 1930 as the Communist party. Ho called for immediate land reforms and a mass uprising against French rule; as a result, the Grand Council viciously suppressed the fledgling Communist movement in its first years.

For the remainder of the decade, native religious sects channeled discontent into more other-worldly outlets. These groups, especially the Hoa Hao, a reform Buddhism, and the Cao Dai, an amalgam of Chinese philosophy, animism, and Christianity, were the only non-Communist organizations that could compete with Ho. During the Japanese occupation of Indochina from 1940 to 1945, however, internal bickering plagued both sects, and they could not counter Ho's skillful building of the Vietminh, a united front of anticolonialists. And when Japan's power disintegrated during early 1945, Vietminh guerrilla forces seized northern border provinces and by August a genuine popular revolution swept the colony. The only tightly organized party uncorrupted by collaboration either with the French or with the Japanese, the Vietminh formed a gov-

593

ernment on September 2, 1945, when Ho Chi Minh declared Vietnam's independence.

Although President Franklin Roosevelt tended to favor an end to colonial rule, Britain had fought World War II in part to protect its empire, not free it, and the new French Republic under General Charles de Gaulle demanded a return of all French possessions. Accordingly, Anglo-French occupation troops forcibly installed a colonial government in Saigon late in 1945; the Vietminh immediately launched a guerrilla counteroffensive against what rapidly became a French war of reconquest. Dreams of imperial glory and a belief in its military superiority led the Fourth Republic to repudiate a compromise agreement worked out with Ho in early 1946.

The French Struggle

The First Indochina War developed in two markedly different stages. From 1947 to 1950 the French demonstrated great military pressure throughout all of Indochina, but still could not break Vietminh dominance in the countryside or growing Communist control over the nationalist movement. Attempts to reestablish the Vietnamese monarchy under Emperor Bao Dai failed because of his obvious domination by the French. Then, from 1950 until 1954 the entire complexion of the war changed: Vietminh military strength flourished and desperate French generals took increasingly ill-advised risks in an effort to defeat the guerrillas. At the same time, Paris began to justify the war not as one of colonial reconquest, but as an anti-Communist effort in support of the legitimate Bao Dai government. French bureaucrats also developed the idea of "association" —a unified Vietnam would exercise semiautonomous powers internally while still associated with the French Union in affairs monetary, diplomatic, and cultural. The refusal to grant political independence or significant economic reform undermined the French military effort as well as the emperor's credibility. In fact, association actually forced nationalists into the Vietminh camp as the only alternative to collaboration.

During this second period events elsewhere lifted the war onto the international stage. Late in 1949 Mao Tse-tung defeated Chiang Kai-shek and established the People's Republic of China. Almost immediately American policy toward Indochina shifted from an apathetic disinterest to a determined effort at blocking further Communist expansion in Asia. When President Truman extended massive military aid to the French in February 1950, the National Security Council justified the new policy largely in "domino" terms: if Indochina were "lost," Thailand would be next; this would upset the balance of power in Southeast Asia, and communism might then reach out for either India or the rich islands of Indo-

nesia. Modeled on the fall of Austria, Czechoslovakia, and other European countries to Hitler after 1938, the simple domino theory substituted communism for fascism and Asia for Europe.

Communist control of the nationalist movement left the United States in a curious dilemma: the best way to defeat the Vietminh would be to replace the French with a non-Communist, nationalist regime, but America's diplomatic needs in Europe required French support, so aid to the French war effort became the only alternative. If cross-purposes muddied America's goals, frustration plagued Western military efforts in Indochina. The French had superior firepower and were well trained in the mode of orderly European combat, but Ho's native forces knew the land and fought an effective guerrilla war of attrition. The French army, under a succession of generals who mistakenly sought only military victory, could not control the countryside—or even move very far from the main roads, for that matter—nor could France oust the Vietminh from their stronghold in the Bac Viet area, the northern provinces outside of Hanoi and Haiphong.

Then, late in 1953, General Vo Nguyen Giap moved the bulk of his Vietminh forces toward Laos in an attempt to win territory and to lure French armies under General Henri Navarre away from their coastal strongholds. Navarre, to prevent future attacks against Laos, converted a

Ho Chi Minh (1890–1969) was the president of North Vietnam from 1954 to 1969. He had a long Communist background, and in this picture is seen visiting Prague, Czechoslovakia to meet with Czech Communist leaders. *United Press International*

small frontier outpost at Dien Bien Phu into a major fortress. By March 1954 when the battle began that would bring the First Indochina War to a stalemate, France had concentrated there nearly 25,000 of its best troops, built an airstrip to supply the fort, and set up massive artillery ranges. Navarre was confident that at last he could wipe out the Communists' main force. Yet Giap's forces not only outnumbered the French two-to-one, but, with the aid of China and thousands of Vietnamese who back-packed ammunition into the remote area, he had assembled superior firepower around the hills of Dien Bien Phu. Though the French retained control of the air, bombing strikes could not destroy the well-hidden Communist embankments which soon knocked out the French airstrip and covered repeated infantry attacks. Then Giap encircled the post; during the first week of May 1954 the garrison fell to the Vietminh army. The French military effort to reassert colonial control had collapsed.

Yet even before this final defeat, two developments had rendered the outcome of battle almost unimportant. While most diplomats moved toward ending the war, Secretary of State John Foster Dulles took the first steps toward prolonging and Americanizing it. The Eisenhower administration seriously considered active military intervention, not only to save the outpost at Dien Bien Phu but also to bolster the entire French effort, which it believed to be an anti-Communist campaign. Washington abandoned ideas of direct interference only after the French government itself refused to continue the war and the military situation in northern Vietnam became hopeless. If the United States were to launch an anti-Communist crusade in Southeast Asia, it would have to find a vehicle other than French colonialism.

Only one day before the fall of Dien Bien Phu, the nations involved in Indochina—France, Britain, Russia, China, the United States, and representatives of Ho Chi Minh's Hanoi-based government and the French puppet regime under Bao Dai—convened in Geneva, Switzerland, to settle the Indochina War. Negotiations were extremely complex: Britain and Russia were interested primarily in France's future military role in Europe; Communist China hoped to secure international recognition; a sulking Dulles wanted no compromise. After six weeks the representatives reached agreement, largely because Russia and China forced Ho Chi Minh to accept Western terms. The Geneva accords granted independence to the three Indochinese states of Laos, Cambodia, and Vietnam. To facilitate military disengagement, Vietnam was temporarily divided at the 17th parallel; nationwide elections within two years would determine the country's permanent political future. None of the new states was to permit foreign troops or bases on its soil or to join an outside alliance.

American Involvement

This outcome satisfied neither Dulles nor Eisenhower. Rather than a compromise, Washington wanted to guarantee the existence of a non-Communist alternative. Thus, the State Department announced that the United States, which had not signed the Geneva accords, would adhere to its terms, but would treat North and South Vietnam as separate entities. Then, in September of 1954, Dulles negotiated the Southeast Asia Treaty Organization (SEATO), a milder version of the NATO alliance, pledging assistance "in accord with constitutional process." The original signatories—France, Great Britain, the United States, Australia, New Zealand, the Philippines, Pakistan, and Thailand—later extended the pact's protection to include Cambodia, Laos, and South Vietnam. Convinced that his only other option was disengagement and the gradual fall of all Southeast Asia to communism, Eisenhower pledged vast economic aid to the native but increasingly elitist South Vietnamese premier, Ngo Dinh Diem. In 1956 the United States supported Diem's open break with the Geneva settlement, and acting on Dulles's explicit approval, the premier called off elections, which the nationalist Communists would probably have won. By this series of actions, Washington committed itself to the creation and then to the defense of a non-Communist government in South Vietnam.

But supporting Diem eventually backfired, for he took American money and built a personalist regime. At first, however, the new leadership seemed altogether viable. Between 1954 and 1957, generously supported by American financial aid, the country made substantial economic growth and even achieved some land reform. The government suppressed gangsters in Saigon and brought under control the religious sects, many of whose leaders had set up independent fiefdoms in the countryside. But Diem never gained broad popular support, and because the rural areas remained in the hands of opponents, he adopted increasingly repressive tactics. In addition, Diem's Catholicism alienated the predominantly Buddhist nation, particularly its intellectuals. In an effort to consolidate personal control, Diem replaced local village elders with his own administrators, launched a "population relocation" program which degenerated into political witch-hunting, and interpreted land reform laws to favor absentee landlords. When the United States protested, the mandarin pointed out that, without his regime, the country would succumb to the Communist insurgency which had broken out in 1957.

According to an analyst in the Department of Defense, Diem's "increasingly oppressive and corrupt regime" had provoked the new revolt, and a united front of anti-Diem factions—nearly all native to South Vietnam—called for genuine land redistribution, representative government, and a decentralized administration. Not until 1959 did the rebellion seriously threaten the Saigon government. Then widespread frustration with Diem, together with surreptitious North Vietnamese support for the rebels, gradually weakened the premier's control over the country. Only American financial aid and military hardware maintained the government in Saigon. As American aid to Diem skyrocketed, so too did Hanoi's support for the insurgents, primarily through training southerners. With its industrial development program accelerated, however, North Vietnam could also send more and more materials to the rebels in the South.

By the end of the decade the Republican administration had dispatched some 685 American "advisory" personnel to Vietnam; but the nonmilitary alternative, land reform and economic growth, collapsed because of Diem's opposition. Ironically, while Eisenhower "could conceive of no greater tragedy than for the United States to become involved in an all-out land war in Asia," his secretary of state announced that "the free world would intervene in Indochina rather than let the situation deteriorate." And if American troops did enter the battle, Dulles argued, "[United States] prestige would be involved to a point where it would have to obtain victory." Eisenhower himself found no answer to the puzzle, which his successors attempted to solve by sending in American troops and firepower. Dulles's reasoning foreshadowed the escalations of the 1960's.

Kennedy and Vietnam

The Diem government approached chaos in the early sixties. All social and economic reform halted, and even retrogressed, as Diem concentrated on maintaining his power and eliminating all opposition. In response, thousands of southern insurrectionists joined the newly organized National Liberation Front (NLF), and many took the trek north for military training. Support from the new Kennedy administration, which eventually sent 16,000 American advisers along with artillery and fighter-bombers to Vietnam, kept the Diem regime alive. Washington also expanded the elaborate clandestine war against North Vietnam, which it first began in 1955. Kennedy now ordered secret agents to sabotage lines of communication throughout the North and American advisers directed military raids across Hanoi's frontiers and into Laos. At first these tactics appeared successful: during 1962 the NLF lost some of its earlier territorial gains. Although some of Kennedy's apologists later insisted that he would have avoided a full-scale conflict, his decisions had enlarged American goals in Vietnam without assuring the achievement of these goals. By 1963 this discrepancy could no longer be ignored. Chief of Staff Maxwell Taylor's hopes for counterinsurgency warfare required popular support and extensive reforms in Vietnam. Yet under Kennedy Washington skirted social and economic problems and concentrated instead upon military victory.

Kennedy escalated the war gradually, perhaps aware that his decisions slowly committed the United States to a military victory. He observed that sending troops to Vietnam was a little like having a drink: the effect wears off and you have to have another. Once the principles of American aid and troop support were well established, the size or character of the military effort could scarcely be held in check. Then, too, American soldiers began to die in Vietnam—sixty by 1963. Advocates of further escalation could employ the effective argument of redemption: for what had these men died? In 1956 Kennedy had declared: "Vietnam represents the cornerstone of the free world in Southeast Asia, the keystone to the arch, the finger in the dike." But Kennedy certainly did have doubts about taking further steps in Vietnam. By September 1963 he said: "In the final analysis it is their war." Yet he still believed that a United States withdrawal could mean the collapse of Southeast Asia. The war in Vietnam, however, was of a sort that the president, Secretary of Defense Robert McNamara, and the chief of staff had anticipated. Their aim was to demonstrate to the Russians that wars of national liberation, in General Taylor's words, were not "cheap, safe, and disavowable" but "costly, dangerous, and doomed to failure." Whether the American army—or the American public—was really ready for such a war is doubtful, as events demonstrated.

The Diem government had aggravated the political situation in the Vietnam countryside, and its persecution of Buddhists sickened the entire world. The ruling family persuaded the legislature to pass laws requiring Buddhists to obey Catholic moral laws, and Diem's Roman Catholic sister-in-law, Madame Nhu, gained notoriety for her cynical dismissal of Buddhist "barbecues"—self-immolation as a form of political protest. Beginning in May 1963, the Buddhists organized strong demonstrations against the Saigon regime; in an attempt to squash this threat, Diem's brother attacked Buddhist temples and pagodas throughout South Vietnam in August. When it became clear that the Diem army raids had alienated the urban middle class, most religious sects, and intellectuals everywhere, the United States abandoned its support of the premier, while Ambassador Henry Cabot Lodge actively collaborated with a cabal of generals. On November 2, 1963, the group assassinated Diem and set up a new government under Major General Nguyen Khanh. The United States acquiesced in and abetted the military coup against Diem not so much because of the regime's corruption but because of its ineffectiveness.

The United States might have used the Diem crisis as a convenient reason for withdrawing from the war. Robert Kennedy urged a course of disengagement during a cabinet meeting, and *Time*'s editors suggested the possibility of neutralizing all of Southeast Asia. But McNamara and Taylor visited Vietnam in September and on October 2 reported that most

American tasks there would be accomplished in fifteen months, with perhaps a thousand troops returning home by the end of 1963. No wonder pursuing the war seemed the practical course—one that prudently weighed cost against advantage.

By the time President Johnson took office in November 1963 he had few political alternatives. He inherited not only the war itself but also Kennedy's principal advisers on foreign affairs; the United States had many troops in the country and South Vietnam's new government was completely dependent on American economic and military aid. In any event, Johnson had long since decided that the "broad lines" of Kennedy's policy were correct. The new president approached Vietnam on the basis of his knowledge of World War II and Korea, quickly identifying the problem as one of halting aggression. If the past coerced his policies, a relative hiatus in cold war confrontations elsewhere freed him to act in Southeast Asia. Johnson, in his later memoirs, *The Vantage Point*, argued that he had helped South Vietnam "to win their contest against the externally directed and supported Communist conspiracy." Contrary to some critics, this view was not an ingenuous rationalization but reflected the president's determination to stand fast "to protect our interests and keep our promises." And since Johnson equated American interests with taking a strong stand, further escalation was inevitable.

Johnson and Vietnam

Diem's legacy of unresolved social and economic problems, together with his elimination of political opponents, had created a political vacuum in South Vietnam. During 1964 a musical chairs of military juntas in Saigon undermined the anti-Communist effort; the Vietcong made rapid, large-scale gains. The *Pentagon Papers* reveal that as Vietcong strength spread, the American administration became more and more interested "in bombing the North as a substitute prosecution of the counterinsurgency campaign in the South." As a result of these pressures, 1964 marked the beginning of the Second Indochina War: Johnson would commit vast resources and wage war throughout the former French colony in order to reach America's goal, a non-Communist South Vietnam.

A pretext to attack North Vietnam—the so-called Gulf of Tonkin crisis—occurred during the first week of August 1964. The navy had helped South Vietnam to conduct extensive operations, code named 34-A, against shore installations in North Vietnam. The spy ship *Maddox*, loaded with electronic equipment, had supported these raids, often cruising inside the twelve-mile limit claimed by Hanoi. After one such incursion, manned by South Vietnamese but supported by Americans, Hanoi apparently decided that it must "show the flag," perhaps to deter further operations. North Vietnam may not unreasonably have assumed that the *Maddox* was part of the last of 34-A and sent several PT boats into the Gulf of Tonkin. The *Maddox*, now over twenty miles from the coast, apparently fired first upon the approaching North Vietnamese ships, which then returned the fire. Two days later, on August 4, as the *Maddox* and another destroyer, the *C. Turner Joy*, cruised in the same general area, they reported a second attack by North Vietnamese boats. Because of intense darkness and malfunctioning sonar and radar equipment, overanxious naval captains may have imagined this second "attack." Although Hanoi may have planned another strike, no material evidence has surfaced that it actually occurred.

But in Washington, Johnson publicly denounced "unprovoked aggression" and used the temporary feeling of crisis to extract congressional approval for a project the administration had contemplated for several months. To insure his freedom of action and demonstrate American unity in an election year, Johnson secured a sweeping authorization "to take all necessary measures . . . to prevent further aggression." Although aware of the 34-A raids, a nearly unanimous Senate adopted the de facto declaration of war, 88-2. Only a few isolated senators, Wayne Morse of Oregon in particular, questioned its ultimate purpose or the advisability of open-ended commitments.

During the next four months the administration moved quickly toward full-scale war. Policy debates in late 1964 revolved around the question of whether to bomb North Vietnam on a regular basis. Initially, the administration announced a "reprisal policy": the United States would attack North Vietnam only after a specific incident of aggression. What amounted to the first reprisal came on August 4, when the air force bombed PT boat bases in North Vietnam in response to the Gulf of Tonkin "incidents." Then, as the political and military situation in the South worsened, Washington made its first major miscalculation: that systematic air attacks against the North would either end Hanoi's support of the southern insurgency or lead to a formal settlement.

By January 1965 the policies and attitudes had crystallized which would, for the next three years, sustain America's escalation of the war, including the use of more and more United States ground combat troops, all-out air attacks upon North Vietnam, and consistent rejection of serious peace talks with the enemy. On one level, the administration anticipated that escalation would improve morale in South Vietnam and bring military victory there. On another level, President Johnson hoped that the conflict would "contain" China and prevent an Indonesia-North Vietnam-North Korea bloc that might squeeze the United States out of East Asia. Johnson saw the war in South Vietnam as a "demonstration" to convince Communists everywhere of America's resolve to deter "aggression." The United States must at all costs avoid defeat, not only because of the supposed domino consequences for Southeast Asia, but also because a withdrawal would produce psychological tremors throughout East Asia and perhaps even Africa and Europe. The Vietnamese war would show America's ability to defend its vision of world order and its international credibility.

Largely because of these considerations, Johnson decided to fight the war tactically somewhere between the extremes of "unmanly withdrawal" and the quick, massive attacks against North Vietnam and the Vietcong advocated by the joint chiefs of staff. He believed that a calculated, steady increase in force would convince his opponents that they could not win. Sustained bombing of North Vietnam began in March 1965, ostensibly in response to a Vietcong attack on an American military base at Pleiku. He sent hundreds of thousands of combat troops into South Vietnam to protect American outposts and to aid Vietnamese units threatened by Vietcong attack. Finally, Johnson authorized independent action by American soldiers; the first "search and destroy" mission involving large numbers of American men took place several miles northwest of Saigon in late June.

Washington military planners soon tripped over some misconceptions. Guerrilla methods often confused generals trained for wars of maneuver; increasing aid did not automatically overwhelm the rebellion. Only a few men, such as Undersecretary of State McGeorge Bundy and some on-the-spot CIA agents, foresaw what the troop needs in Vietnam would be or cautioned that the insurgency might spread as United States support increased. Experts in guerrilla warfare estimated that United States forces would have to outnumber Vietcong-North Vietnamese troops about ten to one. And every time Washington added more soldiers, so too did Saigon's opponents. By early 1968, for example, Hanoi had fielded roughly 135,000 men in the South, the United States about 550,000; double that number would be required just to offset Hanoi's troops.

Initially, optimistic reports from his political and military advisers pressed Johnson toward an ever-widening war. This elusive hope for victory was only one consideration that prevented a compromise settlement; the president's determination to "negotiate from strength" and North Vietnam's own determined militancy scuttled early opportunities to meet at a conference table. As early as July 1964, for example, U Thant, secretary-general of the United Nations, suggested reactivating the Geneva Conference. The French, under the shrewd leadership of De Gaulle, quickly agreed, and so did the Soviet Union, North Vietnam, and even China. But Johnson, fearing that a conference might restrict his maneu-

Modern wars utilize the best of technology and medicine. The United States, in the Vietnam War, first used helicopters on a large scale to evacuate the wounded from battlefields. Getting medical help quicker saved many lives. Soldiers also benefitted greatly from advances in the fields of vascular surgery, amputations, and organ transplants. *United Press International*

verability, answered: "We do not believe in conferences called to ratify terror." A scant nine months later, however, during a speech at the Johns Hopkins University, the president offered to attend a peace conference at any time, and he outlined plans for an Asian Development Bank to rebuild Southeast Asia. Sincere in his hope for peace, Johnson would have negotiated, but he would not jeopardize the war's "demonstration effect," and the demand for a non-Communist regime in Saigon was to the North Vietnamese and Vietcong tantamount to a capitulation. When the Communists not unexpectedly rejected Johnson's terms, he interpreted each rejection as further "proof" of aggression, and could then in good conscience further escalate the war.

Illusory hopes eventually gave way to near cynicism. To check domestic critics and create an aura of peaceful intent, Johnson ordered a halt to the air war, a dramatic thirty-seven-day bombing pause against North Vietnam from December 1965 to January 1966. The president's closest advisers realized that his "terms" were those of victory, not of compromise, and that he undertook the effort largely to justify renewed escalation. But ironically the pause also spread a growing realization that the Rolling Thunder bombing operations against the North had not materially damaged Hanoi's willingness to fight. When bombing resumed in February 1966—because, it was said, Ho Chi Minh refused to negotiate—the case was altered: no longer would the United States attempt to force North Vietnam out of the war; instead, the air force would concentrate on cutting Hanoi's supplies to the Vietcong.

Stymied by the inefficiency of Rolling Thunder and by Hanoi's refusal to cave in at an American bargaining table, Johnson massively escalated the ground war in Vietnam during the spring of 1966. For nearly twenty-four months, the world witnessed America's military attempt to pursue a will-o'-the-wisp victory and to insure a non-Communist South Vietnam. Still, two obstacles remained: the unstable, often arbitrary government in Saigon and a swelling tide of discontent within the United States. In South Vietnam disagreements over military tactics and economic reforms plagued the junta that had replaced Diem. Even after two generals, Nguyen Van Thieu and Nguyen Cao Ky, emerged on top, Saigon could not heal the split between countryside and city which fueled the insurgency, partly because the rebels held much rural territory, partly because the United States command focused on military victory. But at a meeting in Honolulu during February 1966 with President Thieu and Vice-President Ky, Johnson extracted promises that the junta would permit an elected government and begin large-scale land redistribution. It was a delicate diplomatic maneuver, for while Johnson threatened to cut off American aid to force compliance, the two Vietnamese leaders knew

President Johnson and his advisers at a council of war on Guam, March 20, 1967. Front row, left to right: South Vietnamese chief of state Nguyen Van Thieu; President Johnson; and South Vietnamese Premier Nguyen Cao Ky. Back row, left to right: Rear Admiral Horace Bird, commander of U.S. naval forces in the Marinas Islands; Secretary of State Dean Rusk; and Secretary of Defense Robert Mc-Namara. *United Press International*

that they were the president's only option. American insistence upon the appearance, if not the reality, of democracy, together with the temporary eclipse of Communist progress during the massive United States buildup of 1966, finally brought about nationwide elections for a Constituent Assembly. Unfortunately, this "constitutional convention" was rigged: no Communist delegates attended; the regime blocked neutralist candidates; and the generals quickly reasserted their personal control over the new government apparatus.

If Johnson fashioned events in South Vietnam, his own countrymen proved less malleable. After a brief rather positive reaction to their latest military crusade against communism, many Americans increasingly went sour. The inconclusiveness of the struggle was immensely frustrating. The more the United States bombed North Vietnam, for example, the more Ho scattered his factories, infiltrated the South, and whipped up war fever in the North. Indeed, because the country was not heavily industrialized, American bombers quickly discovered that they lacked advantageous targets, and fears about reactions in the Soviet Union and China prevented an assault against the major port of Haiphong. In addition, the air force could not interdict supplies flowing south along the Ho Chi

Disillusion

Minh Trail, for it was a jungle path, not an interstate highway; its location, and even at times its existence, was problematical. The bulk of war material moved at night in small vehicles or on human backs: American "damage" could be easily repaired or simply avoided.

Meanwhile, the ground war in South Vietnam remained locked in a stalemate despite repeated reinforcements. Over half a million American troops guarded major cities and many rural outposts by 1968, but the Communists dominated much of the countryside. When combat units embarked upon "search and destroy" missions, North Vietnamese regulars shunned combat and Vietcong guerrillas hid among the population. Despite vastly improved "kill ratios," American military forces could not keep up with Communist recruitment and North Vietnamese infiltration.

Johnson's program to "win the hearts and minds of the Vietnamese people" was similarly indecisive. To "pacify" the countryside, Washington launched the strategic hamlet program. American troops would move into a village, secure it with a series of fortifications, and leave a garrison of soldiers. Although the tactic protected the village from Vietcong at-

By the end of the 1960's, American disillusionment with the war was growing both at home and in Vietnam. This American soldier, with a half-eaten candy bar still partially wrapped in tin foil, takes aim with a M-79 grenade launcher at Trung Leung, less than a mile south of the DMZ. His hat bears the ironic antiwar slogan, "Kill for Peace." *United Press International*

tack, the spectacle of peasants living under American guns in barbed-wire enclosures provoked memories of concentration camps. It seemed possible that both political and military victory could prove elusive.

If inconclusiveness soured public support for Johnson's policy, a growing antiwar movement within the United States questioned its very purpose. By 1967 Senator J. William Fulbright, who earlier had guided the Gulf of Tonkin resolution through the Senate, now attacked the administration's "arrogance of Power." "Power," observed Fulbright, "tends to confuse itself with virtue." He believed that its history of victory, prosperity, and power gave the United States a dangerous sense of omnipotence and self-righteousness, which, at its worst, could distort reality—as in Vietnam. According to the senator, American "world-saving" in Asia started out by assuming that Western institutions and political methods could establish themselves in an alien culture. While Fulbright and other critics worried about misplaced motives, a mushrooming antiwar coalition directly questioned the war's morality. In October 1967, a rally of 200,000 students, leftists, and "ordinary" Americans demonstrated in a march through the nation's capital. An important portion of the Democratic party had rejected Johnson's leadership. More worrisome, the war fueled the growth of a strident Left that threatened to split the country into doctrinaire factions.

Tet

During 1968 the realities of Vietnam and of domestic disillusionment forced Johnson to shift his tactics, though not his objective. It was plain to most congressional and military leaders that the United States would not be able to win the war in Vietnam for many years, if ever. Despite our bombing, possibly because of it, North Vietnam appeared to be the most stable government in Southeast Asia. In the South the mightiest nation in the world could not, short of nuclear weapons, defeat an army of willful peasants operating without an air force or heavy artillery. To most Americans, it seemed even clearer that the United States was in serious trouble after the Tet offensive of late January–February 1968. On the night of January 29, the American embassy and all the major cities of South Vietnam came under attack. Saigon nearly fell to the enemy and most of the northern city of Hue came under Vietcong control for several days. Only a brutal counteroffensive restored the cities to allied control, though the Vietcong still dominated the rural areas. Their mission had been accomplished in secrecy and dedication; President Thieu's forces appeared inept in contrast.

General Westmoreland immediately flew to the United States and asked for 200,000 more reinforcements, a request that coincided with a major review of war policy in Washington. At this point, Johnson's decision was relatively straightforward: he could not send more men to South Vietnam without endangering America's commitments elsewhere and producing severe strains on the inflated American economy; in addition, the president would have had to mobilize the reserves and increase taxes, but both steps required congressional approval, and he doubted whether Congress or the general public would acquiesce. By this time, Johnson also seemed to have realized the futility of escalation. When Westmoreland explained that he could not guarantee victory even with the additional troops, the president replied: "Then where will it all end?" Dismayed and disillusioned, he entrusted the search for an alternative to a study group chaired by a personal friend, Clark Clifford. Since military victory was not in sight, the Clifford committee turned to "the lesser of evils," diplomacy as a solution for the war.

The decision to reorient American policy was not unexpected. For well over a year, Secretary of Defense Robert McNamara had advocated a negotiated settlement in South Vietnam based upon a coalition government. Former Secretary of State Dean Acheson added his voice of skepticism. Growing disintegration of support for the war at home and a spreading malaise among United States military forces in Vietnam intensified the pressure for negotiation. The disaster of Tet triggered in many military men a hysteria for revenge and a sense of frustration that led to a breakdown in discipline: widespread drug use and even occasional mutinies threatened to destroy morale. Since "body count," not territory, defined the terms of victory in Vietnam, the step was a short one to mass murders of Viet civilians by American soldiers at My Lai and Song My. At these places and elsewhere, company commanders and their troops lost all sense of restraint and committed atrocities not revealed to the American public until 1970 and 1971.

Meanwhile, domestic events further restricted options. When, in March 1968, Senator Eugene McCarthy received nearly 40 percent of the vote in the New Hampshire Democratic primary, voters were rebuking the incumbent president. Soon it appeared that a majority in the party apparently favored someone other than the man who had led the Democrats to a landslide victory only four years earlier. Students throughout the nation, as well as many journalists, teachers, and groups interested in domestic change, more and more protested the course of the war. A desire to unify his party and the country largely motivated the president in his decision to reverse the course of the war.

In a dramatic television appearance on March 31, 1968, Johnson officially announced the results of the Clifford policy review: the United States would halt bombing north of the 19th parallel in an effort to bring about serious peace negotiations; Westmoreland was to receive only a tenth of his troop request. In addition, South Vietnam would take over active prosecution of the war gradually, an approach President Nixon later expanded into "Vietnamization." Yet Johnson's desire for even partial victory imperiled his search for peace; the administration wanted to negotiate, but did not want to compromise along the collaborationist lines suggested by McNamara. Instead, Johnson believed that the Tet offensive had severely weakened Communist ground forces and that a new spirit, a new effectiveness in South Vietnam, would enable the Saigon regime to defeat the Vietcong. The de facto limit on American troops, the bombing restriction, and the beginning of Vietnamization—Thieu promised to raise 135,000 additional troops—were genuine moves toward peace, but still an American peace with American objectives: a non-Communist South Vietnam.

To insure the bombing halt and probably to see what sort of deal the United States contemplated, Hanoi replied favorably to Johnson's offer for talks. For several weeks the two powers debated an appropriate site for the negotiations, each advocating a city sympathetic to its own position. Hanoi finally suggested Paris, presumably to take advantage of De Gaulle's growing anti-Americanism; Johnson could not refuse. On May 10, the peace talks opened at the Majestic Hotel; Xuan Thuy represented Hanoi, Averell Harriman, former ambassador to Moscow, was the chief United States negotiator. Almost immediately, the talks stalled. For five months, the diplomats deadlocked over a question of timing. North Vietnam insisted that meaningful talks could begin only after the United States pledged to stop bombing. Johnson countered that he must continue raids across the Demilitarized Zone (DMZ) to protect American troops; the question of permanent cessation, he argued, should be included in the peace talks, not decided beforehand. The United States position was one of "reciprocity" from Hanoi: a mutual winding down of the war and the participation of both the Saigon regime and the National Liberation Front in any political settlement. By mid-October 1968 the president had accepted an arrangement worked out between Harriman and Thuy whereby the United States would halt all bombing if Hanoi "by its silence" agreed to negotiate with South Vietnam, not increase its aid to the Vietcong, and permit American reconnaissance flights.

If Johnson had hoped to announce the settlement in an effort to boost candidate Hubert Humphrey's chances in the November presidential election, he reckoned without his South Vietnamese allies. The Harriman Thuy plan troubled President Thieu who feared that the inclusion of the NLF in the talks would unduly raise its prestige; in any event, Saigon wanted to prevent, not facilitate, agreement between Hanoi and Washington. Most important, Thieu calculated he could "get a better deal" from a Nixon administration. Stymied by Thieu's reluctance to agree to multilateral talks and despite Thieu's public disclaimers, Johnson announced the total bombing halt anyway. Not only was Harriman's delicate arrangement called into question, but also the obvious disunity prompted a long struggle over procedural details—including the shape of the bargaining table—which preoccupied the Paris talks from November to February 1969. But if Johnson left the incoming president Nixon with a war and an undiluted commitment for a non-Communist South Vietnam, he also left him a diplomatic tool, the Paris peace talks, along with a military and economic weapon, Vietnamization, to pursue that objective.

Nixon's Plan to End the War

During the 1968 campaign, Nixon claimed to have a plan to end the war in Vietnam, which he preferred to withhold lest he upset any progress Johnson might make in the negotiations. After taking office Nixon appointed Henry Cabot Lodge chief American negotiator in Paris. Almost at the outset Lodge insisted on separating the military and political issues in face of North Vietnamese and Vietcong insistence on their inseparability. Although congressional "doves" may have differed from the Nixon stance, they were willing to give him a chance to make some significant moves of his own. Senator George McGovern almost alone attacked the policy in March 1969 as merely a continuation of Johnson's policies. Most opponents of the war, including Senator J. William Fulbright, continued to believe that Nixon would soon end American involvement in Southeast Asia.

On May 7, 1969, the Vietcong offered a ten-point proposal which included American withdrawal, free elections, and a coalition government. In reply, Nixon submitted a phased mutual withdrawal over a twelve-month period, including adding a Communist retreat from Cambodia and Laos. Neither side waivered from these proposals, but Nixon decided to move unilaterally toward disengagement. Scarcely a month later, Secretary of State Rogers remarked that the United States was not wedded to the Saigon regime, thereby raising the possibility of a coalition government. Three days later Nixon announced that he would reduce the 540,000 troops in Vietnam by 25,000 at the end of August, after which he would announce further cuts.

Antiwar demonstrations that fall prompted sarcastic remarks from Vice-President Agnew and Secretary of Transportation Volpe. When the newspapers picked up the story of an earlier American massacre of Vietnamese civilians at Song My, the issue of war crimes heated up debates on the war. Meanwhile, there was still no progress in Paris; Lodge resigned in November. Nixon announced a further substantial reduction of troops in December. Cuts in draft calls and the first draft lottery also lessened opposition to the war.

On March 18, 1970, Prince Sihanouk while visiting Moscow, was overthrown as leader of Cambodia. The government that succeeded him under Lon Nol began to attack North Vietnamese and Vietcong troops, using Cambodian territory as sanctuary. And when American planes attacked gun positions in Cambodia, as they had secretly for many months, France called for a new Indochina conference to prevent the spread of war to all of Southeast Asia. Although both the United States and the Soviet Union expressed cautious interest in the idea, nothing ever came of it. On April 20, Nixon ordered a new cutback of 150,000 troops to take place over an entire year, during which the president could accelerate or reduce the flow of men.

On April 20 and 30, 1970, the United States and South Vietnamese troops began a large-scale troop operation in Cambodia, designed to destroy enemy supplies and sanctuaries. As with earlier offensive actions, the administration defended this tactic on the grounds that it would speed American withdrawal. Such reasoning infuriated war critics: protests and strikes spread throughout the nation, especially on college campuses. In a demonstration against ROTC at Kent State University on May 4, National Guardsmen, called out in response to the burning of an ROTC building the night before, shot and killed four students. National Guard claims of sniper fire (never substantiated) could not suppress the outrage felt across the country; three days later eighty colleges had closed down and hundreds of others undertook various forms of protest, while construction workers attacked a group of war protesters in New York City. To cool the atmosphere, Nixon promised to end his criticism of students. (Only a few days earlier he had referred to campus radicals as "bums" in comparison with American soldiers who were "the greatest.") Even the vice-president, who had been merciless in his criticism of the media and war protesters, decided not to deliver a provocative speech. When nearly 100,000 massed in Washington, the president risked a walk to the protest area at dawn to show his concern for young people. Administration criticism of the antiwar movement upset even some cabinet members. Secretary of Interior Walter Hickel wrote a letter to Nixon asserting he had turned away from the youth of America. Employees of HEW challenged Robert Finch to justify administration policies and allow them to voice their own criticism; soon after Finch resigned to become a White House adviser.

The Democratic Congress launched new attacks on Nixon's Vietnam policies. On June 24, 1970, the Senate voted 81 to 10 to repeal the Tonkin Gulf Resolution. Senators John Cooper and Frank Church formulated an amendment to prohibit the use of American troops in Cambodia; Mark Hatfield and McGovern drew one up to withdraw all troops by June 30, 1971. Both challenged the authority of the president to commit troops in combat without congressional approval. In succeeding months, the Nixon administration argued successfully against any such infringement of executive powers.

As the school year drew to a close, so did the demonstrations, but the war went on. In July David E. K. Bruce took charge of the American delegation in Paris. Negotiations remained on dead center until September, when the Vietcong offered safety to withdrawing troops if the United States would set a pullout date of June 30, 1971. Nixon refused this offer and instead announced on October 12 that 40,000 more troops would be withdrawn as part of 150,000 announced earlier in the spring.

One of the most sensitive issues in the negotiations was the fate of prisoners of war. Many American pilots shot down over North Vietnam had been POWs for four or five years. As their relatives began to insist on concessions to win their release, both pro and antiwar advocates embraced the POW issue for their own ends. On November 23, 1970, the administration authorized massive air strikes on North Vietnam and sent a rescue team to a suspected POW camp. When the news seeped out that no POWs had been rescued, the antiwar people sharpened their criticism, insisting on full withdrawal to win the POWs rapid release. In Paris the Vietcong and North Vietnamese made firm offers to release POWs in return for a definite date on complete American withdrawal from Indochina.

The Nixon administration would not set a date for a final pullout; indeed, in February 1971 the United States and the South Vietnamese launched an offensive in Laos. Although providing air support for South Vietnamese combat forces, the American command insisted that no American combat soldiers aided in the operation. Again Nixon explained the invasion as a means of carrying out Vietnamization and assuring the return home of soldiers by destroying enemy sanctuaries and supply depots. Even though the South Vietnamese soon abandoned the Laos invasion, the administration insisted upon its success. On April 7, 1971, President Nixon announced a further withdrawal of 100,000 troops by December 1971.

Although criticism of the Laos operation did not match the strident denunciation of the invasion in Cambodia a year before, protesters asserted that such a move, along with increased bombing missions, brought neither soldiers nor POWs home. By April demonstrators in Washington and San

Francisco called for a specific date for withdrawal from Southeast Asia. Leading Democratic presidential contenders echoed the sentiment, and a special contingent of Vietnam veterans gathered in the Capitol to discard their medals. Yet Nixon promised to maintain a United States residual force in Vietnam until all POWs were released and until the South Vietnamese could defend themselves. In July the administration rejected a seven-point peace plan that assured the safety of withdrawing troops and promised the release of all prisoners if the United States would pull out by the end of 1971. A few days later, Le Duc Tho, one of the highest ranking North Vietnamese, announced a significant concession: withdrawal and POWs could be negotiated separately. Despite this marked departure from the position that political and military issues were inseparable, Nixon refused the offer.

In the longest court-martial in American history, Lieutenant William Calley was sentenced to life imprisonment for killing twenty-two civilians at My Lai. In this picture Vietnam veterans march in Trenton, New Jersey, protesting Calley's treatment and collecting signatures to send to President Nixon pleading for Calley's release. United Press International

Antiwar Feeling

The president faced serious pressure at home to end American involvement in the war, and at certain junctures specific events increased the demands. One of these was the follow-up on the massacres of civilians at My Lai and Song My. No punitive action had been taken by commanding officers of the American division, and the incident had never been reported to the top echelons of the military. Once the barbaric acts leaked out to the press, however, Lieutenant William Calley received the longest court martial in American military history; the tribunal found him guilty of murdering twenty-two civilians and sentenced him to life imprisonment. A deluge of telegrams induced President Nixon to order Calley confined to quarters pending a full military review of the case. He was a rather low junior officer held responsible for acts carried out in the stress of battle; many felt that Calley was the scapegoat in a situation where high-ranking officers should share the blame and even shoulder the responsibility. Calley's immediate superior, Captain Ernest L. Medina, and commanding officers such as Major General Samuel Koster (although demoted one rank) and Colonel Oren Henderson were all found innocent of complicity, even though they all admitted a failure to pass on complete information about the massacre. The army reduced Calley's sentence to twenty years with a final decision yet to be rendered.

An issue sometimes vaguely associated in the public mind with My Lai was that of drugs. For a long time it had been known that soldiers in Vietnam often used marijuana. In the spring of 1971 stories of epidemic use of "hard drugs" circulated at home. The military established amnesty procedures for addicts, promised treatment without punishment, and tested all returning veterans. War critics pointed out that American soldiers were not only subject to punishment for mistakes committed in the execution of commands, but also were returning as addicts. One way or another "criminals" emerged from Vietnam.

Still another major issue materialized in 1971. On Sunday, June 13, the *New York Times* began serial publication of carefully selected parts of a secret report commissioned by Robert McNamara in 1968 to determine how the United States became involved in the war in Southeast Asia. The Pentagon Papers, as they were soon called, consisted of 3,000 pages of analysis and 4,000 pages of documents, suggesting that American interference started with Truman's decision to give France assistance against the Vietminh. Eisenhower prevented a Communist takeover after 1954 and Kennedy expanded a "limited risk gamble" into a "broad commitment" that left Johnson with the choice of either total withdrawal or increased involvement. The *Times* chose to focus on the build-up in 1964 as the critical period of United States involvement and in so doing cast even more doubt on the credibility of the Johnson administration. Whatever the case, a serious "leak" of security confronted Nixon inasmuch as the Pentagon Papers were supposed to be secret documents.

On June 15, Attorney General John Mitchell asked the *Times* to "refrain" from further publication until the government could assess the strategic importance of the material. When the *Times* "respectfully declined," Mitchell went to court and obtained a restraining order. The

Washington *Post* also had a set of similar documents and began to publish its own series. The *Times* could circumvent the order merely by publishing reports of the *Post* stories. When the Justice Department moved against the *Post*, other papers such as the Chicago *Sun Times* and the Boston *Globe* published their own versions of the Pentagon Papers. Ultimately, on June 25, the Supreme Court agreed to hear the case after the District and Appeals courts had rendered contradictory decisions. After rejecting a government request to hold a secret hearing on the papers, the Court on July 1, 1971, ruled 6 to 3 that the government had failed to meet the "burden" justifying prior restraint. The dissenting opinion complained of the haste with which the case was adjudicated given the possibility of a threat to national security. On the following day the *Times* and *Post* resumed publication of the papers.

The Long Road toward Peace

Nixon continued to withdraw troops from Vietnam at a rate of 13,000 per month (the average since July 1969). On November 12, 1971, he announced a slightly accelerated withdrawal of 45,000 more in the months of December and January. This left 139,000 in Vietnam. Some war critics charged that Nixon was merely trying to make the war invisible to the American public by reducing casualties among combat forces. In addition, they contended that Nixon had not seriously considered North Vietnamese and Vietcong proposals for a release of POWs in return for a firm withdrawal date. But Nixon kept his timetable secret. In January 1972 he announced that 70,000 would be pulled out by May 1. This would leave 69,000; Secretary of Defense Laird conceded that more air power would be used.

Nixon disclosed a new peace plan later in January, which offered total withdrawal within six months of an agreement, an internationally supervised election within the same period, and a general cease-fire after the

UNITED STATES MILITARY FORCES IN SOUTH VIETNAM, 1965–1972

Year	Number
1965	184,300
1966	385,300
1967	485,600
1968	536,100
1969	475,200
1970	334,600
1971	157,800
1972 *	95,500

* First quarter figures.
Source: United States Department of Defense, Office of the Secretary, *Selected Manpower Statistics,* annual and unpublished data.

treaty was signed. The offer stipulated that the United States would support no candidate and abide by the election; finally, it proposed international supervision of the military aspect of the agreement and an international guarantee of its contents. Nixon added that the Thieu government had agreed to resign in advance of the election, which would be arranged by an interim government and the international supervisors. At the same time, Nixon disclosed that Henry Kissinger had visited Paris several times and had held twelve secret meetings with the North Vietnamese who refused to back away from the demand that the Americans withdraw support for the Thieu regime. Nixon said this was impossible before an agreement, and that if the enemy did not accept this offer the United States would continue Vietnamization.

In the months between the spring of 1972 and 1973, public expectations concerning Vietnam rode a see-saw that alternately raised fervent hopes of coming peace and deflated those hopes by dropping back toward seemingly endless fighting. The fruitless negotiations of early 1972 gave way to one of the war's most bitter battles. On April 1, after three days of intense bombardment, North Vietnamese regulars crossed the DMZ to attack South Vietnam with great force. A few days of unsuccessful resistance demonstrated that the South Vietnamese needed help. And on April 6, United States planes began making systematic strikes against North Vietnamese targets, although not bombing above the 20th parallel (about seventy miles south of Hanoi). But nine days later the United States began the first night attacks on the Hanoi-Haiphong area since March 1968 and the first use of B-52's in this region.

News of the fighting leaped once again into the headlines as the "phasing down" of the war suddenly became a cruel joke. Critics charged that American involvement meant simply a change from ground combat to air strikes, an alteration in form but not in substance. Many Americans reawakened to the war's horrors as they watched newscasts detailing the plight of countless South Vietnamese refugees. Adding to the tension, the renewed bombings threatened both President Nixon's scheduled visit to the Soviet Union and the budding relationship with mainland China. A world that had seemed to be moving toward understanding abruptly trembled with the anxieties of reborn conflict. On May 8 President Nixon announced that the United States would mine North Vietnamese ports and systematically attack all supply lines.

Yet, just as a see-saw at its lowest point can only go up, the May 8 speech included new possibilities for negotiation even as the mines were being planted. President Nixon stated two basic conditions for peace: the return of American prisoners of war and an internationally supervised cease-fire. For the first time, the American position mentioned no political requirements for United States withdrawal, at last separating the military and political problems in Vietnam. It soon became clear that the presidential trip to Russia would not be cancelled. From May 22 to 29, Nixon conferred with Soviet leaders, exchanged gifts, addressed the Russian people, and played the tourist; in newspaper headlines ballet replaced battle. Yet the visit was not irrelevant to Vietnam; Russian influence on Hanoi during the next few months, though hard to gauge, was almost certainly significant in pushing for peace.

Even as the war continued, negotiations were clearly underway again by mid-July. Henry Kissinger began slipping out of Washington about every two weeks for secret Paris meetings with North Vietnamese representative Le Duc Tho. Something was happening though few knew precisely what. Kissinger himself described the climate accurately in commenting that "Those who talk don't know, and those who know don't talk."

A flurry of pronouncements near the end of October revealed the progress in Paris. On the twenty-fourth, administration sources stated that bombing north of the 20th parallel had been temporarily halted. The next day North Vietnam announced an agreement that could be signed immediately. Forced by this statement to offer some explanation, Kissinger declared on October 26, "Peace is at hand," and suggested that one more negotiating session should wrap up the cease-fire. But at least one party to the war had not yet agreed to anything. President Thieu of South Vietnam quickly emerged as a major obstacle to immediate accord by demanding the withdrawal of all North Vietnamese troops from the South before any cease-fire. Moreover, it rapidly became clear that Hanoi and Washington did not share the same understanding of several points necessary to the peace. More talks produced only a deterioration in relations. Kissinger charged the North Vietnamese with reopening settled questions and with being obstructive; further meetings were suspended. The seesaw which had risen so buoyantly turned downward once more.

Scarcely two months later, beginning on December seventeenth, the United States launched against North Vietnam the heaviest bombing campaign yet. For two weeks, with only a thirty-six-hour break for Christmas, American planes night after night bombed targets closer to urban populations and to the Chinese border than ever before. Huge B-52's carried on "carpet bombing"—the dropping of bombs by several planes simultaneously in an area over a mile long. This damaged many buildings in Hanoi not themselves targets including foreign embassies and a major hospital. (World opinion reacted with shock.) Many Americans felt heartsick but helpless. Yet Hanoi's reaction to the holocaust seemed restrained, as did that of Peking and Moscow. Renewed signs of North

Vietnam's desire to negotiate, reinforced by the high costs of the bombing in American men and planes, produced an end to the attacks and a reopening of talks in early January.

This time the see-saw rose faster and higher than ever before and stayed up. A peace agreement, signed on January 23, 1973, made possible the separation of military and political questions, a compromise accepted by both sides only within the year. Finally, on March 29, with the release of the last prisoners of war and the departure of the last American troop units from Vietnam, the United States apparently ended its direct military role in Vietnam but not its involvement in Southeast Asia.

Relief but little celebration characterized the American response to the armistice. President Nixon, in his message announcing the peace, did not once use the word "victory," although he continuously reiterated his favorite phrase of "peace with honor." Few would have believed him if he had. The war that was ending had produced, in the words of one journalist, "no famous victories, no national heroes and no stirring patriotic songs." It was a crusade gone sour.

30

The United States emerged from World War II the preeminent world power and the richest nation in world history. It possessed the most advanced technology, a highly trained and productive labor force, and a competitive position in world markets, all without the ugly scars of war that marked the European nations. Many people had feared a depression after the war, but none developed. By the beginning of the 1950's, Americans could take comfort in a new degree of stability and even hegemony, a welcome relief after years of depression and war. Yet the variety of economic and demographic changes spawned by the war initiated vast changes in the social and intellectual life of the 1950's and 1960's.

The Shape of the Economy

With a boost from continued high government defense spending and consumer outlays on goods unavailable under war rationing, the gross national product jumped from $200 billion to $300 billion in the five years after the war. By the end of the 1960's, economic activity reached the dazzling figure of one trillion dollars—aided somewhat by growing inflation. Both profits and wages rose steadily through most of the two postwar decades, although difficulties began to appear in the economy late in the 1960's. Despite temporary recessions, the American economy performed well, at least as measured in sheer quantity.

Advanced industrial nations have an increasingly large number of workers who provide consumer services, and the postwar affluence of the United States originated in part with unparalleled growth in this area. The percentage of the labor force engaged in sales and service occupations—retailing, hotels and motels, restaurants, health spas, movie theaters—leapt sharply upward. Consumers in the 1950's and 1960's were barraged with every sales technique Madison Avenue could devise. Advertising costs in 1970 measured eight times those of 1940, and nearly five times the expenditures of 1945. Almost the sole exception to this growth appeared in network radio advertising, owing, of course, to the growing success of television. To some, consumerism demonstrated the superiority of American life relative to those societies—especially the Soviet Union—where people still struggled to obtain basic necessities. Yet critics like the popular sociologist Vance Packard perceived a strong element of mindless accumulation.

The growth of the American economy encouraged the unprecedented

619

expansion of social services, and government spending on social programs, especially education, increased steadily after World War II. In addition to its political effect, this spending contributed to the swelling professional, technical, and clerical occupations in public education and government bureaucracies. As their numbers increased and the institutions employing them became more stratified and bureaucratized, some public employees turned to unions, with the American Federation of Teachers the prominent example. Additional needs for white-collar workers enlarged a "new middle class," a dynamic element that fueled political movements, influenced cultural styles and tastes, and provided the themes for countless novels and movies from *The Man in the Gray Flannel Suit* to *The Graduate*. C. Wright Mills, an academic sociologist, published in 1951 the first systematic treatment of the "new middle class" and its implications in *White Collar*.

Women—married and single—entered the labor force in record numbers during the postwar era. During World War II, many women held factory jobs, filling vacancies created by the manpower needs of the armed forces. Pushed out of these jobs by returning soldiers, women found that the good times meant widespread opportunities in clerical work, teaching, and nursing—the traditional female fields. But their concentration in low-paying jobs was hardly satisfying; women continued to comprise nearly one-third of unskilled workers, especially in textiles and other light industries. Few business and professional women held the better positions, and in general received less for their work. At the same time, women were having more and more babies. The birth rate per

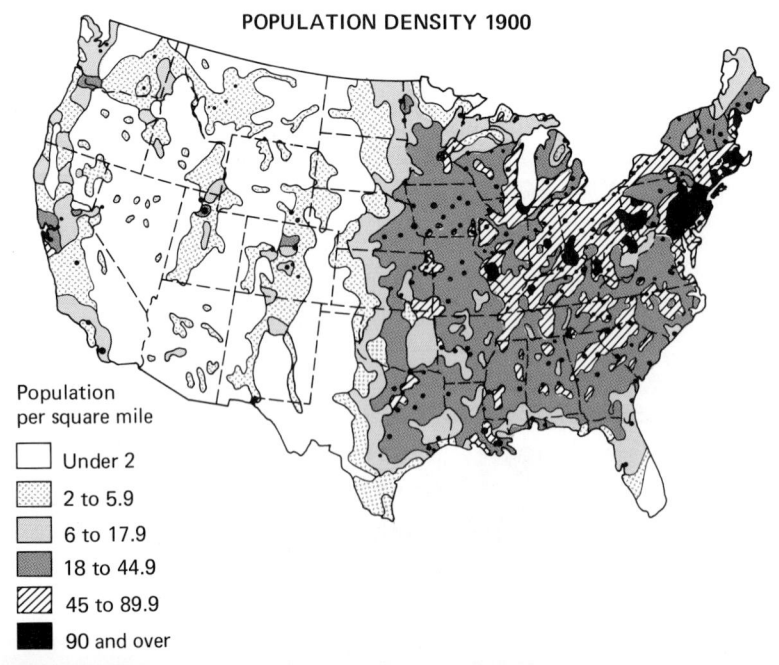

POPULATION DENSITY 1900

Population
per square mile

☐ Under 2
▒ 2 to 5.9
▒ 6 to 17.9
▓ 18 to 44.9
▨ 45 to 89.9
■ 90 and over

1,000 population reached a high 24.1 in 1950 and peaked at 25.0 in 1955 before declining steadily to 17.5 in 1968. This postwar "baby boom" led to a number of important social developments. The bumper crop of children necessitated building programs in the public schools; overcrowded classrooms brought about school financing crises and a national furor over "why Johnny can't read." These postwar children, in elementary school when the Soviet Union launched its Sputnik satellite in 1957, became the target of elaborate programs of curriculum reform with particular emphasis on mathematics and the sciences. More babies also brought about cultural repercussions. They would furnish an immense audience for television and create a record market for rock and roll music. The wave of youth consumption eventually included automobiles, surfboards, clothes, skin creams, magazines, movies, and innumerable other commodities. By the mid-1960's, greater opportunities in public higher education tripled enrollments in publicly controlled institutions as state colleges and community junior colleges multiplied. Finally, the postwar generation created the base for student movements and much of the cultural experimentation of the 1960's. By 1973, the birth rate had fallen sharply, and the median age of the national population was rising.

Mobility continued to characterize Americans. Long-term movements from farms to cities and from parts of the South to the rest of the nation continued, especially into California, which passed New York in the late 1960's to become the nation's most populous state. Black and Spanish-speaking people crowded into decaying inner cities while large numbers of whites fled to the suburbs. Neither slums nor suburbia was a new phe-

POPULATION DENSITY 1970

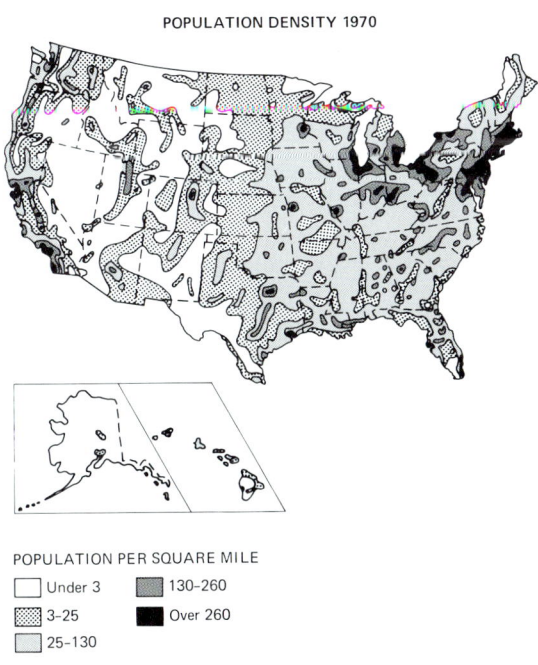

POPULATION PER SQUARE MILE

	Under 3		130–260
	3–25		Over 260
	25–130		

nomenon, but the pace of movement quickened rapidly. New York City proper lost population between 1960 and 1970, and Washington, D.C., showed a black majority by the end of the period. Gary, Indiana; Cleveland; and Newark, New Jersey; elected black mayors for the first time. Income as well as race caused the polarization between city and suburbs; some affluent blacks made inroads into suburbia and many working-class whites remained in the urban enclaves. The "urban crisis" continued unabated despite a succession of renewal programs and President Nixon's announcement in early 1973 that it had been solved.

This urban crisis caused striking and ultimately significant political repercussions in American society. The first major political confrontation of the postwar years, revolving around attempts to deal with a largely imaginary "Communist menace," injected anticommunism and anti-McCarthyism into many areas of American life. The ferreting out of alleged subversives particularly affected the entertainment industry. Folk musicians like Pete Seeger came before the House Un-American Activities Committee for questioning; major studios blacklisted a number of movie screenwriters, collectively known as the "Hollywood Ten," until well into the sixties. At the same time, The Reverend Billy James Hargis, based in Tulsa, Oklahoma, toured the country counterposing Jesus to Stalin; he filled the pages of his *Christian Crusader* with diatribes against the National Education Association and the mass media. Australian-born Dr. Fred Schwartz's Christian Anti-Communist Crusade, with financial backing from Atlantic-Richfield Oil and the Schick Razor Corporation, held massive city rallies. Ex-FBI informer Herbert Philbrick's memoirs served as the basis for the television series, "I Led Three Lives." These cultural flourishes, however, never completely dominated American society.

Opposition to the excesses of anticommunism took a number of forms. The playwright Arthur Miller reacted with *The Crucible* in 1953. Nominally about the Salem, Massachusetts, witchcraft trials of 1692, the play held contemporary meaning as an allegory of Senator Joe McCarthy's own search for alleged Communists. The power of television also came into use as a countermeasure. The Army-McCarthy hearings, broadcast live, illustrated tactics that did not hold up well under the intense scrutiny of television. Later a televised exposé by Edward R. Murrow on "See It Now" contributed to the discrediting of Senator McCarthy.

In another cultural area the upsurge of science fiction during the fifties, both in books and on film, bore a definite if indirect relation to political concerns. A best-selling writer of the period, Robert Heinlein, typically featured a masculine superhero who wiped out the forces of evil with a combination of brute strength and advanced engineering while delivering soliloquies about the effeminacy of the democratic process in time of cri-

Marilyn Monroe with playwright husband Arthur Miller attending a movie premiere in New York (June 1957). Marilyn Monroe was the sex symbol of the fifties, a decade of Sputnik, rock and roll, consumerism, and television. *United Press International*

sis. Heinlein's fiction embodied the political philosophy of Ayn Rand, an Eastern European refugee whose books, widely read among a segment of college students, stressed an ultraindividualist ethic as a counterpoise to socialist but not corporate collectivism. Many science fiction movie plots centered around a threat posed to society (usually American) by an alien force whose characteristics—unemotionalism, lack of individuality, militarism, expansionism—matched those popularly attributed to the Soviet bloc.

All through the postwar period academic social scientists moved in and out of government, notably in the area of foreign policy: the Harvard professor Samuel Huntington essentially wrote the South Vietnamese Constitution, and Henry Kissinger, also a Harvard government professor, progressed from writing European diplomatic history to orchestrating the Vietnam settlement and the détente with China. Other university social scientists turned their attention to the problems raised by the cold war by producing study after study on Soviet and Eastern European affairs, particularly under the auspices of research centers at Columbia, Harvard, and Stanford. Many of the prominent scholars in this field, themselves political refugees from Communist countries, gave their work distinctive vehemence. Drawing on the apparent similarities of communism and fascism —centralized authority, neglect of civil liberties and formal democratic procedures, glorification of mass action—these social theorists grasped the idea of a "totalitarian" society as a menace to "free" society.

Unlike totalitarian societies, America, with its advanced electronic weaponry, had its complement in sophisticated gadgetry for industry and home—copiers, credit card billing, eight-track and cassette tape recorders, direct distance dialing, TV dinners, drive-in banking—a seemingly endless list. Such mechanical innovations had implications reaching far beyond their immediate impact: the copying machine and the cassette recorder, for example, threatened the copyright laws, making it easy for individuals to reproduce materials without paying the original producers, authors, and performers. Inexpensive, high-fidelity recordings of all kinds of music became available, along with improved phonographic equipment. Paperback books, bringing to mass audiences not only a variety of cheap leisure reading but also ready access to serious and scholarly work, vastly improved high school and college curriculums and contributed to what some labeled a knowledge explosion. Factories and stores introduced piped-in Muzak, soothing and cushioning workers and shoppers from the rough edges of everyday life. Air travel for affluent Americans became commonplace, while special fares for young people accustomed them to a convenience that had been a mere fantasy for their parents. Heavy consumer goods reached a far greater market than ever before: by 1970, 99 percent of American households owned at least one television set. But the new technology had a double edge: it meant greater comfort, faster service, and increased leisure for those who could afford it; at the same time, mass-production of comforts and culture brought standardization and homogenization.

Highbrow critics like Dwight MacDonald reacted strongly to the emerging mass culture symbolized by television's situation comedies and popular music's banal lyrics. Newton Minow, chairman of the Federal Communications Commission under President Kennedy, aptly called television a "vast wasteland." Writers for television defended themselves, complaining that sponsor censorship, strict network guidelines on "controversial" subjects, and the difficulties of fitting dramatic action to the precise time segments between commercial breaks restricted originality. The ability of record companies to create rock and roll stars out of adolescents with no musical talent—the most notorious case involving a performer named simply Fabian—unnerved those who placed value on tradition. Some suggested that mass culture might be the harbinger of a dangerous social and political stupor. The sociologist David Riesman called contemporary Americans *The Lonely Crowd*, members of a mass society in which individuals were "other-directed," lacking in personal autonomy, conformist in a thorough-going way. He contrasted this with a picture of an earlier society in which individuals had been "inner-directed," self-motivated, individualistic. Riesman's book contained more loose description than scientific analysis, but it captured one important strain of social criticism.

In 1960 the sociologist Daniel Bell proclaimed the "end of ideology." An advanced industrial society eliminated class conflict, the traditional engine of change, and this, he said, led to "the exhaustion of political ideas in the fifties." Daniel Boorstin, Louis Hartz, and a school of "consensus" historians projected this image back on the American past, finding uniqueness in stability and in the absence of conflict that had characterized European history. These historians provided a useful corrective to more romantic earlier interpretations, but they also seemed to ignore or even denigrate those groups and forces that had fought sharply for change, and they often applied rather tortuous explanations to such obvious conflicts as the Civil War. Such versions of the American past and present came under attack in the 1960's when undeniable social turbulence made judgments of inevitable consensus look somewhat hasty.

In 1967 a series of revelations unveiled the participation of the Central Intelligence Agency in subsidizing and channeling cultural and intellectual life. The CIA and other federal agencies, through an elaborate network of dummy foundations, for years paid the bills for a number of unlikely (and sometimes unwitting) people and groups—Socialist party chairman Norman Thomas, the liberal National Student Association, the literary intellectuals in America and Britain associated with *Encounter* magazine, and the Congress for Cultural Freedom. What the CIA received for its money could not be precisely specified, but the intellectual and academic community had apparently learned a lesson, one which widespread disillusionment with United States policy in Indochina reinforced. Intellectuals grew suspicious of the comfortable and noncritical stance toward government they and their predecessors had adopted in the fifties.

Beyond the confines of both traditional "high" culture and the spreading, popular "mass" culture, a distinctive body of writing originated during the 1950's. The aftermath of World War II, like that of World War I, produced a "lost generation" of disillusioned young adults: the F. Scott Fitzgeralds and the Jazz Age found a counterpart in the beats of North Beach, San Francisco, and Greenwich Village, New York City. The popular press used "beat" as short for beatnik, a spin-off from Sputnik; a few "beats" explained it as short for "beatific," indicating a state of tranquil disengagement from the rat-race America with which they could not identify. Never so self-conscious and organized as the groups of the 1960's, their work did not assume the same commercial importance of some later movements. Yet the beats, their numbers tiny, initiated a literary and cultural flowering. Jack Kerouac gained the largest reputation as a beat spokesman with *On the Road* (1956) and a series of other novels; his effortless, stark prose chronicled beat culture semiautobiographically, detailing the simple pleasures and pains of cross-country hitchhiking, evading the police, appreciating "cool" black jazz, discovering marijuana, dabbling with Zen Buddhism, and generally avoiding the incomprehensible larger society. A revival of Kerouac's novels in the late sixties evidenced a newer generation of alienated youth searching for models and insights. Although Kerouac's novels had the widest audience, the voice of the beat generation spoke in poetry. Allen Ginsberg, coming from a radical middle-class family in Paterson, New Jersey, bummed his way around the world several times before composing the central statement of beat culture, "Howl!" in 1956. Its opening lines clearly expressed the beats' view of oppressive America:

> I saw the best minds of my generation destroyed
>   by madness,
>   starving hysterical naked,
> dragging themselves through the negro streets
>   at dawn looking for
>   an angry fix

Motorcycle youth were a symbol of rebellion in the late fifties and early sixties. Teen-agers took to the roads in hot rods and on motorcycles to find their own identities. Motorcycle gangs, most notably the "Hells Angels," sporting leather jackets and decorated cycles, terrorized towns across the country. *Black Star*

Ginsberg and another poet, Gary Snyder, also popularized Indian and Oriental religion and philosophy among avant-garde groups; they approached Eastern religion with a seriousness and a discipline not matched by the casual borrowings of the Beatles and others in later years. Ginsberg, possibly because of his radical background, maintained a more distinctly political stance than most beats; he became a fixture at antiwar demonstrations in the sixties, chanting rhythmic Indian mantras in an attempt to immobilize the police. With novelist Ken Kesey and satirist Paul Krassner, Ginsberg represented a direct link between the beats and the experimenters of the sixties. Lawrence Ferlinghetti, another beat poet, ran City Lights bookstore and its small publishing company in San Francisco, providing the beat community with publisher, seller, and general meeting place. Their influences radiated outward and appeared in the work of writers such as Kenneth Rexroth, Kenneth Patchen, and William Carlos Williams.

Beat culture, outwardly all exuberance and irreverence, ultimately posed serious questions unnoticed by the majority of apparently frivolous young Americans. By the late fifties, a distinct adolescent subculture emerged, nurtured by a degree of affluence and swelled by the postwar baby boom. Teen-age life revolved around two technological wonders of advanced industrial society—the automobile and the 45 rpm record. The automobile, of course, had been busily reweaving the pattern of American life since Henry Ford introduced the Model T, but only in the fifties could significant numbers of adolescents afford to buy their own cars and modify them in accord with current hot rod styles. Access to automobiles expanded unsupervised dating among adolescents; cars became essential to social success for many high school males and an integral part of masculine identity. James Dean's classic role in the movie *Rebel Without a Cause*—the rebellious, hard-drinking, drag-racing high school stud who defies his middle-class parents and the police in resolving his identity crisis—terrified parents and excited their children.

The adolescent subculture provided a ready market for the musical explosion of rock and roll. Early rock and roll relied on two musical strains with long traditions and independent audiences. The primary appropriation, black "rhythm and blues," gave the drive, the beat, and the solid, earthy feeling of the music. Rhythm and blues, or "race music" as it was called, in turn had its roots in black jazz, gospel, and blues music, all representing an autonomous market for recorded music until the advent of rock and roll. Some rhythm and blues performers—Little Richard, Fats Domino, the Coasters—successfully moved to the newer and larger white audience, but much of black rhythm and blues was simply picked up and bleached by white performers and recording studios without payment or acknowledgment. White country music, the other musical source of rock and roll, contributed some vocal patterns, the distinctive lead guitar sound, and many of the most important performers. The Everly Brothers and Buddy Holly came directly from the country tradition, and Elvis Presley, the dominating figure of early rock, worked as a string bass player on the Grand Ole Opry in Nashville. Before his first major recording contract in 1956 and the release of "Heartbreak Hotel"—a hit with country, popular, and rhythm and blues audiences—Presley had been an acclaimed country performer. Unsophisticated music, its lyrics often ranging from the banal to the ridiculous, rock and roll nonetheless possessed a vitality with which a new generation readily identified.

The adolescent devotees of the rock culture and the hot rod consciously circumscribed themselves by their purposeful separation from the adult world. Most Americans preferred an entirely different range of experience. Neither knowing nor caring about Allen Ginsberg, they read *Reader's Digest*, with a monthly circulation of about ten million copies. The most popular books of the fifties were not Kerouac's novels, but the *Reader's Digest Condensed Books*, abridgments of milder best-sellers, which consistently sold millions of copies. Similarly, the biggest box-office attractions of the fifties were not James Dean films but romantic comedies starring Rock Hudson and Doris Day, and such spectacular movies as *Ben-Hur* and *The Ten Commandments*. Among adult Americans not Elvis but Lawrence Welk ruled, serving waltzlike, romantically light "Champagne Music" over prime-time national television in the late 1950's and 1960's. Instead of drag racing, tens of millions of Americans sat and watched, in a stadium or on television, baseball, football, and horse racing. Most Americans felt reasonably secure in a relatively tranquil society; consequently they responded to passive forms of entertainment, not to the more jarring chords of the teen-agers and beats.

By far the largest commercial culture empire of the fifties was Walt Disney Productions, Inc. In the 1940's Disney achieved success by producing highly innovative animated cartoons and feature movies. By the fifties, he had left the drawing board to oversee a colossal business enterprise, producing cartoons, comic books, a weekly television series, and a host of other projects. "Davy Crockett," a Disney three-part television series, later made into a feature film, ultimately released the largest pre-teen-age merchandising fad ever seen in America. In June 1955 Disney fulfilled his lifelong dream by opening "Disneyland" in Anaheim, California, incontestably the world's greatest amusement park. Drawing on themes and characters from every cartoon and movie Disney had produced, Disneyland created a fantasy world comprehensive enough to appeal to almost everyone. Soviet Premier Nikita Khrushchev was miffed when security problems made it impossible for him to visit Disneyland during his trip to America in 1959—but more than five million Americans did show up annually. The pleasures of Disneyland perhaps evoked a widely shared mood of the fifties—safe, tranquil, vaguely unreal, more than a trifle sugary. But just as Disneyland itself would later be invaded by thousands of antiwar demonstrators, the calm surfaces of mainstream culture would be disrupted by the political tensions of the mid-1960's.

Another comforting fact of the fifties was the steady rise in church membership, increasing more rapidly than the total population. Between 1950 and 1956, Roman Catholics added five million members, Protestants eight million. Actual church attendance also grew, although precise measures of this are difficult to reconstruct. Bishop Fulton J. Sheen conducted a weekly, half-hour television program for several years, blending Catholic doctrine with common sense, wit, and even what might have seemed irreverence—"angels" erased the blackboard he used to illustrate his talks. A central figure in evangelical Protestantism, The Reverend Billy Graham, crusaded across America and throughout the world. Although Graham's origins were orthodox, he presented a nonsectarian image and served as an unofficial "spiritual adviser" to a number of presidents. Graham functioned as a popularizer of Christianity rather than as a theologian; by the mid-1960's he was appropriating the language of the youth culture, letting his own hair grow a bit, and appearing on late-night television talk shows. While organized religion remained a powerful institution, Protestant membership leveled off in the mid-sixties and declined thereafter; the Roman Catholic Church suffered in 1971, for the first time in its history, a small absolute decline in its American membership.

Civil Rights and Student Movements

The rise of the civil rights movement in the later fifties foreshadowed an America of greater conflict. In their struggle for justice, black Americans received early sympathy from many whites, but the campaign inevitably exposed deep-seated inequalities and prejudices that could not be conquered simply by goodwill. Civil rights in particular helped to uncover the problem of poverty in America. The poor had long faced daily poverty, but that fact did not receive national attention at least until the publication in 1962 of Michael Harrington's *The Other America*. Harrington and others demonstrated that more than one-fourth of the population remained underfed and ill-housed, trapped in urban slums or depressed rural areas with no political or economic leverage to improve their situation. As the civil rights movement shifted its focus from formal legal and political demands to challenges for economic equality, resistance stiffened.

At the same time, black intellectuals and artists stressed the cultural separation between blacks and whites. James Baldwin wrote movingly of the black experience in books aptly titled *Another Country* and *Nobody Knows My Name*. Black jazz musicians, for years the leading edge of black culture, began to experiment with new musical forms. The restraint and symmetry in the music of Count Basie and Duke Ellington, or even of Miles Davis and Thelonius Monk, was replaced by the free-form emotional expression of John Coltrane and Ornette Coleman—powerful, discordant expressions of black sensibility; bassist Charles Mingus titled one of his compositions "Fables of Faubus" in scornful memory of the governor of Arkansas. The stirrings of black intellectuals and artists toward a separate cultural identity played a prelude to the strain of political separatism prominent a few years later.

An awareness of racial and economic injustice impelled thousands of white college students to go south in "Freedom Summer," to work for blacks' civil rights, particularly in Mississippi. They met injustice face to face and learned the skills of practical politics. The civil rights movement formed the crucible for several student movements, as politically involved students brought back their experiences and applied them to their universities and to society in general. The civil rights work provided a trained leadership that mobilized campuses around the country during the next few years in massive opposition to the escalating war in Indochina.

The early student movement emerged between the 1962 founding convention of the Students for a Democratic Society (SDS) and the 1964 Free Speech Movement (FSM) at the University of California at Berkeley. The SDS convention convened in Port Huron, Michigan, and developed

The increased fighting in Vietnam required larger draft calls. By the late sixties, when disillusionment with the war reached its peak, many youths resisted the draft and fled the country. The expression on this draftee's face typifies an attitude increasingly prevalent as the decade ended. *The Washington Post*

the "Port Huron Statement" reflecting a mixture of support for American ideals and desire for major changes that characterized the early student movement. SDS called for social reform, not social revolution; the platform coupled its opposition to America's role in the cold war with explicit opposition to communism, a demand for educational reform with a strong belief in the university as a vehicle for social change, and a systematic critique of American society with an insistence on nonviolence. The slogan of SDS during the 1964 presidential campaign, "half the way with LBJ," revealed the group's ambivalence. The Free Speech Movement at Berkeley, though ostensibly revolving around demands for a number of specific political rights such as bringing in speakers and distributing political literature on university property, presented in embryo a challenge to the concept Chancellor Clark Kerr called "The Multiversity." While servicing large numbers of students, Kerr's modern university remained closely tied to business and government, performing the research and analysis tasks that supported defense industries, domestic social policies, and corporate product development. Labeling this orientation a highly sophisticated prop of the status quo, FSM counterposed the somewhat vague and idealistic notion of "a free university in a free society."

Student movements came at a receptive time. In the early 1960's students enrolled in colleges and universities in greater numbers than ever before. Some states advanced an unprecedented one-half of all high school students to some form of college study. California and New York led the nation in the expansion of their universities, state colleges, and two-year junior colleges. Their numbers and a degree of common experience gave some college students a sense of collective identity and potential power. At Berkeley the FSM coalition covered all shades of political opinion; even Young Republicans and Young Americans for Freedom joined in demanding an end to campus restrictions. Surface similarities in dress, hair, and musical taste on some campuses further contributed to an underestimation of the student diversity that splintered college movements a few years later.

SDS in its early years aimed for the creation of "participatory democracy" in America. This vision of a decentralized and debureaucratized community in which everyone affected by any social policy would have a voice in its determination suggested community control of schools, increased student power in universities, citizen control of police forces, and even worker determination of working conditions. SDS initiated in this vein two "model insurgencies" in Newark, New Jersey, and Chester, Pennsylvania, organizing community residents around their local grievances. Increasingly, however, SDS activities on and off campus began to develop other issues in response to the escalation of the war in Vietnam.

The Students for a Democratic Society (SDS) symbolized radical student movements in the late sixties. The large-scale riot at Columbia University in 1968 was a harbinger of clashes at other college campuses, and the beginning of a chasm that was to develop between the police and college students throughout the country. *Black Star*

SDS helped organize the first major antiwar demonstration in Washington in April 1965, and surprised everyone by drawing 25,000 people. Campus SDS chapters began campaigns against research sponsored by the Department of Defense, against recruiting by the Dow Chemical Company, which manufactured napalm, and most important, against ROTC. The training of military officers seemed to many a direct link between the university and American foreign policy; and there were objections to the special status of ROTC courses and staff members. Campus after campus exploded in protest. The shootings at Kent State in 1970 came in the wake of a prolonged struggle over ROTC. On a few leading campuses, successful campaigns produced a denial of academic credit or university facilities to ROTC, which in effect eliminated these programs altogether.

The increased size and militance of student protests coupled with their more sweeping demands produced serious confrontations with college administrators. When small groups resorted to the occupation of buildings and were met with tear gas and police squadrons, broader revolts ensued in 1968 and 1969 at Columbia, Harvard, and San Francisco State College. The size of antiwar demonstrations in major cities escalated immensely. These levels of protest created internal divisions within student movements over the nature of civil rights and antiwar activities, and a proliferation of groups and organizations with differing strategies followed. SDS split into several factions at a stormy convention in 1969. By the beginning of the 1970's, socialist and Marxist ideas competed with participatory democracy and nonviolence for the allegiance of the student.

But in the middle years of the 1960's, the student movement had supported the creation of a self-conscious and many-faceted youth culture. Students and nonstudents worked to reshape themselves, their environment, and ultimately the larger society. The demand for relevant and unprescribed education led to the establishment on some campuses of "free universities"—educational experiments including open registration and courses ranging from traditional academic offerings or political study groups to auto mechanics, transcendental meditation, and macrobiotic cooking. "Underground" newspapers, made possible by technical progress in inexpensive offset printing, appeared in every major city. The Berkeley *Barb*, the Los Angeles *Free Press*, the East Village *Other*, and the Atlanta *Great Speckled Bird* carried a mixed assortment: political analysis and polemics, music reviews, discussions of experimental life-styles, more or less inventive graphic artwork, and excursions into mysticism, Oriental religion, and the effects of "mind-expanding" drugs. Specially developed wire services connected individual papers; the Underground Press Syndicate tied together "anti-Establishment, avant-garde, New Left, youth-oriented periodicals" supplemented by the later, more consciously radical Liberation News Service.

A vocal minority of students found marijuana and eventually other drugs useful tools in their search for spontaneity. Estimates of the number of college students who at least tried marijuana ranged by the late sixties as high as one-half. The stronger drugs which found more limited use—LSD, hashish, mescaline, and amphetamines—were stimulants and "psychedelics" unlike the depressant drugs still popular in the early 1970's. Psychologist Timothy Leary involuntarily left his post at Harvard to preach the necessity to "turn on, tune in, drop out"; novelist Ken Kesey and his band of Merry Pranksters outraged conventional Californians by spiking the punch at rock concerts with the dangerous but not yet illegal LSD.

Rock music remained a major component of the youth culture in the sixties. With the infusion of fresh musical ideas from England via the Beatles and the Rolling Stones, and with the introduction of highly sophisti-

Timothy Leary became the symbol of the drug culture, urging people to discover the "freedom" produced by drugs, and to "drop out" of society in order to find themselves. To Leary, the hallucinogen LSD offered a path to psychedelic ecstasy and religious revelation. *United Press International*

cated electronic equipment for recordings and performances, rock blossomed into a powerful form and a major industry. The beats and the earlier activists who had discovered the strengths of American folk music provided some of the audience for the "urban folk revival" of the late fifties and early sixties which popularized authentic performers like Doc Watson, Mississippi John Hurt, and Jean Ritchie. The revival also produced a number of young, topical folksingers—notably Phil Ochs, Joan Baez, and Bob Dylan—who combined their musical talent with political commentary. Though this resurgence established a permanent audience among college students for folk and country music, its importance increased in 1964–1965 as louder and more commercial rock music became dominant. Bob Dylan was booed off the stage during the 1965 Newport Rock Festival for using electric instruments in his back-up band, but the disapproval of purists hardly slowed his career. Influenced by topical folksongs, rock lyrics often expressed political sentiments and sometimes gave transient support to student causes.

The association of rock with drugs produced innumerable lyrics and a style known as "acid" or "psychedelic" rock—the special province of San Francisco-based groups such as the Grateful Dead, the Jefferson Airplane, and Big Brother and the Holding Company. San Francisco's Haight-Ashbury district became the center of 1967's "summer of love" as thousands of young people swarmed in from across the country. The Grateful Dead gave free concerts in the park; food was distributed by the Diggers, named after a seventeenth-century British sect advocating the abolition of private property. Others pitched in to establish free medical clinics and a host of other services. The "summer of love" also occasioned a minor business boom as hundreds of small entrepreneurs profited from the provision of drug-culture paraphernalia—black-light posters, water pipes, and chrome-plated roach clips. The "head shops" merchandising such items merely foreshadowed a systematic commercialization of youth movements, culminating perhaps in the advertising campaign to "hear the revolution on Columbia Records."

Theodore Roszak's *The Making of a Counter-Culture* (1969) offered a label for what was happening and tried to elevate youthful dissent into a profound social dynamic, suggesting that modern society's technological abundance had spawned an inevitable revolt by its own younger generation. Yale law professor Charles Reich, in a popular but conceptually slippery book, predicted that the emerging culture would lead to *The Greening of America* (1970), a new consciousness transcending the older mentalities of the frontier and of business enterprise.

According to many observers, American society and particularly the young experienced a "sexual revolution" in the postwar years. The Kinsey reports (1948 and 1953), the first major attempt at a systematic investigation of actual sexual practice, based on thousands of interviews, had already presented results that challenged the comfortable presumption of widespread, happy monogamy. The Kinsey methodology was less than airtight, but the report documented an undeniable prevalence of infidelity, pre- and extra-marital sexuality, and practices conventionally labeled "abnormal." Later increased availability of contraceptive information and devices, most notably birth control pills for women, allegedly accelerated sexual permissiveness. Masters and Johnson's *Human Sexual Response* (1966) and *Human Sexual Inadequacy* (1970) became best-sellers though concerned with the dry, clinical presentation of basic sexual physiology. *Human Sexual Response* shattered a number of unexamined myths and helped to legitimize further serious study of the subject. The sixties also saw greater acceptance of male and female homosexuality. Homosexuals, or "gays," became more visible, forming gay power groups to fight against various forms of discrimination.

Whether or not there was a "sexual revolution" in practice, the 1960's encompassed a marked change in the place of sexuality in literature and entertainment. Legitimate commercial movies depicted sexual contact candidly, even leeringly, sometimes becoming nearly indistinguishable from flourishing "hard-core" pornographic films. Network television relaxed controls on program content, and educational television stations in 1972 and 1973 were beginning to flirt with the presentation of partial nudity. A series of Supreme Court decisions virtually eliminated literary censorship while definitions of all four-letter words began creeping into fresh editions of *Webster's New World Dictionary*. The cast of the Broadway musical *Hair* did a nude scene during each performance. Bars and nightclubs began featuring "topless" dancers as an updated form of burlesque. Dozens of photographically illustrated sex manuals appeared, some imported from Scandinavian countries. A few politicians and district attorneys, some church leaders, and even a segment of the Left saw this public expression of sexuality as corrupt and decadent, and campaigned, usually unsuccessfully, for restrictions.

The increased sexual permissiveness of the 1960's seemed a mixed blessing for many American women. The work of Masters and Johnson and later researchers contributed to a more accurate understanding of women's sexuality, exploding repressive stereotypes inherited from the nineteenth century. Contraception provided security against unwanted pregnancy and so allowed freer sexual expression. At the same time, some women found their sex dehumanized, used to entertain men at topless bars, presented half-clad in multimillion dollar advertising campaigns to sell everything from automobiles to shaving cream. Popular music, and especially masculine rock lyrics—witness the Rolling Stones' "Stupid Girl" and "Under My Thumb"—celebrated primarily women's sexuality, never their intelligence, courage, or character. Though the birth control pill was an effective contraceptive, some medical reports began to appear linking it with possibly dangerous side effects; many women in any case resented the assumption that contraception was solely a woman's responsibility. Even within radical political groups, women found themselves treated as typists and lovers; the comment by Stokely Carmichael, militant black leader, that "the only position for women in the movement is prone," aroused understandable outrage.

The Women's Movement

The civil rights, student, and antiwar movements, as well as the "sexual revolution" contributed directly to a movement for women's liberation. The first major literary expression of postwar feminism, Betty Friedan's *The Feminine Mystique* (1962), traced the development of pressures to keep women in the home, the effect of Freudian popularizations in creating stereotypes, and the mindless roles expected of women. Germaine Greer's *The Female Eunuch* (1971) examined the truncated sexuality which she saw affecting both men and women, while Kate Millett's *Sexual Politics* (1970) chronicled the debasement of the female image in modern literature. Also influential was an anthology of shorter writings by less prominent women entitled *Sisterhood Is Powerful*, which presented important articles on housework, the psychology of women, marriage, minority group women, and a broad range of other topics.

Friedan and others formed the National Organization for Women (NOW), still the liberation movement's largest membership organization. NOW concentrated on legal challenges and nonpartisan political action, allowed men to join, and functioned as an umbrella covering many disparate tendencies. Some radical women criticized NOW's excessive concentration on the problems of middle-class professional women, since most women worked as secretaries, factory operatives, or housewives. Many activists avoided permanent organizations, forming ad hoc groups and caucuses to battle within universities, social welfare agencies, neighborhoods, hospitals, and places of employment. Campaigns in several states to legalize abortion argued the right of women to control their own reproduction. In January 1973 the Supreme Court declared abortions legal during the first six months of pregnancy, but in several states official and unofficial resistance made abortions difficult to obtain. The National Women's Political Caucus, formed in 1971, brought together women in electoral politics and public offices to lobby for women's rights within both major parties.

The women's movement operated most successfully and creatively on a decentralized basis, avoiding bureaucratization and conventional leadership. The New York Radical Feminists led the argument for "consciousness raising" as the distinctive vehicle for women's liberation—small, leaderless discussions in which women shared experiences and feelings concerning men, other women, children, jobs, and housework. Many consciousness-raising groups contained activist women, but they generally sought strength and education, not the confrontation of larger political issues. An Equal Rights Amendment to the Constitution passed Congress and began a tortuous journey through state legislatures. Since the amendment would make the formal equality of women a matter of law, some expressed fears that women would consequently be drafted into military service and would be stripped of the benefits of protective legislation in industry.

Congresswoman Bella Abzug of New York and writer Gloria Steinem at the 1972 Democratic convention. The women's liberation movement helped to open new opportunities for women in many areas. Women, as well as minority groups, were especially well represented at the 1972 Democratic convention, showing the effect of such groups as the Women's Political Caucus, formed in 1971. *Black Star*

Writers in the sixties made a critique of middle-class norms less political than that of the women's movement, and more restrained than that of college radicals. Edward Albee's play, *Who's Afraid of Virginia Woolf?*, pictured violence and sadism lurking beneath the respectable exterior of a college professor and his wife whose lives unravel in drunken bouts, screaming quarrels, and hallucinations about a make-believe child. Novelists John Updike and John Cheever chronicled the frustrations and alienation of the successful suburban upper middle class. Philip Roth, the freshest and most popular young writer in the sixties, outraged part of the reading public with the tragicomic sexual misadventures of Alexander Portnoy in *Portnoy's Complaint*. Roth later wrote *Our Gang*, a bitter piece of low farce directed at the Nixon style, verbalizing a fit of pique that revealed Roth's own political frustration.

The novel that best conveyed the chaos of the sixties, *An American Dream* (1964), was written by perhaps the most vocal and visible writer of the decade, Norman Mailer. Writer and novel point up contradictions in American society: romance and moral rhetoric against sex and violence. Mailer's hero, Stephen Rojack, represents the traditional American: a self-made man, successful, handsome, educated, popular. Through Rojack the work examines these success symbols, showing society's obsession with the outward signs rather than the methods of achievement. Law, the presumed corrective to violence, frequently fails; Rojack literally gets away with murdering his wife simply because of who he is. Lurid sexual description attempts to destroy the notion of romantic love.

A scene from Edward Albee's play, *Who's Afraid of Virginia Woolf?* starring Elizabeth Taylor and Richard Burton. *United Press International*

640

Mailer as moralist showed the paradox of the individual in America: if he conforms, he loses the imagination necessary to succeed; and yet nonconformity ostracizes him from society. Violence and sex preoccupy Americans because by definition they are nonconforming acts. The book depicts the violent and often savage responses of individuals and groups who live within a society of paradox.

The Years of Demonstration

All this ferment—feminism, civil rights, rock music, the counter-culture —took on political overtones. Thousands of demonstrators gathered at the 1968 Democratic convention in Chicago, some to demand the nomination of Eugene McCarthy, others to challenge the whole electoral system. Their efforts culminated in running warfare with the police, with hundreds of demonstrators and bystanders gassed and clubbed. Organizers

Roman Catholic priests Philip (left) and Daniel (right) Berrigan watch two baskets of draft board records burn, May 17, 1968, in Catonsville, Maryland. Nine people (five of them priests) removed and burned the records and were then arrested. *United Press International*

of the Chicago protests were later tried on riot conspiracy charges. That same year Martin Luther King, Jr.'s, assassination had reduced the plausibility of nonviolent change for blacks, and the Black Panthers, the most militant revolutionary organization in the black community, was decimated in gun battles with police and weakened by countless arrests of leaders and members, including Bobby Seale, one of the "Chicago 7." At the same time, the largely white antiwar movement, growing but achieving few effects on American policy, felt increasingly frustrated. Shootings of white students at Kent State and black students at Jackson State on consecutive days in the spring of 1970 symbolized the high stakes in dissenting politics.

The political confrontations of the late sixties and the sharp reactions they produced marked a turning point in postwar society. Critics on the left argued that an era of political repression had set in, with its usual

Robert F. Kennedy (1925–1968) and Jacqueline Kennedy at the funeral of her slain husband, President John F. Kennedy. The violence that claimed the president and civil rights leader Medger Evers was soon to claim the young attorney general and Martin Luther King, Jr. *Magnum*

642

deadening effects. Others saw in the decline of experimentation and the apparent retreat from political activity simply a return to normalcy after the chaos of the sixties. All the energy expended on political mobilization and cultural innovation in the preceding decade had not converted any sizable portion of the population to socialism, radicalism, the use of marijuana, or even of health foods. But though the furor of the sixties had left millions of Americans unconvinced, they were not unaffected; Richard Nixon aimed his 1968 election campaign toward those he called "the silent majority," middle- and working-class voters impatient with what they saw as radical excesses on and off campuses. Ethnic group members —Italians, Poles, even some traditionally reformist Jews—expressed a growing concern for preserving their own economic achievements and social identities in the face of the attention being given to blacks and students. The Jewish Defense League, led by Rabbi Meir Kahane, and the

The widow, Coretta King, being comforted by singer Harry Belafonte at her husband's funeral. King was slain on April 4, 1968 in Memphis, where he had gone to support a strike of mostly black garbage workers. His assassination provoked angry blacks to riot in many cities throughout the country. *Magnum*

Italian-American Civil Rights League, organized by reputed Mafia figure Joe Colombo, found surprising support. At the same time, liberal Protestant moral and financial support for the civil rights and antiwar movements disappeared amid a new wave of traditional evangelicalism. Several major denominations cut back their budgets for social programs. In an unprecedented coalition, the Catholic Church joined with Protestant denominations in 1972 to lay the foundations for a coordinated nationwide drive, known as "Key '73," which promised to reach every American household. Religion, Christian and Oriental, appeared in rock lyrics, and a fervent minority of veteran activists turned to fundamentalist religion, proudly proclaiming themselves "Jesus freaks." Rennie Davis, one of the Chicago conspiracy trial defendants, suddenly dropped his political commitments in the spring of 1973 and began proselytizing for an Indian guru, much to the chagrin of old political associates.

The Future Lies Ahead

Other developments also reflected a shift in emphasis from an interest in social change to a desire for personal and interpersonal experience. The largest paperback press run in history occurred for Erich Segal's *Love Story*. Subsequently made into a successful saccharin movie, *Love Story* depicted student life of a traditional sort—no political polemics, no drug-induced visions, but a tragic Ivy League romance. *Jonathan Livingston Seagull* topped the best-seller lists for months, conveying an idiotic vision of tranquillity. The *New York Times* ran a long series of articles portraying a "new mood" on the campus, a quieter, more introspective, even more studious atmosphere. Many political veterans of the New Left retained their commitment but entered a period of study and reflection, particularly as the war in Vietnam reached at least its official end. What the *Times* saw as introspection many radicals saw as long-range planning, a realization that change was difficult but possible. Meanwhile enrollments in psychology courses climbed at most universities, perhaps a formal indicator of a concern with individual growth.

The rebellion of youth seemed past history even by 1971. The "Youth ghettos"—San Francisco's Haight-Ashbury, Berkeley, Cambridge, New York's East Village—suffered from the petty crime waves that inevitably accompanied the drug market. Barbiturates, heavy tranquilizers, and even heroin, which had never been widely used among white youth, replaced the nonaddictive, hallucinogenic drugs. Rock music sacrificed much of its cleverness to a search for higher decibel levels, while the fabled financial success of some rock superstars created hostility between them and their audiences. Many underground papers folded as circulation declined and advertising dried up. The mood of most campuses was in-

deed quieter, to the great relief of administrators and state legislatures. The promise of a rapid and full-blown greening of America seemed discredited. Much of what had been most prominent in the counter-culture either degenerated into escapism—as with drug abuse and religious fanaticism—or was commercialized beyond recognition—as with the transmutation of sexual liberation into pornography.

The black community suffered most from the reaction against radicalism in culture and politics. Contraction of the welfare system joined with persistently high unemployment rates and serious inflation to slow economic progress of black Americans. Heroin addiction reached epidemic proportions in slum areas and law enforcement agencies were unable or, as some blacks charged, unwilling to work seriously at cutting off the major suppliers. The resistance of white parents to busing programs slowed school integration, while slashes in state funds for higher education reduced college opportunities for low-income blacks as well as whites. A debate arose in academic circles over the alleged genetic inferiority of blacks, surfacing in an *Atlantic* article by the psychologist Richard Herrnstein. That the debate arose indicated the changed atmosphere of the early seventies. In the ebullient and even radical days of the sixties, such a note would perhaps not have been struck at all.

The drug culture took its toll when two talented young singers, Jimi Hendrix and Janis Joplin (pictured above) each died of an overdose. Joplin's singing was influenced by 1920's singing star Bessie Smith. *Magnum*

31

In 1969 Richard M. Nixon came to the presidency after eight years of Democratic rule; but his narrow victory hardly represented the landslide he would have liked. With the Democrats bearing the weight of the Vietnam War and its accompanying domestic disruptions, Nixon had boasted a sizable lead early in the campaign—especially after the tumultuous and divisive Democratic convention in Chicago. Then the energetic stumping of Hubert Humphrey coupled with his increasingly antiwar position gradually reduced Nixon's edge, though election day came soon enough to leave him with a withered triumph. A victory of any kind seemed a remarkable feat for a man who could not win the governorship of California six years before.

The new president's political views differed markedly from those of his immediate predecessor, Lyndon Johnson. Although a Southerner, Johnson spearheaded passage of civil rights legislation and backed federal enforcement of antidiscrimination statutes. He advocated social legislation enlarging the federal government's responsibility for the health and welfare of all Americans. Richard Nixon decried a deeper involvement of the federal government in social problems, racial discrimination, or poverty. Instead, Nixon directed his appeals toward a "silent majority" of middle-class people who had tired of paying taxes to support welfarism. Capitalizing on their discomfort and fear over student and black protest on the one hand and a rising crime rate on the other, Nixon followed Alabama Governor George Wallace in appealing for "law and order." For many people he represented a rejection of government activity in social matters, of liberal federal spending, of creeping moral degeneration, and of student and black activism.

Most important, Nixon promised action to a country torn into factions by the Vietnam War. By 1969 millions of college students and hundreds of thousands of older people had participated in a series of rallies and demonstrations against the war. Small radical groups had staged dramatic raids on draft boards or burned draft cards. Many found these acts unpatriotic or even treasonous, assuming that the government's foreign policy should be supported by all Americans. Nixon could be certain that whatever strategy he adopted for Vietnam would arouse both opposition and support. A second problem aggravated by Vietnam challenged Nixon at

President Nixon at his peak, in November 1969, after making his third speech on Vietnam. Piled around him are stacks of telegrams from across the country supporting his Vietnam policy. Despite the president's promises, he did not achieve a cease-fire until January 1973. *United Press International*

**Nixon—
Years of
Triumph**

home: inflation threatened to get completely out of hand. If the president did not act decisively to curb rising prices, he could lose the "silent majority" as quickly as he had gained their approval.

In his inaugural address, Nixon asked that everyone "go forward together." He asserted that the government could not solve all problems and appealed to the young to lower their voices. But his new executive appointments reflected only a narrow segment of American society. The president stocked the White House with long-time followers of homogeneous background whose essential qualification was loyalty to Richard Nixon. The cabinet assembled to heal division and turmoil in the nation contained no blacks, Jews, women, or Democrats. William P. Rogers, one of Nixon's closest friends, took office as secretary of state, and Professor Henry Kissinger of Harvard University succeeded Walter Rostow as head of the National Security Council. Only Walter J. Hickel, designated secretary of the interior, encountered senatorial opposition; his background with Alaskan oil companies suggested to some senators that he might favor corporate over environmental goals. Ironically, Hickel later voiced disagreements with the president and eventually resigned, a victim of the White House penchant for loyalty.

Nixon began to fulfill his promise of aggressive action in foreign policy soon after the inaugural speech in which he observed: "After a period of confrontation, we are entering an era of negotiation." Accordingly, only a month afterward the president flew to Europe to meet with the leaders of friendly nations and to reassert United States commitments. In particular, he attempted to improve relations with Charles de Gaulle, whose resistance to American leadership in Europe had prompted French withdrawal from NATO's military forces and seriously divided the nations of Western Europe.

The first elaboration of the president's foreign policy, the Nixon Doctrine of July 1969, stated that the United States was reducing its military role in Asia but would continue to respect its world obligations. A more comprehensive explanation came in his first "State of the World" message in February 1970. Again he asserted his readiness to negotiate with friend and foe, continuing the major American role but asking our allies to shoulder more of the burden. Concrete applications took the form of troop reductions in Korea, an agreement to return Okinawa to the Japanese, and the apparent goal of disengagement in Vietnam.

But the question that required immediate attention in 1969 was strategic arms limitation talks with the Soviet Union. After the Russian invasion of Czechoslovakia in 1968, the United States had postponed these discussions until tensions eased. Nixon himself preferred to engage in negotiations from a position of strength, and so proposed in March 1969 a modified antiballistic missile plan at a cost of $2.5 billion instead of the $5.5 billion budgeted by Lyndon Johnson. To convince Congress of the need for such a plan, Secretary of Defense Melvin Laird warned repeatedly of Soviet capabilities, pointing to the advanced construction of ABMs around Moscow and the deployment of SS9 missiles with 25-megaton MIRV warheads. Democratic senators objected to the cost and questioned the effectiveness of the program, but the Senate passed ABM by a single vote, 51 to 50 (the tie was broken by Vice-President Agnew). Some who voted in favor believed that Nixon would hold off deployment for fear of jeopardizing talks with the Soviet Union. And the veiled threat of an ABM system seemed to work: in October the Russians did begin SALT talks in Helsinki, Finland; in May 1971 they finally agreed to concentrate on limiting ABMs. America had wanted a more comprehensive agreement covering both defensive and offensive weapons.

The major powers also reached important agreements on Berlin early in 1971, owing in part to the rising prominence of the Social Democrats and Chancellor Willy Brandt in West Germany. Brandt himself began talks with Russia, East Germany, and other Eastern European nations; he softened Germany's stance toward Poland, tentatively recognizing the Oder-Neisse boundary line. An overall agreement on Berlin allowed "unimpeded" access to West Berlin with provisions for two million West Berliners to visit relatives periodically and to transact business in East Germany. The final draft, signed on September 3, 1971, included additional clauses making West Germany the sole representative for West Berlin in international affairs, yet limiting its political activity there.

Closer to home, Latin Americans increasingly demanded economic and political independence from the United States. The government of Peru had seized the American-owned International Petroleum Company in 1968, prompting the administration to enforce laws which cut off aid in the event of insufficient compensation. But Peru nationalized other companies, while Ecuador seized American fishing vessels, claiming they had violated their territorial rights, and Chile elected an ill-fated Marxist president, Salvador Allende, who fell to an army coup in 1973. These events strongly indicated a lessening of United States influence in Latin America. Burdened by commitments in Asia, the Nixon administration could not provide significant economic assistance, especially when Congress consistently reduced the foreign aid budget.

In Africa, Nixon maintained a neutral stance in the Nigerian civil war, but when it ended he tried to provide aid to both sides to ease the suffering and starvation, particularly severe among the Ibos of rebellious Biafra. The Middle East gave Nixon even more problems. The Arab states demanded that the Israelis withdraw from territories occupied in the six-day war of 1967 before any peace settlement. Israel refused to acquiesce without assurance of future security and in turn insisted on face to face negotiations. Some Israelis wanted to hold permanently such key areas as Jerusalem and the west bank of the Jordan. In January 1969 sporadic attacks by Israelis and Arabs occurred almost daily despite a cease-fire. And at times both engaged in large-scale operations—assaults on oil refineries, missile sites, pipelines, and troop emplacements.

President Nasser of Egypt offered a plan in February 1969 that called for Israeli withdrawal and a declaration of nonbelligerency, the territorial integrity of all countries in the Mideast including Israel, freedom of navigation on international waterways, and a just solution to the Palestine problem. On the same day President Nixon accepted a French offer to hold Big Four talks on the Mideast at the United Nations. Israel, however, rejected the Nasser proposal and resisted American pressures to ease their stance on withdrawal. In July 1970 Secretary Rogers proposed a cease-fire which required Egypt to stop the deployment of surface to air missiles near the Suez Canal. Indirect talks resumed through the special UN mission of Gunnar Jarring. Both sides accepted an August 8 cease-fire. This only shifted the focus to Palestinian Arab guerrillas and almost continuous acts of terrorism, including several spectacular airplane hijackings. These led to studied, deadly effective Israeli retaliation. In early 1974, the Israeli-Arab cold war was the most explosive situation in a world otherwise moving slowly toward peace.

In his most surprising reversal of foreign policy goals, Nixon again opened the door to China. In his State of the World message on February 26, 1971, he cited the "People's Republic of China" by name and proposed more trade and the beginning of a "serious dialogue." In early April 1971 the People's Republic invited an American table tennis team and three newsmen to visit Peking. Shortly afterward, Chou En-lai, the Chinese prime minister, stated that more American newsmen would be admitted; at the same time President Nixon announced an easing of the China trade embargo and the removal of American export restrictions on several nonstrategic items. In Nixon's view this was a significant way to "remove needless obstacles" to more contact between the American and Chinese peoples. The contacts with China continued during a brief, embittered war between India and Pakistan in the summer of 1971. Both China and the United States gave their official support to Pakistan, although to no avail. The eastern or Bengali portion of Pakistan seceded and, backed by Indian arms, became the new nation of Bangladesh.

The magnitude of the new thaw became obvious when Nixon announced in a short television address that Henry Kissinger had met with

Chou En-lai in Peking from July 9 to 11. The meeting had been in secret, newsmen having received a bulletin that Kissinger was in bed in Pakistan with a stomach ailment. More dramatic still, Nixon announced a planned visit to Peking to "seek the normalization of relations between the two countries and also to exchange views on questions of concern to the two sides." He stressed that the visit would not be at the expense of old friends, meaning the Nationalists on Formosa. Yet Chiang Kai-shek was displeased. When Nixon suggested that the Nationalist Chinese accept a "dual" formula for the China seat in the UN, both Taipei and Peking rejected it. Subsequently, despite half-hearted American opposition, the General Assembly on October 26, 1971 rejected a resolution that would have required a two-thirds majority vote on the issue. It then voted to seat the People's Republic of China and to expel the Nationalist Chinese.

Before his trip to Peking in February 1972, Nixon ordered an end to all spy flights over China, presumably to avoid any incident such as the U-2 that sabotaged the Eisenhower-Khrushchev meeting and contributed to Nixon's presidential defeat in 1960. After months of preparation, the president finally landed in Peking on Monday, February 20, 1972, where he was greeted by Chou En-lai. During Nixon's five-day visit, Henry Kissinger, Nixon's master diplomat, accompanied him in all meetings with Chou and on an early visit to Mao Tse-tung; Secretary of State Rogers apparently was never present at the secret sessions but met instead with other Chinese officials. At the end of the week Nixon and Chou En-lai issued a joint communique pledging peaceful coexistence and recognizing Taiwan as an "internal" Chinese problem. In effect, Nixon had granted the fact of a single China; he even promised eventual withdrawal of American forces from Taiwan.

The historic trip to China ruffled many feathers. Japanese-American relations, already strained because of economic conflict, steadily worsened. The Soviet Union, aligned against both China and the United States on the India-Pakistani conflict, sensed possible isolation. Moscow had supported Peking's entry into the UN, but this did little to relieve the intense distrust between the two major Communist powers. Yet the Soviet Union and the United States moved toward greater understanding in several areas—the SALT talks, a treaty to ban nuclear weapons from the sea bed, increased cooperation in space, and modernization of the hot line through satellite communications. To cap his new offensive for peace, Nixon announced that he would visit Moscow in May 1972 in order to discuss all major issues that divided the two countries. The trip to Moscow took place as planned, and with considerable fanfare. In the midst of the grave domestic crisis created by the Watergate affair in 1973, Premier Brezhnev made a return visit to the United States.

In contrast to his confident handling of foreign affairs, Nixon faced end-less frustration in dealing with domestic problems. His first major concern had to be an economy threatened by inflation and by increasing deficits in the balance of payments. Nixon appointed Paul McCracken chairman of the Council of Economic Advisers, Arthur F. Burns became his closest economic consultant and head of the Federal Reserve Board, and Robert P. Mayo took over as budget director. Their immediate problem was how restrictive the budget should be to slow down inflation but avoid reces-sion. Unemployment was at a low 3.3 percent, the bond market higher than ever, and interest rates rising steadily. Nixon pared the Johnson bud-get with a $1.1 billion reduction in defense spending and $2.9 in domestic items. His basic policy included the continuation of "tight money" through higher reserve bank rediscount rates, a reduction in Medicaid, in housing, in space programs, and in federal aid for impacted school dis-tricts; a continuation of the 10 percent income tax surcharge; and the en-actment of increased postal rates.

Congress, however, was not about to accept reduced spending. While most Democrats approved of cuts in defense appropriations, they objected to domestic cutbacks. Johnson, after all, had promised guns *and* butter. Representative Wilbur Mills of Arkansas, the powerful chairman of the House Ways and Means Committee, insisted on broad tax reductions with some reforms. In response to Nixon's proposal for a 5 percent in-come tax surcharge and a repeal of the 7 percent investment tax credit, Mills proposed an elimination of all deductions except for charities, a gen-eral lowering of tax rates, and an upward revision of capital gains taxes. While the debate on tax policy rambled on, productivity jerked down-ward. Yet the cost of living continued to rise, in some months by as much as .6 percent. By June 1969 the prime lending rate ballooned to 8.5 per-cent. In Nixon's view the brakes needed steady application in order to ac-complish his purpose.

Two months later the president asked for striking programs of welfare reform and revenue sharing. His welfare proposal guaranteed $1,600 an-nually for a family of four regardless of state contributions. Families could earn an additional $720 a year with no loss in benefits, but beyond this assistance would decrease $.50 on the dollar until wages reached $3,920. The program, to be administered by the Social Security Administra-tion, would have required recipients to register at the nearest unemploy-ment office and to accept suitable jobs or undergo training; no more food stamps would be issued. Not all proponents of welfare reform liked the program. Many, favoring the establishment of a larger guaranteed annual income, objected to Nixon's assertion that such assistance "would under-mine the incentive to work." Nixon's plan for revenue sharing involved turning tax dollars back to state and local governments, many of which were in serious financial difficulty. The mayors of large cities were particularly interested, for the flight of the middle class and businesses to the suburbs had eroded their tax base.

Like Lyndon Johnson, President Nixon could not easily accept criticism. He evidently placed Vice-President Agnew in the political foreground to make scathing remarks about the national news media and campus radicals. In a November 1969 speech to the Mid-West Regional Republican Committee in Des Moines, the vice-president claimed that the three major television networks distorted the news. He especially berated CBS and NBC for their evaluation of Nixon's November third speech calling for public support of his Vietnam policy. On one network Averell Harriman had evaluated the speech negatively; Agnew charged that a network had no business bringing on a man who had swapped "some of the greatest concessions in the history of warfare for an enemy agreement on the shape of a bargaining table." While disclaiming any wish for censorship, Agnew challenged the power of a "small and unelected elite" to control public opinion and warned against allowing such a monopoly in communications.

Nixon explained that Agnew spoke his own mind, that he was not a White House hatchet man, yet Agnew's speech writers belonged to the president's staff. In the weeks following the Des Moines address, Agnew attacked other news media, especially the *New York Times* and the *Washington Post*. Nixon openly appeared much more conciliatory toward the press and war protestors, but later revelations showed his own deep resentment of any form of opposition. Ron Ziegler, his press secretary, conceded that the autumn antiwar demonstration had been peaceful and repeated the claim that the administration intended no censorship.

Agnew was to continue his often colorful attacks during the 1970 campaign, singling out particular senators who had voted against Clement Haynsworth and Harrold G. Carswell—both Nixon nominees who had failed to win confirmation in the Senate to fill vacant Supreme Court seats. Nixon's first appointee to the Court, Chief Justice Warren E. Burger, faced little opposition as the successor to Earl Warren, but labor and civil rights groups fought Nixon's next choices. Haynsworth held stock in a vending machine company which received a favorable decision from his court. He had bought the stock after having made the decision but before publishing it. Senator Robert Griffin who earlier had led the movement against confirming Johnson's appointee Abe Fortas ultimately refused to support Haynsworth. Sixteen other Republicans joined in a 55 to 45 defeat. The same labor and civil rights groups opposed Carswell after hearing of some racist speeches from the 1940's and evidence that the nominee had drawn up the charter of a segregated club. One of the most damaging blows to Carswell was the remark of Nebraska Republican Senator Roman Hruska in defense of the nomination: Hruska insisted Carswell was well qualified but added that mediocre judges and lawyers were entitled to representation on the Court. The Senate refused to confirm by 51 to 47, and thus defeated a second Southerner. Carswell subsequently ran for the Senate but lost in Florida's Republican primary.

Despite Democratic requests for a qualified southern nominee, Nixon angrily contended that the Senate was not interested in "righting" the balance of the Court; he then nominated Harry Blackmun of Minnesota, who won approval 94 to 0. In 1971 the Senate did approve a Southerner, Lewis Powell of Virginia, along with William Rehnquist, an assistant attorney general in the Justice Department and a former Goldwater supporter.

The "new" Supreme Court refused to back down from strong civil rights decisions handed down after 1954. It ruled unanimously on October 29, 1969, that school districts must end segregation "at once" and operate integrated school systems "now and hereafter." This specifically affected thirty-three Mississippi school districts granted a delay by the president. On December 13 the Court decreed that southern school districts had to desegregate by February 1, 1970. In other important decisions, the Court negated residency requirements for welfare recipients, applied a statute of limitations of five years on failure to register for the draft, decided that states had to help the poor pay divorce costs, and held that ethical as well as religious reasons were a sufficient basis for conscientious objection. One of the most significant cases narrowed the landmark Miranda ruling on inadmissible statements: they would now be allowed if the defendant testified in his own defense.

When the Court voted against delays in desegregation, Nixon promised to execute the ruling faithfully. Nevertheless, the United States Commission on Civil Rights, lawyers in HEW, and blacks who had been appointed to high government positions were sharply critical of Nixon's reluctance to push civil rights. The other side also sniped at the president. Senator Strom Thurmond of South Carolina repeatedly contended that Nixon had failed to live up to his campaign promises of greater consideration toward the South, and George Wallace held out the threat of running again in 1972 if Nixon continued to force integration. Wallace made particular use of the issue of school busing, forcing Nixon closer to his own position. On April 20, 1971, however, the Court ruled 9 to 0 that school busing was a proper means to achieve school integration. Nixon

wanted no more busing than the minimum required by law, and the issue was a major one in the 1972 primaries and campaign. As late as 1973 there was simply no concerted attempt to roll back the decisions of the Warren Court. In its first major decision the Court early that year held that states could not deny a woman's right to legal abortion; the vote was a lopsided 7 to 2, with three of Nixon's four appointees in the majority. A later case in 1973 gave localities more power to restrict pornography, but the Court still pursued no clear juristic path.

Other legal issues made headline news. The nation witnessed theatrical courtroom outbursts in the cases of the "Chicago 8," indicted for conspiring to incite riot at the 1968 Democratic Convention in Chicago, and of the "Panther 21," a group charged with conspiracy to blow up buildings in New York City. The trial of the Panthers, postponed for over two months, resumed only when the defendants promised to restrain themselves. In Chicago Bobby Seale, the chairman of the Black Panther party, so infuriated Judge Julius Hoffman that he declared a mistrial and cited Seale for contempt of court. The other seven and their lawyers, although acquitted of the major charge of conspiracy, were convicted on a lesser charge; all received jail sentences on multiple counts of contempt of court, but secured a reversal of these through appeal.

Black Panther party Minister of Defense Huey Newton (left) in China with Premier Chou En-lai (1898–   ), right. Newton visited China to petition Chairman Mao Tse-tung to be chief negotiator to President Nixon, "For the peace and freedom of the oppressed people of the world." *United Press International*

Across the country the Black Panthers were a particular target of arrest and trial, owing in part to fears of a conspiracy to kill policemen. In some large cities gun battles took place between Panthers and police: in December 1969 Chicago police broke into an apartment and killed Fred Hampton, chairman of the Illinois Black Panthers, and Mark Clark, a Panther leader from Peoria. Although an interracial jury declared the killings justifiable, the government eventually dropped felony charges against the surviving Panthers and in August 1972 a grand jury indicted Illinois State's Attorney Edward V. Hanrahan along with thirteen others (including policemen) for conspiring to block the prosecution of police officers responsible for the raid on Hampton's apartment. In fact, in almost every trial of Black Panthers from 1969 to January 1972 the juries failed to return convictions either through direct acquittal or, as in the celebrated case of Seale, by a mistrial.

Although there had been scattered outbreaks of prison violence and related demands for reform, none drew as much attention as that at Attica, New York. On September 9, 1971, one thousand inmates—mostly minority group members—revolted and seized thirty-three guards as hostages. New York's Corrections Commissioner Russell Oswald negotiated with the prisoners for four days and acceded to twenty-eight demands but refused the key request for amnesty. Then, on September 13, with the consent of Governor Rockefeller, who had refused to meet with the prisoners, over a thousand state troopers and deputy sheriffs stormed the prison after helicopters dropped tear gas. Nine hostages and twenty-nine prisoners died. When it was disclosed that gunshot wounds and not slashed throats killed the hostages, a national furor arose over the incident. Although Governor Rockefeller and President Nixon defended the action, many prison officials around the country criticized the way the revolt was handled.

The Attica uprising kindled a debate on rising crime in America that went beyond prison riots to the issue of whether or not prisons either deterred crime or rehabilitated prisoners. The high rate of recidivism strongly indicated that they did not. Once again the whole system of American justice received scrutiny only to reveal long court dockets, crowded jails filled with prisoners awaiting trial, increasing crime rates, and no relief in sight. Nixon's proposed "preventive detention" legislation for those already awaiting trial for felonies only projected a future of bursting jails.

"Law and order" ironically became one of the leading issues in the 1970 congressional campaign. The 1969 local elections had shown only that voters were crossing party lines to split tickets more than ever. Perhaps the best indication came in New York City where Mayor John V. Lindsay, who was defeated in the Republican mayoralty primary, went on to win on the Liberal party ticket against the Democrat Mario Procaccino and Republican John Marchi. In 1970 Vice-President Agnew used his eloquence to denounce "permissive" figures like Senators Charles Goodell, Albert Gore, and Joseph Tydings—all of whom went down to defeat. The Democrats insisted that they too favored law and order but pursued more vigorously the economic issues of inflation and unemployment. Lawrence O'Brien, chairman of the Democratic National Committee, assailed Nixon for a "politics of fear" and for attempting to link the Democrats to violence; Agnew charged that they were trying to panic an electorate with charges of runaway inflation.

The election returns seemed to indicate that the economy had been a more effective issue than law and order. Democrats gained important new Senate seats in Illinois and California; in the House they made significant inroads in California, Florida, Ohio, Illinois, and New Jersey. Democrats also showed surprising strength in southern and midwestern gubernatorial elections, gaining ten additional state houses.

But despite the concern with the economy which swayed election returns in 1970, the excitement surrounding the first live moon landing in July 1969 momentarily obliterated economic worries. As early as December 1968 Apollo 8 had orbited the moon, and the flights of Apollo 9 and 10 followed soon after, testing the lunar module that was to make the landing. On July 16, 1969, Apollo 11 lifted off for the moon with astronauts John Young, Neil Armstrong, and Nelson Aldrin aboard. Five days later Armstrong and Aldrin landed on the moon, and six hours later millions watched on television as Armstrong stepped onto the surface. As John Kennedy had promised, Americans had landed on the moon before the end of the decade. When they returned to earth on July 24, Nixon greeted them on his way to the Far East, but they had to spend eighteen days in quarantine before being cheered and lauded from the White House and across the country. While on the moon, Armstrong and Aldrin set up a seismometer to measure moonquakes, a solar wind screen, and an American flag; they brought home samples of rock showing the moon to be billions of years old. Subsequent flights provided more scientific information. Astronauts Allen Bean and Peter Conrad of the Apollo 12 mission set up a scientific station and inspected an old Surveyor 3 spacecraft. Apollo 13, which was supposed to land in the lunar highlands, ran into trouble when an oxygen tank exploded and a resulting shortage briefly imperiled the lives of the astronauts aboard. But Apollos 14 and 15 made additional successful trips.

Despite the excitement over the conquest of space, many Americans voiced a preference for the application of resources to domestic problems such as poverty and pollution. Public pressure mounted quickest for programs against water and air pollution. Oil spills in the Santa Barbara channel in February 1969 offered an immediate opportunity to take strong action against companies responsible for pollution. Environmentalists, at first upset with Walter Hickel's appointment as interior secretary, were pleased by his call for stiffer laws governing off-shore drilling. In his 1970 State of the Union message Nixon committed himself to improving the "quality of life" by preserving the environment. He first proposed a $10 billion program to clean up the nation's waterways. The federal government would provide $4 billion ($445 million per year) and the states would contribute the other $6 billion. Nixon responded to concern over air pollution by urging legislation to restrict the emission of noxious gases and particles with heavier penalties for violations (up to $10,000 a day); to levy charges against industries using municipal waste treatment plants; to eliminate tetraethyl lead from automobile fuels; to conduct a five-year research project to produce a pollution-free car; and to revise existing water pollution control legislation in order to give the secretary of the interior authority to spend up to one-fifth of appropriated funds "in areas where facilities are most needed." Conceding that the proposals were greater than any made before, most Democrats argued that they were still inadequate.

In contrast to his environmental program, the president's urban and educational programs looked toward a reduced role for the federal government. Nixon had backed away from Johnson's war on poverty although certain popular programs such as Head Start continued under different auspices. He favored returning power to the states and localities and suggested a national population balance to let rural areas survive and hold back the movement toward the suburbs and cities. His education message of March 1970 emphasized his doubts that federal aid could be as effective as improved social and economic circumstances. Probably this was the basis for his veto, in the summer of 1970, of a $4.4 billion education bill —a veto that Congress promptly overrode.

Nixon also faced stiff opposition on defense spending. In addition to those who wished to end the draft, many wanted cutbacks in general troop strength and the closing of unneeded facilities. Nixon responded to many of these demands. He approved the first draft lottery, held December 1, 1970, a basic demand of those who opposed the student exemptions; he closed down numerous military bases; he declared an end to American germ warfare research and turned the army facility at Fort Dietrich, Maryland, over to cancer research. Many of these measures he announced in the course of the debate over ABM.

The results of cutbacks in defense were soon reflected in the economy, which began to cool down as defense contractors who had tooled up for the war or the exploration of space no longer needed so many employees. The Boeing Corporation of Seattle was already in trouble when the debate on a supersonic transport arose. The French had already begun to test their Concorde and the Russians had a quite different SST, while America had spent over $1 billion and did not yet have even a prototype. Scientists and environmentalists alike were beginning to have grave doubts about the potential effects of the plane on the environment. They warned of eliminating ozone from significant areas in the upper atmosphere, and reiterated that steady waves of sonic booms would accompany the plane in flight. In spite of Nixon's contention that the defeat of additional appropriations could lead to the end of United States leadership in the aircraft industry, loss of business to the French and Russians, and widening unemployment, the Senate voted 51 to 46 to end the program.

Boeing laid off seven thousand workers following the demise of the SST. By May 1971 unemployment reached 6.2 percent. Prices continued to rise. With the balance of payments against the United States, foreign banks ceased to support the dollar on the international currency market. West Germany decided to "float" the mark in order to stop the inflow of dollars, which were drastically increasing its money supply. Eurodollars —dollars on deposit in European banks—had grown from $1 billion at the end of the 1950's to over $50 billion.

Finally, on August 15, 1971, Nixon took drastic action by instituting a wage-price freeze for ninety days. He proposed new tax cuts plus programs to add new jobs. In order to right the balance of payments, the president suspended the convertibility of dollars into gold until proper adjustments were made by other nations. (That is, he was refusing to devalue the dollar unless there was some sort of reciprocal change.) In hopes of stemming American spending abroad Nixon proposed a 10 percent import surcharge on existing duties with certain products exempted.

The president established a Cost of Living Council to administer the freeze and called upon corporations to extend it to dividends. At the same time, to stimulate sales and production (and consequently employment) he asked for repeal of the 7 percent automobile excise tax and the activation of the $50 increase in personal tax deductions. The establishment of a 10 percent investment tax credit for one year to be followed by a 5 percent credit on American made machinery and equipment, he believed, would spur investment. Finally, he called for a reduction of federal expenditures by $4.7 billion and a 5 percent cut in federal employment. There were to be a six-month freeze on federal pay hikes, a 10 percent cutback in foreign aid, and a deferral of federal revenue sharing by three months from its effective date. Welfare reform, if passed, would be delayed for one year.

Although the stock market leapt ahead, labor leaders were not pleased. George Meany called the freeze discriminatory against his AFL-CIO workers, whose wages were frozen while industry received tax benefits and unlimited profits. But labor leaders eventually supported the plan even though they insisted that they wanted all pay increases called for in existing contracts. They bridled at Nixon's October 7 proposal of Pay, Price, and Rent Boards, but went along with these, too. No limits were to be set on profits, but the Price Board could seek reductions in the event of "windfall profits." The president also sought authority to impose mandatory controls on interest rates, and asked that lending institutions restrain dividend and interest increases. The freeze slowed but did not stop the pace of inflation.

The economic measures seemed to be most successful abroad. The Japanese agreed to remove their own quotas on certain agricultural products and lowered tariffs on thirty industrial items. But Nixon was looking for more than trade concessions. The yen had been valued at 360 to the dollar before the suspension of gold payments and the Japanese had consistently refused to revalue. In December a ten-nation monetary agreement devalued the dollar by 8.57 percent and sent the price of gold to $38 from its old base of $35. The yen and the mark were revalued upward in relation to the dollar. As other nations also revalued upward, Nixon removed the import surcharge.

The balance of payments problem eased for the moment, but a sluggish economy still plagued the administration. Nixon's 1972 budget had forecast a deficit of only $11.6 billion; it was actually $38.8 billion. His 1973 budget called for expenditures totalling $246.3 billion with receipts of only $220.8 billion. Nixon's first three budgets would have a total deficit of $87 billion. This was a significant turnabout for a man who in 1969 insisted on a budget surplus and who contended that he could meet all needs, cut inflation, and reduce unemployment.

The Election of 1972

In 1972, an election year, many new Nixon proposals sounded unmistakably political. Taking note of high property taxes, he promised a search for alternative methods of financing public schools. He proposed a "joint partnership" between government and industry to encourage new jobs.

He announced lower draft calls, more federal aid to black colleges, greater purchases of farm surpluses, and new authority for the Civil Rights Commission to eliminate discrimination against women.

Aspiring Democratic candidates attacked Nixon for neglecting domestic problems and prolonging the war, even as they began the long, costly primary tour that could lead to a nomination in July. Few voters and even fewer politicians took George McGovern seriously when he began his campaign for the presidency a year and a half before the nominating convention. McGovern, a first-term senator from South Dakota, was not well known; and his main issue, the Vietnam War, seemed nearly exhausted by long exposure. Yet the long-time Democratic front-runner, Senator Edmund Muskie of Maine, made a poor showing in the first primary, in New Hampshire, and went downhill from there. Another presidential contender, Governor George Wallace of Alabama, campaigned vigorously in several states until May 15 when he was shot down and paralyzed by a would-be assassin's bullets. Hubert Humphrey posed a major threat until defeated by McGovern and his devoted precinct workers in the June 6 California primary.

On July 13 George McGovern received the presidential nomination from a convention which, in part as a result of his leadership, gave greater representation to women, minorities, and youth. The candidate's long struggle read like *Cinderella*. But sometime during the convention the clock struck midnight, for the magic of the primary campaign suddenly disappeared. By directing his appeal to the most cohesive and energetic factions within the Democratic party—youth, peace activists, blacks—McGovern won key primaries and the nomination but at the same time gained a vaguely visionary or radical image that almost insured his defeat in November. His unbelievably inept handling of the vice-presidential selection further prejudiced his campaign. Without careful background investigations, McGovern selected Senator Thomas Eagleton of Missouri as his running mate. Ten days later Eagleton, prodded by news-

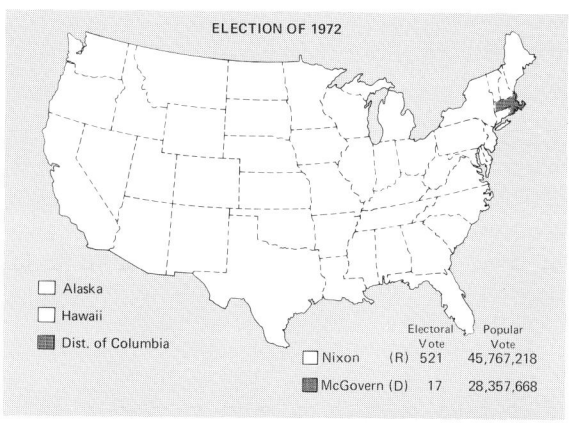

ELECTION OF 1972

Alaska
Hawaii
Dist. of Columbia

	Electoral Vote	Popular Vote
Nixon (R)	521	45,767,218
McGovern (D)	17	28,357,668

paper rumors, admitted earlier hospitalization and shock therapy for severe depression. After first backing Eagleton by "one thousand percent," McGovern eventually forced a crushed Eagleton to withdraw as a candidate. After an embarrassing search for a willing replacement, he finally turned to R. Sargeant Shriver, a Kennedy kinsman and an energetic speaker. This whole fiasco reinforced earlier and exaggerated charges that McGovern was indecisive and weak, even as it seemed to his more idealistic supporters an all too cynical capitulation to political pressure.

President Nixon and Vice-President Spiro T. Agnew (1918–   ) wave to delegates at the final session of the 1972 Republican convention after they accepted the party's nomination for reelection. *Wide World Photos*

Richard Nixon remained calm, his "back-porch" campaign all the more effective because the porch was attached to the White House. No element of suspense invested his renomination on August 23. Some early jockeying over the vice-presidential slot gave way to the matter-of-course choice of Spiro Agnew, who retooled his style for 1972—more poised, restrained, and independent. After the Republican convention, President Nixon cooly sent forth his staff and cabinet members to do battle while protecting and nourishing his image as statesman. He coasted toward November.

One of the most spectacular political incidents in several decades occurred during the summer of the campaign, but although repeatedly brought up by McGovern it aroused little voter reaction. On June 17 five men were captured inside Democratic National Headquarters in Washington while involved in a bugging and spying attempt. Investigators quickly established definite connections between the five and President Nixon's reelection committee, but little more was learned before election day.

Much as the pollsters predicted, Americans on November 7 gave Richard Nixon 60.8 percent of the popular vote and 521 of 538 electoral votes; only Massachusetts and the District of Columbia went to George McGovern. In congressional voting, the Democrats picked up two seats in the Senate to pad their weighty majority and held on to a comfortable margin in the House, while they gained one governorship to increase their statehouse margin of 31 to 19. Nonetheless, President Nixon interpreted the overwhelming victory as a great personal mandate, as a prelude to a triumphant second term.

Bibliography

The two best interpretive books on Eisenhower are those by his speechwriters Emmet John Hughes, *The Ordeal of Power* (New York: Atheneum, 1963), and Arthur Larson, *Eisenhower: The President Nobody Knew* (New York: Scribners, 1968). An overall look at the Eisenhower years, with an excellent bibliography, is Herbert S. Parmet, *Eisenhower and the American Crusades* (New York: Macmillan, 1972). Accounts limited to the president's first term include Robert J. Donovan, *Eisenhower: The Inside Story* (New York: Harper, 1956), Marquis W. Childs, *Eisenhower: Captive Hero* (New York: Harcourt, Brace, 1958), and Merlo J. Pusey, *Eisenhower the President* (New York: Macmillan, 1956). Eisenhower's career during World War II is examined by Stephen E. Ambrose, *The Supreme Commander: The War Years of General Dwight D. Eisenhower* (Garden City, N.Y.: Doubleday, 1970), and his approach to foreign policy during his two presidential terms can be found in *The Eisenhower Presidency and American Foreign Policy*, by David Bernard Capitanchik (New York: Library of Political Studies Service, 1969). Excellent brief essays on Eisenhower are those by Norman A. Graebner, "Eisenhower's Popular Leadership," *Current History* (1960), and Richard H. Rovere, "Eisenhower Over the Shoulder," *American Scholar* (1962); see also the collection of articles edited by Dean Albertson, *Eisenhower as President* (New York: Hill and Wang, 1963), and Richard H. Rovere's collected *New Yorker* columns, *Affairs of State: The Eisenhower Years* (1956). Sherman Adams, the capable assistant to the president until 1958, wrote a memoir, *Firsthand Report* (New York: Harper, 1961), and Ezra Taft Benson has written another, *Cross Fire: The Eight Years with Eisenhower* (Salt Lake City, Utah: Deseret Books, 1962). The president's own memoirs are *Crusade in Europe* (Garden City, N.Y.: Doubleday, 1948), *The White House Years: Mandate for Change, 1953–1956* (Garden City, N.Y.: Doubleday, 1963), and *The White House Years: Waging Peace, 1956–1961* (Garden City, N.Y.: Doubleday, 1965).

For a clarification of the Eisenhower electoral appeal see Angus Campbell, et al., *The American Voter* (New York: John Wiley, 1964), and Samuel Lubell, *The Revolt of the Moderates* (New York: Harper, 1956). Eisenhower's two-time Democratic opponent is the subject of two recent books: Bert Cochran, *Adlai Stevenson: Patrician among the Politicians* (New York: Funk and Wagnalls, 1969), and Herbert J. Muller, *Adlai Stevenson* (London: H. Hamilton, 1968). James L. Sundquist, *Politics and Policy: The Eisenhower, Kennedy and Johnson Years* (Washington, D.C.: Brookings Institution, 1968), is an essential account of legislation in the 1950's and 1960's. Two important sets of documents are *Goals for Americans: The Report of the President's Commission on National Goals* (Englewood Cliffs, N.J.: Prentice-Hall, 1960), and *Peace with Justice: Selected Addresses of Dwight D. Eisenhower* (1961).

Two books that have shaped our understanding of the 1950's are David Riesman, Reuel Denney, and Nathan Glazer, *The Lonely Crowd* (New Haven, Conn.: Yale University Press, 1950), and Daniel Bell, *The End of Ideology*, rev. ed. (New York: The Free Press, 1965). Along with Riesman, et al., the radical sociologist C. Wright Mills (*White Collar*, New York: Oxford University Press, 1953; *The Power Elite*, New York: Oxford University Press, 1956) and the liberal economist John Kenneth Galbraith (*American Capitalism*, Boston: Houghton Mifflin, 1956; *The Affluent Society* (Boston: Houghton Mifflin, 1958) helped to inaugurate the era of political and social muckraking that accompanied the resurgence of liberalism late in the decade. Daniel Bell, ed., *The Radical Right: The New American Right* (Freeport, N.Y.: Books for Libraries, 1955), illustrates the intellectuals' mood in the fifties, which has been criticized by Michael Rogin in *The Intellectuals and McCarthy* (Cambridge, Mass.: M.I.T. Press, 1967).

Paul Goodman's *The Empire City* (Indianapolis, Ind.: Bobbs-Merrill, 1959) and *Growing Up Absurd* (New York: Random House, 1960) present one view of adolescent life in the 1950's; J. D. Salinger's *Catcher in the Rye* (Boston: Little, Brown, 1951) gives another. An academic approach, offering data as well as interpretation, is contained in James S. Coleman's *The Adolescent Society* (New York: The Free Press, 1961) and *Adolescents and the Schools* (New York: Basic Books, 1965). Edgar Z. Friedenberg's *The Vanishing Adolescent* (Boston: Beacon Press, 1964), and James A. Wechsler's *Reflection of An Angry Middle-Aged Editor* (New York: Random House, 1960), anticipate tensions developing between generations. Lawrence Lipton, *The Holy Barbarians* (New York: Messner, 1959), is still the best book on the Beats. Jack Kerouac, *On the Road* (New York: Viking Press, 1957), and Allen Ginsberg, *Howl! and Other Poems* (San Francisco: City Lights Pocket Bookshop, 1956), convey the flavor of the movement. On Ginsberg see Jane Kramer, *Allen Ginsberg in America* (New York: Random House, 1969) and the essay by Richard Kostelanetz in his *Masterminds* (New York: Macmillan, 1969). *The Evergreen Review* of the fifties was the prime media of Beat writers.

Suburbia is the subject of William H. Whyte, *The Organization Man* (Garden City, N.Y.: Doubleday, 1956), John R. Seeley, *Crestwood Heights* (New York: Basic Books, 1956), Robert C. Wood, *Suburbia, Its People and Their Politics* (Boston: Houghton Mifflin, 1959), Marshall Sklare, *Jewish Identity on the Suburban Frontier* (1967), and Herbert J. Gans, *The Levittowners* (New York: Pantheon Books, 1967). Scott Donaldson examines changing views of the suburbs in *The Suburban Myth* (New York: Columbia University Press, 1969).

A Thousand Days (Boston: Houghton Mifflin, 1965), by Arthur Schlesinger, Jr., is a brilliant book, a durable monument to John Kennedy; its very inclusiveness, particularly on the making of foreign policy, gives form to the era. Theodore C. Sorenson's *Kennedy* (New York: Bantam, 1965) is another long book that must be consulted by every student of the period. The work of a third presidential aide, Pierre Salinger, *With Kennedy* (Garden City, N.Y.: Doubleday, 1966), provides important detail. For much more critical assessments of Kennedy see Henry Fairlie, *The Kennedy Promise: The Politics of Expectation* (Garden City, N.Y.: Doubleday, 1973) and Louise Fitzsimons, *The Kennedy Doctrine* (New York: Random House, 1972). The Kennedys' drive to power and their inability to use this power positively because of emotional conflicts and ambivalences is the thesis propounded by Nancy Gager Clinch, *The Kennedy Neurosis: A Psychological Portrait of an American Dynasty* (New York: Grosset and Dunlap, 1973). Tom Wicker's *Kennedy Without Tears* (New York: Morrow, 1964) is uneven, and Victor Laski's *JFK: The Man and the Myth* (1963) is absurdly critical. Early articles on Kennedy include William G. Carleton, "Kennedy in History: An Early Appraisal," *Antioch Review* (1964), and the more critical George Kateb, "Kennedy as Statesman," *Commentary* (1966). See also the valuable collection of pieces edited by Aida Dipace Donald, *John F. Kennedy and the New Frontier* (New York: Hill and Wang, 1966).

Norman Mailer's portrayal of Kennedy as he stirred the national consciousness in 1960 is reprinted in *The Presidential Papers*, rev. ed. (New York: Berkeley Publishers, 1970). More standard accounts of the 1960 campaign include Theodore White, *The Making of the President 1960* (New York: Atheneum, 1961), Paul T. David, et al., *The Presidential Election and Transition 1960–61* (Washington, D.C.: Brookings Institution, 1961). James MacGregor Burns, *John Kennedy* (New York: Harcourt, Brace, 1960) is an essential campaign biography, and Eric Sevareid, ed., *Candidates 1960* (New York: Basic Books, 1959). The impact of the religious question is measured in Philip Converse, et al., "Stability and Change in 1960: A Reinstating Election," *American Political Science Review* (1961); see also Lawrence H. Fuchs, *John F. Kennedy and American Catholicism* (New York: Meredith Press, 1967).

The legislative log-jam of 1962 is the subject of James MacGregor Burns, *The Deadlock of Democracy* (Englewood Cliffs, N.J.: Prentice-Hall, 1963). Robert Lekachman discussed the economy under Kennedy and Johnson in the last chapter of *The Age of Keynes* (New York: Random House, 1966). The confrontation with big steel is examined in Grant McConnell, *Steel and the Presidency—1962* (New York: W. W. Norton, 1963); see also Jim F. Heath, *John F. Kennedy and the Business Community* (Chicago: University of Chicago Press, 1969). A succinct essay touching on the Supreme Court under Kennedy is Alexander Bickel's *The Supreme Court and the Idea of Progress* (New York: Harper and Row, 1970).

The Bay of Pigs is treated in Theodore Draper's *Castroism* (New York: Praeger, 1965), as well as in Schlesinger's *Thousand Days*. Dean Rusk's statements in a period of great importance have been edited by Ernest K. Lindley, *The Winds of Freedom: Selections from Speeches and Statements of Secretary of State Dean Rusk, January 1961–August 1962* (1963). Maxwell Taylor, Kennedy adviser and, by 1963, chairman of the Joint Chiefs of Staff, wrote the influential *An Uncertain Trumpet* (New York: Harper and Row, 1960), and *Responsibility and Response* (New York: Harper and Row, 1967). The Cuban missile crisis is dealt with in the Sorenson book and Robert F. Kennedy gives a fascinating, if highly personal account, of presidential decision-making in *Thirteen Days* (New York: Norton, 1971). For a shrewd contemporary assessment check Henry Pachter, *Collision Course* (New York: Praeger, 1963). The Kennedy policy in Vietnam is covered in the subsequent section on the war, but see especially Roger Hilsman, *To Move a Nation* (Garden City, N.Y.: Doubleday, 1967).

Library shelves are cluttered with books on Kennedy's assassination. One armful might include Thomas G. Buchanan, *Who Killed Kennedy?* (London: Secker and Warburg, 1964), Leo Sauvage, *The Oswald Affair* (Cleveland: World Publishing, 1966), Josiah Thompson, *Six Seconds in Dallas* (New York: Random House, 1967), William Manchester, *The Death of a President* (New York, Harper and Row, 1967), Sylvia Meagher, *Accessories after the Fact: The Warren Commission, the Authorities and the Report* (Indianapolis, Ind.: Bobbs-Merrill, 1967), Mark Lane, *A Citizen's Dissent* (New York: Holt, Rinehart, and Winston, 1968), and Edward Jay Epstein, *Counterplot* (New York: Viking, 1969). Selections from the Warren Report have been edited by *The New York Times* and published by McGraw-Hill as *The Witnesses* (1965).

The Black American

Martin Luther King, Jr., wrote two books that are now highly significant documents of the civil rights movement, *Stride Toward Freedom* (New York: Harper and Row, 1958) and *Why We Can't Wait* (New York: Harper and Row, 1964); see also the biography by John A. Williams, *The King God Didn't Save* (New York: Coward-McCann, 1970), and Gilbert Moore, *A Special Rage* (New York: Harper and Row, 1972). James Baldwin's writings also beautifully evoke that period: *Notes of a Native Son* (Boston: Beacon Press, 1957), *Nobody Knows My Name* (New York: Dial Press, 1961), and especially *The Fire Next Time* (New York: Dial Press, 1963). More militant notes are struck in *The Autobiography of Malcolm X* (New York: Grove Press, 1965), Hamkin A. Jamal, *From the Dead Level: Malcolm X and Me* (New York: Random House, 1972), Claude Brown, *Manchild in the Promised Land* (New York: Macmillan, 1965), Charles V. Hamilton and Stokely Carmichael, *Black Power* (New York: Random House, 1967), and Eldridge Cleaver, *Soul on Ice* (New York: McGraw-Hill, 1967), *Post-Prison Writings and Speeches* (New York: Random House, 1969), and *My Babylon* (1970). For the Black Panthers see Bobby Seale, *Seize the Time* (New York: Random House, 1970), and P. S. Foner, ed., *The Black Panthers Speak* (Philadelphia: Lippincott, 1970). George Jackson's *Soledad Brother* (New York: Coward-McCann, 1970), a collection of his prison letters, and his second book finished just before his death, *Blood in My Eye* (New York: Bantam, 1972), are essential for an understanding of militant black ideology, as is *If They Come in the Morning* (New York: Third Press, 1971), a selection of writings by Angela Y. Davis and others.

A large number of important analytical works appeared during the course of the decade. They include Daniel P. Moynihan and Nathan Glazer, *Beyond the Melting Pot* (Cambridge, Mass.: M.I.T. Press, 1963); Charles Silberman, *Crisis in Black and White* (New York: Random House, 1964); Samuel Lubell, *White and Black: Test of a Nation* (New York: Harper and Row, 1964); Howard Zinn, *SNCC: The New Abolitionists* (Boston: Beacon Press, 1964); Kenneth Clark, *Dark Ghetto* (New York: Harper and Row, 1965); Charles Keil, *Urban Blues* (Chicago: University of Chicago Press, 1966); Lee Rainwater and William L. Yancey, *The Moynihan Report and the Politics of Controversy* (Cambridge, Mass.: M.I.T. Press, 1967); William Brink and Louis Harris, *Black and White* (New York: Simon & Schuster, 1967); Robert Coles, *Children of Crisis* (Boston: Little, Brown, 1967); Harold Cruse, *The Crisis of the Negro Intellectual* (New York: Morrow, 1967) and his *Rebellion or Revolution* (New York: Apollo Editions, 1969); Chuck Stone, *Black Political Power* (New York: Dell, 1970); Lewis M. Killian, *The Impossible Revolution: Black Power and the American Dream* (New York: Random House, 1968); Benjamin Muse, *The American Negro Revolution: From Nonviolence to Black Power, 1963–1967* (Bloomington: Indiana University Press, 1969); and Theodore Draper, *The Rediscovery of Black Nationalism* (New York: Viking Press, 1970). For the black protest and how it is dealt with see Sara Blackburn, comp., *White Justice: Black Experience Today in America's Courtrooms* (New York: Harper and Row, 1971); *Black Protest in the Sixties*, edited with an introduction by August Meier and Elliott Rudwick (New York: Watts, 1970); and James A. Geschwender, *The Black Revolt* (Englewood Cliffs, N.J.: Prentice-Hall, 1971). A controversial interpretation of the black American's fate is Sidney M. Willhelm's *Who Needs the Negro?* (New York: Doubleday, 1971). For other minority groups, see Matt S. Meier and Feliciano Rivera, *The Chicanos: A History of Mexican Americans* (New York: Hill and Wang, 1972), Edward Simmen, ed., *The Chicano: From Caricature to Self-Portrait* (New York: New American Library, 1971), and Wayne Moquin and Charles Van Doren, eds., *A Documentary History of the Mexican Americans* (New York: Praeger, 1971). In addition, Stan Steiner has written on Mexican Americans in *La Raza* (New York: Knopf, 1970) and also *The New Indians* (New York: Dell, 1969). A classic account of Puerto Rican acculturation is Oscar Lewis, *La Vida* (New York: Random House, 1966).

Lyndon Johnson

Two critical but perceptive brief books on Johnson are Michael Davie, *LBJ: A Foreign Observer's Viewpoint* (New York: Duell, Sloan, Pearce, 1966) and Tom Wicker, *JFK and LBJ: The Influence of Personality upon Politics* (Baltimore: Penguin, 1968). A more recent assessment by a foreign journalist is Louis Heren, *No Hail, No Farewell* (New York: Harper and Row, 1970). Other useful studies include the large biography *Sam Johnson's Boy* (New York: Macmillan, 1968), by Alfred Steinberg; Hugh Sidey, *A Very Personal Presidency: Lyndon Johnson in the White House* (New York: Atheneum,

1968); Eric Goldman, *The Tragedy of Lyndon Johnson* (New York: Knopf, 1969); Rowland Evans and Robert Novak, *Lyndon B. Johnson: The Exercise of Power* (New York: New American Library, 1966); Philip Geyelin, *Lyndon B. Johnson and the World* (New York: Praeger, 1966); and Leonard Baker, *The Johnson Eclipse* (1966). On the 1964 election see especially Walter D. Burnham, "American Voting Behavior and the 1964 Election," *Midwest Journal of Political Science* (1966), Milton C. Cummings, ed., *The National Election of 1964* (Washington, D.C.: Brookings Institution, 1966), and Theodore White, *The Making of the President 1964* (New York: Atheneum, 1965). On Goldwater see two essays by Richard Hofstadter in *The Paranoid Style in American Politics* (New York: Knopf, 1965); Richard Rovere, *The Goldwater Caper* (New York: Harcourt, Brace and World, 1965); Stephen Shadeeg, *What Happened to Goldwater?* (New York: Holt, Rinehart, and Winston, 1965); and Clifton White, *Suite 3505: The Story of the Draft Goldwater Movement* (New Rochelle, N.Y.: Arlington House, 1967). Goldwater's own books are *The Conscience of a Conservative* (New York: Manor Books, 1971), *Why Not Victory* (New York: McGraw-Hill, 1962), *Where I Stand* (1964), and *Conscience of a Majority* (Englewood Cliffs, N.J.: Prentice-Hall, 1970).

James Sundquist's *Politics and Policy* (Washington, D.C.: Brookings Institution, 1968) is thorough in its coverage of Great Society legislation. The economy under Johnson is discussed in Robert Lekachman's *Age of Keynes* and by Walter Heller, chairman of the Council of Economic Advisers, in *New Dimensions of Political Economy* (Cambridge, Mass.: Harvard University Press, 1966). A defense of our role in the Dominican Republic by our ambassador to that country under President Kennedy is John B. Martin's *Overtaken by Events* (Garden City, N.Y.: Doubleday, 1966). Johnson's own speeches and messages are to be found in Atheneum publishers' *A Time for Action: A Selection from the Speeches and Writings of Lyndon B. Johnson, 1953–64* (1964), and James MacGregor Burns, ed., *To Heal and to Build: The Programs of President Lyndon B. Johnson* (New York: McGraw-Hill, 1968).

Vietnam

Historical accounts on Vietnam abound. The best include Joseph Buttinger, *Vietnam: A Dragon Embattled*, 2 vols., rev. ed., (New York: Praeger, 1972), George M. Kahin and John W. Lewis, *The United States in Vietnam* (New York: Dial, 1967), and John T. McAlister, Jr., *Vietnam: The Origins of Revolution* (New York: Knopf, 1969). Good introductions to the American role in Vietnam are Ralph K. White, *Nobody Wanted War* (Garden City, N.Y.: Doubleday, 1968) and the slightly more critical Henry Brandon, *Anatomy of Error: The Inside Story of the Asian War on the Potomac, 1954–1969* (Boston: Gambit, 1969).

Critical books also abound. Journalists were among the first critics of the war and prime among them was Bernard B. Fall, killed by a mine explosion while covering Vietnam in 1967. Fall's books include *Street Without Joy: Insurgency in Indo-China, 1946–63* (Harrisburg, Pa.: Stackpole, 1963), *The*

Two Viet-Nams: A Political and Military Analysis (New York: Praeger, 1967), and *Last Reflections on a War* (Garden City, N.Y.: Doubleday, 1967). Other important accounts are Arthur Schlesinger, Jr., *The Bitter Heritage: Vietnam and American Democracy, 1941–1966* (Boston: Houghton Mifflin, 1967), Theodore Draper, *Abuse of Power* (New York: Viking, 1967), and the excellent collection of opinions, Richard M. Pfeffer, ed., *No More Vietnams* (New York: Harper and Row, 1968). Strong critical books include Noam Chomsky, *American Power and the New Mandarins* (New York: Pantheon, 1969) and *At War with Asia* (1970), Mary McCarthy, *Vietnam* (New York: Harcourt, Brace and World, 1967) and *Hanoi* (New York: Harcourt, Brace and World, 1968), Howard Zinn, *Vietnam: The Logic of Withdrawal* (Boston: Beacon, 1967), Bertrand Russell, *War Crimes in Vietnam* (New York: Monthly Review Press, 1967), Jean-Paul Sartre, *On Genocide* (Boston: Beacon, 1968), and the extremely important essay by Carl Oglesby showing the relationship between the cold war and Vietnam, which appeared in Oglesby and Richard Shaull, *Containment and Change*, originally titled *Third World Revolution* (New York: Macmillan, 1967). A more recent examination of America's role in Vietnam is Frances Fitzgerald, *Fire in the Lake* (Boston: Little, Brown, 1972); the Tonkin Gulf resolution is treated in Anthony Austin, *The President's War* (Philadelphia: Lippincott, 1971). Defenses of our role in Vietnam include Frank N. Trager, *Why Vietnam?* (New York: Praeger, 1966), Donald S. Zagoria, *Vietnam Triangle: Moscow, Peking, Hanoi* (New York: Pegasus, 1967), and United States Department of Defense, *Report on the War in Vietnam* [as of June 30, 1968] (1969). Henry F. Graff, *The Tuesday Cabinet* (Englewood Cliffs, N.J.: Prentice-Hall, 1970) contains interviews of administration leaders.

Many books have been written on particular incidents and problems concerning Vietnam. Seymour Hersh's *My Lai 4* (New York: Random House, 1970) recounts the American atrocities there. Seymour Melman's *Pentagon Capitalism* (New York: McGraw-Hill, 1970) updates the "military-industrial complex" argument. On peace efforts see David Draslow and Stuart H. Loory, *The Secret Search for Peace in Vietnam* (New York: Random House, 1968); on international law, Roger H. Hull and John C. Novogrod, *Law and Vietnam* (1967), Richard A. Falk, ed., *The Vietnam War and International Law*, 2 vols. (Princeton, N.J.: Princeton Univ. Press, 1967), and Telford Taylor, *Two Studies in Constitutional Interpretation* (Columbus: The Ohio State University Press, 1969).

Hans Morgenthau's essays, collected in *Truth and Power* (New York: Praeger, 1970), cover a variety of subjects. Among United States senators who have written on the war William Fulbright of Arkansas takes the laurels with *The Arrogance of Power* (New York: Random House, 1967) and *The Crippled Giant* (New York: Random House, 1972). Gale W. McGee of Wyoming has written a defense of our role there in *The Responsibilities of World Power* (Washington, D.C.: 1968). See also Alice Lynd, ed., *We Won't Go: Personal Accounts of War Objectors* (Boston: Beacon, 1968), the North Vietnamese General Vo Nguyen Giap, *Big Victory, Great Task* (New York: Praeger, 1968), and the Brookings report, *Vietnam after the War: Peacekeeping and Rehabilitation* (1968).

The 1968 election is expertly covered by the British journalists Lewis Chester, et al., *An American Melodrama* (New York: Viking, 1969). On President Nixon the best books are his own *Six Crises* (Garden City, N.Y.: Doubleday, 1962); the rambling sometimes incisive *Nixon Agonistes* (Boston: Houghton Mifflin, 1970) by Garry Wills; Earl Mazo and Stephen Hess, *Nixon: A Political Portrait* (New York: Harper and Row, 1967); Joe McGinniss, *The Selling of the President 1968* (New York: Trident, 1969); Jules Witcover, *The Resurrection of Richard Nixon* (New York: G. P. Putnam, 1970); and Ralph de Toledano, *One Man Alone: Richard M. Nixon* (Funk and Wagnalls, 1969). In addition, Bruce Mazlish, *In Search of Nixon* (New York: Basic Books, 1972) is a psychohistorical inquiry, and Leonard Lurie takes a look at the men behind Nixon's reelection in *The Running of Richard Nixon* (New York: Coward MacCann, 1972). Contributions by journalists are Rowland Evans, Jr., and Robert D. Novak, *Nixon in the White House: The Frustration of Power* (New York: Random House, 1971); Paul Hoffman, *The New Nixon* (New York: Tower, 1970); the *New Republic* columnist, John Osborne, has written *The Nixon Watch* (New York: Liveright, 1970), *The Second Year of the Nixon Watch* (New York: Liveright, 1971), and *The Third Year of the Nixon Watch* (New York: Liveright, 1972). Apprehensive conservatives include Allen Drury, *Courage and Hesitation: Inside the Nixon Administration* (Garden City, N.Y.: Doubleday, 1972) and Richard J. Whalen, *Catch the Falling Flag* (Boston: Houghton Mifflin, 1972). The new-money men behind Nixon are examined in an article by Kirkpatrick Sale, "The World Behind Watergate," *New York Review of Books*, May 3, 1973. On Humphrey there are Winthrop Griffith, *Humphrey* (1965), Nelson W. Polsby, *The Citizen's Choice: Humphrey or Nixon* (New York: Grossman, 1968), and Robert Sherill and Harry Ernst, *Drugstore Liberal* (1968). On Robert Kennedy see the senator's own weak books *The Enemy Within* (New York: Harper and Row, 1960) and *To Seek a Newer World* (Garden City, N.Y.: Doubleday, 1969). More useful are Penn Kimball, *Bobby Kennedy and the New Politics* (Englewood Cliffs, N.J.: Prentice-Hall, 1968), William V. Shannon, *The Heir Apparent* (New York: Macmillan, 1967), and Douglas Ross, *Robert F. Kennedy* (New York: Trident, 1968). Eugene McCarthy's own account of the campaign is unrewarding: *The Year of the People* (Garden City, N.Y.: Doubleday, 1968). More important are Jeremy Larner, *Nobody Knows: Reflections on the McCarthy Campaign of 1968* (Garden City, N.Y.: Doubleday, 1970), Arthur Herzog, *McCarthy for President* (New York: Viking, 1969), and Ben Stavis, *We Were the Campaign* (Boston: Beacon, 1969).

Two of the first of undoubtedly many assessments of McGovern and his campaign are Robert Sam Anson, *McGovern* (New York: Harcourt, Brace and World, 1972) and Gary Warren Hart, *Right From the Start* (New York: Quadrangle, 1973).

The fear of avowed radicalism that had gathered strength since mid-decade burst onto the scene in 1968. Basic to the understanding of that year's violence is *The Report of the National Advisory Commission on Civil Disorders* (Washington, D.C., 1968); Hugh Davis Graham and Ted Robert Gurr, *The History of Violence in America* (New York: New American Library, 1969), and Allen D. Grimshaw, ed., *Racial Violence in the United States* (Chicago: Aldine, 1969). See the essay on violence by Richard Hofstadter in *American Violence: A Documentary History* (New York: Random House, 1970), edited by Hofstadter and Michael Wallace. See also, on the Watts riot, Robert Conor, *Rivers of Blood, Years of Darkness* (New York: William Morrow, 1968), and Tom Hayden, *Rebellion in Newark* (1967).

Jack Newfield's *A Prophetic Minority* (New York: New American Library, 1966) is good on the Left during the early sixties. Paul Jacobs and Saul Landau, eds., *The New Radicals* (New York: Random House, 1960) has a useful chronology, and Mitchell Goodman, *The Movement toward a New America* (New York: Alfred A. Knopf, 1970) anthologizes the underground papers. Leslie Fiedler's "The New Mutants," *Partisan Review* (1965), reprinted in David Burner, ed., *The Diversity of Modern America* (New York: Appleton, 1970), is an important early essay, and Kenneth Keniston's *The Uncommitted* (New York: Harcourt, Brace and World, 1965) as well as his excellent work later in the decade, especially his essays in *American Scholar* (1968), (1970), and *Journal* (1970). For a critical view see Irving Howe, ed., *Beyond the New Left* (New York: McCall Publishing Co., 1970). Michael Harrington, *Toward a Democratic Left* (New York: Macmillan, 1968), and Christopher Lasch, *The Agony of the American Left* (New York: Knopf, 1969), are thoughtful books, as is Philip Slater's *Pursuit of Loneliness* (Boston: Beacon Press, 1970). On the establishment American Right see Charles Lam Markmann, *The Buckleys: A Family Examined* (New York: Morrow, 1973).

On the student rebels there is the anthology of sociological studies edited by Edward E. Sampson and Harold A. Korn, *Student Activism and Protest* (San Francisco: Jossey-Bass, 1970). Stephen Spender's *The Year of the Young Rebels* (New York: Random House, 1969) gives an international perspective. For sharp criticism of the students, see George Kennan, *Democracy and the Student Left* (Boston: Little, Brown, 1968), and Oscar and Mary Handlin's polemic against "troublemakers" of the sixties in the final chapter of *Facing Life: Youth and the Family in American History* (Boston: Little, Brown, 1971). On the Berkeley uprising of 1965 there is the anthology edited by Seymour Lipset and Sheldon Wolin, *The Berkeley Student Revolt* (Garden City, N.Y.: Anchor Books, 1965) and that edited by Michael V. Miller and Susan Gilmore, *Revolution at Berkeley* (New York: Dial Press, 1965); on the Columbia riots of 1968 see Roger Kahn, *The Battle for Morningside Heights* (New York: William Morrow, 1970), and Jerry L. Avorn, et al., *Up Against the Ivy Wall* (New York: Atheneum, 1968). See also Kenneth Keniston's assessment of the student radicals of the summer of 1967, *Young Radicals: Notes on Committed Youth* (New York: Harcourt, Brace and World, 1968).

Clark Kerr, *The Uses of the University* (New York: Harper and Row, 1963), describes problems of the new multiversity. David Riesman and Christopher Jencks, *The Academic Revolution* (Garden City, N.Y.: Doubleday, 1968), analyzes changes in higher education. Jacques Barzun, *The American University* (New York: Harper and Row, 1968), calls for more traditionalism, as in its own way does Oscar and Mary Handlin, *The American College and American Culture: Socialization as a Function of Higher Education* (New York: McGraw-Hill, 1970). James Ridgeway, *The Closed Corporation* (New York: Random House, 1968), is a severe attack. Theodore Roszak, ed., *The Dissenting Academy* (New York: Pantheon, 1968), is a collection of critical essays. Works of educational reformers include James B. Conant, *The American High School Today* (New York: McGraw-Hill, 1959), and *Slums and Suburbs* (New York: McGraw-Hill, 1961); Jerome S. Bruner, *The Process of Education* (Cambridge, Mass.: Harvard University Press, 1960) and *Toward a Theory of Instruction* (Cambridge, Mass.: Harvard University Press, 1960); John Holt, *How Children Fail* (New York: G. P. Putnam, 1964), *How Children Learn* (New York: G. P. Putnam, 1967), and *The Underachieving School* (New York: G. P. Putnam, 1969); Jonathan Kozol, *Death at an Early Age* (Boston: Houghton Mifflin, 1967); and Charles Silberman, *Crisis in the Classroom* (New York: Random House, 1970). The problems faced by America's poor are dealt with in Michael Harrington, *The Other America: Poverty in the United States* (New York: Macmillan, 1962). Useful collections of readings on poverty are A. B. Shostak and William Gomberg, eds., *New Perspectives on Poverty* (Englewood Cliffs, N.J.: Prentice-Hall, 1965), and Leo Fishman, ed., *Poverty Amid Affluence* (New Haven, Conn.: Yale University Press, 1966). H. M. Caudill, *Night Comes in the Cumberlands* (Boston: Little, Brown, 1963) is a disturbing and graphic picture of conditions in Appalachia. For the most solid criticism of American health care available see *The American Health Empire: Power, Profits and Politics* (1971), the report from the Health Policy Advisory Center in New York City, and for a view of welfare policy under the Nixon administration by a "participant historian," Daniel P. Moynihan, *The Politics of a Guaranteed Income: The Nixon Administration and the Family Assistance Plan* (New York: Random House, 1973).

Works admired especially by the radical young are Herbert Marcuse, *An Essay on Liberation* (Boston: Beacon Press, 1969), Norman O. Brown, *Life Against Death* (Middletown, Conn.: Wesleyan University Press, 1959) and *Love's Body* (New York: Random House, 1966), R. D. Laing, *The Politics of Experience* (New York: Pantheon, 1967), and Franz Fanon, *The Wretched of the Earth* (New York: Grove Press, 1965). Marshall McLuhan's *Understanding Media* (New York: New American Library, 1971) helps in grasping the new culture. Norman Mailer has been an ally and publicist of the young, from "The White Negro," reprinted in *Advertisements for Myself* (New York: G. P. Putnam, 1959) to *The Armies of the Night* (New York: New

American Library, 1968) and *Miami and the Siege of Chicago* (New York: New American Library, 1971). Lively books by two young spokesmen are Jerry Rubin's *Do It!* (New York: Simon and Schuster, 1970) and Abbie Hoffman's *Woodstock Nation* (New York: Random House, 1969).

The most useful study of the youth culture is Theodore Roszak's *The Making of a Counter-Culture* (1969). Charles Reich's *The Greening of America* (New York: Random House, 1970) is enthusiastic and naïve. Daniel Bell, "Sensibility in the 60's," *Commentary* (1971) is a penetrating essay and Seymour Martin Lipset, "New Perspectives on the Counter Culture," *Saturday Review* (1971) sees the phenomenon as not an entirely new one. Among the other articles on the counterculture the most informative and interesting are Marcia Cavell, "Visions of a New Religion," *Saturday Review* (1970); Daniel Seligman, "A Special Kind of Rebellion," *Fortune* (1969); Peter L. Berger and Brigitte Berger, "The Blueing of America," *New Republic* (1970); and Anthony Scaduto, "Won't You Listen to the Lambs, Bob Dylan?" *The New York Times Magazine*, November 28, 1971. The hippie era is well covered by Warren Hinckle, "A Social History of the Hippies," *Ramparts* (1967), and Lewis Yablonsky, *The Hippie Trip* (New York: Pegasus, 1968). Tom Wolfe's *Electric Kool-Aid Acid Test* (New York: Farrar, Straus, and Giroux, 1968) has many admirers, as does Ken Kesey's fictional *One Flew Over the Cuckoo's Nest* (New York: Viking, 1962). On rock music see Charlie Gillett's *The Sound of the City: The Rise of Rock and Roll* (New York: Outerbridge & Lazard, 1970), and Jerry Hopkins, *The Rock Story* (1970). Erich Goode's anthology, *Marijuana* (New York: Atherton, 1969), covers that ground with scarcely an unbiased essay. Timothy Leary, *The Politics of Ecstasy* (New York: G. P. Putnam, 1968), proselytizes for LSD. Nonliterary sources such as movies are important for an understanding of the youth culture.

Religious currents in the 1960's are suggested by Harvey Cox, *The Secular City* (New York: Macmillan, 1965), and Daniel J. Callahan, ed., *The Secular City Debate* (New York: Macmillan, 1966). Xavier Rhynne (a pseudonym for a participant) reported on Vatican II in *The New Yorker* (1963 to 1965), articles that had wide effect among laity and clerics. Changes in Judaism receive attention in the magazine *Commentary* by such writers as Marshall Sklare.

Women's liberation, although closely related to the new radical culture, also has earlier roots as a revolt against suburban living of the 1950's. Betty Friedan's classic *The Feminine Mystique* (New York: W. W. Norton, 1963) catches this strain. Kate Millett's *Sexual Politics* (Garden City, N.Y.: Doubleday, 1970) is a powerhouse, and among the several anthologies Robin Morgan, ed., *Sisterhood Is Powerful* (New York: Random House, 1970) is probably the best. Other books include Juliet Mitchell, *Women's Estate* (New York: Pantheon, 1971); Shulamith Firestone, *The Dialectic of Sex: The Case for Feminist Revolution* (New York: Bantam, 1970); and Eva Figes, *Patriarchal Attitudes* (New York: Stein & Day, 1970). For the male assessment of women's liberation writings see Richard Sennett's review of Firestone and Mitchell in the *New York Review of Books*, April 20, 1972, and Gore Vidal on Figes, also in the *New York Review of Books*, "In Another Country," July 22, 1971. For a fascinating insight into an intellectual's ambivalent response to the movement see Irving Howe's review, "The Middle-Class Mind of Kate Millett," in *Harper's*, December 1970. Articles on more recent developments include Helen Dudar, "Women's Lib: The War on 'Sexism'," *Newsweek*, March 23, 1970, and Susan Brownmiller, " 'Sisterhood Is Powerful," the *New York Times Magazine*, March 15, 1970. Robert J. Lifton, ed., *The Woman in America* (Boston: Houghton Mifflin, 1965) contains useful essays. The work of William H. Masters and Virginia E. Johnson, *Human Sexual Inadequacy* (Boston: Little, Brown, 1970) has been very influential, especially on women. Martin Hoffman gives homosexuals a fair deal in *The Gay World* (New York: Bantam, 1973).

Summary views of the 1960's, by Richard Rovere and Benjamin DeMott, appeared in the *New York Times Magazine*, December 14, 1969. Other appraisals are David Burner, Robert D. Marcus, and Thomas R. West, *A Giant's Strength: America in the 1960's* (New York: Holt, Rinehart, and Winston, 1971) and William L. O'Neill, *Coming Apart* (Chicago: Quadrangle, 1971). Ronald Berman's *America in the Sixties* (New York: Free Press, 1968) is an excellent intellectual history. Grant McConnell, *Private Power and American Democracy* (New York: Knopf, 1966), and Theodore J. Lowi, *The End of Liberalism* (New York: W. W. Norton, 1969), are major critiques of a body of social thought built up during the sixties. For the new decade, see the editors of *The National Observer*, *The Seventies* (1970), and Leonard Freedman, ed., *Issues of the Seventies* (Belmont, Calif.: Wadsworth Publishing Co., 1970).

EPILOGUE

In the Shadow of Watergate

For recent American presidents, nothing has turned out to be more treacherous and disillusioning than an overwhelming electoral mandate. In three years Harding moved from the glow of an unprecedented election victory to a saddened and ill spectator of an administration in shambles; only death spared him the agony of one unearthed scandal after another. Franklin D. Roosevelt interpreted his awesome victory of 1936 as a license to assault oppositionist federal courts, and in the aftermath of a nasty congressional battle never regained his former legislative influence. In 1964, Lyndon B. Johnson basked in his easy, overwhelming victory over Goldwater, and in fact did use this mandate to push through Congress an unprecedented volume of important domestic legislation, only to flounder in the morass of Vietnam and a United States divided and embittered. In neither case did the debacle have to follow the triumph. No rule applies. The specific circumstances varied widely. Poor judgment had a larger role in each case than fate. Yet, had Richard Nixon been a thoughtful man, this past record might have given him pause.

Just after the January 1973 inauguration, events seemed to conspire in Nixon's favor. Although belatedly, he achieved the promised armistice in Vietnam on January 23, and in February a patchwork truce in Laos, leaving only a confused war in Cambodia. Here Nixon would continue heavy bombings until finally Congress cut off authority and funding in August 1973. Thus he remained at odds with Congress over Indochina policy, even as he remained tough and unyielding in his attitudes toward draft evaders or military deserters. Yet, Nixon was able to celebrate in late March the evacuation of the last American troops from Vietnam. Then, in a carefully orchestrated, almost theatrical drama, he gloried in the returning prisoners-of-war, who on their televised exit from troop planes obligingly read short, patriotic, vaguely proadministration speeches usually written for them by government escorts. In a near orgy of contrived emotionalism, Nixon had his last moments of pride and vindication.

A new Nixon, or possibly a refurbished old one, seemed ready to take full charge of domestic policy in his second term. The problem of reelection no longer confronted him, and he seemed determined to overcome the "lame-duck" disabilities created by the Twenty-second Amendment. Always a very private, even secretive person, Nixon now chose to remain even more aloof, as if to establish the mystique of the lonely leader or the lofty monarch, even as he hinted at parallels between himself and a re-

**The Challenge
to Congress**

vered Charles De Gaulle. Unlike during his first administration, when he had tried to respond to varied interests and confusingly supported varied programs that revealed no coherent goals, Nixon now committed himself to a focused and consistent domestic program—fiscal retrenchment, a critical screening and phased reduction of unsuccessful welfare and anti-poverty programs, the decentralization of political power and responsibility, and a continued retreat from "permissiveness" in national life. He shifted his executive staff, reorganized the federal bureaucracy to the limit of congressional authority, centralized more power in his own hands, relaxed most economic controls, scuttled his earlier proposals for welfare reform, and began to impound appropriated funds in order to cut government costs. In the few brief months before the most damaging Watergate revelations, he seemed ready to defy a Democratic Congress and further expand the power of the presidency, a trend largely begun by his Democratic predecessors. Just as Roosevelt committed his power and prestige to a battle with the courts, so Nixon early and rather defiantly challenged a Democratically controlled and demoralized Congress, which alone seemed to stand in the way of a major reorientation of domestic priorities.

By an early series of executive orders, Nixon provoked what congressional critics soon called a constitutional crisis, and one that Nixon seemed most likely to win. In behalf of what he described as fiscal responsibility he began impounding unspent funds appropriated by Congress, particularly for antipoverty programs and environmental protection. From his perspective, the president had discretionary authority over such expenditures and a responsibility to the public to protect the national interest against reckless congressional spending. Most congressmen disagreed, seeing in such arbitrary presidential action a threat to their power over the purse and a backhanded way for the president to exercise an absolute rather than a conditional veto. Whether Nixon had the legal and constitutional authority for such impounding probably depended upon the exact terms of specific congressional acts or appropriations. In the first test case, a United States District Court in May 1973, ordered a reluctant Nixon administration to resume distribution of water pollution funds to the states in accordance with a specific 1972 congressional authorization which passed over a Nixon veto. Most other litigation supported the congressional position.

Since so much of the impounded money involved the Office of Economic Opportunity and paralleled the dismantling of more vulnerable or radical poverty programs, the conflict had heavy symbolic meaning. Congressmen responded to organized protests by clients of abandoned or unfunded programs, or to environmentalists or academic intellectuals who favored an expanded, not a circumscribed, government role. The Congress could only fume when a Nixon aide suggested that, if it did not like what Nixon was doing, it could always initiate impeachment proceedings, a joke that turned sour in a few months. Nixon seemed increasingly isolated even from Republican congressmen, as if hidden behind a wall erected by such key White House advisers as John Ehrlichman and H. R. Haldeman. Finally, as early Watergate revelations poured out of Washington, Nixon's legal staff briefly appealed to an extreme doctrine of executive privilege to prevent White House aides from testifying before congressional committees. But the very occasion for this confrontation soon deflated the whole executive-congressional contest, for the Watergate affair soon eroded Nixon's popular mandate and forced him to fight, not for new prerogatives, but to save his presidency.

Aftermath of the Watergate Burglaries

On June 17, 1972, the Washington, D.C., police discovered and arrested five gloved burglars in the headquarters of the Democratic National Committee. The location gave its name to the incident and to a vast number of related issues. The offices were in a complex of lush apartments named after the former site of summer concerts on the Potomac, or the Watergate. One did not have to be very cynical to suspect a calculated reelection strategy by Nixon's huge campaign organization, particularly since one of the felons was James McCord, Jr., a security officer for the Committee to Reelect the President (CRP). Some notebooks on the burglars soon led to more highly placed officials—to E. Howard Hunt, Jr., a writer of pulp spy novels, a romantic adventurer, and a former intelligence agent who had already performed some very special assignments for the White House; and to G. Gordon Liddy, a former CIA agent, a strange, violent lawyer who became the legal counsel for the CRP, and who, as later events revealed, masterminded not only the Watergate break-in but a whole repertoire of "dirty tricks" directed against the Democrats.

The Watergate affair soon fizzled as a major campaign issue. After the sensational early account, most newspapers dropped the issue. The seven defendants eventually pleaded guilty, thus avoiding full testimony. The angered trial judge, John J. Sirica, postponed final sentencing in what turned out later to be a successful strategy to get some of the defendants to talk. McGovern probably lost votes by the incredible claim that Nixon headed "the most morally corrupt administration in the history of the United States." The public made no concerted demand for the full truth, as if a seemingly healthy man, on learning of an early but developing cancer, tried to put it out of mind and go about his business as normal, plagued only by vague apprehensions.

By October 1972, the public had access to the broad outlines of the entire Watergate affair. Two young, low-level police reporters for the *Washington Post*, Robert Woodward and Carl Bernstein, pursued every possible lead, every remote clue, in a remarkable, award-winning example of investigative reporting. They slowly reconstructed a story so complex and so sinister that it was simply unbelievable to most readers. The *Post* reported that the Watergate bugging and burglary was only part of a massive campaign of political spying and sabotage directed both by the CRP, headed by former Attorney General John Mitchell, and by Nixon's immediate subordinates in the White House. The *Post* identified most key individuals who would later appear before a federal grand jury and a special Senate committee, revealed the bizarre financing schemes that channeled "laundered" campaign contributions into political espionage and dirty tricks, and noted the continued use of campaign funds by White House employees to buy the silence of the Watergate defendants, or what would later be acknowledged as the very heart of an elaborate coverup conspiracy. The *Post* at first gained not plaudits but resentment for its success. The Nixon administration, in the final weeks of a gloriously successful campaign, rather easily exploited its prestige and power to put down the noxious *Post* and, by implication, all other media still "out to get Nixon." It treated the *Post* reporters as greater criminals than the misguided Watergate seven (much later, after the *Post* accounts proved uncannily accurate, even Nixon apologized for his earlier attacks). Threatened by a loss of two television licenses in Florida, stock prices for the *Post* plummeted after the exposé. Vindication only came in the spring of 1973, when one after another the Watergate conspirators began to talk to

682

federal prosecutors and, through calculated newspaper leaks, to the public.

The big breaks came in late March and early April. On March 23, a trembling, disillusioned James McCord, Jr., gained a postponement of sentencing before Judge Sirica by agreeing to testify fully on the details of the break-in. After this first small crack in the Watergate, with awesome tremors reaching the White House, John Dean III, special counsel to Nixon and a principal architect of an elaborate coverup, began presenting evidence to federal prosecutors and surreptitiously to a now more than interested press. As a climax to all the speculation and rumors,

J. Edgar Hoover (right) and Attorney General John Mitchell (1913–) at the swearing in of four assistant attorneys general, February 14, 1972. *Wide World Photos*

a select Senate committee, chaired by the elderly, intellectually keen "guardian of the Constitution," Sam Ervin of North Carolina, began televised hearings on May 17. It completed the first phase of its hearings—entirely on the Watergate break-ins—by early August, and then resumed less publicized hearings in late September on dirty campaign tricks. By then the main story was clear, although it will take years to determine its fullest implications.

The story began back in 1971, with early campaign plans and financing. Nixon and his immediate advisers chose as their main campaign vehicle the CRP, largely bypassing the Republican National Committee and aggressively soliciting funds from bipartisan although not disinterested benefactors. The CRP eventually collected just over $60 million, and spent about $56 million on the most extravagant election campaign in American history. It raised over $11 million in the weeks before April 7, 1972, after which a more stringent campaign law required the publication

Two faces the American public came to know well as a result of live television coverage of the Watergate hearings, Senator Howard Baker, vice-chairman of the Senate Watergate Committee (left) and Senator Sam Ervin, chairman of the committee. *United Press International*

The Background

684

of the names of major donors to all campaign organizations. In September 1973, as a result of a successful private suit, the CRP had to reveal even the earlier names. Major corporations, with vital government favors at stake, illegally contributed at least $500,000; five of these corporations confessed their guilt in the summer of 1973 in hopes of less stringent penalties from the courts, but each noted the near extortionary pressures applied by CRP fund raisers. In one highly publicized but separate case, International Telephone and Telegraph agreed to finance the Republican convention in San Diego even as it sought administration favors on a proposed merger. The resulting revelations embarrassed Nixon and, joined with strong reservations in San Diego, helped shift the convention to Miami. In another influence-peddling case, a financier and alleged swindler, Robert Vesco, donated $200,000 to the CRP while under SEC investigation. He clearly sought favors, but received nothing but prosecution despite apparent promises of help from the two top CRP officials, director John Mitchell and finance director Maurice Stans, the former secretary of the treasury. In the aftermath, both Mitchell and Stans were indicted for trying to defraud the government, for obstructing justice, and for perjury, the first indictments of former cabinet officials since the Teapot Dome scandals. Other alleged irregularities in finances involved major labor unions, a favor-seeking dairy cooperative, and Las Vegas gambling interests owned by the famous recluse and tycoon, Howard Hughes. Such flagrant abuses only made more dramatic the symbiotic relationship of large corporations and the federal government, and highlighted a political process peculiarly responsive to major contributors. In the aftermath of Watergate, Congress considered several proposed election reforms, most of which included complete federal financing of presidential contests.

The Watergate break-in was only a small incident in a broad CRP effort to subvert the electoral process. Some of the more sinister tricks included a forged letter on the stationery of Senator Muskie, which charged his leading primary opponents of sexual irregularities; phony cables to "prove" that John F. Kennedy ordered the 1963 death of Vietnamese Premier Diem (a stop Ted Kennedy strategy neutralized by his refusal to become a candidate); and detailed investigations into the private lives of prominent Democrats. The plethora of funds invited far-out schemes. So did the ultrasuspicious and vengeful attitudes of so many CRP staffers, who balanced youthfulness and intelligence with a total lack of either ethical sensitivity or an elemental understanding of American politics. Thus, they adopted tactics which, even if undiscovered, promised only slight electoral gains, bungled several of these in execution, and contemptuously, recklessly, at times without much careful thought or consultation,

Senator Edmund Muskie (1914–), a Democratic contender for the 1972 presidential nomination, and one victim of the Committee to Reelect the President (CRP). This letter, which helped end his primary campaign, was forged by the CRP and implied that Muskie had accused his primary opponents of sexual irregularities. *The New York Times*

tried to manipulate and calculate the election results.

The Watergate incident originated as part of an elaborate political intelligence and sabotage plan worked out by G. Gordon Liddy in 1971. In two small meetings chaired by Attorney General John Mitchell, Liddy failed to win approval for his most far-out and ambitious schemes. He progressively reduced his plan and its costs from $1,000,000 to a final $250,000, and at a third rather casual meeting believed that he had secured Mitchell's approval (three witnesses later disagreed as to whether Mitchell rejected the plan a third time, specifically approved it, or remained silent). Whether he approved it or not, Mitchell as well as members of the White House staff accepted and utilized wiretaps and other illegally obtained information gathered by the motley crew assembled by Liddy. Several of his employees were Cuban refugees, with intense ideological reasons for trying to wreck Democratic prospects. Had the arrests not occurred, Liddy planned to continue the electronic surveillance up through the Democratic convention, and some later evidence at least suggests that his employees did continue it in spite of his arrest.

The Implications

Testimony about Watergate opened up a whole series of disturbing issues. The Ervin committee offered the American public an intimate glimpse into the elaborate executive office of the president that had evolved after the Government Reorganization Act of 1939. Here, in the hundreds of White House staff members, was a government within a government. Unlike traditional departments, it had no clear public accountability. In theory, the president controlled the staff. In fact, it often seemed, the staff controlled the president, and even in a sense helped create the president that the American public came to know. For it was the staff that channeled information to Nixon, determined who he would or would not see,

Top presidential aides John Ehrlichman (left) and H. R. Haldeman (right) in a Washington, D.C., courtroom. *United Press International*

and decided what information about the president to release to the newspapers. Nixon's chief staff members—H. R. Haldeman as chief of the White House staff, Henry Kissinger as adviser on foreign affairs, John Ehrlichman as domestic adviser—had much more power than cabinet officers. Except for Kissinger, they did not even deign to be courteous to congressmen. The situation was not new, but seemed more threatening because of the secretive, reclusive proclivities of Nixon and the bluntness and political naïveté of Haldeman and Ehrlichman.

For a people already apprehensive about government invasions of personal privacy and the much reported misuse of military intelligence organizations, the Watergate affair carried clear intimation of an early arrival of 1984. Symbolically, the issue of privacy climaxed in September 1973, with well-supported and later acknowledged charges that Nixon had ordered wiretaps on his sometimes errant brother, Donald Nixon (How close can one come to Big Brother?). This charge fit well within a pattern. Nixon's staff had even compiled an "enemies list," and calculated ways of embarrassing those on it, if not by government harassment at least by withholding government favors. Nixon had long exhibited an exaggerated sensitivity to opposition, and a tendency to fight back at a low level, a tendency that pushed him close to the bounds of legality in earlier campaigns. According to testimony by his closest staff members, he not uncharacteristically equated his own programs and goals with the good of the country, and had difficulty tolerating open opposition, even down to lone demonstrators in front of the White House. In a more sweeping way than his predecessors, he was inclined to use the power of government to bring his enemies to account. Yet, critics who accused him of paranoia too easily overlooked similar traits in Democratic predecessors.

During the demonstrations and campus violence of 1970, and in the wake of the leaked Pentagon Papers, Nixon despaired of the performance of domestic intelligence agencies and actually formed a small, informal White House investigations unit, or what later would be known as the notorious "plumbers" (they plugged leaks) and which included both Hunt and Liddy of Watergate fame. Only the opposition of a jealous J. Edgar Hoover blocked a more ambitious, interagency, super intelligence organization with primary responsibilities in the domestic area. Nixon's plumbers went right to work. In 1971 they burglarized the offices of a California psychiatrist in an unsuccessful effort to find damaging material on Daniel Ellsberg, the person who leaked the Pentagon Papers. John Ehrlichman, who ordered the investigation, later tried to justify such illegal acts on the grounds of national security, and talked vaguely of possible leaks of the Pentagon Papers to the Russian Embassy. In fact, a whole series of documents indicated that the evidence sought was to become part of a major government campaign to discredit Ellsberg in the eyes of the public. Later, the architects of the burglary, including Ehrlichman (he lied about his involvement in early testimony), were indicted by California courts. Such undercover operations against private citizens (no one accused the psychiatrist of any crime, although he exercised his right of refusing to cooperate with FBI interrogators), coupled with the elaborate use of bugging and surveillance by the CRP, seemed to establish the federal government, or at least the White House branch of it, as the leading violator of civil liberties.

Just as disturbing, although not as unprecedented, were attempts to compromise independent federal agencies. In the aftermath of the Watergate arrests, White House officials desperately tried to get the CIA to provide cover. To its credit, the CIA refused to claim the seven arrested culprits or even to block an investigation into CRP campaign funds "laundered" through Mexican banks, after even Nixon expressed a concern that such a bothersome investigation might endanger foreign intelligence operations. But the CIA did overstep its legal jurisdiction by outfitting Hunt and Liddy with its latest intelligence devices and providing false identification papers for their domestic "plumbing." The FBI, seemingly so independent under Hoover, succumbed to political pressures under his interim successor, a well-meaning but naïve L. Patrick Gray III. Gray conducted the original investigation of the Watergate affair, but passed on much of his raw data to John Dean and thus to the very White House group managing the coverup. More embarrassing, he accepted from Dean and Haldeman some extremely sensitive papers taken from the White House safe of E. Howard Hunt and, following what he took to be a clear although oblique order, eventually destroyed them and with them the most damaging evidence on Liddy's various schemes. By his confession of this poor judgment, Gray lost any chance of Senate approval as permanent FBI director. Because of his fumbling, and at times all too honest testimony, Nixon soon lost all confidence in Gray but, instead of firing him, allowed him to suffer through weeks of public humiliation.

With Gray's career wrecked, the FBI position was again open and available as a desperate tool to facilitate the coverup of illegal government activities. In the critical 1973 trial of Daniel Ellsberg, the federal government lost any possible chance of conviction through a series of prosecution blunders that led the judge to declare a mistrial. Always belatedly, and under pressure from Judge W. Matthew Bryne, Jr., the prosecution eventually submitted a large body of secreted information vital to the defense. This included records from an FBI wiretap of a phone used by Ellsberg in preparing his defense, but above all the startling revelation about Ellsberg's psychiatrist. In what seemed an obvious White House effort to prevent this damaging revelation, John Ehrlichman twice contacted Judge Bryne about his availability for the vacant FBI directorship. He gave him the clear impression that he was Nixon's first choice, and during a trial recess even invited him to San Clemente where he briefly chatted with Nixon.

Not as shocking, and not as unusual, the Nixon administration tried, without great success, to use the Internal Revenue Service to punish enemies and reward friends. They succeeded in quashing some audits and initiating others, tactics used successfully by preceding administrations. Even as the Watergate hearings made all the headlines, another Senate committee probed the procedures of the IRS. It uncovered a whole spectrum of favors for the wealthy, and a frequent abuse of IRS authority in dealing with small, unrepresented, and easily intimidated taxpayers. Later revelations about Nixon's own finances seemed to make him first among the privileged.

In the summer of 1973, as the Ervin committee slowly, repetitiously, but grippingly elicited the most sordid details on Watergate, one big question remained tantalizingly in the foreground—how responsible was Nixon? As revealed in endless polls, a majority of a now cynical public seemed assured that he knew quite a bit, and that he had refused to "come clean" in two lame television speeches. By late July Nixon's confidence rating dropped from an inauguration high of 68 percent to a low of 31 percent, the lowest rating for any president since the darkest days of the Truman administration. Amidst growing talk of impeachment, a few daring congressmen began preparing bills. Nixon seemed to do little to help his own case. He appeared more defensive and beleaguered as the summer advanced, and inspired little confidence by dissembling speeches that had to be inaccurate at least on small details. He called no press conferences. Yet, he did respond to the pressures, particularly in reluctantly dismissing Ehrlichman and Haldeman, and in appointing a special, completely independent Watergate prosecutor—Harvard law professor Archibald Cox. With his most loyal staff disgraced, he desperately shuffled his cabinet and tried to rebuild an effective White House organization.

Through all this, Nixon was completely consistent on one point—he had no prior knowledge of the Watergate break-in, and until March of 1973 knew nothing of any coverup. He condemned the illegal deeds, took ultimate but no proximate responsibility for what happened, dismissed but did not repudiate his more loyal and "overzealous" staff members, and by August tried to place much of the blame for Watergate on an infectious climate of "lawlessness" that began with the antiwar movement. In his counterattack on the recessed Ervin committee, Nixon deplored the con-

tinued rooting in the mire of Watergate, asked that the issue be left with
the courts, and begged support for administrative efforts to solve pressing
domestic and foreign problems. He quite correctly noted that no one had
produced any evidence of his prior knowledge of Watergate. In a chal-
lengeable argument, he also stressed that only John Dean, the one defec-
tor among the immediate White House staff, had testified to his early
knowledge and complicity in a coverup. In their testimony, Ehrlichman
and Haldeman supported Nixon on every point. But Dean contended
that certain Nixon remarks as early as September 1972, indicated his
knowledge of efforts to limit the public disclosures to the convicted
Watergate seven. He also interpreted later Nixon comments about possible
executive clemency as further proof of complicity. The earliest alleged
proof of presidential responsibility, unanswered by Nixon, came from
L. Patrick Gray. Three weeks after the break-in Gray claimed that he
placed an urgent call to the president to complain of early efforts by
the White House staff to block his full FBI investigation, but received
only an evasive and casual reply. Thus, the issue of presidential guilt
came down to conflicting testimony, which in ordinary circumstances
could never be resolved. Enter the White House tapes.

John Dean III, former
White House counsel, tes-
tifying before the Senate
Watergate Committee.
His wife, Maureen, is in
the rear. In March 1973
James McCord, Jr., leaked
the information that
cracked the Watergate case
wide open. In April, Dean
began presenting evi-
dence to federal prosecutors and to the press.
Wide World Photos

In the most startling, because least expected, revelation of the Ervin committee, a White House employee stated that the Secret Service had wired Nixon's three principal White House offices and his phones in order to record all conversations. Haldeman and Ehrlichman also had recording devices. This revelation was disconcerting news for Americans, who usually identified such devices only with totalitarian countries. Congressmen who had talked fully and frankly with Nixon were incensed, while civil libertarians worried over both the existence of such tapes and their safekeeping. Nixon lamely justified the recordings as a means of preserving an official record of his presidency, apparently not so much for historians as for his own later use. The very existence of the tapes meant that much of the controverted testimony about Nixon's personal involvement in the Watergate coverup (by now this was an almost obsessive concern of the Ervin committee) might now be resolved. Accordingly, both the Senate committee and Special Prosecutor Cox requested, and then subpoenaed, a selected list of tapes. Nixon refused to surrender them. He insisted that they would generally support his position as against Dean, although he admitted ambiguities that could lead different people to conflicting inferences. He also believed it vital for him to protect other, off-guard comments made by himself or his staff. Possibly he also wanted to hide from the public his much respected command of profanity and obscenity, by all reports as rich and varied as that of Lyndon Johnson or even Dwight Eisenhower. Nixon stressed that the confidentiality of presidential consultation outweighed the possible evidential value of the tapes. When Judge Sirica ruled that Nixon had to turn over to him certain of the tapes, Nixon appealed the decision and promised, a bit ambiguously, to abide by a "definitive" ruling of the Supreme Court.

The tapes posed several issues, most with no clear precedents to guide the courts. In his most appealing argument, Nixon suggested that confidentiality within his official staff was necessary for the effective functioning of the presidency, and at least as deserving of constitutional protection as the privacy of confessions to a priest, revelations to a psychiatrist, or privileged sources for a newsman. Nixon was on strong ground in refusing the tapes to the Ervin committee, for the independence of the executive branch surely set limits on the legislative power of investigation. But Nixon faced almost insurmountable odds in his effort to keep the tapes away from the courts. He had already weakened his own case by lending several crucial tapes to Haldeman after his resignation from the White House staff; this meant that a private citizen had already heard the tapes and probably used them so as more ably to present an administrative position and to discredit John Dean, who had no access to them. Cox only requested selected tapes that directly related to criminal prosecutions. His goal was hardly the discovery of confidential information, but only the testing of conflicting testimony that, in its totality, had already bared the nature of White House conversations. Since the tapes were material evidence for major crimes, the courts possibly faced insurmountable difficulties in convicting anyone without such evidence (in October 1973, lawyers for John Mitchell alleged that certain tapes were necessary for developing an adequate defense in the Vesco case, an allegation sure to appear again and again). Finally, Nixon considerably weakened his legal case by earlier waiving executive privilege and permitting his staff to testify freely about the controverted conversations. If not privileged before, how could the information become privileged later? Thus, the most unfriendly critics of Nixon argued that he had assumed a position above the law. Even Republican congressmen, and apparently a majority of the public, believed he should have surrendered the specified tapes without necessarily implicating the ultimate constitutional issues and without conceding any legal obligation. Such a voluntary action need not have threatened either a balanced separation of powers or the necessary prerogatives of an effective executive.

The Watergate crimes exemplified a new type of political scandal, and by far the most serious in our history. Those responsible had tried to effect a coup, to assure their own continuance in power by illegal means. The conspirators were rarely motivated by private greed. Most probably believed that the ends justified even their most sordid means, or else they suppressed concern over the means as they kept their minds on details and on future achievements. John Mitchell in effect admitted complicity in the coverup because of the transcending importance of a Nixon victory. Rather than face even the remote possibility of defeat, the CRP leadership (youthful, rarely experienced in politics, drawn directly from law offices or campuses) chose not only to manipulate but by their very excesses to subvert the existing electoral system. As they so often lamented in the aftermath, they were surely not the first. And, indeed, much that was ugly in Watergate had long been at least a minor element in American politics, a recourse of desperate men in both parties. To an extent, Watergate was an overreaction to past political defeats, or to the easy success of Democratic candidates. Nixon had suffered from the finesse, the cold and calculated use of power by Kennedy in 1960, and possibly lost that election because of some old-fashioned voting frauds in Illinois. This past rankled, and helped lead to Nixon's artless efforts to master the political game. Not surprisingly, the Nixon administration suffered from one of the immediate consequences of its artless abuse of power—a much more searching and critical scrutiny of the whole political process than journalists and commentators had ever dared under Nixon's Democratic predecessors. Soon everyone was talking about disturbing revelations of privilege in high places, or about the monarchial trappings of the presidency, issues that never made the news in the glory days of the Nixon administration.

The Naked Emperor

Few feudal kings were as pampered and indulged as the contemporary American president. His private life now belies every traditional ideal of social equality, and is a standing affront to the memory of a Jackson or even a Calvin Coolidge. The president occupies a lavish mansion, has a retinue of servants to cater to his every need, receives the best medical care without cost, has a built-in guarantee of great private wealth, enjoys a fleet of limousines, helicopters, and airplanes to carry him on both public and private trips. He enjoys tax privileges denied ordinary citizens, and even in a four-year reign collects invaluable private gifts. He owns his own personal papers, even though the public invests them with their high commercial value, and can automatically collect enormous advances from publishers for his memoirs, which ghost writers usually compose. Nixon inherited these privileges. But more conspicuously than his predecessors, he enjoyed them to their fullest, occasionally pushing some of them to the very limits of legality. As his luster dimmed during Watergate, he had to fend off a series of damaging accusations about his Florida and California estates, about government expenditures at each, and about complicated financial transactions between him and a few wealthy benefactors.

Unlike former presidents, Nixon established two vacation White Houses; his palatial ocean-front home in San Clemente, California, and his vacation compound at Key Biscayne, Florida. In addition, he frequently enjoyed the government provided retreat at Camp David, Maryland, and even a government protected but privately owned hideaway at Grand Cay in the Bahamas. In 1973 an increasingly beleaguered and defensive Nixon seemed to alternate between all these sites, thus requiring the use of his $80 million jet fleet, his dozen large helicopters, the elaborate communications equipment, and the hundreds of people involved in serving and protecting him. No one could estimate the millions spent on his trips. Even clearer was the $10 million spent by the government at the Nixon properties. This financed major changes at both San Clemente and Key Biscayne, changes made in the name of security, but a security that embraced health and comfort as much as protection against assassins. Much of the new landscaping, the new heating facilities, the den furniture, the heat for swimming pools, the improved access roads, the special wooden fences, and even golf carts represented valuable and enduring private assets, yet apparently gifts exempt from normal taxation. Newsmen sus-

pected chicanery in many of the seemingly nonsafety improvements. Nixon, who insisted that he did not personally order any of the changes, felt unfairly slandered by the detailed newspaper reports, particularly since some of the changes reflected overly elaborate security precautions that often frustrated Nixon more than anyone else. These grew out of the Kennedy assassination. But Nixon was at least vulnerable for taking advantage of so much governmental generosity at so many sites, and for seeming to exploit every built-in privilege of his office. His expensive private trips accompanied a gasoline shortage and government appeals for consumer restraint. He even over air-conditioned his White House office in order to enjoy his fireplace during summer months.

Nixon also faced probing questions about his real estate investments. At the very least, he seemed devious in so long concealing or countenancing false accounts about his private finances. Perhaps the fairest judgment is that Nixon, who grew up in modest circumstances, always carefully attended to his personal finances, freely availing himself of the best tax and investment advice and frequently accepting loans and gifts from wealthy friends and patrons. The presidency multiplied his financial opportunities and added to his patrons. Two of his closest and most wealthy confidants, Robert Abplanalp and Charles G. Rebozo, helped him acquire both his estates. With minimal funds of his own, and a friendly $625,000 loan, Nixon purchased his twenty-nine-acre San Clemente property for about

Gathered in the living room of the western White House in San Clemente, California (January 6, 1971) are dinner guests of the Nixons'. Left to right: Bob Hope; Tricia Nixon; the first lady; Gerald Ford, now vice-president, then minority leader of the House; Mrs. Ford; the president; Mrs. Hope; Henry Kissinger, now secretary of state, then assistant to the president on national security; and golfer Arnold Palmer. *United Press International*

$52,000 an acre. Then, in a complicated deal, he officially sold twenty-three acres, but not the mansion, to Abplanalp and Rebozo for $54,000 an acre, canceling the loan and most of the mortgage indebtedness. Thus, with a net investment of approximately $300,000, Nixon acquired a mansion worth up to $3 million by local estimates, and in addition retained the use of the whole acreage. Meanwhile, he more than doubled his money on real estate investments in the Miami area. These deals, made possible by obliging friends, and savings from his salary and investments, enabled Nixon to triple his wealth in his first five presidential years, and even by his own conservative estimate to become a millionaire by 1974.

To disarm critics and to refute some widely circulating rumors about financial indiscretions, Nixon decided upon an unprecedented action for an American president—a full accounting of his private wealth and full details on his federal tax returns during his presidential years. The revelations, given to the public just before the Christmas holidays of 1973, defused the wildest rumors, won Nixon plaudits for his candor, but only helped reinforce Nixon's reputation for tricky deals and for an overly zealous pursuit of self-interest. Particularly embarrassing was his payment of only $792.81 in federal income taxes in 1970 and only $878.03 in 1971, and this on a salary of $200,000 plus an additional expense account of $50,000, which Nixon also declared, perhaps illegitimately, as salary in order to increase his allowable charitable deductions. The one major deduction (Nixon gave only a pittance to churches or to organized charities) was a gift of a part of his vice-presidential papers, hurriedly appraised by a so-called "expert" for $576,000, to the National Archives. He used an income tax loophole indulged by several prominent Americans until Congress closed it in 1969. By pro-rating this gift over three years, Nixon virtually escaped any federal liability. Yet, the gift itself may not have been legal. Much of the evidence indicated Nixon did not fully meet the 1969 deadline in completing the conveyance of the papers. Nixon agreed to submit this and other questionable tax issues to a congressional committee and to abide by its final ruling.

In other tax decisions Nixon at least pushed at the limits of legality. As most Americans in similar circumstances, he quite legitimately postponed payment of capital gains taxes from the sale of his New York apartment in 1969 by using the money to help buy his San Clemente estate. Despite this, and despite his voting in California, as president he never filed or paid California state income taxes, on the excuse that he was not a resident of California for tax purposes. Since the District of Columbia exempts elected federal officials from local income taxes, Nixon was able to escape all the burdens of state citizenship. Finally, Nixon paid no capital gains tax on the later notorious and very profitable sale of twenty-three acres of his San Clemente estate. His tax accountant, guided by the exact amount received in the sale, conveniently estimated the value of the remaining estate so low as to cancel any gains. Even Nixon's later private audit, which still drastically undervalued the estate, showed a capital gain of $117,370, an amount that Nixon seemed willing to declare, belatedly, for tax purposes.

And Agnew Too

After a summer of travail, Nixon surely welcomed the almost unbelievable but diverting tribulations of Vice-President Spiro Agnew. Suddenly America had a new scandal that was so traditional and old-fashioned as to seem almost comforting. During a detailed federal investigation of influence-peddling in Maryland, originally aimed at Democratic politicians, the Department of Justice heard extended and completely persuasive testimony implicating Agnew in bribery and extortion. In late September 1973, it began presenting its evidence to a federal grand jury in Baltimore, in expectation of an early indictment. The evidence indicated that, for over a decade, as executive of Baltimore County, as governor of Maryland, and as vice-president, Agnew had received periodic payments from engineering firms as required compensation for lucrative county or state contracts. Agnew collected well over $100,000, mostly in periodic, small payments. He continued to accept furtive envelopes with cash payments through 1972, but was never able to deliver on major federal contracts. As Agnew later lamented, he simply followed a traditional pattern for awarding professional contracts in Maryland, a state with a long tradition of informal, personalized politics. Unlike more artful politicians, Agnew never exploited the legal even if questionable roads to wealth so brilliantly exploited by a Lyndon Johnson or a Richard Nixon. He asked for bribes in order to meet social obligations and higher living standards that he believed to be necessitated by the offices he held.

Agnew at first responded to early newspaper leaks about the investigation with righteous indignation. He publicly denied any wrongdoing and condemned the compromising of secret grand jury proceedings. His open and frank news conferences, and a particularly bitter but fighting speech in California, seemed to point up Nixon's more defensive and cautious response to the Watergate revelations. Agnew rallied his large Republican constituency, gained standing in popularity ratings, and talked vaguely about a frame-up by Nixon's own Justice Department. In early October he vowed to fight his case before the courts and before the public until completely exonerated, and won considerable sympathy by admitting that even the suggestion of major scandal had probably doomed his presidential ambitions. To the later shock of most of his friends, this surface posturing concealed a long and difficult bargaining process.

The Justice Department kept Nixon informed of its Agnew investigation. By late summer of 1973 Nixon knew the gravity of the charges and the weight of the evidence. He was confident that, sooner or later, Agnew would have to surrender his office, and he believed the sooner the better. In early September Agnew's attorneys tried to arrange a plea bargain with the Justice Department, but could not gain their key demand —that Agnew avoid any jail sentence as a reward for his resignation. Nixon's lawyers joined the bargaining, but also failed to find any mutually acceptable compromise. The Justice Department was sure of its ability to prosecute successfully, and anxious to show its independence after its seeming failures in the early prosecution of the Watergate conspirators. For almost a month, Agnew held out for a minimal, nonjail sentence while the Justice Department insisted upon a guilty plea and at least a short incarceration.

Agnew was always in a strong bargaining position. In a vain hope that he could shift the inquiry from the federal courts, he appealed unsuccessfully for a nonimpeachment investigation by the House of Representatives. His lawyers also asked a federal judge for an injunction to squash

Spiro T. Agnew on nationwide television after resigning his post as vice-president of the United States. In his television address he denied all wrongdoing, praised Vice-President designate Gerald Ford, and called for political reform. Agnew ended the broadcast with the words, "Thank you, good-night, and farewell." *Wide World Photos*

the grand jury proceedings. They cited not only the prejudicial effects of the preindictment publicity, but also argued an unresolved but quite persuasive constitutional position—that a vice-president could not be indicted or tried on criminal charges until impeached and removed from office (otherwise, a vice-president might succeed to the presidency while on trial). These legal moves, tied to his tough public stance, suggested long, agonizing months of litigation all the way up to the Supreme Court, or precedent-setting impeachment proceedings, neither welcomed by the Nixon administration. Under White House pressure, Attorney General Elliot Richardson finally capitulated. Plea bargaining resumed on October 6. Agnew quickly accepted a more lenient bargain.

On October 10, 1973, in one of the most unusual and dramatic moments of American history, the vice-president of the United States and the attorney general confronted each other in a Baltimore courtroom. Before a federal judge, Agnew pleaded *nola contendere* (an equivalent of guilty) to a single charge of income tax evasion. In a brief statement, he admitted receiving $29,500 in 1967, which he used for personal expenses and did not declare on his income tax return. The judge assessed a $10,000 fine and a three-year, unsupervised probation, or an almost unbelievably light sentence for such a major felony. As an obvious concession to disappointed and hard-working prosecutors, the court also released a detailed, forty-page summary of the evidence against Agnew, or the part of the bargain most damaging to Agnew, who still faced possible state criminal charges and civil action by the Internal Revenue Service. Almost simultaneous with his court appearance, Agnew submitted his formal resignation from the vice-presidency. Both the judge and the attorney general excused the light sentence on grounds of national interest. But it was clear that this was the price they had to pay for his resignation. Thus Agnew, the very symbol of law and order, a long-time enemy of permissive courts, became the most notable beneficiary of plea bargaining and a very permissive sentence, all to the anger and bitterness of those Americans who had suffered jail sentences for relatively minor crimes.

On October 12 Nixon nominated Representative Gerald Ford of Michigan as the new vice-president. At a special White House gathering of cabinet, Congress, and diplomatic corps, Nixon seemed his old, confident self. Almost gone were the lines of care deposited by Watergate, as he seemed to thrive on the pomp and pageantry of the occasion. Briefly forgotten were the still unresolved legal issues surrounding the presidential tapes, and remote but still conceivable impeachment proceedings against Nixon. During the formal presentation, Nixon never once mentioned Agnew, but the man and the name still haunted the proceedings, for never before had a vice-president had to resign under pressure and on the verge of conviction for major crimes. Ford seemed a good antidote for the lingering bad taste engendered by Agnew. As most of Nixon's appointments, he possessed neither brilliance nor charisma, and seemed unlikely to become a presidential candidate in 1976. A loyal Republican, sympathetic to Nixon's domestic and foreign policies, and well-liked in the Congress, Ford promised better lines of communication between the administration and Congress. By the terms of the Twenty-fifth Amendment, both houses had to approve the Ford nomination. Neither acted quickly, using their vote as a lever to pressure Nixon on the White House tapes. Ford finally took the oath of office in a ceremony at the Capitol on December 6, 1973.

The Tapes— Phase Two

Almost unnoticed during the most intense moments of the Agnew drama, the Federal Court of Appeals for the District of Columbia rendered its decision on the contested White House tapes. It upheld Judge Sirica's right to hear them, and in partial justification cited Nixon's earlier waiver of executive privilege for his staff. The decision invited the Supreme Court to overrule Nixon on the specific, contested tapes, yet without specifically rejecting the general principle of confidentiality. Everyone expected Nixon to appeal. He did not. In a bid to avoid such an ultimate confrontation, on October 19 he negotiated a seeming compromise with the chairman and vice-chairman of the Senate Watergate Committee— Senators Ervin and Howard Baker. Unfortunately, the major participants could not later agree on the exact terms of the compromise. Ervin and Baker, already rebuffed by the lower courts in their attempt to gain the tapes for their committee, believed Nixon had agreed to surrender, both to their committee and to the courts, edited transcripts of the controverted tapes, excluding only extraneous or national security materials. Senator John Stennis of Mississippi was to hear all the tapes in order to certify the integrity and completeness of the transcripts. But as Nixon's lawyers interpreted the deal, Nixon was to prepare summaries of the tapes, possibly including some direct quotations, and provide these to the committee and the courts. The ailing and elderly Stennis, a long-time supporter of Nixon, but a Democrat too well respected in the Senate to elicit major opposition, was to certify only the accuracy of the summaries. Later, it seemed, the crucial difference of interpretation involved not the critical content of the tapes, but the often blunt and crude language that Nixon wanted to share only with Stennis. Whatever the exact terms of the bargain, however, it blew up almost as soon as announced, precipi-

tating the most explosive political crisis of a hectic year and one of the
gravest in American history.

Special Prosecutor Cox was the key figure in the explosion. For several weeks Nixon's lawyers, who privately doubted a favorable ruling by
the Supreme Court, had worked to secure a compromise on the nine contested tapes. Attorney General Richardson helped explore possible terms,
and particularly tried to find a formula acceptable to Cox, who was not
averse to compromise but who was very careful to protect the evidential
value of the tapes and to keep open his access to other White House records. He even accepted the idea of a referee, but preferred someone who
could assess the evidential value of the material (he or Judge Sirica were
best qualified for this). Cox was particularly suspicious of frequent White
House appeals to a vaguely defined "national security," which if accepted
as an excuse for concealment gave the administration the unilateral right
to screen all released tapes and documents. Richardson failed in his media-

Attorney General Elliot
Richardson (right) and
Special Watergate prose-
cutor Archibald Cox (left)
at the start of the Senate
Judiciary Committee hear-
ings in May 1973. *Wide
World Photos*

tion. Nixon, already apprehensive about Cox and his staff of bright young lawyers, resentful of Cox's investigation of his private finances or those of close friends, became convinced that Cox was partisan, out to discredit his administration rather than conduct an impartial inquiry. Since Cox seemed likely to reject any compromise acceptable to the administration, Nixon went ahead with his private bargain with an amenable Senate committee. He surely suspected that Cox would resent or even repudiate the compromise. He took the risk, since he welcomed a clear excuse to fire Cox and terminate his investigation.

After winning his compromise with Ervin and Baker, Nixon ordered Cox, as an employee of the executive branch, to cease all his efforts in the courts to obtain the tapes or other presidential materials. Cox immediately repudiated the compromise. In a tense but fluent news conference on the next day, October 20, he announced that, in accordance with the commitments made to the Senate at the time of his appointment, he would advise Judge Sirica that Nixon had not complied with the court order asking for the tapes, and that continued noncompliance would, in his opinion, place Nixon in contempt of court. Cox thus openly defied Nixon, upholding what he defined as his obligations to a system of law. He explained that summaries of the tapes would probably not serve as admissible evidence in the courts, that the tapes were no more crucial in his successful prosecution of the guilty than other, more extensive documentary material still in the White House, and that the Nixon administration, despite promises of cooperation, had so far not surrendered a number of requested items, thus delaying and impeding his investigation. A troubled and tense America awaited Nixon's response to Cox. It came in a few hours. He asked Attorney General Richardson to fire Cox. Richardson, a friend of Cox, sure of his integrity as special prosecutor, and mindful of his earlier commitment to the Senate, resigned rather than comply. Assistant Attorney General William Ruckelshaus, in a display of rare political courage, likewise refused the order; Nixon fired him before he could resign. Finally, a virtually unknown solicitor general became acting attorney general and promptly fired Cox. Nixon abolished the office of special prosecutor. Within an hour FBI agents surrounded Cox's offices and secured all his files.

Nixon surely did not bargain for the intense public reaction, which he later blamed on the media. Richardson and Cox, appointed in the midst of the first Watergate crisis, invested with a special role by the Senate, symbolized detachment, political independence, and fairness. During all the sinister revelations about a government that had so compromised law and elementary principles of fair play, the sweeping probe by Cox, the promise of coming indictments of high officials, had provided an elemental assurance for otherwise disillusioned Americans. The system still worked. It could cleanse itself. Now they lost even this assurance. Upon his dismissal, Cox expressed the pervasive concern—was America to remain a government of law or would it become a government of men? The FBI agents around Cox's former office seemed all too reminiscent of Nazi Germany. Foreign correspondents weighed the possibilities of a military coup, and some Americans for the first time tried to face up even to this possibility. The intermittent talk of impeachment, a minor chord during the summer of 1973, now swept the country. An early poll showed over 40 percent of Americans favored early impeachment. Over the Veteran's Day weekend congressmen plowed through stacks of telegrams, almost all demanding Nixon's impeachment or resignation. Although a majority of cautious House members did not commit themselves to immediate impeachment proceedings, only a handful openly opposed it. Other congressmen joined in appeals for Nixon's resignation, or supported a new, special prosecutor to be created by congressional action.

Judge Sirica represented Nixon's last hope. If he accepted the earlier compromise, then Nixon would be in no danger of contempt and the House would lose its one, best excuse for impeachment. On Tuesday, October 24, Sirica reconvened his two grand juries, stressed their continuing responsibilities, and made clear he would ask presidential lawyers to show cause why Nixon should not be held in contempt. On that same afternoon, presidential Counsel Charles A. Wright appeared in Sirica's courtroom, in the second dramatic court confrontation in a month. Much more was now at stake than in the Agnew case. A group of youthful lawyers from Cox's former staff clustered together in the courtroom, half gloating, half frightened, waiting to hear what they assumed would be arguments to support Nixon's noncompliance with a court order. Instead, Wright announced that Nixon would surrender the tapes as ordered. He seemed to have capitulated to all the pressure. This crisis seemed over, so suddenly and so unexpectedly as to leave most Americans in a state of shock. With less haste, and diminished enthusiasm, the House Judiciary Committee proceeded with its preimpeachment inquiry, but short of new revelations of wrongdoing almost no one believed it would ever eventuate in a vote favoring impeachment.

The crisis over the tapes paralleled the climax of a renewed Arab-Israeli war. Once again, Nixon was able to use a seeming success in diplomacy to counter intense domestic criticism. On October 25, even as the United Nations tried to implement a cease-fire agreed to by both Israel and Egypt, and secured through the cooperation of the United States and the Soviet Union, Egypt asked both major powers to send troops to police the existing boundaries. Nixon emphatically rejected such big-power involvement. Already, the two powers had resupplied the two sides and had maintained a rough military balance. This balance seemed threatened when the Soviet Union made early moves to send her own troops into the area despite American opposition. In what he later called a precautionary move, Nixon alerted American military forces. Kissinger helped persuade Soviet leaders, who claimed to be perplexed by all the unwarranted excitement, to reject any direct military involvement and to continue their cooperation in seeking a negotiated settlement. In the wake of a short, intense, and indecisive war, some type of negotiation between the warring parties seemed closer than ever before, and would indeed begin in Geneva in December.

Nixon followed this seeming diplomatic success (many believed he overreacted, or called the military alert to divert attention from the firing of Cox) with an embittered, often tense news conference. He reacted angrily to rumors of his poor health or mental instability. He alleged that the United States had met and mastered the greatest challenge since the Cuban missile crisis. In the most bitter denunciation of the press and television ever offered by an American president, he decried the vicious and distorted interpretation of his motives in offering a compromise on the tapes. In a move to block a new investigation by a special prosecutor appointed either by Sirica or by act of Congress, Nixon promised that his Justice Department would appoint a new prosecutor within a week, and that his administration would fully cooperate with him.

On November 1, Nixon jointly nominated Republican Senator William Saxbe of Ohio as attorney general, and a respected Houston lawyer, Leon Jaworski, as special prosecutor. The selections maximized the chances of some type of carefully qualified Senate approval, lessened the chances of a separate congressionally authorized prosecutor, but scarcely mollified new suspicions of Nixon created by the final, most incredulous surprise in the long battle over the tapes. According to embarrassed White House lawyers, two of the most crucial tapes did not exist. By their account, even Nixon did not know they were missing until after he consented to turn them over to Sirica. White House technicians offered a detailed explanation—Nixon received a vital, post-Watergate call from John Mitchell on an untapped phone, and an expired tape prevented a record of a crucial Nixon conversation with John Dean. After all the seeming evasions of the past, such testimony did little to suppress widespread assumptions of just another devious trick, and this at a time when Nixon's popularity had already reached an all-time low (only a 22 percent confidence vote in one late October poll).

This was not the end. In late November an embarrassed White House lawyer had to inform Judge Sirica that a crucial eighteen-minute segment

of a June 20, 1972 tape (a conversation between Nixon and Haldeman about Watergate) had apparently been accidently erased. Sirica began an extensive hearing to ascertain the facts. Nixon's beleaguered legal staff desperately hinted at sinister and unknown forces, but clearly sought a scapegoat in Nixon's private secretary, Rose Mary Woods. Miss Woods, in testimony before the court, acknowledged playing and transcribing the tape, and even conceded the possibility that she accidentally erased a short segment while answering a phone. Her "boo-boo," or Rose Mary's "stretch," became an occasion of much humor and many cartoons, for a reenactment of her mistake showed that in order to have effected the erasure she needed the agility of an acrobat. An unsatisfied Sirica submitted the tapes to a panel of technical experts. After six weeks of testing, the panel reported on January 15, 1974 that the missing segment had been erased, not in one continuous re-recording, but in five to nine shorter, often overlapping segments. No accident by Miss Woods could account for it. It seemed almost certain that someone had played a part of the tape, reversed it, and deliberately erased that segment by re-recording over it, and then continued the same procedure for the remaining segments, or in fact through all the Watergate conversations. Marks on the tape identified the segments, while a few erasures did not quite overlap, leaving minute but unintelligible segments of the earlier voices. Since only Nixon and possibly four staff members had ever had access to the tapes, the testimony

United States District Court Judge John J. Sirica, named *Time* magazine's "Man of the Year" for 1973, has taken a hard line with all Watergate defendants. *Wide World Photos*

was particularly damaging. More than any earlier testimony, it challenged the integrity of the White House. The new revelations almost coincided with the belated beginnings of an impeachment inquiry by the House Judiciary Committee, and considerably increased the likelihood of House impeachment. Most estimates indicated a lengthy investigation, with no final vote on impeachment until the summer of 1974.

Nixon's desperate but unsuccessful efforts to put Watergate behind him, or to dissipate the thirst for scandal by the Agnew affair, were not entirely self-serving. By the summer of 1973 the United States faced some of the most troubling economic problems since the depression of the thirties. By August, the United States suffered a rate of inflation not even duplicated in the aftermath of World War II and by the winter of 1973–1974 by an energy crisis not duplicated since World War II. Food prices led an upward spiral that prodded a 1973 cost of living increase of over 8 percent (the index rose by almost 2 percent in August alone and by an annual rate of 9.6 percent in the second half of 1973). Retail food prices in August rose by 6.1 percent, or the largest increase since 1933. Overall wholesale prices rose 5.8 percent, led by farm products, up an astounding 23.1 percent in only one month, or the sharpest rise in this century. Fortunately, some of the most dramatic increases were temporary aberrations, based on short-term scarcities and worsened by food hoarding. While retail prices continued to rise, overall wholesale prices fell by 1.8 in September, again led by a 6 percent drop in farm and food prices (for all of 1973, wholesale prices rose by 18.2 percent, promising even higher retail prices in 1974). In all of 1973 price increases easily outpaced increases in personal income, meaning an overall loss in living standards of at least 1 percent, and by some calculations by over 3 percent. For over two years several categories of wage-laborers had suffered a decline in real income as a result of inflation. Americans with fixed incomes, including many retired people, faced a drastic loss of purchasing power, and if inflationary trends continued they could only look forward to financial disaster.

The Nixon administration failed in its anti-inflation measures largely because of built-in pressures beyond its control, but in part because it failed to adopt a consistent economic policy. Early in 1973, Nixon heralded a relaxation of most economic controls. Phase III quickly ran aground on a wave of spring price increases (wholesale prices leaped by an annual rate of 21.9 percent in the first quarter, 23.4 in the second). This almost forced Nixon to reinstitute temporary price controls on most consumer goods, and to formulate a new, Phase IV program of regulated but flexible prices and wages. For most items, this went into effect in mid-August (meat and gasoline remained frozen into September), but the wage and price boards almost immediately faced overwhelming pressures for increases. Angry gasoline dealers closed stations on several weekends and soon gained the higher prices and profits they believed necessary to remain in business. All these efforts to slow inflation succeeded in only one sense—they did not so crudely dampen the economy as to increase unemployment or lead to any drop in production outside the one critical area of housing, where high interest rates and spiraling construction costs had already priced most middle-income people out of the new housing market. Corporate profits reached new highs in 1973, although the insecurities of inflation, increasing energy shortages, and unpredictable government policies depressed stock prices and eroded business confidence. It seemed that government vacillation among tight controls, no controls, and flexible controls had increased economic anxieties and exaggerated the response of corporations and consumers to actual or rumored scarcities.

Back of the inflation lay some hard realities. Although the gross national product will continue to rise, it is quite possible that Americans have already reached or passed the peak of consumer affluence, at least measured quantitatively. At the very least, the rate of growth in private consumption will slow. More and more of our product will have to go into social overhead, including rising costs to preserve or improve our environment, or be exchanged for much dearer foreign goods. By early 1974 it seemed likely that limited energy resources and higher costs would force most Americans to accept smaller automobiles and to use them less; that permanently higher food costs would lead to a stable or lowered per capita consumption of red meats and dairy products; and that narrowed differences in productivity would continue to reduce differences in living standards among advanced countries to the relative detriment of the United States. This was joined with falling birth rates, the prospect of a more stable but relatively older population, and necessary but difficult shifts in occupational patterns, a shift already all too apparent to teachers. These changes do not mean a lowered quality of life, provided anyone could come close to agreement on what that means. A lowering of private consumption in certain areas might accompany cleaner air and streams, better public transportation, and even a more equal distribution of income and wealth. The opportunities and challenges at least equaled the hazards, but the much discussed issue of living quality always begged a critical question—did Americans share enough similar tastes to agree on what makes for a more desirable style of life?

The economic woes of 1973 reflected major international readjustments. The United States changed from a nearly self-contained economy before 1941 to a much more interdependent economy in 1973, as the share of goods imported approximately doubled. The very magnitude of postwar economic growth, the vast expenditure of productive energy for defense and for domestic consumption, drained away vital resources (particularly oil, gas, and vital minerals) which we will increasingly have to import. The growth of multinational corporations or cartels and the development of cooperative trading blocks may stabilize international trade but will lessen the role of both competition and diplomatic bargaining in controlling prices and supplies. Even more than large national corporations, which already frustrate most efforts at effective governmental regulation, the huge international firms may be almost impossible to control in behalf of any national priorities. Increasingly, the American standard of living will depend in a hundred areas upon the type of bargains American political or business leaders will be able to negotiate with foreign governments or foreign producers. Unfortunately for Americans, their bargaining position drastically worsened in the seventies, and more than anything else this required the inflationary belt-tightening of 1973.

By the mid-sixties the United States suffered a growing and troubling balance-of-payments deficit (more dollars left the country than came in). For a time we continued to sell more goods than we bought, but a large export of capital in other forms (military commitments abroad, foreign aid, foreign investments) helped create the growing deficits. Finally, in 1971, our trade balance also moved into the red. In 1972 our payments deficit ballooned to a horrendous $10 billion, our trade deficit to over $6 billion. Our gold reserves, our credit standing, the prestige of the dollar could not long sustain such heavy losses. One possible answer seemed to be more efficient production, and thus a better bargaining position on the international market. This hope proved chimerical except in a few agricultural areas, and for reasons disillusioning to many Americans. In many industries our plant facilities were old and inefficient in comparison to those in Germany and Japan (railroads were only the most dramatic example). Our labor efficiency, although still very high, rose less rapidly than in competing countries, and seemed to have reached a near plateau by the seventies, whether this primarily reflected a lack of technological innovation, bad management, the enervating effect of union featherbedding, too much or too little government regulation, or even a significant decline in what many too loosely referred to as the work ethic. Short of more efficient production, two alternatives competed at the political level: Firstly, a vast reduction of foreign military obligations and of our dwindling commitment to foreign economic assistance, a position increasingly appealing to congressional Democrats. Or, secondly, negotiated or unilateral policies in the area of tariffs, quotas, and currency exchange designed to favor American exports, a position adopted by a Nixon administration that did not make clear its sure implications—higher profits for exporters and producers of export commodities, but higher prices and reduced living standards for consumers.

Devaluation and a New Scarcity

Even as public attention centered on Phases I through IV of Nixon's new economic controls, he used the strongest available weapon—currency devaluation—to better our trade position. In December 1971, the United States had officially devalued the dollar by 8.6 percent by raising the official price of gold to $38 an ounce. This devaluation, tied to temporary import duties, almost forced Germany and Japan to revalue their currency in relation to the dollar. But the official exchange rates still understated the declining fortunes of the dollar. Commercial gold prices, as stated in dollars, rose throughout 1972 and well into 1973, peaking at over $100 an ounce. In February 1973, Nixon approved another official devaluation of 10 percent. Already, several countries floated their currency in relation to the dollar (they let market competition determine the rate of exchange), leading to periodic fluctuations in exchange rates. This official and unofficial devaluation drastically lowered the price of American products in foreign markets, and slowly raised the cost of foreign goods in America. As intended, this concealed but severe tax on consumption helped stabilize the dollar, lessened the drain of gold from the United States, and drastically reduced the balance-of-payment deficits. By the end of 1973 the United States had achieved both trade and payments surpluses. By 1974 the dollar had become so strong as to invite devaluation by other countries.

In 1973 dollar devaluation coincided with worldwide food shortages. To compound the problems, bad weather in the fall of 1972 cut American corn production and destroyed a large proportion of unharvested and vital soy beans, a heavy export crop and the leading source of protein for animals and poultry. Our wheat crop, although normal, paralleled major failures in other parts of the world and overwhelming foreign demand. Our agricultural program, geared to surpluses and low world prices, lagged behind changed realities. In 1972 the Nixon administration, pursuing older priorities and using export subsidies, negotiated a major wheat sale with the Soviet Union, a sale soon greeted by charges of favoritism to major exporters and an irresponsible lack of concern for domestic needs as Americans watched cereal and bread prices soar. Actually, the Soviet sale was only an unexpected addition to normal wheat sales abroad, which included shipments to China. Dollar devaluation boosted agricultural exports by lowering the prices required of foreign purchasers, including those countries that had a developed dependence on American farm products. Embargoes on all food exports might have aided domestic consumers (Nixon did partially embargo soy beans, to the consternation of Japan), but such an embargo would have ruined our efforts to improve our balance-of-payments, and would have curtailed the profits of already angry farmers. New harvests in 1973 and the ingenuity of farmers promised some relief from domestic shortages in 1974, but soaring world populations and acute droughts in Africa and Asia, as well as greater affluence in industrial states, guaranteed continuing pressures on food supplies and continued high prices for American consumers.

Food prices only led the inflationary boom, although they directly affected the most people and led to the most bitter consumer protests. After electric "brownouts" during several summers, near exhausted heating oil and propane supplies during the mild winter of 1972 led to regional shortages. The very effort to meet this demand by refineries helped create a real or fabricated gasoline shortage in the summer of 1973. Diversion of refinery capacity to gasoline, in turn, left dangerously low heating oil supplies for the winter of 1973–74. The purported national gasoline shortage, and quite real shortages at gasoline stations during the most busy tourist season, led to a complicated and continuing controversy. Many congressmen argued that the major oil companies, with unprecedented profits and continued exports of petroleum products, had contrived the local shortages, particularly in highly competitive areas where independent dealers had operated low-margin outlets and provoked unending price wars. Since the independents bought surplus gasoline from major refineries, the curtailed supplies forced many of them to close, and this in turn allowed the major companies to raise prices to their local stations and, in some areas, force gasoline prices up by as much as ten cents a gallon. The large companies also had clear political goals for promoting a shortage—early congressional approval of a pipeline across Alaska, less pressure from environmentalists, and broader public acceptance of high profit levels and unique tax privileges.

Even if the petroleum shortages of the late summer were more illusory than real, the Arab-Israeli war of October precipitated a worldwide energy crisis and seemed to threaten vital even though marginal American imports of Arab oil. The Arab states, by a surprise attack on a Jewish holiday, Yom Kippur, gained an early advantage in the war and at least regained a sense of pride from early conquests. But in just over a week Israel regained the initiative and pushed across Suez into Egypt and well along the Damascus road in Syria. Despite these victories, Israel lost diplomatic support and, pressured by the United States, accepted an early cease-fire and eventually agreed to serious negotiation, or what seemed another brilliant diplomatic achievement by Henry Kissinger. Oil, not weapons, proved the most decisive weapon in this brief war. The Arab oil states more than doubled crude oil prices (at least officially), cut production, and attempted a boycott of "unfriendly" states, including the Netherlands and the United States. Japan and most countries of Western Europe were almost completely dependent on Arab oil. Soon, the United States was almost alone in its open support of Israel, as our former allies capitulated to Arab blackmail. Meanwhile, in Europe and in Japan the price of scarce gasoline soared, leading to rationing in some countries, to driving bans in others, and in all the Western world to the prospect of a severe recession.

In the United States the Arab oil policies, coming in the wake of mar-

Waving flags, signs, and a sword, Jews rally in Lafayette Park across the street from the White House during the Arab-Israeli six-day war of 1967. The demonstration was a plea for the future security of Israel. The 15,000-person demonstration turned into an emotion-packed victory celebration at news of the Arab acceptance of the UN cease-fire. *United Press International*

ginal domestic shortages during the summer, precipitated the great energy crisis of the winter of 1973–1974. The crisis was real enough for those who experienced it, whether or not it rested on a realistic assessment of existing oil supplies or realistic projections of future needs. As winter began, the oil companies predicted dire scarcities ahead, the rumors soon competing with facts. Both Congress and President Nixon began developing allocation and even rationing plans, while both the oil companies and the government launched a tremendous energy conservation crusade, even as the government surveyed alternative energy sources or ways of increasing domestic oil production. Homeowners, businesses, and schools reduced their thermostats to 68° or lower; most gasoline stations closed on Sundays, and airlines cut out their more unprofitable flights. By government permission, regulated heating oil and gasoline prices rose by up to 33 percent in only two months, with some American drivers paying over 50 cents a gallon for gasoline. Most Americans seemed at first to respond to the crisis with ingenuity and zest, or even with enthusiasm and a secret relish for still largely token sacrifices. But they also contemplated with forebodings all the possible changes, in layoffs, discomfort, inconveniences, and changed life styles. Since early forecasts indicated a long-term shortage, many people began to assume something like a siege mentality. Prophets of economic doom proliferated. In mid-January 1974, the Nixon administration used new congressional authority to make many of the voluntary cutbacks mandatory, not by direct rationing but by cutting heating oil supplies to consumers enough to force a 6° lowering of thermostats, and by allowing gasoline retailers no more gasoline than they received in 1972. The government also prepared stand-by rationing coupons for possible but unlikely use by spring. Yet, by January of 1974, much of the crisis seemed contrived or at least to be based on grievous miscalculations. This lent credence to growing charges of deceit and selfishness on the part of major oil companies. The Arab embargo simply never held; oil imports in November and December exceeded those for the same months of 1972. In part because of mild weather and private restraint, yearend stocks of crude oil and heating oil were also larger, and gasoline comparable, to those of a year earlier. Only small refineries seemed short of crude oil, and then only because of their dependence on the large companies. With these revelations, confusion seemed to reign, with escalating charges and countercharges between Congress and the president, and between the oil companies and angry consumer advocates, such as Ralph Nader. A perplexed and increasingly cynical public could only hope that several congressional investigations would lead to some of the needed facts.

By early 1974, half the goods on the market seemed either to be in short supply or so rumored. Petroleum products alone furnished vital ingredients for hundreds of consumer items. Lumber, scarce and expensive, followed the same pattern as wheat—currency devaluation increased foreign sales and drove up domestic prices. Even the price of money soared to all-time highs. The Federal Reserve Board tried to facilitate Nixon's anti-inflation controls, and at the same time help avert rationing and rigid price controls. It used credit restraints to help drive prime interest rates up to an astounding 10 percent by August 1973 and again in early 1974. Yet, inflation-hedging buying or limited hoarding of foodstuffs overrode even this impediment. Thus, monetary policy did not lead to the intended goal—lowered demand and a slackening of price increases—or to the possible hazard—such a severe dampening of demand as to lead to a serious recession. But the much discussed energy crisis did lead to serious layoffs in January 1974, particularly in the lagging automobile industry, and promised more retrenchment in coming months. Although estimates varied, almost all economists predicted an economic slowdown for 1974. Some forecast a major recession.

Retrospect on the Nixon Administration

Nixon, as most presidents, eventually formulated a lofty even if typically fuzzy dream for his administration, an ennobling rationalization of all his efforts. Nothing in his puzzling past, in his enigmatic personality, suggested the exact content of his matured aspiration, of his aggressive and insecure bid for great political achievement, or for the deserved plaudits accorded our most successful presidents. Despite early promises to the contrary, he let Vietnam pull him into its cruel lair, with its personal fruits of executive secrecy, duplicity, and arbitrary initiatives, and its social and political fruits of congressional suspicion, popular disquietude, and widespread campus revolt. Such opposition could only strike a vulnerable Nixon as unfair or even treasonable. Many of the dark secrets of Watergate lay in the nature of that opposition and in Nixon's inability to suffer or learn from it. Belated peace in Vietnam, the end of the draft, the detente with China and the Soviet Union finally helped defuse the explosive potential of foreign policy and gain Nixon a broad basis of popular support. Whatever the value one gave to these diplomatic accomplishments, he clearly presided over a major shift in the alignments dating from World War II. The consequences of these changes are not yet apparent.

Despite his achievements in foreign policy, Nixon lost his bid for major domestic achievements during the calamitous events of 1973. As he began his second term, he effectively responded to deeply felt apprehensions and articulated vaguely perceived new priorities. He well expressed a growing popular apprehension about the Leviathan in Washington, and a growing support for the decentralization of political power. Yet events soon disclosed an administration that had pushed federal power to frightening, undreamed of excesses—in secret, deceitfully concealed air operations in Indochina, in new domestic intelligence schemes, in the willful subversion of electoral integrity, in a near contempt for law and court procedures. Nixon talked often, and appealingly, about a needed revival of moral standards, a regained respect for law and order, yet Watergate revealed among his closest friends and advisers a flagrant violation of law and a completely cynical and amoral use of power.

Ironically, Watergate led to a searching critique of federal power and to a healthy distrust of the executive branch of government, of intelligence agencies, of vague appeals to national security. It stimulated a far-ranging discussion of political ethics, of basic moral and constitutional principles. But Nixon, instead of receiving credit for these new concerns, became the leading victim of them. His near apology for an Ehrlichman or a Haldeman, his less than candid public discussions of Watergate, his later duplicity in trying to avoid disclosure of the White House tapes, made it impossible for him to continue his pleas for honesty and morality. Had fate decreed his plight, had courage or heroism inadvertently trapped him, had strength and wisdom betrayed him, he would have seemed our most tragic president. As it was, by the end of 1973 he seemed merely our most pathetic, a living illustration of the terrible temptations, the severe tests of character and ability, the demands for almost preternatural wisdom, that confront all men who willingly bid for great power and follow the dictates of great ambition.

Index

722

735